FIFTH EDITION

INTERNATIONAL ACCOUNTING AND MULTINATIONAL ENTERPRISES

FIFTH EDITION

INTERNATIONAL ACCOUNTING AND MULTINATIONAL ENTERPRISES

LEE H. RADEBAUGH

Brigham Young University

SIDNEY J. GRAY

University of New South Wales

JOHN WILEY & SONS, INC.

Acquisitions Editor	Mark Bonadeo
Production Editor	Sandra Russell
Assistant Editor	Ed Brislin
Marketing Manager	Keari Bedford
Designer	Kevin Murphy
Production Management Services	Hermitage Publishing Services

This book was typeset in 10/12 ITC New Baskerville by Hermitage Publishing Services and printed and bound by Hamilton Printing Company. The cover was printed The Lehigh Press, Inc.

The paper in this book was manufactured by a mill whose forest management programs include sustained yield harvesting of its timberlands. Sustained yield harvesting principles ensure that the number of trees cut each year does not exceed the amount of new growth.

This book is printed on acid-free paper. ∞

Library of Congress Cataloging in Publication Data:

Radebaugh, Lee H.
    International accounting & multinational enterprise/Lee H. Radebaugh, Sidney J.
Gray. — 5th ed.
        p. cm.
    Rev. ed. of: International accounting and multinational enterprises/Lee H. Radebaugh,
Sidney J. Gray. 4th ed. c1997.
    Includes bibliographical references and index.
    ISBN 0-471-31949-X (alk. paper)
    1. International business enterprises—Accounting. 2. Comparative accounting. I. Gray,
S. J. II. Radebaugh, Lee H. International accounting and multinational enterprises. III. Title.

HF5686.I56 A76 2001
657'.96—dc21   2001026446

Printed in the United States of America.

10 9 8 7 6 5 4 3 2 1

ABOUT THE AUTHORS

Lee H. Radebaugh, MBA, DBA (Indiana)

Professor Radebaugh is the Director of the School of Accountancy and Information Systems and KPMG Professor of Accounting at Brigham Young University. In addition, he is the Executive Director at the BYU Center for International Business Education and Research (CIBER). He received his MBA and Doctorate from Indiana University. He previously taught at Penn State University from 1972 to 1980. In 1975 he was a visiting professor at Escuela de Administración de Negocios para Graduados (ESAN), a graduate business school in Lima, Peru. In 1985, he was the James Cusator Wards visiting professor at Glasgow University in Scotland. He was Associate Dean of the Marriott School of Management from 1984 to 1991.

Lee Radebaugh is the author of *International Business: Environments and Operations* (Addison-Wesley, ninth edition) with John D. Daniels, *Global Accounting and Control* (John Wiley & Sons) with Sidney J. Gray and Stephen Salter, *Introduction to Business: International Dimensions* (South-Western Publishing Company) with John D. Daniels, and is the co-editor of books on Canada-U.S. trade and investment relations. He has also published several other monographs and articles on international business and international accounting in journals such as the *Journal of Accounting Research,* the *Journal of International Business Studies,* the *Journal of International Financial Management and Accounting,* and the *International Journal of Accounting.*

His primary teaching interests are international business and international accounting. He is an active member of the American Accounting Association, the European Accounting Association, and the Academy of International Business, having served on several committees, and as the President of the International Section of the AAA and the Secretary-Treasurer of the AIB. He is also active with the local business community as former President of the World Trade Association of Utah and member of the District Export Council. In 1998, he was named the "Outstanding International Accounting Educator" of the International Section of the American Accounting Association and "International Person of the Year" by the World Trade Association of Utah.

Sidney J. Gray, BEc (Sydney), Ph.D. (Lancaster), FCCA, CPA, ACIS, MIMgt

Professor Gray received his economics degree from the University of Sydney and his Ph.D. in international accounting from the University of Lancaster. He teaches and researches international business strategy, cross-cultural management and international accounting at the University of New South Wales, Sydney, Australia, where he is a Professor and Head of the School of International Business. He was formerly a Professor at the University of Warwick in England and the University of Glasgow in Scotland.

Sidney Gray has published in many leading journals around the world including *Journal of Accounting Research, Abacus, Journal of International Business Studies, Journal of International Financial Management and Accounting, Accounting and Business Research, European Accounting Review, International Journal of Accounting,* and the *Journal of Business Finance and Accounting.* He is the author/co-author of more than 20 books and monographs and 100 articles. His books include *Global Accounting & Control* (John Wiley & Sons) with Stephen Salter and Lee H. Radebaugh and *Financial Accounting: A Global Approach* (Houghton Mifflin) with Belverd E. Needles, Jr.

He is active in many academic and professional organizations. He has served as President of the International Association for Accounting Education and Research (IAAER), Chairman of the British Accounting Association, and Secretary General of the European Accounting Association. He has served as a member of the Accounting Standards Committee for the U.K. and Ireland and as a member of the Consultative Group to the International Accounting Standards Committee. In 1994, he received from the American Accounting Association's International Section the award of "Outstanding International Accounting Educator." He is currently a Vice President of the Australia–New Zealand International Business Academy.

PREFACE

The global challenges of doing business in the twenty-first century require accountants and managers who are more aware of the international financial complexities involved and who have knowledge and understanding relevant to solving problems arising from the ever-increasing pace of international business, finance, and investment.

TARGET AUDIENCE

Our aim in writing this book is to contribute to the development of internationally competent people in accounting and business. The target audience at senior undergraduate level includes both accounting and business students, and at Master's level those students looking to broaden their horizons. In addition, this book should be helpful to practicing accountants, managers, and consultants who wish to become more involved in the international aspects of accounting.

A STRATEGIC APPROACH

This book presents international accounting within the context of managing multinational enterprises (MNEs). We focus on the business strategies of MNEs and how accounting applies to these strategies. This unique approach gives students the opportunity to learn about international accounting from a perspective similar to what they will experience in the business world. The book also discusses accounting issues in the context of different countries. We discuss the key factors that influence accounting standards and practices in different countries, and how those factors impact the harmonization of standards worldwide. In particular, we have tried to concentrate on culture and its unique contribution to accounting standards and practices. Our emphasis is on the needs of users of financial and accounting information across borders with the aim of enhancing their understanding of how to use information and therefore make more informed decisions in an increasingly complex and dynamic international business environment.

CONTENTS OF THE BOOK

This book emphasizes the international business context of international accounting and financial decision making. In this latest edition of the book we have restructured the text to provide a better flow of material and also to present it more succinctly. At the same time, an in-depth and balanced coverage is provided of key issues relevant to users at both the internal and external levels of international business activity:

- Chapter 1 examines international accounting issues in the context of international business.
- Chapter 2 reviews the development of accounting in the global economy.
- Chapter 3 provides a comparative international analysis of financial accounting especially from a cultural perspective.
- Chapter 4 focuses on the use of financial statements across borders by managers and investors alike and the problems of understanding the meaning of financial information in different national contexts.
- Chapter 5 examines issues associated with corporate transparency and disclosure in an international context and the pressures for both traditional as well as more market-oriented approaches to disclosure.
- Chapter 6 focuses on the participants and factors involved in the global harmonization of accounting and reporting including recent developments in International Accounting Standards.
- Chapter 7 analyzes the concepts, issues, and practices involved with the often controversial areas of international business combinations, goodwill, and intangibles.
- Chapter 8 provides an analysis and review of issues and developments relating to international segment reporting.
- Chapter 9 deals in some detail with the problems and impact of foreign currency transactions including hedging and the use of derivatives in an environment of changing exchange rates.
- Chapter 10 examines the issues involved with exchange rate changes and the foreign currency translation of financial statements.
- Chapter 11 analyzes the problems of accounting for price changes internationally and provides a comparative analysis of practices around the world.
- Chapter 12 provides an examination of auditing issues relevant to the multinational enterprise, a review of audit standards internationally, and an update on international harmonization efforts.
- Chapter 13 looks at the theory and practice of management organization and control across borders and explores the variety of national and cultural influences at work.
- Chapter 14 examines some of the special problems of budgeting and performance evaluation in the multinational enterprise with particular reference to the complexities of foreign exchange and transfer pricing.
- Chapter 15 concludes the book with a discussion of the challenges of coping with the complexities of taxation across borders and the need for effective tax planning.

CHAPTER MATERIALS

Each chapter provides objectives and concludes with a summary of the main points of the chapter. In addition, discussion questions, exercises, and cases are provided. Throughout the book, reference is made in the text to relevant research and items of special interest are highlighted either in tables or exhibits.

INSTRUCTORS' MANUAL

This book is accompanied by an instructors' manual that includes: (1) suggested course outlines; (2) solutions for the discussion questions, exercises, and cases; (3) a multiple-choice test bank. Also available, new to this edition, are Powerpoint Presentations for each chapter.

ACKNOWLEDGMENTS

We would like to thank our many colleagues from around the world for their contributions to the international business and accounting literature. Their research has been of great benefit to us and has helped to ensure the relevance and reliability of the subject matter. Many individuals have been helpful in the process of producing the book. We especially would like to thank Grace Setiawan at the University of New South Wales and Mark Bonadeo and his team at John Wiley & Sons for their assistance.

LEE H. RADEBAUGH
SIDNEY J. GRAY

CONTENTS

FIFTH EDITION

INTERNATIONAL ACCOUNTING AND MULTINATIONAL ENTERPRISES

CHAPTER ONE

INTERNATIONAL ACCOUNTING AND INTERNATIONAL BUSINESS

Chapter Objectives

- Identify the key trends in the development of accounting through history
- Introduce some of the key national differences in accounting systems worldwide
- Highlight the evolution of business to modern times
- Discuss the important accounting dimensions of global business and the major topics that comprise the field of international accounting
- Introduce the chapters in the book

INTRODUCTION

What an exciting time to study international accounting as we enter the new millennium! We are closer than ever to having a uniform set of international accounting standards that firms can use as they list on stock exchanges all over the world. International business activity is increasing dramatically through traditional exporting and importing of goods and services as well as foreign direct investment. Capital markets are opening up and becoming more transparent and capital flows freely around the world at a quicker pace. Stock markets are linking up with each other just as firms are doing to increase their global competitiveness, and accounting will be one of the key areas that will help determine how successful cross-border stock market linkages become. Companies are finding that they need to move quickly outside of their home country capital market if they want to be a truly multinational corporation, and the U.S. stock market has risen quickly as the location for new

1

issues of foreign corporations. A new currency, the euro, was introduced in Europe in 1999, changing forever the notion of foreign exchange risk in Europe and changing the way European companies keep their accounts. And now the euro is even turning out to be a competitor for the U.S. dollar in global currency markets. To embark on our journey into the new millennium of international accounting, we will first trace the international development of accounting, highlight some of the critical factors that determine national differences in accounting systems, provide an initial perspective on these differences and their importance for accountants in the modern world, and outline the focus of the book. In addition, we will examine some of the key elements of international business and how they affect company strategy and the accounting function within that strategy.

THE INTERNATIONAL DEVELOPMENT OF THE ACCOUNTING DISCIPLINE

Many books have been written on the origin of accounting, but no one has been able to establish when it really began. Clearly, accounting is a function of the business environment in which it operates, and it originated in order to record business transactions. The origin of accounting and its subsequent changes are therefore best studied in the context of the history of commercial transactions. Although the recording of transactions is probably as old as the history of record keeping, we tend to think of the establishment of double-entry accounting, the basis for modern accounting, as the key event. In 1994, the seventeenth annual congress of the European Accounting Association (EAA) was held in Venice to celebrate the 500-year anniversary of the publication of the first printed book on double-entry accounting by Luca Pacioli. Why were the Italians so influential in the development of double-entry accounting, and could it have developed elsewhere?

Early Italian Influence

Record keeping, the foundation of accounting, has been traced back as far as 3600 B.C., and historians know that mathematical concepts were understood in various ancient civilizations from China, India, and Mesopotamia—often referred to as the "Cradle of Civilization"—to some of the ancient native cultures of Central and South America. Business transactions in different areas around the world, including the city-states of central and northern Europe, probably gave rise to the recording of business transactions.

However, double-entry accounting was probably developed in the Italian city-states between the thirteenth and fifteenth centuries. The most significant influences on accounting took place in Genoa, Florence, and Venice. There is no defining moment when double-entry accounting was born, but it seems to have evolved independently in different places, responding to the changing nature of business transactions and the need to record them properly. The Genoese system was probably a development of the ancient Roman system. Commercial activity had been flourishing in Genoa for a long time, and Genoa was at the height of her wealth and power during the fourteenth century. The Genoese system assumed the concept of a business entity. Because it recorded items in terms of money, it was the first to imply that unlike items could be compared in terms of a common monetary unit. The system also implied some understanding of the distinction between capital and income in that it included both expenses and equity accounts. The oldest double-entry books were the Massari (treasury officials) ledgers of the Commune of Genoa, dating from 1340. Given that they were written in perfect double-entry form, it stands to reason that the concepts must have originated and evolved earlier than that. In fact, the government of the Commune of Genoa decreed in 1327 that government accounts had to be kept in the same way that the banks kept their accounts, so it would seem natural that double-entry accounting existed with Genoese banks prior to 1327, even though we have no records of Genoese banks prior to 1408.

Florentine commerce also flourished in the thirteenth and fourteenth centuries, giving rise to double-entry accounting there as well. In 1252, Florence coined the gold florin, soon accepted as the standard gold piece all over Europe. A major achievement in Florence was the development of large associations and *compagnie* (partnerships) that pooled capital, initially within family groups and then from outside the family groups. Given the nature of Florence as an artistic center, it is easier to find manuscripts relating to the development of bookkeeping. The account books of the fourteenth century reflect the partnership contracts of the *compagnie*, which identified the capital of the separate partners, made provisions for the division of profits and losses, clearly defined the duties of each partner, and provided for the dissolution of the *compagnie*. Records were often kept in great detail, almost in narrative form. Until the influence of the Venetians, Florentine accounts listed debits above credits rather than on separate pages. Separate columns for transactions were needed to record which monetary value was used.

However, the key influence on double-entry accounting, not so much for its development as its spread, came from Venice. Venice was the key commercial city of the Renaissance because of its commercial empire and advantages as a port. The Venetians may not have developed double-entry accounting before the Genoese and Florentines, but Venice "developed it, perfected it, and made it her own, and it was under the name of the Venetian method that it became known the world over" (Peragallo, 1938).

Luca Pacioli

Luca Pacioli, who was born in San Sepolcro in the Tuscany region of Italy in 1447, was not an accountant but was educated as a mathematician by Franciscans and actually became a Franciscan monk himself. In 1464, he became the tutor of the three sons of a Venetian merchant, then left Venice to study mathematics. After becoming a Franciscan monk, he accepted a teaching position at the University of Perugia, then traveled extensively and taught at the Universities of Florence, Rome, Naples, Padua, and Bologna. In 1494, in Venice, he published the first significant work on accounting up to that point, *Summa de Arithmetica, Geometria, Proportioni et Proportionalita,* more commonly known as *Summa de Arithmetica.* His discussion of accounting comprises one of the chapters in the *Summa de Arithmetica.* Given the extreme detail included in the book and the fact that Pacioli was not a merchant or bookkeeper, many historians believe he got his information from somewhere else. In fact, Pacioli did not claim that his ideas were original, just that he was the one who was trying to organize and publish them. His objective was to publish a popular book that could be used by all, following the influence of the Venetian businessmen rather than the bankers. Wherever his ideas originated, the Venetian method became the standard for not only the Italians but also the Dutch, German, and English authors on accounting.

Pacioli introduced three important books of record: the memorandum book, the journal, and the ledger. The memorandum book included all information on a transaction. From the memorandum book, a journal entry was made into the journal. Information was then posted to the ledger, the center of the accounting system. Pacioli felt that all transactions required both a debit and credit in order for the transaction to remain in equilibrium.

Subsequent Developments

The growing literature on accounting represented an attempt to describe good practices rather than challenge underlying assumptions or develop a general theory of accounting. The literature began to change during the 1550s to reflect new commercial and political realities. The rise of nation-states and the need to manage public finances increased the importance of good accounting practice. However, a major change was the decline of Italy as a world commercial power. As commercial traffic shifted from the ports of Venice to the Atlantic shipping routes, Italy slipped in importance and relatively few new developments took place in accounting. It is true that changing business forms that emphasized large-scale business enterprises caused a change in focus, but accounting authors still clung to the old forms of accounting, and no new theories developed.

The French Revolution in the late 1700s marked the beginning of a great social upheaval that affected governments, finances, laws, and customs. Italy came under the influence of the French and then the Austrians, and their system of double-entry accounting was also influenced. It is interesting to note that Napoleon was surprised at how efficient the Italian system of accounting was. The serious study of accounting and development of accounting theory also began in this period and has continued to the present day. However, the influence of the Arabs, Genoese, Florentines, and Venetians continues to be felt in the double-entry system we use today. Even the British, who acquired their knowledge of double-entry accounting soon after Pacioli's *Summa de arithmetica* was published, did not begin adopting double-entry accounting quickly until the Industrial Revolution of the period 1760–1830. At that point, the importance of accounting grew substantially.

As the scale of enterprises increased following technological breakthroughs such as mass production, and as fixed assets grew in importance, it became necessary to account for depreciation, the allocation of overhead, and inventory. In addition, the basic form of business organization shifted from proprietorships and partnerships to limited liability and stock companies and ultimately to stock exchange listed corporations. Accounting had to adapt to satisfy these new needs. Increased government regulation of business made new demands on firms, which also generated new accounting systems. Most notable was the increased taxation of business and individuals, which brought with it new tax accounting systems and procedures.

Since the early 1900s, the rapidity of change and the increasing complexity of the world's industrial economies necessitated still more changes in accounting. Mergers, acquisitions, and the growth of multinational corporations fostered new internal and external reporting and control systems. With widespread ownership of modern corporations came new audit and reporting procedures and new agencies became involved in promulgating accounting standards: namely, stock exchanges, securities regulation commissions, internal revenue agencies, and so on.

Finally, with the dramatic increase in foreign investment and world trade and the formation of regional economic groups such as the European Union, problems arose concerning the international activities of business. This phenomenon remains particularly complex, for it involves reconciling the accounting practices of different nations in which each multinational operates, as well as dealing with accounting problems unique to international business.

NATIONAL DIFFERENCES IN ACCOUNTING SYSTEMS

One might infer that these historical developments had a uniform effect on accounting systems throughout the world, yet nothing could be further from the truth. Despite some similarities, there are at least as many accounting systems as there are countries, and no two systems are exactly alike. The underlying reasons for these differences are essentially environmental: accounting systems evolve from and reflect the environments they serve, just as in Genoa, Florence, and Venice in the 1400s. The reality of the world is that environments have not evolved uniformly or simultaneously. Countries today are at stages of economic development ranging from subsistence, barter economies to highly complex industrial societies.

While accounting practices evolved there were, for example, differences in the amount of private ownership, the degree of industrialization, the rate of inflation, and the level of economic growth. Given these differences in economic conditions, differences in accounting practices should not be surprising. Just as the accounting needs of a small proprietorship are different from those of a multinational corporation, so are the accounting needs of an underdeveloped, agrarian country different from those of a highly developed industrial country.

Economic factors, however, are not the only influences. Educational systems, legal systems, political systems, and sociocultural characteristics also influence the need for accounting and the direction and speed of its development. For example, in some Muslim countries where religious doctrine does not permit the charging of interest, there are unlikely to be elaborate accounting procedures related to interest.

The ways in which environmental factors affect the evolution of accounting practices are covered in greater detail in Chapter 2. For the moment, it is sufficient to acknowledge their role and the fact that in each country their unique combination results in a unique system of accounting.

Implications of National Differences in Accounting

There is some benefit to understanding how different nations do things. After all, there is always something to be learned from the experiences of others. As a case in point, consider inflation. Suppose a country has never experienced any significant inflation and has therefore never developed accounting procedures related to inflation. What would happen the first time the country experienced substantial and persistent inflation?

It could independently try to devise appropriate accounting procedures, or it could benefit from the experiences of other countries, which, having experienced significant inflation for some time, have developed inflation accounting procedures that work and make sense. However, it also must be acknowledged that one country's solution may not be appropriate or feasible for another country. The nature of the inflation may be different, its effects may be different, and the other country's practices for dealing with inflation may be incompatible or inconsistent. On the other hand, if another country's practices are suitable and feasible, they could significantly shorten the time it would take a country to adapt its system so as to account properly for the effects of inflation. In this sense, accounting is a form of technology that can be borrowed or shared, depending on its suitability.

At the present time, the most important reason for understanding different national accounting systems lies in the increasingly internationalized world of business in which people buy and sell, invest and disinvest, from one country to another. For example, if an enterprise is considering granting credit to or acquiring a company in another country, it must be able to assess the financial position of that company—not an easy thing to do.

When the foreign company offers a balance sheet and income statement for analysis, several things become immediately evident. First, the language and the currency are different. Second, the terminology is different; certain terms (accounts) have no counterparts in the other language or accounting system, or they mean different things. Third, the types and amount of information disclosed are likely to be different. In addition, there are a host of less obvious but perhaps more important differences. For example, the procedures that were followed to arrive at the final figures are likely to be different and less likely to be explained. Differences in procedures, such as rules of valuation, recognition, or realization, render the financial statements meaningless unless the analyst is familiar with the foreign country's accounting system.

THE EVOLUTION AND SIGNIFICANCE OF INTERNATIONAL BUSINESS

International business can be traced back to several centuries B.C. As far as anyone can tell, the reasons and motives were the same then as they are today: people wanted something they did not have in their own country, and they found someone in another country able to provide them with what they wanted. But trade on a major and planned scale did not really begin until the Greeks started exporting inexpensive, mass-produced goods around the fifth century B.C. By the end of the Greek period, there was sufficient trade to have permitted not only full-time professional traders but even some traders who specialized by area of the world or by commodities.

During the Roman period, traders roamed freely through the empire, and with better transportation, political stability, and few tariffs and trade restrictions, trade flourished. In fact, the Roman Empire established the feasibility and desirability of what is now known as the European Union.

During the Middle Ages, international business flourished in some areas of the world. For example, it flourished in Byzantium (present-day Istanbul) until the Crusades, facilitated by the development of banking and insurance and by the first large-scale international trade fairs. However, international trade did not fare as well in Europe until much later. Wars, plagues, and a generally anticommercial religious doctrine hindered commerce both domestically and internationally. It was not until the twelfth century that commercial activity and trade broke out of their undeveloped state. With their resurgence came laws and regulations regarding commerce and trade. Initially developed by guilds, then by city-states, and then much later by nation-states, international commercial regulations have continued to proliferate to the present day.

The Preindustrial Period

As Europe emerged from the Dark Ages, merchants sought ways to increase international business. By that time, however, the right to trade had become a privilege granted by the state, a phenomenon that has persisted to modern times. The privilege was based on what was to be known as mercantilism, a concept by which each state sought to become more pervasive and powerful militarily, economically, and politically than its rivals. During this period of mercantilism, the state was the driving and controlling force behind domestic and international economic activity.

The sixteenth and seventeenth centuries saw the first major foreign investments, under the rubric of colonialism. Governments invested directly in colonies, or gave individuals the right to do so, with the express purpose of obtaining first raw materials, then products, in a near-monopolistic control of trade. Finally, during this period of mercantilism the center of commercial and financial activity shifted steadily westward, from Byzantium to Italy, to the Netherlands and Belgium, and ultimately to Britain. This dominating influence of Western Europe was to last until the twentieth century.

The Industrialization Period

The Industrial Revolution, which began in the latter half of the eighteenth century, continued to have a major impact on international business throughout the nineteenth and twentieth centuries. The Industrial Revolution and its accompanying technologies gave rise to mass production and standardization of products and required sizable capital investments on an unparalleled scale. The emergence of large-scale, limited-liability companies combined with large-scale infrastructure projects such as railroads, canals, and power generating systems often necessitated obtaining capital from other countries—a major form of international business that has continued to the present. To exploit scale economies of production fully, the exporting of mass-produced goods became a necessity for many firms located in countries with small domestic markets. Simultaneously, industrialization often required an increase in the importation of raw materials and capital goods in many countries that did not possess them in sufficient quantity or quality. The multinational firm as it is known today emerged in this period, with early overseas expansion by firms such as Singer, Ford, Dunlop, and Lever Brothers.

The industrialization process also brought with it growing trade restrictions as many nations sought to protect their "infant industries." Although there was relatively little U.S. government interference or involvement with international trade or investment during this period, there was growing foreign government involvement, particularly in trade. This prompted many firms to begin replacing exports with direct investments in the more protectionist countries in order to keep their established markets. Despite the continued increase in both trade and investments, a trend was established: foreign investments were becoming much more influential.

The Post–World War II Period

The Great Depression and World War II stunted the growth of international business. The reasons are fairly obvious: drastic reductions in income; the bankruptcy of individuals, companies, and governments; then war, the destruction of property, and an end to the stability of money. Throughout this period, trade protectionism and the regulation of capital flows were on the rise, which, when combined with the other factors just mentioned, slowed the growth of international business activity.

At the end of World War II, there was a tremendous pent-up demand for products and services. With some semblance of order restored to international politics and the international monetary system, both trade and investment increased sharply.

The remnants of 1930s and early 1940s protectionism conspired to emphasize investment. The formation of the European Economic Community in the late 1950s (now the European Union), with its strong economy and the elimination of its internal trade restrictions, resulted in significant growth of U.S. manufacturing investment abroad. During the 1970s and 1980s, this trend had slowed considerably, but it was followed by an equally significant increase of foreign investment in the United States. However, the move to a more unified European Union resulted in significant interest in Europe once again.

The Multinational Era

The proliferation of multinational enterprises and their activities has constituted perhaps the most significant development in international business. Their wealth and influence are significant, yet the impressive role that they now play is far from the whole story of the growth in international business. For virtually all of the world's economies, international trade and foreign investment have increased in importance as a percentage of total economic activity.

Reasons for International Involvement

International business includes all business transactions that involve two or more countries. These transactions can be conducted exclusively in the private sector, or they can also involve the public sector. Companies get involved in international business for a variety of reasons. The major reason is to expand sales, perhaps because a firm has excess capacity and does not have additional sales opportunities at home. Thus, it needs to sell products abroad to utilize its capacity more efficiently. International sales can also be profitable.

A second reason to get involved in international business is to gain access to raw materials or other factors of production. Mining and agricultural companies operate in countries where natural resources or climate allow them to pursue their activities. On the other hand, manufacturing companies have found many developing countries in Eastern Europe, Asia, and Latin America to be ideal for doing business because of cheap labor and overhead-type expenses. Thus, they have expanded abroad to gain production efficiencies.

A third incentive for international activity is to gain access to knowledge. Learning about new technology quickly can make a big difference in a company's ability to compete in global markets. New technology is being developed worldwide, so companies cannot rely on their domestic market to keep abreast of new developments.

Forms of International Involvement

When companies, and especially the market seekers, first begin to expand beyond domestic markets they usually get involved in exports and imports. Merchandise exports are goods sent out of a country, and merchandise imports are goods brought into a country. Exports and imports can also involve services as well as goods. Service exports refer to the receipt of earnings from the performance of services abroad. If KPMG sent auditors to different countries to perform an audit and received a fee for those services, that work would be considered a service export. The country where the work was performed would experience a service import, which would result in an outflow of cash to the exporting country. Other examples of services are travel, tourism, and transportation.

In addition to exporting and importing, companies can expand abroad through one of several types of strategic alliances. A strategic alliance is used to describe a wide variety of collaborations, which are of strategic importance to one or more of the parties involved. Strategic alliances include licensing agreements, franchising, management contracts, custom contracts, and shared ownership of foreign companies. The choice of the type of strategic alliance depends on legal factors, cost, experience, competition, risk, control, and product complexity.

Two similar strategic alliances involve a licensing agreement and a franchise agreement. A licensing agreement exists when one company grants rights to intangible property to another company for a specified period of time in return for a royalty. The intangible property might involve a production process, formula, design, pattern, patent, or invention. Companies enter into licensing agreements to earn a return on their intellectual property without having to undertake the risk of expanding abroad using their own capital. A franchise, such as those of Holiday Inn or McDonald's, involves the use of a trademark that is an essential asset but also provision of assistance on a continual basis in running the business. Holiday Inn, for example, provides a reservation service for franchisees and continual audits on quality, and so on. Sometimes companies will cooperate in the development of new technology or in producing goods and services.

Companies can also invest abroad. A direct investment occurs when a company assumes some degree of control over a foreign corporation in order to influence management decisions. The decision can occur in the form of an acquisition of existing stock in a local firm or in the establishment of a "greenfield investment," which is the establishment of a new firm in a foreign location. If the investor owns 100 percent of the stock in the local firm, that firm becomes a wholly owned subsidiary. If two or more firms are involved in establishing a venture, the operation is known as a joint venture, another form of strategic alliance. Joint ventures often occur because the investor lacks financial or managerial expertise or because the investor needs to rely on the local knowledge of the partner in the venture.

Global Enterprises

There are a variety of terms used to describe companies involved in international business. The most frequently used term is multinational enterprise (MNE), which refers to companies that have a worldwide view of production, the sourcing of raw materials and components, and final markets. There is no consensus as to how much of a company's sales, assets, earnings, and employees must be abroad for the firm to be considered an MNE, but anything less than 10 percent of these indicators would probably disqualify a company from the elite group of MNEs. More than 10 percent implies that the companies are operating in at least two countries, and most MNEs have significant geographical spread. Companies that are not committed to doing business abroad simply lack a global vision. Another indicator of multinational involvement is the degree of international experience of key executives.

Although we use the term *MNE* in this book, other terms are often used as well. *MNC,* or multinational corporation, has been used extensively, but it is narrower than *MNE* in that it refers to the corporate form of organization and would exclude other forms, such as partnerships. The UN favors the use of transnational corporations (TNC) to reflect the fact that such companies transcend national boundaries. Theorists have also distinguished MNEs as either global or multidomestic. Global companies tend to integrate their operations worldwide, whereas multidomestic companies treat operations in different countries as being relatively independent. This is a crucial distinction and is discussed more fully in Chapter 13. In that chapter, we will also look at some of the more recent theories to emerge on the strategy and structure of companies engaged in international business. In this book, we will tend to use the term MNE more extensively to preserve the broader sense of companies doing business internationally.

Large MNEs

It is difficult to identify precisely the largest MNEs in the world because there are different definitions of size. The two most commonly used measures for size are sales and market value. In addition, other measures, such as profits and return on shareholders' equity, are often used to compare worldwide. Many argue for stock market valuations because they reflect the opinions of investors from around the world. In recent years, high-technology stocks have risen and fallen dramatically, with Microsoft replacing General Electric as the largest company in the world in market value in 1999, but by early 2000, Cisco Systems had jumped ahead of Microsoft with General Electric again taking the number-one position. Large swings in stock prices in 2000 and 2001 created havoc with the rankings of the largest companies in the world. Exhibit 1.1 identifies the top global corporations in 2000 by market value.

Even though the large MNEs are the ones most noticed and discussed, a company does not have to be large to be engaged in international business. The probability that a firm will engage in international transactions increases with firm size and as the firm begins to saturate the domestic environment. However, even small companies can export or import or get involved in licensing agreements. This is especially true of high-tech start-up companies that often get involved in international business immediately. In addition, some companies such as Nike design products in the domestic market but manufacture all of their products offshore—in countries outside their home country. Although the top MNEs in Exhibit 1.1 are from the industrial countries, there are many MNEs from developing countries as well. They come primarily from Asia and Latin America and are in a variety of industries.

Exhibit 1.1   2000 Leaders—The *Business Week* Global 1000

RANK			MARKET VALUE	RANK			MARKET VALUE
2000	1999		Billions of U.S. dollars	2000	1999		Billions of U.S. dollars
1	2	GENERAL ELECTRIC	U.S. 520.25	46	34	HSBC HOLDINGS	Britain 93.30
2	8	INTEL	U.S. 416.71	47	28	ROCHE HOLDING	Switzerland 92.38
3	9	CISCO SYSTEMS	U.S. 395.01	48	25	BERKSHIRE HATHAWAY	U.S. 89.13
4	1	MICROSOFT	U.S. 322.82	49	36	BELLSOUTH	U.S. 87.88
5	4	EXXON MOBIL	U.S. 289.92	50	69	WALT DISNEY	U.S. 87.66
6	70	VODAFONE AIRTOUCH	Britain 277.95				
7	6	WAL-MART STORES	U.S. 256.66				
8	27	NTT DOCOMO	Japan 247.24				
9	38	NOKIA	Finland 242.19				
10	5	ROYAL DUTCH/SHELL GROUP	Neth./Britain 213.54				
11	15	CITIGROUP	U.S. 209.86				
12	10	BP AMOCO	Britain 207.51				
13	122	ORACLE	U.S. 204.01				
14	3	INTERNATIONAL BUSINESS MACHINES	U.S. 192.49				
15	13	NIPPON TELEGRAPH & TELEPHONE	Japan 189.16				
16	23	DEUTSCHE TELEKOM	Germany 187.25				
17	16	LUCENT TECHNOLOGIES	U.S. 183.34				
18	17	AMERICAN INTERNATIONAL GROUP	U.S. 173.50				
19	12	MERCK	U.S. 172.87				
20	18	PFIZER	U.S. 171.52				
21	32	TOYOTA MOTOR	Japan 170.52				
22	77	LM ERICSSON	Sweden 158.05				
23	84	NORTEL NETWORKS	Canada 152.39				
24	31	SBC COMMUNICATIONS	U.S. 149.03				
25	43	FRANCE TELECOM	France 148.71				
26	11	COCA-COLA	U.S. 131.97				
27	82	EMC	U.S. 126.19				
28	21	JOHNSON & JOHNSON	U.S. 124.55				
29	20	AMERICA ONLINE	U.S. 121.76				
30	33	HEWLETT-PACKARD	U.S. 120.14				
31	91	SUN MICROSYSTEMS	U.S. 119.62				
32	96	TEXAS INSTRUMENTS	U.S. 118.23				
33	141	TOTALFINAELF	France 116.32				
34	41	HOME DEPOT	U.S. 112.38				
35	37	DELL COMPUTER	U.S. 111.55				
36	7	AT&T	U.S. 109.10				
37	19	BRISTOL-MYERS SQUIBB	U.S. 108.80				
38	14	WORLDCOM	U.S. 107.57				
39	29	NOVARTIS	Switzerland 105.96				
40	76	WARNER-LAMBERT	U.S. 105.92				
41	42	TIME WARNER	U.S. 103.65				
42	30	GLAXO WELLCOME	Britain 102.12				
43	24	BANK OF AMERICA	U.S. 94.86				
44	171	VIACOM	U.S. 94.41				
45	26	BRITISH TELECOMMUNICATIONS	Britain 93.70				

Source: Business Week, July 10, 2000, p. 49.

The Decision to Become Global

The decision to become global depends on how effectively management assesses two different but interactive dimensions: the external environment and the internal capabilities of the firm.

Environmental Constraints   Environmental constraints strongly influence the elements of the management process, which in turn affect management and managerial effectiveness, which determines firm efficiency (Farmer and Richman, 1965). Figure 1.1 identifies the major international and local constraints that affect the MNE. The environmental constraints are grouped into four categories: educational, sociological (or sociocultural), political and legal, and economic. The educational characteristics include the level of literacy, the availability of specialized and higher education, the attitude toward education, and the match of education with skill requirements in the economy. Sociocultural characteristics include the attitude toward managers and authority, interorganizational cooperation, the attitude toward achievement and work, class structure and individual mobility, and the attitudes toward wealth, rationality, risk taking, and change.

Among the major political and legal characteristics are the relevant legal rules of the game and flexibility in their application, defense and foreign policy, political stability, and political organization. Key economic characteristics are the general economic framework, fiscal and monetary policy, economic stability, capital markets, factor endowments, and market size.

These constraints are labeled C_1 (educational), C_2 (sociocultural), C_3 (legal-political), and C_4 (economic). The basic idea behind Figure 1.1 is that management operating in the home country is influenced in its operating decisions by the environmental constraints in that country. Any company, domestic or foreign, needs to be aware of those constraints. When operations are set up in a foreign country, the constraints change. There are economic constraints in both the home and foreign country, but those constaints may be different.

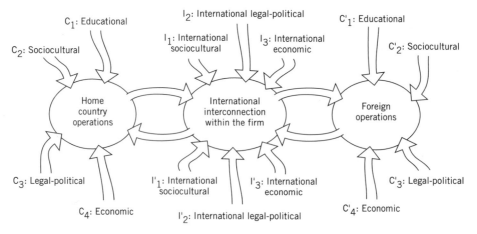

Figure 1.1   International and Local Constraints Affecting a Multinational Firm

As Figure 1.1 shows, there is also a list of international environmental constraints, and, each country has its own unique set. Firms that cross national boundaries must adjust to the new set of environmental constraints in the host country. However, the mere crossing of boundaries introduces a different set of international environmental constraints. The sociological constraints (I_1) include national ideology, the attitude toward foreigners, and the nature and extent of nationalism. The attitude toward investments by U.S. MNEs, for example, may be very different in the United Kingdom than it is in Iran. Important legal-political constraints (I_2) are relevant legal rules for foreign business—such as import-export restrictions, foreign investment restrictions, profit remission restrictions, and exchange control restrictions. Economic constraints (I_3) include the general balance-of-payments position, international trade patterns, and membership and obligations in international financial organizations.

Environmental constraints can rarely be changed by the MNE, so management has to decide whether or not those constraints would permit successful foreign investment. Sometimes, management becomes overwhelmed with the differences and takes a polycentric attitude, which implies that all operating policies and procedures must be adjusted to the local environment. This is especially true of MNEs from the Western hemisphere investing in Asia. In other cases, management takes an ethnocentric attitude, which means that everything the MNE does in the home country can be transferred to the foreign country, in spite of the environmental differences. Although the MNE can act as an agent of change in many circumstances, the ethnocentric attitude is usually a little extreme.

An important dimension of the environmental constraints is that some countries might have country-specific advantages, also known as location-specific advantages, that might strongly influence foreign investment. For example, the existence of a key natural resource; the availability of a plentiful, cheap labor supply; or the presence of a large market are country-specific advantages and are reasons why an MNE might want to invest in a particular location. These country-specific advantages would exist as incentives, rather than barriers, to investment.

Firm-Specific Advantages   The firm-specific advantages, also called ownership-specific advantages, relate primarily to the intangible assets that the firm possesses. In many cases, MNEs are basically in oligopolistic industries. However, smaller firms may have a firm-specific advantage because of a market niche or unique product capability. Typically, these firm-specific advantages are not easily duplicated by competitors, except in the long run or at very high costs. Thus, "The core skill of the MNE can be some element of its management structure, marketing techniques, or overall strategic planning that leads to a firm-specific advantage. These firm-specific advantages are modeled as endogenous to the MNEs, since their internal markets permit the MNEs to control them" (Rugman, Lecraw, and Booth, 1985).

A firm with a set of firm-specific advantages has a variety of options available for their productive use. As we mentioned earlier, the firm could exploit this advantage through exports. However, barriers to exports then lead the firm to explore other options. Selling the firm-specific advantage to another firm is a possibility, but the gains from the sale would not be as high as they would if the firm were to use the firm-specific advantage internally. A firm that decides to use the firm-specific advantages rather than sell them to other firms internalizes the firm-specific advantages.

ACCOUNTING ASPECTS OF INTERNATIONAL BUSINESS

A firm's first exposure to international accounting usually occurs as a result of an import or export opportunity. In the case of exports, a domestic company may receive an unsolicited inquiry or purchase order from a foreign buyer. Assuming the domestic company desires to make the sale, it needs to investigate the foreign buyer, particularly when the buyer asks for the extension of credit. This procedure is often not as easy as it appears.

First, the buyer may not be listed in any of the international credit rating directories, such as Standard & Poor's. If not, the seller may need to ask its bank to have its foreign affiliates check on the buyer's creditability. Alternatively, it may ask the buyer to supply financial information. The buyer may be willing to supply financial statements, but these statements may be difficult for the domestic company to interpret. The statements may be in a foreign language and may be based on accounting assumptions and procedures unfamiliar to the company's accountants. Most companies new to international business must then get help, either from a bank or from an accounting firm with international expertise. If the foreign buyer pays in its own currency, the selling company must become familiar with the potential gains and losses from changes in the exchange rate that may occur between the time the order is booked and the time the payment is received.

The selling company must also deal with a host of other international details—special international shipping and insurance documents, customs declaration forms, international legal documents, and so on. Once again, the services of lawyers, shippers, bankers, and accountants with international expertise are needed.

In the case of a potential import, the international accounting aspects are not as involved because most of the details are the responsibility of the foreign seller. However, if the foreign seller requires payments in his or her currency or if the domestic buyer wants information about the reliability of the foreign supplier, the buyer may need to consult an international bank, lawyer, or accounting firm.

Establishing an Internal International Accounting Capability

As the firm becomes increasingly involved in trade, the international accounting activity increases, and so do the costs of using outside expertise. At some point it becomes feasible for the company to develop the international capabilities of its own staff, including its own accountants.

The next major development that is likely to necessitate increased international accounting skills is the creation of a separate organization within the company to handle international trade. This may be an export department. Special accounting systems and procedures must be established in control, reporting, and taxation areas.

Typically, the next evolutionary step is the establishment of a foreign operation of some kind. In the minimal case, the company may decide to license a foreign manufacturer to produce its product or some part of its product. This involves selecting a potential licensee, analyzing its reliability and capability, and drawing up a contract. It also involves developing an accounting system to monitor contract performance and royalty and technical payments and to handle the foreign money flows into the company's tax and financial statements.

At the other end of the spectrum, the company may establish a wholly owned subsidiary in a foreign country. Accounting for the foreign subsidiary would include (1) meeting the requirements of the foreign government, which would be based on procedures and practices different from those in the parent company's country; (2) establishing a management information system to monitor, control, and evaluate the foreign subsidiary; and (3) developing a system to consolidate the foreign subsidiary's operating results with those of the parent for financial and tax-reporting purposes.

Between these extremes are a host of alternatives: setting up a sales office, setting up a warehouse, forming a joint venture with another company, and buying into an existing company. Each brings with it new international dimensions and requirements for management and, more specifically, for the company's accountants. It should also be pointed out that, before any of this takes place, a thorough study of market conditions—legal, economic, political, and sociocultural—should be made, including detailed feasibility studies and risk analysis. All of these steps require the collection and appropriate analysis of information in both quantitative financial terms and qualitative terms.

During a first venture into any of these more advanced areas, the international expertise of outside groups can be indispensable because of the money and risks involved in international trade. However, using outside international experts in no way lessens the need to develop in-house international capabilities, not only in accounting but in other functional areas as well.

Finally, some knowledge of international accounting may be necessary even if a firm is not involved in international business per se—for example, if the firm wishes to borrow money or to buy or sell stocks or bonds outside its home country. In some cases, it may be cheaper to borrow money or issue stocks or bonds abroad because interest rates are lower or exchange rate movements are favorable. In order to take advantage of these situations, the firm needs to know not only the relevant foreign laws, regulations, and customs but also the domestic legal, tax, and accounting treatments of any of these transactions. Alternatively, there may be better investment opportunities abroad for short-term liquid funds because of higher returns, predicted exchange rate movements, or both.

From an investment standpoint, the firm must know exactly what it is doing as well as know all the attendant risks. This entails an understanding of the financial statements, the terms of the foreign offer, and foreign currency movements. And as was the case with raising capital abroad, the investing firm must understand both the foreign and domestic laws and the tax and accounting treatments of the transaction being considered.

THE FIELD OF INTERNATIONAL ACCOUNTING

The study of international accounting involves two major areas: descriptive/comparative accounting and the accounting dimensions of international transactions/ multinational enterprises.

The first area is fascinating because it is truly fundamental to an understanding of the nature and uses of accounting. However, it would be impossible to study accounting for each country in the world in the same depth that one does for one's own country. Although some description is necessary when studying accounting in different countries, the important issues are the forces and conditions that create international differences. Some countries, such as the United States, the United Kingdom, Germany, France, and, more recently, Japan, are key countries to study because of their strong influence on the rest of the world. Colonial ties and direct investment require a basic understanding of those countries and their accounting systems.

We have described the issues relating to international transactions and multinational enterprises earlier. Obviously, there are firms that are not considered multinational enterprises that are involved in import/export transactions and require special attention. However, multinational enterprises have these problems and a host of others. Financial reporting problems, translation of foreign currency financial statements, information systems, budgets and performance evaluation, audits, and taxes are some of the major problems faced by these firms.

OVERVIEW OF THE TEXT

We believe that international accounting should be studied in the context of MNEs from a strategic perspective. Thus, we focus on the strategies of MNEs and how accounting is relevant to those strategies. However, this focus on the strategic context of the MNE does not imply that we are ignoring other important international accounting perspectives. For example, international accounting can be discussed from a descriptive/comparative point of view, irrespective of the activities of MNEs. Chapters 2, 3, and 6 discuss accounting development, comparative accounting and international harmonization. International financial reporting issues are discussed from an MNE and comparative perspective in Chapters 7 to 11, where we identify key accounting issues, such as business combinations and goodwill and other intangibles; segmental reporting; foreign exchange accounting; and accounting for price changes.

Chapter 1 not only sets up the logic for the book, but it also provides the general background on MNEs for students who have never taken an international business class.

Chapter 2 discusses the environmental influences on accounting development. In this chapter, we discuss how the international environment, especially culture, has a strong influence on accounting and control systems. We discuss the nature of external environmental influences and show how they influence accounting systems and practices.

Chapter 3 shows how companies need to be aware of the different accounting systems and accounting traditions they face in different parts of the world. We concentrate on some important studies that have attempted to explain why accounting systems differ from one country to another. This chapter emphasizes the importance of understanding similarities and differences in accounting systems, particularly in the context of multinational strategy. We conclude with a discussion of some of the unique accounting traditions and underlying roots of practice in a number of important countries of the world with different cultural backgrounds.

Chapter 4 introduces techniques for comparing financial statements of companies from different countries. We examine the extent to which international differences in accounting principles have an impact on measures of earnings and assets. Foreign companies that list their securities on a U.S. stock exchange must provide a reconciliation of their earnings and stockholders' equity to U.S. GAAP earnings and stockholders' equity, an important point of discussion in this chapter.

Chapter 5 deals with a number of important international transparency and disclosure and reporting issues, some of which are discussed in more detail later (e.g., segment reporting).

Chapter 6 examines the key international harmonization issues at work in the world today. In particular, the International Accounting Standards Committee is stepping forward to challenge the major national standard setters, such as the Financial Accounting Standards Board in the United States. Will the IASC win out, or will the existing fragmentation of capital markets allow national standard setters to rule? Or will the national standard setters give up a little sovereignty in order to allow capital markets to be even more open and attractive?

Chapter 7 is the first of several chapters that examines important financial reporting issues. In particular, we discuss different consolidation methods that are used around the world, the importance of the equity versus the cost method, and the issue of whether or not companies should consolidate operations, especially foreign operations. In addition, we deal with some of the current issues arising in cross-border mergers and acquisitions. Issues involved in accounting for goodwill and intangible assets are also discussed, especially the advantages and disadvantages of alternative accounting methods relating to goodwill, brands and trademarks, and research and development costs.

Chapter 8 on segment reporting concentrates on the reasons why companies are required to provide line-of-business and geographic segment information. New standards worldwide have caused this area to change dramatically in recent years.

Chapter 9 dealing with accounting for foreign currency transactions begins with a discussion of foreign exchange and then moves into issues surrounding accounting for foreign currency transactions. Then we move to Chapter 10 to continue the discussion of foreign exchange by examining how MNEs translate the results of their foreign operations and consolidate those results with domestic operations.

Chapter 11 concludes our discussion of key accounting concepts by looking at accounting for price changes and inflation. This is especially relevant in the context of foreign operations and foreign exchange accounting. Although inflation in general has fallen in recent years, it is never far away and needs to be addressed.

Chapter 12 on the international auditing of foreign operations concentrates on three key issues that relate to auditing: the nature of the accounting and auditing profession worldwide, the organization of international public accounting firms, and the harmonization of auditing standards and practices.

Chapter 13 on management organization and control of global operations introduces our discussion of major managerial accounting issues. Particular emphasis is placed on organizational structure, information systems, and the importance of the control process.

Chapter 14 focuses on international budgeting and performance evaluation issues and trends including the problems of dealing with foreign currency changes.

In Chapter 15, the final chapter, we focus on the multinational enterprise as it attempts to satisfy the tax codes in its own country and to operate in different tax environments around the world. We discuss some key issues relating to the taxation of exports and imports as well as the earnings of foreign operations. This chapter ends with a discussion of how firms can plan their operations internationally in a complex taxation environment.

Selected References

Daniels, John D. and Lee H. Radebaugh. 2001. *International Business Environments and Operations*. Ninth Edition. Upper Saddle River, NJ: Prentice Hall.

Edwards, J. R. 1989. *A History of Financial Accounting*. London: Routledge.

Farmer, Richard N. and Barry M. Richman. 1965. *Comparative Management and Economic Progress*. Homewood, IL: Irwin.

Gray, S. J. and C. B. Roberts. 1997. "Foreign Company Listings on the London Stock Exchange," in T. E. Cooke and C. W. Nobes, eds. *The Development of Accounting in an International Context*. London: Routledge.

Hill, C. W. 2000. *International Business*. New York: McGraw-Hill.

McMickle, Peter L. and Richard G. Vangermeersch. 1987. *The Origins of a Great Profession*. Memphis, TN: Academy of Accounting Historians.

Parker, R. H. 1989. "Importing and Exporting Accounting: The British Experience," in Hopwood, A. G., ed., *International Pressures for Accounting Change*. Englewood Cliffs, NJ: Prentice-Hall.

Peragallo, Edward. 1938. *Origin and Evolution of Double Entry Bookkeeping*. New York: American Institute.

Rugman, Alan M., Donald J. Lecraw, and Laurence D. Booth. 1985. *International Business: Firm and Environment*. New York: McGraw-Hill.

Seidler, Lee J. 1967. "International Accounting—The Ultimate Theory Course," *Accounting Review* 41, 4 (October): 775–81.

Ten Have, O. 1976. *The History of Accountancy*, translated by A. van Seventer. Palo Alto, CA: Bay Books.

United Nations. 1997. *World Investment Report 1997: Transnational Corporations, Market Structure and Competition Policy*. New York: UN.

CHAPTER TWO

ACCOUNTING DEVELOPMENT IN THE GLOBAL ECONOMY

Chapter Objectives

- Identify the key environmental influences on business and accounting
- Discuss the major factors influencing the development of accounting and information disclosure in the global economy
- Examine some of the important accounting issues that distinguish MNEs from purely domestic corporations
- Discuss culture as an important determinant of accounting systems worldwide
- Identify the major international pressures for accounting change

INTRODUCTION

To a large extent, accounting is a product of its environment; that is, it is shaped by, reflects, and reinforces particular characteristics unique to its national environment. This chapter investigates factors influencing the development of national accounting systems and the accounting and information disclosure practices of corporations, especially MNEs. First, however, we will examine the impact of environmental influences on business practices in general.

ENVIRONMENTAL INFLUENCES ON BUSINESS AND MANAGEMENT

The significance of environmental influences on business and management practices was recognized by Richard Farmer and Barry Richman (see Chapter 1) in their book *International Business*, published in 1965, a classic analysis of educational, sociocultural, legal, and political and economic factors in the operation of global businesses. Most important, an understanding of such influences can help to explain why business is conducted differently from one country to another. In other words, differences in national environments can help explain differences in business operations. For example, if one country has a law that prohibits making employees redundant after a certain length of service while another country has no such law, then—other things being equal—employment practices are likely to be different in the two countries. Similarly, if there is an extensive capital market (e.g., a major stock exchange) in one country but none in another, the principal methods of obtaining capital for business ventures are likely to be different.

We should note, however, that a corporation need not passively adapt to the environment in which it operates. The corporation itself can modify or change the environmental characteristics of the country, thereby bringing about changes that would permit it to operate more efficiently and effectively. For example, if a law bans some desired business activity, the corporation could bring about a change in that law by supporting candidates who would change it or by lobbying for the change.

Two essential points should be drawn from this brief discussion of environmental influences. First, environmental analysis can be a valuable tool in explaining and understanding differences in the ways businesses operate in different countries. The second point concerns "cultural relativism," which means that the rationality of any behavior should be judged in terms of its own cultural context and not that of an outsider. Put another way, we cannot judge the rationality of behavior in Japan using the customs and values of the United States or vice versa. There are many business practices around the world that may appear to be illogical and irrational (e.g., approaches to negotiations); yet when there is an understanding of the culture in which the behavior takes place, it is usually found that the seemingly irrational behavior is in fact quite rational. More important, it may be the only truly rational way of doing things in that country.

Too often incorrect assumptions are made that the "other people" simply do not know any better, that the home ways of doing business are better than the foreign ways, and that the home ways, if transplanted to another country, would be more successful. In case after case, this assumption has been proved false at considerable financial loss to the corporations involved.

ENVIRONMENTAL INFLUENCES ON ACCOUNTING

Like business in general, corporate accounting and information disclosure practices are influenced by a variety of economic, social, and political factors. A model of the environmental influences is presented in Figure 2.1. These include the nature of enterprise ownership, the business activities of the enterprise, sources of finance and the stage of development of capital markets, the nature of the taxation system, the existence and significance of the accounting profession, the state of accounting education and research, the nature of the political system, the social climate, the stage of economic growth and development, the rate of inflation, the nature of the legal system, and the nature of accounting regulation. The nature of

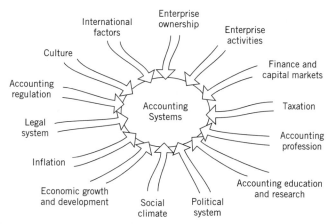

Figure 2.1   Environmental Influences on Accounting Development

accounting systems at the country level will vary according to the relative influence of these environmental factors, and such systems will, in turn, tend to reinforce established patterns of behavior.

With respect to enterprise ownership, the need for public accountability and disclosure will be greater where there is a broad ownership of shares compared to family ownership. Where there is state ownership, the influence of centralized control on the nature of accounting systems will tend to override the serving of microeconomic objectives. The activities of enterprises will also influence the nature of the accounting system depending on whether the business is agricultural, extractive, or manufacturing; whether it is diversified; whether it is multinational; and whether it is a large group of companies or a small business.

The sources of finance are another important influence. Clearly, there will be more pressure for public accountability and information disclosure when finance is raised from external shareholders via stock exchanges rather than banks or family sources, where information will be available more directly.

Taxation is a very important factor in situations where accounting systems are strongly influenced by state objectives; that is, in countries like France and Germany public accounting reports are used as a basis for determining tax liabilities. In the United States and the United Kingdom, on the other hand, the published accounts are adjusted for tax purposes and submitted separately from the reports to shareholders.

Where there is a more developed accounting profession there is likely to be more developed, judgmentally based public accounting systems rather than more centralized and uniform systems. Furthermore, the development of professional accounting will depend on the existence of a sound infrastructure of accounting education and research, which is often lacking in, for example, developing countries.

The political system is obviously a very important influence on accounting in that the nature of the accounting system will reflect political philosophies and objectives (e.g., central planning versus private enterprise). The social climate, that is, attitudes toward informing and consulting employees and toward environmental concerns, will also be influential. In Europe, for example, there is a much more positive approach to the disclosure of information relating to such matters than in the United States.

The nature and extent of economic growth and development will also be influential insofar as a change from an agricultural to a manufacturing economy will pose new accounting problems, such as the depreciation of machinery, leasing, and so on. In many countries, services are now becoming more important, and thus problems related to how to account for intangible assets such as brand names, goodwill, and human resources have become significant. Inflation is often associated with economic growth and is a major influence on accounting where hyperinflation has been rife (e.g., in South America) to the extent that alternative systems to the traditional historical cost approach are often used.

The legal system is also important in determining the extent to which company law governs the regulation of accounting. In countries, such as France and Germany, with a tradition of codified Roman law (or civil codes)—versus common law as in the United Kingdom and the United States—accounting regulations tend to be detailed and comprehensive. Furthermore, the influence of the accounting profession in setting accounting standards tends to be much less in such countries compared to countries, such as the United Kingdom and the United States, where company law is supplemented by professional regulation.

In addition, the influence of culture (i.e., societal or national values) on accounting traditions and practices needs to be taken into account. International factors are also bringing about changes in the environment that are creating harmonization in international accounting in contrast to the constraining influences operating at national levels.

Naturally, the influence of these factors is dynamic and will vary both between and within countries over time. Moreover, an evolutionary process of some complexity appears to be at work that is reflected in a growing number of international and regional influences. These include the activities of MNEs and intergovernmental organizations such as the United Nations (UN), the Organisation of Economic Cooperation and Development (OECD), and the European Union (see Chapter 6). In the European context, the European Union is an especially significant influence in that any agreement on the harmonization of accounting and information disclosure eventually becomes legally enforceable through a process of implementation in the national laws of the member countries.

While there are many differences in national environments, with correspondingly varying effects on accounting systems, there are also many similarities. Attempts to classify countries and identify patterns or groupings are still very much in the early stages. However, such efforts appear to be a useful way to gain a better understanding of the key factors influencing the development of accounting systems and thus help us predict likely changes and their impact.

Accounting systems in socialist economies tend to be quite different from those in developed market economies such as the United States, Japan, and the EU countries. In the former socialist economies of Russia and Eastern Europe, for example, accounting is making a transition to a market approach. As far as public accounting and reporting in the market economies are concerned, however, a number of distinct models of accounting appear to be identifiable, including, at the very least, the British-American and continental European traditions. But given the factors of change at work, making accurate assessments or predictions about the future evolution of accounting is difficult. Because of the activities of many national and international organizations and the changing nature of business and especially multinational operations, accounting today is in a state of flux. It may well be that new models or patterns of accounting and reporting are being formed. The British and continental European traditions, for example, are now being coordinated and to some extent fused through EU efforts to harmonize accounting. Efforts to identify international patterns of accounting are discussed further in Chapter 3.

We will now discuss in greater detail some of the factors having the greatest influence on the development of accounting and information disclosure by corporations.

MAJOR DEVELOPMENTAL FACTORS

Corporations as Legal Entities

The emergence of corporations, the separation of ownership and control, and the development of securities markets have been particularly important for accountability and disclosure. There is little doubt that a highly influential factor in the United States, the United Kingdom, and other market economies was the recognition of corporations as legal entities with the public ownership of shares and the legal right of limited liability.

The characteristics of these early corporations necessitated disclosure to protect two groups in particular. First, as a consequence of limited liability, the resources available to creditors if the corporation were liquidated were limited to those of the corporation itself. Given that the liability of the shareholders was limited to their investment, disclosure was seen as a necessary means of regulation. Information disclosure, or "transparency," would help creditors determine the extent to which they were prepared to commit resources to the corporation as well as the use of resources they had already committed.

The second major reason for the close relationship between limited liability and disclosure was the protection of shareholders. The emerging entrepreneurs often came from backgrounds that did not give them easy access to the capital necessary to launch and expand individual projects. The introduction of limited liability removed a major disability. Those who owned capital often were unwilling to become involved in what frequently were risky projects because they stood to lose not only their investment but the rest of their personal wealth as well. Limited liability restricted the potential loss to the investment in the corporation. As many of these investors were not directly involved in the running of the business, it was considered essential for their protection that they should have access to information on a regular basis.

Accountability to those with a direct financial relationship with corporations has been strongly influenced by two other developments—the growth of professional management and the emergence of securities markets.

Professional Management

The separation of ownership and control of corporations appears to have resulted from the emergence of professional management composed of individuals whose positions of power within corporations stemmed from their possession of administrative and/or technical skills rather than ownership of the corporation's capital. The growth in size and increasing complexity of business is the basis for the growth in the importance of management. At the same time, in many countries (e.g., Italy, Greece, Switzerland) most businesses are still family owned and financed and, even where they are listed, control is retained by family holdings.

Whether, and to what extent, the separation of ownership from management and the division of the corporation into two essentially distinct groups result in behavior different from that of a corporation owned and controlled by the same persons is a matter of considerable controversy. Concern over the possibility of a conflict of interest when owners and management were different people and the bad experience of individual cases were further reasons for maintaining and expanding accounting and information disclosure. Owners could now be reassured that management was not behaving in a manner detrimental to the owners' interests.

Securities Markets

Corresponding to the growth in the number, size, and complexity of corporations was the demand for finance in the form of shares, or what is termed equity investment, as well as loans. This gave rise to the development of capital markets where the raising of finance could be facilitated. A major factor influencing accounting was the emergence of stock exchanges or securities markets, which have their origins in the desire of shareholders to trade their investments without liquidating the company, and the need for a mechanism to raise new finance in an efficient manner. The former reason, the exchangeability of shares, occupies the major portion of the market's time and energy, especially in countries such as the United States, the United Kingdom, and Japan. The relative market capitalization of the world's major developed securities markets is shown in Exhibit 2.1, from which it can be seen that the United States is dominant with a 46 percent share followed by Japan at 13 percent, to the U.K. at 8 percent, and France and Germany at 4 percent each.

There is also a growing number of securities markets that have been termed "emerging" markets (e.g., in China, Eastern Europe, and the developing countries of Africa). Indeed, securities markets are seen to be fundamental elements of the transition to a market economy, which necessarily involves the privatization of state-owned enterprises and the need to attract foreign investment.

The growth of securities markets necessitated the expansion of information availability to a wider audience: in particular, potential investors interested in buying and selling shares. As most private shareholders were not capable of comprehensively analyzing the financial disclosures of corporations, they tended to rely on specialist advisers and financial analysts. These analysts now act as interpreters of corporate reports for many investors, current and potential. In this way the information needs of investors, and financial analysts in particular, have acted as a constant pressure on corporations to increase both the quality and the quantity of their disclosures. Further, it has often been in the interests of corporations, and their managers, who are concerned to raise capital at favorable rates and to maximize the value of their corporation, to respond to such pressures. Thus, the emergence of securities markets has served to both deepen and broaden disclosure.

Exhibit 2.1   World Stock Market Capitalization: Major Markets (as of the end of 1999)

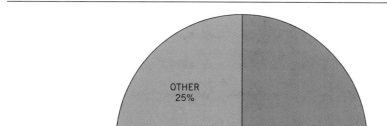

The importance of the information used by potential investors and the recommendations of financial analysts has meant that the financial disclosures of public corporations whose shares are traded have become publicly accessible. Corporate reports are available to groups other than investors and creditors not because of any pressure directly exerted by these groups but because of the necessity of available corporate information for unidentifiable potential investors.

The predominant influence of securities markets and their regulatory bodies in determining the quality and quantity of publicly available information in corporate reports is reflected in the strong correlation between well-developed markets and the degree of financial disclosure in corporate reports. Countries with active and well-developed markets (e.g., the United States and United Kingdom) generally have a greater degree of public financial disclosure than those with relatively less-developed markets.

Why is it that securities markets and the interests of shareholders/investors appear to have been the predominant force behind the emergence of public corporate disclosure? We have already argued that the existence of an active market necessitates the publication of financial information for share-trading decisions by shareholders and potential investors. What distinguishes shareholders from other finance providers is that most shareholders are "outsiders." Despite being nominal owners of the corporation, they have perhaps the least access to private information and arguably the least control unless they are institutional investors with significant shareholdings. The bargaining power of other finance providers (e.g., bankers) is such that these participants do not have to rely on published reports exclusively, if at all. In France and Germany, for example, the public ownership of shares in corporations is much less widespread than in the United States and the United Kingdom. In France, the government has played a major role in the supply of finance to corporations. In Germany, the banks are a significant source of loan finance and are often major equity investors in their own right.

These "other" finance providers generally have, as a result of their power, the ability to obtain considerably more detailed and up-to-date information than "outsiders." Therefore, disclosure to finance providers can be seen as a spectrum: at one end, that of least disclosure, are shareholders and investors (with the exception of those who are directly involved with the company). Toward the other end, information disclosure is less restricted and varies in its nature depending on the purpose for which it is required and the power of the finance provider.

The myth that shareholders control public corporations still persists nevertheless. While this may be the case for small private corporations where the number of investors is limited, it does not apply, in the normal course of events, to large public corporations. Private investors in public corporations, where there is usually a widespread dispersion of share ownership, tend to exert little direct influence on the running of a corporation. These shareholders are usually passive, exercising their "power" on the advice and initiative of management (i.e., the board of directors).

While the possibility of adverse changes in share prices may exert some indirect discipline on management, on account of their effect on financing potential and the possibility of takeover, this is unlikely to be significant in countries where there are few shareholders and where securities markets are of relatively less importance as sources of finance (e.g., in many continental European countries).

Reinforcing the relative lack of influence of shareholders in many countries has been the influence of governments, as in France and Sweden, in the development and use of accounting systems that facilitate the provision of information for national economic planning and control. In France, for example, a uniform for national accounting system was developed over the years as a basis for macroeconomic planning and corporate taxation. For many governments, including France, Germany, Italy, and Japan, the collection of taxes is closely linked to information disclosed by companies in their published accounts, and hence the tax rules have had a major influence on the accounting methods used. This is an entirely different orientation from the United States and the United Kingdom, where professional accountants have played a preeminent role in the development of accounting systems and forms of corporate reporting directed primarily to shareholders.

A Wider Audience

Accountability and information disclosure by corporations has developed historically in response to those with direct financial investment. In recent years, however, there has been an increasing acknowledgment that since finance providers, such as shareholders, bankers, lenders, and creditors, are not the only group affected by the actions of a corporation, there is an obligation to report to a wider audience, which includes employees, trade unions, consumers, government agencies, and the general public. There are a variety of reasons for this widespread belief that companies should explicitly disclose information to groups other than finance providers. One of the most significant is the development and growth of the influence of trade unions and employees in most developed countries. They have been instrumental in voicing the view that those who are significantly affected by decisions made by institutions in general must be given the opportunity to influence those decisions. Furthermore, there is growing public concern about the impact of corporations, especially in relation to so-called externalities (e.g., pollution of the environment and the influence of large corporations on national economic and social policies).

These developments, among others, have expanded the concept of "accountability" and the desire of various groups in society to monitor and influence the behavior of business corporations. Wider corporate accountability thus has become an issue of major interest in recent years. To what extent has it affected corporate reports? The development of accounting by corporations has been constrained by restrictions on both the supply and demand sides.

On the supply side, the goal divergence—where it exists—between corporation management and finance providers operates within a common framework. Differences are usually measurable and controllable. However, explicit acknowledgment of the "rights" of nonfinance providers, such as trade unions, to information may, for some corporations, mean that they would be committed to pursue goals other than those they have traditionally followed. From a managerial perspective, this could endanger the growth or survival of the corporation. The extent to which corporations have in practice been influenced in their behavior by the goals of nonfinance providers is another matter. But many corporations, regardless of what they actually do, have been reluctant to formally acknowledge the influence of other "stakeholders."

Corporate reports may be used as a source of information helpful for making decisions and reporting on management's stewardship. To the extent that the goals of finance providers and management are seen as not being completely compatible with those of nonfinance providers, increasing information disclosure may, therefore, be seen as increasing the power of the recipients to influence the behavior of the corporation as well as providing material for criticism of the corporation's performance.

A further constraint is that many of the expectations of nonfinance providers are not clearly defined—the techniques to measure them do not exist. While the information requests of finance providers relate to the periodic financial resources and position of a corporation and the results of its operations, many of the information requirements of nonfinance providers appear to relate to a corporation's social as well as economic performance. Not only are measurement techniques often unavailable or underdeveloped but often there is not even general agreement on the broad elements of accountability involved.

On the demand side, to the extent that nonfinance providers wish to use information, that which is made available for finance providers may in fact partially or even completely satisfy their information needs. Thus, in attempting to identify the special or unique information needs of nonfinance providers, there has been a tendency to ignore the possibility that they may wish to obtain or use information aimed at finance providers.

The ability of nonfinance providers to influence corporate behavior varies considerably. Those with limited or no influence can exert little direct pressure for increased disclosure, whereas those with some power may be able to bypass the published corporate report and obtain information directly, and in greater detail, in special reports. In many European countries, especially Germany and France, trade unions or employee representatives have, through various forms of "codetermination" or collective bargaining, obtained access to information. In Germany, for example, this right to disclosure is established in law with works councils given access to a wide range of financial and nonfinancial information. The philosophy behind this is that such access will promote mutual trust between employers and employees. The availability of information for bargaining with corporations can be double-edged, however, in the sense that the information may not substantiate opinions previously held and could therefore reduce rather than enhance the influence of the user group concerned.

An acknowledgment of a right of access to information implies certain political values—essentially those of liberal democracies, like those established in Western Europe. In countries where democracy is not as well established (e.g., in some African countries), the conditions necessary for increased accountability and disclosure are considerably less well developed.

An Evolutionary Process

Public accounting and disclosure in corporate reports has in the main been a spin-off from the evolution, over a considerable period of time, of accountability and disclosure to finance providers. The major impetus has been provided by the growth of active and well-developed securities markets. In many countries, such markets are not well developed, and while their limited maturity in this respect may not ultimately prevent wider disclosure, it would necessitate measures significantly different from those experienced in many of the developed countries.

ACCOUNTABILITY AND MULTINATIONAL ENTERPRISES

While we have considered the evolution of information disclosure by enterprises, we have not yet distinguished between those whose ownership and operations remain essentially in one country (i.e., domestic enterprises) and those that operate simultaneously in a number of countries (i.e., MNEs). What differentiates MNEs from domestic firms and how do, or should, these factors affect the accountability and reports of MNEs?

Foreign direct investment (FDI) by MNEs entails certain benefits and costs for host countries. In this context, the demand for greater disclosure from MNEs may be viewed as part of a bargaining process—an effort by host countries, and developing countries in particular, to improve their bargaining powers. The fact that MNEs operate in a number of different nation-states has given them an opportunity to take actions in their own best interest that are not available to others. This is the basis for a conflict of perspectives between that of a national view of various groups within the nation-state and the multinational view of the MNEs. While business activities in a single country are for many MNEs just a part of their global operation, this is the part that is of primary concern for most of those affected in the host country.

The multinationality, "size," and complexity of MNEs have enabled some of them to undertake actions detrimental to a host country. Cases of tax avoidance bordering on evasion, political interference, discriminatory practices, and so on are well documented. Whether these are exceptions or whether they represent more general practice is a matter of debate. The known cases, however, have been sufficient when combined with other factors to increase the pressure for greater accountability and disclosure.

Accountability by MNEs thus may be differentiated from accountability by domestic corporations, though both are business organizations with many features in common. A domestic corporation's primary operations are in one country and its cross-frontier relationships are with unrelated parties. On the other hand, MNEs operate in a number of countries with different laws and currencies, and there is usually a significant volume of transactions between units located in different countries. The common control of these globally dispersed operations provides the opportunity to coordinate pricing, sourcing, and location decisions in a manner that, while increasing the net return of the group, may be detrimental or, alternatively, advantageous to individual nation-states. This special impact of MNEs appears to have given rise to pressure for more accountability and information disclosure.

We will now look at the global environmental context in which MNEs operate and the influence of culture and international forces for change on the development of accounting internationally.

CULTURE AND THE GLOBAL ENVIRONMENT

Business and managerial behavior is strongly influenced by culture (i.e., shared value systems or attitudes) (Hofstede, 1980). National differences in culture patterns have emerged over long periods of time and have often maintained their stability over many generations. How does this happen and how does change occur?

The origins of culture, or societal values, can be found in a variety of factors affecting the ecological or physical environment. Societal values lead to the development and maintenance of institutions in society, which include family systems, social class structures, the political system, the legal system, the financial system, the nature of business ownership, the education system, and so on. These institutions, once developed, tend to reinforce societal values and the factors giving rise to such values. However, when change at the national level occurs, it is mainly as a result of external forces, through the forces of nature or the forces of people. With respect to the latter, international trade and investment (and multinational enterprises) are potent factors as are the major upheavals of war and colonization. In addition, scientific discovery (i.e., new technology) is a major factor for change. Such external forces affect societal values primarily through the physical environment, but they may also have an impact on the functioning of institutions in the short term by imposed force. Whether or not societal values will change in practice, however, is more likely to be the result of longer-term shifts in environmental conditions.

Culture, or societal values, at the national level may be expected to permeate organizational and occupational subcultures as well, though with varying degrees of integration. Accounting systems and practices can influence and reinforce societal values. With this in mind, we can perhaps obtain more fundamental insights than we have hitherto into why there are differences between national systems of accounting and reporting, both internal and external.

Figure 2.2 shows a model of the process whereby societal values influence the accounting subculture. The figure also shows the influence of societal values on the

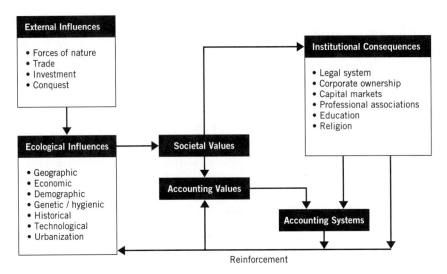

Figure 2.2 Culture, Societal Values, and the Accounting Subculture

Source: S. J.Gray, "Towards a Theory of Cultural Influence on the Development of Accounting Systems Internationally," *Abacus* (March 1988): 7.

institutional framework for the development of accounting, for example, the legal system, professional associations, and so on. Accordingly, the value system or attitudes of accountants are shown as being related to and derived from societal values and particularly work-related values. Accounting "values" or attitudes, for example, conservatism, will, in turn, have an impact on the development of accounting systems in the individual country. This is particularly true for measurement and disclosure practices and the approach to regulation, that is, statutory versus professional or self-regulation.

INTERNATIONAL PRESSURES FOR ACCOUNTING CHANGE

It may also be possible to appreciate the potential impact of forces for change that arise from international factors. Accordingly, the model developed by Gray (1988) to elaborate the process of accounting change is shown in Figure 2.3, which identifies a number of important international pressures affecting accounting change, including growing international economic/political interdependence, new trends in FDI, changes in multinational corporate strategy, the impact of new technology, the rapid growth of international financial markets, the expansion in business services, and the activities of international regulatory organizations.

Let us consider briefly some of the pressures for change that arise from growing international interdependencies and from concerns to harmonize the regulatory framework of international economic and financial relationships. Although basic distinctions have been made and may to some extent still be made between East and West (i.e., socialist countries and Western capitalist countries) and North and South (i.e., developed and developing countries), there are dramatic changes occurring at

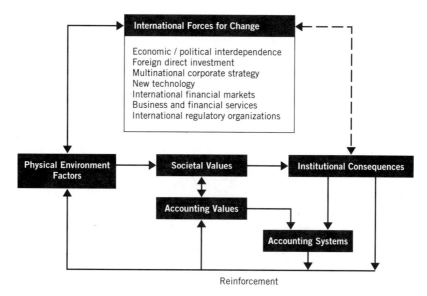

Figure 2.3   Change and Development of Accounting Values and Systems Internationally

Source: S. J. Gray, "International Accounting Research: The Global Challenge," *International Journal of Accounting 23*, no. 4 (Winter 1989): 294.

the political level, which in turn are causing economic changes that are restructuring the landscape of international business and accounting. Most notably, the hitherto centrally planned economies of the former Soviet Union and Eastern Europe are embracing a more Western market-oriented approach to economic development, as is the People's Republic of China. Furthermore, the growing worldwide trend toward the deregulation of markets and the privatization of public sector corporations in many developing as well as developed countries has opened up new opportunities for international investment and international joint ventures and alliances.

Economic groupings, such as the European Union (EU), have been a major influence in promoting economic integration through the free movement of goods, people, and capital between countries. To achieve its goals, the EU has embarked on a major program of harmonization, including measures to coordinate the company law, accounting, taxation, capital market, and monetary systems in the EU countries. While the goal of removing all nontariff barriers has proved elusive, the European Union has emerged as a major economic and, to some extent, political force in recent years. The European Union now has a membership of 15 nations and a potential market of 350 million consumers. Not only this, the EU is also committed to helping the process of economic integration on a broader Europe-wide scale following the events and reforms that have taken place in Eastern Europe. In time, the EU is likely to become further enlarged to accommodate even more European countries.

International organizations, such as the UN and the OECD, are also deeply involved in the development of international business on a global scale. The UN is responsible for the emergence of organizations such as the World Bank Group, the

International Monetary Fund (IMF), the UN Conference on Trade and Development (UNCTAD), the Conference on the Law of the Sea, the General Agreement on Tariffs and Trade (GATT), the World Trade Organization (WTO), and the Economic and Social Council (ECOSOC). UNCTAD includes the work of the former Commission on Transnational Corporations, which was designed to promote an effective international framework for the operations of transnational corporations and to monitor the nature and effects of their activities. In particular, the UNCTAD and its Intergovernmental Working Group of Experts on International Standards of Accounting and Reporting (ISAR) has been involved, among other things, in initiatives to develop international standards of accounting and reporting and to promote accounting education in Russia and Africa.

The OECD, in contrast to the UN, is focused mainly on the development of the industrialized countries of the world. The major objective of the OECD is to foster international economic and social development, and to this end a "Code of Conduct," including information disclosure guidelines, has been issued relating to the operations of multinationals to encourage them to develop positive relationships with host countries.

Although the relationships between MNEs and host countries have become less antagonistic and more pragmatic and businesslike in recent years, there are a number of areas of continuing concern. There is little doubt that MNEs exert a significant impact on the culture and social development of host countries. Employment and consumption patterns are often significantly influenced by MNEs. As a result, there is pressure for more accountability to employees and consumers and for some consultation with the parties affected by the decisions of MNEs.

The environmental impact of MNEs is also an area of major and growing importance in terms of accountability. Whereas developed countries have a growing array of regulations, developing countries tend to have lower standards, and are more concerned with improving economic conditions. At the same time, many MNEs have increased their awareness of pollution, safety procedures, and the need for stronger community relations. In this context, both the UN and OECD have been concerned with providing guidelines to MNEs, including the disclosure of relevant information, to encourage positive relationships with host countries.

At the level of international financial markets there has been concern to harmonize differences in tax regimes, exchange controls, restrictions on foreign investments, and accounting and disclosure requirements, which still provide obstacles to the globalization of securities markets. The OECD and especially the European Union have been influential in efforts to harmonize the minimum requirements for the admission of securities to listing and the content of prospectuses. In addition, the International Coordinating Committee of Financial Analysts Societies and the International Organization of Securities Commissions (IOSCO), both private organizations, are seeking to promote the internationalization and integration of securities markets on a global basis.

As to the internationalization of accounting and auditing standards, the International Accounting Standards Board (IASB) and the International Federation of Accountants (IFAC) are both involved in the harmonization effort and provide a professional counterpoint to the activities of intergovernmental organizations such as the UN, OECD, and the European Union.

This brief discussion of some of the international pressures for change high-lights the dynamic nature of accounting globally. National traditions and practices will be increasingly challenged in the years ahead as new problems are identified and the pressures for global harmonization escalate.

SUMMARY

1. Business and management practices are influenced by a variety of educational, sociocultural, legal, political, and economic factors.

2. Accounting is similarly influenced by a variety of environmental factors. These factors shape, reflect, and reinforce accounting characteristics unique to each national environment.

3. Major factors promoting the development of corporate reporting internationally include the ownership of stocks (shares) by the public, the growth of professional management, and the emergence of securities markets.

4. At the same time, major factors constraining public reporting and disclosure include the financing of business by banks and government agencies, the design of accounting information systems for government planning and control, and the influence of tax rules.

5. In recent years, a wider audience for corporate reports has been recognized including employees, trade unions, consumers, government agencies, and the general public.

6. Accountability and disclosure pressures on MNEs are different from those on domestic corporations because of the global reach, size, and complexity of MNE operations.

7. Culture is an important factor underlying the evolution of accounting systems internationally. Collective or societal values at the national level are likely to influence the attitudes of accountants and the development of accounting systems.

8. Major international forces for change are at work in the global environment including a growing international economic/political interdependence, new trends in FDI, changes in multinational corporate strategy, the impact of new technology, the rapid growth of international financial markets, the expansion in business services, and the activities of international regulatory organizations.

Discussion Questions

1. How is the business and cultural environment changing in your country? Are international factors becoming more important? Is accounting changing in response to changes in environmental influences? If so, in what way and with what effect?
2. How important is the stock market in your country? Is it getting more important? If so, how and why?
3. What international pressures for change in accounting do you think are going to be most important during the early years of the twenty-first century?
4. How important a constraint on change are national cultural differences likely to be? Are cultures themselves changing? In what way?

Exercise: National Accounting Development

Form into groups of three or four students and have each group select two countries for comparison from different regions of the world. Using a variety of country sources assess: (1) the major factors influencing accounting development in each country, (2) the relative importance of these factors.

Selected References

Baydoun, N. and R. Willett. 1995. "Cultural Relevance of Western Accounting Systems to Developing Countries," *Abacus* (March): 67–92.

Berle, A. Jr. and G. C. Means. 1932. *The Modern Corporation and Private Property.* New York: Macmillan.

Chatfield, Michael. 1977. *A History of Accounting Thought.* New York: Kreiger; Lee T. A. and R. H. Parker, 1979. *The Evolution of Corporate Financial Reporting.* London: Nelson.

Choi, Frederick D. S. 1974. "European Disclosure: The Competitive Disclosure Hypothesis," *Journal of International Business Studies* (Fall).

Edwards, J. R. 1989. *A History of Financial Accounting.* London: Routledge.

Farmer, R. and B. Richman. 1965. *International Business: An Operational Theory.* Homewood, IL: Irwin.

Galbraith, John K. 1967. *The New Industrial State.* Boston: Houghton Mifflin.

Gray, S. J. 1980. "The Impact of International Accounting Differences from a Security Analysis Perspective: Some European Evidence," *Journal of Accounting Research* (Spring).

Gray, S. J. 1998. "Towards a Theory of Cultural Influence on the Development of Accounting Systems Internationally," *Abacus* (March).

Gray, S. J. 1989. "International Accounting Research: The Global Challenge," *International Journal of Accounting,* 23 (4) (Winter).

Gray, S. J. and A. G. Coenenberg, eds. 1984. *EEC Accounting Harmonisation: Implementation and Impact of the Fourth Directive.* Amsterdam: North-Holland.

Hofstede, Geert. 1980. *Culture's Consequences: International Differences in Work-Related Values.* Beverly Hills: Sage.

Hofstede, Geert. 1991. *Cultures and Organisations: Software of the Mind.* London: McGraw-Hill.

Michael C. Jensen and William H. Meckling, 1976. "Theory of the Firm: Managerial Behaviour, Agency Costs, and Ownership Structure," *Journal of Financial Economics* (October).

Mueller, Gerhard, G. 1967. *International Accounting.* New York: Macmillan.

Nair, R. D. and Werner G. Frank. 1980. "The Impact of Disclosure and Measurement Practices on International Accounting Classifications." *Accounting Review* (July).

Nobes, C. W. 1983. "A Judgmental International Classification of Financial Reporting Practices," *Journal of Business Finance and Accounting* (Spring).

Organisation for Economic Cooperation and Development. 1976. *International Investment and Multinational Enterprises.* Paris: OECD, revised.

Perera, H. 1994. "Culture and International Accounting: Some Thoughts on Research Issues and Prospects," *Advances in International Accounting,* 7: 267–85.

Radebaugh, Lee H. 1975. "Environmental Factors Influencing the Development of Accounting Objectives, Standards and Practices in Peru." *International Journal of Accounting* (Fall).

United Nations Conference on Trade and Development. 1978. *Dominant Positions of Market Power of Transnational Corporations—Use of the Transfer Pricing Mechanism.* New York: UN.

United Nations. 1977. *International Standards of Accounting and Reporting.* New York: UN.

United Nations. 1988. *Conclusions on Accounting and Reporting by Transnational Corporations.* New York: UN, revised.

Zeff, S. A. 1972. *Forging Accounting Principles in Five Countries.* Champaign, IL: Stipes.

CHAPTER THREE

COMPARATIVE INTERNATIONAL FINANCIAL ACCOUNTING

Chapter Objectives

- Discuss different ways to identify and classify accounting systems internationally
- Examine the key dimensions of national culture and how they influence behavior in work situations
- Identify accounting values that influence comparative accounting practice
- Show how cultural values and accounting values relate to each other in the development of accounting standards and practices worldwide
- Compare accounting systems in the Anglo-American, Nordic, German, Latin, and Asian countries

INTRODUCTION

While there is a growing awareness of the varying influences of environmental factors on accounting development in a global context, many experts also realize that there may be systematically different patterns of accounting behavior applicable to various groups of countries. In this chapter we will examine the extent to which we can identify and classify accounting systems internationally. To assess whether there are systematic similarities or differences in accounting systems that may enable certain countries to be classified together, it is necessary to determine an appropriate scheme of classification. In essence, the classification of accounting and reporting systems, as in the case of political, economic, and legal systems, should sharpen our ability to describe, analyze, and predict the development of accounting systems. Such information is likely to provide useful input for strategic planning and control decisions and for formulating policies to harmonize international accounting systems.

PURPOSES OF INTERNATIONAL CLASSIFICATION

The classification process should help us describe and compare international accounting systems in a way that will promote improved understanding of the complex realities of accounting practice. The classification scheme should contribute to an improved understanding of (1) the extent to which national systems are similar to or different from each other, (2) the pattern of development of individual national systems with respect to each other and their potential for change, and (3) the reasons why some national systems have a dominant influence while others do not. Classification should also help policymakers assess the prospects and problems of international harmonization. Policymakers at national level will thus be in a better position to predict likely problems and identify solutions that may be feasible given knowledge of the experience of countries with similar development patterns. Developing countries seeking to choose an appropriate accounting system will also be better informed about the relevance for them of the systems used by other countries. The education of accountants and auditors who operate internationally would also be facilitated by an appropriate classification system. Similarly, such a system would enable problems involving the establishment of appropriate accounting and control systems for MNEs to be better understood and solved.

CLASSIFICATION OF ACCOUNTING AND REPORTING SYSTEMS

Research into the international classification of accounting systems has taken two main forms. In the deductive or judgmental approach, relevant environmental factors are identified and, by linking these to national accounting practices, international groupings or development patterns are proposed. In the inductive or empirical approach, individual accounting practices are analyzed, development patterns or groupings are then identified, and finally explanations keyed to a variety of economic, social, political, and cultural factors are proposed.

The Deductive Approach

The environmental analysis performed by Gerhard Mueller in his book *International Accounting* published in 1967 provides a pioneering starting point for discussing the deductive approach to accounting classification. Mueller identified four distinct approaches to accounting development.

1. In the *macroeconomic pattern,* business accounting correlates closely with national economic policies. The goals of the corporation usually follow rather than lead national economic policies. Here, accounting income might be smoothed to promote economic and business stability, depreciation rates adjusted to stimulate growth, special reserves created to pro-

mote investment, and social responsibility accounting developed to meet macroeconomic concerns. Mueller gave Sweden, France, and Germany as examples of this approach.

2. In the *microeconomic pattern,* accounting is viewed as a branch of business economics. In this pattern, a fundamental orientation exists toward individual economic entities. Here, accounting concepts are derived from economic analysis. A fundamental concept is concerned with the maintenance in real terms of the monetary capital invested in the corporation. Replacement-value accounting as used by some companies in the Netherlands is often assumed to fit the microeconomic approach, together with developments in segmental reporting and the disclosure of employee costs, pensions, long-term commitments, and so on.

3. In the *independent discipline* pattern, accounting is viewed as a service function and is derived from business practice. A deep-seated respect for pragmatism and judgment exists here. Accounting is considered to be capable of developing its own conceptual framework, derived on a piecemeal basis from its own successful business practices. Income is a pragmatic measure that seems useful in practice, and full and fair disclosure is a "generally accepted accounting principle" that has evolved over the years. Mueller cited the United States and the United Kingdom as comprehensive examples of this approach.

4. In the *uniform accounting* pattern, accounting is viewed as an efficient means of administration and control. Here, a more scientific approach to accounting is adopted whereby a uniform approach to measurement, disclosure, and presentation will promote ease of use and a means of control for all types of businesses by all kinds of users including managers, governments, and tax authorities. Centrally planned economies, as well as other countries with a strong government involvement in economic planning such as France, Germany, Sweden, and Switzerland, are given as typical examples.

While Mueller perceived all these judgmentally assessed patterns or approaches as closely linked to economic or business factors, he recognized a wider set of influences, such as legal system, political system, and social climate as relevant to accounting development, though without offering precise specification. Mueller, however, gave no explicit recognition to cultural factors, which were presumably subsumed within the set of environmental factors he identified.

Mueller's further contribution to the research on classifying international accounting was his categorization of business environments, which he then linked to different types of accounting systems. Using assessments of economic development, business complexity, political and social climates, and legal systems, Mueller identified 10 country groupings. Although Mueller pointed out that different business environments need different accounting systems, he did not empirically assess accounting differences in practice.

Mueller's environmental analysis was adapted and extended by Nobes (1983), who based his hypothetical classification on an evolutionary approach to the identification of measurement practices in developed Western nations. Nobes adopted a hierarchical scheme of classification (see Figure 3.1) to lend more subtlety and discrimination to the assessment of country differences. However, like Mueller, he made no explicit mention of cultural factors. Nobes made a basic distinction between microeconomic and macroeconomic systems, and a further disaggregation between business economics and business practice orientations under the micro-based classification. Under the macro-uniform based classification, he made a disaggregation between a government/tax/legal orientation and a government/economics orientation. He then hypothesized further disaggregations between U.K. and U.S. influences under the business practices orientation and between tax-based and law-based systems under the government/tax/legal orientation. The increased discrimination permitted by this analysis, however, is balanced by the problems of allocating countries to categories; for example, to tax-based or law-based families when both aspects are influential, as with France versus Germany. Japan is also difficult to categorize given the macro-based continental European influences of tax as well as the micro-based U.S. influence on the securities laws.

Nobes then tested this classification system by means of a judgmental analysis of measurement and valuation reporting practices in 14 developed countries. He used a structural approach to accounting practices whereby he assessed major features such as the importance of tax rules, the use of prudent/conservative valuation procedures, the making of replacement cost adjustments, and so on (see Exhibit 3.1). Nine factors were identified as those likely to predict which countries would be grouped together, and Nobes then scored these factors based on questionnaires and personal judgment.

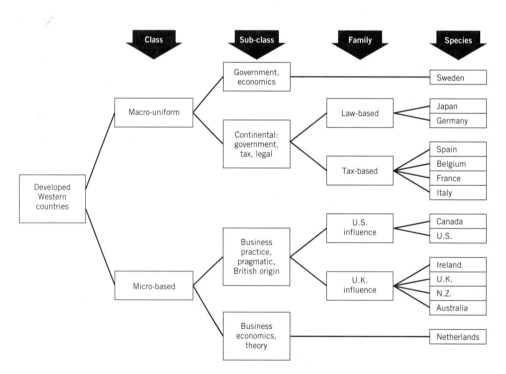

Figure 3.1   A Hypothetical Classification of Financial Reporting Measurement Practices in Developed Western Countries

Exhibit 3.1 Factors for Differentiation of Accounting Systems

1. Type of users of the published accounts of the listed companies
2. Degree to which law or standards prescribe in detail and exclude judgment
3. Importance of tax rules in measurement
4. Conservatism/prudence (e.g., valuation of buildings, stocks, debtors)
5. Strictness of application of historic cost (in the historic cost accounts)
6. Susceptibility to replacement cost adjustments in main or supplementary accounts
7. Consolidation practices
8. Ability to be generous with provisions (as opposed to reserves) and to smooth income
9. Uniformity between companies in application of rules

Source: C. W. Nobes, "A Judgmental International Classification of Financial Reporting Practices," *Journal of Business Finance and Accounting* (Spring 1983): 8.

While his statistical analysis provided strong support for the classification of countries as either micro-based or macro-based, it went little beyond this. Nevertheless, empirical research by Doupnik and Salter (1993) on a larger number of countries also provided broad support for Nobes' classifications. In a study of 50 countries, communist as well as capitalist, the macro/micro classification was clearly supported by both measurement and disclosure practices.

More recently, Nobes, (1998) has updated his classification scheme to distinguish between strong and weak equity market and shareholder orientations (see Figure 3.2). This incorporates changes that are taking place internationally whereby some companies in countries such as Germany and Japan are accounting on a basis consistent with U.S. generally accepted accounting principles (U.S. GAAP) or International Accounting Standards (IASs).

The Inductive Approach

By way of contrast to the studies discussed in the previous section, the inductive approach to identifying accounting patterns begins with an analysis of individual accounting practices. Perhaps the most important contribution of this type was by Nair and Frank (1980), who carried out a statistical analysis of international accounting practices using the Price Waterhouse surveys of 1973 and 1975. They made an empirical distinction between measurement and disclosure practices because these were considered to have different patterns of development.

The empirical results, using factor analysis applied to individual practices, showed that with respect to the Price Waterhouse (1973) data it was possible to identify four measurement groupings characterized broadly as the British Commonwealth, Latin American, continental European, and U.S. models. This is a result that seems plausible and fits quite well with prior research on national accounting systems. Regarding disclosure, however, seven groupings were identified that could not be plausibly described nor any explanation offered for the differences between them and the measurement groupings.

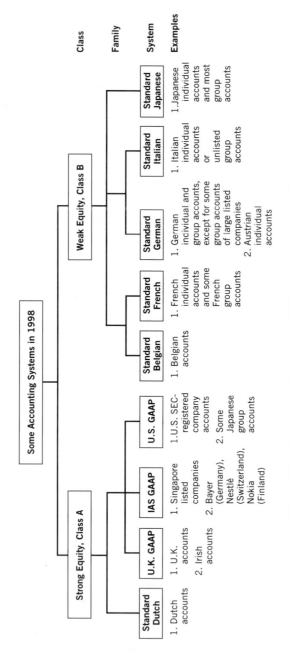

Figure 3.2 Reasons for International Differences in Financial Reporting

With respect to the Price Waterhouse (1975) data, it was possible to identify five measurement groupings of countries, with Chile as a single-country "group" (see Exhibit 3.2). However, the number of groupings increased to seven when disclosure practices were considered, the same number as in the results of the 1973 data analysis. The measurement groupings were characterized broadly, in this case, as the British Commonwealth, Latin American/south European, northern and central European, and U.S. models. The disclosure groupings, on the other hand, could not be similarly described nor any plausible description or explanation offered.

Subsequent to the identification of country groupings, Nair and Frank attempted to assess the relationships of these groupings with a number of explanatory variables. While relationships were established with respect to some of the variables—which included language (as a proxy for culture), various aspects of economic structure, and trading ties—it was clear that there were differences between the measurement and disclosure groupings. Moreover, the hypotheses that cultural and economic variables might be more closely associated with disclosure practices and trading variables might be more closely associated with measurement practices were not supported.

One problem with this type of research is the lack of reliability and relevance in the data for the research problem under investigation. There were problems in the Price Waterhouse surveys with respect to data errors, misleading answers, swamping of important questions by trivial ones, and exaggeration of differences between the United States and the United Kingdom. Perhaps the fundamental

Exhibit 3.2   Measurement Groupings (1975 Survey)

I British Commonwealth Model	II Latin American/ South European Model	III Northern and Central European Model	IV United States Model	V
Australia	Argentina	Belgium	Bermuda	Chile
Bahamas	Bolivia	Denmark	Canada	
Fiji	Brazil	France	Japan	
Iran	Colombia	Germany	Mexico	
Ireland	Ethiopia	Norway	Philippines	
Jamaica	Greece	Sweden	United States	
Malaysia	India	Switzerland	Venezuela	
Netherlands	Italy	Zaire		
New Zealand	Pakistan			
Nicaragua	Panama			
Rhodesia	Paraguay			
Singapore	Peru			
South Africa	Spain			
Trinidad	Uruguay			
United Kingdom				

Source: R. D. Nair and W. G. Frank, "The Impact of Disclosure and Measurement Practices on International Accounting Classifications," *Accounting Review* (July 1980): 433.

weakness of the surveys was that there was some confusion between the rules (mandatory and nonmandatory) and actual practices, which are often different.

From this review of some of the major studies in international classification it seems clear that research in this area is still in a relatively early stage with only very broad country groupings or accounting patterns so far identified. Furthermore, only very general relationships between environmental factors and accounting systems have been established.

Also noteworthy is the fact that in all this classification research, little explicit attention has been given to the influence of culture as a possibly more fundamental factor underlying differences in international accounting systems.

CULTURAL INFLUENCES ON ACCOUNTING SYSTEMS

In accounting, the importance of culture and its historical roots is now increasingly being recognized. While there has been a lack of attention to this dimension in the past in the international classification literature, Harrison and McKinnon proposed a methodological framework incorporating culture for analyzing changes in corporate financial reporting regulation at the nation-specific level. The use of this framework to assess the impact of culture on the form and functioning of accounting was demonstrated through an analysis of Japan's accounting system. Culture is considered an essential element in the framework for understanding how social systems change because "culture influences: (1) the norms and values of such systems; and (2) the behavior of groups in their interaction within and across systems."

Complementing this approach is the proposal by Gray (1988), briefly discussed in Chapter 2, that a theoretical framework incorporating culture could be used to explain and predict international differences in accounting systems and to identify patterns of accounting development internationally. More specifically, Gray explored the extent to which the cultural values identified by Hofstede (1980) from his cross-cultural research into work-related values could be helpful in this task.

CULTURE, SOCIETAL VALUES, AND ACCOUNTING

Structural Elements of Culture that Affect Business

Hofstede's pioneering research was aimed at detecting the structural elements of culture and particularly those that most strongly affect known behavior in the work situations of organizations and institutions. In perhaps one of the most extensive cross-cultural surveys ever conducted, psychologists collected data about "values" from the employees of an MNE located in more than 50 countries. Subsequent statistical analysis and reasoning revealed four underlying societal value dimensions— that is, collective values at the national level along which countries could be positioned. These dimensions, with substantial support from prior work in the field, were labeled Individualism, Power Distance, Uncertainty Avoidance, and Masculinity. Subsequent research by Hofstede and Bond (1988) into Chinese values revealed a fifth dimension: a short-term versus long-term orientation or what was termed Confucian Dynamism. Such dimensions, which we will discuss shortly, were perceived to represent elements of a common structure in cultural systems. It was also shown how countries could be grouped into culture areas, on the basis of their scores on the four value dimensions, using cluster analysis and taking into account geographical and historical factors. Exhibit 3.3 shows the countries within each of the identified culture areas and any identifiable subgroups of countries within each group.

If societal value orientations are related to the development of accounting systems, given that such values permeate a nation's social system, then—as Gray suggests—there should be a close match between culture areas and patterns of accounting systems internationally.

Exhibit 3.3   Culture Areas

More-developed Latin	Less-developed Latin	More-developed Asian
Belgium	Colombia	Japan
France	Ecuador	
Argentina	Mexico	
Brazil	Venezuela	
Spain	Costa Rica	
Italy	Chile	
Less-developed Asian	Guatemala	
	Panama	**African**
Indonesia	Peru	East Africa
Pakistan	Portugal	West Africa
Thailand	Salvador	
Taiwan	Uruguay	
India	**Near Eastern**	**Asian-colonial**
Malaysia	Arab countries	Hong Kong
Philippines	Greece	Singapore
	Iran	
	Turkey	
	Yugoslavia	
Germanic	**Anglo**	**Nordic**
Austria	Australia	Denmark
Israel	Canada	Finland
Germany	Ireland	Netherlands
Switzerland	New Zealand	Norway
	United Kingdom	Sweden
	United States	
	South Africa	

Source: G. Hofstede, *Culture's Consequences* (Beverly Hills: Sage, 1980), p. 336.

Further, assuming that Hofstede has correctly identified Individualism, Power Distance, Uncertainty Avoidance, Masculinity, and Confucian Dynamism as significant cultural value dimensions, it can then be argued that it should be possible to establish their relationship to "accounting values." If such a relationship exists, then a link between societal values and accounting systems can be established and the influence of culture assessed.

However, before an attempt can be made to identify significant accounting values that may be related to societal values, it is important to understand the meaning of the four value dimensions initially identified by Hofstede. These dimensions are well described by Hofstede (1984) as follows.

Individualism versus Collectivism. Individualism stands for the preference for a loosely knit social framework in society wherein individuals are supposed to take care of themselves and their immediate families only. Its opposite, collectivism, stands for the preference for a tightly knit social framework in which individuals expect their relatives, clan, or other in-group to look after them in exchange for unquestioning loyalty (the word "collectivism" is not used here to describe any particular political system). The fundamental issue addressed by this dimension is the degree of interdependence a society maintains among individuals. It relates to people's self-concept: "I" or "we."

Large versus Small Power Distance. Power Distance is the extent to which the members of a society accept that power in institutions and organizations is distributed unequally. This affects the behavior of the less powerful as well as the more powerful members of society. People in Large Power Distance societies accept a hierarchical order in which everybody has a place that needs no further justification. People in Small Power Distance societies strive for power equalization and demand justification for power inequalities. The fundamental issue addressed by this dimension is how a society handles inequalities among people when they occur. This has obvious consequences for the way people build their institutions and organizations.

Strong versus Weak Uncertainty Avoidance. Uncertainty Avoidance is the degree to which the members of a society feel uncomfortable with uncertainty and ambiguity. This feeling leads them to beliefs promising certainty and to maintain institutions protecting conformity. Strong Uncertainty Avoidance societies maintain rigid codes of belief and behavior and are intolerant of deviant persons and ideas. Weak Uncertainty Avoidance Societies maintain a more relaxed atmosphere in which practice counts more than principles and deviance is more easily tolerated. The fundamental issue addressed by this dimension is how a society reacts to the fact that time only runs one way and that the future is unknown, and whether it tries to control the future or just lets it happen. Like Power Distance, Uncertainty Avoidance has consequences for the way people build their institutions and organizations.

Masculinity versus Femininity. Masculinity stands for the preference in society for achievement, heroism, assertiveness, and material success. Its opposite, Femininity, stands for the preference for relationships, modesty, caring for the weak, and the quality of life. The fundamental issue addressed by this dimension is the way in which a society allocates social (as opposed to biological) roles to the sexes.

The fifth dimension, labeled Confucian Dynamism, refers to a short-term versus long-term orientation. This dimension is described as Confucian because the values involved seem to be identifiable with the teachings of Confucius, a legendary

Chinese intellectual of the sixth century B.C. The short-term orientation emphasizes respect for tradition; respect for social and status obligations regardless of cost; social pressure to "keep up with the Joneses," even if it means overspending; small savings levels and so little money for investment; a concern to get quick results; a concern for appearances; and a concern for truth rather than virtue. The long-term orientation, on the other hand, emphasizes the adaptation of traditions to meet modern needs; a respect for social and status obligations within limits; a thrifty and sparing approach to resources; large savings levels and so funds available for investment; perseverance toward achieving gradual results; a willingness to subordinate personal interests to achieve purpose; and a concern for a virtuous approach to life.

Accounting Values

Having identified societal values, is it possible to identify significantly related accounting values at the subcultural level of the accountant and accounting practice? Gray (1988) proposed the identification of four accounting values, derived from a review of accounting literature and practice, as follows:

1. *Professionalism versus statutory control:* This value reflects a preference for the exercise of individual professional judgment and the maintenance of professional self-regulation as opposed to compliance with prescriptive legal requirements and statutory control.

2. *Uniformity versus flexibility:* This value reflects a preference for the enforcement of uniform accounting practices between companies and for the consistent use of such practices over time, as opposed to flexibility in accordance with the perceived circumstances of individual companies.

3. *Conservatism versus optimism:* This value reflects a preference for a cautious approach to measurement that enables one to cope with the uncertainty of future events as opposed to a more optimistic, laissez-faire, risk-taking approach.

4. *Secrecy versus transparency:* This value reflects a preference for confidentiality and the disclosure of information about the business only to those who are most closely involved with its management and financing as opposed to a more transparent, open, and publicly accountable approach.

What arguments are there to support these accounting value dimensions? How do they relate to societal values? What impact are they likely to have on the development of national accounting systems?

Professionalism versus Statutory Control   Gray proposed this as a significant accounting value dimension because accountants are perceived to adopt independent attitudes and to exercise their individual professional judgments, to a greater or lesser extent, throughout the world.

A major controversy in many Western countries, for example, surrounds the issue of the extent to which the accounting profession should be subject to public regulation or statutory control or should be permitted to retain control over accounting standards as a matter of private self-regulation.

The development of professional associations has a long history, but they are much more firmly established in the Anglo-American countries, such as the United States and the United Kingdom than in some of the continental European countries (e.g., France, Germany, and Switzerland, and in many of the less developed countries).

In the United Kingdom, for example, the concept of presenting "a true and fair view" of a company's financial position and results depends heavily on the judgment of the accountant as an independent professional. This is so to the extent that accounting information disclosures beyond, and sometimes contrary to, what is specifically required by law may be necessary. This contrasts with the traditional position in France and Germany, where the professional accountant's role has been concerned primarily with the implementation of relatively prescriptive and detailed legal requirements. With the implementation of the EU directives in the 1980s, this situation was changed to the extent that there is some movement, if not convergence, toward a more statutory approach.

To what extent then can professionalism be linked to the societal values of Individualism, Power Distance, Uncertainty Avoidance, Masculinity, and Long-Term Orientation? Professionalism can be linked perhaps most closely with the individualism and uncertainty-avoidance dimensions. A preference for independent professional judgment is consistent with a preference for a loosely knit social framework where there is more emphasis on independence, a belief in individual decisions, and respect for individual endeavor. This is also consistent with weak uncertainty avoidance where practice is all important, where there is a belief in fair play and as few rules as possible, and where a variety of professional judgments tend to be more easily tolerated. There also appears to be a link, if less strong, between professionalism and power distance in that professionalism is more likely to be accepted in a small power-distance society where there is more concern for equal rights, where people at various power levels feel less threatened and more prepared to trust each other, and where there is a belief in the need to justify the imposition of laws and codes. Professionalism would also seem to be linked with masculinity and short-term orientation to the extent that this implies a concern with individual assertiveness and social status.

Uniformity versus Flexibility   This is a significant accounting value dimension because attitudes about uniformity, consistency, or comparability are a fundamental feature of accounting principles worldwide. This value is open to different interpretations, ranging from a relatively strict intercompany and intertemporal uniformity, to consistency within companies over time and some concern for comparability between companies, to relative flexibility of accounting practices to suit the circumstances of individual companies.

In countries like France and Spain, for example, a uniform accounting plan as well as the imposition of tax rules for measurement purposes have long been in operation because there has been a concern to facilitate national planning and the pursuit of macroeconomic goals. In contrast, in the United Kingdom and the United States there has been more concern with intertemporal consistency and some degree of intercompany comparability because of a perceived need for flexibility.

To what extent can uniformity be linked to societal value dimensions? Uniformity can be linked perhaps most closely with the uncertainty-avoidance and individualism dimensions. A preference for uniformity is consistent with a preference for strong uncertainty avoidance, which leads in turn to a concern for law and order and rigid codes of behavior, a need for written rules and regulations, a respect for conformity, and the search for ultimate, absolute truths and values. This value dimension is also consistent with a preference for collectivism, as opposed to individualism, with its tightly knit social framework, belief in organization and order, and respect for group norms. There also seems to be a link, if less strong, between uniformity and power distance: uniformity is more easily facilitated in a large power-distance society in that the imposition of laws and codes promoting uniformity are more likely to be accepted.

Conservatism versus Optimism   This is a significant accounting value dimension because it is arguably "the most ancient and probably the most pervasive principle of accounting valuation" (Sterling, 1967).

Conservatism or prudence in asset measurement and the reporting of profits is seen as a fundamental attitude of accountants the world over. Moreover, conservatism varies according to country, ranging from a strongly conservative approach in Japan and some continental European countries (such as France, Germany, and Switzerland) to the much less conservative, risk-taking attitudes of accountants in the United States, the United Kingdom, and, to some extent, the Netherlands.

The varying impact of conservatism on accounting measurement practices internationally has also been demonstrated empirically. Such differences appear to be reinforced by the relative development of capital markets, the differing pressures of user interests, and the influence of tax laws on accounting practice in the countries concerned.

To what extent, then, can conservatism be linked to societal value dimensions? Conservatism can be linked perhaps most closely with the uncertainty-avoidance dimension and the short-term versus long-term orientations. A preference for more conservative measures of profits and assets is consistent with strong uncertainty avoidance that stems from a concern with security and a perceived need to adopt a cautious approach to cope with the uncertainty of future events. A less conservative approach to measurement is also consistent with a short-term orientation where quick results are expected and hence a more optimistic approach is adopted relative to conserving resources and investing for long-term results. There also seems to be a link, if less strong, between high levels of individualism and masculinity, on the one hand, and weak uncertainty avoidance on the other, to the extent that an emphasis on individual achievement and performance is likely to foster a less conservative approach to measurement.

Secrecy versus Transparency   This is a significant accounting value dimension that stems as much from management as it does from the accountant because of the influence of management on the quality and quantity of information disclosed to outsiders. Secrecy, or confidentiality, in business relationships is nevertheless a fundamental accounting attitude.

Secrecy also appears to be closely related to conservatism. Both values imply a cautious approach to corporate financial reporting in general, but secrecy relates to the disclosure dimension and conservatism relates to the measurement dimension. The extent of secrecy appears to vary across countries, with lower levels of disclosure—including instances of secret reserves—evident in Japan and continental

European countries such as France, Germany, and Switzerland than in the United States and United Kingdom. These differences also seem to be reinforced by the differential development of capital markets and the public ownership of shares, which often provide incentives for the voluntary disclosure of information.

To what extent then can secrecy be linked to societal value dimensions? A preference for secrecy is consistent with strong uncertainty avoidance because the latter stems from the need to restrict the disclosure of information to outsiders to avoid conflict and competition and to preserve security. A close relationship between secrecy and power distance also seems likely in that high power-distance societies are likely to be characterized by the restriction of information to preserve power inequalities. Secrecy is also consistent with a preference for collectivism, as opposed to individualism, in that its concern is for the interests of those most closely involved with the firm rather than external parties. A long-term orientation also suggests a preference for secrecy that is consistent with the need to conserve resources within the firm and ensure that funds are available for investment relative to the demands of shareholders and employees for higher payments. A significant but possibly less important link with masculinity also seems likely to the extent that in societies where there is more emphasis on achievement and material success there will be a greater tendency to publicize such achievements and success.

A matrix showing the nature of the relationships of accounting values with societal values is shown in Exhibit 3.4.

Accounting Values and International Classification

Having related societal values to international accounting values, it is possible, as Gray argues, to make a useful distinction between the authority for accounting systems on the one hand—that is, the extent to which such systems are determined and enforced by statutory control or professional means—and the measurement and disclosure characteristics of accounting systems, on the other. In this way, accounting values can be linked to specific accounting system characteristics (see Figure 3.3).

The accounting values that are most relevant to the professional or statutory authority for accounting systems as well as their enforcement appear to be professionalism and uniformity. Both are concerned with regulation and the degree of enforcement or conformity. Accordingly, these can be combined and the classification of culture areas hypothesized on a judgmental basis, as shown in Figure 3.4. In making these judgments, we will refer to the relevant correlations between value dimensions and the clusters of countries identified from the statistical analyses carried out by Hofstede. From this classification it seems clear that the Anglo and Nordic culture areas can be contrasted with the Germanic and more-developed Latin culture areas as well as the Japanese, near Eastern, less-developed Latin, less-developed Asian, and African culture areas. The former colonial Asian Countries are separately classified because they represent a mixture of influences.

The accounting values most relevant to the measurement practices used and the extent of information disclosed are, self-evidently, the conservatism and secrecy dimensions respectively. These can therefore be combined and the classification of culture areas hypothesized on a judgmental basis, as shown in Figure 3.5. As before,

Exhibit 3.4   Matrix of Relationship of Accounting Values with Societal Values

Basic Value System	Professionalism	Statutory Control	Uniformity	Flexibility	Conservatism	Optimism	Secrecy	Transparency
Individualism	Positive	Negative	Negative	Positive	Negative	Positive	Negative	Positive
Collectivism	Negative	Positive	Positive	Negative	Positive	Negative	Positive	Negative
Large Power Distance	Negative	Positive	Positive	Negative	n/a	n/a	Positive	Negative
Small Power Distance	Positive	Negative	Negative	Positive	n/a	n/a	Negative	Positive
Strong Uncertainty Avoidance	Negative	Positive	Positive	Negative	Positive	Negative	Positive	Negative
Weak Uncertainty Avoidance	Positive	Negative	Negative	Positive	Negative	Positive	Negative	Positive
Masculinity	Positive	n/a	n/a	n/a	Negative	Positive	Negative	Positive
Femininity	Negative	n/a	n/a	n/a	Positive	Negative	Positive	Negative
Short term	Positive	Negative	n/a	n/a	Negative	Positive	Negative	Positive
Long term	Negative	Positive	n/a	n/a	Positive	Negative	Positive	Negative

Note: n/a = not applicable.

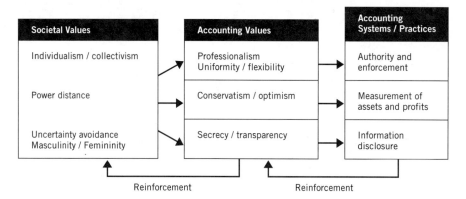

Figure 3.3 Culture and Accounting Systems in Practice

in making judgments about these classifications, we have again referred to the relevant correlations between value dimensions and the resultant clusters of countries identified from the statistical analysis carried out by Hofstede. Here again, there appears to be a sharp division of culture area groupings with the former Asian-colonial group relating more closely with the Anglo and Nordic groupings. This can be contrasted with the Germanic and more-developed Latin groupings, which

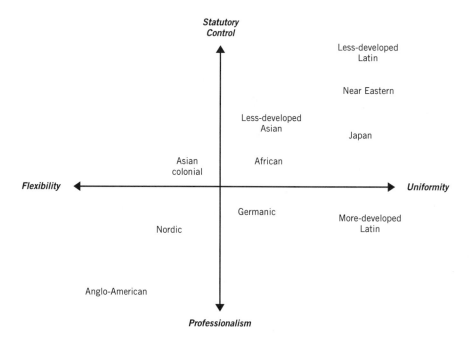

Figure 3.4 Accounting Systems: Authority and Enforcement

Source: S. J. Gray, "Towards a Theory of Cultural Influence on the Development of Accounting Systems Internationally," *Abacus* (March 1988): 12.

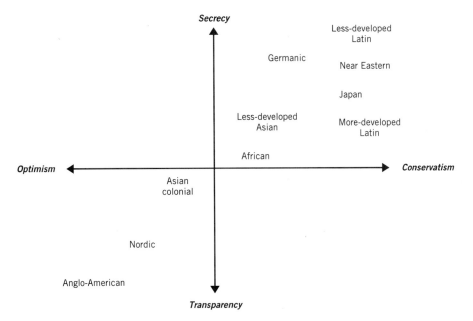

Figure 3.5   Accounting Systems: Measurement and Disclosure

Source: S. J. Gray, "Towards a Theory of Cultural Influence on the Development of Accounting Systems Internationally," *Abacus* (March 1988): 13.

are related to the Japanese, less-developed Asian, African, less-developed Latin, and Near Eastern-area groupings. In broad terms, countries can be grouped as either relatively optimistic and transparent or relatively conservative and secretive.

This classification of country groupings by culture area can be used as a basis for further assessing the relationship between culture and accounting systems. This classification is particularly relevant for understanding systems authority and enforcement characteristics, on the one hand, and measurement and disclosure characteristics, on the other.

In the wake of Gray's analysis, further research is needed to test the extent to which culture influences the development of international accounting practices and whether the hypothesized country groupings can be empirically supported. The research findings to date do tend to support the significance of culture as an influential factor in the development of accounting. Salter and Niswander (1995) concluded from an empirical study of twenty-nine countries that Gray's model "provided a workable theory to explain cross-national differences in accounting structure and practice which is particularly strong in explaining different financial reporting practices." To explain professional and regulatory structures, however, Salter and Niswander suggested that the inclusion of variables such as the development of financial markets and levels of taxation enhances the explanatory power of the model.

With respect to the conservatism dimension, empirical studies of profit measurement practices in France, Germany, the Netherlands, Sweden, the United Kingdom, and the United States indicate the existence of significant differences that support the importance of this dimension internationally.

The significance of the secrecy/transparency dimension has also received some support from recent research findings on information disclosure practices in some major countries, including Canada, France, Germany, Japan, the Netherlands, Switzerland, the United Kingdom, and the United States.

COMPARATIVE ACCOUNTING SYSTEMS

In this section we will outline the accounting systems of a selection of countries using the cultural classification identified earlier as the basis for discussion. Accordingly, we will review the accounting systems of the United States and the United Kingdom as major countries in the Anglo-American culture area, the Netherlands and Sweden as representatives of the Nordic countries, Germany and Switzerland as representatives of the Germanic countries, France, Italy, and Brazil as representatives of the Latin countries, and China and Japan as representatives of the Asian countries.

ANGLO-AMERICAN ACCOUNTING

There is no doubt that Anglo-American accounting can be distinguished from accounting in continental Europe, Asia, Latin America, and many other parts of the world. It is practiced not only in the United States and United Kingdom but also to an important extent in countries and regions where, for example, the United Kingdom has had a major colonial influence, such as in Australia, Canada, Hong Kong, India, Ireland, Kenya, Malaysia, New Zealand, Nigeria, Singapore, and South Africa. Anglo-American accounting tends to be relatively less conservative and more transparent than that of the Germanic and Latin countries and Japan.

United States

Accounting in the United States is very similar to the United Kingdom, as might be expected given the importance of the historical and investment connections between the two countries. Just as the language and legal system of the United States were exported from the United Kingdom, so too were the founding fathers of U.S. accounting, including pioneers such as Arthur Young (a Glasgow University graduate of the 1880s). Nevertheless, the United States has adapted rather than adopted the United Kingdom's accounting tradition. Indeed, recent historical and environmental circumstances of the United States have given rise to some significant distinguishing features.

In the United States, accounting is focused very much on large corporations and the interests of investors, though the needs of creditors and other users are recognized. The relevance of information to business decisions is paramount subject to the constraint of reliability.

The securities markets are the dominant influence on accounting regulation in the United States. Dealings in securities and investor protection are regulated and enforced at the federal government level under the Securities Act of 1933 and the Securities Exchange Act of 1934, which were passed in response to the stock market crash of 1929 and subsequent financial crises.

The Securities and Exchange Commission (SEC) was established with the legal authority to enforce the securities laws and also to formulate as well as enforce accounting standards. However, the SEC recognizes as authoritative the "Generally Accepted Accounting Principles" (GAAP) embodied in standards issued by an independent Financial Accounting Standards Board (FASB), which was established in 1973 following criticism of the standard-setting procedures of the American Institute of Certified Public Accountants. Thus, the standard-setting role has been delegated to the FASB with the SEC acting in only a supervisory capacity unless it deems it necessary to intervene, which it has done only on rare occasions (e.g., with respect to oil and gas accounting). Corporations are required to follow FASB standards, otherwise the SEC will refuse registration and hence trading in their securities. It should be noted that only listed corporations (a minority of U.S. corporations) are required to comply with the very detailed regulations imposed by the SEC for investor protection purposes.

The FASB has a very open approach to standard-setting known as operating "in the sunshine." All meetings are open to the public and a variety of opinions are sought in an elaborate "due process" to ensure that the public interest is properly served. To help formulate new standards and improve existing ones, the FASB has developed an explicit conceptual framework of objectives and qualitative characteristics for financial reporting in its series of statements on financial accounting concepts. The FASB's pronouncements on accounting practice are issued as Statements of Financial Accounting Standards (SFAS). More than 135 of these had been issued by 2000. Taken together, the FASB standards are quite detailed and voluminous compared to, for example, U.K. standards. This suggests that while the United States is similar in many ways to the United Kingdom, it is unique in having perhaps the most comprehensive system of accounting regulations in the world, at least as far as securities markets are concerned.

United Kingdom

In the United Kingdom, as in the United States, primacy of place is given to the information needs of investors. It is expected, however, that most of the needs of other groups will be similar to those of investors and will thus be satisfied in any event. The special needs of other groups are usually met privately or on a voluntary basis (e.g., a value-added statement for employees).

Like the United States, the securities markets of the United Kingdom have a significant influence on accounting practice, but they do not dominate the process of accounting regulation. Company law in the United Kingdom has a much wider remit than the U.S. securities laws as far as the provision of accounting information is concerned. The U.K. Companies Act of 1985, which consolidated all previous extant companies acts and was amended by the companies act passed in 1989, includes accounting requirements for *all* limited liability companies, not just large companies or those listed on stock exchanges. In addition, the accountancy profession and, to a lesser extent, the stock exchange are involved in the accounting regulatory process.

There have been a number of substantial revisions to U.K. company law in recent years, primarily to implement the EU Fourth Directive on company accounts and the Seventh Directive on consolidated accounts, in 1981 and 1989, respectively. Prior to the 1980s, company law was perceived as providing little more than a framework for accounting regulation within which the accounting profession could set more detailed accounting rules or standards as appropriate. While company law did in fact incorporate specific requirements, these were mainly concerned with disclosure, thus leaving matters of accounting treatment to the judgment of the profession. This flexible approach is still enshrined in the legal requirement that company accounts must present "a true and fair view" of a company's results and financial position. This is a principle that overrides the detailed requirements of the law, and accounting standards for that matter, to the extent that additional or, in exceptional circumstances, alternative information should be provided. The principle that accounts should present a true and fair view has also been adopted by the EU in its accounting directives.

The accounting profession in the United Kingdom has enjoyed a substantial amount of independence since professional associations were first formed in the 1850s. Accounting was very much an "independent discipline" derived from the needs of individual businesses. Accountants were independent professionals making judgments, either as company accountants or as auditors, on the appropriate method to be used in individual accounts. This accounting tradition has now evolved to a much more regulated state as a result of criticisms concerning the flexibility of professional accounting standards used in the preparation of company accounts as well as governmental pressures and developments in EU harmonization.

In 1970, to stave off government intervention and the creation of a U.S.-style SEC, the profession set up its own self-regulatory organization, the Accounting Standards Steering Committee (ASSC), which was subsequently renamed the Accounting Standards Committee (ASC). The aim of the ASC was to develop Statements of Standard Accounting Practice (SSAPs) with adoption and enforcement being the responsibility of the six professional bodies involved. A total of 25 SSAPs were issued by the ASC under this system up until 1990 when, following sustained criticism of its effectiveness in curbing "creative accounting," a new standard-setting framework was established. An independent Accounting Standards Board (ASB), similar to the FASB in the United States, was set up, guided by a Financial Reporting Council (FRC), which represented a wide constituency of interests.

The new ASB has the power to issue Financial Reporting Standards (FRSs) on its own authority. There is also a legal sanction for companies that do not comply with FRSs in that any departures from accounting standards must be explained and the financial effects disclosed. The FRC's Financial Reporting Review Panel and the Department of Trade and Industry are also empowered to investigate complaints about departures from accounting standards that do not appear to result in a true and fair view and to go to the courts, if necessary, to require a company to revise its accounts. The ASB recognizes that the requirement to give a true and fair view may justify a departure from accounting standards, but it is imposing a stricter regime than in the past that is consistent with the statement that "because accounting standards are formulated with the objective of ensuring that the information resulting from their application faithfully represents the underlying commercial activity, the Board envisages that only in exceptional circumstances will departure from the requirements of an accounting standard be necessary in order for financial statements to give a true and fair view" (Foreword to Accounting Standards, June 1993, paragraph 18).

NORDIC ACCOUNTING

Accounting in the Nordic countries is in some respects similar to that of the Anglo-American countries, but there are some important Germanic influences, especially regarding the significance of taxation. This group includes the Netherlands, Denmark, Sweden, and Finland (all members of the European Union) as well as Norway. Nordic accounting tends to be less conservative and more transparent than the Germanic and Latin countries, but not as much as the Anglo-American group of countries.

The Netherlands

The Netherlands is famous for its business economics approach to accounting. While investors have pride of place as users of accounts, the information needs of other users and especially employees are recognized on a voluntary basis. The practice of social reporting has been established since the 1970s and involves disclosures mainly about employment and personnel policies in both annual reports and special reports.

Accounting in the Netherlands is similar in many ways to that of the United Kingdom and the Anglo-American approach as a whole. Company law and the accounting profession are the major influences, and although the number of companies listed on the stock exchange is relatively small, there is more of a tradition of public ownership of shares and an international business outlook than in many other continental European countries.

Company law in the Netherlands is incorporated in the Civil Code, which is based on the Roman law system. It is similar to most continental European countries except that the Civil Code traditionally has not provided a detailed framework. Governments have had a somewhat laissez-faire attitude to commerical matters, much like the United Kingdom. However, the influence of company law has grown steadily since 1970 through the Act on the Annual Accounts of Enterprises and the implementation of the EU Fourth and Seventh Directives, in 1983 and 1988, respectively. Before 1970 there was a virtual absence of legislation on accounting, a gap that was filled by the influential Dutch accounting profession now known as the Royal Nederlands Institut van Registeraccountants (NIVRA).

Despite the currently fairly detailed provisions of the Civil Code, the overriding criterion is the application of "generally acceptable accounting principles," which is more or less the Dutch equivalent of the U.K. "true and fair view." Guidelines as to what are "acceptable"—as opposed to the U.S. "accepted"—principles are provided by the Council for Annual Reporting, which consists of representatives of the employers, users, employees, and the accounting profession (NIVRA). While these guidelines, which complement and supplement the law just as the accounting standards in the United Kingdom do, are not mandatory, they are followed by most companies.

A novel feature of regulation in the Netherlands is the Civil Code provision that interested parties, including shareholders, employees, works councils, and trade unions may complain to the Enterprise Chamber (Ondernemingskamer) of the Court of Justice in Amsterdam if they believe that the accounts do not comply with the law. Hence, through this means the company law is being supplemented by a body of interpretative case law. This is perhaps another example of the unique Dutch compromise between the continental European and Anglo-American legal traditions and culture.

Sweden

The accounting tradition in Sweden gives preference to the information needs of creditors, government, and the tax authorities. However, this situation has been changing quite fast because of the growing involvement of major Swedish companies in international mergers and acquisitions and their need to seek finance in international financial markets. The Swedish stock market has also grown in importance and is a potential focal point for the Nordic countries. Recent developments suggest the emergence of a two-tier approach to corporate reporting, with the accounts of individual companies prepared on a traditional basis in contrast to the consolidated accounts of major groups, which may be focused more on shareholder information needs and the standards applicable in an international capital market context.

While the development of accounting in Sweden, as in France and Germany, has been strongly influenced by legal and taxation requirements, there is also a tradition in Sweden of involvement by the accounting profession in the standard-setting process. The influence of the stock exchange is also important with respect to accounting and disclosure by large corporations. Many of these corporations are multinationals and are thus exposed to international capital market pressures. But in contrast to the Netherlands, the overriding influence in Sweden has been the state, which has been committed, in general, to the use of accounting information for the purpose of macroeconomic planning and policy making. In this regard, the Swedish tax system has been used aggressively to promote macroeconomic objectives and as such has encouraged a more conservative approach to income measurement.

Company law governing accounting is embodied in the 1975 Companies Act, the 1976 Accounting Act, and the 1981 Act on the Annual Accounts in Certain Forms of Business Enterprise. While the Accounting Act required that generally accepted accounting principles be followed, these principles were not defined. However, this situation was changed somewhat following the New Accounting Act of 1995, which implemented the EU Accounting Directives. Over the years, the law has tended to provide a framework rather than detailed requirements. This flexibility has enabled the Swedish accounting profession, the Foreningen Auktoriserade Revisorer (FAR), founded in 1923, to play an influential role by making recommendations on accounting matters. However, in 1976, the government established the Bokforingsnamnden (BFN), or Accounting Standards Board, to make recommendations on accounting matters within the framework of company law.

More recently, in 1991, an Accounting Council (Redovisningsradet) was established to take over the standard-setting role of the FAR but in the form of a body that is representative of a broader constituency (i.e., industry, government, and the profession) and also independent of the accounting profession, like the FASB in the United States. The stock exchange supports both the new Accounting Council and BFN and, in addition, encourages listed companies to disclose additional information about their performance, prospects, financial goals and strategies, and the company's business environment. It is noteworthy that the recommendations issued by the Accounting Standards Board and the Accounting Council are not mandatory but advisory in the context of company law. In practice, therefore, the approach to accounting standard-setting in Sweden seems to be very much consensus oriented and somewhat flexible despite the legalistic and taxation influences at work.

GERMANIC ACCOUNTING

In many respects, the Germanic group of countries differs significantly from the Anglo-American and Nordic groups. The influences of company law and taxation are paramount. The Germanic group includes Germany and Austria (members of the European Union) as well as Israel and Switzerland. Germanic accounting has also had some influence in France, Japan, and a number of former European colonies in Africa. Germanic accounting tends to be relatively conservative and secretive compared to Anglo-American accounting.

Germany

The accounting tradition in Germany gives preference to the information needs of creditors and the tax authorities. However, large listed corporations and especially MNEs are now aiming to present more shareholder-oriented corporate reports.

Company law seems to be the predominant influence on accounting in Germany. The legal system in Germany is highly codified and prescriptive because it is based on the Roman law system as opposed to the Anglo-American common law system. The laws on accounting in Germany amend the Commercial Code (Handelsgesetzbuch). A tradition of uniformity in accounting has dominated Germany and has led to the development of uniform accounting in France. The German tax laws are also a strong influence to the extent that the annual accounts form the basis for the tax accounts. This principle is known in Germany as the "Massgeblichkeitsprinzip." Thus, any allowance or deduction claimed for tax purposes must be charged in the annual accounts.

The accounting profession is relatively small, and professional pronouncements have much less status than do those, for example, in the United States, the United Kingdom, and the Netherlands. The German stock market is still relatively small, reflecting the fact that the major sources of finance have been the banks along with the government and family interests. Those corporations that are listed tend to be quite closely held by these interested parties. Nevertheless, the stock market is becoming more important in Germany, and many German MNEs are listed in other European countries with a growing number also listed in the United States. This is influencing corporate reporting behavior and encouraging some voluntary disclosure of information.

The Commercial Code sets out the detailed accounting requirements governing limited liability corporations. This was revised by the Accounting Directives Law of 1985, which implemented the EU Fourth and Seventh Directives. While the concept of "a true and fair view" was incorporated in the EU directives, this seems to have been interpreted for German purposes as a requirement to present transparent and reliable financial statements in accordance with the legal provisions. In practice, the tax rules tend to dominate legal decisions on accounting issues, and hence the development of accounting principles within the legal framework can be traced to this source rather than to the accounting profession, which consists of the Institut der Wirtschaftsprüfer in Deutschland (IDW) and the Wirtschaftsprüferkammer. Most recently, however, a German Accounting Standards Board has been established similar to the FASB in the United States and the Commercial Code revised to permit consolidated accounts to be prepared on the basis of U.S. GAAP or International Accounting Standards.

Switzerland

Much like Germany, the accounting tradition in Switzerland gives preference to the information needs of creditors and the authorities. However, the importance of the Swiss securities market is growing, and many large Swiss companies are seeking capital in international financial markets. As a result, a growing number of large companies are making extensive voluntary disclosures of information consistent with internationally accepted practice.

The secrecy of the Swiss is world renowned, and Swiss accounting is among the most conservative and secretive in Europe and the world today. As in Germany, Swiss accounting practice is dominated by company law and the tax regulations governing the accounting profession, which is small and still in the early stages of setting accounting standards. However, in contrast to Germany, the legal requirements relating to accounting are modest and still permit the creation of secret reserves. Further, only listed companies, banks, insurance companies, and railways are required to file or publish annual accounts. However, this is not surprising given that most companies are small and family owned and managed.

Nevertheless, times are changing, albeit rather slowly, and Swiss corporations face increasing competition in international business and financial markets. Company law has been revised with changes inspired by the EU Fourth and Seventh Directives. An accounting standards board has also been established to make accounting and reporting recommendations for Swiss companies.

The existing Swiss Commercial Law (Code of Obligations) provides the general principles of bookkeeping practice to be followed by all enterprises as well as other rules specifically on accounting for limited liability companies. However, these accounting rules are very conservative and focus primarily on the interests of creditors. In effect, they institutionalize the practice of secret reserves by permitting assets to be undervalued. The essential feature of the law is a concern with the maintenance of share capital in nominal terms (i.e., historical costs). Accordingly,

Italy

As in France, the interests of government and the taxation authorities take precedence over those of shareholders, although the balance is now changing somewhat as major Italian companies become more involved in international financial markets.

In Italy, the influences of company law (the Civil Code) and the taxation regulations on accounting are similar to those in a number of other continental European countries and especially France, Belgium, and Spain. Italian accounting in practice is in many respects comparable with that of its European neighbors despite the fact that the EU Fourth and Seventh Directives were only implemented, somewhat belatedly, in 1991. This is especially true for listed companies, which are subject to additional legal and stock exchange regulations. Furthermore, a number of major MNEs make voluntary disclosures of information in response to international capital market pressures.

While the origins of double-entry bookkeeping can be traced to Italy in the thirteenth century, the filing of annual accounts by limited liability companies has been required by law only since 1882. Following amendments to the Civil Code in 1942 and 1974, an increasingly stricter regime was imposed, which in 1991 was updated by the implementation of the EU Directives.

Given that the accounts are used as the basis for taxation, as in most continental European countries, there has been a tradition of conservatism to minimize taxable profits and distributions to shareholders. It is also not uncommon for Italian companies to present different sets of accounts for management, the taxation authorities, and shareholders, but the scope for this has been reduced in recent years. In this regard, listed companies have been subject to additional regulation primarily by the Commissione Nazionale per le Società e la Borsa (CONSOB), which is more or less the equivalent of the U.S. SEC. The CONSOB was established in 1974 and has been responsible for a number of important developments including the requirement that, in addition to the statutory audit, listed companies have a more extensive audit by an approved auditing firm. The CONSOB also had the authority to require the filing of consolidated accounts by groups of companies, but in practice companies were encouraged rather than required to do so.

Implementation of the Fourth and Seventh EU Directives has brought about a change of emphasis in Italian accounts with the introduction of the true and fair view concept and the requirement that consolidated accounts be presented. Italy has been slow to adopt the EU directives because the interests of external users of accounts and the protection of shareholders have not been considered as important as the need to support and develop the interests of major family or state-owned industrial enterprises. This has been reinforced by the legal heritage of the nineteenth century, which has tended, like the Swiss, to protect the right of companies to keep the secrets of their business from competitors and outsiders, including until recently external shareholders.

The professional accounting bodies in Italy, the Consiglio Nazionale dei Dottori Commercialisti and the Consiglio Nazionali dei Ragioneri, are essentially advisory. There is a joint body that issues recommendations on accounting principles. The accounting bodies have recommended the use of IASC standards for matters not covered by them. It is also noteworthy that the CONSOB has recommended that listed companies adopt the profession's statements on accounting principles.

Brazil

As in France and Italy, the accounting tradition in Brazil gives preference to the information needs of creditors and the tax authorities. While the interest of domestic and foreign investors in Brazilian companies listed on the stock exchange has grown, this is still of minor significance as far as attitudes to accounting and disclosure are concerned.

As in other Latin countries, the influences of government, company law, and the taxation regulations on accounting are of fundamental importance. In this, Brazil's cultural heritage of Portuguese colonization is a significant underlying factor. While the basic commercial code was established in 1850, the corporation law of 1976 contains the basic requirements governing the preparation of financial statements and disclosures for public companies. In addition, the Commissão de Valores Mobiliarios (CVM), the Securities Exchange Commission, prescribes accounting standards for listed companies. While the stock market is small relative to those in the United States and the United Kingdom, it is one of the major markets in Latin America and growing in importance. Indeed, a number of Brazilian companies are now listed on U.S. stock markets.

The accounting profession in Brazil is not as well developed as in the Anglo-Saxon countries, but the institute for Brazilian accountants, the Instituto Brasileiro de Contadores (IBRACON), and the Conselho Federal de Contabilidade, or Federal Accounting Council, issue accounting standards that form the basis of generally accepted accounting principles. If such standards are approved by the CVM, they become obligatory for listed companies, and in general it appears that the CVM tends to rely on the accounting profession to develop accounting standards.

ASIAN ACCOUNTING

The Asian group of countries have cultures quite distinct from the Anglo-American, Nordic, Germanic, and Latin groupings. However, as far as accounting is concerned many have a colonial history, such as Indonesia (Netherlands); India, Pakistan, Hong Kong, Singapore, and Malaysia (United Kingdom); and the Philippines (Spain/United States). China has been influenced by both Western ideas and the socialist uniformity of the former Soviet Union. Even in Japan, with its unique culture, it appears that both German and U.S. influences have been important in establishing the Japanese accounting tradition. Asian accounting tends to be relatively more conservative and secretive compared to the Anglo-American countries.

China

A major shift of emphasis is under way in China from a primary focus on the information needs of government, that is, involving national planning and taxation, to a broader view of user needs that includes those of investors, creditors, and enterprise management. A more micro-oriented decision-making approach is thus being encouraged that retains a measure of macroeconomic control—a difficult balance to strike given China's tradition of uniformity and detailed regulation. Moreover, this tradition appears to be consistent with established Chinese cultural values and hence will be difficult to change.

The People's Republic of China (PRC) is a communist country and hence government, through laws passed by the National People's Congress, is the major influence on accounting and auditing. While the history of accounting in China can be traced back 2000 years or so, it was only in the early 1900s that double-entry bookkeeping was introduced. By the 1940s, Western-oriented accounting systems were established in large corporations, and teaching in the universities was increasingly influenced by ideas from the United Kingdom and the United States. However, the founding of the PRC in 1949 led to a dramatic change of approach with the introduction of Soviet Union-style accounting and an emphasis on uniformity and centralized control for national planning purposes. But since 1978, this approach has been increasingly modified following China's new "open door" policy to the outside world and its ambitious program for modernization. Once again, ideas and information from Western countries and indeed all over the world were sought to help China promote its concept of a socialist market economy based on public ownership and central planning, but with the market now playing an increasingly important role.

With economic reform and moves to a more market-oriented economy have come a series of accounting reforms. The Accounting Law of the People's Republic of China, adopted in 1985 and revised in 1993 and again in 1999, established general principles concerning the nature and role of accounting and empowered the Ministry of Finance (MOF) to issue accounting standards.

In 1992, the Basic Accounting Standard for Business Enterprises, the conceptual framework of PRC accounting, was issued. From 1993, specific accounting standards were developed on a variety of topics with 10 final standards issued to date. In 1998, the old rules applicable to joint stock companies were replaced by the issuance of the Accounting System for Joint Stock Limited Enterprises. Following the revision of the accounting law in 1999, the PRC State Council also issued Financial Accounting and Reporting Rules (FARR) for Enterprises which updates the definitions of assets, liabilities, owners' equity, revenues, and expenses that were previously set out in the Basic Standard. The FARR also specifies the components of the financial statements including a cash flow statement as well as balance sheet and income statement.

The new accounting standards, structured as a basic standard and a series of specific standards, represent a major change of approach in Chinese accounting in that *all* enterprises are now required to comply with a unified set of accounting principles. However, what is most significant is the *content* of the new accounting standards. It represents a new era in Chinese accounting, one based on a Western market-oriented approach rather than the old Soviet Union style. Fund accounting, based on the equality of fund sources with fund applications, has been abolished and replaced by the accounting equation, where assets equal liabilities plus capital or owners' equity. In making this change, the interests of a wider group of users beyond government have been recognized, namely, investors, creditors, and enterprise management. Accounting information must now meet much more than the requirements of national macroeconomic control. So that an enterprise's financial position and operating results can be understood and financial practices and administration strengthened, accounting information must also now meet the needs of external users and management.

While the government, through the MOF and its official accounting agency, the Department of Administration of Accounting Affairs (DAAA), has been decisive in reforming accounting, it is fair to say that accounting organizations, notably the Accounting Society of China, a body that fosters research on accounting theory, practice, and education, have played an important advisory role. The society, established in 1980, set up a research group in 1987 on accounting theory and standards with the majority of its members comprised of university professors. International accounting firms, notably Deloitte Touche Tohmatsu, have also been influential.

With respect to the practicing side of the profession, the auditing function, having been abolished after the founding of the PRC, was resumed only in 1983 with the establishment of the government's Audit Administration. Similarly, the Chinese Institute of Certified Public Accountants was reestablished by the government only in 1988. With the rapid pace of accounting reform there is currently a serious shortage of accountants.

Japan

Despite the significance of the stock market, the accounting tradition in Japan gives preference to the information needs and priorities of creditors and the tax authorities.

The government has been a major influence on all aspects of accounting in Japan. The Commercial Code, modeled after the German commercial code of the nineteenth century, was introduced in 1890 with the objective of protecting creditors. After World War II, the Commercial Code was revised to protect the interests of investors as well, following U.S. practice. Further, in 1948, a new securities and exchange law was introduced, modeled on the U.S. securities laws of 1933 and 1934, to protect investors in public corporations listed on stock exchanges or with stocks (shares) traded on the over-the-counter market.

The corporation tax law is another major, if not overriding, influence on income measurement practices in that corporate tax returns must be based on the annual accounts approved by shareholders. Much like France and Germany, tax-deductible expenses including depreciation cannot be claimed for tax purposes unless they are charged in the individual company accounts. Thus, there is a tendency toward very conservative accounting in Japan.

Government institutions are directly involved in accounting standard-setting. The Business Accounting Deliberation Council (BADC), which establishes Financial Accounting Standards for Business Enterprises, is an advisory body within the Ministry of Finance (MOF). The MOF is responsible for the securities and exchange law and its related accounting regulations. On the other hand, the Ministry of Justice is responsible for the application of the Commercial Code. With accounting systems under the jurisdiction of two government institutions, there is no unified approach to regulation. In fact, a number of large listed corporations are obliged to prepare two sets of financial statements, one required by the

Commercial Code and the other by the Securities and Exchange Law, though it is the form of presentation rather than the substance that must be different. The Commercial Code also requires only nonconsolidated financial statements. The Securities and Exchange Law, on the other hand, requires consolidated financial statements and an independent audit, but such statements have been regarded as supplementary information to the parent company accounts.

The accounting profession in Japan is small and has lacked influence in the accounting standard-setting process, but it provides recommendations on the practical application of the legal accounting regulations. The Japanese Institute of Certified Public Accountants was established by law in 1948, although an earlier body had been in existence since 1927. In 1991, a new body, the Corporation Finance Research Institute (COFRI), was also established with the purpose of providing authoritative advice to the BADC in the MOF. A special interest in the international aspects of accounting regulation appears to be an important motivation for this new development.

While the traditional sources of finance in Japan were the banks, which dominated the Zaibatsu industrial groups up until the end of World War II, there was a substantial broadening of share ownership and development of the securities market following the subsequent breakup of the Zaibatsu by the American postwar administration. However, since then, new *Keiretsu* groupings have emerged involving a number of listed companies. These are supported by a member bank that acts as a principal source of funds. They also maintain cross-holdings in each other to ensure control, and employ a variety of other mutually beneficial informal relationships. In general, there tends to be a secretive approach in Japan, with a lack of public information disclosure.

There is also an interesting international dimension to accounting in Japan. Many Japanese companies prepare an additional set of financial statements in English for the foreign readers of accounts, which are often referred to as "convenience translations." Further, approximately 30 Japanese companies listed in the United States prepare their consolidated financial statements in accordance with U.S. GAAP (generally accepted accounting principles) rather than reconcile Japanese GAAP income and shareholders' equity with U.S. GAAP as permitted under the Form 20F filing required by the SEC. The main reason for this appears to be that when Japanese corporations were first listed in the United States, there were no Japanese consolidation requirements, and hence it was considered appropriate to adopt U.S. GAAP. Indeed, these major MNEs often go beyond U.S. requirements in response to competitive pressures in the international capital marketplace. Most recently, an accounting standards board has been established in Japan similar to the FASB in the United States. Japan now appears poised to participate more fully in the international standard-setting process than it has done in the past.

SUMMARY

1. Patterns of international accounting development can be identified using a classification scheme to assess similarities and differences.

2. International accounting classification helps to describe and compare accounting systems in a way that will promote improved understanding of the nature and problems of accounting practice.

3.   International classification research has been both deductive, whereby relevant environmental factors are identified and linked to accounting practices, and inductive, whereby accounting practices are analyzed and development patterns identified.

4.   Although international classification research is still at an early stage, it is possible to identify some broad country groupings and patterns of accounting development. At the very least a macro/micro or strong/weak equity market pattern can be observed. Within that framework, U.S., U.K., and continental European models can be identified.

5.   Cultural influences on accounting development are now increasingly being recognized. Their importance for explaining fundamental accounting differences internationally seems clear and has received some support from recent empirical research.

6.   It is possible to identify key accounting values derived from societal cultural influences: professionalism, uniformity, conservatism, and secrecy. An international classification of accounting systems can be made on the basis of the link between accounting values, on the one hand, and accounting system characteristics, on the other.

7.   The accounting values of professionalism and uniformity are linked to the authority and enforcement characteristics of accounting systems. Conservatism is linked to the measurement of assets and profits. Secrecy is linked to the nature and extent of information disclosure.

8.   A comparative analysis of accounting systems reveals distinctive patterns of accounting but also unique features that are applicable to each country depending on its history and culture.

9.   Anglo-American accounting is clearly distinguishable from other country groups especially with respect to the emphasis on investor interests and disclosure to the stock market.

10.   Nordic accounting has many features that are comparable with Anglo-American accounting, but it also has some similarities to Germanic accounting.

11.   Germanic and Latin accounting have many similar features, particularly with respect to the influences of company law and taxation, but they are also distinguishable in a number of respects, especially in the emphasis given to uniform accounting.

12.   In Asia, Chinese accounting strongly reflects its communist heritage but is becoming increasingly open to Anglo-American influences.

13.   Japanese accounting is unique despite being influenced by both the Anglo-American and Germanic traditions.

14.   The major factors of government, the stock markets, company law, the accounting profession, the taxation authorities, and accounting conservatism and secrecy, tend to influence the development of accounting to a greater or lesser degree depending on the history and culture concerned.

15.   The growing internationalization of business and securities markets is bringing about some convergence of accounting practice at the level of consolidated accounts prepared by MNEs that are listed on stock exchanges—and especially those competing for capital in the international context.

Discussion Questions

1. To what extent is the strong/weak equity market distinction a useful way to identify different patterns of accounting development?

2. Do cultural influences impact more on accounting measurement compared to disclosure practices?

3. To what extent do you think culture explains the relative importance of stock exchanges and professional accounting associations around the world?

4. Where does your country fit in terms of "professionalism/statutory control" "Uniformity/Flexibility," "Conservatism/Optimism," and "Secrecy/transparency"?

5. To what extent are countries changing with respect to national cultures and "accounting values"?

6. What are the prospects for the global convergence of accounting systems?

7. Which countries have the greatest potential for accounting change? What are your reasons for thinking this?

Exercise

Form into small groups and have each group select *two* countries from different culture areas (as defined by Hofstede).

1. Identify and compare each country's societal and accounting values

2. Locate each country in Gray's "Authority and Enforcement" and "Measurement and Disclosure" frameworks. How do the countries compare?

3. Comment on the relevance and reliability of your findings.

Selected References

Achleitner, Ann-Kristin. 1995. "Latest Developments in Swiss Regulation of Financial Reporting," *European Accounting Review,* 4, (1).

Bailey, D. 1995. "Accounting in Transition in the Transitional Economy." *European Accounting Review,* 4 (4): 595–623. (Entire issue devoted to accounting in Eastern Europe and the former U.S.S.R.)

Banerjee, B. 2000. "Regulation of Accounting in India: Issues and a Suggested Framework." *Indian Accounting Review,* 4 (2) 21–35.

Barrett, M. Edgar. 1976. "Financial Reporting Practices: Disclosure and Comprehensiveness in an International Setting," *Journal of Accounting Research* (Spring).

Chen, Y., P. Jubb and A. Tran. 1997. "Problems of Accounting Reform in the People's Republic of China," *The International Journal of Accounting,* 32 (2): 139–53.

Choi, F. D. S. and K. Hiramatsu, eds. 1987. *Accounting and Financial Reporting in Japan.* Princeton, NJ: Van Nostrand Reinhold.

Chow, Lynne Min-Ying, Gerald Kun-Kwai Chau, and Sidney J. Gray. 1995. "Accounting Reforms in China: Cultural Constraints on Implementation and Development," *Accounting and Business Research,* 26 (1) (Winter).

Cooke, T. E. 1988. *European Financial Reporting: Sweden.* London: Institute of Chartered Accountants in England and Wales.

Cooke, T. E. and M. Kikuya. 1992. *Financial Reporting in Japan: Regulation, Practice, and Environment.* Oxford: Basil Blackwell.

Cooke, T. E. and R. H. Parker, eds. 1994. *Financial Reporting in the West Pacific Rim.* London: Routledge.

Cooke, T. E. and M. Kikuya. 1992. *Financial Reporting in Japan.* Oxford: Basil Blackwell.

Doupnick, T. S. and Salter, S. B. 1993. "An Empirical Test of a Judgmental International Classification of Financial Reporting Practices," *Journal of International Business Studies* (first quarter).

Doupnik, T. S. and Salter, S. B. 1995. "External Environment, Culture, and Accounting Practice: A Preliminary Test of a General Model of International Accounting Development, *International Journal of Accounting*, 30 (3): 189–207.

Enthoven, A. J. H., Y. V. Sokolov, S. M. Bychkova, V. V. Kovalev, and Semenova, M. V. 1998. *Accounting, Auditing, and Taxation in the Russian Federation.* Institute of Management Accountants. Montvale: NJ and University of Texas at Dallas (Richardson: TX).

Fortune Global 500. www.fortune.com/fortune/global500/

Frost, C. A. and G. Pownall. 1994. "Accounting Disclosure Practices in the United States and the United Kingdom." *Journal of Accounting Research* (Spring): 75–102.

Gordon, P. D. and S. J. Gray. 1994. *European Financial Reporting: United Kingdom.* London: Routledge.

Gray, S. J. 1980. "The Impact of International Accounting Differences from a Security Analysis Perspective: Some European Evidence," *Journal of Accounting Research* (Spring).

Gray, S. J. 1985. "Cultural Influences and the International Classification of Accounting Systems" (paper presented at the European Institute for Advanced Studies in Management workshop on "Accounting and Culture," Amsterdam, June).

Gray, S. J. 1988. "Towards a Theory of Cultural Influence on the Development of Accounting Systems Internationally," *Abacus* (March).

Gray, S. J. and A. G. Coenenberg, eds. 1984. *EEC Accounting Harmonisation.* Amsterdam: North-Holland.

Gray, S. J., Coenenberg, A. G., and Gordon, P. D. 1993. *International Group Accounting: Issues in European Harmonization,* London: Routledge.

Gray, S. J. and H. M. Vint. 1995. "The Impact of Culture on Accounting Disclosures: Some International Evidence," *Asia-Pacific Journal of Accounting* 2.

Harrison, G. L. and J. L. McKinnon. 1986. "Culture and Accounting Change: A New Perspective on Corporate Reporting Regulation and Accounting Policy Formulation," *Accounting, Organizations and Society,* 11 (3).

Hofstede, Geert. 1980. *Culture's Consequences: International Differences in Work-Related Values.* Beverly Hills: Sage.

Hofstede, Geert. 1984. "Cultural Dimensions in Management and Planning," *Asia Pacific Journal of Management* (January).

Hofstede, Geert and Michael H. Bond. 1988. "The Confucius Connection: From Cultural Roots to Economic Growth," *Organizational Dynamics* 16 (4).

Hofstede, Geert. 1991. *Cultures and Organizations.* Maidenhead, England: McGraw-Hill.

Hove, M. R. 1986. "Accounting Practices in Developing Countries: Colonialism's Legacy of Inappropriate Technologies," *International Journal of Accounting*, 21 (1): 81–100.

International Association for Accounting Education and Research. www.iaaer.org

International Accounting Standards Board www.iasb.org.uk

Jaggi, B. C. 1975. "The Impact of the Cultural Environment on Financial Disclosures," *International Journal of Accounting* (Spring).

Jermakowicz, E. and D. F. Rinke. 1996. "The New Accounting Standards in the Czech Republic, Hungary, and Poland vis-à-vis International Accounting Standards and European Union Directives," *Journal of International Accounting, Auditing & Taxation,* 5 (1): 73–87.

Jordan, W. & Son. *International Corporate Procedures.* Bristol, England: Jordan Publishing, 2000, continuing.

Lefebvre, C. and Liang-vi Lin. 1990. "Internationalization of Financial Accounting Standards in the People's Republic of China," *International Journal of Accounting*, 25.

McKinnon, J. L. 1986. *The Historical Development and Operational Form of Corporate Reporting Regulation in Japan.* New York: Garland.

Mueller, Gerhard G. 1967. *International Accounting.* New York: Macmillan.

Mueller, Gerhard G. 1968. "Accounting Principles Generally Accepted in the U.S. versus Those Generally Accepted Elsewhere," *International Journal of Accounting* (Spring).

Nair, R. D. and Werner G. Frank. 1980. "The Impact of Disclosure and Measurement Practices on International Accounting Classifications," *Accounting Review* (July).

Nobes, C. W. 1981. "An Empirical Analysis of International Accounting Principles: A Comment," *Journal of Accounting Research* (Spring).

Nobes, C. W. 1983. "A Judgmental International Classification of Financial Reporting Practices," *Journal of Business Finance and Accounting* (Spring).

Nobes, C. W. 1984. *International Classification of Financial Reporting.* London: Croom Helm.

Nobes, C. W. 1998. "Towards a General Model of the Reasons for International Differences in Financial Reporting," *Abacus,* 34 (2).

Nobes, C. W. and R. H. Parker, eds. 2000. *Comparative International Accounting,* 6th ed. Englewood Cliffs, NJ: Prentice-Hall.

Ordelheide, D. and D. Pfaff. 1994. *European Financial Reporting: Germany.* London: Routledge.

Parker, R. H. 1989. "Importing and Exporting Accounting: The British Experience," in *International Pressures for Accounting Change,* edited by A. G. Hopwood. Englewood Cliffs, NJ: Prentice-Hall.

Puxty, A. G., H. C. Willmott, D. J. Cooper, and A. Lowe. 1987. "Modes of Regulation in Advanced Capitalism: Locating Accountancy in Four Countries," *Accounting, Organizations, and Society,* 12 (3): 273–91.

Riccaboni, A. and R. Ghirri. 1994. *European Financial Reporting: Italy.* London: Routledge.

Rivera, J. M. and A. S. Salva. 1995. "On the Regional Approach to Accounting Principles Harmonization: A time for Latin American Integration?," *Journal of International Accounting Auditing & Taxation,* 4 (1): 87–100.

Salter, Stephen and Frederick Niswander. 1995. "Cultural Influence on the Development of Accounting Systems Internationally: A Test of Gray's (1988) Theory," *Journal of International Business Studies* (second quarter): 394.

Saudagaran, S. M. and J. G. Diga. 1997. "Financial Reporting in Emerging Capital Markets: Characteristics and Policy Issues," *Accounting Horizons,* 11 (2): 41–64.

Saudagaran, S. M. and J. G. Diga. 1997. "The Impact of Capital Market Developments on Accounting Regulatory Policy in Emerging Markets: A Study of ASEAN." *Research in Accounting Regulation* (Supplement 1): 3–48.

Saudagaran, S. M. and J. G. Diga. 2000. "The Institutional Environment of Financial Reporting Regulation in ASEAN," *The International Journal of Accounting,* 35 (1): 1–26.

Scheid, J.-C. and P. Walton. 1992. *European Financial Reporting: France.* London: Routledge.

Shahrokh Saudagaran and Gary Biddle. 1992. "Financial Disclosure Levels and Foreign Stock Exchange Listing Decisions," *Journal of International Financial Management and Accounting* (Summer).

Sterling, Robert R. 1967. "Conservatism: The Fundamental Principle of Valuation in Traditional Accounting," *Abacus* (December).

Street, D. L., N. B. Nichols, and S. J. Gray. 2000. "Assessing the Acceptability of International Accounting Standards in the US: An Empirical Study of the Materiality of US GAAP Reconciliations by Non-US Companies Complying with IASC Standards," *The International Journal of Accounting,* 35 (1): 27–64.

Tang, Y. W. L. Chow, and B. J. Cooper. 1994. *Accounting and Finance in China.* Hong Kong: Longman.

Taylor, Peter and Stuart Turley. 1986. *The Regulation of Accounting.* London: Basil Blackwell.

Walton, P., ed. 1995. *European Financial Reporting: A History.* London: Academic Press.

Walton, P., ed. 1996. *Country Studies in International Accounting—Europe.* Cheltenham, U. K., Edward Elgar.

Weetman, P. and S. J. Gray. 1990. "International Financial Analysis and Comparative Corporate Performance: The Impact of U.K. versus U.S. Accounting Principles on Earnings," *Journal of International Financial Management and Accounting* (Summer/Autumn).

Weetman, P. and S. J. Gray. 1991. "A Comparative Analysis of the Impact of Accounting Principles on Profits: The U.S.A. versus the U.K., Sweden, and the Netherlands," *Accounting and Business Research* (Autumn).

Xiao, Z. and A. Pan. 1997. "Developing Accounting Standards on the Basis of a Conceptual Framework by the Chinese Government," *The International Journal of Accounting*, 32 (3): 279–99.

Zeff, S. A. 1972. *Forging Accounting Principles in Five Countries*. New York: Stipes.

Zeff, S. A. 1995. "A Perspective on the U. S. Public/Private-Sector Approach to the Regulation of Financial Reporting," *Accounting Horizons* (March): 52–70.

Zeff, S. A., F. Van der Wel, and K. Camfferman. 1992. *Company Financial Reporting: A Historical and Comparative Study of the Dutch Regulatory Process*. Amsterdam: North-Holland.

Zeff, S. A., F. Van der Wel, and K. Camfferman. 1997. *Company Financial Reporting: A Historical and Comparative Study of the Dutch Regulatory Process*. Amsterdam: North-Holland.

Zhou, Zhong Hui. 1988. "Chinese Accounting Systems and Practices," *Accounting, Organizations and Society*, 13, (2).

CHAPTER FOUR

INTERNATIONAL FINANCIAL STATEMENT ANALYSIS

Chapter Objectives

- Assess the importance of international accounting differences from the perspective of financial analysts and other users of financial statements

- Identify major differences in accounting principles around the world that affect financial results

- Provide a quantitative analysis of how differences in accounting principles can impact on the reported earnings of U.S. and U.K. firms and the analysis of comparative performance

- Show how reported earnings are affected by differences in accounting principles in other parts of the world, with special reference to continental Europe and Japan

- Review developments in the effort to achieve global accounting harmonization

INTRODUCTION

The purpose of this chapter is to examine the importance of differences in international accounting from the perspective of financial statement analysis. We will also assess the extent to which there are systematic differences across countries as a result of the differential impact of accounting principles on measures of earnings and assets. For the purposes of financial analysis it is necessary not only to be aware of international differences in accounting but also to be able to assess their impact on earnings and assets and the key indicators and ratios involved, for example, earnings per share, return on equity, leverage (gearing), and so on. In doing so, we will look at the impact of differences in accounting principles around the world, with special reference to a selection of major countries. We will also attempt to assess the differential impact of "conservatism" on measurement practices, as discussed in Chapter 3, in the context of cultural influences on accounting.

INTERNATIONAL ACCOUNTING DIFFERENCES AND FINANCIAL STATEMENT ANALYSIS

Just as business and financial markets have become increasingly internationalized, so has the significance of differences in international accounting become more important from the perspective of international financial statement analysis. The key question concerns the extent to which international accounting differences impact on assessments of earnings and future cash flows and their associated risks and uncertainties.

These assessments are important to portfolio investors making their stock (share) valuations. They are also important to corporations concerned with foreign direct investment (FDI), which involves the valuation of potential acquisitions and participating interests/joint ventures or the raising of capital or the listing/trading of stocks (shares) on foreign stock exchanges. A growing number of corporations are listed internationally (see Exhibit 4.1), with London being the most popular stock exchange, and many more are seeking to become so. In addition, there has been a dramatic increase in emerging stock markets and competition for international investment.

Exhibit 4.1   International Stock Market Comparisons of International Company Listings on Foreign Exchanges

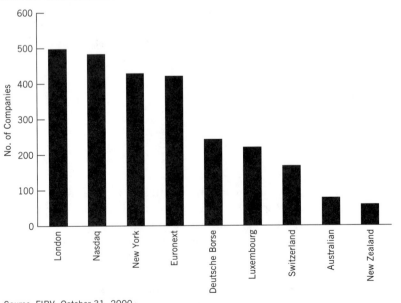

Source: FIBV, October 31, 2000.

International accounting differences pose a number of problems from a financial analysis perspective. First, in attempting to value a foreign corporation, there is likely to be a tendency to look at earnings and other financial data from a home country perspective, and hence there is a danger of overlooking the effects of accounting differences. Unless significant differences are taken into account, possibly with some restatement involved, this could have very serious consequences. Second, an awareness of international differences suggests the need to become familiar with foreign accounting principles to better understand earnings data in the context in which such measures are derived. Third, issues of international comparability and accounting harmonization become highlighted in the context of considering alternative investment opportunities. In this regard, Choi and Levich (1991) provide a useful framework for analyzing the impact and relevance of accounting diversity in similar or dissimilar economic environments (see Exhibit 4.2). In dissimilar economic environments or situations, accounting diversity is illogical and leads to noncomparable results (box C). Logical practice suggests similar accounting treatments (box A). Where economic environments are dissimilar, however, as is likely in the case of international investment (boxes B and D), accounting diversity may well be justified, especially where the sources of such dissimilarity are in the company laws, tax regulations, sources of finance, business customs, accounting culture, and so on (box D). On the other hand, similar accounting treatments may be justifiable where such factors are of similar significance (box B). The importance of understanding environmental and cultural factors is thus emphasized (see Chapters 2 and 3).

In a survey to explore how capital market participants respond to accounting diversity, Choi and Levich sampled the opinions of institutional investors, MNEs issuing securities, banks underwriting international securities, and regulatory bodies. While only 48 percent of those interviewed were apparently affected by international accounting diversity (see Exhibit 4.3) it seems that the 52 percent of

Exhibit 4.2 Accounting Diversity and Economic Environments

| | | Economic Situation of Two Firms | |
		Similar	Dissimilar
Accounting Treatment	Similar	Logical Practice Results Comparable (A)	May or May Not Be Logical Results May or May Not Be Comparable (B)
	Dissimilar	Illogical Practice Results Not Comparable (C)	Logical Practice Results May Not Be Comparable (D)

Source: F.D.S. Choi and R. M. Levich, "International Accounting Diversity and Capital Market Decisions," in *Handbook of International Accounting,* edited by F.D.S. Choi (New York: John Wiley, 1991), p. 7.4.

Exhibit 4.3   Capital Market Effects of Accounting Diversity: Summary Findings for Investors, Issuers, Underwriters, Regulators, and Others

	Yes	No	N.A.	Total
Investors	9	7	1	17
Issuers	6	9		15
Underwriters	7	1		8
Regulators	0	8		8
Raters and others	2	1		3
Total	24	26	1	51[a]

Key Questions
Does accounting diversity affect your capital market decisions?

[a]The International Accounting Standards Committee was interviewed, but their answers are not included here.

Source: F.D.S. Choi and R. M. Levich "International Accounting Diversity and Capital Market Decisions," in *Handbook of International Accounting,* edited by F.D.S. Choi (New York: John Wiley, 1991), p. 7.16.

respondents claiming to be not affected were in fact coping by various means, including (1) restating accounts to their own GAAP, (2) developing foreign GAAP capabilities, (3) using other sources of information, and (4) using different investment approaches, for example, a "top-down" macroeconomic approach to country selection coupled with stock diversification within a country. Similar approaches were used by those respondents whose investment decisions were apparently affected by accounting diversity. For the investor group, Exhibit 4.4 shows the wide-ranging nature of the effects arising both from GAAP differences and from disclosure differences. The results of this study suggest that the problems and costs arising from international accounting diversity are very real and need to be investigated further to assess whether and how they might be resolved. At the least, there is a clear need to assess the extent of such diversity and its impact on measures of earnings and performance.

Exhibit 4.4   Capital Market Effects of Accounting Diversity: Investors

	From GAAP Differences	From Disclosure Differences
Geographic spread of investments	3	3
Types of companies/securities selected	6	7
Information processing costs	5[a]	2[b]
Assessment of security returns or valuation	8	8

[a] Two reported these costs were significant.

[b] Both feel this cost is significant.

Source: F.D.S. Choi and R. M. Levich, "International Accounting Diversity and Capital Market Decisions," in *Handbook of International Accounting,* edited by F.D.S. Choi (New York: John Wiley, 1991), p. 7.18.

MAJOR DIFFERENCES IN ACCOUNTING PRINCIPLES AROUND THE WORLD

The extent of accounting diversity around the world is undoubtedly significant enough to make the job of the financial analyst a very difficult one in terms of making international comparisons.

If we now focus on some key measurement issues in a selection of major countries, that is, the United States, the United Kingdom, the Netherlands, Sweden, Germany, Switzerland, France, Italy, Brazil, China, and Japan, we can gain some insight into the variety of accounting principles in use that can impact differentially on earnings and assets.

For these countries, which are representative of the culture classifications identified earlier and whose accounting systems have been discussed in Chapter 3, the accounting principles relating to a selection of key measurement issues are presented on a comparative basis in Exhibit 4.5. From this summary, it can be seen that there are some important differences across countries.

With respect to the measurement basis used, the conservative application of historical cost is generally required in the Germanic, Latin, and Asian countries. However, in the Anglo-American and Nordic countries, there tends to be a more flexible approach, especially in the United Kingdom and the Netherlands. In those two countries, historical cost is frequently modified by revaluations to market value or replacement cost, especially in the case of land and buildings and to a lesser extent plant and equipment. At the same time, the United States retains a conservative historical cost approach while permitting market valuations in accounting for acquisitions and certain intangibles such as brands, publishing rights, and so on.

Depreciation accounting in the Anglo-American and Nordic countries tends to be based on the concept of useful economic life, whereas in the Germanic, Latin, and Asian countries, the tax rules generally encourage more accelerated methods.

Inventory measurement is generally based on the principle of "lower of cost and market" but with some variation as to the meaning of *market,* that is, net realizable value or replacement cost. LIFO (last-in, first-out) is sometimes permitted for tax purposes, for example, in the United States and Japan, but more often it is not, for example, in the United Kingdom, Germany, France, Italy, and Brazil. Construction contracts are generally accounted for using the percentage-of-completion method in the Anglo-American and Latin countries, but the more conservative completed contract method tends to be used in the Germanic countries.

R&D costs are usually expensed immediately in the Anglo-American and Germanic countries, though capitalization of development expenses is permitted in the United Kingdom. In the Nordic, Latin, and Asian countries a more flexible approach is generally adopted. A permissive approach is also generally adopted toward capitalizing the borrowing costs of assets.

The treatment of retirement benefits varies somewhat, with the Anglo-American, Nordic, and Germanic countries generally accounting for costs on the basis of accrued and/or projected benefits likely to be payable to employees, in contrast to the more pay-as-you-go approach of some Latin and Asian countries.

Exhibit 4.5   International Differences in Accounting Principles: Some Key Measurement Issues

	Anglo-American Accounting	
Accounting Issues	United States	United Kingdom
Measurement Basis		
• Property	Historical cost required	Periodic revaluations
• Plant and Equipment	Historical cost required	Revaluations permitted
• Inventories	• Lower of cost and Market (Net realizable value)	• Lower of cost and market (Net realizable value)
	• LIFO permitted	• FIFO; LIFO not permitted
Depreciation Accounting	Usually straight line—based on useful economic life	Usually straight line—based on useful economic life
Construction Contracts	Percentage-of-completion method	Percentage-of-completion method
Research and Development Costs	Expensed immediately	Development costs may be capitalized
Borrowing Costs of Assets	Treated as cost of the asset	Usually expensed immediately
Exchange Rates for Income Statement Translation	Actual or average rates	Usually closing rates
Retirement Benefits	Costs based on accrued benefits	Costs based on accrued or projected benefits
Deferred Taxation	Full deferral	Partial deferral
Business Combinations	Pooling not permitted	Pooling required in specified circumstances
Goodwill (Positive)	Non-amortization method required—subject to impairment tests	Amortization method required—no maximum period but impairment tests required
Intangibles (brands publishing rights, patents)	Non-amortization method required—subject to impairment tests	Capitalization without amortization permitted

	Nordic Accounting	
Accounting Issues	Netherlands	Sweden
Measurement		
• Property	Revaluations permitted at current replacement cost	Historical cost but exceptional revaluations permitted
• Plant and Equipment	Revaluations permitted at current replacement cost	Historical cost
• Inventories	• Lower of cost and market (current replacement cost)	• Lower of cost and market (net realizable value or current replacement cost)
	• LIFO permitted	• Usually FIFO

Exhibit 4.5 (*Continued*)

	Nordic Accounting	
Accounting Issues	Netherlands	Sweden
Depreciation Accounting	Straight line—based on useful economic life	Straight line—based on useful economic life
Construction Contracts	Completed contract and percentage-of-completion methods	Completed contract method
Research and Development Costs	Capitalization permitted	Capitalization permitted
Borrowing Costs of Assets	Treatment as cost of the asset permitted	Treatment as cost of the asset
Exchange Rates for Income Statement Translation	Average or closing rates	Usually average rates
Retirement Benefits	Costs based on projected benefits	Costs based on accrued benefits
Deferred Taxation	Full deferral	Accounting income influenced by tax rules
		Deferred taxes in consolidated accounts
Business Combinations	Pooling permitted in specified circumstances	Pooling required in specified circumstances
Goodwill (positive)	Immediate write-off permitted	Amortization method required—maximum of 20 years
Intangibles (brands, publishing rights, patents)	Capitalization permitted subject to amortization	Capitalization permitted subject to amortization

	Germanic Accounting	
Accounting Issues	Germany	Switzerland
Measurement Basis		
• Property	Historical cost required	Usually historical cost but lower valuations permitted
• Plant and Equipment	Historical cost required	Usually historical cost
• Inventories	• Lowest of historical cost, replacement cost, net realizable value	• Lower of cost and market
	• Usually average cost method	• Various method permitted
Depreciation Accounting	Accelerated methods permitted	Accelerated methods permitted
Construction Contracts	Completed contract method	Completed contract method permitted
Research and Development Costs	Expensed immediately	Usually expensed immediately

(continues)

Exhibit 4.5   (*Continued*)

Germanic Accounting		
Accounting Issues	Germany	Switzerland
Borrowing Costs of Assets	Treatment as cost of the asset permitted	Treatment as cost of the asset permitted
Exchange Rates for Income Statement Translation	Usually average rates	Usually average rates
Retirement Benefits	Costs based on accrued benefits	Costs based on accrued or projected benefits
Deferred Taxation	Accounting income strongly influenced by tax rules	Accounting income strongly influenced by tax rules
Business Combinations	Pooling permitted in specified circumstances	Pooling permitted in specified circumstances
Goodwill (positive)	Immediate write-off permitted	Immediate write-off permitted
Intangibles (brands, publishing rights, patents)	Capitalization permitted subject to amortization	Capitalization permitted subject to amortization

Latin Accounting			
Accounting Issues	France	Italy	Brazil
Measurement Basis			
• Property	Historical cost required	Historical cost required	Historical cost plus inflation adjustments
• Plant and Equipment	Historical cost required	Historical cost required	Historical cost plus inflation adjustments
• Inventories	• Lower of cost and market (Net realizable value) • Weighted Average or FIFO; LIFO permitted only in consolidated accounts	• Lower of cost and market (Net realizable value) • Usually LIFO permitted only in consolidated accounts	• Lower of cost and market (Net realizable value) • Weighted Average or FIFO; LIFO not permitted.
Depreciation Accounting	Accelerated methods permitted	Accelerated methods permitted	Usually straight-line
Construction Contracts	Percentage-of-completion method	Completed contract permitted method	Percentage-of-completion method
Research and Development Costs	Capitalization permitted	Capitalization permittted	Capitalization permitted
Borrowing Costs of Assets	Treatment as cost of the asset permitted	Treatment as cost of the asset permitted	Treatment as cost of the asset permitted
Exchange Rates for Income Statement Translation	Average or closing rates	Usually average rates	Average or closing rates

Exhibit 4.5 (*Continued*)

Latin Accounting			
Accounting Issues	France	Italy	Brazil
Exchange Rates for Income Statement Translation	Average or closing rates	Usually average rates	Average or closing rates
Retirement Benefits	Costs based on accrued or projected benefits	Costs expensed as paid	Costs expensed as paid
Deferred Taxation	Accounting income strongly influenced by tax rules	Accounting income strongly influenced by tax rules	Accounting income strongly influenced by tax rules
Business Combinations	Purchase method normally required	Some elements of pooling permitted	Purchase method normally required
Goodwill (positive)	Amortization method required	Amortization method required	Amortization method required
Intangibles (brands, publishing rights, patents)	Capitalization permitted subject to amortization	Capitalization permitted subject to amortization	Capitalization permitted subject to amortization

Asian Accounting		
Accounting Issues	China	Japan
Measurement basis		
• Property	Historical cost required	Historical cost normally required but land can be revalued
• Plant and Equipment	Historical cost required	Historical cost required
• Inventories	• Provisions for losses permitted	• Normally at cost • Lower of cost and market permitted (replacement cost or net realizable value)
	• Various methods permitted including LIFO	• LIFO permitted
Depreciation Accounting	Usually straight-line	Accelerated methods permitted
Construction Contracts	Completed contract and percentage-of-completion methods permitted	Completed contract and percentage-of-completion methods permitted
Research and Development Costs	Development costs may be capitalized	Capitalization permitted
Borrowing Costs of Assets	Treatment as cost of the asset permitted	Treatment as cost of the asset permitted
Exchange Rates for Income Statement Translation	Average rates	Average or closing rates
Retirement Benefits	Costs expensed as paid	Costs based on accrued or projected benefits

(continues)

Exhibit 4.5   (*Continued*)

	Asian Accounting	
Accounting Issues	China	Japan
Deferred Taxation	Accounting income strongly influenced by tax rules	Accounting income strongly influenced by tax rules
Business Combinations	Purchase method normally required	Some elements of pooling permitted
Goodwill (positive)	Amortization method required	Amortization method required—maximum of five years
Intangibles (brands, publishing rights, patents)	Capitalization permitted subject to amortization	Capitalization permitted subject to amortization

The treatment of taxation is a major area of differentiation between the Anglo-American and Nordic countries, on the one hand, and the Germanic, Latin, and Asian countries, on the other. In particular, the latter group's approach to the measurement of accounting income is strongly influenced by the tax rules.

The treatment of business combinations around the world varies to the extent that the pooling-of-interests method is required or permitted in certain specified circumstances. Generally, however, the purchase method is required. But with the purchase method comes a major area of differentiation and controversy between countries, that is, the treatment of goodwill. In the Latin and Asian countries, the more conservative amortization method is required in contrast to the Anglo-American, Nordic, and Germanic countries where there is some variety of approach and some flexibility, especially in countries such as the Netherlands.

Related to goodwill is the issue of intangibles, such as brands, publishing rights, and patents, where there is generally a flexible approach to capitalization but subject usually to amortization.

Finally, the issue of foreign currency translation is important in that earnings measures are impacted by the choice between average or closing rates. Here, there would seem to be some flexibility in general, though average rates are prescribed in the United States.

Although there is a growing awareness of this diversity of measurement principles and practices internationally, there is much less that is known about the overall impact of accounting differences on earnings and shareholders' equity. After all, differences with respect to various aspects of measurement may well compensate for each other to the extent that their overall impact may not be significant. The important question is whether accounting differences impact systematically on measures of income. In other words, do these differences really matter?

While there has been a relatively limited amount of research into the quantitative impact of international accounting differences, there is now some evidence available concerning relationships between U.S. accounting principles and those in the United Kingdom, a number of continental European countries, and Japan.

THE IMPACT OF U.S.–U.K. ACCOUNTING DIFFERENCES: A QUANTITATIVE ANALYSIS

Let us first examine the question of whether there is an overall quantitative impact on earnings arising from differences between U.S. and U.K. accounting principles. Using U.S. GAAP as the yardstick, it is possible to make an assessment of the relationship between U.K. earnings reported under U.K. GAAP and U.K. earnings adjusted in accordance with U.S. GAAP. Given that "conservatism" is a major influence on measurement practices (see Chapter 3), then this relationship can be described in terms of relative conservatism.

Accordingly, an index of conservatism can be calculated, as shown by Gray (1980), using the following formula:

$$1 - \left(\frac{RA - RD}{|RA|} \right)$$

where
RA = adjusted earnings (or returns)
RD = disclosed earnings

In the case of U.S. versus U.K. accounting principles, this becomes

$$1 - \left(\frac{\text{U.S. GAAP Earnings} - \text{U.K. GAAP Earnings}}{|\text{U.S. GAAP Earnings}|} \right)$$

An index value *greater than* 1 means that U.K. GAAP earnings are *less* "conservative" than the U.S. GAAP measure would have been. An index value *less than* I means that U.K. earnings are *more* "conservative" than the U.S. measure would have been. An index value exactly *equal to* 1 indicates neutrality between the two systems with respect to the effect of accounting principles. The denominator has been taken as U.S. GAAP earnings to provide a benchmark against which U.K. GAAP earnings can be compared.

To illustrate the effect of the index, take two examples:

Example 1: U.K. GAAP earnings £110 million   Example 2: U.K. GAAP earnings £90 million
U.S. GAAP earnings £100 million   U.S. GAAP earnings £100 million

Index $1 - \left(\dfrac{100 - 110}{100} \right)$ $1 - \left(\dfrac{100 - 90}{100} \right)$

= 1.1   = 0.9

Note: The data can also be restated in $ terms as required.

Having established an overall index of conservatism, it is then possible to establish the relative effect of the various individual adjustments by constructing partial indices of adjustment using the formula:

$$\text{Partial index of "conservatism"} = 1 - \left(\frac{\text{partial adjustment}}{|\text{ U.S. GAAP Earnings }|}\right)$$

For example:

	Millions of Pounds
U.K. GAAP earnings	120
Adjustments for U.S. GAAP:	
Deferred taxation	(15)
Goodwill amortization	(5)
Adjusted earnings per U.S. GAAP	100
Overall index of "conservatism"	1.2
Partial index for deferred taxation	$1 - \left(\frac{-15}{100}\right) = 1.15$
Partial index for goodwill	$1 - \left(\frac{-5}{100}\right) = 1.05$

An opportunity to compare earnings resulting from U.K. accounting principles with those that would have resulted under U.S. accounting principles is given by those U.K. corporations obliged to report to the SEC in the United States. The Form 20-F report to the SEC contains a reconciliation of U.K. earnings with the earnings that would have been reported under U.S. GAAP. The effect of each accounting policy, which differs between the two countries, is quantified separately. In addition to the quantified difference, the accounting policies as they affect the corporation are explained by way of note, which occasionally gives further insight into the differences between U.K. and U.S. accounting practice. British Telecom is an example of a U.K. corporation reporting under 20-F (See Exhibit 4.6 where the Form 20-F reconciliation is reproduced in the corporate annual report.)

The reconciliations disclosed in Form 20-F can be used to test whether U.K. GAAP earnings before extraordinary items are systematically *less* conservative than they would be if U.S. GAAP were applied or, conversely, whether U.S. reporting practices are *more* conservative than U.K. reporting practices. This data is, of course, much more reliable than any independent attempt to adjust company accounts for international differences because it is provided by the company itself and subject to audit.

The SEC requires a report on Form 20-F where the corporation sponsors an ADR (American Depositary Receipt), which is traded on one of the national stock exchanges such as the New York Stock Exchange (NYSE), the American Stock Exchange (AMEX), or the National Association of Securities Dealers Automated Quotations (NASDAQ).

Based on the analysis of 37 United Kingdom corporations providing reconciliations on Form 20-F, Weetman and Gray (1990) found that statistically, significant differences existed and that United States GAAP measures of earnings for the period 1985–87 were much *more* "conservative" than United Kingdom GAAP earnings. More specifically, it was evident that United Kingdom earnings were, on average, between 9 and 25 percent *higher* than United States earnings as a result of differences in accounting principles.

Exhibit 4.6   British Telecom (U.K.)

British Telecom: Notes to the Accounts:
United States Generally Accepted Accounting Principles

The group's consolidated financial statements are prepared in accordance with accounting principles generally accepted in the United Kingdom (U.K. GAAP), which differ in certain significant respects from those applicable in the United States (U.S. GAAP). The following statements summarise the material estimated adjustments, gross of their tax effect, which reconcile net income from that reported under United Kingdom GAAP to that which would have been reported had United States GAAP been applied.

Net income	**1999**	1998	1997
YEAR ENDED 31 MARCH	**£m**	£m	£m
Net income applicable to shareholders under UK GAAP	**2,983**	1,702	2,077
Adjustments for:			
Pension costs	**(104)**	(66)	83
Redundancy charges	**(284)**	(253)	156
Capitalization of interest, net of related depreciation	**(19)**	(38)	(23)
Goodwill amortisation	**(85)**	(71)	(73)
Mobile licenses, software and other intangible asset capitalization and amortization, net	**(226)**	42	77
Investments	**(6)**	5	–
Deferred taxation	**220**	163	(148)
Other items	**(60)**	(37)	–
Net income as adjusted for U.S. GAAP	**2,589**	1,447	2,149
Basic earnings per American Depositary Share as adjusted for U.S. GAAP	**£4.02**	£2.27	£3.39
Diluted earnings per American Depositary Share as adjusted for U.S. GAAP	**£3.93**	£2.23	£3.36

Differences between United Kingdom and
United States generally accepted accounting principles

The following are the main differences between United Kingdom and United States GAAP which are relevant to the group's financial statements.

(a) Pension costs

Under United Kingdom GAAP, pension costs are accounted for in accordance with United Kingdom Statement of Standard Accounting Practice No. 24, costs being charged against profits over employees' working lives. Under United States GAAP, pension costs are determined in accordance with the requirements of United States Statements of Financial Accounting Standards (SFAS) Nos. 87 and 88. Differences between the United Kingdom and United States GAAP figures arise from the requirement to use different actuarial methods and assumptions and a different method of amortising surpluses or deficits.

(b) Accounting for redundancies

Under United Kingdom GAAP, the cost of providing incremental pension benefits in respect of workforce reductions is taken into account when determining current and future pension costs, unless the most recent actuarial valuation under United Kingdom actuarial conventions shows a deficit. In this case, the cost of providing incremental

(continues)

Exhibit 4.6   (*Continued*)

pension benefits is included in redundancy charges in the year in which the employees agree to leave the group.

Under United States GAAP, the associated costs of providing incremental pension benefits are charged against profits in the period in which the termination terms are agreed with the employees.

(c) Capitalisation of interest

Under United Kingdom GAAP, the group does not capitalise interest in its financial statements. To comply with United States GAAP, the estimated amount of interest incurred whilst constructing major capital projects is included in fixed assets, and depreciated over the lives of the related assets. The amount of interest capitalised is determined by reference to the average interest rates on outstanding borrowings. At March 31, 1999 under United States GAAP, gross capitalised interest of £499m (1998 – £525m) with regard to the company and its subsidiary companies was subject to depreciation generally over periods of 2 to 25 years.

(d) Goodwill

Under United Kingdom GAAP, in respect of acquisitions completed prior to April 1, 1998, the group wrote off goodwill arising from the purchase of subsidiary undertakings, associates and joint ventures on acquisition against retained earnings. The goodwill is reflected in the net income of the period of disposal, as part of the calculation of the gain or loss on divestment. Under United States GAAP, such goodwill is held as an intangible asset in the balance sheet and amortised over its useful life and only the unamortised portion is included in the gain or loss recognised at the time of divestment. Gross goodwill under United States GAAP at March 31, 1999 of £1,957m (1998 – £925m) was subject to amortisation over periods of 3 to 20 years. Goodwill relating to MCI was unchanged for the period from October 31, 1997 when the investment ceased to have associated company status until disposal on September 15, 1998. The value of goodwill is reviewed annually and the net asset value is written down if a permanent diminution in value has occurred. Under United Kingdom GAAP, goodwill arising on acquisitions completed on or after April, 1, 1998 is generally accounted for in line with United States GAAP.

(e) Mobile cellular telephone licences, software, and other intangible assets

Certain intangible fixed assets recognised under United States GAAP purchase accounting requirements are subsumed within goodwill under United Kingdom GAAP. Under United States GAAP these separately identified intangible assets are valued and amortised over their useful lives.

(f) Investments

Under United Kingdom GAAP, investments are held on the balance sheet at historical cost. Under United States GAAP, trading securities and available-for-sale securities are carried at market value with appropriate valuation adjustments recorded in profit and loss and shareholder's equity, respectively. The net unrealised holding gain on available-for-sale securities for the year ended March 31, 1999 was £76m (1998 – £1,315m relating primarily to the investment in MCI, 1997 – £nil).

(g) Deferred taxation

Under United Kingdom GAAP, provision for deferred taxation is generally only made for timing differences which are expected to reverse. Under United States GAAP, deferred taxation is provided on a full liability basis on all temporary differences, as defined in SFAS No. 109. At March 31, 1999, the adjustment of £1,424m (1998 – £2,095m) reconciling ordinary shareholders' equity under United Kingdom GAAP to the approximate amount under United States GAAP included the tax effect of other United States GAAP adjustments. This comprised an adjustment increasing non-current assets by £59m (1998 – £76m decrease); an adjustment increasing current assets by £50m (1998 – £68m increase); £nil adjustment (1998 – £184m decrease) to current liabilities; an adjustment decreasing minority interests by £11m (1998 – £3m decrease) and an adjustment increasing long-term liabilities by £1,544m (1998 – £2,274m increase).

(h) Dividends

Under United Kingdom GAAP, dividends are recorded in the year in respect of which they are declared (in the case of interim or any special dividends) or proposed by the board of directors to the shareholders (in the case of final dividends). Under United States GAAP, dividends are recorded in the period in which dividends are declared.

The most frequently occurring adjustments were found to be those dealing with amortization of goodwill and deferred taxation. Of the two, the amortization of goodwill was the *dominant* effect when measured as a percentage of United States reported earnings. In fact, up to 18 percent of the difference between United States and United Kingdom-based earnings, on average, was taken up by goodwill amortization, which was generally not found in U.K. profit and loss accounts at that time. In a follow-up study, Weetman, Jones, Adams, and Gray (1998) discovered that the tendency for U.K. GAAP to result in higher earnings had continued. In 1988, U.K. earnings were, on average, 17 percent higher than U.S. earnings and that the gap had widened to 25 percent by 1994 (see Exhibits 4.7 and 4.8).

In summary, the differences between U.S. and U.K. accounting principles show that in practice U.K. GAAP is significantly *less* conservative, or the United States *more* conservative, as far as the quantitative impact on earnings is concerned. While this is contrary to what might be expected from two major Anglo-American countries with *similar* accounting traditions, an important question still to be addressed is this: how different are the United States and United Kingdom from other countries with quite *different* accounting traditions?

A GLOBAL PERSPECTIVE ON EARNINGS MEASUREMENT

While the evidence available suggests that earnings measured under U.K. accounting principles tend to be systematically higher or less conservative than earnings measured under U.S. accounting principles, what do we know about the relative impact of Anglo-American accounting principles on earnings compared to those of continental Europe and Japan?

Continental Europe

The importance of understanding how accounting differences can affect the interpretation of company accounts in Europe has been emphasized again recently. It is not so clear, however, how the net effect of such differences has an impact on earnings. An early attempt to quantify, in practice, the impact of French and German accounting principles compared to U.K. accounting principles was made by Gray (1980) in an empirical study of 15 French, 28 German, and 29 U.K. companies for the period 1972–75. The database for this study was provided by DAFSA Analyse of

Exhibit 4.7   Number of Companies Making Each Category of Adjustment to Profit, Together with Mean and Median Index of Comparability for 1988 and 1994

Nature of Adjustment to Profit	1988 *Count*	1988 *Mean*	1998 *Median*	1994 *Count*	1994 *Mean*	1994 *Median*
Overall	25	1.17	1.10	25	1.25	1.18
Goodwill	24	1.13	1.06	23	1.21	1.15
Deferred tax	22	1.06	1.01	23	1.00	1.00
Pensions/post-retirement benefits/insurance	10	1.01	1.01	19	1.02	1.02
Asset/expense	14	0.98	0.99	14	1.12	1.01
Historic cost/revalued asset	13	0.95	0.98	18	0.98	0.99
Intangibles	3	1.08	1.07	5	1.34	1.06
Restructuring	—	—	—	5	0.80	0.88
Foreign currency translation	5	1.00	1.01	4	0.94	0.99
Financial instruments	2	1.26	1.26	4	0.98	1.04
Leasing	2	1.05	1.05	4	1.16	1.15
Revenue recognition	3	1.02	1.00	3	0.95	0.99
Extraordinary items	12	0.95	1.05	—	—	—
Miscellaneous	5	1.01	1.03	13	0.98	1.01

The following outliers were excluded from calculation of the mean values of profit in respect of the 1994 data:

1. ICI Group plc (Overall index of comparability and partial index of comparability for pension costs and retirement benefits)

2. WPP Group plc (overall index of comparability and partial index of comparability for amortization of goodwill)

Source: P. Weetman et al., *Accounting and Business Research* (Summer 1998): 196.

Paris with its data bank of European company accounts adjusted according to the "European Method" used by financial analysts. Using this adjusted basis of earnings as the yardstick for comparison, a "conservatism" index was calculated for each company as in the U.S.-U.K. comparative analysis, and the summarized results are shown in Exhibit 4.9.

From this it appears that earnings tend to be more conservative or understated in France and Germany than in the United Kingdom. The statistical significance of this hypothesis was supported by the results of a series of statistical (chisquare) tests as shown in Exhibit 4.10. It should be noted in this regard that there were no significant differences between France and Germany.

A more recent study by Simmonds and Azières (1989) provided support for these results and some further insight into measurement differences following the EU harmonization initiative, which was embodied especially in the EU Fourth Directive on Company Accounts (1978). A simulation exercise was carried out on a case study basis using a simplified version of the accounts of a multinational group. The overall results of this study demonstrate, as Exhibit 4.11 shows, that the highest most likely net profit and return on assets occurs in the United Kingdom and

Exhibit 4.8 Frequency Table of Distribution of Values of Index of Comparability for Profit

Level of Materiality	Index Values	1988	1994
Adjustment to U.K. profit is – 10% or more of the amount of US profit	≤0.90	5	4
Adjustment to U.K. profit between – 5% and – 10% of the amount of U.S. profit	0.91 – 0.94	1	1
Adjustment to U.K. profit within +/– 5% of U.S. profit	0.95 – 1.04	3	2
Adjustment to U.K. profit is between +5% and +10% of the amount of U.S. profit	1.05 – 1.09	3	1
Adjustment to U.K. profit is +10% or more of the amount of the U.S. profit	≥ 1.10	13	17
Total		25	25
Range (excluding outliers): lowest value		0.65	0.75
highest value		1.79	2.76

The following outlying index values were eliminated before calculating the t-statistic presented in Table 7

Name:	Index value eliminated	Year	Cause
ICI Group plc	3.36	1994	Large pension expense adjustment
WPP Group plc	10.77	1994	Low U.S. profit figure

Source: P. Weetman et al., *Accounting and Business Research* (Summer 1998): 197.

the lowest most likely net profit and return on assets in Spain, closely followed by Belgium and Germany.

Weetman and Gray (1991) using data disclosed to the SEC under Form 20-F, have also examined the impact of accounting differences on earnings in practice in the Netherlands, Sweden, and the United Kingdom. The research results tended to suggest that the Netherlands is at the less conservative end of the spectrum, similar to, but not as extreme as, the United Kingdom, while in Sweden there was a tendency to be more conservative than U.S. GAAP.

Japan

We suggested in Chapter 3 that accounting in Japan is the subject of many influences with a unique outcome. Despite the growing internationalization of Japanese accounting standards, the influence of taxation, creditor interests, and a "conservative" culture have ensured that measures of earnings are relatively understated compared to the United States. A study by Aron (1991) concluded that Japanese earnings in 1990 are understated by 33.9 percent, on average, compared to earnings measured under U.S. GAAP. This estimate was calculated for stock market

Exhibit 4.9   A Comparative Analysis of Profits-Measurement Behavior in France, Germany, and the United Kingdom, 1972–75

Reported Profits Classified Using an Index of Conservatism		France	Germany	United Kingdom	Total Disclosures
I.	0.50	12	12	2	26
II.	0.50–0.74	20	35	10	65
III.	0.75–0.94	14	37	5	56
Pessimistic (<0.95)		46 (77%)	84 (75%)	17 (14%)	147
IV.	0.95–0.99	4	4	11	19
V.	1.00	1	1	4	6
VI.	1.01–1.05	0	4	17	21
Neutral (0.95–1.05)		5 (8%)	9 (8%)	32 (28%)	46
VII.	1.06–1.25	3	6	37	46
VIII.	1.26–1.50	2	6	20	28
IX.	1.50	4	7	10	21
Optimistic (>1.05)		9 (15%)	19 (17%)	67 (58%)	95
Total Disclosures		60 (100%)	112 (100%)	116 (100%)	288

Source: S. J. Gray, "International Accounting Differences from a Security Analysis Perspective: Some European Evidence," *Journal of Accounting Research* (Spring 1980): 68.

listed companies taken as a whole by making adjustments, on a judgmental basis, for the impact of tax deductible reserves, consolidation practices, and depreciation. After making further adjustments for cross-holdings and differences in capitalization, it was suggested that the average Japanese price-earnings ratio becomes 12.51 and not 34.30 as reported by Morgan Stanley Capital International Perspective. Thus, the mystery of relatively high Japanese price-earning ratios was resolved to some degree. However, it should be noted that differences in financial ratios such as corporate liquidity and gearing (leverage) are not just the result of accounting differences but also differences in the financial systems and norms of countries. In Japan, for example, higher levels of gearing and short-term payables are considered normal relative to the United States because of longer-term relationships with

Exhibit 4.10   Comparative Analysis of Profits-Measurement Behavior: Chi-Square Test Statistics 1972–75 (2 × 2 Analysis, One-Tailed Test)

Comparative Analysis	1972	1973	1974	1975
France/United Kingdom	6.67[a]	10.40[b]	16.30[b]	11.54[b]
Germany/United Kingdom	9.27[b]	19.36[b]	16.97[b]	9.53[b]
France/Germany	0.05	0.003	0.30	0.67

[a] Significant at the 0.01 level.
[b] Significant at the 0.001 level.

Source: S. J. Gray, "International Accounting Differences from a Security Analysis Perspective: Some European Evidence," *Journal of Accounting Research* (Spring 1980): 69.

Exhibit 4.11 Comparative Analysis of the Impact of Accounting Measurement Differences in the European Union

Millions of European Currency Units	Belgium	Germany	Spain	France	Italy	Netherlands	U.K.
Net Profit	135	133	131	149	174	140	192
Net Assets	726	649	722	710	751	704	712
Return (%)	18.6	20.5	18.2	21.0	23.2	19.9	27.0

Source: A. Simmonds and O. Azières, *Accounting for Europe: Success by 2000 AD?* (Brussels: Touche Ross Europe, 1989), p. 42.

bankers and suppliers. Similarly, a longer-term view tends to be taken of profitability, with much more emphasis placed on achieving growth in sales and market share.

Data at the corporate level on the impact of Japanese/U.S. GAAP differences is not readily obtainable because most Japanese companies listed in the United States report in accordance with U.S. GAAP. However, a study by Cooke (1993) provides some interesting case evidence. Tokio Marine and Fire Insurance Company, for example, reveals that Japanese GAAP income is 50 percent and 48 percent of U.S. GAAP income for 1990 and 1991, respectively (see Exhibit 4.12).

Exhibit 4.12 Reconciliation Statement: The Tokio Marine and Fire Insurance Company

	31 March 1991	31 March 1990
Net income (Japanese GAAP)	40,253	37,031
Add:		
Excess of change in underwriting reserves in report to stockholders over change in unearned premiums in the financial statements	32,379	33,934
Deferred policy acquisition costs	19,576	13,973
Other	7,540	5,552
Deduct:		
Additional provision for losses incurred but not reported	(2,593)	(6,380)
Income taxes (deferred taxation)	(9,300)	(2,200)
Other	(4,619)	(7,969)
Net Income (U.S. GAAP)	83,236	73,941
Japanese/U.S. =	48.36%	50.08%

Note: A reconciliation was not provided for 1989 although the net income reported to shareholders using Japanese GAAP was ¥44,092 m and the comparable figure based on U.S. GAAP was ¥92,978 m. The Japan/U.S. comparison is 47.41 percent.

Source: T. E. Cooke, "The Impact of Accounting Principles on Profits: The U.S. versus Japan," *Accounting and Business Research* (Autumn 1993): 469.

Exhibit 4.13   The Comparative Impact of
International Accounting
Differences on Earnings:
Earnings Adjustment Index
Based on U.S. GAAP

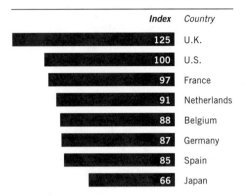

Index	*Country*
125	U.K.
100	U.S.
97	France
91	Netherlands
88	Belgium
87	Germany
85	Spain
66	Japan

A COMPARATIVE GLOBAL ANALYSIS

While there is a pressing need for further research in this area, the research to date
provides a global perspective that indicates that U.S. accounting principles are significantly *more* conservative than the United Kingdom but significantly *less* conservative than Japan and many continental European countries in terms of their
impact on earnings. If the United States is taken as the yardstick with an index number of 100, then its relationship, on average, with the United Kingdom, Belgium,
France, Germany, the Netherlands, Spain, and Japan can be shown as it is in Exhibit
4.13. Of course, this is very much a judgmental impression based on the limited evidence available.

Taken overall, clearly, the United Kingdom is significantly less conservative
than other countries, with Japan at the other extreme reporting only 66 percent of
U.S. earnings and 53 percent of U.K. earnings, on average, on the basis of differences in accounting principles. The continental European countries, on the other
hand, are largely bunched together in a more conservative group compared to the
United States. This suggests that significantly different approaches to accounting
measurement persist despite the continued international harmonization efforts to
achieve global comparability.

INTERNATIONAL ACCOUNTING
DIFFERENCES AND THE STOCK MARKET

While the persistence of significant measurement differences internationally poses
problems for financial analysts and those concerned with international harmonization, there is an important question concerning how stock prices react to earnings
calculated under different GAAPs. While the evidence on this issue is so far limited,
some early research by Meek (1983) indicated that U.S. stock prices react to foreign
GAAP earnings. More recently, research by Pope and Rees (1992) suggests that in

the case of U.K. corporations listed in the United States and also reporting under U.S. GAAP, there is significant incremental explanatory power given by the U.S. GAAP earnings adjustment information. Further, research by Amir, Harris, and Venuti (1993) of Form 20-F reconciliations for companies in 20 countries supports the value relevance of the U.S. GAAP information. However, more recent research by Rees (1995, 1996), Barth and Clinch (1996), and Fulkerson and Meek (1998) is less clear with mixed results.

FACTORS INFLUENCING MEASUREMENT DIFFERENCES

The reasons for measurement differences can be found in the environmental and cultural factors influencing accounting principles in these countries (as discussed in Chapters 2 and 3). In the United States and the United Kingdom, it seems that the stock market is a dominant influence, with the information needs of investors encouraging a more "optimistic" view of earnings and hence higher share prices. At the same time, accounting principles are relatively flexible, the accounting profession is relatively independent of government, and the tax rules have only a limited influence on accounting practice. Underlying cultural values tend to both motivate and reinforce a *less* conservative approach to measurement taken overall (see Chapter 3).

In continental Europe and Japan, on the other hand, it appears that taxation and sources of finance are relatively major influences compared to the stock market. In these countries, there is a tradition of commercial codes and accounting plans. Moreover, it is common for the tax authorities to allow for tax purposes *only* those items charged in the accounts and to tax earnings as reported in the accounts. This tends to lead to a more conservative application of accounting principles in order to report lower earnings for tax purposes. In addition, the significance of creditors and loan finance relative to equity provides a further conservative influence in that lower earnings will tend to better meet the interests of creditors and lenders vis-à-vis shareholders. The legal requirements relating to accounting are also usually more detailed, with the result that professional influence is relatively low and is limited mainly to the audit function. Finally, underlying cultural values tend to both motivate and reinforce a *more* conservative approach to measurement.

GLOBAL ACCOUNTING HARMONIZATION

Although a number of organizations around the world, including the UN and EU, have been concerned with harmonizing international differences in accounting and reporting, the most important body in recent years has been the International Accounting Standards Committee (IASC). The IASC was established in 1973 by leading professional accounting organizations in Australia, Canada, France, Germany, Ireland, Japan, Mexico, the Netherlands, the United Kingdom, and the United States.

The main aim of international accounting standards has been to achieve a degree of comparability that will help investors make their decisions while reducing the costs of MNEs in preparing multiple sets of accounts and reports. It is also fair to say that the IASC saw itself as playing a major role in coordinating and harmonizing the activities of the many agencies involved in setting accounting and reporting standards. The IASC's standards are also intended to provide a useful model for developing countries wishing to establish accounting standards for the first time.

In the early days of IASC, international standards were developed allowing substantial flexibility to accommodate different national interests but since the late 1980s, there has been growing pressure to develop more uniform standards to facilitate cross-border capital raisings and stock exchange listings. A core standards program to promote the development of more uniform and high-quality standards was initiated in cooperation with the International Organization of Securities Commissions (IOSCO) and was completed in 1998. The IASC is now hoping that IOSCO's recent endorsement will lead to a greater recognition of International Accounting Standards and the promotion of global harmonization at least among MNEs. The IASC has so far approved 41 International Accounting Standards and has already gained acceptance by many stock exchanges around the world though often subject to certain conditions. A growing number of companies are also electing to follow IAS's though compliance is not always as comprehensive in practice as claimed (Street, Gray, and Bryant, 1999).

As of May 2000, IOSCO recommended acceptance of IAS's subject to supplemental treatments where necessary. The key question now is whether IOSCO members, and especially the United States, will accept IAS's wholeheartedly as "global" standards with equal, if not greater, status compared to domestic standards. A crucial part of this acceptance is the recent restructuring of the governance of IASC, (and its renaming as the International Accounting Standards Board (IASB)) effective 2001, to make it a more independent body with a status consistent with the global authority required to set standards at this level. Further analysis of global accounting harmonization issues is provided in Chapter 6.

SUMMARY

1. The significance of international accounting diversity for the global investment community and the problems of international financial statement analysis have received increasing recognition.

2. There are many significant differences in accounting principles around the world that impact on reported earnings and financial position.

3. Research into the quantitative impact of U.S.-U.K. accounting differences reveals that such differences are systematic and that they do matter. U.K. earnings are significantly higher or *less* conservative than U.S. earnings on the basis of GAAP differences.

4. The impact of U.K. GAAP on earnings also seems to be significantly *less* conservative compared to France, Germany, the Netherlands, Sweden, and a number of other continental European countries.

5. Accounting principles in Japan are significantly *more* conservative than those in the United States and the United Kingdom with respect to their impact on earnings and assets.

6. When making comparisons between the United States and the United Kingdom, on the one hand, and continental Europe and Japan, on the other, it is clear that while accounting measurement practices in the United States are signifi-

cantly *more* conservative than the United Kingdom, they are significantly *less* conservative than Japan and many continental European countries.

7. The impact of differences in accounting principles tends to reflect the dominant stock market focus of the United States and United Kingdom versus the taxation/creditor emphasis still important in continental Europe and Japan. At the same time, these differences seem to be motivated and reinforced by underlying differences in cultural attitudes toward conservatism or prudence in accounting measurement.

8. While research on the reaction of stock prices to international accounting differences is still somewhat limited, findings tend to support the value relevance of such differences to investors.

9. Efforts to achieve global accounting harmonization have been made since the early 1970s, notably by the International Accounting Standards Committee (IASC), now renamed as the International Accounting Standards Board (IASB) following a restructuring of the governance of the IASC in 2001.

10. Recent endorsement of International Accounting Standards by IOSCO is a promising step forward towards acceptance of a global set of accounting standards.

Discussion Questions

1. To what extent is it possible for investors to cope with international accounting differences *without* making any adjustments or reconciliations to their home country GAAP?

2. How desirable are reconciliations such as those required under the SEC's Form 20-F regulations for foreign corporations?

3. If accounting principles around the world are harmonized, will this necessarily eliminate the diversity of earnings measurements practices?

4. Do you think it inevitable that pressures for the globalization of measurement principles and practices will overcome local environmental and cultural influences? If so, when?

Case: *The Japanese Puzzle*

Tom Griffen was puzzled. He had just completed a standard financial ratio analysis of the translated financial statements of a major Japanese manufacturing company. He knew that the company was an acknowledged leader in its industry and one of the largest and most successful in terms of world market share. What puzzled him was that the company appeared to be on the verge of bankruptcy—at least according to his calculations of the various financial ratios and indicators commonly employed in the United States. In comparing the financial statements of the Japanese firm to its U.S. counterpart with comparable sales, employment, and market share, he observed the following differences.

Balance Sheet Comparisons

The Japanese firm had two and a half times as much cash, deposits, and securities, 50 percent more notes and accounts receivables, and overall 30 percent more current assets, despite having 25 percent less inventory than the U.S. firm. In terms of fixed assets, operating fixed assets of the Japanese firm were only 23 percent of total assets versus 38 percent for the U.S. firm, while its long-term investments accounted for 11 percent of total assets versus only 6 percent for the U.S. firm.

As for liabilities, the Japanese firm had two and a half times more short-term borrowings, and its debt was nearly double that of the U.S. firm. Finally, the equity base of the Japanese firm was less than half that of the U.S. firm, whereas its debt-to-equity ratio was roughly three times larger.

Income Statement

Over a four-year period, the reported income of the Japanese firm was generally only about half that of its U.S. counterpart but had remained remarkably stable as a percentage of sales while that of the U.S. firm had fluctuated significantly from year to year. Its earnings per share were also consistently lower, despite having less equity.

Although Tim knew that there were significant differences between U.S. and Japanese cultures and business environments, he was not certain how these differences might be affecting the Japanese company's financial statements. Perhaps something was wrong with his use of the standard financial ratio analysis.

Questions

1. In general, what are the problems with applying one country's standard financial analysis techniques to the analysis of financial statements of a company from another country or with making other comparisons to firms in other countries?

2. In this specific case, what conditions or factors in Japan might be causing the puzzling financial analysis results?

3. What might Tom do to assess the true financial position of this company?

Case: *Matterhorn (Switzerland)*

Jack Stone is in a real quandary. He has only two weeks in which to make a final recommendation on the acquisition of Matterhorn, a Swiss manufacturer of high-quality mountain climbing equipment. Jack is on the international acquisitions staff of Leisure, Inc., a large U.S. company that specializes in recreational consumer goods for an increasingly fitness-conscious U.S. population. Leisure, Inc. has little experience in the international market but believes that Western Europe has potential. Jock Hancock, Leisure's president and founder, heard about Matterhorn from a mutual friend while skiing in Switzerland and asked his acquisitions staff to look into the matter.

Matterhorn is a Swiss corporation, with a large percentage of the stock owned by Hans Groberg and his family. Hans started the business 30 years ago and is anxious to sell so he can retire. He has two sons and a daughter who manage various Matterhorn subsidiaries but none of them is anxious to take over the business. Since beginning the business, some of the stock has been sold to nonfamily members, so Hans's personal holdings are less than 15 percent. However, his control over Matterhorn has never been questioned by other shareholders. The banks have provided substantial financing for Matterhorn and control most of the proxy votes of other shareholders at the annual meetings.

Part of Jack's dilemma is that he has no idea what to offer Matterhorn shareholders for their stock. The Swiss company law requires that financial statements be prepared, but the information disclosed is rather limited. Jack computed a price-earnings ratio for Matterhorn and discovered that it was four times that of a similar company in the United States, and he suspects that Matterhorn's earnings were understated in comparison with U.S. GAAP. On the balance sheet, he noticed that certain fixed assets were carried at a value of one Swiss franc, even though their insured value was several million Swiss francs. In talking with a CPA who had experience in Switzerland, Jack found out that hidden reserves, which tend to understate the value of assets and overstate expenses, were allowed. Jack tried to get Matterhorn's accountant to show him how the hidden reserves really affected the books, but the accountant was hesitant to do so.

Another problem is trying to get a picture of the whole corporation. Matterhorn's financial statements—such as they are—contain the results of only the parent. Jack knows that at least 10 subsidiaries controlled by Hans's children were not consolidated with Matterhorn's operations. Jack has tried to get copies of the financial statements of the subsidiaries and a summary of intercompany transactions but still has not received a response.

Questions

1. What are the major problems Jack faces in trying to evaluate this investment opportunity?
2. Why is the consolidation issue so tricky here?
3. What are some major differences in disclosure between Switzerland and the United States as brought out in this case?
4. Why are the Swiss so conservative and secretive in their accounting?

Case: *Hanson and* ICI (*United Kingdom*)

In May 1991, Hanson, the United Kingdom's most notoriously acquisitive corporation, purchased a 2.8 percent stake in ICI, the United Kingdom's largest manufacturer and the world's fourth largest chemical corporation. Amid speculation about the possibility of a takeover bid, the comparative performance of the two companies was a significant issue because of the claims of the respective management concerning their relative efficiency and success.

From an accounting perspective, it is possible to assess performance in terms of both U.S. and U.K. GAAPs because Hanson and ICI are listed in the United States and are required by the SEC, under Form 20-F, to provide reconciliation data. Exhibit 4.14 shows net income and shareholders' equity data for the period 1986–90 in accordance with both U.K. and U.S. GAAPs together with the data for long-term debt.

Questions

1. Calculate the "conservatism" index and returns on equity for Hanson and ICI for the period 1986–90 under both U.K. and U.S. GAAPs.
2. Does it appear that U.S. GAAP is more or less conservative than U.K. GAAP? What could be the main reasons for this?
3. To what extent do the results affect your assessments of comparative corporate performance?
4. Calculate the debt-equity (leverage or gearing) ratio for both corporations under both U.K. and U.S. GAAPs.

5. To what extent are the results likely to affect your assessment of the comparative riskiness of investing in Hanson and ICI?

Exhibit 4.14 Hanson and ICI: Comparative Data Under U.K. and U.S. GAAP

(in £)	1986	1987	1988	1989	1990
Hanson					
Net Income					
U.K. GAAP	365	572	1121	1101	1000
U.S. GAAP	332	542	880	927	950
Shareholders' Equity					
U.K. GAAP	1439	1730	2192	1046	2834
U.S. GAAP	2715	3083	3691	4825	6632
Long-term Debt	1972	1727	2124	4971	4258
ICI					
Net Income					
U.K. GAAP	557	760	838	1057	670
U.S. GAAP	589	734	800	860	650
Shareholders' Equity					
U.K. GAAP	3665	3445	3925	5014	4671
U.S. GAAP	3785	3939	4480	5469	5397
Long-term Debt	1897	1876	2046	2210	2373

Source: Hanson, ICI, Annual Reports

Case: Daimler-Benz (Germany)

Daimler-Benz (now DaimlerChrylser) was one of Germany's largest companies in 1993 with interests in automobiles, microelectronics, rail systems, energy systems, automation technology, and aerospace. The business had become increasingly global, with total sales of 98 billion deutsche marks, of which 60 billion are outside Germany.

On October 5, 1993, Daimler-Benz became the first German company to be listed on the New York Stock Exchange. While this opened up new opportunities for raising capital, stock marketability, and publicity for the corporation and its products, it also heralded a new era of financial reporting and disclosure to comply with SEC regulations in the United States. In accordance with the Form 20-F filing requirement, Daimler-Benz provided a reconciliation of earnings and equity to U.S. GAAP. This reconciliation was reproduced in its 1993 annual report and accounts (see Exhibit 4.15). It was also stated that Daimler-Benz is in the process of adapting its methods of accounting and valuation as closely as possible to U.S. GAAP.

Questions

1. Discuss the arguments for and against Daimler-Benz listing its shares in the United States.

2. Identify and discuss the major differences between U.S. and German accounting principles.

3. Calculate the "conservatism" index and returns on equity for 1992 and 1993 under both German and U.S. GAAP.

4. Does it appear that German GAAP are more or less conservative than U.S. GAAP? How can you explain your findings?

Exhibit 4.15   Daimler-Benz (Germany)

Valuation in Consolidated Financial Statements Adjusted to U.S. Accounting Principles

We began to conform our balance sheet accounting and valuation methods to international conventions with the 1989 consolidated financial statements, in order to simplify comparison with other companies as well as to improve our method of reporting. We were the first German company to list its stock on the New York Stock Exchange, and therefore reconciled net income and stockholders' equity to generally accepted accounting principles in the United States (U.S. GAAP). It became apparent that there were still substantial differences between our accounting principles and the U.S. accounting principles, which have a decisive influence on financial reporting.

In the 1993 consolidated financial statements, we have therefore adapted our methods of accounting and valuation as closely as possible to U.S. GAAP. These measures, which at the same time achieve substantial alignment between the German commercial balance sheet and the German tax balance sheet, have generated a one-time income before tax of DM 2.6 billion in the German consolidated financial statements. This amount is classified as extraordinary income. The balance of the differences are from rules and regulations regarding obligatory accounting and valuation procedures.

Our annual report includes a reconciliation of the net income and stockholders' equity determined according to the principles of the German "Handelsgesetzbuch" (Commercial Code) to those amounts reported under U.S. GAAP.

Additional Information in Accordance with the "U.S. Generally Accepted Accounting Principles" (U.S. GAAP)

With the introduction of Daimler-Benz stock on the New York Stock Exchange, we are filing an annual report as a "Form 20-F" with the Securities and Exchange Commission (SEC). Much of the content of this filing is information taken from our annual report; however, additional data and financial information is provided determined on the basis of U.S. accounting principles. In the following section we have set forth what we consider to be the most important information from the "Form 20-F." Since there are substantial differences, especially in the annual net income and stockholders' equity, the reconciliations are required to convert certain financial data from the German consolidated financial statements to the values calculated by using U.S. generally accepted accounting principles.

Differences in Accruals as a Result of the Change in the Treatment of Provisions and Valuation Methods

U.S. accounting principles do not allow the formation of the extensive loss provisions as permitted by German law. The excess German loss provisions have to be dissolved, which has an effect on the net income as well as stockholders' equity. According to U.S. GAAP, the stockholders' equity increased by DM 5.8 billion during 1993 as a result of the dissolution of certain loss provisions which also changed the inventory and receivables value. We use the term *Appropriated Retained Earnings* to disclose to the American investors that such retained earnings are not available for distribution as dividends. This term also establishes a bridge between the two different accounting cultures.

Long-Term Manufacturing

Customer deposits and manufacturing costs are reported under German law in accordance with the completed contract method, whereas U.S. principles generally require that the percentage-of completion method be used. The majority of contracts within the group require partial prepayment as well as partial recognition of profits based upon payments received. Contracts of this nature are also customary in the United States, and are recognized under its accounting regulations. The resulting differences therefore are not material.

Goodwill and Acquisition of Investments in Businesses

Under German accounting regulations, goodwill can be allocated to stockholders' equity, or capitalized and amortized generally over the expected useful life, which in Germany ranges between 5 to 15 years. Under U.S. GAAP, the difference between acquisition costs and market value must be capitalized and amortized over a period not exceeding 40 years.

Disposal of Investment in Businesses

Under German accounting principles, sales of subsidiaries and shareholdings in businesses must be allocated to the period in which the contract is signed. According to U.S. GAAP, the gain or loss on investment cannot be recognized until after the actual monetary exchange of the investment.

Pension Provisions

According to U.S. accounting principles, the determination of provisions for old-age pensions requires, among other things, a determination for anticipated increases in wages and salaries. The calculation is not based on the discount rate of 6 percent for unaccrued interest, which is applicable under German tax law but incorporates the respective actual interest rates. Another difference is a result of the requirement that health care costs for retirees be actuarially calculated and accrued for in the United States.

Currency Translation and Financial Instruments

Unrealized exchange profits and losses on financial instruments are treated differently in the two accounting systems. Under German law, according to the imparity principle, only unrealized losses are to be recorded, whereas under U.S. GAAP unrealized profits as well as losses must be recorded.

Other Differences in Valuation

Additional differences between German and American accounting methods may occur with respect to inventories, minority interests, and leasing activities.

Deferred Taxes

Under German accounting regulations, deferred tax assets are established only for the elimination processes in consolidation. Under U.S. accounting principles deferred tax assets can also be recorded for valuation adjustments and existing tax loss carryforwards.

Reconciliation of Consolidated Net Income and Stockholders' Equity to U.S. GAAP

	1993	1992
	in millions of DM	
Consolidated Net Income in Accordance with German Commercial Code	**615**	1,451
% Minority interest	(**13**)	(33)
Adjusted net income under German regulations	**602**	1,418
+/− Changes in appropriated retained earnings: provisions, reserves, and valuation differences	(**4,262**)	774
	(**3,660**)	2,192
Additional adjustments		
+/− Long-term contracts	**78**	(57)
Goodwill and business acquisitions	(**287**)	(76)
Business dispositions	—	337
Pensions and other postretirement benefits	(**624**)	96
Foreign currency translation	(**40**)	(94)
Financial instruments	(**225**)	(438)
Other valuation differences	**292**	88
Deferred taxes	**2,627**	(646)
Consolidated net income (loss) in accordance with U.S. GAAP before cumulative effect of changes in accounting principles in accordance with U.S. GAAP	(**1,839**)	1,402
Cumulative effect of changes in accounting in accordance with U.S. GAAP for postretirement benefits other than pensions (net of tax of 33 million DM)	—	(52)
Consolidated Net Profit in Accordance with U.S. GAAP	(**1,839**)	1,350
Earnings (loss) per share in accordance with U.S. GAAP	**DM (39.47)**	DM 29.00[1]
Earnings (loss) per American Depositary Share[2] in accordance with U.S. GAAP	**DM (3.95)**	DM 2.90
Stockholders' Equity in Accordance with German Commercial Code	**18,145**	19,719
% Minority interest	(**561**)	(1,228)
Adjusted stockholders' equity under German regulations	**17,584**	18,491
+/− Appropriated retained earnings/ (provisions, reserves, and valuation differences)	**5,770**	9,931

		23,354	28,422
Additional adjustments			
+/− Long-term contracts		**207**	131
Goodwill and business acquisitions		**2,284**	1,871
Pensions and other postretirement benefits		(**1,821**)	(1,212)
Foreign currency translation		**85**	(342)
Financial instruments		**381**	580
Other valuation differences		(**698**)	(1,708)
Deferred taxes		**2,489**	(138)
Stockholders' Equity in Accordance with U.S. GAAP		**26,281**	27,604

[1] Includes the negative effect of the change in accounting for postretirement benefits other than pensions of 1.12 DM per share (0.11 DM per American Depositary Share).

[2] Corresponds to one-tenth of a share of stock of 50 DM per value.

Source: Daimler-Benz, 1993 Annual Report.

Case: News Corporation (Australia)

News Corporation is one of Australia's largest media companies with newspapers, magazines, film, and TV operations around the world. As it is listed in the United States, a Form 20F filing is required by the SEC with a reconciliation of net income and stockholders equity from Australian GAAP to U.S. GAAP (see Exhibit 4.16).

Exhibit 4.16   The News Corporation Limited and Subsidiaries Notes to Consolidated Financial Statements

Note 18 – United States Generally Accepted Accounting Principles

	Year Ended June 30 (in millions)		
	1996	1997	1998
Net income as reported in the consolidated statements of operations	A\$ 1,020	A\$ 720	A\$ 1,682
Items increasing (decreasing) reported income before minority interest:			
Amortization of publishing rights, titles and television licenses	(256)	(318)	(552)
Net deferred taxes related to the amortization of publishing rights, titles and television licenses	(30)	(32)	(40)
Amortization of excess of cost over net assets acquired	16	13	17
Equity in earnings of associated companies	(51)	(235)	(288)
Revaluation of noncurrent assets	(76)	–	–
Developing business start-up costs	(59)	(239)	(145)

Other, net	(28)	(32)	(32)
Net decrease in reported income before minority interest	(484)	(843)	(1,040)
Approximate income before minority interest in accordance with accounting principles generally accepted in the United States	536	(123)	642
Minority interest	(53)	(76)	(87)
Approximate net income in accordance with accounting principles generally accepted in the United States	A$ 483	A$ (199)	A$ 555

	As of June 30 (in millions)	
	1997	1998
Stockholders' equity as reported in the consolidated balance sheets	A$ 22,234	A$ 27,211
Items increasing (decreasing) reported equity:		
Publishing rights, titles and television licenses:		
Revaluation and other	(4,188)	(5,366)
Amortization	(1,988)	(2,441)
Excess cost over net assets acquired:		
Effect of adopting SFAS No. 109 and other	1,991	2,397
Amortization	169	186
Accounts payable and other—noncurrent:		
Effect of adopting SFAS No. 109 and other deferred taxes	(2,445)	(2,923)
Other	(156)	(190)
Investments:		
Elimination of associated company's interest in TNCL	(530)	–
Associated companies reserve	(744)	(1,050)
Reclassification of minority interest in subsidiaries	(2,930)	(1,951)
Other	(121)	(160)
Net decrease in reported stockholders' equity	(10,942)	(11,498)
Approximate stockholders' equity in accordance with accounting principles generally accepted in the United States	A$ 11,292	A$ 15,713

Questions

1. Calculate the "conservatism" index for net income and stockholders' equity for 1997 and 1998

2. Calculate the returns on equity for 1997 and 1998 under both Australian GAAP and U.S. GAAP. (*Note:* Use the stockholders' equity figure as at June 30, 1997 and 1998 for the purpose of calculating 1997 and 1998 returns.)

3. Explain the reasons for the different results and discuss how these differences might be resolved.

Selected References

Adams, C. A., P. Weetman, E. A. E. Jones, and S. J. Gray. 1999. "Reducing the Burden of U.S. GAAP Reconciliations by Foreign Companies Listed in the United States: The Key Question of Materiality," *The European Accounting Review*, 8 (1): 1–22.

Amin, E., T. S. Harris, and E. K. Venuti. 1993. "A Comparison of the Value-Relevance of U.S. versus non-U.S. GAAP Accounting Measures using Form 20-F Reconciliations," *Journal of Accounting Research* 31, supplement.

Aron, Paul H. 1991. "Japanese P/E Ratios in an Environment of Increasing Uncertainty," in *Handbook of International Accounting*, edited by F. D. S. Choi. New York: John Wiley.

Barth, M. and G. Clinch. 1996. "International Accounting Differences and Their Relation to Share Prices: Evidence from U.K., Australian and Canadian Firms," *Contemporary Accounting Research* (Spring): 134–170.

Bhushan, R. and D. R. Lessard. 1992. "Coping with International Accounting Diversity: Managers' Views on Disclosure, Reconciliation and Harmonization," *Journal of International Financial Management and Accounting,* 4(2): 149–64.

Brown, R. R., V. E. Soybel, and C. P. Stickney. 1997. "Achieving Comparability of U.S. and Japanese Price Earnings Ratios," in *International Accounting and Finance Handbook,* edited by F. D. S., Choi, 2nd ed. New York: John Wiley, pp. 7.1–7.18.

Choi, F. D. S., S. K. Min, S. O. Nam, H. Hino, J. Ujiie, and A. I. Stonehill. 1983. "Analyzing Foreign Financial Statements: The Use and Misuse of International Ratio Analysis," *Journal of International Business Studies* (Spring–Summer): 113–31.

Choi, F. D. S. and K. Hiramatsu. 1987. *Accounting and Financial Reporting in Japan.* New York: Van Nostrand Reinhold.

Choi, F. D. S. and R. M. Levich. 1990. *The Capital Market Effects of International Accounting Diversity.* Homewood, IL: Dow Jones-Irwin.

Choi, F. D. S. and R. M. Levich. 1991. "International Accounting Diversity and Capital Market Decisions," in *Handbook of International Accounting*, edited by F. D. S. Choi. New York: John Wiley.

Cooke, T. E. 1989. "Voluntary Corporate Disclosure by Swedish Companies," *Journal of International Financial Management and Accounting* (Summer): 171–95.

Cooke, T. E. 1993. "The Impact of Accounting Principles on Profits: The US versus Japan," *Accounting and Business Research* (Autumn).

Fortune Global 500. www.fortune.com/fortune/global500/

Frost, C. A. and G. Pownall. 1996. "Interdependencies in the Global Markets for Capital and Information: The Case of SmithKline Beecham plc," *Accounting Horizons* (March): 38–57.

Fulkerson, C. L. and G. K. Meek. 1998. "Analysts Earnings Forecasts and the Value Relevance of 20F Reconciliations from Non-US to US GAAP," *Journal of International Financial Management and Accounting* (9): 1–15.

Gray, S. J. 1980. "International Accounting Differences from a Security Analysis Perspective: Some European Evidence," *Journal of Accounting Research* (Spring).

Harris, T. S., M. Lang, and H. P. Möller. 1994. "The Value Relevance of German Accounting Measures—An Empirical Analysis," *Journal of Accounting Research* (Autumn) 32 (2): 187–209.

International Accounting Standards Board. www.iasb.org.uk

International Organization of Securities Commission. www.iosco.org

Meek, G. 1993. "U.S. Securities Markets Responses to Alternative Earnings Disclosures of Non-US International Corporations," *Accounting Review* (April).

Nobes, C. W. 1988. *Interpreting U.S. Financial Statements.* London: Butterworths.

Nobes, C. W. 1989. *Interpreting European Financial Statements: Towards 1992.* London: Butterworths.

Norton, J. 1995. "The Impact of Financial Accounting Practices on the Measurement of Profit and Equity: Australia versus the United States," *Abacus* (September) 31 (2): 178–200.

Pope, P. F. and W. P. Rees. 1992. "International Differences in GAAP and the Pricing of Earnings," *Journal of International Financial Management and Accounting* (Autumn).

Radebaugh, L. H., G. Gebhardt, and S. J. Gray. 1995. "Foreign Stock Exchange Listings: A Case Study of Daimler-Benz," *Journal of International Financial Management & Accounting,* 6 (2): 158–92.

Rees, L. L. 1995. "The Information Contained in Reconciliations to Earnings Based on U.S. Accounting Principles by Non-U.S. Companies," *Accounting and Business Research* (25): 301–10.

Rees, L. L. 1996. "A Comparison of Investors' Abilities to Assimilate U.S. GAAP Disclosures," *Journal of Accounting and Public Policy* (15): 271–87.

Samuels, J. M., R. E. Brayshaw, and J. M. Craner. 1995. *Financial Statement Analysis in Europe.* London: Chapman & Hall.

Sherman, R. and R. Todd. 1997. "International Financial Statement Analysis," in *International Accounting and Finance Handbook,* edited by F. D. S. Choi, 2nd ed. New York: John Wiley, pp. 8.1–8.61.

Simmonds, A. and O. Azières. 1989. *Accounting for Europe: Success by 2000 AD?* Brussels: Touche Ross Europe.

Street, D. L., S. J. Gray, and S. M. Bryant. 1999. "Acceptance and Observance of International Accounting Standards," *The International Journal of Accounting,* 34 (1): 11–48.

Weetman, P., E. A. E. Jones, C. A. Adams, and S. J. Gray. 1988. "Profit Measurement and UK Accounting Standards: A Case of Increasing Disharmony in Relation to US GAAP and IASs," *Accounting and Business Research* (Summer).

Weetman, Pauline and S. J. Gray. 1990. "International Financial Analysis and Comparative Corporate Performance: The Impact of U.K. versus U.S. Accounting Principles on Earnings," *Journal of International Financial Management and Accounting* (Summer–Autumn).

Weetman, Pauline and S. J. Gray. 1991. "A Comparative International Analysis of the Impact of Accounting Principles on Profits: The USA versus the UK, Sweden and the Netherlands," *Accounting and Business Research* (Autumn).

CHAPTER FIVE

INTERNATIONAL TRANSPARENCY AND DISCLOSURE

Chapter Objectives

- Explain the importance of corporate transparency and information disclosure
- Show how annual report disclosures are an important way of communicating to stakeholders in the company
- Evaluate the incentives to disclose information and the costs involved
- Review international disclosure regulation and reporting trends
- Highlight important issues found in corporate reports, such as the chairperson's statement, the review of corporate strategy and results, external and unusual events, acquisitions and disposals, human resources, social responsibility, R&D, capital investment, and future prospects
- Describe other types of corporate disclosures, such as the review of operations, including segmental information and the review of financial position and results
- Review issues relating to the frequency and timeliness of corporate reporting internationally.

INTRODUCTION

In this chapter we examine differences in transparency and disclosure practices by MNEs and across countries. The lack of "transparency" of company accounts and reports is a major issue and concern in many countries around the world consistent with the growing need to attract and retain foreign capital and facilitate capital raisings internationally. This issue was highlighted recently with the Asian financial crisis in 1997 and the suggestion that higher levels of disclosure would have helped to prevent the crisis occurring in the first place (Choi, 1998).

DISCLOSURE IN CORPORATE REPORTS

The amount of information disclosed by MNEs in corporate reports has expanded considerably in recent years. The major source of pressure for increased disclosures has been the financial and investment community. Both MNEs and standard-setting bodies in countries with well-developed securities markets, such as the United States, the United Kingdom, France, Germany, and Japan, have been concerned primarily with responding to pressures from this direction. There has also been something of an explosion in the demand for information by a wide range of other participant groups including, most important, governments, trade unions, employees, and the general public.

We will examine the pressures for information disclosure, why disclosure is important, the incentives and costs to management to make disclosures, and the types of disclosure in different countries.

The Pressures for Information Disclosure

Not surprisingly, MNEs are concerned about the manner in which apparently ever-increasing requirements for information disclosure are determined by regulatory bodies and standard-setting agencies at both governmental and professional levels. The pace at which regulation has accelerated since the early 1970s is such that it is sometimes suggested that only a time lag separates a request from its eventual declaration as a required disclosure. Such a view may vastly oversimplify the technical and political process through which standards are established—a process in which many companies directly or indirectly participate. But the ultimate result, albeit at times postponed or slowed down, has been increasing accounting and disclosure requirements.

The acceleration in the demand for information for investment purposes might well appear to be unsustainable and hence must eventually decline. However, the increasing internationalization of financial markets and share ownership, combined with a concurrent growth in awareness of the considerable diversity of accounting principles and practices in different countries, has fueled the demand for additional information disclosures to increase both the quality and comparability of MNE reports.

Apart from the investor group, there is a growing belief among other groups—such as governments and trade unions—that both an increased availability and an improved quality of information are essential. It can be argued that many of these demands are general, vague, and imprecise. However, as the demand has grown, so too has its precision at both the national and international levels. International organizations such as the UN, OECD, European Union, and IASB are now issuing more detailed requirements and recommendations.

At a time when some may have thought that, for MNEs headquartered in countries with well-developed securities markets, the demand for information might have eased, there has been a growing and articulated demand from a range of nontraditional information users for more information, some of it already available to and directed at investors—some demanded by emerging user groups.

Users with the ability or power to obtain "tailor-made" reports, such as trade unions at national levels with adequate bargaining power and organizational ability, are apparently learning the limitations of corporate annual reports. They are increasingly concentrating their energies on obtaining special purpose reports more in line with their specific information needs. While this has the effect of reducing the demands on the annual publication of the general purpose corporate report, it increases the pressures on corporations to improve the availability of more comprehensive information through other channels.

Thus, the increased supply of information appears in some respects to have actually increased, rather than reduced, the demand for additional information. If the demand for information were fixed, corporations could include this as one of the benefits to be matched against the costs of information disclosure. However, this is clearly not possible in the current dynamic context of information demand. But to what extent is the information demanded likely to be used and understood—and by whom?

Communicating to Users

The decisions of corporations and/or regulatory bodies as to which groups have a right to or should be provided with information are a major determinant of the content of corporate reports—and influence in particular the *range* of information. Equally important is the decision about whom within these groups the information is aimed at; this determines its *depth*. Despite the long history of information disclosure by corporations, only recently have systematic efforts been made to assess the ability of supposed users actually to use corporate annual reports. There is growing evidence that these reports are neither read nor understood by a considerable percentage of those whom they are supposed to inform, especially the layperson investor.

The direct users are apparently the relatively small number of experts who have the necessary ability and experience to analyze financial information. No group is without its information analysts. Many investors and shareholders do not make investment decisions alone but rely on the advice of experts. They may do this by buying advice or by consulting the financial press or other sources of interpretation.

Why do only a minority directly use corporate reports? The fact is that corporations, of even moderate size, are complex organizations. A comprehensive corporate analysis necessitates not only the use of financial information but additional data as well as to assess current and future trends. In the main, MNEs are especially complex and so too are their corporate reports. Not only do MNEs produce a variety of products, but, most important, they operate in a number of countries and therefore in different operating environments with a variety of risks, opportunities, and pressures. Accordingly, MNE corporate reports have some characteristics rarely, and sometimes never, found in those of domestic corporations. Their worldwide consolidated financial statements are usually drawn up according to the accounting standards and practices of one country only, usually that of the MNE's headquarters. Few users are familiar with the accounting practices of more than one country, and there is an inevitable tendency by many users to interpret MNE corporate reports as if they were drawn up according to the practices of their own rather than the source country.

Limiting or reducing (by simplifying) the information in annual accounts may make them superficially more intelligible to a wider audience. But it may well result in the omission of essential information useful to the direct users—the experts. To suggest otherwise is to confuse corporate annual reports with the underlying reality they attempt to portray. This is not to say that the clarity of such reports cannot be improved, nor that some information provided may not be superfluous. However, if corporate reports were to be pitched at the level of the layperson they would have to be reduced substantially in size. This would mean foregoing important elements in the accounting and information message and lowering the standard of analysis of those who actually, rather than ideally or hypothetically, use them.

In order to make informed decisions about corporations, an ability to analyze information is essential —those who cannot do so are precluded from making such decisions. The U.S. Financial Accounting Standards Board (FASB) was quite definite about this when it stated, "clearly investors ... have varying understanding of matters such as security markets, business enterprises and financial statements, and financial statements cannot directly help investors and creditors who know little about those matters."

The tension between the need for more detailed and complex information for decision-making purposes and information that can be readily understood by the layperson for stewardship purposes has led to much ambiguity. The 1973 U.S. Trueblood Report, for example, stated that

> accounting information should be presented so that it can be understood by reasonably well-informed, as well as by sophisticated, users. In effect, presenting information understandable only to sophisticated users establishes a bias ... no valid users' needs should be ignored. Information that can be understood, and is needed, by sophisticated users should not be diluted to eliminate what less able users cannot understand.

However, this means trying to achieve the impossible—providing something for everyone. This ambiguity and lack of consensus, while possibly acting as a constraint on increasing disclosure requirements, has not in practice prevented regulatory bodies from requiring extensions in disclosure. The effective demand has come from those who actually use and desire more information (i.e., the experts, especially investment analysts active in the securities market) and not from those who some may wish did so. Many MNEs nevertheless appear to regard widespread usage of their reports as desirable and view the current level of complexity, and even more the additional information now demanded, as inhibiting or preventing this. Demanding expanded disclosures, often in the name of greater accountability, is contradictory to them. Increased information means greater complexity, thus making corporate accounts and reports even less accessible than before to all but a few. A minority argument is to regard corporate reports as information, which of necessity is, and can only be, appropriately used by experts. Accordingly, no amount of reduction, or alteration, would compensate for the absence of adequate analytical skills, knowledge, and experience in laypersons.

Just as the majority of information providers considers questions regarding the comprehensiveness of information to be within the ambit of the conventional wisdom, "information for all with a legitimate interest," so too on the demand side there is a failure to appreciate the difference between actual users of information and those on whose behalf the information is used. The OECD, for example, refers to information that should "improve public understanding." Such a distinction is unnecessary, however, because what ultimately matters, from the user's perspective, is the expanded *availability* of relevant information. Ironically, what might appear elitist—aiming information at the experts—is likely to be the most democratic. In this way the information needs of the many groups affected by the operations of MNEs are perhaps best served in practice. At the same time, there is presumably some limit to the quantity of information that can be conveniently analyzed even by experts.

The view that does not differentiate between different levels of interpretive abilities within groups, but sees them as homogeneous, has tended to dominate the disclosure debate. A major objective of corporate reports is, or perhaps should be, to "serve primarily those users who have limited authority, ability, or resources to obtain information and who rely on financial statements as their principal source of information." As we have suggested, however, this is probably best achieved through the medium of expert users, in that they are likely to be able to make the most effective use of the information disclosed. While attempts to help the unsophisticated *directly*, by simplifying corporate reports, may be worth investigating, the danger is that this approach may be ineffective, misleading, and a waste of resources. On the other hand, the provision of simplified information on a *supplementary* basis as a means of improving firm-participant communications could prove to be a worthwhile option that will in no way diminish the supply of information for the expert user.

The Importance of Information Disclosures

While there is no doubt about the continuing significance of accounting measurement issues, the importance of information disclosed in financial statements and accompanying reports is being increasingly recognized by multinational corporations. This information provides an important input to the financial analysis process of evaluating the *quality* of earnings and financial position, both current and prospective. A particularly important motivation for voluntary information disclosures by MNEs is that the annual report provides the opportunity to communicate more policy and future-oriented information about the corporation. This may better inform or influence investors in the increasingly globalized securities markets. It is interesting, for example, that more than 400 of the fortune Global 500 firms now provide financial and other corporate information on the Internet. This is a trend that is likely to have an increasing impact on the disclosure practices of stock exchange-listed companies around the world.

It is generally accepted that the costs of providing information should not exceed the benefits derived by the users of the information. In particular, the need for MNEs to maintain business confidentiality in sensitive areas and to avoid jeopardizing their competitive position should be taken into account. At the same time, this need must be weighed against the interests of analysts, investors, and the public in the transparency of multinational business operations. In practice, it appears that the more specific and the more future oriented—and especially the more quantitative—the information proposed for disclosure, the more sensitive becomes the attitude of MNEs toward its provision.

Managerial Incentives to Disclose Information

Management provides information both voluntarily and in response to regulation. There may be incentives for the management of an MNE to disclose information voluntarily if it perceives it to be in its own interests and that of the corporation, to respond to the information demands of users and participant groups. Research by Meek and Gray (1989) and others has shown, for example, that voluntary disclosures are forthcoming when corporations are competing for finance from investors, especially in a cross-border context. Where governments and trade unions exert an influence over the environment the MNE operates in, there will also be strong influences on the MNE to disclose information to compete with other MNEs for investment opportunities or to exchange it to maintain existing rights or avoid potential constraints on their operations.

On the other hand, if management decides that the information demands are unreasonable or inimical to their interests or those of the MNE (e.g., when the information is unfavorable or contains "bad news"), they must either achieve some compromise or accept the consequences, if any, of nondisclosure. Thus a diverse and complex set of factors influence corporate disclosures (see Figure 5.1).

Costs of Information Production

The disclosure of information has a direct monetary cost. MNEs are understandably unwilling to incur increased costs through expanded disclosures unless they are

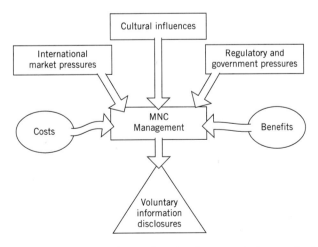

Figure 5.1   The Costs and Benefits of Voluntary Disclosures by MNCs

required to do so or the potential benefits exceed the estimated costs. The direct cost of information disclosure to a corporation is the value of the resources used in gathering and processing the information as well as in its audit and communication.

The direct costs of such disclosures will preeminently depend on the internal structure of the MNE and information generated in order to manage this structure. The closer existing information is to the disclosure requested, the lower will be the actual direct cost of producing the information. Because the information needs of management are not always identical with those of other groups, the absence of complete harmony between internal and external information needs is inevitable.

Apart from the direct costs of disclosure there are the indirect costs relating to competitive disadvantage (see next section), with its associated disincentives to innovate or invest, as well as the costs resulting from interference or regulation by governments.

Competitive Disadvantage of Disclosure

The most frequently cited objection to increased disclosure requirements is that of competitive disadvantage (i.e., the use of the additional information by competitors to the detriment of the corporation disclosing the information). It is a major basis for the resistance to expanded disclosures.

In some circumstances disclosure of information could be damaging to MNEs. As a general rule, the more specific or future oriented a disclosure is, the greater the potential competitive disadvantage for the disclosing corporation.

What of the relatively small percentage of possible disclosures that hypothetically could cause damage to the discloser? Should this danger definitively rule out their release? Information that allows competitors to increase their well-being at the expense of the discloser is damaging for the latter but profitable for the former.

The dilemma is to distinguish between disclosures, which, for the economy as a whole, result in aggregate competitive advantages exceeding aggregate competitive disadvantages. What is detrimental or beneficial to the economy in the short term may, in some circumstances, have the opposite effect in the longer term. Increased competition through disclosure could lead to greater vigor in the economy. It could also lead to a decline in business incentives as a result of the appropriation of rewards by competitors facilitated by expanded disclosures.

The relative importance of various possible costs of disclosure was explored in a study by Gray, Radebaugh, and Roberts in 1990. The study found general agreement by both U.S. and U.K. financial executives (see Exhibit 5.1) that the indirect cost of competitive disadvantage was the most important cost factor constraining voluntary disclosures. However, the results of the tests showed that, overall, there were significantly different perceptions in the responses concerning the impact of several of the types of costs involved, including the possibility of claims from employees or trade unions and technical processing problems.

Managerial Attitudes to Voluntary Disclosures

Demands for additional information disclosures have come from both international organizations (in particular the UN, OECD, European Union, and IASB) and

Exhibit 5.1   Cost Factors Constraining Voluntary Information Disclosure as
Perceived by U.K. and U.S. Financial Executives

	Rank	
	U.K.	U.S.
Cost of competitive disadvantage	1	1
Cost of data collection and processing	2	2
Cost of auditing	3	3
Possibility of claims from employees or trade unions	4	9
Threat of takeover or merger	5	6
Cost of publication	6	5
Technical processing problems	7	3
Possibility of intervention by government agencies	8	8
Possibility of claims from political or consumer groups	9	10
Possibility of intervention by taxation authorities	10	7

Note: Items with higher ranks have greater constraints
Source: S. J. Gray, L. H. Radebaugh, and C. B. Roberts, "International Perceptions of Cost Constraints on Voluntary Information Disclosures," *Journal of International Business Studies* (Winter 1990): 602.

the host governments and societies in which MNEs operate. However, the growing globalization of capital markets indicates the presence of significant market pressures for additional information about MNE operations as well as the existence of prospects for and concern about the international coordination of capital market regulations. It is against this background that MNE management must weigh the costs and benefits of voluntary information disclosures.

Gray, Radebaugh, and Roberts (1990) also examined the extent to which there are perceived net costs or benefits for disclosing specific items of information voluntarily, the types of costs involved, and the significance of cost constraints with respect to specific disclosures. The results of the study showed that, on average, the respondents tended to perceive most voluntary or discretionary disclosure items as giving rise to a net cost (see Exhibit 5.2). At the same time, there was a wide range of views depending on the specific item of information concerned. However, items perceived as giving rise to major net costs in both the United States and the United Kingdom were inflation-adjusted profits, quantified forecasts, and narrowly defined segment information.

In terms of voluntary disclosure practices by MNEs, a study by Meek, Roberts, and Gray (1995) examined the factors influencing the voluntary disclosures of 226 MNEs from the United States, the United Kingdom, and continental Europe. A wide range of information disclosures were examined and categorized into three types: strategic, nonfinancial, and financial. A common benchmark of voluntary disclosures was established that would apply to all countries, and a disclosure score was calculated for each company. The means and standard deviations for all companies and for the U.S., the U.K., and the continental European groupings are shown in Exhibit 5.3. Scores for these groupings are also given for the internationally listed and domestically listed samples; from these it can be seen that the internationally listed MNEs tend to disclose more information voluntarily.

Exhibit 5.2 The Net Costs or Benefits of Disclosure of Specific Items Perceived by U.K. and U.S. Financial Executives—Items with Highest Net Costs

	Rank	
	U.K.	U.S.
LoB profits; narrow definition	1	2
Describe major legal proceedings	2	9
Quantitative forecasts; sales and profits	3	7
LoB sales; narrow definition	4	4
Geographical profits; narrow definition	5	3
Inflation-adjusted profits	6	5
LoB segment transfers	7	12
Geographical segment transfers	8	13
Describe major patents and expiry dates	9	8
Foreign assets by country	10	10
Geographical sales data; narrow definition	11	6
Employment information	23	2
Value-added statements	24	1

Source: S. J. Gray, L. H. Radebaugh, and C. B. Roberts, "International Perceptions of Cost Constraints on Voluntary Information Disclosures," *Journal of International Business Studies* (Winter 1990): 602.

Taken overall, the results show that all MNEs regardless of size or home country provide more information in their annual reports than the regulations require. With respect to the factors influencing voluntary disclosure, statistical support was found for size, international listing status, country or region of origin, and industry. A relatively weak multinationality effect was also detected. The results also indicate that the factors explaining voluntary annual report disclosures differ by information type. The largest MNEs are those that set the trends in providing voluntary disclosures of nonfinancial and financial information. There are also industry patterns to these two types of disclosures, suggesting that MNEs pay attention to what their closest competitors disclose when making decisions about such disclosures. Nonfinancial information is also a European phenomenon. Finally, strategic information disclosures are a special feature of continental European MNEs and, generally speaking, are also significant for internationally listed MNEs.

INTERNATIONAL DISCLOSURE REGULATION

As indicated earlier, management's disclosure pattern may be set not only by its own preferences and cultural tendencies but also by regulation. International information disclosure requirements concerned specifically with the form and content of the directors' report in the EU center primarily on the Fourth (1978) and Seventh (1983) Directives on company annual accounts and consolidated accounts respectively. In the case of MNEs, the EU Seventh Directive, which has been imple-

Exhibit 5.3 Voluntary Disclosure Scores by Multinationals

	Strategic Information		Nonfinancial Information		Financial Information		Overall Disclosures	
	Mean	Standard Deviation	Mean	Standard Deviation	Mean	Standard Deviation	Mean	Standard Deviation
All Companies	21.03	13.81	18.06	11.01	16.62	8.89	18.23	7.49
U.S. All Companies	17.22	10.52	11.89	7.10	16.54	6.81	15.20	5.40
U.S. International	20.03	10.98	14.50	7.41	17.27	7.12	17.09	5.55
U.S. Domestic	14.41	9.32	9.27	5.73	15.81	6.46	13.32	4.56
U.K. All Companies	16.83	8.52	25.70	9.15	14.58	9.30	18.73	6.78
U.K. International	17.41	9.70	25.71	10.28	16.92	10.44	19.87	7.95
U.K. Domestic	16.24	7.27	25.69	8.03	12.24	7.44	17.60	5.24
Cont. Euro. All Companies	36.52	16.56	23.01	12.41	19.67	11.83	25.16	8.30
Cont. Euro. International	36.51	17.54	21.87	13.28	23.19	9.34	26.23	8.36
Cont. Euro. Domestic	36.53	15.05	24.16	11.65	16.15	13.16	24.09	8.29

Source: G. K. Meek, C. B. Roberts, and S. J. Gray, "Factors Influencing Voluntary Annual Report Disclosures by U.S., U.K., and Continental European Multinational Corporations," *Journal of International Business Studies* (third quarter, 1995): 564.

mented in all member countries, is especially relevant. Under Article 36 of the Directive, the annual report of the Board of Directors must include a "fair review of the development of the business" together with an indication of any important events that have taken place since the end of the year and any "likely future development." An indication must also be given of activities in the field of Research and Development. So far as individual companies, as opposed to groups of companies, are concerned, the Fourth Directive incorporates similar requirements.

Also relevant here are the information disclosure requirements in the United States. The SEC requires a "management discussion and analysis" of the financial statements to be provided in annual reports. This is expected to include discussion of the results of operations, liquidity and capital resources, and, preferably, the impact of inflation. In addition, the disclosure of future-oriented information is considered desirable. The discussion of these topics on a segmental basis for each business segment is also encouraged. The purpose of the SEC requirements is to provide a framework for discussion that allows management some flexibility to comment on the specific features of the corporation and its industry and that encourages innovation in presentation (e.g., the mixing of narrative commentary and quantitative date) to promote effective communication. The aim is to provide users with an understanding of management's own insights into strategy and performance. This example has been followed in the United Kingdom with the non-mandatory statement by the Accounting Standards Board recommending the provision of an "Operating and Financial Review."

The relative strength of disclosure regulation internationally can be estimated using a 1992 study by Adhikari and Tondkar (see Exhibit 5.4). This study revealed significant variations in the overall quantity and level of detail of disclosure (both financial and nonfinancial) that are required as part of the listing and filing requirements of stock exchanges around the world. Disclosure scores were calculated on a weighted as well as unweighted basis for a total of 35 stock exchanges. The weighted scores were based on the relative importance of the disclosures to stock market analysts. The New York Stock Exchange is clearly the leader in terms of disclosure requirements, with London not far behind.

The study found that size of the equity market was significant in determining the level of disclosure and clearly those countries with more developed stock markets tend to have higher levels of disclosure regulation compared to those in some of the emerging economies (e.g., India and Pakistan), although Switzerland has one of the lowest levels of disclosure consistent with its reputation for "secrecy." However, no significant relationships were found for the other variables examined, that is, degree of economic development, type of economy, activity on the equity market, and dispersion of stock ownership.

A further study of disclosure levels by Saudagaran and Biddle (1995) provided information on the relative rankings of eight major stock markets according to the judgments of a wide range of interested parties such as corporate managers, investment bankers, public accountants, stock exchange officials, attorneys, and academics. The survey included an assessment of capital market expectations as well as statutory and stock exchange reporting requirements. As Exhibit 5.5 shows, the United States ranked highest, with Canada and the United Kingdom not far behind. Switzerland is clearly perceived to have the lowest disclosure level, which is consistent with its reputation for "secrecy."

Exhibit 5.4   Accounting Disclosure Requirements of Global
Stock Exchanges

Weighted and Unweighted Disclosure Scores

Stock Exchange (Country)	Disclosure Scores	
	Weighted	Unweighted
1. Sydney (Australia)	74.60	74.64
2. Vienna (Austria)	54.17	53.52
3. Rio de Janeiro (Brazil)	67.28	68.75
4. Toronto (Canada)	79.00	78.64
5. Bogota (Colombia)	54.58	54.48
6. Copenhagen (Denmark)	67.20	66.86
7. Cairo (Egypt)	49.02	48.02
8. Helsinki (Finland)	70.54	71.05
9. Paris (France)	76.20	76.16
10. Frankfurt (Germany)	67.20	66.86
11. Athens (Greece)	60.00	59.41
12. Hong Kong (Hong Kong)	77.04	75.77
13. Bombay (India)	58.23	58.84
14. Milan (Italy)	68.46	68.39
15. Tokyo (Japan)	77.68	77.68
16. Seoul (Korea)	71.43	72.00
17. Luxembourg (Luxembourg)	66.62	66.64
18. Kuala Lumpur (Malaysia)	75.69	75.41
19. Mexico (Mexico)	70.55	70.68
20. Amsterdam (Netherlands)	73.19	72.84
21. Wellington (New Zealand)	67.13	65.91
22. Oslo (Norway)	60.63	60.59
23. Karachi (Pakistan)	55.71	55.82
24. Lisbon (Portugal)	65.68	65.50
25. Singapore (Singapore)	80.89	80.32
26. Johannesburg (South Africa)	74.50	73.48
27. Madrid (Spain)	68.84	68.36
28. Stockholm (Sweden)	60.54	60.05
29. Zurich (Switzerland)	52.24	52.39
30. Taipei (Taiwan)	72.19	71.70
31. Bangkok (Thailand)	74.78	75.41
32. Istanbul (Turkey)	50.68	50.68
33. London (United Kingdom)	86.21	84.86
34. New York (United States)	90.31	90.75
35. Caracas (Venezuela)	73.67	73.32

Source: A. Adhikari and R. H. Tondkar, "Environmental Factors Influencing
Accounting Disclosure Requirements of Global Stock Exchanges," *Journal of
International Financial Management and Accounting* (Summer 1992): 105.

Exhibit 5.5   Disclosure Level Survey Results[a] (Based on 142 responses)

	Mean Ranks				
	Statutory Reporting Requirements	Exchange Reporting Requirements	Capital Market Expectations	Overall Disclosure Levels	Disclosure Level Rank (DLR)
United States	7.27	7.29	7.17	7.28	8
Canada	6.48	6.38	5.91	6.41	7
United Kingdom	5.84	5.87	6.09	6.02	6
Netherlands	4.68	4.80	4.50	4.75	5
France	4.11	4.50	4.13	4.17	4
Japan	3.82	4.04	4.22	3.83	3
Germany	3.96	3.90	4.04	3.81	2
Switzerland	2.70	2.78	3.17	2.60	1

Spearman Rank Correlation between Overall
Disclosure Levels and:

Statutory Reporting Requirements	.976
Exchange Reporting Requirements	1.000
Capital Market Expectations	.952

[a] Ranks are in descending order with '8' ('1') indicating highest (lowest) disclosure level.
Source: S. M. Saudagaran and G. C. Biddle, "Foreign Listing Location: A Study of MNCs and Stock Exchanges in Eight Countries," *Journal of International Business Studies* (second quarter, 1995): 331.

REPORTING TRENDS

In the following review of trends, we will discuss the information disclosures in directors' reports in the context of three fairly well-accepted categories of disclosure: we will label these the *corporate review,* the *operations review,* and the *financial review.* The chapter concludes with a discussion of additional information disclosures.

The *corporate review* includes information disclosures relevant to the overall performance of a corporation. This group of items includes:

1. The chairperson's statement
2. The review of corporate strategy and results
3. External and unusual events information
4. Acquisitions and disposals information
5. Human resources information (including information about management and organizational structure and labor employment information)
6. Social responsibility information
7. Research and Development information
8. Investment program information
9. Future prospects information.

The *operations review,* on the other hand, includes:

1. A more detailed discussion and analysis of operations
2. Disaggregated analysis by business and geographical segment

The *financial review* includes the discussion and analysis of

1. Results
2. Liquidity and capital resources
3. Asset valuations and inflation

Corporate Review Information

The corporate review is a review of the business activities of the corporation as a whole and is consistent with the scope of the requirements of the EU Fourth (1978) and Seventh (1983) Directives. The content of the corporate review typically includes:

1. The Chairperson's Statement   This statement provides a platform for insights from the chairperson or chief executive in his or her leadership role about the overall performance and prospects of the corporation.

2. A Review of Corporate Strategy and Results (including also a Mission Statement) MNEs invariably provide some narrative commentary and data that are relevant to a review of corporate strategy and results. A mission statement or statement of objectives is increasingly included (see, for example, the statement by Unilever in Figure 5.2). Statements of corporate values (often including some corporate objectives) are also sometimes presented as in the case of Telstra (see Figure 5.3).

More information tends to be disclosed in this review of corporate strategy and results when stock market pressures exert themselves (e.g., when corporations are changing their strategy or are subject to the threat of a takeover bid). The merger of Daimler with Chrysler, for example, in 1998 prompted substantial discussion in the DaimlerChrysler annual report about the strategy of the new company and gave rise to a new mission statement (see Figure 5.4).

3. Comments on External and Unusual Events   MNEs also tend to provide some commentary on the impact of external events such as exchange rates, interest rates, government policy, market conditions, foreign competition, and so on. Many cor-

---

Our purpose in Unilever is to meet the everyday needs of people everywhere—to anticipate the aspirations of our consumers and customers and to respond creatively and competitively with branded products and services which raise the quality of life.

Our deep roots in local cultures and markets around the world are our unparalleled inheritance and the foundation for our future growth. We will bring our wealth of knowledge and international expertise to the service of local consumers—a truly multi-local multinational.

Our long-term success requires a total commitment to exceptional standards of performance and productivity, to working together effectively and to a willingness to embrace new ideas and learn continuously.

We believe that to succeed requires the highest standards of corporate behavior toward our employees, consumers, and the societies and world in which we live.

This is Unilever's road to sustainable, profitable growth for our business and long-term value creation for our shareholders and employees.

Figure 5.2   Unilever's Corporate Purpose

OUR COMPANY VALUES

PREAMBLE

- The Values outlined below are those originally adopted by the Senior Management Team to guide their behavior, and which are now adopted as Values for the whole Company.

- These Values guide our behavior in all our business activities, whether onshore or offshore.

- We shall continually monitor our own behavior against these Values.

VALUES

We believe in these key Values:

- **The Customer Comes First**
  Our customers dominate our priorities; we aim to meet customers' needs, on time every time.

- **Respect for Individuals**
  We encourage constructive, candid, open communications. We are accessible. We always treat our people with fairness and equality. We trust our colleagues.

- **Highest Standards of Integrity**
  We always act honestly. We say what we mean; we mean what we say.

- **Business Success**
  Business success secures our future. Our profits permit us to invest for long-term customer satisfaction, a rewarding future for our people, and a return to the shareholder.

- **Continual Improvement**
  We seek new ways of doing things, taking risks where necessary in pursuing new opportunities.

- **Teamwork**
  We acknowledge our interdependence; we give recognition for a job well done.

- **Bias for Action**
  We have a bias for action, and for achieving results for our customers.

Figure 5.3   Telstra

OUR PURPOSE *is to be a global provider of automotive and transportation products and services, generating superior value for our customers, our employees and our shareholders.*

OUR MISSION *is to integrate two great companies to become a world enterprise that by 2001 is the most successful and respected automotive and transportation products and services provider.*

We will accomplish this by constantly delighting our customers with the quality and innovation of our products and services, resulting from the excellence of our processes, our people and our unique portfolio of strong brands.

Figure 5.4   DaimlerChrysler

porations also report unusual events affecting the corporation, such as factory explosions, fraud, and litigation.

4. Acquisitions and Disposals Information Discussion and analysis of acquisitions and disposals are not widespread. While disclosure levels are relatively high in the United States and United Kingdom, information on acquisitions and disposals is rarely comprehensive or well presented elsewhere.

5. Human Resources Information Many MNEs provide information that is relevant to an assessment of human resources. This area of disclosure often includes information about management and organizational structure as well as labor and employment. Information about senior management (e.g., names, experiences, responsibilities, but excluding the directors) and organizational structure tends to be provided by only a minority of MNEs. However, disclosure levels for these areas are relatively high in Australia and New Zealand, France, Sweden, and the United States.

Disclosures about labor and employment are made by a majority of MNEs, with disclosure levels relatively high in France, Germany, the Netherlands, Sweden, Switzerland, and the United Kingdom. The nature and extent of narrative commentary and data vary considerably and include such topics as labor relations, training, welfare benefits, and safety. It is interesting to note that France requires a separate *bilan social* (social balance sheet or social report) containing details of pay structure, health and safety conditions, hours worked, absenteeism, strikes, industrial relations, and so on. This encourages some French MNEs (e.g., Pernod Ricard) to include employment information in their annual reports.

6. Value-Added Information While it is regarded by U.S. companies as a costly disclosure, value-added information often proves quite interesting and useful reading. Value-added statements show, in financial terms, the contribution of all stakeholders, and especially employees, to business performance. A minority of MNEs—primarily European firms—provides this information. An example of a value-added statement is given by Electrolux (Sweden) (see Figure 5.5).

The purpose of the value-added statement, which shows the value added to materials and services purchased externally, is to present the results of a corporation's operations that are attributable to the efforts of a more broadly defined group of participants, rather than just the investor group, and to show the distribution of wealth created to all stakeholders.

7. Social Responsibility Information The term *social responsibility* refers to accountability to society as a whole with respect to matters of public interest such as community welfare, public safety, and the environment. An increasing number of MNEs disclose social responsibility information such as environmental protection and clean-up information. This information is also often available from other sources. Figure 5.6 gives an example of environmental disclosure from SmithKline Beecham (U.K.).

8. Research and Development Information It is generally accepted that R&D is a critical element of corporate success in the longer term. Information about R&D

Statement of Added Value

Added value represents the contribution made by a company's production, i.e. the increase in value arising from manufacture, handling, etc. within the company. It is defined as sales revenues less the costs of purchased goods and services.

Sales revenues for the Electrolux Group in 1997 totaled SEK 113,000m (110,000). After deduction of purchases of goods and services, the value added by the Group amounted to SEK 32,977m (35,309), a decrease of 7% (–4) from the previous year. The decrease refers mainly to the provision for the restructuring program. During the past five years, added value has increased at an average annual rate of 4.5% (5.8).

In 1997, SEK 3,628m (5,536) of the value added remained within the Group and was utilized among other things for capital expenditure as well as product development and marketing Dividend payments to shareholders accounted for 3% (3) of added value in 1997. or 4% (3) of the Group's total payroll costs.

The added value generated within the Group over the past two years and its distribution are shown in the tables below:

CALCULATION OF ADDED VALUE	1997 SEKm	%	1997 per Employee, SEK ·000	1996 SEKm	%
Total revenues	113,000	100	1,067	110,000	100
Cost of purchased goods and services	–80,023	–71	–756	–74,691	–68
Added value	32,977	29	311	35,309	32

CALCULATION OF ADDED VALUE	1997 SEKm	%	1997 per employee, SEK ·000	1996 SEKm	%
To employees					
Salaries	19,883	60	188	20,249	58
Employer contributions	6,185	19	58	6,174	17
	26.068	79	246	26,423	75
To State and municipalities					
Taxes	944	3	9	1,237	3
To credit institutions					
Interest, etc.	1,422	4	13	1,198	3
To shareholders					
Dividend payments (1997: Proposed)	915	3	9	915	3
	3,281	10	31	3,350	9
Retained in the Group					
For wear on fixed assets (depreciation)	4,255	13	40	4,438	13
Other	–627	–2	–6	1,098	3
	3,628	11	34	5,536	16
Added value	32,977	100	311	35,309	100

Figure 5.5 Electrolux

Environment & Safety

As we manufacture and deliver high-quality healthcare products around the world, we are committed to conducting ourselves in a manner that protects both people and the environment. To manage that commitment, we work according to established environment and safety practices and policies that are integrated into the very fabric of our business. Key achievements during 1999 include:

Environmental Goals After a detailed review of our long-term environmental performance goals, we identified new opportunities for improvement, including a ten-fold increase in the amount of waste recycled. The revised goals, based on specific facility projects, are detailed in our Environment and Safety Report.

Behavioral Safety Program Our Behavioral Safety Program empowers employees to encourage and counsel each other on safe work practices. The program has been formally launched and will be phased into all manufacturing operations. We expect this innovative approach to safety to help SB achieve further reductions in lost time injury and illness incidence rates, which have been reduced by more than 20% each year over the last three years for a total improvement of 59%.

Control Matrices In support of our manufacturing processes, we introduced structured control systems that provide a standardized approach for categorizing hazards and defining the corresponding level of administrative and engineering controls required for safe and environmentally responsible handling and production of SB materials.

Environment and Safety Management Implementation of our Environment and Safety Management System, which assists and supports compliance with SB and legislative requirements, continues on schedule. With implementation nearing completion at most of our sites, we will explore the possibility of external company-wide certification. We also continued to integrate environment and safety issues into key business processes such as research and development, capital review, contract manufacturing and site acquisition and divestiture.

Sustainable Development At SB, we believe that it is important to continue to move toward sustainable business practices. We integrate innovative product design and development, excellent economic performance, demonstrated social responsibility and strong commitment to safety and the environment into the fabric of our business. Doing so enables us to maintain a strong competitive advantage and achieve our goal of helping to make people's lives everywhere healthier.

Performance Corporate Environment and Safety reviews site performance on a three-year schedule using a new scored system. An Environment and Safety Report is available and posted on the World Wide Web at www.sb.com. The report highlights SB's environment and safety activities and key performance indicators.

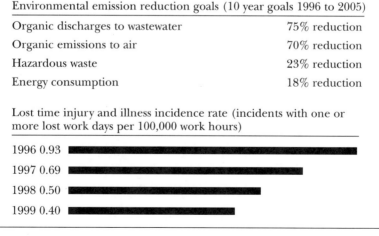

Environmental emission reduction goals (10 year goals 1996 to 2005)

Organic discharges to wastewater	75% reduction
Organic emissions to air	70% reduction
Hazardous waste	23% reduction
Energy consumption	18% reduction

Lost time injury and illness incidence rate (incidents with one or more lost work days per 100,000 work hours)

1996 0.93	
1997 0.69	
1998 0.50	
1999 0.40	

Figure 5.6   SmithKline Beecham

activities is disclosed by only a small majority of MNEs. While the nature and extent of the information, both narrative commentary and data, vary substantially, disclosure levels are relatively high in Germany, Japan, the Netherlands, Switzerland, the United Kingdom, and the United States.

9. Investment Program Information   It is generally accepted that the quality of a corporation's capital expenditures, as opposed to acquisitions of ongoing businesses from other corporations, is a critical factor in corporate success in the longer term. However, information about the corporation's investment program, including the nature, location, and significance of capital expenditure tends to be provided by only a small majority of MNEs. Disclosure levels are relatively high in Australia and New Zealand, the Netherlands, Switzerland, and the United Kingdom.

10. Future Prospects Information   While users are interested in improving their understanding of the current and past activities of MNEs, they are also, often primarily, interested in the corporation's future prospects. Information about future business prospects is disclosed by a majority of MNEs. However, this information is usually provided in the form of narrative commentary—as might be expected given the sensitive nature from a competitive disadvantage perspective of quantitative, future-oriented information. The nature and extent of the information provided vary substantially and are often general and very limited. Disclosure levels, however, are relatively high in Germany, Hong Kong, the Netherlands, the United Kingdom, and the United States.

Operations Review

The operations review relates to the activities of the various segments of the corporation's operations. This is where a more detailed review of business activities is provided on a disaggregated basis. Segmental reporting is now a well-established practice in information disclosures by MNEs, but the focus of attention has been on quantitative rather than qualitative information. In practice, the majority of MNEs provide additional narrative commentary, and sometimes quantitative data, on a segmental basis in their operations review.

1. Review of Business Segments   It is common practice for MNEs to provide a review of operations categorized by business segment, and a substantial majority of them do so. These reviews are often extensive, containing both narrative commentary and quantitative data. In countries where requirements governing the disclosure of quantitative segmental data have only recently been introduced or do not exist (e.g., Italy, Japan, Switzerland), this data often has been incorporated voluntarily into the operations review. The United States and Canada have recently provided for segmental disclosure on a management basis with disclosure being provided along the lines of the corporate organization.

In countries where quantitative disclosure requirements are effective, the business segments reviewed tend to be consistent with the quantitative data disclosed, and in some cases the operations review provides even more disaggregated and extensive information.

2. Review of International Operations and Geographical Segments   In contrast to business segments, a review of operations categorized by geographical segment is less common in practice. However, a discussion of activities on a geographical basis is frequently incorporated into the analysis of business segments. Some MNEs provide a review of international or geographical segment operations in addition to a review of business segment operations. Whether or not this information is provided seems to depend on the organizational structure of the corporation or the directors' aim of emphasizing international operations, which, for example, seems quite common in the case of Japan.

The discussion and analysis of international operations are an important area of information because the business activities of MNEs are becoming increasingly complex and geographically diversified.

Financial Review

The financial review relates to the discussion and analysis of the financial results and position of the corporation as a whole. The topics discussed include results, liquidity and capital resources, and asset valuations and inflation. The scope of this review is broadly consistent with the requirements in the United States to provide a "management discussion and analysis" of matters relevant to an improved understanding of the factors influencing a corporation's performance. Items included are:

1. An Analysis of Results   U.S. MNEs, consistent with SEC requirements, generally provide a more extensive discussion of events with a potential impact on earnings. Also included are the correlation of past trends with current sales and earnings, the reconciliation of underlying causes and economic influences with any changes in sales in the current year, and the disclosure of any matters that are expected to impact future operations.

2. An Analysis of Liquidity and Capital Resources   Disclosure levels are relatively high in France, Germany, Italy, the Netherlands, the United Kingdom, and the United States. Notably, U.S. MNEs generally provide a more extensive discussion, consistent with SEC requirements, and deal with funding obligations under existing contracts and expectations regarding future contracts, including the funding of projected business expansions. Plans to remedy liquidity problems are also discussed by some corporations.

3. An Analysis of Asset Values and Inflation   Apart from South America, requirements in the area of asset values and inflation are limited, despite some experience of inflation accounting in a number of countries. A discussion of asset valuations and the impact of inflation is provided in practice by only a small minority of MNEs. It is noteworthy, however, that disclosure, in terms of both narrative commentary and data, is especially evident in the Netherlands, Sweden, Switzerland, and the United Kingdom.

FREQUENCY AND TIMELINESS OF REPORTING

A further major disclosure issue concerns the timeliness and frequency of corporate reporting by MNEs. The need for information to be updated more frequently is becoming increasingly important to investors in the dynamic context of international securities markets. In practice, the development from reporting annually to a more frequent half-yearly and even quarterly basis has been somewhat slow (see Exhibit 5.6). In the United States and Canada, quarterly reports are required,

Exhibit 5.6 Interim Reports—Frequency

Argentina	Quarterly (most) Half-yearly (some)
Australia	Quarterly
Austria	Half-yearly
Belgium	Half-yearly
Brazil	Half-yearly
Canada	Quarterly
Chile	Quarterly
Colombia	Quarterly
Denmark	Half-yearly
France	Half-yearly
Germany	Half-yearly
Hong Kong	Half-yearly
India	Half-yearly
Ireland	Half-yearly
Israel	Quarterly
Italy	Half-yearly
Japan	Half-yearly (some) Quarterly (some)
Malaysia	Half-yearly
Mexico	Quarterly
Netherlands	Half-yearly
New Zealand	Half-yearly
Norway	Quarterly
Pakistan	Half-yearly
Peru	Quarterly
Philippines	Quarterly
Portugal	Half-yearly
Singapore	Half-yearly
South Africa	Half-yearly
Spain	Half-yearly
Sweden	Quarterly (some) Half-yearly (some)
Switzerland	Half-yearly
Thailand	Quarterly
United Kingdom	Half-yearly
United States	Quarterly

Source: Adapted from IASC *Interim Financial Reporting* (1996), p. 94.

though listed foreign companies are exempt if their local requirements specify only biannual reports. In Europe, the EU Directive on Interim Reports issued in 1982 required listed companies to provide half-yearly reports, but this was limited to abridged statements of income together with some brief commentary on operations. Many MNEs go beyond this to provide a full income statement and balance sheet. A number of MNEs also voluntarily provide unaudited quarterly reports in response to stock market and investor pressures (e.g., Volvo, ICI, Sony, Unilever).

The timeliness of reporting, whether it be annual, half-yearly, or quarterly, is a related issue, and here requirements and practices vary, though the norm for the publication of annual reports is usually set at a limit of six months from the financial year-end.

GROWING PRESSURES FOR TRANSPARENCY

There is growing pressure around the world to promote greater "transparency" and disclosure consistent with the importance of cross-border capital raisings and the growth of world trade and investment. Disclosure regulation varies internationally and there is often a lack of transparency, especially in the emerging economies.

Although many MNEs tend to be willing to disclose additional information, a growing number of major MNEs are more enlightened and often perceive it to be in their own interests to make voluntary disclosures likely to be relevant to external stakeholders, particularly investors. However, the nature of the disclosures would seem to depend not only on international capital market factors but also on local national concerns and traditions. The IASB is endeavoring to raise the standard of disclosure globally. One of the most important areas concerns segmental disclosures where the latest IAS endeavors to reveal the returns and risks of MNE operations on a more strategic and hence more insightful basis.

SUMMARY

1.   Information disclosure in MNE annual reports is an important complement to the financial statements. Additional information helps users gain a better understanding of the nature and effects of the activities of MNEs and to better analyze and assess the quality of earnings and financial position.

2.   At the same time, MNEs need to consider the costs involved, maintain business confidentiality in sensitive areas, and avoid jeopardizing their competitive position. In practice, the more specific and future oriented the item of information disclosure, the less likely are MNEs to want to make disclosures.

3.   There are significant variations in the overall quantity and level of detail of disclosure required by stock exchanges around the world.

4.   In practice, MNEs voluntarily disclose a wide range of additional narrative and quantitative information, though this tends to vary in volume, type, and quality according to the size of the MNE, its international stock exchange listing status, the geographical location of its headquarters, and the nature of its business operations.

5.   The largest MNEs tend to be the trendsetters in providing voluntary disclosures of nonfinancial and financial information. There are also industry pat-

terns to these two types of disclosure. Nonfinancial information disclosure is also a European phenomenon. Strategic information disclosures are a special feature of continental European MNEs and are also significant for internationally listed MNEs in general.

6.   Additional voluntary information disclosures by MNEs in their annual reports relate to a wide range of information disclosed in the corporate review. Examples include information relevant to the overall performance and prospects of a corporation, including the chairperson's statement, corporate strategy and results, external and unusual events, acquisitions and disposals, human resources, social responsibility, R&D, investment program, and future prospects.

7.   Information disclosed by MNEs in the operations review often includes a discussion and analysis of operations disaggregated by business and geographical segment.

8.   Information disclosed in the financial review often includes a discussion and analysis of results, liquidity and capital resources, and asset valuations and inflation.

9.   The frequency and timeliness of reporting varies around the world with quarterly reports required in North America and half-yearly reports required in Europe.

Discussion Questions

1.   To what extent are information disclosures by MNEs in directors' annual reports, as opposed to the financial statements, likely to be useful to financial analysts and investors?

2.   What are the likely costs and benefits to MNEs of making additional voluntary information disclosure?

3.   In which countries are stock exchange disclosure regulations most stringent? less stringent? What are the reasons for this?

4.   Are MNEs always likely to have a competitive advantage relative to smaller domestic companies with respect to information disclosures about their business activities?

5.   Discuss the kinds of information you would like to see in the corporate review, the operations review, and the financial review sections of an MNEs directors' report.

6.   Discuss the relevance to financial analysts and investors of additional disclosures by MNEs with regard to corporate strategy and related issues.

7.   Why is information relevant to future prospects likely to be of interest to financial analysts and investors? What are the constraints on MNEs providing such voluntary disclosures in practice?

Exercise

In groups of three or four students, select three major companies from different countries with operations in oil and gas field *or* pharmaceuticals. Access information about their social responsibility and environmental disclosures from annual reports, Web sites, and other public sources. Prepare a comparative and critical analysis of their corporate disclosures.

Case: *Infosys Technologies* (India)

One of India's new high-technology companies is Infosys, specializing in software development. Infosys is now listed on the NASDAQ, the first Indian company to be listed in the United States. While Infosys discloses more information than most Indian companies, as required by the SEC, the company discloses a substantial amount of additional information voluntarily including a value-added statement, an economic value added statement, and an "Intangible Assets Scoresheet" (see Exhibit 5.7).

Exhibit 5.7   Infosys (India)

Intangible Assets Scoresheet

			Knowledge Capital					
Our Clients (External Structure)			Our Organization (Internal Structure)			Our People (Competence)		
	1998– 99	1997– 98		1998– 99	1997– 98		1998– 99	1997– 98
Growth/Renewal								
Revenue growth over previous year (%)	97	81	IT investment/ value added (%)	11.71	14.12	Education index of all staff	10,731	7,326
Percentage of revenue from image-enhancing clients	49	46	R&D/value added (%)	2.62	2.88			
Percentage of revenue from exports	98	96	Total investment in organization/ value added (%)	19.16	18.52			
No. of new clients added during the year	39	45						
Efficiency								
Sales/Client (Rs. in lakhs)	407	243	Average proportion of support staff (%)	14.90	17.10	Value added per software engineer (Rs. in lakhs)	13.69	10.67
			Sales per support staff (Rs. in lakhs)	107	72	Value added per employee (Rs. in lakhs)	11.65	8.84
Stability								
Repeat-business revenue/total revenue (%)	90	83	Average age of support staff (Years)	30.88	31.15	Average age of all employees (Years)	26.14	26.56
Sales from the five largest clients/total revenue (%)	28	35						

(continues)

Exhibit 5.7   (*Continued*)

		Knowledge Capital			
Our Clients (External Structure)		Our Organization (Internal Structure)		Our People (Competence)	
1998–99	1997–98	1998–99	1997–98	1998–99	1997–98
Sales from the ten largest clients/total revenue (%)					
44	50				

The figures above are based on Indian GAAP financial statements.

Questions

1. Discuss the reasons why Infosys might want to disclose additional information voluntarily.

2. Explain and discuss the relevance of the information items disclosed in the intangible assets scoresheet. How would you interpret the changes from 1997–98 to 1998–99?

3. Under what circumstances could voluntary disclosures give rise to a competitive advantage rather than disadvantage?

Selected References

Accounting Standards Board. ASB Statement. 1993. *Operating and Financial Review*. London: ASB (July).

Adams, C. A., W. Y. Hill, and C. B. Roberts. 1998. "Corporate Social Reporting Practices in Western Europe: Legitimating Corporate Behaviour," *British Accounting Review*, (30): 1–21.

Adhikari, A. and R. H. Tondkar. 1992. "Environmental Factors Influencing Accounting Disclosure Requirements of Global Stock Exchanges," *Journal of International Financial Management and Accounting*, 4 (2): 75–105.

Beets, S. D. and C. C. Souther. 1999. "Corporate Environmental Reports: The Need for Standards and an Environmental Assurance Service," *Accounting Horizons* (June): 129–45.

Buzby, S. L. 1975. "Company Size, Listed vs. Unlisted Stocks, and Extent of Financial Disclosure," *Journal of Accounting Research* (Spring).

Choi, F. D. S. 1998. "Financial Reporting Dimensions of Asia's Financial Crisis," *Indian Accounting Review*, 2 (2): 1–11.

Chow, C. W. and A. Wong-Boren. 1987. "Voluntary Financial Disclosure by Mexican Corporations," *The Accounting Review*, 62 (3) (July): 533–41.

Cooke, T. E. 1991. "An Assessment of Voluntary Disclosure in the Annual Reports of Japanese Corporations," *International Journal of Accounting*, 26 (3): 174–89.

Cooke, T. E. 1989. "Voluntary Corporate Disclosure by Swedish Companies," *Journal of International Financial Management and Accounting* (Summer).

Craig, R. and J. Diga. 1998. "Corporate Accounting Disclosure in ASEAN," *Journal of International Financial Management & Accounting*, 9 (3): 246–74.

European Union. 1978. *Fourth Directive for the Co-ordination of National Legislation Regarding the Annual Accounts of Limited Liability Companies*. Brussels: EC.

European Union. 1983. *Seventh Council Directive on Consolidated Accounts*. Brussels: EC.

European Union. 1983. *Seventh Council Directive on Consolidated Accounts*. Brussels: EC.

Firth, M. A. 1979. "The Impact of Size, Stock Market Listing, and Auditors on Voluntary Disclosure in Corporate Annual Reports," *Accounting and Business Research* (Autumn).

Fortune Global 500. www.fortune.com/fortune/global500/

Frost, C. A. and K. P. Ramin. 1997. "Corporate Financial Disclosure: A Global Assessment," in *International Accounting and Finance Handbook,* edited by F. D. S. Choi, 2nd ed. New York: John Wiley.

Gray, S. J. and C. B. Roberts. 1989. "Voluntary Information Disclosure and the British Multinationals: Corporate Perceptions of Costs and Benefits," in *International Pressures for Accounting Change,* edited by A. G. Hopwood. Englewood Cliffs, NJ.: Prentice-Hall.

Gray, S. J., L. H. Radebaugh, and C. B. Roberts. 1990. "International Perceptions of Cost Constraints on Voluntary Information Disclosures: A Comparative Study of U.K. and U.S. Multinationals," *Journal of International Business Studies* (Winter) 21 (4): 597–622.

Healy, P. M. and K. G. Palepu. 1993. "The Effect of Firms' Financial Disclosure Strategies on Stock Prices", *Accounting Horizons,* 7 (March): 1–11.

International Accounting Standards Board. www.iasb.org.uk

International Accounting Standards Committee, 2000. *International Accounting Standards Committee, Objectives and Procedures.* London: IASC.

International Organization of Securities Commissions. www.iosco.orgMcCleay, S. J. 1983. "Value Added: A Comparative Study," *Accounting Organizations and Society,* 8 (1).

McNally, G., L. Eng, and C. Hasseldine. 1982. "Corporate Financial Reporting in New Zealand: An Analysis of User Preferences, Corporate Characteristics, and Disclosure Practices for Discretionary Information," *Accounting and Business Research* (Winter).

Meek, G. K. and S. J. Gray. 1988. "The Value Added Statement: An Innovation for U.S. Companies?," *Accounting Horizons* (June).

Meek, G. K. and S. J. Gray. 1989. "Globalization of Stock Markets and Foreign Listing Requirements: Voluntary Disclosures by Continental European Companies Listed on the London Stock Exchange," *Journal of International Business Studies* (Summer) 20 (2): 315–36.

Meek, G. K., C. B. Roberts, and S. J. Gray. 1995. "Factors Influencing Voluntary Annual Report Disclosures by U.S., U.K. and Continental European Multinational Corporations," *Journal of International Business Studies* (third quarter), 26 (3): 555–72.

Nobes, C. W. and R. H. Parker, eds. 2000. *Comparative International Accounting.* Englewood Cliffs, NJ; Prentice-Hall.

Organisation for Economic Cooperation and Development. 1976. *International Investment and Multinational Enterprises.* Paris.

Roberts, C. B. and S. J. Gray. 1997. "Corporate Social and Environmental Disclosures," in *International Accounting and Finance Handbook,* edited by F. D. S. Choi. New York: John Wiley.

Salter, S. B. 1998. "Corporate Financial Disclosure in Emerging Markets: Does Economic Development Matter?," *The International Journal of Accounting,* 33 (2): 221–34.

Saudagaran, S. M. and G. C. Biddle. 1995. "Foreign Listing Location: A Study of MNCs and Stock Exchanges in Eight Countries," *Journal of International Business Studies* (second quarter).

United Nations, 1988. *Conclusions on Accounting and Reporting by Transnational Corporations.* New York: UN (revised 1994).

United Nations. 1993. *Transnational Corporations in World Development.* New York: UN.

Wallace, R. and K. Naser. 1995. "Firm-specific Determinants of the Comprehensiveness of Mandatory Disclosure in the Corporate Annual Reports of Firms Listed on the Stock Exchange of Hong Kong," *Journal of Accounting and Public Policy,* (14): 311–68.

Zarzeski, M. T. 1996. "Spontaneous Harmonization Effects of Culture and Market Forces on Accounting Disclosure Practices," *Accounting Horizons* (March): 18–37.

CHAPTER SIX

GLOBAL HARMONIZATION OF ACCOUNTING AND REPORTING

Chapter Objectives

- Identify the impact on MNEs of the different pressures leading to accounting harmonization and disclosure

- Show how governments get involved in the harmonization of accounting directly or indirectly through groups such as the UN, the OECD, and the European Union

- Discuss how trade unions and employees are interested in harmonizing accounting to get information that will help them formulate policy concerning MNEs

- Describe how the International Organization of Securities Commissions (IOSCO) is representing investors in pushing for harmonization of accounting to facilitate cross-border comparisons of financial statements

- Examine how accountants, through the International Accounting Standards Board (IASB), are pushing for harmonization

INTRODUCTION

The previous chapters have explored the significance of differences in international accounting and the factors giving rise to them. We will now look at the pressures for the global harmonization of accounting and reporting, with special reference to the impact on MNEs.

International pressures for improvement in the comparability of accounting and information disclosure by corporations, especially MNEs, arise from the diverse interests and concerns of a wide range of participant groups and organizations. Underlying these pressures is the fundamental belief that improvements in comparability will facilitate more informed international comparisons of corporate performance and prospects, with consequent economic benefits. The role and impact of MNEs will be revealed more clearly and will thus assist in monitoring and, if necessary, in controlling MNE behavior. Further, national and international policy making is expected to be enhanced by a more comprehensive accountability for large and complex organizations.

MNE corporate reports are clearly an important current and potential source of information and are required for a wide range of purposes.

Pressures for the harmonization of international accounting as a means to achieve comparability are growing, but the term *harmonization* is often used rather loosely and sometimes interchangeably with *standardization*. To clarify these concepts it is helpful to think of a spectrum ranging from total flexibility and diversity to total uniformity. Harmonization implies a more flexible approach compared to standardization, which in turn suggests a more strict approach that results ultimately in a state of uniformity. As we will see, different organizations have different approaches to the achievement of international comparability.

Which groups of users and organizations are interested in the affairs of MNEs and the harmonization or standardization of international accounting? The power and global reach of MNEs is such that most nations and many people are affected, directly or indirectly, by their operations. It is possible, however, to distinguish a number of groups that, while having some common concerns, have other concerns that are unique. Why is it that they want information relating to MNEs? What is the nature of the information that they desire or need to satisfy their decision requirements? Why do they wish to influence the behavior of MNEs with respect to accounting and information disclosure? The major participant groups are as follows:

- governments
- trade unions and employees
- investors (including financial analysts)
- bankers and lenders
- accountants and auditors

Here we will be concerned, in particular, with the activities and influences of international intergovernmental, trade union, professional accounting, and investment/banking organizations involved in the setting of international standards for accounting and reporting. A simplified model of the participants and pressures involved in the demand for information disclosure by MNEs is set out in Figure 6.1. National and international participant groups are distinguished, though clearly there is likely to be considerable interaction between these two levels as well as between and within groups at all levels.

While the focus of our discussion will be on major participant groups, broadly defined, it is also recognized that there will be differences in information needs not only between groups but to some extent within them as well.

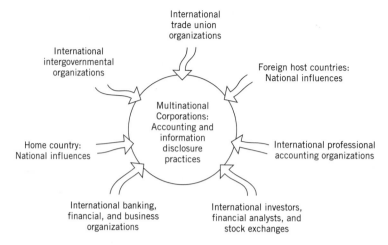

Figure 6.1 Multinational Corporations: Participants and Pressures for International Harmonization

GOVERNMENTS

Both the role of government in determining the content and nature of corporate reports and, especially, the extent of government involvement in the process have been widely studied. The extent of government involvement is comprehensive in some countries, especially those with a tradition of detailed prescriptive legislation (e.g., France and Germany), in contrast to the Anglo-American countries where the emphasis is on delegation to autonomous or quasiautonomous private professional bodies. The literature on the role of government as an actual or potential user of corporate reports, however, is very sparse. Much of the discussion contains little more than assertions that governments are users of such reports. The report of the UN's Group of Experts, for example, specifies governments, together with a long list of other users, including investors, lenders, suppliers, and so on, but provides little further elaboration other than to mention the needs of home and host countries and especially developing countries.

The information governments require of corporations varies and is influenced by, for example, the extent of government planning and regulation. However, such information is often vast and far too extensive to be included in a corporate annual report, which would, if it contained all such information, become totally unwieldy. Moreover, in addition to the question of quantity, much of the information is mutually regarded by both supplier and receiver as confidential and is thus limited to restricted special purpose reports. While the relative power of corporations (and MNEs in particular) and governments is a matter of controversy, it is evident that governments usually have the authority to demand and receive whatever information they need from MNEs. The extensive, and mainly confidential, information needs of governments, both home and host, combined with their power to obtain such information, would thus seem to support the view that governments are not important users of published corporate reports. Yet a great deal of the pressure for increasing the amount of information disclosure by MNEs has come from governments (e.g., through their participation in and support of the UN's activities). This apparent paradox may be explained by identifying certain specific, rather than general, circumstances wherein governments may in fact be users. These circumstances reflect the transnational nature of MNEs, the role of intergovernmental bodies, the heterogeneous nature of governments, the limited expertise of some governments, and the relative power distribution between MNE and host country.

First, information relevant to an MNE subsidiary's operations may not be available from the subsidiary but only from outside the country, for example, from the parent corporation or elsewhere within the MNE group. In such circumstances, a government may have limited authority to obtain the information. While some MNEs may supply information where and when requested, there may be others that do not or do so only to a limited extent. Where such information is not provided, governments may be unable or unwilling to press for it. Accordingly, they may, in some circumstances, use the MNE's worldwide consolidated annual financial statements together with segmental information to provide an insight, albeit limited, into the performance of subsidiaries at the country level.

Second, the important role of MNEs in world trade and development has meant that many governments wish to evaluate and monitor directly, or through international intergovernmental organizations, the strategy, performance, behavior, and consequences of MNE operations as a whole. A major source of such global information is the MNEs' corporate financial reports. Information that is not drawn up on a similar basis, as with MNEs based in many different countries, cannot be adequately aggregated. Thus, the governmental need for evaluation is reflected in demands not only for increased availability of information but also for greater comparability of the information so it can be aggregated.

Third, unlike investors but to some extent like trade unions, governments are neither single individuals nor organizations. The varying roles of governments are performed by a large range of departments or agencies. Special reports supplied to one unit (e.g., taxation authorities) are usually not available to other sections of government. The existence of discrete governmental units requires that some of them rely on corporate reports rather than on the more detailed information available only to other units. In some circumstances, what is available in corporate reports may be adequately comprehensive for the analytical purposes in question.

Finally, while governments are often characterized as having adequate power to require whatever information is needed from MNEs, this power is not unlimited and is often overstated. There is no doubt that it is extensive in many countries. However, in some "host developing countries," which are especially dependent on MNEs, requests for some types of information (e.g., social and environmental) may receive a negative response from the MNE. Increased availability of information in MNE corporate reports would mean that governments would have direct access to the information without having to bargain for it and thus possibly offend each MNE. Uniform disclosure requirements would also prevent MNEs from playing one potential host country against another in the competition for investment, thereby pressuring them to reduce their information disclosure requirements.

Governments would, therefore, seem to have an interest in gaining access to more information disclosure concerning extranational operations—that is, for accountability and predictive purposes their concern is to place the operations of the MNE subsidiary into the context of MNE operations as a whole. Accordingly, both worldwide aggregated and geographically disaggregated financial information is likely to be useful for this purpose. Moreover, the demand for greater international comparability of MNE information disclosure seems to be motivated by the desire of governments at the national level, especially in host countries, or through intergovernmental organizations such as the UN, OECD, and the European Union, to monitor the activities of MNEs in general as a basis for policy formulation.

Many governments believe that their bargaining power to obtain sufficient comparable information from MNEs is likely to be enhanced by involvement in intergovernmental organizations.

United Nations

The UN first became involved in the information disclosure debate in 1976 when a group of experts were appointed through the activities of the Commission on Transnational Corporations (now included in the work of the UNCTAD) to formulate proposals following a study of the impact of MNEs on development and international relations. Not only did this study identify a problem in international comparability with respect to the information provided by MNEs, it also revealed an apparently serious lack of information, both financial and nonfinancial. As a result, the Group of Experts concentrated on the development of lists of minimum items of financial and nonfinancial information to be disclosed by MNEs in their general purpose corporate reports, both at the level of the MNE group as a whole and through its individual member corporations. The outcome of those deliberations was a comprehensive and detailed set of proposals incorporating, most importantly, worldwide consolidated financial statements, segmental or disaggregated information, and a wide range of nonfinancial and "social" information. These proposals were meant to be used as the basis for developing a set of international standards in the context of a code of conduct for MNEs, and in 1979 this process was taken a step further with the establishment of an ad hoc intergovernmental "working group of experts" from 34 countries, including 22 countries from Africa, Asia, and Latin America. It is the UN's comprehensive spread of membership that ensured such strong representation from the developing countries compared to those of the industrialized West and Eastern Europe. This emphasis on developing countries tended also to suggest a prime concern to monitor and, if necessary, control MNE activities. From a political standpoint, they also represented quite different interests from those of the OECD, which is composed of developed countries, and the IASC (now IASB), which represented professional accounting interests.

While a major aim of this group would seem to have been to recommend international standards that member countries would agree to support and, if necessary, to enforce by law, progress in reaching agreement was slow and in some cases, particularly regarding nonfinancial information, impossible. In October 1982, the majority of countries recommended that the group continue its work in a more permanent form. There was general consensus that any group established

> should serve as an international body for the consideration of issues of accounting and reporting falling within the scope of the work of the Commission on Transnational Corporations in order to improve the availability and compara-

bility of information disclosed by transnational corporations; the Group should review developments in this field including the work of standard setting bodies; the Group should concentrate on establishing priorities, taking into account the needs of home and host countries, particularly those of developing countries.

This proposal was accepted by the UN, and the Intergovernmental Working Group of Experts on International Standards of Accounting and Reporting (ISAR) held its first session in 1983. Since then, sessions have been held every year on a variety of issues, including accounting for inflation, pension accounting, intangible assets, joint ventures, privatizations, and environmental reporting. In 1988, the Group of Experts published its agreed-upon *Conclusions on Accounting and Reporting by Transnational Corporations* (revised in 1994), and in 1989 the Group's contribution to the conceptual framework debate was published as *Objectives and Concepts Underlying Financial Statements.*

While the group does not appear to have had much direct influence on the development of international accounting standards, either at the professional or at the MNE level, it seems to have had a useful monitoring role in officially endorsing, where appropriate, desirable international standards. At the same time, there have been some useful contributions to the debate on a number of important questions (e.g., intangible assets, environmental reporting, etc.). A noteworthy recent development is the UN's involvement in accounting education and development, with special reference to Russia and the developing countries of Africa.

Organization for Economic Cooperation and Development

The OECD has a much more limited membership of countries compared to the UN. With only 24 members, as opposed to the UN's more than 180, the OECD represents the interests of an industrialized and substantially Western group of nations, including Australia, Canada, France, Germany, Japan, the Netherlands, the United Kingdom, and the United States. These countries are home for most of the world's MNEs. In 1976, following consultations with business and trade union interests, a set of *Guidelines for Multinational Enterprises* was approved with the aim of strengthening confidence between MNEs and governments and to meet criticisms about MNE activities. The intention was to encourage the positive contributions of MNEs to economic growth and social progress while minimizing or resolving problems. Governments agreed to recommend these guidelines, which related to financing, taxation, competition, and industrial relations, as well as information disclosure, to MNEs. In practice, however, only a handful of MNEs appear to have taken serious notice of the guidelines. The recommendations relating to information disclosure are outlined in Exhibit 6.1. Compared to the UN's *Conclusions,* the OECD's *Guidelines* are very brief and general and are concerned with information disclosure by the MNE as a group entity.

While the information recommendations were left essentially unchanged in the 1979 revision of the *Guidelines,* it was decided that the OECD should continue its efforts in this area by establishing a working group as a basis for contributing to and participating in the international standard-setting process. The OECD did not, however, attempt to establish itself as a standard-setting body in its own right. In this regard, a survey of accounting standards in OECD member countries was carried

Exhibit 6.1 OECD Guidelines for Multinational Enterprises: Disclosure of Information

Enterprises should, having due regard to their nature and relative size in the economic context of their operations and to requirements of business confidentiality and to cost, publish in a form suited to improve public understanding a sufficient body of factual information on the structure, activities, and policies of the enterprise as a whole, as a supplement, insofar as necessary for this purpose, to information to be disclosed under the national law of the individual countries in which they operate. To this end, they should publish within reasonable time limits, on a regular basis, but at least annually, financial statements and other pertinent information relating to the enterprise as a whole, comprising in particular:

  i. the structure of the enterprise, showing the name and location of the parent company, its main affiliates, its percentage ownership, direct and indirect, in these affiliates, including shareholdings between them;

  ii. the geographical areas where operations are carried out and the principal activities carried on therein by the parent company and the main affiliates;

  iii. the operating results and sales by geographical area and the sales in the major lines of business for the enterprise as a whole;

  iv. significant new capital investment by geographical area and, as far as practicable, by major lines of business for the enterprise as a whole;

  v. a statement of the sources and uses of funds by the enterprise as a whole;

  vi. the average number of employees in each geographical area;

  vii. research and development expenditure for the enterprise as a whole;

  viii. the policies followed in respect of intragroup pricing;

  ix. the accounting policies, including those on consolidation, observed in compiling the published information.

Source: Organisation for Economic Cooperation and Development *International Investment and Multinational Enterprises* (OECD, 1976, revised 1979).

out in 1980 to assess the diversity of practice and the potential for harmonization. Further studies have been made on topics such as consolidations, segmental disclosures, and intangible assets. In general terms, it seems that the OECD aims to work toward promoting international understanding and agreement on a variety of issues as a basis for improving the comparability and harmonization of accounting and reporting standards.

European Union

As of 2001, the European Union (EU) consists of 15 nations (Austria, Belgium, Denmark, Finland, France, Germany, Greece, Italy, Ireland, Luxembourg, the Netherlands, Portugal, Spain, Sweden and the United Kingdom). The European Union has been involved in the international harmonization of accounting and reporting standards since the middle 1960s as part of its program of company law harmonization, which was undertaken after the Treaty of Rome (1957). The activities of the European Union have taken place in the context of promoting the goal of European economic integration and development whereby corporations, including MNEs, should have the freedom to become more international by being able to do business and compete within a common framework of law, taxation, and financial resources.

As far as company law is concerned, the basic principle is that no corporation should be at a competitive disadvantage as a result of legal differences between countries. An important part of the company law harmonization process is the public disclosure of comparable and reliable financial information to protect the interests of shareholders, lenders, suppliers, and other interested parties. The harmonization of accounting and reporting in the European Union is especially significant for MNEs because, in contrast to the UN and OECD, any agreement that takes the form of a directive has the force of law and each member country has the obligation to incorporate such directives into its respective national law. Regulations, on the other hand, become law throughout the European Union without having to go through the national legislative process. The major position with respect to EU directives and regulations relevant to accounting and information disclosure as of 2000 is shown in Exhibit 6.2.

We will now briefly outline those directives that have special relevance, paying particular attention to the Fourth and Seventh Directives, which are arguably fundamental to EU accounting harmonization. The First and Second Directives were approved in 1968 and 1976, respectively, and were concerned with basic issues such as the publication of accounts, minimum capital, and so on.

Fourth Directive The Fourth Directive was approved in 1978, adding detailed requirements relating to information disclosure, classification and presentation of information, and methods of valuation. Implementation has taken some time, however, with Italy finally amending its company law only in 1991.

Agreement on the Fourth Directive involved a long and difficult period of consultation and negotiation, especially in view of the fact that the United Kingdom and Ireland, along with Denmark, joined the European Union (which was then composed of Belgium, France, Germany, Italy, Luxembourg, and the Netherlands) only in 1973, and with quite different traditions of accounting and information disclosure policy. The result was a compromise between the continental European and Anglo-American systems with perhaps more emphasis placed on disclosing the nature and effect of differences between countries than on removing them.

The intention of the Fourth Directive was not necessarily to produce uniformity but rather to bring about a coordination or harmonization of existing legal requirements. Nevertheless, the Fourth Directive does provide a broadly uniform structure for the classification and presentation of information, albeit with different layouts permitted for the balance sheet and profit and loss account, incorporating some choice of presentation. Of particular interest is the scope allowed for a more analytical approach in the balance sheet (see Exhibit 6.3) and in the choice between analyzing costs on an operational basis or by type of expenditure in the profit and loss account (see Exhibits 6.4–6.5). A modified balance sheet (showing account headings only) is also permitted provided that the detailed information required is given in the notes.

A significant feature of the Fourth Directive is its detailed requirements concerning the principles and application of conventional historical cost accounting. There is substantial flexibility, however, concerning inventory valuation, depreciation, and the treatment of goodwill. At the same time, alternative valuation approaches such as current replacement cost, revaluations to market value, and price level adjustments are permitted either in the main accounts or in supplementary statements.

Exhibit 6.2   EU Directives and Regulations Relevant to Corporate Accounting
and Disclosure

Directives on Company Law	Date Adopted	Subject
First	1968	Publication of accounts, ultra vires rules
Second	1976	Separation of private from public companies, minimum capital, limitation on distribution
Third	1978	Mergers/fusions
Fourth	1978	Annual accounts, content, valuation, presentation rules
Fifth	(Drafts 1972, 1983, 1988)	Structure, management, and audit of companies
Sixth	1982	Demergers/spin-offs
Seventh	1983	Consolidated accounts, including associated companies
Eighth	1984	Qualifications and work of auditors
Ninth	(Predraft stage)	Links between public company groups
Tenth	(Drafts 1985, 2000)	International mergers of public companies
Eleventh	1989	Disclosure relating to branches
Twelfth	1989	Single-member companies
Thriteenth	1989	Mergers
—	(Drafts 1980, 1983)	Employee information and consultation
—	1979	Admission of securities to listing
—	1980, 1982, 1987	Listing particulars
—	1982	Interim reporting by listed companies
—	1986	Accounts of banks
—	1991	Accounts of Insurance companies
Regulations		
European company statute	(Drafts 1970, 1975, 1989)	Proposals for a European company subject to EU laws
European economic interest grouping	1985	Proposals for a business form facilitating joint ventures

The directive also incorporates disclosure requirements that have significantly increased the level of information disclosed in many of the EU countries. The impact of the directive has been felt most sharply in countries like Italy and in some relatively new EU member states (e.g., Finland, Greece, Portugal, and Spain) where information disclosures have been relatively less developed than in France, Germany, and the United Kingdom.

Another important feature of the Fourth Directive is the adoption of the U.K. concept of a "true and fair view." However, whether or not this has had any major

Exhibit 6.3   EU Fourth Directive

Balance Sheet: (Analytical Layout)

A. Called-up Share Capital Not Paid   X

B. Fixed Assets

I. Intangible Assets

1. Development costs	X		
2. Concessions, patents, licenses, trade marks, and similar rights and assets	X		
3. Goodwill	X		
4. Payments on account	X̲		
		X	

II. Tangible Assets

1. Land and buildings	X		
2. Plant and machinery	X		
3. Fixtures, fittings, tools, and equipment	X		
4. Payments on account and assets in course of construction	X̲		
		X	

III. Investments

1. Shares in group companies	X		
2. Loans to group companies	X		
3. Shares in related companies	X		
4. Loans to related companies	X		
5. Other investments other than loans	X		
6. Other loans	X		
7. Own shares	X̲		
		X̲	
(total of B)			X

C. Current Assets

I. Stocks

1. Raw materials and consumables	X	
2. Work-in-progress	X	
3. Finished goods and goods for resale	X	
4. Payments on account	X̲	
	X̲	

II. Debtors

1. Trade debtors	X	
2. Amounts owed by group companies	X	
3. Amounts owed by related companies	X	
4. Other debtors	X	
5. Called-up share capital not paid	X	
6. Prepayments and accrued income	X̲	
	X̲	

(continues)

Exhibit 6.3 (*Continued*)

III. Investments

1. Shares in group companies	X
2. Own shares	X
3. Other investments	X
	X

IV. Cash at Bank and in Hand

	X

(total of C)	X

D. Prepayments and Accrued Income (Total of C and D)

	X
	X

E. Creditors: Amounts Falling Due Within One Year

1. Debenture loans	(X)	
2. Bank loans and overdrafts	(X)	
3. Payments received on account	(X)	
4. Trade creditors	(X)	
5. Bills of exchange payable	(X)	
6. Amounts owed to group companies	(X)	
7. Amounts owed to related companies	(X)	
8. Other creditors including taxation and social security	(X)	
9. Accruals and deferred income	(X)	(X)

F. Net Current Assets (Liabilities) (C + D − E)

	X

G. Total Assets Less Current Liabilities (A + B + F)

	X

H. Creditors: Amounts Falling Due after More Than One Year

1. Debenture loans	(X)	
2. Bank loans and overdrafts	(X)	
3. Payments received on account	(X)	
4. Trade creditors	(X)	
5. Bills of exchange payable	(X)	
6. Amounts owed to group companies	(X)	
7. Amounts owed to related companies	(X)	
8. Other creditors including taxation and social security	(X)	
9. Accruals and deferred income	(X)	(X)

I. Provisions for Liabilities and Charges

1. Pensions and similar obligations	(X)	
2. Taxation, including deferred taxation	(X)	
3. Other provisions	(X)	(X)

Exhibit 6.3   (*Continued*)

J. Accruals and Deferred Income	$\frac{(X)}{X}$

K. Capital and Reserves

I. Called-up Share Capital	X

II. Share Premium Account	X

III. Revaluation Reserve	X

IV. Other Reserves

1. Capital redemption reserve	X	
2. Reserve for own shares	X	
3. Reserves provided for by the articles of association	X	
4. Other reserves	X	X

V. Profit and Loss Account	X
	X

impact in other EU countries is not clear. The application of this concept would have an overriding effect in that it might require the disclosure of additional, or in exceptional circumstances, different information from that required specifically by the Fourth Directive. It seems, however, that continental European countries have not yet been much affected in practice by this strictly British philosophy.

Taken overall, the Fourth Directive seems to have been very much a starting point in the harmonization process. Its inherent flexibility concerning measurement and valuation principles and its lack of comprehensiveness with respect to issues such as foreign currency translation, leases and funds, or cash flow statements leaves much to be desired. On the other hand, the directive has done much to raise the level of information disclosure and transparency throughout the EU countries.

Seventh Directive   In 1983 the Seventh Directive on consolidated accounts was adopted. This raised issues of special relevance to MNE operations and was the subject of some controversy. Of particular importance were issues concerning the definition of a "group." Here, the U.K. approach, based on share ownership and legal rights to control other corporations, was contrasted with the German approach, which was based on effective management control as well as share ownership criteria. This was resolved by a compromise whereby control criteria other than ownership could be applied by member countries on an optional basis. There were also issues relating to the measurement of performance and financial position of the

Exhibit 6.4 EU Fourth Directive

Profit and Loss Account (Operational Basis)		
1. Turnover		X
2. Cost of sales		(X)
3. Gross profit or loss		X
4. Distribution costs		(X)
5. Administrative expenses		(X)
6. Other operating income		X
7. Income from shares in group companies		X
8. Income from shares in related companies		X
9. Income from other fixed asset investments		X
10. Other interest receivable and similar income		X
11. Amounts written off investments		(X)
12. Interest payable and similar charges		(X)
13. Tax on profit or loss on ordinary activities		(X)
14. Profit or loss on ordinary activities after taxation		X
15. Extraordinary income	X	
16. Extraordinary charges	(X)	
17. Extraordinary profit or loss		X
18. Tax on extraordinary profit or loss		(X)
19. Other taxes not shown under the above items		(X)
20. Profit or loss for the financial year		X

MNE group. Further questions included the extent to which consolidation requirements should be applied to MNEs that were based outside the European Union but had groups of subsidiaries in one or more EU countries.

While the first proposal was issued in 1976 and revised in 1979, it was only in 1983 that agreement was reached, following substantial further revisions. These allowed for some flexibility of interpretation and the availability of options, which could be adopted by the decision of individual member countries. While this would seem to undermine somewhat the objectives of comparability, the Seventh Directive is a major development. It requires worldwide consolidations, the use of a "fair value" approach when accounting for assets purchased through acquisitions, the equity treatment of associated corporations, and segmental disclosures of turnover by line of business and geographical area. It appears likely that the extent of information disclosure throughout the European Union has been substantially enhanced as a result of this directive. The United Kingdom and to a significant extent the Netherlands are, however, the exceptions to this given this the Seventh Directive has essentially adopted Anglo-American consolidation principles. While this directive has now been adopted in all EU member countries, some countries have been slower than other to implement it (e.g. Italy adopted the directive only in 1991).

The Eighth Directive, adopted in 1984, is another important directive in that it deals with the qualification and work of auditors across the EU member countries,

Exhibit 6.5   EU Fourth Directive

Profit and Loss Account (Type of Expenditure Basis)		
1. Turnover		X
2. Change in stocks of finished goods and in work-in-progress		(X)
3. Own work capitalized		X
4. Other operating income		X
5. a. Raw materials and consumables	(X)	
b. Other external charges	(X)	(X)
6. Staff costs:		
a. Wages and salaries	(X)	
b. Social security costs	(X)	
c. Other pension costs	(X)	(X)
7. a. Depreciation and other amounts written of tangible and intangible fixed assets	(X)	
b. Exceptional amounts written off current assets	(X)	(X)
8. Other operating charges		(X)
9. Income from shares in related companies		X
10. Income from shares in related companies		X
11. Income from other fixed asset investments		X
12. Other interest receivable and similar income		X
13. Amounts written of investments		(X)
14. Interest payable and similar charges		(X)
15. Tax on profit or loss on ordinary activities		(X)
16. Profit or loss on ordinary activities after taxation		X
17. Extraordinary income	X	
18. Extraordinary charges	(X)	
19. Extraordinary profit or loss		X
20. Tax on extraordinary profit or loss		(X)
21. Other taxes not shown under the above items		(X)
22. Profit or loss for the financial year		X

including the setting of minimum educational requirements, to encourage the mobility of professional auditors.

A further important and highly controversial proposed directive, which was issued in 1980 and subsequently shelved, concerned employee information and consultation with special reference to MNEs. This proposed directive, usually referred to as the "Vredeling proposals," called for the regular provision of information to employees in subsidiary corporations about the activities of the MNE at group level as well as at the level of the individual subsidiary. The information disclosures proposed covered areas such as organization structure; employment; the economic and financial situation; probable development in production, sales, and employment; rationalization plans; and plans for new working methods or other methods that could have "a substantial effect" on employee interests. Furthermore, under the proposed directive, employees would need to be consulted when decisions proposed by management were likely to affect their interests (e.g., in the case of a factory closure or any change in the activities of the subsidiary corporation). While this proposed directive met with considerable opposition from MNEs and some governments, the issues involved have been raised again in the context of implementing the EU's "Charter of Fundamental Social Rights," which was approved in 1990.

Related to developments in accounting harmonization are those concerned with the harmonization of stock exchange regulations and securities laws. These were designed to ensure that both existing and potential investors have access to sufficient information in the context of promoting the development of a "European" capital market with active and well-developed stock exchanges in all the EU countries. A number of relevant directives have been approved, including the minimum conditions for listing and the disclosure of information (listing particulars) for the admission of shares to official stock exchange listing. These directives were adopted in 1979 and 1980, respectively. Further, a directive on interim reports, adopted in 1982, required listed corporations to publish half-yearly reports of financial results together with information on trends and likely future developments in the current year of operations.

As far as future EU accounting harmonization efforts are concerned, it seems that, consistent with the deregulation fervor of the 1992 initiative to remove nontariff barriers, there are no plans to issue any new accounting directives. In fact, rather than attempt to achieve further harmonization, it is now considered more effective to adopt a "mutual recognition" approach to accounting and disclosure requirements. This is a process whereby the regulations in one country are accepted as equivalent in another, subject to the minimum standards set in the Fourth and Seventh Directives. In 1990, a European Accounting Advisory Forum was established by the EU Commission to encourage consultation between professional and governmental standard-setting agencies as well as other interested parties. The forum's purpose was to deal with new or unresolved issues in the context of promoting international harmonization in the EU and the world at large. While the forum did not set accounting standards, it was hoped that any consensus on such matters as foreign currency translation, for example, would serve as guidelines for adoption by national standard-setting agencies throughout the EU countries.

Although the EU harmonization effort has been successful in raising the level of information disclosure internationally, it seems to have made little progress in resolving differences in measurement practices across the EU countries. Such differences reflect the variety of national environmental circumstances and cultural traditions in the European Union, which persist despite the moves toward economic integration.

In 2000, however, the European Commission signaled a major change of stance on international harmonization by announcing a proposal to require all *listed* companies in the European Union to publish consolidated financial statements in accordance with International Accounting Standards (IAS) beginning in 2005. This proposal is understood to have the support of the EU member states as it is consistent with the aim to use one set of accounting standards that will be recognized globally. The European Commission will be proposing the issuance of a regulation that will enforce IASB throughout the EU. Although this is a very important vote of support for the IASB, there is some concern that this development may lead to a European version of IAS.

This brief review of the activities and influence of international, intergovernmental organizations such as the UN, OECD, and European Union in accounting and information disclosure demonstrates an international concern not only to harmonize accounting measurement and presentation practices but also to ensure the disclosure of sufficient comparable information internationally. This process is perceived to be essential as a basis for promoting fair competition and a degree of protection for investors and other parties and for ensuring that policy making is informed and that control, where necessary, is exercised. Intergovernmental involvement is seen to be influential in this process. Such a process is not necessarily detrimental to the interests of MNEs in that there is clearly an intergovernmental concern to promote international business and the growth of MNEs as much as to regulate their activities. However, there are likely to be differences in emphasis and approach according to the membership and objectives of the intergovernmental organization concerned.

TRADE UNIONS AND EMPLOYEES

The term *trade union* encompasses a number of different but related organizations. The trade union organizations that participate at intergovernmental levels are the international trade union confederations (ITUCs)—for example, European Trade Unions Confederation (ETUC), the International Confederation of Free Trade Unions (ICFTU), and the World Confederation of Labor (WCL). These represent the national central trade union organizations. In addition, there are international trade union secretariats each of which concentrate on a specific industry and represent internationally those trade unions involved with the relevant industrial category. Their direct contact with MNEs, albeit limited, is with individual MNEs rather than intergovernmental organizations. In the national context, trade union attempts to influence the behavior of MNEs may take place at a variety of levels ranging from activities at shop-floor level to influencing national government policy. The relationships of trade unions with MNEs are considerably more complex and varied than, for example, those of investors in the context of stock markets. The perceived information needs of trade unions will depend on the specific point of contact with MNEs and the purpose for which information is required.

Trade unions are primarily grounded in the national territory within which they operate. It is within national states that trade unions have developed and where their power exists. While MNEs have grown beyond the limits of national territories, trade unions have done so only to a very limited extent. The growing gap between the location of international business and national trade unions is in the eyes of the latter a potential, and in some instances actual, disability for them.

In 1977, the ICFTU, WCL, and ETUC issued their own set of accounting and information disclosure requirements. The focus of this document was on MNEs and the need for international harmonization, with recommendations on taking a more uniform approach to accounting as well as comprehensive and detailed disclosures of financial and nonfinancial information. The ICFTU had also issued an earlier "multinational charter" in 1975, which emphasized the need for MNEs to be more publicly accountable and called for legal regulation to require the disclosure of more information, including a report about matters of a social nature and information about future prospects, investment, and employment.

Their purpose in these proposals, however, was not to facilitate interfirm comparisons—although this may be of some limited interest—but rather to provide a reliable basis for the formulation of policy concerning MNEs. Such policy development is inhibited not only by gaps in the availability of information for obtaining an accurate aggregate picture of their activities and impact but also by the variation in the methods of measurement used and a lack of what is considered necessary information.

The main national trade union concern, shared by international trade union organizations as well, centers on an increase in information disclosure relating to the operations of MNE subsidiaries. Of particular concern to trade unions in relation to MNE information disclosures are the consequences of the transfer pricing policies of each MNE's subsidiaries.

The relationship between an MNE subsidiary and other units of the MNE, especially those outside that subsidiary's country of location, may affect the relevance and reliability of the financial position and performance reported by the MNE subsidiary. While the impact of MNE intragroup transactions is of concern to a range of interested groups, many of them (e.g., revenue and taxation authorities) do not rely on corporate reports for their information because they have access to greater amounts of information directly from the corporation concerned. For those who are interested in the affairs of MNE subsidiaries but who have to rely wholly, or mainly, on corporate reports for financial information (e.g., trade unions), the impact of such subsidiaries' transactions with related parties is of crucial interest. Because the primary concern of most regulatory bodies and accounting commentators is with the information needs of investors, MNE subsidiary transactions have received little attention to date.

While trade unions and employees require information about the performance and future prospects of MNEs just as much as other groups do, information regarding the terms, conditions, scale, security, and location of employment are of special concern to them. Their primary interest is with the national situation of each MNE subsidiary and its relationship with other subsidiaries in the MNE group. International trade union organizations are also concerned with obtaining information about related party transactions and transfer pricing practices as a basis for formulating overall policy toward MNEs.

INVESTORS

Investors, including financial analysts, are those who have access to corporate reports and use them and other publicly available information as a basis for making investment decisions. Investors are "outsiders" to the MNE and range from the sophisticated to the layperson, from the active to the passive, and from the diversified to the nondiversified. Primarily, investors own or are potential owners of shares in the MNE parent corporation, though there may also be a limited number of investors in MNE subsidiaries.

The interests of investors in obtaining more information from MNEs are represented by international organizations of financial analysts and to some extent by bodies such as the International Organization of Securities Commissions (IOSCO), which is involved with the regulation of stock exchanges.

Besides additional information disclosure, especially information about the future prospects of MNEs on a worldwide basis such as up-to-date measurements relating to earnings and asset values, investors and financial analysts are concerned about the lack of comparability of much of the information that is currently provided. At the same time, some observers argue for a shift of emphasis in the stock market toward an information approach. There, the concern would be to ensure the disclosure of a wide range of relevant information relating to earnings prospects as opposed to an emphasis on the calculation and prediction of earnings on a standardized basis.

While such a change in emphasis may be desirable, particularly with respect to the needs of expert financial analysts in well-developed and efficient securities markets, international financial analysts, professional accountancy organizations, and governments continue to be concerned in practice with the lack of international comparability of corporate reports for investor purposes. The perceived problem is that even across countries where extensive corporate reporting requirements exist (e.g., the United States and the United Kingdom), the corporate annual reports of corporations may not be comparable—the variety of measurement methods and disclosures thwart effective comparative evaluation of financial position and performance. Even in the European Union, the Fourth and Seventh Directives effectively allow corporations a choice of accounting alternatives in many instances, including basic valuation principles.

What are the reasons for such concern with comparability between corporations? The purpose of comparisons is to evaluate alternatives and is, therefore, especially relevant to those who wish to choose between corporations in an international context. Investor decisions are characterized by a choice between alternative corporations in the process of buying, holding, or selling the shares of different corporations. For the diversified investor holding a portfolio of shares, however, it is a corporation's risk and return relative to the market as a whole and its effect on overall portfolio risks and returns that will be of special concern.

To facilitate the analysis and comparison of MNE reports based on different accounting influences at the national level and to enhance understanding of those from other than the user's country, investors and financial analysts—for example, the International Coordinating Committee of Financial Analysts Associations (ICC-FAA)—support progress toward international accounting harmonization.

Another important organization in the context of securities market regulation and the protection of investors is IOSCO. This is the leading organization for securities regulatiors and has as its mission the global coordination of stock exchange rules so as to encourage both multilisting by corporations and international securities trading. The international standardization of accounting regulations together with sufficiently detailed information disclosures is an important factor in achieving these objectives. IOSCO has developed a close relationship with the International Accounting Standards Committee (now IASB) as discussed later.

It should be emphasized that the evident concern by investor-related groups with comparability does not necessarily indicate uniformity, at least in the short term, but rather a degree of standardization and a minimum of information disclosure concerning accounting differences, enough to enable comparisons to be made. Evidence concerning the operations of well-developed securities markets such as in the United States and the United Kingdom suggests that there is a tendency for such markets to be "efficient" in the sense that expert or sophisticated investors will ensure that share prices quickly reflect all publicly available information. In setting share prices, it is believed that experts will allow for the effect of differences in accounting methods, to the extent that this is possible with the available information. Of course, even the experts will not be able to allow for differences that are not disclosed, or generally known about, nor will they be able to compensate for any absence of relevant information, which is not otherwise obtainable from alternative sources. Even if the experts were able to unravel the differences there may well be a cost saving if corporations were able to adopt a degree of standardization that did not entail any loss of information content.

With regard to the information to be disclosed, it has been suggested that investors are only concerned with overall MNE results, as reported in worldwide consolidated financial statements and thus are not interested in segmental or disaggregated information. However, an analysis of aggregate results often requires an understanding of the profitability, degree of risk, relative performance, and potential for growth of the component parts. As a diversified corporation's performance and future prospects are the sum of those of its various parts, investors are also likely to be interested in disaggregated, or segmental, information.

Geographical segmentation is of special relevance to MNEs, which are, by definition, diversified across national boundaries. Segmental information on an industrial, line of business (LOB), or product line basis is also relevant to those MNEs active in a number of industries, but it is not exclusive to them in that such a corporation may confine its operations to one country. This interest in segmental information is not to say that aggregate financial information is necessarily of any less importance to investors. On the contrary, knowledge of the total results of operations, including resources and obligations, of the MNE on a worldwide basis is also essential to an overall assessment of risks and returns. Worldwide consolidations are, however, by no means the norm in all countries.

In summary, the kind of disclosure relevant to investors and financial analysts would appear to include information relating to the performance and future prospects of the worldwide operations of the MNE group and, in particular, geographical and line of business segmentation. In the absence of a sufficient degree of international accounting harmonization, there is a demand for additional information disclosures that will assist in determining the validity and effect of MNE measurement practices and so facilitate international comparisons.

BANKERS AND LENDERS

Like investors, the information needs of bankers and lenders appear to be focused on corporate information relating to financial position, performance, and future prospects. There is, however, a difference in emphasis in that there is likely to be particular concern with the security of loans advanced (i.e., the risk of default on obligations to pay loan interest and to refund the loans when due). It would seem that in countries where bankers and other lenders are more significant than shareholders as financiers of corporations, as in France, Germany, and Japan, this is likely to have a conservative influence on the measurement of publicly disclosed financial performance and wealth. At the same time, this group of information users is likely to have more direct access to the required information and does not, therefore, have to rely primarily on publicly available corporate reports.

In the context of international accounting harmonization, international banking organizations are apparently involved to the extent that they support the goal of requiring more comparable information from their clients, including governments, financial institutions, and corporations. Of particular importance here are the international development banks (e.g., the Asian Development Bank, the European Investment Bank, the European Bank for Reconstruction and Development, the International Bank for Reconstruction and Development, and the World Bank, with special reference to the International Finance Corporation [IFC]). In addition, a host of banks are involved in international lending in the Eurocurrency markets and newly emerging international markets in Singapore, Hong Kong, Japan, and and Middle East.

International banks often require special financial reports, and the IFC has gone so far as to issue detailed instruction booklets on accounting and reporting standards, which are likely to have an impact on practice in a number of developing countries. MNEs are also often motivated to increase the quantity of information disclosed in their corporate reports voluntarily through the process of competing for funds in the Eurocurrency and other international capital markets.

ACCOUNTANTS AND AUDITORS

The role of accountants, as the preparers and users of information in MNEs, is an extremely important one with respect to technical skills, influence, and responsibility. This is reinforced by the role of the accountant as the auditor or verifier of corporate reports issued by MNEs to external parties.

While international firms of accountants, which have grown primarily in response to the growth of MNEs, are active in the international harmonization of accounting and reporting, it is at the level of international professional organizations that most of the developments are taking place, notably the Internatinal Accounting Standards Committee (IASC), now renamed as the International Accounting Standards Board (IASB).

International Accounting Standards Board

The IASC, while closely related to the International Federation of Accountants (IFAC), was granted an independent responsibility for the development of international *accounting* standards. The IFAC on the other hand, concerned itself primarily with the promulgation of international *auditing* guidelines or standards.

The IASC was established in 1973 by leading professional organizations in Australia, Canada, Germany, Ireland, Japan, Mexico, the Netherlands, the United Kingdom, and the United States. The IASC had a membership comprising 143 organizations from 104 countries (as of January 2000), including the founder members, most of whom maintained membership of the governing board and thus retained a significant measure of influence. When compared with the membership of the UN, however, it is clear that the membership of the IASC has been relatively limited and, of course, has been bounded by the need for the existence of a professional accountancy organization—something that has often been outside the experience of socialist and emerging economies. However, in May 2000, the IASC was formally restructured and a new constitution adopted. The IASC was also renamed as the International Accounting Standards Board (IASB). The main reason why the IASC felt the need to restructure was that pressure had grown for the IASC to become more independent of professional accounting bodies from around the world, with the aim of working more closely with those who actually set local standards (i.e., the national standard setters) to reach agreed solutions. It was also felt that the IASC exists to serve a wider public interest and that greater assurance should be given of that objective. Accordingly, the governance of IASC was vested in a board of trustees with a new standards board empowered to make decisions on international accounting standards (see Exhibit 6.6).

The stated objectives of the IASC are "(a) to formulate and publish in the public interest accounting standards to be observed in the presentation of financial statements and to promote their worldwide acceptance and observance, and (b) to work generally for the improvement and harmonization of regulations, accounting standards, and procedures relating to the presentation of financial statements."

In practice, the main aim of international accounting standards is to achieve a degree of comparability that will help investors make their decisions while reducing the costs of MNEs in preparing multiple sets of accounts and reports. It is also fair to say that IASC was seen itself as having a global role to play in coordinating and harmonizing the activities of the many national agencies involved in setting accounting and reporting standards. It has been suggested too that the IASC's standards provide a useful model for developing countries wishing to establish accounting standards for the first time.

The position of the IASC (as of January 2001) regarding standards is shown in Exhibit 6.7. A total of 41 standards have been issued as well as a number of

Exhibit 6.6   The IASC's New Governance Structure

TRUSTEES

- 19 individuals with diverse geographic and functional backgrounds
- Trustees will:
- appoint the Members of the Board, the Standing Interpretations Committee and the Standards Advisory Council.
- Monitor IASC's effectiveness.
- Raise its funds.
- Approve IASC's budget.
- Have responsibility for constitutional change.

| STANDARDS ADVISORY COUNCIL | BOARD • 14 Members, 12 full-time 2 part-time | STANDING INTERPRETATIONS COMMITTEE |

Exhibit 6.7   International Accounting Standards

In effect at January 2001

International Accounting Standards deal with most of the topics that are important in published financial statements of business enterprises. They set out principles that can be applied in consistent ways in different countries. They require like transactions and events to be accounted for in a like way wherever they take place—and different transactions and events to be accounted for in a different way.

IAS 1	Presentation of Financial Statements	IAS 22	Business Combinations
IAS 2	Inventories	IAS 23	Borrowing Costs
IAS 3	(No longer effective. Superseded by IAS 27 and IAS 28)	IAS 24	Related Party Disclosures
		IAS 25	(No longer effective. Superseded by IAS 39 and IAS 40)
IAS 4	(No longer effective. Superseded by IAS 16, IAS 22 and IAS 38)	IAS 26	Accounting and Reporting by Retirement Benefit Plans
IAS 5	(No longer effective. Superseded by IAS 1)	IAS 27	Consolidated Financial Statements and Accounting for Investments in Subsidiaries
IAS 6	(No longer effective. Superseded by IAS 15)	IAS 28	Accounting for Investments in Associates
IAS 7	Cash Flow Statements		
IAS 8	Net Profit or Loss for the Period, Fundamental Errors and Changes in Accounting Policies	IAS 29	Financial Reporting in Hyperinflationary Economies
IAS 9	(No longer effective. Superseded by IAS 38)	IAS 30	Disclosures in the Financial Statements of Banks and Similar Financial Institutions
IAS 10	Events After the Balance Sheet Date	IAS 31	Financial Reporting of Interests in Joint Ventures
IAS 11	Construction Contracts	IAS 32	Financial Instruments: Disclosure and Presentation
IAS 12	Income Taxes		
IAS 13	(No longer effective. Superseded by IAS 1)	IAS 33	Earnings Per Share
IAS 14	Segment Reporting	IAS 34	Interim Financial Reporting
IAS 15	Information Reflecting the Effects of Changing Prices	IAS 35	Discontinuing Operations
		IAS 36	Impairment of Assets
IAS 16	Property, Plant and Equipment	IAS 37	Provisions, Contingent Liabilities and Contingent Assets
IAS 17	Leases	IAS 38	Intangible Assets
IAS 18	Revenue	IAS 39	Financial Instruments: Recognition and Measurement
IAS 19	Employee Benefits		
IAS 20	Accounting for Government Grants and Disclosure of Government Assistance	IAS 40	Investment Property
		IAS 41	Agriculture (effective January 1, 2003)
IAS 21	The Effects of Changes in Foreign Exchange Rates		

Source: www.iasb.org.uk

revised standards. These cover a wide range of issues including the disclosure of accounting policies, consolidated financial statements, funds statements, segment reporting, accounting for changing prices, accounting for leases, accounting for the effects of changes in foreign exchange rates, related party disclosures, and financial instruments.

In restrospect, the IASC has made remarkable progress toward its goal of achieving worldwide agreement on accounting standards since its formation in 1973, given the very different national cultures and accounting traditions that have evolved in countries around the world for centuries. Indeed, as the IASC, now IASB, entered 2001 it embarked on a new era of global standard setting. It is now a restructured, independent standard setter that has widespread support from governments, standard-setting agencies, securities commissions, and professional accounting associations worldwide.

In May 2000, the IASC also received an endorsement from the International Organization of Securities Commissions (IOSCO), following completion in December 1998 of a core set of standards as agreed with IOSCO in 1995 (IOSCO, 2000a). The 1995 agreement between IASC and IOSCO followed growing recognition of the need for global accounting standards that could be used for cross-border listings and national listings alike. Business preparers were motivated by the possibility of cost savings and investors by the need for more comparable financial information internationally. The recent Asian financial crisis also highlighted the problems caused by a lack of confidence in accounting in the countries concerned and created pressure for the adoption of a set of globally recognized standards. As Arthur Levitt, chairman of the SEC in the United States, has said, "The significance of transparent, timely and reliable financial statements and its importance to investor protection has never been more apparent. The current financial situations in Asia and Russia are stark examples of this new reality. These markets are learning a painful lesson taught many times before: investors panic as a result of unexpected or unquantifiable bad news" (Levitt, 1998).

Furthermore, also in 2000, as noted earlier, the European Commission announced that it will introduce legislation requiring all EU listed companies to prepare consolidated financial statements based on IAS by 2005. Indeed, in some countries, such as Belgium, France, Germany, and Italy, companies are now permitted to use IAS already in their consolidated financial statements. Street, Gray, and Bryant (1999) show that a growing number of companies, including multinationals such as Bayer, Essilor, Nestlé, and Pirelli, have also voluntarily adopted IAS though many have done so noting exceptions.

Nevertheless, the IASB continues to face major obstacles to achieving its goal of worldwide recognition and acceptance of IAS and their effective use in practice. In particular, the hard-won IOSCO endorsement announced at its annual meeting in Sydney in May 2000 fell short of expectations. Following an assessment of IAS, IOSCO recommended that its members allow multinational companies to use 30 core IAS for the purposes of cross-border listings and capital raisings. However, IOSCO members were also permitted to require reconciliation of certain items, call for supplementary information, and eliminate some of the options that still exist in IAS (see Exhibit 6.8).

Together with this somewhat limited and modest endorsement of IAS, IOSCO's Technical Committee published a report summarizing its assessment work and noting numerous outstanding issues that members are expected to address

Exhibit 6.8   IOSCO Press Release (Extract) Sydney, Australia—17 May 2000

Resolution Concerning the Use of IASC Standards for the Purpose of Facilitating Multi-national Securities Offerings and Cross-border Listings

The following resolution was approved by the Presidents Committee of IOSCO:

In order to respond to the significant growth in cross-border capital flows, IOSCO has sought to facilitate cross-border offerings and listings. IOSCO believes that cross-border offerings and listings would be facilitated by high quality, internationally accepted accounting standards that could be used by incoming multinational issuers in cross-border offerings and listings. Therefore, IOSCO has worked with the International Accounting Standards Committee (IASC) as it sought to develop a reasonably complete set of accounting standards through the IASC core standards work program.

IOSCO has assessed 30 IASC standards, including their related interpretations ("the IASC 2000 standards"), considering their suitability for use in cross-border offerings and listings. IOSCO has identified outstanding substantive issues relating to the IASC 2000 standards in a report that includes an analysis of those issues and specifies supplemental treatments that may be required in a particular jurisdiction to address each of these concerns.

The Presidents Committee congratulates the IASC for its hard work and contribution to raising the quality of financial reporting worldwide. The IASC's work to date has succeeded in effecting significant improvements in the quality of the IASC standards. Accordingly, the Presidents Committee recommends that IOSCO members permit incoming multinational issuers to use the 30 IASC 0200 standards to prepare their financial statements for cross-border offerings and listings, as supplemented in the manner described below (the "supplemental treatments") where necessary to address outstanding substantive issues at a national or regional level.

Those supplemental treatments are:

- **reconciliation:** requiring reconciliation of certain items to show the effect of applying a different accounting method, in contrast with the method applied under IASC standards;

- **disclosure:** requiring additional disclosures, either in the presentation of the financial statements or in the footnotes; and

- **interpretation:** specifying use of a particular alternative provided in an IASC standard, or a particular interpretation in cases where the IASC standard is unclear or silent.

In addition, as part of national or regional specific requirements, waivers may be envisaged of particular aspects of an IASC standard, without requiring that the effect of the accounting method used be reconciled to the effect of applying the IASC method. The use of waivers should be restricted to exceptional circumstances such as issues identified by a domestic regulator when a specific IASC standard is contrary to domestic or regional regulation.

The concerns identified and the expected supplemental treatments are described in the Assessment Report.

IOSCO notes that a body of accounting standards like the IASC standards must continue to evolve in order to address existing and emerging issues. IOSCO's recommendation assumes that IOSCO will continue to be involved in the IASC work and structure and that the IASC will continue to develop its body of standards. IOSCO strongly urges the IASC in its future work program to address the concerns identified in the Assessment Report, in particular, future projects.

IOSCO expects to survey its membership by the end of 2001 in order to determine the extent to which members have taken steps to permit incoming multinational issuers to use the IASC 2000 standards, subject to the supplemental treatments described above. At the same time IOSCO expects to continue to work with the IASC, and will determine the extent to which IOSCO's outstanding substantive issues, including proposals for future projects, have been addressed appropriately.

through supplemental treatments (IOSCO, 2000b). Hence, in practice, members of IOSCO, including the Securities and Exchange Commission (SEC) in the United States (U.S.), will now individually determine whether or not to endorse IAS for cross-border listings. In this respect, the SEC has a key role to play as guardian of the world's largest capital market.

The SEC currently requires the reconciliation of IAS financial statements to U.S. GAAP and it remains to be seen whether this barrier to IAS recognition will be lifted or at least moderated. Recent research by Street, Nichols, and Gray (2000) suggests that the gap between IAS and U.S. GAAP is narrowing. Major areas of difference appear to be limited to property, plant and equipment revaluations, deferred taxes (where partial rather than comprehensive allocation has been used), goodwill (where goodwill has been charged to reserves contrary to U.S. requirements or different amortization periods have been used), and capitalized borrowing costs (where borrowing costs are expensed rather than capitalized).

In addition, the changes in IAS following completion of the core standards work program indicate that these differences have been reduced further as IAS moves closer to U.S. GAAP. This is so much so that it could be argued that IAS are now, in practice, sufficiently close to U.S. GAAP to be acceptable to the SEC. Alternatively, the SEC may consider it necessary that additional disclosures be provided where companies utilize certain IAS alternatives that have historically yielded material and significant deviations from U.S. GAAP such as the revaluation of property, plant, and equipment. However, the number of IAS subject to additional disclosures is likely to form an increasingly short list.

In addition to sharing the concerns of IOSCO about some of the "quality" issues raised, the SEC in the United States has argued that a comprehensive infrastructure must be in place so that high-quality global accounting standards can be used, interpreted, and enforced consistently around the world. In this regard, the International Federation of Accountants (IFAC) has stated that companies and auditors are asserting that financial statements comply with IAS when in fact the accounting policies used and notes indicate otherwise.

Research suggests that noncompliance with IAS is indeed problematic despite the revision of IASI Presentation of Financial Statements in 1997 (effective for accounting periods beginning on or after July 1, 1998). IASI Revised requires that "Financial Statements should not be described as complying with International Accounting Standards unless they comply with all the requirements of each applicable Standard and each applicable Interpretation of the Standards Interpretation Committee. Inappropriate treatments are not rectified either by disclosure of the accounting policies used or by notes or by explanatory material."

Recent research by Street and Gray (2000) found that of 162 companies referring to IAS in their 1998 and 1999 accounts, only 124 (77 percent) stated that they were fully in compliance with IAS. While a number of companies had responded to IASI Revised by no longer stating exceptions to IAS, 13 companies had decided to no longer refer to IAS, with 11 companies referring only to national GAAP and 2 companies adopting U.S. GAAP. More troubling for the IASC was that 15 companies violated the revised IASI by referring to the use of IAS with exception in 1999.

All of these companies were audited by Big 5+2 international accounting firms. Six of the Big 5+2 audit reports only made reference to national GAAP. The remaining nine audit reports stated the accounts are "in accordance with IAS" and for seven of these nine, the Big 5+2 auditors specified exceptions to IAS in the audit report. Thus while it appears that the international accounting firms are aware of IAS, they are not consistently supporting the enforcement process. It is important that auditors worldwide take a firm stand and insist on full compliance with IAS for those companies claiming compliance with IAS. In particular, actions should support the vision of the Big 5+2 auditors that global accounting standards should be developed and applied on a consistent worldwide basis.

These findings highlight the importance of ongoing efforts by several organizations including the IASC, IFAC, and the newly formed International Forum on Accountancy Development (IFAD) to raise the standard of accounting and audit practices worldwide.

The recent restructuring of the IASC should assist in addressing the noncompliance problems identified as, most importantly, the new IASB board includes seven members that will also serve as liaisons to national accounting standard-setting boards. The idea is that these members will work to harmonize their national standards with IAS, thereby making it possible for more companies to accurately state that their financial statements are in compliance with both IAS and national GAAP. Currently, differences between national GAAP and IAS often make this impossible.

The U.S. SEC has also noted some situations where a foreign registrant's footnotes assert that financial statements comply in all material respects with IAS or are consistent with IAS, yet the company has applied only certain IAS or omitted information without explaining the reasons for exclusion. The SEC has stated that it will challenge such assertions and where they cannot be sustained will require either changes to the financial statements to conform with IAS or removal of the assertion of compliance with IAS.

Other notable efforts in 2000 to address compliance problems facing the IASC included the formation of the IFAD and the restructuring of IFAC. IFAD was established following the Asian financial crisis when the accounting profession was criticized for not doing enough to enhance the accounting capabilities of developing and emerging nations. Following discussions between the World Bank and IFAC, it was agreed to form IFAD, representing an alliance of accountancy groups and firms across the world. IFAD is intended to be a means by which regulators, international financial institutions, investors, and representatives of the accountancy and auditing profession come together to ensure that economic downturns such as the Asian financial crisis are not repeated.

IFAD has been undertaking country-by-country reviews of accounting standards, ethics and disciplinary procedures, corporate governance, banking, and company law. IFAD has benchmarked information collected through these individual country reviews against international standards and will finance consultants to visit countries to help close the gaps wherever these may be identified. IFAD is firmly committed to encouraging conformity and consistency of national accounting standards with IAS. Successful implementation of IFAD's vision would go far in addressing the key problem of noncompliance with IAS.

Further, in May 2000, IFAC agreed to a restructuring plan where, as part of the restructuring, IFAC and the large international accounting firms have undertaken a major new initiative. A key aspect of this effort is the establishment of a new IFAC-sponsored grouping of accounting firms that will work closely with IFAC in developing and encouraging implementation of international accounting and auditing standards. Only time will tell if the combined efforts of the IASB, IFAD, and IFAC can overcome national, cultural, and other barriers and achieve global acceptance and enforcement of IAS around the world.

THE INTERNATIONAL HARMONIZATION AND DISCLOSURE DEBATE

To what extent MNEs create net benefits for host countries is still a matter of some controversy. However, many governments perceive that accounting harmonization and disclosure may help redress any competitive imbalance between MNEs and host-country domestic corporations and improve the bargaining position of host governments. Naturally, this will be effective only at a cost both to the MNE and the home country. Thus, it may be expected that governments from the industrialized countries, where a significant number of MNEs are based, will not be totally supportive of increased regulation, as indeed is evidenced by the relatively soft approach of the OECD compared to the UN. Whether regulation is necessary as an alternative or supplement to the pressures of market forces in individual host countries, in the home country, and in international financial markets would, therefore, seem to depend on the extent to which a more competitive international environment is considered an acceptable goal.

As far as economic development in the context of regional intergration is concerned, there seems little doubt that the long-term goal is to remove market imperfections and that in a community such as the European Union there is a serious commitment to eliminating regulatory barriers despite the short-term costs likely to be incurred in some member countries.

Moving from a regional to a wider international level is, however, an entirely different matter. It is by no means evident that there is a commitment to worldwide economic integration, with its implications for a more competitive environment in which trade and investment would flow freely—the objective of the European Union. On the country, many governments appear to be more concerned with protecting the interests of their own business community, including MNEs, at the expense of others.

If this is so, there certainly does not seem to be any broad support for the need to develop worldwide accounting standards for *all* corporations, as envisaged by the IASB. What is left is a set of arguments that relate more to the self-interest of MNEs, professional accounting firms, and members of the business, financial, and investment community. All tend to subscribe to a more harmonized approach to accounting and financial reporting, largely from the dual perspective of minimizing cost and maximizing shareholder wealth in the context of an international capital market.

Furthermore, evidence suggests that national differences in accounting and financial reporting are to a considerable extent a function of differences in priorities concerning domestic needs, which are the product of a variety of environmental factors of an economic, political, and cultural nature. Thus, in the case of domestic corporations with no significant international operations or financing, there is little reason to be concerned that worldwide standards serve international objectives, which may well be irrelevant or, at most, of minor significance compared with domestic objectives.

International classification research has also shown that distinct patterns of accounting and country groupings have emerged over some considerable time, and hence it seems likely that any natural coordination will be a lengthy process. At the same time, the impact of regional economic groupings such as the European Union, and perhaps also international intergovernmental organizations such as the UN and OECD, may well be significant though their influence has yet to become effective. The IASB also has the potential to become a more important influence in the future, particularly with the support of the IOSCO. The current situation is thus highly dynamic, and it may well be that new models or patterns of accounting are in the process of being formed that are bringing together disparate traditions, with a consequent enhancement of worldwide accounting harmony.

If it is accepted that MNEs are, and are likely to remain, the most important motivation for international standards, future developments seem likely to be concerned with the resolution of a number of significant accounting and reporting problems specific to MNE operations and their involvement in international securities markets. As far as corporate reporting by MNEs is concerned, limited progress has been made in the conceptual and technical development of such key areas as accounting for intangible assets, foreign currency translation, group accounting, segmental reporting, accounting for related party transactions, and nonfinancial disclosures such as social and environmental reporting. There is substantial scope for innovation here if we are to develop corporate reporting systems that can cope more effectively with the complexity of MNE operations.

While reporting requirements at the national level have become more detailed and complex, particularly in the United States, large corporations, and MNEs in particular, have also become more complex. It may well be that in practice there is now less, rather than more, effective information disclosure, contrary to popular belief. This raises the question of whether adequate reporting systems exist to match the growing complexity of MNE operations. Judging from the controversy surrounding issues such as group accounting, accounting for intangibles, accounting for inflation, financial instruments, and foreign currency translation, it seems certain that there is much to be resolved internationally as far as external reporting is concerned, despite the undoubted sophistication of many MNE internal accounting systems.

The disclosure of information on the basis of what is used internally is, of course, prima facie desirable on the presumption that what is useful for management will be useful to external users. This does not mean, however, that it is necessarily an easy task to adapt internal reporting to a form suitable for external reporting or that the costs, especially those relating to competitive disadvantage, are insignificant. A major problem is that national regulation determines to a greater or lesser extent what is reported externally, with incompatible differences the possible result. Moreover, to the extent that information is disclosed voluntarily, there are likely to be differences over the content, classification, measurement, and presentation of information between MNEs.

There is a need, therefore, for further research to help develop more innovative external reporting systems that can cope with the complexity of MNE operations as well as tackle problems concerning the feasibility and extent of global harmonization. Currently, the potential for using alternative forms of reporting is restricted, as is knowledge of the costs and benefits involved.

SUMMARY

1.   Regardless of the merits of the various interests and claims of the many participants in the process of setting international standards for accounting and corporate reporting, there is clearly a well-articulated demand internationally for both additional and more comparable information by a wide range of organizations and user groups.

2.   Major user groups interested in international standard-setting include governments and international intergovernmental oranizations, trade unions and employees, investors and financial analysts, bankers, lenders, creditors, and, last but not least, accountants and auditors.

3.   While there are some similarities between the information needs of user groups, there are also a number of significant differences involving the quantity of information that should be disclosed, the basis upon which the information should be measured, the degree of uniformity such information should have, and the extent to which information disclosures should be mandatory.

4.   Furthermore, the power to influence international accounting and information disclosure practices varies considerably, from the legal force of EU directives throughout the European Union to the guidelines of the OECD and UN and the recommendations of the IASB.

5.   The international harmonization of accounting is complex and dynamic. For example, international organizations have the potential to strongly influence whether national governments decide to implement any international agreements by incorporating them into national law.

6.   A major objective of accounting and information disclosure so far as international intergovernmental and trade union organizations are concerned is to monitor and, if necessary, control MNE operations. At the very least, it seems that international accounting standards may be relevant to improving the competitive bargaining power of those involved in economic and social relationships with MNEs.

7.   From the standpoint of investors, financial analysts, bankers, lenders, and creditors, it appears that the prime objective of international accounting standards is additional and comparable information about the financial position, performance, and prospects of corporations, and especially MNEs, to be used as a basis for investment and lending decisions and to satisfy accountability objectives.

8.   Accountants and auditors also have a vital role to play as preparers, users, and verifiers of information disclosed by MNEs and are, in the form of the IASB, themselves heavily involved in the standard-setting processes which influence international accounting and reporting behavior.

9.   The development of international accounting and disclosure standards—especially those for MNEs—is an essentially political process, with a variety of organizations, both public and private, involved in setting standards that affect MNEs. All these organizations have differing objectives, scope, and powers of enforcement.

10.   Recent developments suggest a more consultative approach to international accounting harmonization, and, with the support of IOSCO, the IASB has the potential to be recognized as the global standard-setting authority.

11.   Accountants and accounting organizations are an essential part of the international standard-setting process and provide the innovations, technical development, and implementation skills necessary to introduce desired standards of accounting and information disclosure.

Discussion Questions

1.   Discuss the likely future of the European Union's involvement in accounting standard-setting in a global context.

2.   How can global pressures for international accounting harmonization be reconciled with local pressures for addressing national needs and priorities?

3.   Discuss the advantages and limitations of the IOSCO endorsement.

4.   Why are many MNEs voluntarily adopting IAS rather than U.S. GAAP?

5.   Discuss the problems and prospects of enforcing IAS.

Exercise

Form into groups of three or four students representing the various participants in international accounting standard-setting, including the IASB, the IOSCO, the United States, the European Union, developing countries, and MNEs. In particular, discuss the following questions:

1.   Should international accounting standards be set for the world or be restricted to MNEs interested in raising finance from international investors?

2.   Should international accounting standards be set on the basis of a philosophy of "uniformity" or a philosophy of "mutual recognition," where some differences are tolerated?

3.   If the goal is "uniformity," how can the "right" answers be found?

4.   Should the IASB have the authority to set international accounting standards or should standards be the outcome of a more collaborative/consultative exercise?

5.   How can international accounting standards be enforced?

Selected References

Adhikari, A. and R. H. Tondkar. 1995. "An Examination of the Success of the EC Directives to Harmonize Stock Exchange Disclosure Requirements," *Journal of International Accounting Auditing & Taxation*, 4 (2): 127–46.

Coenenberg, A. G. and S. J. Gray, eds. 1984. *EEC Accounting Harmonization: Implementation and Impact of the Fourth Directive*. Amsterdam: North-Holland.

Commission of the European Community. 1980. *Proposal for a Directive on Procedures for Informing and Consulting the Employees of Undertakings with Complex Structures, in Particular Transnational Undertakings*. Brussels: EC, October, revised 1983.

Dumontier, P. and B. Raffournier. 1998. "Why Firms Comply Voluntarily with IAS: An Empirical Analysis with Swiss Data," *Journal of International Financial Management & Accounting*, 9 (4): 216–45.

Emenyonu, E. N. and S. J. Gray. 1992. "European Community Accounting Harmonisation: An Empirical Study of Measurement Practices in France, Germany, and the United Kingdom," *Accounting and Business Research* (Winter): 49–58.

Emenyonu, E. N. and S. J. Gray. 1996. "International Accounting Harmonization in Major Developed Stock Market Countries: An Empirical Study," *International Journal of Accounting,* 31 (3): 269–79.

European Community. 1978. *Fourth Council Directive for Coodination of National Legislation Regarding the Annual Accounts for Limited Liability Companies.* Brussels: EC.

European Community. 1983. *Seventh Council Directive on Consolidated Accounts.* Brussels: EC, June.

Goeltz, R. K. 1991. "International Accounting Harmonization: The Impossible (and Unnecessary) Dream," *Accounting Horizons,* 5 (1): 85–88.

Gray, S. J. (with L. B. McSweeney and J. C. Shaw). 1984. *Information Disclosure and the Multinational Corporation.* New York: John Wiley.

Gray, S. J., A. G. Coenenberg, and P. D. Gordon, eds. 1993. *International Group Accounting: Issues in European Harmonization.* London: Routledge.

Hegarty, J. 1997. "Accounting for the Global Economy: Is National Regulation Doomed to Disappear?," *Accounting Horizons* (December): 75–90.

Herrmann, D. and W. Thomas. 1995. "Harmonisation of Accounting Measurement Practices in the European Community," *Accounting and Business Research* (Autumn): 253–65.

International Forum on Accountancy Development. www.ifad.net

International Federation of Accountants. www.ifac.net

International Accounting Standards Committee. International Accounting Standards, Shaping the New Millenium, Annual Review 1999.

International Accounting Standards Committee. International Accounting Standards, Annual Review 2000.

International Accounting Standards Committee. 2000. International Accounting Standards 2000. London: IASC.

International Accounting Standards Board. www.iasb.org.uk

International Organizations of Securities Commissions. www.iosco.orgIOSCO, 2000a. *Resolution Concerning the Use of IASC Standards for the Purpose of Facilitating Multinational Securities Offering and Cross-Border Listings.* Sydney, Australia, May 17, 2000.

IOSCO Technical Committee, 2000b. *IASC Standards—Assessment Report,* Report by the Technical Committee, May 2000.

Levitt, Arthur. 1998. "The Numbers Game." Presentation at the New York University Center for Law and Business, New York (September 28).

McGregor, W. 1999. "An Insider's View of the Current State and Future of International Accounting Standard Setting," *Accounting Horizons* (June): 159–68.

Mueller, G. G. 1967. *International Accounting.* New York: Macmillan.

Mueller, G. G. 1997. "Harmonization Efforts in the European Union," in *International Accounting and Finance Handbook,* edited by F. D. S. Choi, 2nd ed. New York: John Wiley.

Nobes, C. W. and R. H. Parker, eds. 2000. *Comparative International Accounting.* Englewoods Cliffs, N.J.: Prentice-Hall.

Organisation for Economic Cooperation and Development. 1976. "International Investment and Multinational Enterprises," *Guidelines for Multinational Enterprises.* Paris: OECD, revised 1979.

Organisation for Economic Cooperation and Development. 1976. *International Investment and Multinational Enterprises.* Paris: OECD, revised 1979; International Confederation of Free Trade Unions, European Trade Union Confederation, World Confederation of Labour. 1977. *Trade Union Requirements for Accounting and Publication by Undertakings and Groups of Companies.* Brussels.

Saudagaran, S. M. and J. G. Diga. 1998. "Accounting Harmonization in ASEAN: Benefits, Models and Policy Issues," *Journal of International Accounting Auditing & Taxation,* 7 (1): 21–45.

Street, D. L. and K. A. Shaughnessy. 1998. "The Evolution of the G4+1 and Its Impact on International Harmonization of Accounting Standards," *Journal of International Accounting Auditing & Taxation,* 7 (2): 131–61.

Street, D. L., S. J. Gray, and Bryant, S. M. 1999. "Acceptance and Observance of International Accounting Standards: An Empirical Study of Companies Claiming to Comply with IASs," *International Journal of Accounting,* 34 (1): 11–47.

Street, D. L., N. B. Nichols, and S. J. Gray. 2000. "Assessing the Acceptability of International Accounting Standards in the U.S.: An Empirical Study of the Materiality of U.S. GAAP Reconciliations by Non-U.S. Companies Complying with IASC Standards." *The International Journal of Accounting,* 35 (1): 27–63.

Street, D. L. and S. J. Gray. 2000. "IAS 1 Compliance Survey: Challenging Times." *Accountancy* (December): 104–06.

Tay, J. S. W. and R. H. Parker. 1990. "Measuring International Harmonization and Standardization," *Abacus,* 26 (1): 71–88.

Taylor, Stephen and Stuart Turley. 1986. *The Regulation of Accounting.* London: Basil Blackwell.

United Nations. 1988. *Conclusions on Accounting and Reporting by Transnational Corporations.* New York: UN, revised 1994.

Van Hulle, K. 1992. "Harmonization of Accounting Standards: A View from the European Community," *European Accounting Review,* 1 (1): 161–72.

Wallace, R. S. O. 1990. "Survival Strategies of a Global Organization: The Case of the International Accounting Standards Committee," *Accounting Horizons,* 4 (2): 1–22.

Walton, P. 1999. "European Harmonization," in *International Accounting and Finance Handbook,* 2nd ed., 1999 Supplement, edited by F. D. S. Choi. New York: John Wiley, pp. 11.1–11.14.

CHAPTER SEVEN

INTERNATIONAL BUSINESS COMBINATIONS, GOODWILL, AND INTANGIBLES

Chapter Objectives

- Show how countries aggregate information through the process of consolidating financial statements

- Differentiate between acquisition and merger accounting

- Describe the treatment of nonconsolidated subsidiaries

- Discuss the various efforts at harmonization of consolidation practices by the International Accounting Standards Committee (IASC) and also in the European Union

- Compare the different attitudes toward the cash-flow statement worldwide

- Identify the issues involved in joint-venture accounting worldwide

- Examine the conceptual issues involved in accounting for goodwill and other intangible assets

- Identify the major approaches to accounting for goodwill: asset without amortization, asset with systematic amortization, and immediate write-off

- Describe the different national practices of accounting for goodwill and the major international efforts at harmonizing these practices

- Examine the choice of accounting methods, national practices, and harmonization efforts with respect to brands, trademarks, patents, and related intangibles

INTRODUCTION

The financial performance and future prospects of the MNE as an economic entity are of interest to a wide range of groups, including investors, bankers, employees, and managers. It is in this context that a corporate report on the group of corporations controlled and coordinated by the MNE parent corporation is relevant. Subsidiary corporations may have been established for strategic purposes by the MNE in the process of organic growth or acquired in the context of merger and takeover activity. In addition, the parent may have interests or investments in associated corporations, joint ventures, and alliances that are not controlling interests but are nevertheless significant to its overall financial performance. In this chapter, we will discuss issues relating to consolidated financial statements, including goodwill and intangibles We will also examine the accounting treatment of joint ventures. National and international developments will also be reviewed in both a comparative and a harmonization context.

CONSOLIDATED FINANCIAL STATEMENTS

While there is a recognized need for information about MNE operations on a worldwide basis, it is a matter of some controversy how best to report this information. Consolidation is currently accepted in practice as the best means of accounting for groups and business combinations internationally. Consolidated reports are relevant not only to external users, notably investors, but also to managers as a basis for overall control and evaluation of performance. Consolidation involves aggregating, on a "line-by-line" basis, information about the assets, liabilities, revenues, and expenses of the MNE's many individual legal entities into income, financial position, and funds or cash flow statements relating to a single economic entity.

At the same time, it is increasingly recognized that the complexity of MNE operations is such that consolidations are likely to be less than revealing without some disaggregation of the information accumulated; hence, the corresponding demand for segment (disaggregated) information by lines of business and geographical markets. Consolidated and segment statements are thus complementary forms of reporting—each appears to be necessary to make an informed appraisal of MNE operations. Paradoxically, just as consolidations are now becoming accepted in practice as appropriate for groups operating in the international environment, so too are their limitations becoming apparent: they do not reveal any significant differences in the risks and returns applicable to the various operations of the MNE.

Apart from the United Kingdom and the United States—and, more recently, the EU countries—legal and professional requirements relating to group accounts are not perhaps as comprehensive or widespread as might be expected, though the number of countries with regulations in this area is growing. Japan, which first introduced regulations to publish consolidated financial statements in 1976, provides a case study of the significance of such disclosure requirements. Toshiba is a Japanese firm that reported 1976 earnings of U.S.$130 million on a nonconsolidated basis but a loss of U.S.$13 million when its foreign and other subsidiaries were consolidated.

Clearly, nonconsolidation can be highly misleading as to overall financial performance, and this is especially so for MNEs with complex foreign operations.

There is no doubt that, in practice, the quality and quantity of consolidated
information vary considerably both between and within countries. In the United
Kingdom, a parent company balance sheet is always provided in addition to a consolidated balance sheet and income statement. In contrast, in the United States,
only consolidated financial statements are provided. In Germany, it is normal practice for both parent company and worldwide consolidated financial statements to
be provided.

An alternative to full consolidation on a line-by-line basis is proportional consolidation, where only the ownership share of assets and liabilities is consolidated
on a pro rata or proportional basis. This is typically considered appropriate for joint
ventures.

With respect to associated or affiliated corporations, where there is a significant influence but not controlling interest, the majority of MNEs use the equity
method, whereby a share of profits is consolidated on a "one-line" basis according
to the equity owned by the MNE. The assets and liabilities of the associate are not
consolidated. Instead, the investment amount in the MNE parent's books is
adjusted to reflect the MNE's share in equity. The more conservative cost method—
whereby only dividends received and receivable are included in the results for the
year—is widely used, however, in countries such as Australia and Sweden.

Different consolidation methods impact differently on the balance sheet and
income statement, as a simplified example of a 50 percent-owned foreign company
shows (see Exhibit 7.1) It can be seen from Exhibit 7.1 that the balance sheet under
full consolidation eliminates the investment amount for the foreign company and
instead includes all the assets of the foreign company, with the 50 percent minority
interests in them shown separately under shareholders' equity. Under proportional
consolidation, 50 percent of the fixed assets and inventory are brought in, compared to the equity method, which merely restates the cost of the investment in the
foreign company from $M75 to $M80 to reflect the 50 percent share of equity
(including the share of income for 2001). In the income statement, net income is
the same under each method but presented differently. Under full consolidation,
the minority interest share is deducted from gross income, whereas under proportional consolidation, the share of income is incorporated in the proportionate revenues and expenses included in the income statement. The equity approach, on
the other hand, is to subsequently add the share of income of the associated company to the parent company's net income. This example excludes issues relating to
foreign currency translation, which are discussed in Chapter 10.

Purchase versus Pooling-of-Interests Accounting   There are also some considerable differences between countries regarding the methods of full consolidation
used for business combinations resulting from mergers and takeovers. For example,
the purchase method of consolidation (termed the acquisition method in the
United Kingdom) is normally used, whereby assets are generally revalued to "fair
value" as of the date of acquisition of the subsidiary, and the difference between the
purchase cost and the revalued net assets is described as goodwill on consolidation.
However, in some countries, the pooling-of-interests method (termed the merger
method in the United Kingdom) is also permitted in certain circumstances. In this

Exhibit 7.1   MNE Consolidation Alternatives

	MNC Parent ($m)	Foreign Company ($m)	Full Consolidation ($m)	Proportional Consolidation ($m)	Equity Method ($m)
Consolidation Method					
Balance Sheet as at December 31, 2001					
Fixed assets	250	130	380	315 (250 + 65)	250
Investment in foreign company (50 percent)	75	—	—	—	80 (50% × 160)
Inventory	50	30	80	65 (50 + 15)	50
	375	160	460	380	380
Share capital	350	150	350	350	350
Net income—1995	25	10	30	30	30
Shareholder's equity	375	160	380	380	380
Minority interests	—	—	80	—	—
	375	160	460	380	380
Income Statement for 2001					
Revenues	50	20	70	60 (50 + 10)	50
Expenses	25	10	35	30 (25 + 5)	25
	25	10	35	30	25
Income from foreign associate company	—	—	—	—	5 (50% × 10)
	25	10	35	30	30
Minority interests	—	—	5	—	—
Net income	25	10	30	30	30

case, assets are not revalued, no goodwill arises, and there is no distinction between pre- and postacquisition earnings. Under purchase accounting, the acquired company contributes to group profits only after the combination, whereas under pooling-of-interests accounting all the precombination profits are included. This tends to provide an artificial incentive to use pooling, when permitted, to show enhanced profits.

Furthermore, under purchase accounting, the investment by the holding company is recorded at market value, and the assets and liabilities of the acquired company are generally revalued to fair value, as already mentioned, as of the date of the business combination. Under pooling, however, the investment is recorded at nominal value, and assets and liabilities are not revalued. The effect of this difference is that, under the acquisition approach, profits subsequent to combination may be decreased by increased depreciation charges relating to revalued assets. Profits may also be decreased by the amortization of goodwill. Thus, there is a further incentive to use the pooling-of-interests method where this is a permitted alternative to purchase accounting.

The potential for enhancing reported earnings, however, does not rest entirely with pooling. A pessimistic view of asset valuations, in the context of fair value adjustments, could be taken. Furthermore, provisions for reorganization and anticipated future losses (included in the cost of the purchase) could increase goodwill, and, with the immediate write-off of such goodwill against reserves (permitted in the Netherlands but not the United States), could well encourage a preference for purchase accounting.

In a conventional accounting principles context, the rationale for choosing between these two approaches is not well developed. However, what rationale there is seems to reflect the questionable assumption that the nature of ownership is of paramount importance regardless of the economic substance of the business combination. In this context, where one company purchases another and the shareholders of the acquired company cease to have ownership rights, the purchase method is considered appropriate. On the other hand, if there is a continuity of ownership through an exchange of shares, the pooling-of-interests method is considered appropriate. An assumption underlying merger accounting is that all that has changed is the size of the business to be accounted for, with both constituents of the group continuing as before; in other words, there is a uniting of interests. In contrast, purchase accounting treats the business combination from the viewpoint of the shareholders of the acquired company. The subsidiary is also treated as if its assets, liabilities, and goodwill have been purchased separately and contribute to the business from the date of combination. Thus, assets and liabilities are revalued to reflect their purchase values, or new "historical costs," as at the date of acquisition.

In practice, the pooling-of-interests method is used by only a small minority of companies worldwide. In Australia and Hong Kong, for example, it is not permitted. Interestingly, pooling is *required* in Canada, Singapore, Sweden, the United Kingdom, and the United States in certain restricted circumstances and permitted in countries such as France, Germany the Netherlands, and Switzerland (see

Exhibit 7.2   Accounting for Business Combinations

	Pooling Method if Uniting of Interests	Purchase Method if Uniting of Interests
Australia	Not permitted	Required
Canada	Required	Not permitted
France	Permitted	Preferred
Germany	Permitted	Permitted
Hong Kong	Not Permitted	Required
Japan	Permitted	Permitted
Netherlands	Permitted	Permitted
Singapore	Required	Not Permitted
Sweden	Required	Not Permitted
Switzerland	Permitted	Permitted
United Kingdom	Required	Not Permitted
United States	Required	Not Permitted

Exhibit 7.2). In the United States, pooling is a minority practice used in fewer than 10 percent of new business combinations, but where a U.S. combination satisfies the criteria for pooling, it *must* be accounted for using the pooling-of-interests method. In the United Kingdom, practice has now been brought into line with that of the United States with the issuance of FRS 6 *Acquisition and Mergers,* which has the objective of ensuring that "merger accounting" is used only for those business combinations that are not, in substance, the acquisition of one entity by another but the formation of a new reporting entity as a substantially equal partnership where no party is dominant.

The Treatment of Nonconsolidated Subsidiaries   Subsidiaries may be nonconsolidated for various reasons. In this regard, the impact on earnings will depend on whether they are accounted for using the equity method or the cost method. If the equity method is used, then reported earnings will tend to be higher because the MNE's share of earnings rather than dividends is included.

In Japan, the United Kingdom, and the United States, the equity method is required. But this is not the case, for example, in Australia, Sweden, and Switzerland. In both the United States and the United Kingdom, recent changes in regulation require the consolidation of all material subsidiaries. Because it is mainly financial subsidiaries that have been affected by these changes, the latter have had the effect of increasing leverage or gearing.

A major problem in Japan, however, is that it is not easy to identify a subsidiary in the first place. The legal criterion of majority share ownership is misleading. Corporate groups in Japan are significantly different from groups in the United Kingdom and the United States. Ownership patterns in U.K.-U.S. groups generally reflect a majority shareholding either directly or indirectly via the parent corporation. In contrast, there is a complex pattern of decentralized cross-holdings in Japanese groups (see Figure 7.1).

These groups are known as *keiretsu* (i.e., headless combinations). Legal relationships are not the critical factor here. Relationships concerning the supply of raw materials and technology, market outlets, source of debt finance, and inter-

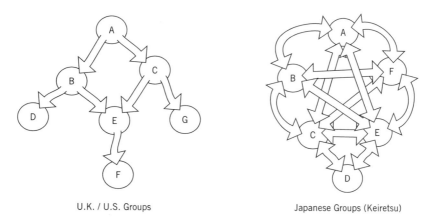

U.K. / U.S. Groups   Japanese Groups (Keiretsu)

Figure 7.1   Corporate Group Share Ownership Patterns

locking directorships are also very important. Group consciousness is the key, built on a system of cooperation based on mutual trust and loyalty.

Hence, Japanese consolidated accounts are not necessarily an accurate reflection of group results—both earnings and assets may be seriously understated. Many companies may report compliance with U.S. GAAP for U.S. listing purposes, but they are not strictly comparable with U.S. consolidated accounts.

Fair Value Adjustments Under acquisition accounting, both the United States and the United Kingdom require the revaluation of the assets acquired to fair value, or updated purchase price, usually based on current values. However, this is not required, for example, in Japan or Switzerland where book values are retained even though they may be in excess of fair value.

The financial impact of *not* restating assets to fair value is that earnings will be relatively overstated on account of lower depreciation charges and assets will be understated where fair value exceeds book value. In the case of many acquisitions, however, the fair value of assets may be lower than book value—hence, the reverse will apply in countries not requiring restatement (i.e., earnings will be understated).

Accounting for Goodwill There are a variety of practices for treating goodwill arising from the consolidation of subsidiaries on a worldwide basis. Majority practice worldwide is to treat goodwill as an asset subject to systematic amortization. However, a significant minority adopt the method of immediate write-off against reserves. Only a small minority retained goodwill permanently as an asset.

The most restrictive approaches to goodwill can be seen in countries such as Australia, Canada, Japan, Sweden, and the United States, where immediate write-off against reserves is not permitted. Further, maximum amortization periods of between 5 and 40 years are required. Some other countries, however, are more flexible, including notably the Netherlands.

International Accounting Standards

In International Accounting Standards 27 (1994) and 28 (1998), the IASC states that worldwide consolidated financial statements should be provided along with information about a group's member corporations, including its associated corporations. Such consolidations should include all subsidiaries, foreign and domestic. Associated corporations, where the investor corporation holds a significant interest, are to be accounted for by the equity method except when the investment is acquired and held exclusively with a view to its disposal. The standards also specify criteria for the exclusion of subsidiaries from the consolidation (i.e., if control is temporary or severe long-term restrictions on the transfer of funds impairs control by the parent). Uniform accounting policies for all corporations consolidated are required, or at least there must be disclosure of any differences in accounting policy.

The IASC's IAS 22 on *Accounting for Business Combinations,* issued in 1983, also included requirements relating to the treatment of business combinations and accounting for goodwill. However, this was revised in 1993 and 1998 to impose much stricter requirements than existed hitherto.

Under the original IAS 22, either the purchase method for acquisitions *or* the pooling-of-interests method for a merging or uniting of interests could be used. But the revised standard (para. 8) tightens up the criteria for pooling as follows: "A uniting of interests is a business combination in which the shareholders of the combining enterprises combine control over the whole, or effectively the whole, of their net assets or operations to achieve a continuing mutual sharing in the risks and benefits attaching to the combined entity such that neither party can be identified as the acquirer." Regarding goodwill, the revised IAS 22 now stipulates that goodwill *must* be recognized as an asset (where goodwill is the excess of the cost of acquisition over the fair value of net identifiable assets acquired) and *must* be amortized against revenues on a systematic basis over its useful life. The amortization period should not exceed 20 years, unless a longer period can be justified. The method of immediate write-off against reserves has been eliminated by the IASC—it is now an unacceptable alternative.

A major problem with the revised standard is that it is difficult to establish the theoretical superiority of the amortization method over alternative approaches, though there would seem to be majority support in practice for treating goodwill as an asset subject to systematic amortization. In many respects, the IASC would seem to have been influenced by U.S. practice and the preference for a more uniform accounting treatment of goodwill.

What chances of success does the IASC have to achieve compliance on a worldwide basis? In practice, a number of countries adopt a flexible approach and permit the immediate write-off of goodwill against shareholders' equity. There are also theoretical arguments to support both the asset-with-amortization and immediate write-off methods. In consequence, enhanced transparency concerning the treatment of goodwill is likely to be more important than the uniformity introduced by the IASC.

Problems and Prospects

While demand for MNE consolidated financial statements has been growing, there has not been a rapid response in practice. Many large MNEs based in countries such as India, Italy, and Switzerland have not provided worldwide consolidated information, though the situation has changed with the relatively recent introduction of new laws. On the other hand, many MNEs have been voluntarily disclosing consolidated information (e.g., Ciba-Geigy in Switzerland and Fiat in Italy). In some countries, such as India and Saudi Arabia, consolidated accounts are still not required. Further developments must be expected with the continuing involvement of the IASC, now IASB, in the setting of international accounting standards, though the European Union has undoubtedly been more influential in the short term in that the Seventh Directive has legal force throughout the EU countries.

Just beneath the surface, however, are many problems to be resolved internationally, especially those relating to determining the appropriate concept of group identification and the relevant techniques of consolidation, including the treatment of associated corporations. Further issues include the disclosure of details of ownership in, and activities of, members of the group. Given the wide variety of participants interested in MNEs, there appears to be pressure to develop disclosure and measurement practices that will provide information to satisfy a number of perspectives. From a governmental and trade union standpoint, for example, additiona subgroup consolidated financial statements at "country" level may be useful, whereas investors who tend to be more concerned with the MNE as a total economic entity may well be satisfied with a group consolidation on a worldwide basis.

A final issue concerns the relevance of the consolidation process itself in the context of MNE operations, with its variety of geographical locations, differential rates of inflation, exchange rates, and political risk. How meaningful is aggregate information of this kind? There seems to be room for experimentation with alternative forms of presentation and disclosure, including the further development of segmental reporting.

Now consider the funds or cash flow statement. This statement may be viewed as one of the required consolidated financial statements, but because it is something of an innovation in many countries, we will discuss it separately.

FUNDS AND CASH FLOW STATEMENTS

The funds statement, or statement of changes in financial position, is becoming increasingly recognized as an important and integral part of the consolidated financial statements. It provides an analysis of the sources and uses of funds accruing to the corporation during the period. The statement shows the inflow of funds from operations and from such items as new loans, equity capital, or the sale of assets together with the outflow of funds for dividends, loan repayments, and new investment. It should be emphasized that the term *funds* does not necessarily imply "cash" flows, though some presentations emphasize the net change in cash/liquid balances as opposed to changes in working capital (i.e., stocks, trade debtors, and creditors).

The purpose of funds and cash flow statements is to provide further insight into the financial performance, stability, and liquidity prospects of the MNE—matters of common concern to all user groups. However, in the context of MNEs, the usefulness of a consolidated funds statement may be extremely limited without additional information on a disaggregated basis. Of special interest from a risk-analysis perspective is the geographical location of the sources and uses of funds—information that is effectively denied by a consolidated statement.

While there is nothing new about the use of funds and cash flow statements, especially by financial analysts and bankers, they appear to be something of an innovation as far as regulation is concerned, despite voluntary disclosures by a significant number of major corporations.

A funds statement is legally required in France, in accordance with the Plan Comptable Général, as well as in Sweden. In other countries, for example, Brazil, Canada, and the Philippines, legal requirements also exist. In addition, a number of economies, including Australia, Hong Kong, New Zealand, and the United States, have professional requirements. Interestingly, in the United States, the funds statement requirement was replaced in 1987 by the pioneering SFAS 95 on cash flow statements. In the United Kingdom, a professional accounting standard on funds statements (SSAP 10) was similarly replaced by a cash flow statement requirement, Financial Reporting Standard No. 1 (FRS 1), issued by the Accounting Standards Board (ASB) in 1991.

It is also noteworthy that a few countries, including Fiji, Malaysia, Nigeria, and Singapore, have adopted the International Accounting Standard on cash flow statements (IAS 7, revised 1992) in the absence of national requirements. Stock exchange requirements may also be influential, as in Australia. But in many countries there are no requirements to present a funds or cash flow statement. These include, most notably, Belgium, Germany, India, Italy, Saudi Arabia, and Switzerland.

Despite the relative lack of regulation governing funds and cash flow statements, they clearly are increasingly provided in practice and in particular by large corporations, including MNEs, on a voluntary basis.

International Accounting Standard 7 (IAS 7), issued in 1977 and revised in 1992, now requires a cash flow statement. The statement must report cash flows during the period classified by operating, investing, and financing activities. Consistent with the U.K and U.S. standards, companies are permitted to use either the direct method, whereby major classes of gross cash receipts and payments are disclosed, or the indirect method, whereby net profit or loss is adjusted for the effects of transactions of a noncash nature. The direct method is encouraged by IAS 7 on the grounds that this is likely to be more useful in estimating future cash flows. Interestingly, the requirements of IAS 7 have now been endorsed and accepted by the IOSCO and the SEC in the United States.

Problems and Prospects

While a funds or cash flow statement is a relative newcomer to published corporate reports and is considered to be an innovation in many countries, it is rapidly becoming accepted as an essential and primary financial statement. There is growing pressure from the IASC for the publication of such a statement. On the other hand, it has been omitted from EU requirements presumably because funds or cash flow statements have not been featured widely in the laws of the member countries, and thus the question of harmonization does not arise from a legal perspective. Looking at the world as a whole, accounting regulation in this area is growing but has a tendency to be highly flexible. Many MNEs are voluntarily providing funds or cash flow statements, especially in Germany and Switzerland. However, the presentation of funds or cash flow statements is not well developed in practice, and there is some confusion and doubt about their purpose, effective presentation, and use. With respect to funds statements, there is considerable variation in the definition of *funds* used, in the items disclosed, in the measurement of funds from operations, and in the form of presentation of the statement. The use of funds statements for comparative purposes is thus likely to be limited. It also seems that the existing forms of the funds statement need to be critically evaluated in the light of potential uses. Certainly, the consolidation form is of limited usefulness for understanding the complexity of MNE operations where the geographical location and currency of sources and uses of funds are essential information. There is also the question of whether a cash flow statement could be more useful than a funds statement in an international context, as recently introduced in the United States and United Kingdom and endorsed by the IASC.

JOINT VENTURE ACCOUNTING

This has become an increasingly important issue with the rapid growth in joint venture arrangements, both between MNEs themselves and between MNEs and host country corporations or governments. In this regard, there are problems involving how to coordinate different cultural and accounting traditions in a way that resolves issues relating to financial control, the measurement of profit, and the valuation of joint venture investments. Relatively little is currently known about either the control processes employed or how best to measure the performance of joint ventures. In the context of joint ventures in Russia, Eastern Europe, and China, major problems have arisen from the fact that the accounting systems used in socialist economies have been very different from those of Western, market-oriented countries. Accounting in a centrally planned context has had primarily a record-keeping function and has not been decision oriented or concerned with efficiency at the enterprise level. Instead, it has been used as a means of centralized control. At the same time, there has been a tendency to emphasize the receipts and payments approach rather than the accruals approach used in Western accounting systems, with resulting differences in measurements of profit. There have also been differences in terms of asset valuation, depreciation, the treatment of liabilities, and the use of fund accounting for a variety of purposes, including new investment and social and employee benefits. While changes to a more Western accounting-oriented approach are now taking place, differences in accounting tradition and culture persist and can give rise to problems and misunderstandings.

The recent wave of international joint ventures has also posed a variety of questions concerning financial reporting by the multinational corporation. In this regard, the IASC has attempted to resolve the issues involved from the venturer's perspective in IAS 31 (revised 1998) on *Financial Reporting of Interests in Joint Ventures*. This can be contrasted with the problems of accounting *by* joint ventures, which involves decisions about the accounting principles to be used in the joint venture financial statements themselves.

In IAS 31, a joint venture is defined as "a contractual arrangement whereby two or more parties undertake an activity which is subject to joint control." This joint control must involve a contractually agreed sharing of control over an economic activity.

Joint ventures may take many forms, but three broad types are typical: jointly controlled operations, jointly controlled assets, and jointly controlled entities. With respect to joint ventures involving operations and assets rather than entities, IAS 31 requires recognition of the venturer's involvement on the basis of its share in the operations or assets. However, with jointly controlled entities, a choice of two alternatives is provided for preparing consolidated financial statements. The reason for this is that this issue is still a matter of some controversy internationally.

The "Benchmark Treatment" recommended by the IASC is to use the proportionate consolidation approach by either combining its share of the joint venture's assets, liabilities, income, and expenses on a line-by-line basis with the consolidated group amounts or by including separate line items for its joint ventures in the consolidated financial statements. The "Allowed Alternative Treatment" is to use the equity method, whereby the share of net income and net assets in joint ventures is brought into the accounts as a single-line item with further information given about the various joint ventures involved in the notes to the accounts.

Whatever method is used, information disclosures are required for contingencies and capital commitments as is a listing and description of the venturer's interests in significant joint ventures and the proportion of ownership interest it holds in controlled entities. Furthermore, where a venturer uses the line-by-line method of proportionate consolidation or equity method, there must be disclosures of the aggregate amounts of current assets, long-term assets, current liabilities, long-term liabilities, and income and expenses relating to its joint venture interests.

GOODWILL AND INTANGIBLES

The Significance of Intangible Assets

There has been a dramatic growth in the significance of intangible assets relative to the tangible assets of MNEs. A number of major factors are responsible for this, including the continuing wave of international mergers, the pursuit of global market leadership often through the development or acquisition of famous brand names, the worldwide expansion of the services sector, the speed and extent of technological change with special reference to the impact of information technology, and the growing sophistication and integration of international financial markets.

As a result, the problems of how corporations should account for intangibles including goodwill, brands, patents, R & D, and so on have been highlighted and have aroused considerable controversy. Many of these problems have yet to be resolved in theory or in practice, and there is currently a variety of accounting treatments that are considered acceptable in the international corporate context.

Accounting for intangibles is an issue of major international significance and cannot be dealt with in national isolation. If the problems that are arising are to be resolved, a substantial effort will be needed in research and experimentation as well as in consultation among all parties concerned internationally. Research and experimentation will likely promote a better understanding of the nature of practice, the reasons underlying the choice of particular valuation methods and disclosures, and the feasibility of new approaches. Wide-ranging consultation and negotiation among standard-setting agencies are also necessary if an international agreement is to be reached on an appropriate regulatory framework for intangible assets.

A statement of the objectives and concepts underlying financial statements—or a conceptual framework—may be useful in providing a basis for evaluating alternative methods of accounting for intangible assets. In this respect, the conclusions of the International Accounting Standards Committee (IASC), in *Framework for the Preparation and Presentation of Financial Statements* (1989), provided some guidance.

In the IASC's framework it is generally accepted that the objective of financial statements is to provide useful information to a wide range of users for decision-making purposes and to keep management accountable for the resources entrusted to them. Such information must be "relevant and reliable." In addition, "accrual accounting" should be used subject to the application of "prudence" when appropriate. Furthermore, the information provided should be "comparable" and "understandable."

The purpose of the balance sheet is to provide an indication of the financial strength of a company in a way that should help users to judge the ability of the company to meet its obligations. In this context, a key issue is whether the balance sheet should reflect the purchase cost of assets or their value in economic terms, or both. Unfortunately, this question is not resolved by the IASC's conceptual framework—indeed, there appears to have been a conscious attempt to avoid tackling what is undoubtedly a matter of some controversy.

A key concept governing the reporting of assets in the balance sheet is that of "recognition." This requires not only the expectation of future economic benefits but also the measurement of the assets with sufficient reliability, keeping in mind the need to exercise prudence in judging the uncertainty of future outcomes.

Because intangible assets tend to lack physical substance, an important criterion influencing recognition is that intangibles can be identified as resources that indicate the financial strength of a company and its ability to meet its obligations. In this context, the "separability" of the asset would seem likely to weigh heavily in the identification decision in that this would indicate the potential for realization without necessarily threatening the viability of the business as a going concern. At the same time, the criterion of reliable measurement is important but necessarily becomes more judgmental and problematic in the case of intangible assets.

There is no doubt that the implementation of objectives and concepts governing financial statements requires considerable interpretation and judgment, especially when concepts conflict. The fundamental, unresolved problem is how to decide on an appropriate trade-off between "relevance" and "reliability" in the provision of useful information to investors and other users. It is therfore difficult to be optimistic that the conceptual framework approach will resolve the problems of intangible assets.

The Stock Market Perspective

Efficient market theory suggests that in highly developed securities markets, such as the United Kingdom and the United States, share prices quickly reflect all publicly available information. The research findings on this issue have tended to show that this is in fact the case. The implication of these findings is that it is not the accounting treatment of items such as intangible assets that really matters (i.e., whether they are capitalized or not, how amortized, and so on). More important is the disclosure of relevant information about intangibles and how they have been accounted for. Irrespective of accounting treatment, the economic substance of the information disclosed will be incorporated in share prices provided that there is full disclosure. Following from this, it is important to ensure that sufficiently detailed information is disclosed about the nature and treatment of intangible assets so that users can make their own assessments about the treatment adopted and evaluate the likely effects of using alternative treatments.

On the other hand, not everyone is convinced that markets are efficient and that financial analysts are capable of adjusting for differences in accounting treatments across companies and also countries. This skepticism is increased regarding assessments over time. There is evidence, however, that reported corporate earnings are adjusted by analysts to exclude profits/losses on the sale of property and amortization/valuation adjustments, where these occur, with respect to goodwill. For stock (share) valuation purposes, it would seem the focus is on recurring profits and future cash flow. In addition, there is no doubt that market participants draw on a wide range of information in making their recommendations and decisions. There is also a strong psychological element involved. The securities markets are also significantly affected in general terms by economic and political factors at both the national and international levels.

Irrespective of views of market efficiency, it is important for companies to disclose as much information as possible about their affairs, within competitive limits, and to communicate this information effectively in a variety of ways. Such information should not be restricted to accounting information in the financial statements but extended to include qualitative information and quantitative nonfinancial information. In this way, any limitations inherent in financial statements and accounting conventions should be largely overcome and fairer stock (share) prices set.

GOODWILL

The dramatic growth of international mergers and acquisitions together with the major expansion in the service industries, where intangible assets are much more significant, has highlighted the significance of goodwill and the problem of how to account for it. Goodwill, in this context, is the excess of the purchase price for the company as a whole over the fair (current) value of the net assets acquired by the bidding company. This is commonly referred to as "purchased goodwill" and is, in effect, a premium paid to reflect the future earning capacity of the acquisition. Goodwill may, of course, be negative if the purchase price is less than the fair value of the net assets acquired. Another way of looking at goodwill is to define it as the difference between the value of a company or business taken as a whole and the value of its individual assets less liabilities.

With respect to business combinations. it should be noted that goodwill only arises in the context of purchase accounting. Where the pooling-of-interests method is used, the nominal value of the shares issued rather than the market value of the consideration is recognized, with the result that goodwill does not become an issue.

The crux of the problem with goodwill is that it is unlike other assets (i.e., it incorporates the value of future earnings and it relates to the valuation of the business as a whole). Accordingly, it is currently a matter of considerable controversy to whether goodwill should be treated as an asset for accounting purposes and, if so, whether or not it should be amortized against future earnings. This is an important issue because profits are used as a significant indicator of business performance. Moreover, if assets are indicators of financial strength, then the question arises whether the "value" of goodwill is relevant in contrast to the traditional emphasis on the existence and cost of tangible assets.

Choice of Accounting Methods

In practice, a variety of approaches is evident in many countries and, depending on the accounting requirements concerned, companies may be able to write off the cost of goodwill directly against reserves (shareholders' equity) or capitalize good-will as an asset, with or without amortization.

Asset Without Amortization   Proponents of this method argue that purchased goodwill should be capitalized on the grounds that future economic benefits are expected for which valuable consideration has been given, and in a successful business the value of goodwill does not decline because it is being continuously maintained. If goodwill were to be amortized, then this would be double counting (i.e., the cost of maintaining the goodwill plus the amortization cost). Thus, there is no need to amortize goodwill against earnings. Goodwill is also part of the cost of the investment and to amortize it against the earnings from the investment is to confuse the measurement of earnings with that of the capital invested. It is recognized, however, that periodic revaluations of goodwill may be necessary to recognize any reductions in the value of capital and that in such cases these amounts should be treated as charges against equity or earnings.

Opponents of this method argue that it is inconsistent to treat purchased goodwill as an asset but not internally generated goodwill. Further, purchased goodwill should not be retained indefinitely as an asset because such goodwill is being continuously replaced by new goodwill generated internally since acquisition. It is also argued that the recoverability of purchased goodwill has a high degree of uncertainty, in that such goodwill relates to the future of the company as a whole.

Asset with Systematic Amortization   Proponents of this method view purchased goodwill as an asset embodying future economic benefits for which consideration has been given. They believe, however, that goodwill is a cost of resources that will be used up and that, therefore, should be systematically amortized against earnings. Consistent with the accrual accounting concept, it is argued that costs should be matched against revenues. Goodwill is viewed as similar to other assets that are consumed or used up in the production of future earnings. If goodwill is not amortized, then future earnings would be overstated because there would be a failure to include all the costs incurred to generate such earnings. Further, where any permanent diminution in value occurs, then the effect of any such revaluation should be charged against earnings immediately.

Opponents of this method argue that double counting occurs because expenditures to maintain goodwill are made at the same time as the amortization of purchased goodwill. Further, it is very difficult to estimate when the goodwill will be exhausted, if at all, and hence the period of amortization will be arbitrary, with a consequently arbitrary and potentially severe impact on earnings. It is argued that amortization, in any event, represents an unrealized loss, not a cash outflow.

Immediate Write-Off   This method is favored by those who argue that purchased goodwill is not an asset for the purposes of financial statements. Goodwill is not separable or independently realizable but exists only by virtue of a valuation of the company or business as a whole. It is not a resource consumed or used up similar to other productive resources. Further, the true value of goodwill has no predictive relationship to the costs paid on acquisition in that its value will fluctuate over time according to a variety of economic factors and changes in investor opinion. Comparability between firms is also enhanced in that neither purchased nor internally generated goodwill are recognized as assets. Accordingly, goodwill is written off against equity (i.e., realized or unrealized reserves including retained earnings) with no charges made against current earnings. Alternatively, the write-off can be shown in a special reserve as a separate negative amount or as a "dangling debit" in the liabilities section of the financial statements, which in effect reduces the equity of the company. A variant of this approach, however, is to write off goodwill immediately against current earnings but usually as an extraordinary or nonrecurring item.

Opponents of this method argue that purchased goodwill is indeed an asset embodying expected future benefits and should be treated as such either with or without amortization. Further, there are likely to be problems with writing off large amounts of goodwill, especially in the case of service companies (with limited tangible assets) and highly acquisitive companies, to the extent that equity may become depleted or even negative and gearing or leverage unduly high. In such situations, the stated financial position would be a misleading indicator of the financial strength of the company.

Comparative National Practices

A variety of approaches to accounting for goodwill is evident in many countries. In a review of countries from different parts of the world, it is clear that the regulations in most countries are fairly flexible, with companies permitted to either treat goodwill as an asset subject to systematic amortization or to write it off immediately against equity (see Exhibit 7.3). Only in a minority of countries (e.g., Switzerland) is goodwill permitted to be capitalized without amortization.

Where the amortization treatment is adopted, a maximum period of amortization is stated in only a minority of cases with the maximum ranging from 5 years in Japan, 20 years in Australia and Sweden, and 40 years in Canada. Many countries specify only that amortization should be based on the criterion of "useful economic life." In practice, companies adopt a variety of amortization periods to suit their circumstances.

Where an arbitrary period is stated, it is not necessarily the period used in practice. In Japan, the majority of companies immediately write off goodwill on consolidation against current earnings, the incentive being that it is deductible for tax purposes. It should be noted, though, that these amounts have tended to be small because of the relatively lower number of mergers taking place, compared to the United States and the United Kingdom, and the potential for more nonconsolidated subsidiaries in accordance with the existing regulations. In the United States, it seems that a 5- to 10-year amortization period is common, though most large companies have used up to 40 years, especially those making significant acquisitions. In this context, it is interesting to note a number of MNEs based, for example, in France, Germany, Italy, Sweden, and Switzerland adopting a 40-year amortization period consistent with practice in the United States. Electrolux in Sweden, for example, adopted a 40-year period for its American acquisitions, apparently contrary to Swedish law and professional standards, on the grounds that this was in accordance with international practice. However, this was before a new Swedish

Exhibit 7.3 Accounting for Purchased Goodwill

	Asset with Amortization	Immediate Write-off against Reserves
Australia	Yes—maximum period 20 years	No
Brazil	Yes	No
Canada	Yes—maximum period 40 years	No
France	Yes	No
Germany	Yes	Yes
Greece	Yes	Yes
Hong Kong	Yes	Yes
India	Yes—maximum period normally 5 years	No
Italy	Yes	Yes
Japan	Yes—maximum period 20 years	No
Kenya	Yes	Yes
Philippines	Yes—maximum period 40 years	No
South Africa	Yes	Yes
Spain	Yes	No
Sweden	Yes—maximum period 20 years	No
Switzerland	Yes	Yes
Thailand	Yes	Yes
United Kingdom	Yes—subject to impairment tests	No
United States	No—subject to impairment tests	No
European Union	Yes	Yes
IASC	Yes—maximum period normally 20 years	No

accounting standard was issued that imposed a 20-year maximum period of amortization and prohibited the immediate write-off method.

In Australia, Canada, France, Japan, the Philippines, Spain, Sweden, and the United States, for example, the method of immediate write-off against equity is *not* permitted. On the other hand, the majority European practice, along with many other economies, including Brazil, Hong Kong, Kenya, Malaysia, Nigeria, South Africa, and Thailand, tends to be more flexible. Prior to the European Union's Seventh Directive on consolidated accounts it was common practice in France and Germany for goodwill, arising from consolidation, to be capitalized as an asset without amortization in the balance sheet. With the implementation of the EU Seventh Directive, this practice has been eliminated. Companies now have a choice between the systematic amortization of goodwill against earnings over a period not exceeding the useful economic life of the asset or its immediate write-off against equity.

In the United Kingdom, prior to 1998, the immediate write-off method became the preferred method in practice, mainly because of its favorable effect on reported future earnings. Not only was no amortization of goodwill charged, but the flexible U.K. approach permitted provisions for reorganization costs and anticipated future losses to be offset against the value of net assets acquired, thus enhancing the amount of goodwill to be written off with a further beneficial effect on future earnings. However, these provisions, other adjustments to fair values, and changes in accounting policy must now be disclosed and any provisions relating to the organization must be treated as part of the postacquisition results of the business combination. The majority of large companies in Germany and the Netherlands followed the U.K. trend toward using the immediate write-off method. On the other hand, the U.K. approach was criticized by U.S. companies on the grounds that U.K. companies had a competitive advantage in making takeover bids internationally because they escaped the burden of goodwill amortization against future earnings hitherto required in the United States. In this regard, the differences between U.K. and U.S. rules were highlighted by Blue Arrow (U.K.) (now Manpower-U.S.) in reporting earnings for 1989 of £65 million under U.K. rules but losses of £686 million under U.S. rules, the main reason being that any goodwill amortization or write-downs in the United States had to be charged against earnings. U.S. concern over this issue has been mitigated recently, however, by the decision to allow goodwill amortization charges to be tax deductible in certain circumstances. Most recently (2001) the FASB has required that amortization of goodwill be dependent on annual impairment tests; that is, if the value of goodwill is less than that capitalized, there would be a charge against income equivalent to the impairment amount concerned.

The problem in the United Kingdom was that with the dramatic growth in merger activity the amounts written off against equity became so large that many companies became concerned about the effect on the perceived strength of the balance sheet and the degree of gearing of leverage. For example, Saatchi and Saatchi, with negative shareholders' equity, and Hanson, with a negative profit and loss account reserve, both reinstated purchased goodwill in pro forma accounts for the purposes of calculating borrowing limits. This problem would also seem to have motivated some companies, especially in the services sector where the treatment of goodwill has had the most impact, to review their policy toward intangibles and, for example, to treat brands, together with trademarks, patents, licenses, copyrights, publishing rights, and so on, as assets for balance sheet purposes.

In the United Kingdom, the Accounting Standards Board (ASB) has now imposed more restrictive requirements on companies, whereby the amortization method is the only method permitted for the treatment of goodwill. This includes a presumed maximum period of amortization of 20 years, except in special circumstances where purchased goodwill has an indeterminate life believed to be greater than 20 years. In such cases, it can be accounted for as an asset subject to an annual review of its value and assessment of any impairment losses to be charged against income.

International Accounting Standards

The International Accounting Standards Committee (IASC) in its revisions of IAS 22 (1993 and 1998), concerning "business combinations," has dealt with the goodwill issue by eliminating the immediate write-off method and adopting the asset-with-amortization method. The standard now requires systematic amortization (usually on a straight-line basis) over a period not exceeding 20 years, unless a longer period can be justified. The IASC also required that where goodwill is amortized over a period exceeding 20 years, then at the end of each financial year the recoverable amount of goodwill should be estimated and any impairment recognized as a charge against income.

Conclusions

Accounting for goodwill continues to be a major issue of growing significance and controversy, with a variety of treatments in many countries. While capitalization without amortization is a minority practice, many countries adopt a flexible approach and permit either capitalization with systematic amortization or immediate write-off against equity. In practice, many larger MNEs treat goodwill as an asset subject to systematic amortization. However, only in a small number of countries is a maximum period of amortization specified, the norm being to require amortization over the useful economic life of the asset.

Applying the criterion of "separability," goodwill would not seem to qualify as an asset in the conventional accounting context given that goodwill is the difference between the value of a business taken as a whole and the sum of its individual assets and liabilities. The problem is that goodwill cannot be unbundled from the business and disposed of as a separate asset. On the other hand, the measurement of purchased goodwill can be carried out with a reasonable degree of certainty, which seems to meet the "reliability" criterion, although this becomes more difficult when deciding on an appropriate period of amortization. Further, because goodwill is a cost incurred with the expectation of future economic benefits, it does appear to meet the "relevance" criterion for asset recognition. Clearly, there is no easy solution to the debate given the persuasive arguments supporting each of the methods proposed.

At the same time, proposals involving the arbitrary treatment of goodwill do not appear desirable in that there could be negative and unforeseen economic consequences relating to stock market reaction, managerial motivation, takeover activity, and financing policy. Given the controversy involved, we suggest that at the present time a flexible approach to goodwill appears to be preferable, permitting either immediate write-off against equity or capitalization as an asset, with or without amortization, depending on the nature of the goodwill concerned. However, such flexibility should be subject to full disclosure of the method used; the reasons for using it; and the assumptions, calculations, and amounts involved to the extent that the data will permit the application of alternative methods. This approach is consistent with the view that from a securities market perspective it is disclosure of the relevant information not its treatment that really matters.

Further, given the growing significance of goodwill, corporations should be permitted to incorporate goodwill as an asset in the balance sheet *without* amortization where this can be justified—but subject to annual review on a systematic basis and, when necessary, appropriate write-down. In other words, a more valuation-oriented approach to the balance sheet could be encouraged. This approach is also consistent with the view that goodwill amortization should not be charged against earnings because the cost of maintaining goodwill is already being accounted for. In any event, financial analysts will eliminate goodwill amortization in making their own valuations of a business. Further, if the value of goodwill is maintained and its life is sufficiently long, it is questionable whether there should be any necessity to amortize it in accordance with the regulations. Clearly, where write-downs or amortization are necessary, such amounts should be identified separately and their details reported.

We also suggest that information disclosures relevant to goodwill and its maintenance, both internally generated and purchased, should be made, within competitive limits. Included here could be information about brands, advertising, market share, innovation, human resources including management, and so on. Consideration could also be given to the presentation of goodwill adjustments, irrespective of method, in a separate statement of total gains and losses incorporating other equity adjustments such as asset revaluations, foreign currency translation adjustments, and so on.

BRANDS, TRADEMARKS, PATENTS, AND RELATED INTANGIBLES

The pursuit of "globalization" by many MNEs has become associated with the acquisition of famous brand names, as well as trademarks, patents, licenses, franchises, publishing titles, and so on, as a means of rapidly obtaining market share, especially in the service industries. The purchase price of acquired brands is commonly included in the payment of goodwill. Thus, the accounting treatment of brands and related intangibles is closely associated with issues arising in the context of goodwill.

The identification of brand accounting as an issue has arisen from the practice in some countries, notably Australia, France, and the United Kingdom, of putting a separate valuation on acquired brands and including them as assets in the balance sheet. While this is controversial enough, there have also been instances of homegrown as well as acquired brands being capitalized. In some cases, entity as well as product brand names have also been capitalized.

It has been argued that a major reason for capitalizing brands is the result of the controversy over goodwill and, in particular, the practice of immediate write-off, which has the consequence of depleting shareholders' funds. Incorporating brand valuations in balance sheets would restore equity and enhance borrowing capacity. In so doing, it could also, in the U.K. context, facilitate takeovers without consultation with shareholders as required by the London Stock Exchange rules for major transactions as such transactions are defined in terms of size relative to corporate assets. Another reason for capitalizing brands is that some corporations perceived themselves to have been undervalued by the stock market, and thus vulnerable to takeover, because they did not explicitly recognize the value of their brands. This view was highlighted by the Nestlé (Switzerland) takeover of Rowntree (United Kingdom), where it was claimed that the hostile bid succeeded because of the stock market's lack of appreciation of brand values.

Choice of Accounting Methods

In practice, a wide variety of approaches to accounting for brands and related intangibles is evident, with companies in some countries able to capitalize brands as assets, with or without amortization.

Asset without Amortization   Proponents of this method argue that acquired brands, and similar intangibles, should be capitalized on the grounds that future economic benefits are expected for which valuable consideration has been given. Further, the value of brands does not decline because it is being continuously maintained through advertising expenditure, sales promotion, and so on. Thus, there is no need to amortize brands against earnings. Brands are considered to be identifiable intangible assets, which can be valued albeit with some judgment involved. It is recognized, however,that there may be instances where either amortization is appropriate or revaluations are necessary with consequent write-downs. The principle of capitalizing brands can also be extended to homegrown brands on the grounds of consistency, comprehensiveness, and comparability.

Opponents argue, however, that while brands are valuable assets, it is impossible to assess the expected future economic benefits with a reasonable degree of certainty. Furthermore, it is very difficult to identify and assess the value of a brand as a separate asset. Although a brand may have legally separable property rights attached, such as trademarks, patents, and designs, they are not themselves the entire brand but only a part of it. There is also a variety of alternative valuation methods that can be used, including historical cost, market valuation, current cost, the allocation of the purchased cost of goodwill, discounted cash flow, and the use of earnings multiples, all of which involve varying degrees of subjective judgment.

Asset with Systematic Amortization   Proponents of this method argue that while acquired brands may be viewed as assets embodying future economic benefits, they are a cost incurred that will be used up in generating future earnings. Such costs should be systematically amortized against earnings consistent with the accrual accounting concept.

On the other hand, opponents argue that if the value of brands is being continually maintained by advertising expenditure and other means, then amortization is inappropriate unless there is evidence to the contrary. If amortization *is* appropriate, then it should be over the useful economic life of the asset, not an arbitrary period.

Immediate Write-Off   The immediate write-off approach is supported by the argument that brands and related intangibles are not assets for balance sheet purposes because they are not separable from other associated assets, both tangible and human, nor independently realizable. Further, it is not possible to assess the future economic benefits of brands with a reasonable degree of certainty. It is argued, therefore, that "prudence" should govern the "recognition" decision. Accordingly, the cost of brands should be written off immediately against equity or earnings consistent with the treatment of goodwill. This treatment would also enhance comparability between firms.

Opponents of this method, however, argue that brands are indeed assets and should be recognized as such with or without amortization. It is argued that a valuation approach is desirable because it is more relevant to users in providing information about the substance of the business.

Although many countries recognize the cost of acquired trademarks, patents, and similar intangibles as assets, the issue of accounting for "brands" is relatively new and controversial. The controversy has arisen from the recent practice of some large companies, especially in Australia, France, and the United

Kingdom of identifying brands as intangible assets. In Australia, it has been accepted practice for some time now to value licenses, copyrights, and publishing rights, with a similar practice now being followed more recently in the United Kingdom.

While most companies have valued only acquired brands, usually on the basis of allocating an appropriate proportion of the cost of goodwill, there have been companies that have valued both homegrown and acquired brands. The valuation approach used here was apparently based on a "current cost" approach and permitted by U.K. company law under the alternative valuation rules introduced following the EU Fourth Directive (1978). Curiously, these rules do not permit a market valuation to be used. Where current cost is the valuation basis, then annual revaluations are necessary. The capitalization of homegrown brands and other intangibles except goodwill is also permitted. This is now common practice among those companies valuing brands. While a valuation approach seems more relevant, one problem is that the companies concerned have provided very little information about the valuation process involved. This makes the valuations difficult to interpret, with the resulting uncertainty likely to undermine confidence from a securities market perspective.

Although accounting for brands does not yet appear to have become a major issue elsewhere, the treatment internationally of intangibles such as trademarks, patents, licenses, and so on, tends to be flexible. In continental Europe, for example, the normal practice is for such items to be recognized as assets and then systematically amortized over their useful economic lives. On the other hand, many companies write off intangibles immediately against equity. In the European Union, the Fourth Directive states that intangible assets, including internally developed assets, may be recognized in the balance sheet. Under the directive, trademarks, patents, licenses, and similar rights are specifically permitted to be included. But, if so, they must be systematically amortized over their useful economic lives or written down to reflect any reductions in value. In some countries, (e.g., France), capitalization without amortization is acceptable if there is no limit to the useful life of the asset concerned. Under the alternative valuation rules of the Fourth Directive (Article 33), it appears that a current cost valuation of intangible assets is permitted as an alternative to historical cost.

In Canada and the United States, identifiable intangible assets such as trademarks, patents, licenses, copyrights, and so on, are recognized as assets and treated similarly to goodwill. Internally developed intangibles, on the other hand, must be written off immediately against earnings.

International Accounting Standards

In 1998, the ISSC issued IAS 38 "Intangible Assets" which superseded IAS 4 and IAS 9 on "Depreciation" and "Research and Development Costs," respectively. Intangible assets such as brands, trademarks, patents, and so on are permitted to be recognized only if it is probable that the future economic benefits that are attributable to the asset will flow to the enterprise and that the cost of the asset can be measured reliably. In this regard, internally generated brands, mastheads, publishing titles, customer lists, and similar items should *not* be recognized as assets (para. 51).

For those assets that are recognized, systematic amortization is required over their useful lives subject to the rebuttable proposition that this will not exceed 20 years. The amortization period should be reviewed at the end of each financial year and any impairment losses to the recoverable amount of the assets recognized as a charge against income.

Conclusions

Accounting for brands, trademarks, patents, and similar intangible assets is currently a highly controversial issue. These assets are treated in a variety of ways in many countries. Problems associated with the treatment of these kinds of intangibles would seem to be closely linked to the goodwill issue. The capitalization of brand names has become an issue, particularly in countries where there is a more flexible approach to accounting practice in general and the treatment of goodwill has impacted seriously on either earnings or equity. So far as the accounting treatment of brands is concerned, the majority practice is to capitalize them as assets without amortization, including in some cases homegrown brands, but subject to revaluation on a periodic basis as appropriate. Trademarks, patents, and similar intangibles tend to be treated as assets subject to systematic amortization but are retained permanently as assets subject to revaluation where they are viewed as having an unlimited life. A minority of companies adopt the method of immediate write-off against equity.

Applying the criterion of "separability," brand names, especially those purchased, may well qualify as assets. Much will depend on the circumstances of each case to determine whether or not brands can be identified separately for valuation purposes. As regards the "reliability" of measurement, there are many problems involved in making an assessment in that the value of goodwill usually includes the value of brands. While there is an expectation of future economic benefits, there are a number of alternative approaches to the valuation of brands that can be considered acceptable at the present time. Thus, there is considerable debate as to whether brands can be measured with a reasonable degree of certianty. Again, the problem of striking an appropriate balance between "relevance" and "reliability" needs to be resolved.

We suggest that brands, trademarks, patents, and related intangibles, including those developed internally, should be permitted to be capitalized as assets where they can be identified separately. Such valuations would be subject to annual review and, where necessary, appropriate write-down. In some cases, it may be appropriate for brands to be systematically amortized over their useful economic lives. The significance of brands and similar intangibles is such that a valuation-oriented approach could be encouraged, at least in terms of providing supplementary information. Given the variety of valuation methods available (e.g., economic value, net realizable value or market value, and current cost), comprehensive information should be given about the method used, the basis of revaluation, if any, and the basis for the amortization period adopted where applicable. In the case of brands not identified, for balance sheet purposes, additional information could be disclosed, within competitive limits, including market share, advertising support, and so on.

RESEARCH AND DEVELOPMENT

Technological change, and in particular change in information technology, has been a dramatic feature of recent decades and MNEs have played a major role in new developments. The significance of R&D expenditures in the overall business context has increased.

R & D expenditures include direct and indirect costs related to the creation and development of new processes, techniques, applications, and products. It has been suggested that three categories of expenditure can be identified.

1. Pure research, which is directed primarily toward the advancement of knowledge in general and not toward any specific practical aim or application.

2. Applied research, which is directed primarily toward exploiting the knowledge obtained in pure research and to applying it in an area of business interest.

3. Development, which is work directed toward the introduction or improvement of specific products or processes.

A variety of expenditures can be classified under the heading of R&D expenditures, including expenditures on tangible fixed assets, which could be subject to the usual requirements relating to such assets, personnel costs, materials and services, software costs, relevant overhead costs, and the amortization of patients and licenses.

Market research and advertising expenditure may also be considered similar to R&D expenditure and treated accordingly.

A variety of approaches to accounting for, R&D is evident around the world (see Exhibit 7.4). It is clear, however, that there is a tendency to adopt a relatively prudent approach to asset recognition and the assessment of expected future economic benefits. While the immediate write-off method is widely accepted, there are varying degrees of acceptance of the alternative method of capitalizing and amortizing R&D expenditures.

The most prudent approach is found in countries such as Germany and the United States, where all costs are required to be written off against earnings immediately, unless, of course, tangible assets with alternative uses are involved—such assets being amortized against earnings in the usual way. In the United States, there is also an exception permitted in the case of computer software development costs subject to specified criteria concerning recognition. In many other countries, including Canada, India, Malaysia, the Philippines, South Africa, and the United Kingdom, all research costs must be written off immediately, but development costs may be capitalized in certain specified circumstances and amortized to match the future revenues generated by the asset. The usual specified circumstances include the need to have a clearly identifiable project and related expenditures as well as the satisfaction of criteria concerning the technical feasibility and commercial and financial viability of the project. All the technical, commercial, and financial issues would need to be assessed with a reasonable degree of certainty for the development expenditure to be carried as an asset. Such expenditure is also permitted to be carried forward where a company has been contracted to carry out work for which it is to be reimbursed. In practice, only a minority of large MNEs capitalize

Exhibit 7.4 Comparative National Practices of Accounting for Research and Development

Country or Area	Asset with Amortization	Maximum Amortization Period	Immediate Write-off Against Earnings
Australia	Yes	No specified	Yes
Brazil	Yes	Not specified	Yes
Canada	Development costs only[a]	Not specified	Yes
France	Yes	Not specified	Yes
Germany	No	Not applicable	Yes
Greece	Yes	5 years	Yes
Hong Kong	Yes	Not specified	Yes
India	Development costs only[a]	Not specified	Yes
Indonesia	Yes	Not specified	Yes
Italy	Yes	5 years	Yes
Japan	Yes	5 years	Yes
Kenya	Yes	Not specified	Yes
Malaysia	Development costs only[a]	Not specified	Yes
Netherlands	Yes[b]	Not specified	Yes
Philippines	Development costs only[a]	Not specified	Yes
South Africa	Development costs only[a]	Not specified	Yes
Spain	Yes	Not specified	Yes
Sweden	Yes	5 years	Yes
Switzerland	Yes	Not specified	Yes
Thailand	Yes	Not specified	Yes
United Kingdom	Development costs only[a]	Not specified	Yes
United States	No[c]	Not specified	Yes
European Union	Yes	5 years	Yes
IASC	Development costs only[a]	Not specified	Yes[d]

[a] Permitted in specified circumstances in the case of development costs only.
[b] A reserve must be established if R&D costs are capitalized.
[c] Exceptions permitted in specified circumstances in the case of computer software development costs.
[d] Unless development costs satisfy asset recognition criteria, in which case they must be capitalized.

development costs. This is probably not surprising in view of the difficult judgments involved, which can lead to problems if circumstances change.

A small number of countries, including Greece, Italy, Japan, and Sweden, permit the capitalization of R&D expenditure, but they require such amounts to be amortized within a maximum period of five years. In the Netherlands, it is necessary to establish a reserve to match the R&D amounts capitalized. It is pertinent to note here that the EU Fourth Directive on company accounts indicates a maximum amortization period of five years, which does not seem to have been observed, at least in terms of national regulation, in most of the member countries. In contrast, in many economies such as Australia, Brazil, Hong Kong, India, Indonesia, Kenya,

Spain, Switzerland, and Thailand, there would seem to be a flexible approach to the treatment of R&D expenditure in that there is often a lack of regulation on the issue, and various methods are practiced.

International Accounting Standards

International Accounting Standard 38 (issued in 1998) deals with "Intangible Assets" including research and development and requires the immediate write-off against earnings of research expenditures. In the case of development costs, these should be similarly expensed unless the development project satisfies specified criteria, including the technical feasibility of the product, the separable identification of the costs involved, the existence of a future market or internal usefulness if it is to be used by the enterprise itself, the existence of adequate resources to develop the product and the expectation that the costs can be recovered from future revenues from the project. If *all* these criteria are met, the development costs must be recognized as an asset and amortized on a systematic basis over their useful economic life with a rebuttable presumption that this will not exceed 20 years. The same requirements regarding the review of amortization periods and the recognition of impairment losses applies as in the case of all other intangibles.

Conclusions

Accounting for R&D expenditures has become an issue of increasing importance given the rate of technological change and the significance of such expenditures for many companies. A variety of treatments are used in many countries. While the immediate write-off method is widely accepted, there are varying degrees of recognition across countries of the alternative method of capitalizing R&D expenditures subject to systematic amortization. In this context, a significant number of countries permit capitalization with amortization, but only in the case of development costs and where the technical feasibility and commercial and financial viability of the development project can be assessed with a reasonable degree of certainty. In only a small number of countries is a maximum period of amortization specified. In practice, however, only a minority of companies capitalize development costs.

Applying the criterion of separability, R&D expenditure does not appear to qualify as an asset except in cases where development projects are sufficiently advanced to produce assets such as brands, trademarks, patents, or other assets that can be identified separately from their associated tangible assets and the business as a whole. In such cases, the "relevance" criterion is satisfied. Furthermore, at the development stage of a project it may be possible, irrespective of separability, to assess the future economic benefits of the costs incurred with a reasonable degree of certainty, thus meeting the "reliability" criterion.

We suggest that R&D expenditures should be capitalized but only to the extent of development costs. Capitalization should be subject to evidence concerning a project's technical feasibility and commercial and financial viability. In such cases, systematic amortization would be required over the useful economic life of the project together with annual reviews and periodic revaluation according to the circumstances of the company concerned. In addition, full disclosure should be made of the reasons for the capitalization and the assumptions, calculations, and amounts involved. Additional information about the nature of the projects involved also seems desirable, within competitive limits.

SUMMARY

1. Consolidation is the accepted means of accounting for MNE groups and business combinations. The method of full consolidation involves the aggregation, on a line-by-line basis, of information about the assets, liabilities, revenues, and expenses of the MNE's many individual legal entities into income, financial position, and funds or cash flow statements relating to the MNE as a single economic entity.

2. The methods of proportional and equity consolidation may also be used as an alternative to full consolidation, depending on the involvement of the MNE in the investee corporation.

3. While efforts are being made to develop international accounting and disclosure harmonization relating to consolidated financial statements, there is a variety of regulations and practices at national level.

4. Major problem areas include accounting for mergers and acquisitions, criteria for the consolidation of subsidiaries, fair value adjustments, accounting for goodwill, funds or cash flow statements, accounting for associated companies and joint venture accounting.

5. A major area of controversy at the international level has been the treatment of goodwill and related intangibles.

6. While funds statements are increasingly being provided by MNEs, a recent trend is to either emphasize cash flows or to replace funds statements with a cash flow statement.

7. Joint venture accounting has become a major issue with the growth of strategic alliances and joint ventures by MNEs, including those with governments and corporations in Russia, Eastern Europe, and China. Accounting for the venturer's interest is a controversial issue but usually takes the form of a choice between proportionate consolidation or the equity method, including supplementary disclosures about joint venture interests.

8. Accounting for intangible assets is an issue of major international significance in the twenty-first century. The continuing wave of international mergers, the pursuit of globalization, the dramatic expansion in services, and the revolution in information technology have all contributed to the realization that there are fundamental problems in this area that need to be addressed.

9. Much controversy has surrounded the challenge to traditional accounting concepts and practices, which are currently based on the treatment of physical tangible assets.

10. There is no doubt that theory and practice concerning the treatment of intangible assets is in a state of flux, with a variety of practices evident worldwide. Harmonization efforts are also at an early stage. No easy solutions are available, nor is there any clear consensus on the issues involved.

11. If company accounts are to reflect the needs of the new millennium, it can be argued that a major change in thinking is required whereby the nature and

importance of intangible assets are given much more weight in the theory and practice of accounting and information disclosure.

12.   A more valuation-oriented approach, at least in terms of supplementary information, seems desirable. The balance of argument is thus tipped more in favor of "relevance" in contrast to "prudence" and "reliability." A more positive attitude to intangibles would result in the recognition of goodwill, brands, and, in certain cases, R&D as assets in the balance sheet, subject to annual review, and write-down or amortization as appropriate, subject to a careful assessment of the current commercial realities.

13.   The competitive pressures of securities markets internationally suggest the need for companies to be much more open in terms of information disclosure about intangible assets and to place more emphasis on effective communications with the investment community.

Discussion Questions

1.   Compare and contrast the different forms of presentation of consolidated financial statements internationally, making reference to the use of full, proportional, and equity methods of consolidation.

2.   Outline the arguments for and against the use of purchase accounting versus pooling-of-interests accounting for business combinations.

3.   Why has accounting for goodwill become such a significant problem internationally?

4.   While the trend among MNEs around the world is to prepare consolidated financial statements, it has been suggested by experts that such statements may hide more than they reveal. Do you agree?

5.   Discuss the relevance of funds and cash flow statements, making reference to recent developments in regulation and practice internationally.

6.   How important an issue is joint venture accounting? Why is it so difficult to agree on a harmonized approach to this issue?

7.   Why is it so difficult to resolve the debate over the appropriate accounting treatment of goodwill?

8.   What kinds of MNEs are concerned about the valuation of intangible assets? Should a more flexible approach to this issue be adopted by regulators?

9.   To what extent are issues concerning intangible assets important in developing countries?

Case: *Multigroup (Switzerland)*

Multigroup, a pharmaceuticals MNE based in Switzerland, decided to prepare consolidated financial statements for the first time. As there were no Swiss legal requirements regarding consolidation, Multigroup had to decide what accounting principles to use for its subsidiaries, joint ventures, and associates around the world. Multigroup's subsidiaries, all majority owned, were located in the United States, the United Kingdom, France, and Germany. A 50 percent-owned joint venture was located in the Netherlands. There were also interests in Associated Corporations at 30, 35, and 40 percent in the United States, the Netherlands, and Japan, respectively. In addition, there had been the recent acquisition of Bizcorp in the United States for a cash consideration of 750 million Swiss francs. The book value of the net assets of Bizcorp at the date of acquisition were 600 million Swiss francs, but at fair value they were valued at 670 million Swiss francs.

Questions

1. Discuss the possible alternative accounting treatments of Multigroup's subsidiaries, making special reference to U.S., U.K. and IASC GAAPs. What is your recommended treatment?
2. Discuss the possible alternative accounting treatments of Multigroup's joint venture in the Netherlands. What is your recommended treatment?
3. Discuss the possible alternative accounting treatment for Multigroup's associated corporations. What is your recommended treatment?
4. Discuss the possible alternative treatments of goodwill in the case of the recent Bizcorp acquisition, making special reference to U.S. and U.K. GAAPs. What is your recommended treatment?
5. Discuss the likely effects on Multigroup's financial statements of the decisions made concerning the treatment of subsidiaries, the joint venture, the associated corporations, and the recent acquisition. How do you think the securities markets would react to the disclosure of consolidated information?

Case: *Bonanza* (United States)

Bonanza Group acquired the Bargain Company at the beginning of 2001 for a purchase price of $300 million. The book value of the net assets was stated at $200 million, but at "fair value" this was restated at $220 million. Bonanza's policy is to depreciate assets subject to revaluation on a straight-line basis over a 10-year period. Bonanza Group's earnings before charging for any goodwill amortization or additional depreciation were $50 million. Bonanza's management was wondering whether a change of headquarters might be a good idea from a reported earnings perspective and decided to consider the position in Japan Sweden, Switzerland, and the Netherlands compared to the United States.

Questions

1. Prepare a comparative schedule showing the net earnings after any goodwill or depreciation adjustments in accordance with generally accepted accounting principles in each of the following countries:
    a. United States (assume goodwill non-amortization)
    b. Japan (assume goodwill amortization over 5 years)
    c. Sweden (assume goodwill amortization over 20 years)
    d. Switzerland (assume goodwill amortization over 8 years)
    e. Netherlands (assume immediate write-off of goodwill against reserves)
2. Compare and contrast your findings across the five countries and discuss the significance of the results from the perspective of both Bonanza's management and international financial analysts.

Case: SmithKline Beecham (United Kingdom)

In 1989, SmithKline of the United States and Beecham of the United Kingdom agreed to a merger, which was accounted for on a merger accounting (or pooling-of-interests) basis as permitted under U.K. GAAP. However, under U.S. GAAP, the purchase accounting method, requiring the recognition of goodwill, would have to be used. The effect of this difference in practice was revealed as SmithKline Beecham was required to file a reconciliation to U.S. GAAP under Form 20F required by the SEC as it was listed in the United States. This information was also disclosed for the benefit of U.S. investors in the 1989 annual report (see Exhibit 7.5).

Exhibit 7.5. SmithKline Beecham Plc: Additional Information for U.S. Investors

The group prepares its consolidated accounts in accordance with generally accepted accounting principles ("GAAP") in the U.K.

U.K. GAAP differs in certain respects from those applicable in the U.S. The effect of such differences of a material nature is set out below. There is a fundamental difference between U.K. and U.S. GAAP in the accounting for the merger. Under U.K. GAAP, the combination has been accounted for using merger accounting principles, whereas under U.S. GAAP the transaction would have been accounted for using the purchase accounting method. For the purposes of this reconciliation to U.S. GAAP, it has been assumed that SmithKline is the acquiree.

	Year Ended 31 December	
	1989 (£m)	1988 (£m)
Income Statement Data		
Net income after extraordinary items per U.K. GAAP	130	367
U.S. GAAP adjustments (net of taxation):		
Elimination of SmithKline results prior to merger	(144)	(62)
Merger transaction and SmithKline restructuring costs	281	—
Goodwill—Beecham	(26)	(36)
Deferred taxation:		
due to timing differences	(3)	(6)
due to ACT	(27)	(5)
Other, net	6	(1)
Purchase accounting:		
Amortization of intangible assets	(60)	—
Amortization of goodwill	(28)	—
Depreciation and other	(42)	—
Net income per U.S. GAAP	87	257
Represented by:		
Income before nonrecurring charges and taxes on income	349	412
Nonrecurring charges	(115)	—
Taxes on income	(162)	(181)

(continues)

Exhibit 7.5.   (*Continued*)

	Year Ended 31 December	
	1989 (£m)	1988 (£m)
Income from continuing operations	72	231
Income from discontinued operations (net of taxes)	15	26
Net income per U.S. GAAP	87	257
Per-Share Data		
Average number of A and B ordinary shares in issue	951.5m	665.2m
Per ordinary share per U.S. GAAP		
Income from continuing operations	7.5p	34.7p
Net income	9.1p	38.6p
Per Equity Unit per U.S. GAAP		
Income from continuing operations	37.5p	173.5p
Net income	45.5p	193.0p
Balance Sheet Data		
Shareholders' equity per U.K. GAAP	(297)	1,360
U.S. GAAP adjustments:		
Elimination of SmithKline equity prior to merger	—	(98)
Goodwill—Beecham	461	441
Capitalization of interest	37	7
Dividends	50	74
Deferred taxation:		
due to timing differences	(66)	(61)
due to ACT	5	32
Revaluation reserve	(156)	(108)
Other, net	(12)	—
Purchase accounting:		
Property, plant and equipment	69	—
Intangible assets	754	—
Goodwill	2,665	—
Other, net	35	—
Shareholders' equity per U.S. GAAP	3,545	1,647

Source: Extract from SmithKline Beecham annual report, 1989.

    a.   *Goodwill:* Under U.K. GAAP, goodwill may be amortised over its useful life through the profit and loss account or eliminated directly against reserves. Under U.S. GAAP goodwill is capitalised and amortised by charges against income over the

Exhibit 7.5. (*Continued*)

period that, it is estimated, is to be benefited. Goodwill eliminated directly against reserves in the U.K. accounts has been reinstated and amortised over a 40-year period, which is the estimated useful life for the purpose of U.S. GAAP.

b. *Capitalization of interest:* Under U.K. GAAP, the capitalization of interest is not required, and the group does not capitalise interest in its financial statements. U.S. GAAP requires interest incurred as part of the cost of acquiring fixed assets to be capitalised and amortised over the life of the asset.

c. *Deferred tax:* Under U.K. GAAP, provision is made for deferred tax under the liability method where it is probable that a tax liability will become payable or a tax asset will crystallize within the foreseeable future. In the U.S., Accounting Principles Board Opinion No. 11 requires deferred tax to be provided in full under the deferral basis.

Under U.K. GAAP, the group writes off any Advance Corporation Tax ("ACT") which is not considered to be recoverable. However, if deferred taxation is provided, such ACT may be available for offset against the balance on the deferred taxation account. As deferred taxation is provided under U.S. GAAP on all timing differences, the deferred tax account has been reduced by the appropriate amount of ACT.

d. *Extraordinary items:* Under U.K. GAAP, the costs or credits relating to the restructuring of the group, including the disposal of operations, may be classed as extraordinary items. Under U.S. GAAP, such disposals and one-time charges are treated as nonrecurring items, except that in the case of the restructuring charges of SmithKline, these are treated as part of the quantification of the fair value of the separable net assets under the purchase accounting adjustments.

e. *Discontinued operations:* Under U.K. GAAP, income earned from both continuing operations and discontinued operations up to the date of sale is aggregated in the consolidated income statement; material gains and losses arising on the sale of discontinued operations may be shown as extraordinary items. Under U.S. GAAP, gains or losses on the sale of those activities that comply with the U.S. GAAP definition of discontinued operations are not shown as extraordinary items but are shown under the heading "discontinued operations," and income from continuing operations and discontinued operations normally is disclosed separately for each year presented.

f. *Ordinary dividends:* Under U.K. GAAP, dividends are provided for in the fiscal year in which they are declared by the board of directors. Under U.S. GAAP such dividends are not provided for until formally declared by the board of directors.

g. *Property revaluation:* Under U.K. GAAP, properties are carried either at original cost or at subsequent valuation, less related depreciation, calculated at the revalued amount where applicable. Any surplus on the revaluation of a property is taken directly to shareholders' equity. Under U.S. GAAP, revaluations of properties are not permitted.

h. *Purchase accounting adjustments:* Under U.K. GAAP, the combination is being accounted for using merger accounting principles, pursuant to which the assets and liabilities of the group are the sum of the historical net assets of Beecham and SmithKline. Under U.S. GAAP, the combination has been accounted for using the purchase method. For purposes of this reconciliation, SmithKline has been treated as the acquiree. Under the purchase method, the aggregate purchase price is allocated to the assets and liabilities of SmithKline based on their fair values, with the remainder allocated to goodwill. The aggregate purchase price of £3,205 million is based on the trading values of the Equity Units based on the mid-market price shown in the Stock Exchange Daily Official List on July 27, 1989

(continues)

Exhibit 7.5. (*Continued*)

(being the first full day of trading in the Equity Units), less an assumed value for the Preferred Shares (based on the liquidation preference), plus transaction costs. Goodwill arising of £2,693 million is being amortised over 40 years. Allocation of the purchase price is based on independent appraisals and other studies.

i. *Future developments:* SFAS No. 96, *Accounting for Income Taxes,* was issued in December 1987 and subsequently amended in December 1989. The standard, which becomes effective no later than the 1992 fiscal year, requires a change in accounting for income taxes from the deferral method to the liability method, for the purposes of U.S. GAAP.

The group is currently studying this U.S. Accounting Standard to determine the effect it may have on its reconciliation of net income and shareholders' equity between U.K. and U.S. GAAP.

Source: SmithKline Beecham, 1989 Annual Report.

Questions

1. Discuss the impact of purchase accounting versus merger accounting on earnings and equity, with specific reference to the treatment of goodwill.

2. Quantify the net effects of using purchase accounting on SmithKline Beecham's 1989 earnings as per U.K. GAAP.

3. To what extent is the treatment of goodwill responsible for SmithKline Beecham's negative shareholders' equity in 1989 as per U.K. GAAP?

4. Compare and contrast the return on equity for 1988 and 1989 under both U.K. and U.S. GAAP. If Beecham had used the asset with amortization method rather than the immediate write-off method for the treatment of goodwill, what would the return on equity figures be? Comment on your results.

5. Discuss the pros and cons of treating goodwill by using the asset-with-amortization method versus the immediate write-off method.

Selected References

Bailey, D. T., ed. 1988. *Accounting in Socialist Countries.* London: Routledge.

Barwise, P., C. Higson, A. Likierman, and P. Marsh. 1989. *Accounting for Brands.* London: London Business School and the Institute of Chartered Accountants in England and Wales.

Choi, F. D. S. and C. Lee. 1991. "Merger Premia and National Differences in Accounting for Goodwill," *Journal of International Financial Management and Accounting,* 3 (3): 219–40.

Diggle, G. and C. W. Nobes. 1994. "European Rule Making in Accounting: The Seventh Directive as a Case Study," *Accounting and Business Research* (Autumn). 24(96): 319–33.

Egginton, Don A. "Towards Some Principles for Intangible Asset Accounting," *Accounting and Business Research* (Summer 1990).

European Community. 1983. *Seventh Council Directive on Consolidated Accounts.* Brussels: EC.

Gray, S. J. 1988. "Acquisition and Merger Accounting: A United Approach," *Accountant's Magazine* (July).

Geringer, J. N. and L. Hebert. 1989. "Control and Performance of International Joint Ventures," *Journal of International Business Studies* (Summer).

Gray, S. J. 1989. "Accounting for Brands: A Mission Impossible?" *Investment Analyst.* (April).

Gray, S. J., A. G. Coenenberg, and P. D. Gordon, eds. 1993. *International Group Accounting: Issues in European Harmonization.* London: Routledge.

International Accounting Standards Committee. 1989. *Framework for the Preparation and Presentation of Financial Statements.* London: IASC.

International Accounting Standards Committee. 1992. IAS 7, *Cash Flow Statements.* London: IASC, revised 1989.

International Accounting Standards Committee. 1994. IAS 27, *Consolidated Financial Statements and Accounting for Investments in Subsidiaries.* London: IASC, reformatted.

International Accounting Standards Committee. IAS 28, *Accounting for Investments in Associates.* London: IASC, revised 1998.

International Accounting Standards Committee. 1998. IAS 22, *Business Combinations.* London: IASC, revised.

International Accounting Standards Committee. 1998. IAS 31, *Financial Reporting of Interests in Joint Ventures.* London: IASC, revised.

International Accounting Standards Committee. 1998. IAS 38, *Intangible Assets.*

Needles, Belverd E. Jr., *Financial Accounting*, 8th ed. (Boston: Houghton Mifflin, 2000).

Nobes, C. W. and J. E. Norton. 1996. "International Variations in the Accounting and Tax Treatments of Goodwill, and the Implications for Research," *Journal of International Accounting, Auditing and Taxation,* 5 (2).

Taylor, P. A. 1987. *Consolidated Financial Statements.* New York: Harper & Row.

U.S. Financial Accounting Standards Board. 1987. "Statement of Financial Accounting Standards No. 94." *Consolidation of All Majority-Owned Subsidiaries.* Stamford, CT: FASB.

U.S. Financial Accounting Standards Board. 1987. "Statement of Financial Accounting Standards No. 95," *Statement of Cash Flows.* Stamford, CT: IASC.

United Nations. 1988. *Conclusions on Accounting and Reporting by Transnational Corporations.* New York: UN, revised 1994.

U.K. Accounting Standards Board. 1991. FRS 1, *Cash Flow Statements.* London: ASB (September).

U.K. Accounting Standards Board. 1994. FRS 6, *Acquisitions and Mergers.* London: Accounting Standards Board (September).

CHAPTER EIGHT

INTERNATIONAL SEGMENT REPORTING

Chapter Objectives

- Identify the major uses and users of segment information
- Discuss the major benefits of segment disclosure from the perspective of predictive ability tests and stock market studies
- Highlight the costs of segment disclosures from the standpoint of preparation and disclosure of information to competitors
- Review the segment reporting requirements of the International Accounting Standards Committee (IASC)
- Compare the different regulations for segment disclosures around the world, especially in the United States and the United Kingdom.
- Examine the problems of segment reporting in practice and discuss ways to make segment disclosures more useful

In this chapter we discuss issues relating to segment reporting. Segment reporting is the counterpoint to consolidated information in that it involves the disaggregation of the consolidated financial statements.

In recent years there has been a continuing trend toward diversification by MNEs, especially with regard to geographical activity. This has raised questions as to whether consolidated financial statements are adequate where the corporation's operations consist of a number of activities in a variety of locations with different profitability, risk, and growth characteristics. Furthermore, are individual subsidiary financial statements adequate where different types of operations are contained within a single legal entity or where a single business activity is carried out across a number of legal entities?

To the extent that there is a lack of correspondence between the financial statements of the reporting entity and the nature of the corporation's activities, there appears to be a need for disaggregated information in segment reports. Such information would ensure that overall performance, risks, and prospects can be better evaluated by investors, other users, and management and that a more comprehensive accountability can be achieved. Let's consider the users and uses of segment information, the benefits and costs involved, the regulatory environment, and the problems of segment reporting in practice.

USERS AND USES OF SEGMENT INFORMATION

Investors are likely to be interested in the future cash flows they may obtain by investing in a company as well as the risk or uncertainty of those cash flows. They are, therefore, interested in the performance of an MNE as a whole rather than the performance of any specific element of the corporation's activities. However, this does not mean that only consolidated information is valuable to them. Both the size and uncertainty of future cash flows are likely to be affected by many factors, including those related to the industries and countries in which a MNE operates. Different industries and different countries have a variety of profit potentials, degrees and types of risk, and growth opportunities. Different rates of return on investment and different capital needs are also likely to exist throughout the various segments of a business. Because of this diversification of operations, there has been a demand for MNEs to report key items of disaggregated information, especially turnover and profits. Such disaggregated or segment data is typically provided for both geographical areas and lines of business.

Segment information is likely to help investors by allowing them to combine company-specific information with external information, thus allowing a more accurate assessment of both the risk and the potential for future growth. In addition, investors can gain an idea of the success of past operations by comparing them with the performance of similar corporations. However, for most diversified MNEs such external yardsticks are not available. In principle, the provision of disaggregated data may allow investors to compare the success of individual segments with those of other corporations; however, given the very large degree of latitude MNEs have in deciding what constitutes a reportable segment, such an advantage of comparability may be more apparent than real. This is the case especially when comparing profit measures: not only is there discretion in the choice of segments but also in the methods used for common cost allocations and transfer pricing.

Other users often have a direct relationship, not with the MNE as a whole, but with a part of it. Disaggregated data regarding the performance of that segment of the company is then relevant to employees, creditors, and host governments. All these groups are likely to be interested in, not only the MNE as a whole, but also that sector of the company that most affects themselves. They will often require information that is even more disaggregated than that currently provided. For example, employees are likely to want information at the plant level, host governments at the individual country level, and creditors at the level of the individual subsidiary or legal entity. However, segmentally disaggregated information will go some way toward meeting these information needs. This is especially important for those groups such as employees and developing-country host governments that often lack the power to demand specific information relevant to themselves.

But are the benefits of segment reporting likely to exceed the costs? Is regulation of the reporting process necessary? If so, what form should it take? How should segments be identified? What should be the content of segment reports? How should the items disclosed be measured and presented? First, let's consider the arguments for and against segment reporting and the research findings available so far.

THE BENEFITS OF SEGMENT REPORTING

The possible benefits of segment data have been examined using a variety of research techniques. Many of the earliest attempts simply asked users whether they required such information. While this approach might have provided some valuable insights, however, it also suffered from several major problems or limitations. Particularly important are the problems of ignorance and "gaming." If information is not currently provided or is provided by only a few companies, people may inaccurately assess either the value they would derive from such information or the problems and limitations inherent in its use. *Gaming* can occur if the users of financial statements perceive the information contained in them to be costless or a free good; if this is the case, it is in their best interests to overstate the value of any information to persuade companies to provide it. Because of these problems, more direct tests of usefulness are necessary. Such tests are of two types: (1) predictive ability (forecasting) tests and (2) stock market reaction tests (i.e., how the market views the information disclosed).

Predictive ability tests compare the accuracy of forecasts of future sales or earnings based on consolidated data to that of forecasts based on disaggregated data. Because future earnings are one of the main variables investors are interested in, it is assumed that useful information is any information that helps to predict earnings. However, such an approach implicitly assumes that at least some shareholders are not only capable of using but also will use the information provided in this way. Whether or not this is true is unclear, and thus the implications drawn from these indirect tests of usefulness must be considered with some caution. The alternative approach—stock market reaction testing—appears to have somewhat greater validity. The idea is that if information has an effect on the stock market, that information must have been used, and so the usefulness of the data is tested directly. If the information has no effect, it is either irrelevant or has already been obtained from other sources so there is no need for disclosure.

Research studies concerned with the prediction of earnings have all concluded that forecasts are more accurate if they are based on line-of-business (LOB) segmental data rather than consolidated earnings. Studies using U.S. data have also found that forecasts based on segment earnings are more accurate than forecasts based on segmental turnover. However, this finding has not been supported by U.K. data. In addition, there is some evidence that the relative accuracy of segment-based forecasts may depend on the size of the corporation, with such disclosures being more useful for smaller corporations. There have been few prediction studies relating to geographical segment disclosures, but recent research by Roberts (1990), using U.K. data, and Balakrishnan, Harris, and Sen (1990), using U.S. data, found similar results to those involving LOB disclosures (i.e., segment-based forecasts outperformed consolidated-based forecasts).

With respect to stock market studies, there is evidence that disclosure of both LOB and geographical segment data result in a decrease in market assessments of risk of the disclosing corporation (i.e., a decrease in variability of stock [share] prices relative to the overall market). However, some of this evidence is inconclusive, with conflicting studies suggesting that such a relationship does not hold. Accounting-based risk measures formed from both geographical disclosures and LOB asset data appear to be correlated to market risk measures. However, LOB disclosures appear not to have affected the average risk-equalized market returns of the disclosing corporations, although there is some evidence that they have resulted in a decrease in the variability of such returns.

With regard to geographical disclosures, recent research using both U.S. and U.K. data has shown a significant relationship between such disclosures and market risk assessments.

THE COSTS OF SEGMENT REPORTING

Several arguments against segment disclosures have been put forward; some apply to all corporations, others only in certain situations. It has been argued that the cost of compiling, processing, and disseminating such information will exceed the benefits. However, no evidence is available regarding either the costs of disclosure or any precise quantification of the benefits. At any rate, the excessive cost argument has doubtful validity in most cases. MNEs need disaggregated information for internal planning and control purposes and so produce some such information already. Even if the information used internally is not in a form suitable for external reporting, it seems unlikely, given the extensive use of computerized information systems, that the generation of such information will be particularly expensive. This is especially true when one realizes just how much discretion companies have in deciding what constitutes a reportable segment. This means that, to a large extent, segments can be identified in such a way as to suit the already existing internal information system.

Another, and potentially more serious, cost is that of disseminating information that is likely to benefit existing or potential competitors. This argument of competitive disadvantage is often used by MNEs to press for less restrictive information disclosure requirements. While this may apply at the corporation level, especially if the same requirements do not apply to corporations of other nationalities, it may not be a problem at the level of the entire economy. If such information aids competition and investor evaluation, it might be considered an advantage rather than a cost to society. Whether this is so will depend on attitudes regarding the desirability of aiding competition and will tend to be largely case-specific, depending on the characteristics of the industries and corporations involved. It does appear, however, that such information may be advantageous when seen in the wider societal perspective.

Another argument against the competitive disadvantage rationale for nondisclosure is that such disclosures are only an attempt, and not a very successful one, to tip the balance back in favor of corporations operating in a single industry or country. The point is that such corporations disclose far more information about their single segment than do any multisegment MNEs.

The major argument against segment information is that in some cases it may be inappropriate and therefore potentially misleading. The disclosure of segment information implicitly assumes that the segments reported are relatively autonomous and independent of each other. This means that the figures reported for any one segment can be assessed independently of a consideration of the performance of the rest of the company. If, instead, the company is highly integrated, not only are relatively large transfers between the segments likely, but the segment results cannot be understood or considered in isolation from the rest of the company. At the extreme, if the company is highly integrated, any disaggregated results are arbitrary enough to be meaningless. Unfortunately, little evidence is available regarding either the extent to which most companies are integrated or what level of interdependence between parts of the company would invalidate segment information. Thus, although this appears to be a significant problem for some companies, it is difficult to gauge its incidence in practice.

INTERNATIONAL ACCOUNTING STANDARDS

The IASC issued a standard (IAS 14) in 1981 that followed fairly closely the requirements in the United States at that time. Thus, it required (for both LOB and geographical segments) information on sales, with internal and external revenues shown separately; operating results and identifiable assets, in either absolute or relative terms; and a reconciliation statement to the consolidated accounts. IAS 14 applied to all listed companies that provided consolidated statements. However, in practice, compliance by non-U.S. MNEs has often been only partial. In 1997, following a review, the IASC issued a revised IAS 14 "Segment Reporting" which limits the scope for managerial discretion in segment identification. The IASC approach looks to a company's organization structure and internal reporting system as the basis for identifying segments as this should normally provide the best evidence of an enterprise's predominant source of risks and returns. This will determine whether the "primary" segment reporting format will be business segments or geographical segments, with a higher level of disclosure relative to the secondary reporting format. If risks and returns are strongly affected by both and this is reflected in a "matrix" approach to management, then business segments should be used as the primary segment reporting format. The IASC, however, does not prohibit a "matrix" presentation with full segment disclosures on each basis. If neither approach is reflected in the internal organizational and management structure, then either business segments or geographical segments should be chosen as the primary format. Reportable segments are those where the majority of revenue is earned from external customers and where segment revenue is 10 percent or more of total revenue.

The disclosure requirement for primary segments (see Exhibit 8.1) comprises revenues (external and intersegment shown separately), operating result (before

Exhibit 8.1 Schedule A—Information About Business Segments (All amounts million)

	Paper Products 20×2	Paper Products 20×1	Office Products 20×2	Office Products 20×1	Publishing 20×2	Publishing 20×1	Other Operations 20×2	Other Operations 20×1	Eliminations 20×2	Eliminations 20×1	Consolidated 20×2	Consolidated 20×1
Revenue												
External sales	55	50	20	17	19	16	7	7				
Inter-segment sales	15	10	10	14	2	4	2	2	(29)	(30)		
Total revenue	70	60	30	31	21	20	9	9	(29)	(30)	101	90
Result												
Segment result	20	17	9	7	2	1	0	0	(1)	(1)	30	24
Unallocated corporate expenses											(7)	(9)
Operating profit											23	15
Interest expense											(4)	(4)
Interest income											2	3
Share of net profits of associates	6	5					2	2			8	7
Income taxes											(7)	(4)
Profit from ordinary activities											22	17
Extraordinary loss: uninsured earthquake damage to factory		(3)										(3)
Net profit											22	14
Other Information												
Segment assets	54	50	34	30	10	10	10	9			108	99
Investment in equity method associates	20	16					12	10			32	26
Unallocated corporate assets											35	30
consolidated total assets											175	155
Segment liabilities	25	15	8	11	8	8	1	1			42	35
Unallocated corporate liabilities											40	55
Consolidated total liabilities											82	90
Capital expenditure	12	10	3	5	5	3	4	3				
Depreciation	9	7	9	7	5	2	3	4				
Non-cash expenses other than depreciation	8	2	7	3	2	2	2	1				

Source: IASC. IAS14 *Segment Reporting* (revised 1997).

interest and taxes), carrying amount of segment liabilities, cost incurred to acquire property, plant, equipment and intangibles, depreciation and amortization, significant non-cash expenses, and share of profit or loss of associates or joint ventures. The secondary segment information required comprises revenues (external and intersegment shown separately) carrying amount of segment assets, and cost incurred to acquire property, plant, equipment and intangibles. It should be noted here the loss of information about profits for secondary segments in contrast to the original IAS 14 which required the same information for both business and geographical segments.

REGULATIONS AROUND THE WORLD

U.S. Requirements

To date, the United States has the most extensive accounting requirements in the world. The SEC has required LOB segment disclosures since 1969, but in 1976 the FASB introduced more comprehensive requirements in SFAS 14, *Financial Reporting for Segments of a Business Enterprise.* This required, for both LOB and geographical segments, the disclosure of revenues from unaffiliated customers, intragroup transfers, operating profit or loss or net income, or other profitability measures, and identifiable assets. In addition, for industry segments, companies were required to disclose depreciation, capital expenditure, and equity in the net income and assets of associates. Unfortunately, these requirements did not provide a clear definition of identifiable segments. For example, SFAS 14 stated:

> Foreign geographical areas are individual countries or groups of countries as may be determined to be appropriate in an enterprise's particular circumstances. Factors to be considered include proximity, economic affinity, similarities in business environments and the nature, scale and degree of interrelationship of the enterprise's operations in the various countries (Para. 34).

Vaguer guidance was provided for determining what constitutes an identifiable LOB segment:

> No single set of characteristics is universally applicable in determining the industry segments of all enterprises, nor is any single characteristic determinative in all cases. Consequently determination of an enterprise's industry segments must depend to a considerable extent on the judgement of the management of the enterprise (Para. 12).

Once the segments had been identified, however, clear guidance was given as to what constituted a reportable segment. For geographical segments, these would be reported if segment sales accounted for at least 10 percent of total sales or if identifiable assets accounted for at least 10 percent of total identifiable assets. Similarly, LOB segments would be separately disclosed if either of these requirements were met or if segment profits or losses accounted for at least 10 percent of the profits or losses of all segments that incurred a profit or loss, respectively.

Following a recent review of SFAS 14, the FASB (working jointly with the Canadian Accounting Standards Board) issued a new standard SFAS 131 in 1997, which limits managerial discretion in segment identification by requiring segments to be consistent with a company's organization structure and internal reporting system. This is very similar to the IASC's recently revised IAS 14 (1997).

The new standard was issued following criticisms of the lack of guidance offered by SFAS 14 on segment identification resulting in vague and unduly aggregated segment reporting behavior. The new SFAS 131 requires disclosures for each reportable segment similar to IAS 14. Reportable segments may be based on lines of business, geographic location, or a combination of both. Additional information is required about the geographic areas of operations if the reportable segment disclosures do not provide this. This second tier of reporting is referred to as enterprise-wide disclosures. While revenue and asset disclosures are required at this level, profits disclosures are not, thus resulting in a loss of information compared to SFAS 14 similar to the IASC's original IAS 14 (Nichols, Street, and Gray, 2000).

U.K. Requirements

In the United Kingdom, segment disclosure requirements were first introduced by the London Stock Exchange in 1965 and were subsequently incorporated in the 1967 Companies Act with respect to LOB disclosures of sales and profits.

Following the EU Fourth and Seventh Directives, the Companies Acts of 1981 and 1989 (now incorporated in the 1985 Companies Act, as amended) require the disclosure of geographical segment turnover, together with LOB disclosure of both sales and profit before tax. Geographical profits disclosures were not required although they were specified as a required disclosure, albeit with some flexibility, by the London Stock Exchange. The Companies Act also states that if any market or class of business is immaterial (a term not defined), it may be combined with another. Even more discretion is given to companies in the additional statement that "if disclosure is seriously prejudicial to the interest of the company that information need not be disclosed" (Schedule 4, para. 55[5]), it being sufficient instead to state that such disclosures have not been made. The only guidance the Companies Act provides regarding segment identification is the statement, "the directors of the company should have regard to the manner in which the company's activities are organized" (para. 55[3]).

The most important new requirement is that such information should be provided in the notes to the accounts, thus falling within the scope of the audit. However, the Companies Act still fails to tackle the more serious problem of segment identification: there are no definitions of what "material" is or what a reportable segment is; consequently, either lack of disclosure or misleading disclosures is possible. Emmanuel and Gray (1977) have shown that leaving this to the discretion of management has led to inadequate or inconsistent disclosures by many large U.K. corporations. Even if such discretion does not encourage deliberate manipulation, "no amount of sophisticated data can remedy the damage caused by segments wrongly identified in the first place."

More recently, a new standard SSAP 25, *Segmental Reporting*, was issued. This extended existing requirements by requiring the disclosure of segment net assets for both LOB and geographical segments. In addition, geographical segmentation of sales was required both by source, that is, location of production or service facilities, and destination. Geographical segmental profits disclosures were also required unequivocally, in contrast to the London Stock Exchange's somewhat flexible existing requirement, which mandated disclosure only when segment profits from a geographical area were "abnormal" (i.e., substantially out of line with the normal ratio of profit to sales). These changes brought the scope of U.K. regulation to a level similar to that of the United States, if not in the same amount of detail.

Requirements in Other Countries

Many other countries also require segment information (see Exhibit 8.2). Notably, Australia and Canada have extensive requirements comparable to those in the

Exhibit 8.2   Segment Disclosure Requirements

	Line of Business			Geographical		
	Sales	Profits	Assets	Sales	Profits	Assets
Australia	Yes	Yes	Yes	Yes	Yes	Yes
Brazil	No	No	No	No	No	No
Canada	Yes	Yes[a]	Yes	Yes	Yes[b]	Yes
China	Yes	Yes	Yes	Yes	Yes	Yes
France	Yes	No	No	Yes	No	No
Germany	Yes	No	No	Yes	No	No
Greece	Yes	No	No	Yes	No	No
Hungary	Yes	No	No	Yes	No	No
India	No	No	No	No	No	No
Italy	Yes	No	No	Yes	No	No
Japan	Yes	Yes	Yes	Yes	Yes	Yes
Netherlands	Yes	No	No	Yes	No	No
Philippines	Yes	Yes	Yes	Yes	Yes	Yes
Singapore	Yes	Yes	Yes	Yes	Yes	Yes
South Africa	Yes	Yes	Yes	Yes	Yes	Yes
Spain	Yes	No	No	Yes	No	No
Sweden	Yes	Yes	No	Yes	No	No
Switzerland	No	No	No	No	No	No
Thailand	Yes	Yes	Yes	Yes	Yes	Yes
United Kingdom	Yes	Yes	Yes	Yes	Yes	Yes
United States	Yes	Yes[a]	Yes	Yes	Yes[b]	Yes
European Union	Yes	No	No	Yes	No	No
IASC	Yes	Yes[a]	Yes	Yes	Yes[b]	Yes

[a] Only if LOB is the primary basis of reporting.
[b] Only if geographical area is the primary basis of reporting.

United Kingdom and the United States. In the EU countries, the EU Fourth (1978) and Seventh (1983) Directives have set a minimum requirement of disclosure (i.e., sales by line of business and geographical area). While the United Kingdom goes well beyond this, most European countries have adopted a more secretive approach though in practice many MNEs go beyond the minimum (e.g., Philips in the Netherlands [see Exhibit 8.3]).

Exhibit 8.3   Philips – Segment Data (1999)

Sales, Sales Growth, and Number of Employees by Product Sector				1999
	Sales (to third parties)	% Growth		Number of Employees
		Nominal	Comparable	
Lighting	4,548	2	1	47,453
Consumer Products	12,437	0	6	47,970
Components	3,754	(2)	3	41,709
Semiconductors	3,796	18	5	29,952
Professional	5,186	15	4	25,187
Origin	1,056	0	0	16,690
Miscellaneous	682	(27)	(11)	11,181
Unallocated				6,732
Total	**31,459**	**3**	**4**	**226,874**

Product sectors					1999
	Segment Revenues	Ebitda[a]	Income (loss) from Operations	As % of Segment Revenues	Income (loss) from Operations[b]
Lighting	4,597	772	602	13.1	631
Consumer Products	12,781	847	555	4.3	519
Components	5,325	661	286	5.4	311
Semiconductors	4,557	1,195	614	13.5	612
Professional	5,479	261	100	1.8	125
Miscellaneous	769	(9)	(91)	(11.8)	(83)
Unallocated		(365)	(412)		(416)
Total intersegment revenues	**35,243** **3,784**	**3,555**	**1,751**	**1,796**	
Sales income from operations as a % of sales	**31,459**		**8.5**		**5.7**

Data by product sector (the data included in this report are unaudited).

[a] In Philips's definition, Ebitda represents income from operations before depreciation and amortization charges.

[b] Excluding restructuring.

(continues)

Exhibit 8.3   (*Continued*)

Product sectors					1999
	Total Assets	Net Operating Capital	(In)tangible Fixed Assets	Capital Expenditures	Depreciation
Lighting	2,849	1,875	1,275	176	161
Consumer Products	4,500	1,689	884	296	285
Components	5,179	2,078	3,197	259	364
Semiconductors	5,188	3,194	2,917	622	467
Professional	3,432	1,780	916	99	84
Origin	683	240	275	56	68
Miscellaneous	913	318	328	68	79
Unallocated	6,752	(728)	362	86	40
Total	**29,496**	**10,446**	**10,154**	**1,662**	**1,548**

Data by geographic area
(the data included in this report are unaudited)

Sales, Sales Growth, and Number of Employees by Main Country				1999
	Sales (to third parties)	% Growth Nominal	% Growth Comparable	Number of Employees
Netherlands	1,619	(2)	(1)	43,153
United States	7,535	5	9	26,282
Germany	2,727	(2)	2	13,964
France	1,962	(6)	(8)	12,521
United Kingdom	2,281	18	16	7,938
China (incl. Hong Kong)	2,023	8	4	22,097
Other countries	13,312	3	2	100,919
Total	**31,459**	**3**	**4**	**226,874**

Geographic Areas 1999

	Segment Revenues	Ebitda[a]	Income (loss) from Operations	As % of Segement Revenues	Income (loss) from Operations[b]
Netherlands Europe excl.	12,452	927	513	4.1	565
Netherlands	16,600	1,118	611	3.7	622
United States and Canada	9,310	507	82	0.9	60
Latin America	1,642	15	(41)	(2.5)	(31)
Africa	107	3	1	0.9	1
Australia and New Zeland	424	4	1	0.2	1

Exhibit 8.3   (*Continued*)

Geographic Areas 1999

	Segment Revenues	Ebitda[a]	Income (loss) from Operations	As % of Segment Revenuses	Income (loss) from Operations[b]
Total	**51,723**	**3,555**	**1,751**		**1,796**
Interregional revenues	**(20,264)**				
Sales Income from operations as a % of sales	**31,459**		**5.6**		**5.7**

[a] In Philips's definition, Ebitda represents income from operations before depreciation and amortization charges.

[b] Excluding restructuring.

Main Countries   1999

	Total Assets	Net Operating Capital	(In)tangible Fixed Assets	Capital Expenditures	Depreciation
Netherlands	7,452	2,439	1,811	435	370
United States	5,139	2,839	2,476	249	228
Germany	1,558	86	632	134	147
France	1,118	164	392	92	113
United Kingdom	1,041	607	321	55	53
China (incl. Hong Kong)	1,570	635	635	91	123
Other countries	11,618	3,676	3,887	606	514
Total	**29,496**	**10,446**	**10,154**	**1,662**	**1,548**

In Japan, segment reporting requirements were only introduced in 1990 and were initially limited to sales, profits, and assets disclosures by line of business but are now broadly consistent with International Accounting Standards. While many other countries have aligned themselves with international standards, there are others (e.g., Brazil and India) that have no segment disclosure requirements.

SEGMENT REPORTING PROBLEMS

Segment information now must be audited in many countries, which presents a problem regarding the verifiability of the information. Particular problems involve common cost allocations, intragroup transfers, and transfer pricing. While these problems mean that the information may not be as verifiable as other items of financial information, a trade-off between verifiability and relevance is required.

Another problem facing the auditor is segment identification. In the absence of clear guidelines, the task of the auditor in assessing whether the segments disclosed are reasonable is extremely difficult. As we noted earlier, U.K. company law leaves segment identification to the discretion of the directors of each corporation on the grounds that what is relevant and reportable will depend on the unique characteristics of each company. In contrast, the FASB in the United States provides detailed and prescriptive rules regarding what constitutes a reportable segment. However, the decision on what constitutes an *identifiable,* and thus potentially reportable, segment is a function of each corporation.

In practice, there are differing approaches to geographical segment identification in various countries, for example, U.S. and U.K. MNEs tend to aggregate sales and profits by continent. However, there have also been cases of multicontinental aggregation, referring, for example, to Europe, the Middle East, and Africa as one segment. Such an approach is unlikely to be informative given the different economic and political environments and risk factors involved. In contrast, MNEs in some continental European countries (e.g., Aga in Sweden) voluntarily disclose additional segmental data, at least with respect to sales and employees, on a much more disaggregated geographical basis.

The general lack of guidance regarding segment identification implies that the advantage of comparability between corporations has been sacrificed in favor of relevance and the opportunity to provide more useful information specific to each corporation. However, it also means that corporations can manipulate disclosures to present the best possible picture of their operations and thus manage external perceptions of corporate success. For example, they can hide the poor performance of one area of their operations by aggregating it with another that has done particularly well. The apparent lack of consistency of disclosures in practice suggests that the comparability of information has been sacrificed for an advantage that may be more apparent than real.

It is difficult to know how to overcome the problems of segment identification. Segmentation along organizational lines is desirable in that it provides the important advantage that the management's internal accounting and control system will presumably be consistent with the firm's organizational structure and will make the provision of segmental information to external users a relatively easy and inexpensive task. But, more significantly, management will be disclosing its own view of segments with significant differences in risk and return. If the management accounting reports "are the best that management can produce to guide their own decisions, then there is an initial presumption that the same statements, or less detailed versions of them, are likely best to serve the investor in making his investment and dis-investment decisions" (Solomons, 1968).

Of course, it may be that management is misguided or inefficient and that the organization of the firm therefore may not be an accurate indicator of significant risk and return differences. This is especially likely when the firm is going through a rapid development phase or when the management has not responded adequately to changing business conditions. In addition, diverse activities may be combined organizationally through historical accident or the influence of powerful personalities. On the other hand, combinations may be deliberate because of common demand elasticities, the use of joint production facilities, or interdependence of product. Hence, there may be sound managerial reasons behind a particular organizational structure. Moreover, the breaking down of organizational units into smaller or different components will necessitate the allocation of common costs. Information from segments thus classified may therefore be questionable at least in terms of profits and the segments identified unlikely to reflect the company's actual diversification strategy, which is information that would appear to be useful in evaluating and predicting managerial performance.

The Dual-Yardstick Proposal

In support of an organizational approach, similar to that now required by the IASC and in the United States, Emmanuel and Gray (1978) suggested requiring disclosures on an industry (or LOB) and geographical basis, which would be at the same time consistent with the MNE's organizational structure. This would provide a discipline on the disclosures supplied, enhance the potential for verification, and ensure an insight into managerial strategy. If the industry/geographical groupings identified internally were then related to an external standard industrial classification (i.e., a dual yardstick), this would not only improve communication, it would also be an invaluable aid to prediction insofar as segmental data from the firm could then be compared with aggregate, external industrywide, or geographical data.

Emmanuel and Gray suggested a decision criterion to the effect that an organizational unit is a segment for reporting purposes if *all* of the following apply:

1. More than 50 percent of its physical sales volume is sold externally.
2. Revenue and profitability information is accumulated regularly for this unit.
3. Responsibility for the unit's operating performance resides with the immediate manager of the unit.

Effectively, the conditions of a profit center are applied to the organizational units of the corporation. Due to the size of the corporation, different organizational units must be recognized, but this should not be taken to mean that each is run as a separate business activity. The extent of the coordination of the activities can be roughly gauged by the degree of internal versus external trade. Let's consider the application of the proposal to an organization structure such as that of MNE XY in Figure 8.1.

At the first organizational level, assume the identified units are not consistent with the government's Standard Industrial Classification (SIC) at the desired level of disaggregation. At the next tier, assume there is a partial consistency. With respect to the paper and packaging division, if less than 50 percent of the sales volume of the paper and board department is sold internally and the units are treated as profit centers for internal purposes, then two reportable segments can be identified. For the engineering division, a further tier of the organization structure must be uncovered. The electronics and telephone units are consistent with the SIC at the desired level of disaggregation, and if the three conditions for a profit center are satisfied, two further reportable segments are discovered. On the mechanical engineering side, however, the corporation's organization is inconsistent with the SIC, where pumps, valves, and compressors are presumed to constitute a single heading. The corporation now has a choice regarding the identification of reportable segments given that the sub-

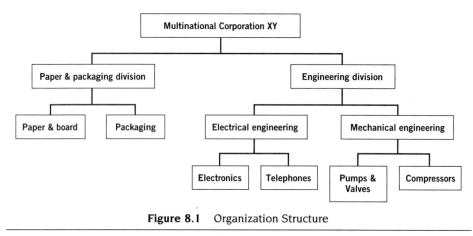

Figure 8.1 Organization Structure

Source: C. R. Emmanuel and S. J. Gray, "Segmental Disclosures by Multibusiness, Multinational Companies: A Proposal," *Accounting and Business Research* (Summer 1978): 175.

units conform to the definition of a profit center. The corporation's executives can decide whether the gains from disclosing information for pumps, valves, and compressors separately will outweigh any possible competitive disadvantages. Should separate disclosure not take place, the results of a reportable segment called "Mechanical engineering: Pumps, valves, and compressors" would be disclosed. For MNE XY, given the assumptions about the individual unit's degree of dependence on internal trade, five segments can thus be identified and reported on.

Along with the dual yardstick for identifying segments is the desirability of a requirement for *all* corporations to provide information about managerial responsibilities, organization structure (preferably in the form of a chart showing both the business and geographical elements), and volume of internal transactions. This seems feasible, judging by the best examples of current practice, and would also facilitate auditor verification of the quality of segmental disclosures. Such additional information may also be significant as an indicator of corporate strategy.

The proposal, therefore, attempts to identify reportable segments by combining management's method of operating a corporation's diverse activities with a standard industrial classification. The rigid use of the SIC to identify reportable segments is avoided by initially focusing on the corporation's organization structure, and hence a balance is struck between the use of managerial discretion and a potentially inflexible classification system. The reportable segments identified under the proposal are significant for external users because of the identification process. Successive tiers of the organization structure are uncovered only when disclosure is not consistent with the SIC. The process of disaggregation starts at the top and proceeds downward. It is also unlikely that the proposed process of disaggregation will stop short of identifying segments that have a material effect on the enterprise's operating results. Furthermore, the absence of a quantitative significance criterion reduces the scope for manipulation inasmuch as modifications of the organization structure will carry serious implications for internal control and behavior. The proposal therefore appears to satisfy criteria relating to the identification of realistic, material segments.

In addition to the business activities thus far considered, an international analysis, both by location and markets, also requires consideration. Emmanuel and Gray suggest that the primary yardstick should be the organization structure, identified in the same way as outlined earlier, but that disclosure should be made consistent with the geographical areas considered significant by management, consistent with its risk-return perceptions. In this respect a clear-cut disclosure by continent or country should be made, depending on the organization of the corporation concerned and the emphasis of its activities. A mixing-up of geographical locations with the markets served from such locations obviously should be avoided.

Emmanuel and Gray acknowledge that this approach to identifying reportable geographical segments is not entirely satisfactory because of the discretion given to management. However, the use of significance criteria or other arbitrary rules is unlikely to be of universal application and thus could result in the dissemination of misleading information.

Considerations of integration on an international scale also must be accounted for so that if external sales—in terms of physical volume—for any international segment corresponding to a specific organizational unit are less than 50 percent, the separate disclosure of that segment can be omitted. A more complex situation arises when more than one organizational unit appears within an identified geographical segment. When the external sales of each unit are less than 50 percent, only the total geographical segment need be disclosed. This indicates that the proposal, with regard to a LOB analysis, can be applied primarily to the organization structure if that structure initially identifies business activities, or it can be applied secondarily to the case where the organization structure initially shows geographical locations. Hence, an international analysis also should be disclosed irrespective of whether the organization structure is business dominated or is some mixture or combination of both. A crucial distinction concerns the disclosure of home country performance from foreign performance in that this will assist the monitoring of national performance. In exceptional cases, the 50 percent rule would have to be relaxed so that home country performance could be distinguished from other geographical reportable segments.

An application of geographical disclosure relating to location can be illustrated with reference to the business-dominated organization structure of MNE XY (see Figure 8.2)

It is first necessary to establish whether geographical segments exist relating to the business segments already identified from the organization structure. If less than 50 percent of the sales volume of the German or French locations of the paper and board department is sold internally and the units are treated as profit centers for internal purposes, then three reportable geographical segments can be identified. A similar identification procedure can be adopted in the case of packaging; electronics; telephones; and pumps, valves, and compressors. If, for example, in the case of telephones the Canadian unit were selling internally more than 50 percent of its volume to the U.S. unit, then a choice would have to be made whether to aggregate Canada with the United States into a segment entitled North America or to disclose the Canadian unit separately with other similar units as "nonsegmented operations." The appropriate choice seems to depend on the nature of the firm's other activities in the United States, and because there is a separate electronics operation it could be more informative to keep U.S. activities as a separate disclosure.

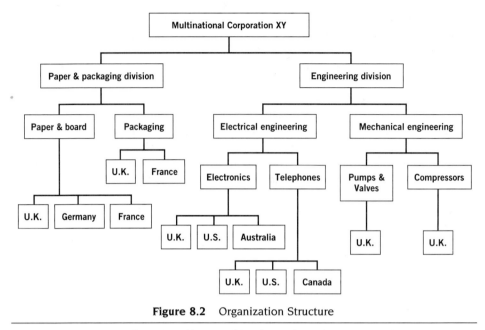

Figure 8.2   Organization Structure

Source: C. R. Emmanuel and S. J. Gray, "Segmental Disclosures by Multibusiness, Multinational Companies: A Proposal," *Accounting and Business Research* (Summer 1978): 176.

Clearly, the auditor's task is an important one in this context, just as in the case of a LOB analysis. He or she is responsible for judging the meaningfulness of the segmental disclosures in the light of the company's international activities, and risk factors involved, and the organization of responsibilities to match such activities. It should be emphasized, however, that the examples given serve only to illustrate this proposal. In practice, a complex variety of organization structures are likely to be found, which will challenge judgment and ingenuity to a greater degree than exhibited here.

Matrix Presentation

From our earlier discussion of regualtion it is evident that in many countries corporations are required to disclose both LOB and geographical segmental data. However, most corporations provide such information separately rather than in a matrix form of presentation that gives information on the interrelationship of the two types of segments (see, for example, BOC of the United Kingdom in Exhibit 8.4). The general lack of a matrix presentation presents another problem to the users of segment information. Both risk and expected return are dependent on the extent to which specific industry activities are committed to specific countries. A matrix presentation would mean that a more accurate assessment of business prospects is possible. This is because the effect of changes in political, economic, or social conditions in any country will depend on the specific lines of business carried on by the corporation in the country concerned.

Exhibit 8.4 BOC (United Kingdom)

Notes to the Financial Statements

1. Segment Information

a) Turnover 2000

	Gases and Related Products £ Million	Vacuum Technology £ Million	Distribution Services £ Million	Total £ Million	Discontinued Operations £ Million	Total Group by Origin £ Million	Total Group by Destination £ Million
		Continuing Operations					
Europe	603.1	152.1	225.3	980.5	–	980.5	948.9
Americas	931.0	308.9	–	1,239.9	–	1,239.9	1,160.6
Africa	500.8	–	–	500.8	–	500.8	499.9
Asia/Pacific	1,058.8	97.7	1.1	1,157.6	–	1,157.6	1,269.4
Turnover	3,093.7	558.7	226.4	3,878.8	–	3,878.8	3,878.8
1999							
Europe	605.9	94.7	251.6	952.6	–	952.2	943.4
Americas	821.1	185.1	–	1,006.2	–	1,006.2	963.2
Africa	386.7	–	–	386.7	–	386.7	386.7
Asia/Pacific	903.1	61.0	2.4	966.5	–	966.5	1,018.3
Turnover	2,716.8	340.8	254.0	3,311.6	–	3,311.6	3,311.6
1998							
Europe	667.5	104.8	312.4	1,084.7	76.7	1,161.4	1,120.5
Americas	831.8	177.0	–	1,008.8	114.3	1,123.1	1,076.6
Africa	333.9	–	–	333.9	–	333.9	335.4
Asia/Pacific	864.1	41.3	1.5	906.9	24.6	931.5	1,017.4
Turnover	2,697.3	323.1	313.9	3,334.3	215.6	3,549.9	3,549.9

(continues)

Exhibit 8.4 (*Continued*)

		Continuing Operations					
	Gases and Related Products £ Million	Vacuum Technology £ Million	Distribution Services £ Million	Total £ Million	Total £ Million	Discontinued Operations £ Million	Total Group £ Million
b) Business Analysis 2000							
Total operating profit before exceptional items	**467.9**	**64.8**	**29.4**	**(1.5)**	**560.0**	–	**560.6**
Exceptional items	**(21.6)**	**(4.2)**	**1.5**	**19.9**	**(4.4)**	–	**(4.4)**
Capital employed[1]	**3,764.1**	**265.1**	**98.6**	**12.5**	**4,140.3**	–	**4,140.3**
Capital expenditure	**356.6**	**38.3**	**16.8**	**2.0**	**413.7**	–	**413.7**
Depreciation and amortization	**276.4**	**17.5**	**17.1**	**2.3**	**313.3**	–	**313.3**
1999							
Total operating profit before exceptional items	428.1	29.7	28.7	(6.6)	479.9	–	479.9
Exceptional items	(56.7)	(6.6)	(1.1)	(5.0)	(69.4)	–	(69.4)
Capital employed[a]	3,431.9	179.4	106.5	4.0	3,721.8	–	3,721.8
Capital expenditure	470.3	14.4	17.1	3.6	505.4	–	505.4
Depreciation and amortization	233.7	13.6	21.0	2.5	270.8	–	270.8
1998							
Total operating profit before exceptional items	418.5	32.4	27.9	(4.9)	473.9	6.0	479.9
Exceptional items	(174.9)	(27.2)	(33.7)	(23.2)	(240.6)	–	(240.6)
Capital employed[a]	3,115.7	165.5	131.1	3.2	3,389.1	–	3,389.1
Capital expenditure	523.1	21.5	39.1	3.2	586.9	9.3	596.2
Depreciation and amortization	220.2	14.9	23.0	2.1	260.2	10.5	270.7

[a] Capital employed comprises the capital and reserves of the Group, its long-term liabilities and all current borrowings net of cash and deposits.

Continuing Operations

	Europe £ Million	Americas £ Million	Africa £ Million	Asia/Pacific £ Million	Total £ Million	Discontinued Operations £ Million	Total Group £ Million
c) Regional Analysis 2000							
Total operating profit before exceptional items	**201.4**	**122.6**	**68.6**	**168.0**	**560.6**	–	**560.6**
Exceptional items	**22.9**	**(25.4)**	**(0.6)**	**(1.3)**	**(4.4)**	–	**(4.4)**
Capital employed[a]	**1,267.5**	**1,275.1**	**309.5**	**1,288.2**	**4,140.3**	–	**4,140.3**
Capital expenditure	**127.2**	**121.9**	**31.8**	**132.8**	**413.7**	**–**	**413.7**
1999							
Total operating profit before exceptional items	170.9	104.8	61.0	143.2	479.9	–	479.9
Exceptional items	(38.1)	(11.2)	(5.8)	(14.3)	(69.4)	–	(69.4)
Capital employed[a]	1,186.6	1,111.8	304.9	1,118.5	3,721.8	–	3,721.8
Capital expenditure	141.8	146.2	32.9	184.5	505.4	–	505.4
1998							
Total operating profit before exceptional items	199.2	89.4	60.5	124.8	473.9	6.0	479.9
Exceptional items	(139.0)	(36.2)	(8.7)	(56.7)	(240.6)	–	(240.6)
Capital employed[a]	1,246.6	1,040.9	237.1	864.5	3,389.10	–	3,389.1
Capital expenditure	269.7	170.2	31.3	115.7	585.9	9.3	596.2

[a] Capital employed comprises the capital and reserves of the group, its long-term liabilities and all current borrowings net of cash and deposits.

(continues)

Exhibit 8.4 (*Continued*)

	Joint Ventures[c]		Associates[c]	
	Americas £ Million	Asia/Pacific £ Million	Africa £ Million	Asia/Pacific £ Million
d) Joint Ventures and Associates Analysis 2000				
Turnover	**43.1**	**214.9**	**20.1**	**21.0**
Operating profit	**12.6**	**35.5**	**3.2**	**5.3**
Capital employed[b]	**45.4**	**182.0**	**7.5**	**36.5**
Capital expenditure	**120.7**	**90.2**	**4.0**	**2.4**
Group share	**36.6**	**45.1**	**1.1**	**0.7**
Other partners	**84.1**	**45.1**	**2.9**	**1.7**
Depreciation and amortization	**6.5**	**17.3**	**0.5**	**2.8**
1999				
Turnover	33.8	182.1	17.9	25.1
Operating profit	7.6	31.7	2.7	8.0
Capital employed[b]	40.0	145.1	7.2	38.7
Capital expenditure	280.5	81.4	1.8	21.2
Group share	85.2	40.6	0.7	7.0
Other partners	195.3	40.8	1.1	14.2
Depreciation and amortization	4.5	14.6	0.4	3.2
1998				
Turnover	38.9	179.9	10.6	25.7
Operating profit before exceptional items	7.2	38.7	1.2	6.4
Exceptional items	–	(7.7)	–	(1.2)
Capital employed[b]	46.7	127.9	1.2	26.8
Group Share	89.7	39.7	1.1	10.4
Others partners	197.1	39.7	1.6	22.9
Depreciation and amortization	4.5	14.8	0.3	2.8

[b] Capital employed comprises the Group's share of the net assets of joint ventures or assaociates.

[c] All of the Group's joint ventures and associates are principally engaged in the gases and related products business.

SUMMARY

1. The growth of large diversified MNEs presents problems for both MNEs and the users of accounts, especially in terms of assessing a corporation's future cash flows and the risk or uncertainty associated with those future cash flows. Segment reporting (i.e., the disclosure of disaggregated data) is likely to be somewhat effective in meeting the information needs of investors and other users.

2. Results of studies of predictive ability have shown that both LOB and geographical segmental data are more useful than consolidated data for the prediction of earnings.

3. Stock market research relating to risk assessment suggests that disclosure of LOB and geographical segment data results in a decrease in a company's riskiness as perceived by investors.

4. Although regulation is growing internationally, with important new developments by the IASC and in the United States, the major problem of segment identification is still prevalent. The scope for managerial discreption provides substantial potential for the dissemination of misleading information.

5. Potential constraints on the disclosure of segment data reporting include the costs of compiling, processing, and disseminating information and, more significantly, the costs of competitive disadvantage. The major argument against such disclosure is that in some cases, where the company is highly integrated, it may be inappropriate and therefore potentially misleading.

6. While companies often use the competitive disadvantage argument to counter attempts at further regulation or to justify nondisclosures, there may be wider investment and societal benefits from segment reporting.

7. There is scope for introducing segment disclosure guidelines that encourage disclosures and yet do more to control their quality so they are truly informative.

8. The application of a "dual yardstick" based on internal organizational criteria and an external scheme of industrial/geographical classification seems desirable and is supported by recent developments at the IASC and in the United States.

9. A matrix analysis of LOB and geographical segment disclosures is likely to provide more insight into risk-return relationships and future prospects than single-dimension disclosures.

Discussion Questions

1. Critically evaluate the benefits of segment reporting with particular reference to the results of predictive ability and stock market research.

2. Critically evaluate the costs of segment reporting.

3. Discuss the major problems concerning the content and presentation of segment information that have been identified in practice.

4. To what extent are MNE concerns that segment reporting will give rise to competitive disadvantage likely to be justified? Discuss specific situations and items of information.

5. If the risks of operating in a foreign country (e.g., Mexico) are high, should MNEs be required to disclose information about the operations and assets involved even if they comprise a relatively minor part of the total, for example, 5 percent?

6. Is it possible to rely on international capital market pressures to stimulate the disclosure of useful segment information by MNEs, or is more focused and detailed regulation necessary?

7. What are the advantages of a "matrix" approach to segment reporting?

Case: BMW (Germany)

BMW is a German-based automobile company with a strong worldwide brand name. Besides automobiles, BMW manufactures motorcycles and is involved in aircraft engine production, software, and financial services. In 1999, BMW disclosed segment information by both line of business and geographical area as shown in Exhibit 8.5, some of it on a voluntary basis.

Questions

1. Why do you think BMW would disclose segment information voluntarily when there is no compulsion to do so?

2. Critically evaluate the meaning and significance of the geographical segments identified by BMW and the segment information disclosed. How useful is financial statement analysis based on these segments likely to be?

3. What explanations might there be for BMW's approach to geographical segment identification?

4. Discuss some alternative bases for identifying geographical segments. What criteria could you use to support your choice?

Exhibit 8.5   BMW

Segment Information by Business Fields	External Sales		Intersegment Sales		Total Sales	
In Euro Million	1999	1998	1999	1998	1999	1998
BMW Automobiles	19,673	17,946	4,937	4,034	24,610	21,980
Rover Automobiles	7,427	7,739	1,211	727	8,638	8,466
BMW Motorcycles	767	652	2	1	769	653
Financial Services	5,748	5,512	405	259	6,153	5,771
Miscellaneous, consolidated companies	787	431	−6,555	−5,021	−5,768	−4,590
BMW Group	**34,402**	**32,280**	–	–	**34,402**	**32,280**

Exhibit 8.5 (*Continued*)

Segment Information by Business Fields	Segment Result		Financial Result		Result from Ordinary Business Activities	
In Euro Million	1999	1998	1999	1998	1999	1998
BMW Automobiles	2,001	1,947	105	56	2,106	2,003
Rover Automobiles	–992	–755	–215	–202	–1,207	–957
BMW Motorcycles	18	16	–	–	18	16
Financial Services	752	642	–436*	–344*	316	298
Miscellaneous, consolidated companies	–337	–415	215	116	–122	–299
BMW Group	**1,442**	**1,435**	**–331**	**–374**	**1,111**	**1,061**

* Interest expense from the financing of leasing business.

Segment Information by Business Fields	Assets		Capital Expenditure		Depreciation/ Write-downs	
In Euro Million	1999	1998	1999	1998	1999	1998
BMW Automobiles	10,108	9,792	1,609	1,466	1,199	1,146
Rover Automobiles	6,277	5,705	625	729	694	623
BMW Motorcycles	313	303	40	35	32	48
Fincnaical Services	20,530	15,827	9	6	8	7
Miscellaneous, consolidated companies	279	–988	–128	–57	–109	55
BMW Group	**37,507**	**30,639**	**2,155**	**2,179**	**2,042**	**1,859**

Segment Information by Regions	Assests		Capital Expenditure		External Sales	
In Euro Million	1999	1998	1999	1998	1999	1998
Germany	11,543	11,033	1,086	1,016	9,206	9,271
Great Britain	9,394	7,126	630	733	4,826	5,615
Rest of Europe	3,658	3,140	79	75	8,118	7,194
North America	8,900	5,159	320	281	8,098	6,413
Asia	1,723	1,291	8	4	2,534	2,212
Miscellaneous, consolidated companies	2,289	2,890	32	70	1,620	1,575
BMW Group	**37,507**	**20,639**	**2,155**	**2,179**	**34,402**	**32,280**

Case: Nestlé

Questions

Examine the segment data reported by Nestlé in the company's 1999 annual report and accounts as given below (Exhibit 8.6). Nestlé claims to have prepared its report in accordance with IAS 14 (revised 1997). Please answer the following questions based on your study of these disclosures:

1. What is the primary basis and what is the secondary basis of segment reporting by Nestlé?
2. To what extent has Nestlé complied with IAS 14?
3. To what extent has Nestlé voluntarily disclosed information beyond the requirements of IAS 14?

Exhibit 8.6   *Nestlé*

Key Figures by Management Responsibility and Geographic Area
(in millions of Swiss francs)

	1999
Sales	
Food:	
• Europe	27,098
• Americas	22,045
• Africa, Asia, and Oceania	13,611
Other Activities	11,906
	74,660
Results	
Food:	
• Europe	2,671
• Americas	2,799
• Africa, Asia, and Oceania	2,185
Other Activities	1,675
	9,330
Unallocated items[a]	(1,416)
Trading profit	7,914
Capital Expenditure	
Food	
• Furope	923
• Americas	718
• Africa, Asia, and Oceania	381
Other Activities	665
	2,687
Unallocated items[b]	119
	2,806

(continues)

Exhibit 8.6   (*Continued*)

Key Figures by Product Group	
Sales	
• Beverages	20,859
• Milk products, nutrition and ice cream	19,411
• Prepared dishes and cooking aids (and miscellaneous activities)	20,185
• Chocolate and confectionery	10,195
• Pharmaceuticals	4,010
	74,660
Results	
• Beverages	3,764
• Milk products, nutrition and ice cream	2,168
• Prepared dishes and cooking aids (and miscellaneous activities	1,850
• Chocolate and confectionery	882
• Pharmaceuticals	1,077
	9,741
Unallocated items[a]	(1,827)
Trading profit	7,914
Capital Expenditure	
• Beverages	618
• Milk products, nutrition and ice cream	366
• Prepared dishes and cooking aids (and miscellaneous activities)	464
• Chocolate and confectionery	280
• Pharmaceuticals	91
	1,819
Administration, distribution, research and development	987
	2,806

[a] Mainly corporate expenses, research and development costs as well as amortization of intangible assets.

[b] Corporate and research and development fixed assets.

Selected References

Ajinkya, B. B. 1980. "An Empirical Evaluation of Line of Business Reporting," *Journal of Accounting Research* (Autumn).

Balakrishnan, R., T. S. Harris, and P. K. Sen. 1990. "The Predictive Ability of Geographic Segment Disclosures," *Journal of Accounting Research* (Autumn).

Collins, D. W. and R. Simonds. 1979. "SEC Line of Business Disclosure and Market Risk Adjustments," *Journal of Accounting Research* (Autumn).

Edwards, P. and Smith, R. A. 1996. "Competitive Disadvantage and Voluntary Disclosures: The Case of Segmental Reporting," *British Accounting Review* (June): 28 (2): 155–72.

Emmanuel, C. R. and S. J. Gray. 1977. "Segmental Disclosures and the Segment Identification Problem," *Accounting and Business Research* (Winter).

Emmanuel, C. R. and S. J. Gray. 1978. "Segmental Disclosure by Multibusiness Multinational Companies: A Proposal," *Accounting and Business Research* (Summer).

Emmanuel, C. R. and R. Pick. 1980. "The Predictive Ability of U.K. Segment Reports," *Journal of Business Finance and Accounting* (Summer).

Financial Accounting Standards Board. 1997. *SFAS 131: Financial Reporting for Segments of a Business Enterprise.* Stamford, CT: FASB.

Gray, S. J. and L. H. Radebaugh. 1984. "International Segment Disclosures by U.S. and U.K. Multinational Enterprises: A Descriptive Study," *Journal of Accounting Research* (Spring).

Gray, S. J. and C. B. Roberts. 1988. "Voluntary Information Disclosures and the British Multinationals," in *International Pressures for Accounting Change* edited by A. G. Hopwood. Englewood Cliffs, NJ: Prentice-Hall.

Herrmann, D. 1996. "The Predictive Ability of Geographic Segment Information at the Country, Continent and Consolidated Level," *Journal of International Financial Management and Accounting* (Spring), 7 (1): 50–73.

Institute of Chartered Accountants in England and Wales. 1990. SSAP 25, *Segmental Reporting.* London: ICAEW.

International Accounting Standards Committee. 1997. *IAS 14 Segment Reporting.* London: IASC.

Meek, G. K. and S. J. Gray. 1989. "Globalization of Stock Markets and Foreign Listing Requirements: Voluntary Disclosures by Continental European Companies Listed on the London Stock Exchange," *Journal of International Business Studies* (Summer).

Mohr, R. M. 1983. "The Segment Reporting Issue: A Review of Empirical Research," *Journal of Accounting Research* (Spring).

Nichols, N., D. L. Street, and S. J. Gray. 2000. "Geographical Segment Disclosures in the United States: Reporting Practices Enter a New Era," *Journal of International Accounting, Auditing and Taxation,* 9 (1): 27–63.

Prodhan, B. K. 1986. "Geographical Segment Disclosures and Multinational Risk Profile," *Journal of Business Finance and Accounting* (Spring).

Prodhan, B. K. and M. C. Harris. 1989. "Systematic Risk and the Discretionary Disclosure of Geographical Segments: An Empirical Investigation of U.S. Multinationals," *Journal of Business Finance and Accounting* (Autumn).

Senteney, D. L. and M. S. Bazaz. 1992. "The Impact of SFAS 14 Geographic Segment Disclosures on the Information Content of US-Based MNE's Earnings Release," *International Journal of Accounting* (3).

Radebaugh, Lee H. 1987. *International Aspects of Segment Disclosures: A Conceptual Approach,* Research Monograph No. 2. Glasgow: University of Glasgow.

Roberts, C. B. 1989. "Forecasting Earnings Using Geographical Segment Data: Some U.K. Evidence," *Journal of International Financial Management and Accounting* (Winter).

Roberts, C. B. and S. J. Gray. 1995. "Segmental Reporting," in *Comparative International Accounting,* edited by C. W. Nobes and R. H. Parker. Englewood Cliffs, NJ: Prentice-Hall.

Solomons, David. 1968. "Accounting Problems and Some Proposed Solutions," *Public Reporting by Conglomerates,* edited by A. Rappaport, P. A. Firmin, and S. A. Zeff. Englewood Cliffs, NJ: Prentice-Hall.

Street, D. L., N. Nichols, and S. J. Gray. 2000. "Segment Disclosures Under SFAS 131: Has Business Segment Reporting Improved?" *Accounting Horizons,* 14 (3) (September): 259–85.

Thomas, W. B. 2000. "The Value-relevance of Geographic Segment Earnings Disclosures Under SFAS 14," *Journal of International Financial Management & Accounting,* 11 (3): 133–55.

United Nations. 1988. *Conclusions on Accounting and Reporting by Transnational Corporations.* New York: revised 1994.

CHAPTER NINE

FOREIGN CURRENCY
TRANSACTIONS

Chapter Objectives

- Examine exchange rates and the nature of the foreign exchange market
- Describe the foreign exchange derivatives market, especially in the context of forward contracts, swaps, and options
- Identify the different ways that companies can account for transactions denominated in a foreign currency
- Discuss how companies can account for forward contracts, swaps, and options in the context of foreign currency transactions, commitments, and anticipated future transactions.

INTRODUCTION

In May 2000, the U.S. Federal Reserve raised interest rates by 1/2 percent, the fifth increase in interest rates in less than one year, with promises to raise rates more to combat U.S. inflation. On that news, the U.S. dollar rose against most major currencies, following a trend that had begun in late 1999 and was expected to continue as markets reacted to the relatively higher U.S. interest rates and prospects that financial investments in the United States would be worth more than similar investments in countries with lower interest rates. A big loser was the euro, the new currency of Europe that was introduced on January 1, 1999. The euro had fallen by 23 percent against the dollar since it was introduced, due in part to the fact that a net of $160 billion in capital had fled Europe in 1999 seeking higher returns in the hot U.S. stock market and U.S. economy. But just as the dollar has risen recently against currencies, it can fall as well, and it is likely that the euro will stabilize and recover as it gains more experience in foreign exchange markets and as the dollar weakens.

What does this have to do with accounting? In the next two chapters, we will discuss foreign exchange and its impact on the way companies account for foreign currency transactions and the translation of foreign currency financial statements. In addition, we will look at foreign exchange derivatives and how they can be used to hedge foreign exchange exposures. But first, let's examine exchange rates and their determinants.

FOREIGN EXCHANGE

Basic Markets

Foreign exchange can either be traded "over-the counter" (OTC) or on an exchange. The OTC market is composed of commercial banks, such as Citibank, and investment banks, such as Merrill Lynch. Each OTC trader has a trading room with individuals who specialize in specific currencies. The exchanges where foreign currencies are traded are securities exchanges such as the Philadelphia Stock Exchange, the London International Financial Futures Exchange, and the Chicago Mercantile Exchange, where certain types of foreign exchange instruments, such as futures and options are traded.

The traditional foreign exchange instruments that comprise the bulk of foreign exchange trading are the spot, outright forward, and FX swap markets. Spot transactions involve the exchange of currency the second day after the date on which the two foreign exchange traders agree to the transaction. The rate at which the transaction is settled is the spot rate. Outright forward transactions involve the exchange of currency three or more days after the date on which the traders agree to the transaction. It is the single purchase or sale of a currency for future delivery. The rate at which the transaction is settled is the forward rate and is a contract rate between the two parties. The forward transaction will be settled at the forward rate no matter what the actual spot rate is at the time of settlement. In a FX swap, one currency is swapped for another on one date and then swapped back at a future date. Most often, the first leg of an FX swap is a spot transaction, with the second leg of the swap a future transaction. For example, assume that Toyota (Japan) receives a dividend in U.S. dollars from its subsidiary in the United States but has no use for dollars for another 30 days. Toyota could enter into an FX swap with a Japanese bank where it sells the dollars for yen in the spot market and agrees to buy the dollars with yen in 30 days at the forward rate.

In addition to the traditional foreign exchange instruments, there are other instruments, such as futures and options. Futures are traded on an exchange, whereas options can be traded OTC or on a securities exchange, such as the Philadelphia Stock Exchange. A futures contract is an agreement between two parties to buy or sell a particular currency at a particular price on a particular future date as specified in a standardized contract to all participants in that currency futures exchange. Options are the right but not the obligation to trade foreign currency in the future. All of these instruments that are not considered spot foreign exchange are also known as derivatives. In addition to the foreign exchange derivatives, there are other financial derivatives such as interest rate swaps. However, we will focus only on a few foreign exchange derivatives in this chapter.

Spot Market

Most foreign currency transactions take place with the foreign traders of banks. Therefore, rates are quoted from the trader's perspective. Ordinarily, the trader will offer two quotes—the bid and the offer price of a foreign currency. For example, the quote for British pounds sterling may appear as follows:

$$\$1.5495/05$$

which means that the trader will buy pounds for $1.5495 (bid) and sell pounds for $1.5505 (offer or ask). The difference between the two quotes is the profit margin for the trader.

Exchange rate quotes can be obtained from a number of sources, such as the *Wall Street Journal* (United States) and the *Financial Times* (United Kingdom) and from one of several online services, such as CNN (see the markets section and the currency markets within that section at the following site: http://cnnfn.com). In addition to getting quotes on the Internet, you can also trade on the Internet. Chase Manhattan offers an on-line, real-time Windows-based FX payments and trading system, allowing clients to buy and sell more than 65 currencies, perform cross-currency trades, and purchase currency for forward value dates in a completely automated fashion. Exhibit 9.1 provides the May 16, 2000, rates published

Exhibit 9.1   Currency Trading

CURRENCY TRADING

Tuesday, May 16, 2000

EXCHANGE RATES

The New York foreign exchange mid-range rates below apply to trading among banks in amounts of $1 million and more, as quoted at 4 p.m. Eastern time by Reuters and other sources. Retail transactions provide fewer units of foreign currency per dollar. Rates for the 11 Euro currency countries are derived from the latest dollar-euro rate using the exchange ratios set 1/1/99.

	U.S. $ equiv.		Currency per U.S. $	
Country	Tue	Mon	Tue	Mon
Argentina (Peso)	1.0002	1.0002	.9998	9998
Australia (Dollar)	.5772	.5743	1.7324	1.7414
Austria (Schilling)	.06546	.06626	15.277	15.092
Bahrain (Dinar)	2.6525	2.6525	.3770	.3770
Belgium (Franc)	.0223	.0226	44.7848	44.2445
Brazil (Real)	.5498	.5484	1.8190	1.8235
Britain (Pound)	1.4948	1.5065	.6690	.6638
1-month forward	1.4955	1.5072	.6687	.6635
3-months forward	1.4971	1.5086	.6680	.6629
6-months forward	1.4998	1.5112	.6668	.6617
Canada (Dollar)	.6733	.6726	1.4853	1.4867
1-month forward	.6738	.6731	1.4842	1.4856
3-months forward	.6748	.6741	1.4820	1.4835
6-months forward	.6763	.6756	1.4786	1.4802
Chile (Peso)	.001933	.001931	517.45	517.85
China (Renminbi)	.1208	.1208	8.2772	8.2777
Colombia (Peso)	.0004890	.0004900	2045.00	2041.00
Czech. Rep. (Koruna)				
Commercial rate	.02470	.02467	40.486	40.531

	U.S. $ equiv.		Currency per U.S. $	
Country	Tue	Mon	Tue	Mon
Denmark (Krone)				
Ecuador (Sucre)				
Floating rate	.00004000	.00004000	24999.50	24999.50
Finland (Markka)	.1515	.1533	6.6009	6.5212
France (Franc)	.1373	.1390	7.2823	7.1945
1-month forward	.1376	.1393	7.2669	7.1783
3-months forward	.1382	.1399	7.2379	7.1499
6-months forward	.1390	.1408	7.1917	7.1045
Germany (Mark)	.4606	.4662	2.1713	2.1451
1-month forward	.4615	.4672	2.1667	2.1403
3-months forward	.4634	.4691	2.1581	2.1318
6-months forward	.4664	.4721	2.1443	2.1183
Greece (Drachma)	.002677	.002710	373.52	369.02
Hong Kong (Dollar)	.1284	.1284	7.7902	7.7896
Hungary (Forint)	.003479	.003520	287.44	284.12
India (Rupee)	.02277	.02263	43.925	44.195
Indonesia (Rupiah)	.0001166	.0001151	8575.00	8685.00
Ireland (Punt)	1.1438	1.1577	.8743	.8638
Israel (Shekel)	.2412	.2411	4.1457	4.1483
Italy (Lira)	.0004652	.0004709	2149.62	2123.69
Japan (Yen)	.009120	.009134	109.65	109.48
1-month forward	.009173	.009189	109.01	108.83
3-months forward	.009276	.009290	107.80	107.64
6-months forward	.009446	.009455	105.87	105.76
Jordan (Dinar)	1.4073	1.4085	.7106	.7100
Kuwait (Dinar)	3.2446	3.2499	.3082	.3077
Lebanon (Pound)	.0006627	.0006604	1509.00	1514.25
Malaysia (Ringgit)	.2632	.2632	3.8000	3.8000
Malta (Lira)	2.2528	2.2712	.4439	.4403

(continues)

Exhibit 9.1 (*Continued*)

Country	U.S. $ equiv. Tue	U.S. $ equiv. Mon	Currency per U.S. $ Tue	Currency per U.S. $ Mon	Country	U.S. $ equiv. Tue	U.S. $ equiv. Mon	Currency per U.S. $ Tue	Currency per U.S. $ Mon
Mexico (Peso)					Spain (Peseta)	.005414	.005480	184.72	182.42
Floating rate	.1052	.1049	9.5050	9.5300	Sweden (Krona)	.1097	.1103	9.1144	9.0660
Netherland (Guilder)	.4087	.4137	2.4465	2.4170	Switzerland (Franc)	.5811	.5859	1.7209	1.7069
New Zealand (Dollar)	.4757	.4746	2.1022	2.1070	1-month forward	.5830	.5879	1.7152	1.7010
Norway (Krone)	.1104	.1114	9.0578	8.9794	3-months forward	.5865	.5913	1.7051	1.6912
Pakistan (Rupee)	.01927	.01928	51.898	51.870	6-months forward	.5917	.5966	1.6900	1.6763
Peru (new Sol)	.2855	.2855	3.5025	3.5025	Taiwan (Dollar)	.03248	.3256	30.790	30.710
Philippines (Peso)	.02403	.02405	41.620	41.575	Thailand (Baht)	.02538	.02544	39.395	39.315
Poland (Zloty) (d)	.2254	.2291	4.4370	4.3650	Turkey (Lira)	.00000162	.00000163	618090.00	614940.00
Portugal (Escudo)	.004493	.004548	222.57	219.89	United Arab (Dirham)	.2723	.2723	3.6729	3.6729
Russia (Ruble) (a)	.03537	.03539	28.270	28.260	Uruguay (New Peso)				
Saudi Arabia (Riyal)	.2666	.2666	3.7504	3.7504	Financial	.08365	.08372	11.955	11.945
Singapore (Dollar)	.5770	.5769	1.7330	1.7335	Venezuela (Bolivar)	.001471	.001473	679.61	679.00
Slovak Rep. (Koruna)	.02099	.02125	47.650	47.053	SDR	1.3084	1.3116	.7643	.7624
South Africa (Rand)	.1417	.1416	7.0550	7.0625	Euro	.9008	.9118	1.1101	1.0967
South Korea (Won)	.0008974	.0008969	1114.35	1115.00					

Special Drawing Rights (SDR) are based on exchange rates for the U.S., German, British, French, and Japanese currencies. *Source:* International Monetary Fund.

a-Russian Central Bank rate. Trading band lowered on 8/17/98. b-Government rate. d-Floating rate; trading band suspended on 4/11/00.

Key Currency Cross Rates (Late New York Trading May 16, 2000)

	Dollar	Euro	Pound	SFranc	Guilder	Peso	Yen	Lira	D-Mark	FFranc	CdnDir
Canada	1.4853	1.3380	2.2202	0.8631	.60711	.15627	.01355	.00069	.68406	.20396	...
France	7.2823	6.5599	10.8856	4.2317	2.9766	.76615	.06641	.00339	3.3539	...	4.9029
Germany	2.1713	1.9559	3.2457	1.2617	.88751	.22844	.01980	.00101	...	.29816	1.4619
Italy	2149.6	1936.4	3213.2	1249.1	878.65	226.16	19.604	...	990.01	295.18	1447.3
Japan	109.65	98.77	163.90	63.717	44.819	11.536	...	.05101	50.500	15.057	73.823
Mexico	9.5050	8.5621	14.208	5.5233	3.8851	...	.08668	.00442	4.3776	1.3052	6.3994
Netherlands	2.4465	2.2038	3.6570	1.4216	...	.25739	.02231	.00114	1.1267	.33595	1.6471
Switzerland	1.7209	1.5502	2.5724	...	.70341	.18105	.01569	.00080	.79257	.23631	1.1586
U.K.	.66900	.6026	...	.3887	.27345	.07038	.00610	.00031	.30810	.09186	.45040
Euro	1.11010	...	1.6594	.64508	.45376	.11679	.01012	.00052	.51127	.15244	.74741
U.S.	...	.9008	1.4948	.58109	.40875	.10521	.00912	.00047	.46055	.13732	.67326

Source: Reuters

Source: Wall Street Journal, May 17, 2000, pp. C16 and C22.

in the *Wall Street Journal.* Two different rates are quoted for each day. The first two columns contain a direct quote (also referred to as "U.S. terms"), which is the amount of local currency equivalent (in this case U.S. dollars) to one unit of the foreign currency. The second two columns contain an indirect quote (also referred to as "European terms"), which is the amount of foreign currency required for one unit of the local currency. For example, in Exhibit 9.1 the exchange rate for U.S. dollars and Italian lira is as follows:

$.0004652 per lira (direct) or

ItL12149.62 per U.S. dollar (indirect)

Our discussion thus far has centered on exchange rates between the U.S. dollar and other currencies. Rates are generally quoted this way because most foreign currency transactions take place in dollars, even when two currencies other than the dollar are directly involved. For example, a Mexican company selling goods to a Swiss company may denominate the sale in dollars such that the Swiss importer converts francs into dollars, and the Mexican exporter converts dollars into pesos. The exchange rate between the peso and the Swiss franc is called a cross rate, the rate between two nonquoted (in this case two nondollar) currencies.

Cross Rates

When discussing exchange rates from a U.S. perspective, a cross rate is the relationship between two nondollar currencies. For example, the number of deutsche marks per British pound would be considered a cross rate. One way to determine the cross rate is to divide the deutsche mark indirect quote by the British pound indirect quote from the spot rate quotes in Exhibit 9.1 (2.1713/.6690 = 3.2456 deutsche marks per pound). Another way is to use the cross rate table found at the bottom of Exhibit 9.1. The cell where the Germany row intersects the pound column is the cross rate for deutsche marks per pound. The cross rate is helpful for countries that trade significantly with each other, such as Germany and the United Kingdom or France.

Outright Forward Market

A forward contract is a contract between a foreign currency trader and client for future sale or purchase of foreign currency. The forward contract is a derivative because its future value is based on the current spot exchange rate. During a period of foreign exchange stability, there may be relatively little difference between the current spot and forward rate. In Exhibit 9.1, for example, forward rates are quoted for several currencies. The London *Financial Times* quotes forward rates for far more currencies than does the *Wall Street Journal* and is thus a good source to consult for other rates. In addition, it provides quotes in terms of British pounds and in terms of U.S. dollars. In the *Wall Street Journal,* the spot rates are given for midrange rates (the average of the buy and sell rates) that apply to trading among banks in amounts of $1 million or more, as quoted at 4:00 P.M. Eastern time. However, the *Financial Times* provides the mid-rate (the average of the buy and sell rate) at the close of the trading day in London and also provides the bid/offer spread at that time. The spot and 90-day forward rates quoted for pounds in the *Wall Street Journal* are as follows:

	British Pounds
90-day forward	$1.4971
Spot	1.4948
Points	+ 23

The spread in pounds is +.0023 or 23 points. Because the forward rate is greater than the spot rate, the pound is selling at a premium of 23 points. If the forward rate had been less than the spot rate, the pound would have been selling at a discount in the forward market.

The premium or discount is normally quoted at the number of points above or below the spot rate, but it could also be expressed in annualized percentage terms. The formula used to determine the percentage is as follows:

$$\text{Premium (discount)} = \frac{F_o - S_o}{S_o} \times \frac{12}{N} \times 100$$

where F_o is the forward rate on the day that the contract is entered into, S_o is the spot rate on that day, N is the number of months forward, and 100 is used to convert the decimal to percentage amounts (i.e., $0.05 \times 100 = 5\%$).

Using the British pound example,

$$\text{Premium} = \frac{1.4971 - 1.4948}{1.4948} \times \frac{12}{3} \times 100 = .15\%$$

which means that the pound sterling is selling at a .15 percent premium over the dollar spot rate, which is a very small premium.

Swaps

One of the fastest growing and most popular derivatives of foreign exchange is the swap. A swap is a simultaneous spot and forward transaction. For example, assume that a U.S. company has just received a dividend from a French subsidiary, but it has no use for the French francs for 30 days. It could take the French francs and deposit them in a French bank for 30 days to earn interest, or it could enter into a swap transaction. In a swap, the U.S. company would take the French francs to its bank and convert them into U.S. dollars to use for 30 days in the United States. At the same time, it would enter into a forward contract with the bank to deliver dollars in 30 days in exchange for French francs at the forward exchange rate.

A variation on the spot/forward swap is a foreign currency swap that is entered into because of interest rate differentials. To illustrate this type of swap, suppose that a Japanese company would like to borrow floating-rate (a floating-rate note, or FRN) U.S. dollars to finance a foreign investment in the United States, but the company is not very well known outside Japan. Also, suppose that a U.S. company would like to borrow fixed-rate Japanese yen to fund an investment in Japan but is also not well known in Japan. A financial intermediary, such as an investment bank, could put the two companies together through a currency swap. The Japanese company issues a fixed-rate yen bond, turns the yen proceeds over to the U.S. company, and agrees to pay the U.S. company its dollar coupon on principal obligations on a U.S. dollar FRN that the U.S. company would issue. In addition, the U.S. company would turn the proceeds of the dollar FRN over to the Japanese company. At the end of the swap agreement, the Japanese company would return the dollars to the U.S. company, and the U.S. company would return the yen to the Japanese company. The swap exchange rate is the rate at which the two companies agree to exchange yen for dollars.

Options

Another derivative is an option, which is the right but not the obligation to trade foreign currency at a given exchange rate on or before a given date in the future.

Options can be traded on an exchange, such as the Philadelphia Stock Exchange, or with financial intermediary, such as an investment banker like Goldman Sachs.

There are two parties to an option, the writer of the option and the holder of the option. The writer of the option sells the option, and the holder of the option buys the option from the writer. The holder has the power to exercise or execute the option, that is, to elect to make the exchange made possible by the option. The holder of the option must pay an up-front fee (premium) to the writer of option, but it is the holder, not the writer, that determines whether or not the option will be exercised.

An option can be either a put option or a call option. A put option gives the holder the right to sell foreign currency to the writer of the option, and a call option gives the holder the right to buy foreign currency from the writer of the option.

The cost of the option is composed of a premium and a brokerage fee. The premium must be paid by the holder to the writer of the option as soon as the option is entered into, and no refund of the premium is given to the holder if the option is not exercised. The premium is like an insurance premium—you pay it whether you collect or not. If the option is written on an exchange, such as the Philadelphia Stock Exchange, a fee must be paid to the stockbroker at the time the option is entered into and must also be paid if the option is exercised.

To illustrate the cost of an option, assume that a U.S. company enters into a **put** option on June 1 on the Philadelphia Stock Exchange to sell Japanese yen (¥) for dollars on September 30. Assume that the yen is trading at $0.009251 per yen on June 1 or 108.10 per dollar, and that the size of the options contract is ¥6,250,000 or $57,819 at the spot rate on June 1. Also, assume that the strike price, the price at which the option will be settled, is 93 or $0.0093 per yen (¥107.53 per dollar) and that the premium is $0.000179 per yen.

In addition to the premium, there is also a brokerage fee for entering into an exchange-traded contract. If the holder exercises the option, there is another brokerage fee charged at the exercise date. Although there is no set brokerage fee, we assume for our example that the cost is $25 per contract. If we need to sell ¥100 million, we need to buy 16 contracts of ¥6,250,000 each (¥100 million/6,250,000 = 16). For a strike price of 93, each contract would cost

$$¥6,250,000 \times \$0.000179 = \$1,118.75$$

Brokerage cost   =   25.00

Total $1,143.75

For 16 contracts, the total cost is $1,143.75 × 16 = $18,300. This means that if we want to hold a put contract to sell ¥100 million at a strike price of 93, it will cost $18,300. If we decide to exercise the option, it will cost an additional $400 (16 × $25), and we will receive $930,000 for our ¥100 million. By the expiration date in September, we need to decide whether or not to exercise the option. If the spot rate on the expiration date is equal to the strike price ($0.0093), the option is considered to be "at-the-money," and we do not need to exercise the option. Thus we will walk away from the premium of $18,300, but we do not have to pay the addition $400. If the spot rate on the expiration date is greater than $0.0093, the yen would be stronger against the dollar than at the strike price, and we would receive more dollars for ¥100 million than if we exercised the option. Therefore, the option is considered "out-of-the-money" because the strike price is unfavorable relative to the market price.

For example, if the spot rate at the exercise date in September were $0.0098, we would not exercise the option, and we would receive the following amount of yen:

$$¥100,000,000 \times \$0.0098 = \$980,000$$

which is greater than the $930,000 at the strike price. Since the premium and initial brokerage expense are sunk costs, they do not factor into the decision on whether or not to exercise the option.

On the other hand, if the spot rate were less than $0.0093, the yen would be weaker against the dollar than at the strike price, and we would receive fewer dollars from the yen than if we exercised the option. Therefore, the option is considered to be "in-the-money" because the strike price is favorable relative to the market price, and we would exercise the option.

Therefore, the option sets a lower limit on what will be received for the ¥100 million. If the spot at the end of September were $0.0090, we would exercise the option and incur another brokerage cost, and we would receive the following for the yen:

$$¥100,000,000 \times \$0.0093 \quad = \$930,000$$
$$\text{Brokerage cost to exercise} = \underline{\quad -400}$$
$$\text{Total proceeds} \qquad\qquad = \$929,600$$

Of course, we also paid a premium of $18,300, so our net proceeds would be $911,300. Without the option, we would have received $900,000, which is still less than the net proceeds above. The weaker the yen becomes against the dollar, the better the option looks. Thus, the option ensures that the least we will ever receive for the yen is $911,300 ($929,600 less the initial brokerage cost and premium of $18,300), an effective exchange rate of $0.009113 (¥109.7 per dollar).

Foreign Exchange Markets

Foreign exchange is traded 24 hours a day around the world by a variety of institutions. According to a Central Bank survey of foreign exchange market activity by the Bank for International Settlements in Basel, Switzerland, global net turnover of foreign exchange is estimated to be $1.5 trillion per business day.

Foreign exchange is traded among banks in the interbank market, through foreign exchange brokers, through securities brokers on different securities exchanges, and over the counter by nonbank financial institutions, such as investment banks. The interbank market is the most important market in trading foreign exchange.

In addition to dealing directly with each other, banks also deal indirectly with each other through specialists called foreign exchange brokers. For example, if a bank were holding British pounds ("long in pounds") and they wanted to sell the pounds, they could contact a broker who would find a bank willing to buy the pounds. Traders execute about 40 to 50 percent of their trades with other banks through computers, another 10 percent through telephones, and the remaining 30 to 40 percent through brokers. The most significant change in trading activity is the movement to more computer-based trades as banks begin to link together to facilitate trading.

Outside of bank trades, foreign exchange is also traded through specialized markets such as the International Monetary Market of the Chicago Mercantile Exchange, the London International Financial Futures Exchange, and the Philadelphia Stock Exchange. The listed exchanges tend to specialize in derivatives such as futures and options, and one must deal through a securities broker to effect the trades. The brokers make deals on the exchange floor rather than over the telephone. In contrast, the over-the-counter market involves investment banks such as Goldman Sachs and Bankers Trust and is a rapidly growing source of derivatives for the corporate customer.

The most widely traded currency in the world is the U.S. dollar, which figures on one side of 87 percent of net reported turnover (each currency trade involves two currencies). However, the dollar is more important in some currency trades (such as the Canadian dollar, Australian dollar, and Japanese yen) than in others (such as the European currencies). As we noted earlier, each currency trade is a pair, involving two currencies. Seven of the 10 largest currency pairs involve the U.S. dollar. The top two are the dollar/deutsche mark (20.2 percent of total trades), the dollar/yen (18.5 percent). The world's dominant currencies are the U.S. dollar, the deutsche mark, and the yen. That should change with the introduction of the euro, because the deutsche mark is only one of the currencies that make up the euro. Thus the dollar/euro pair should rise in importance relative to the dollar/yen pair.

As Figure 9.1 shows, the most important countries in which foreign exchange is traded are the United Kingdom, the United States, and Japan. However, other significant markets are Singapore, Switzerland, Hong Kong, and Germany. It is interesting to note the importance of London as a trading center, even though the

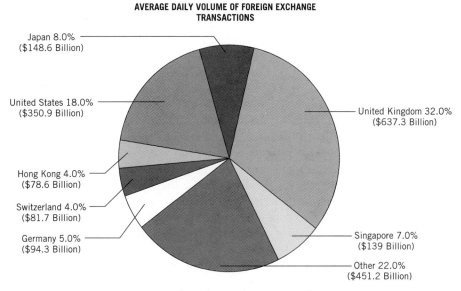

Figure 9.1 Average Daily Volume of Foreign Exchange Transactions

Source: Bank for International Settlements. *Central Bank Summary of Foreign Exchange Market Activity* (Basel:BIS, March 1993), p. 14.

British pound is not a dominant trading currency like the dollar, deutsche mark, or yen. However, more dollars and deutsche marks are traded in London than are British pounds, and more of those currencies are traded in London than in their home markets.

Currency Convertibility

Not all currencies are convertible—or exchangeable—into another currency. Convertible currencies are typically strong or relatively stable in value in comparison with other currencies, and their value tends to be set by market forces, which are relatively independent of direct government intervention. Countries with weak currencies whose values are artificially maintained by government intervention tend to have black markets where the value is set more by market forces than by government fiat.

Nonconvertible currencies tend to have trading restrictions and government controls. For example, a government may require that firms wanting to gain access to foreign exchange get a government license for that privilege. That way the government can decide what it wants to use scarce foreign exchange for and can ration its use. Governments may also establish multiple exchange rates where one rate is used for one transaction and another for another transaction. For example, the exchange rate on luxury items may be much higher than for essentials, requiring the importer to come up with more local currency to get the foreign exchange.

The International Monetary System

Although foreign currencies are traded quite freely, there is a form of supranational influence that tries to encourage a certain amount of order. The International Monetary Fund (IMF) was created in 1944 with the primary objective of promoting exchange stability. At that time, the currencies of 133 member countries were assigned a fixed exchange rate or par value based on gold and the U.S. dollar; gold was worth $35 an ounce, and currencies were quoted on that basis. Currencies were allowed to float freely in a band of 1 percent on either side of par value. However, stability did not last forever. Countries like Brazil were constantly devaluing their currency—permanently decreasing the par value in terms of gold and the dollar. Others were experiencing periodic changes, such as the British pound in 1967. But the major trading currencies were still adhering fairly well to par values. In December 1971, after significant pressure against the U.S. dollar, the IMF allowed the U.S. dollar to formally devalue and also allowed currencies to float $2\frac{1}{4}$ percent on either side of par value without a formal devaluation or revaluation.

Continued pressure on the dollar in early 1973 forced another devaluation, and subsequent instability finally forced the major trading countries of the world to break loose from the fixed rate system for one of greater flexibility.

Exchange Rate Arrangements   As part of the move to greater flexibility, the IMF permitted countries to select and maintain an exchange arrangement of their choice, as long as they properly communicated their arrangement to the fund.

Each year, the fund receives information from the member countries and classifies each country into one of several categories. In several of the categories, countries lock the value of their currency onto another currency and allow the currency to vary by plus or minus 1 percent against that value. Several currencies in Latin America have dollarized their currencies by locking them onto the dollar. Similarly, several countries in Africa have locked their currencies onto the French franc. A few countries follow the same procedure as described above but allow their currencies to vary by $2\frac{1}{4}$ percent instead of only 1 percent.

Another large group of countries adopt a free float or a managed float. In both cases, market forces basically set the value of the currency. In the case of the managed float, the government intervenes to influence the value of the currency, but in the context of market forces.

Government Intervention   Although exchange rates change on the basis of supply and demand, governments try to influence rates. In 1999, the Japanese yen began to strengthen dramatically against the U.S. dollar, which forced the Central Bank of Japan to intervene in currency markets to drive down the yen against the dollar. In July 1999, the Bank of Japan tried to convince the U.S. Treasury to endorse its policy of intervention to weaken the yen, but Treasury was not interested, believing that sound economic policy rather than intervention would lead to an appropriate exchange rate. Coordination of central bank intervention can take place on a bilateral or multilateral basis. The preceding example illustrated an attempted bilateral negotiation. Multilateral coordination will take place in the European Union as the euro Central Banks meet to determine intervention policies with the rest of the world.

The Determination of Exchange Rates

There are a variety of political and economic factors that affect exchange rates and their relative values, and among the most important are the following:

- purchasing power parity
- interest rates
- trade balance
- capital flows
- foreign exchange reserves
- economic growth and employment
- confidence—political and economic
- government reactions
  - domestic versus international concerns
  - intervention in foreign exchange markets

Purchasing power parity (PPP) refers to relative prices in one country versus those of another. According to PPP, a change in relative inflation must result in a change in exchange rates in order to keep the prices of goods in two countries fairly similar. In essence, the exchange rate should make the cost of a product the same in one country as it is in another, taking into consideration transportation costs. However, PPP is more useful as a long-run indicator of exchange rate differences than it is a short-term predictor of exchange rates. Country A with a higher rate of inflation should have a weakening currency or consumers in Country B would never buy products from Country A. Conversely, countries with relatively low rates of inflation should have a stronger currency.

The Big Mac index published each year by *The Economist* is a good example of purchasing power parity. Exhibit 9.2 shows how the price of a Big Mac can be used to estimate the exchange rate between the dollar and another currency. Since the Big Mac is sold in more than 100 countries, it is easy to compare prices. PPP suggests that the exchange rate should leave hamburgers costing the same in the United States as abroad. However, sometimes the Big Mac costs more, and sometimes it costs less, demonstrating how far currencies are under- or overvalued against the dollar. Looking at Exhibit 9.2, in 2000, a Big Mac cost an average of $2.51 in the United States and FFr18.50 in France. Dividing the franc price of the Big Mac by the dollar price of the Big Mac yields a purchasing power exchange rate of FFr7.37 per dollar. However, the actual exchange rate was FFr7.07, so the franc was overvalued against the dollar by 4 percent. Based on the actual exchange rate, the Big Mac costs $2.62 in France, so Big Macs are not a big bargain in France. At the same time that the franc was overvalued against the dollar, many other currencies, such as the Chinese yuan and Brazilian real were undervalued against the dollar.

Interest rates in two countries are related to each other through inflation and exchange rate differences. According to the Fisher Effect, if the nominal interest rate in Country A is lower than that in Country B, Country A's inflation is expected to be lower so real interest rates are equal. Taking that one step further, the country with the higher nominal interest rate should have a higher rate of inflation, so its currency would be expected to weaken in the future against the low-interest-rate (and therefore low-inflation) country. However, this gets complicated in practice in that there is no universal understanding about what the real rate of interest should be worldwide. As a result, interest rate differentials also involve investors' perceptions of potential returns.

The trade balance between two countries, such as the United States and Japan, can also affect exchange rates. The balance of payments of a country summarizes all international transactions between domestic residents and foreign residents. Transactions are separated into a current account and a capital account. The current account includes merchandise trade, services trade, and unilateral transfers (such as foreign aid that one country sends another without expecting a reciprocal transaction). The capital account includes private and government short-term and long-term capital flows. In the case of the United States, the trade deficit in 1999 was huge, especially with Japan. Partly as a result of the trade deficit with Japan, the dollar remained weak against the yen over much of 1999 and early 2000, even though it was strong agaist most other countries in the world.

Capital flows are a part of the balance of payments and reflect investment decisions by private and government investors. When the United States was suffering a balance-of-trade deficit in the late 1990s, a number of foreigners invested funds in the United States by investing in U.S. companies, starting up new companies, or purchasing U.S. treasury bills. This large inflow of capital helped to strengthen the dollar.

Exhibit 9.2   The Big Mac Index

The Golden-Arches Standard

	Big Mac Prices		Implied PPP[a] of the Dollar	Actual $ Exchange Rate 25/04/00	Under (−)/ Over (+) Valuation Against the Dollar, %
	In Local Currency	In Dollars			
United States[b]	$2.51	2.51	−	−	−
Argentina	Peso2.50	2.50	1.00	1.00	0
Australia	A$2.59	1.54	1.03	1.68	−38
Brazil	Real2.95	1.65	1.18	1.79	−34
Britain	£1.90	3.00	1.32[c]	1.58[c]	+20
Canada	C$2.85	1.94	1.14	1.47	−23
Chile	Peso1,260	2.45	502	514	−2
China	Yuan9.90	1.20	3.94	8.28	−52
Czech Rep	Koruna54.37	1.39	21.7	39.1	−45
Denmark	DKr24.75	3.08	9.86	8.04	+23
Euro area	#eu2.56	2.37	0.98[d]	0.93[d]	−5
France	FFr18.50	2.62	7.37	7.07	+4
Germany	DM4.99	2.37	1.99	2.11	−6
Italy	Lire4,500	2.16	1,793	2,088	−14
Spain	Pta375	2.09	149	179	−17
Hong Kong	HK$10.20	1.31	4.06	7.79	−48
Hungary	Forint339	1.21	135	279	−52
Indonesia	Rupiah14,500	1.83	5,777	7,945	−27
Israel	Shekel14.5	3.58	5.78	4.05	+43
Japan	¥294	2.78	117	106	+11
Malaysia	M$4.52	1.19	1.80	3.80	−53
Mexico	Peso20.90	2.22	8.33	9.41	−11
New Zealand	NZ$3.40	1.69	1.35	2.01	−33
Poland	Zloty5.50	1.28	2.19	4.30	−49
Russia	Rouble39.50	1.39	15.7	28.5	−45
Singapore	S$3.20	1.88	1.27	1.70	−25
South Africa	Rand9.00	1.34	3.59	6.72	−47
South Korea	Won3,000	2.71	1,195	1,108	+8
Sweden	SKr24.00	2.71	9.56	8.84	+8
Switzerland	SFr5.90	3.48	2.35	1.70	+39
Taiwan	NT$70.00	2.29	27.9	30.6	−9
Thailand	Baht55.00	1.45	21.9	38.0	−42

Source: "Big MacCurrencies," *The Economist,* April 29, 2000, p. 75.

[a]Purchasing-power parity: local price divided by price in the United States.

[b]Average of New York, Chicago, San Francisco, and Atlanta.

[c]Dollars per pound.

[d]Dollars per euro.

Foreign exchange reserves also flow from balance-of-payments transactions. The balance of payments reflects flows in a given year, whereas foreign exchange reserves reflect the balance of reserves at a given time.

Economic growth and employment affect exchange rates in two different ways. In 1999 and early 2000, the strong U.S. economy was attracting a lot of capital from abroad, which helped to strengthen the U.S. dollar. However, the strong economy also resulted in record levels of imports, which led to a worsening of the balance of payments and pressure on the dollar.

We have discussed the confidence factor, especially on the economic side, earlier. However, political confidence can also affect the exchange rate. In late 1989, the Japanese stock market began to decline, and inflationary pressures began to rise, putting downward pressure on the Japanese yen. In early 1990, there was open debate between the Ministry of Finance of Japan and the Bank of Tokyo over what the interest rate policy should be. That debate drove the stock market down even further and shook investors' confidence in the Japanese government's ability to manage the economy and therefore the exchange rate, pushing down the yen even more. In the Mexican case, political assassinations and civil unrest in the state of Chiapas, Mexico, in 1994 led to a lack of confidence in the new government's ability to retain political control. That instability, coupled with the balance-of-payments and foreign exchange reserves problems, resulted in the December 1994 devaluation of the peso.

Government reactions to different events can also affect exchange rates. When the Brazilian government decided to put the clamp on inflation in June 1994, the real (the name of the Brazilian currency) stabilized and actually strengthened against the U.S. dollar. Black market dealers who had previously preferred to hold dollars as a hedge against inflation suddenly were unloading their dollars in favor of the stronger real. In 1995 when the U.S. dollar fell against the deutsche mark and yen, there was significant pressure on the U.S. government to raise interest rates to support the dollar, but President Clinton was concerned about the domestic economy and did not want to raise interest rates and run the risk of starting a recession, especially so close to an election year. Finally, as we discussed earlier, governments can directly intervene in currency markets.

FOREIGN CURRENCY TRANSACTIONS

Conceptual Issues

Foreign currency transactions are transactions denominated in a currency other than the reporting currency of the firm. The reporting currency is the currency in which the firm's financial statements are issued. For example, a sale by a U.S. firm to a Canadian firm for which payment is to be received in Canadian dollars is considered to be a foreign currency transaction for the U.S. firm. If the payment is to be received in U.S. dollars, the transaction would not be a foreign currency transaction for the U.S. firm, even though the buyer is not a U.S. firm. Foreign currency transactions may involve the buying and selling of goods and services, the borrowing or lending of funds, or the receipt or payment of dividends.

No accounting problem arises as long as the transactions are denominated in the firm's domestic currency. However, when a transaction is denominated in a foreign currency, the firm needs to resolve four accounting problems:

- the initial recording of the transaction
- the recording of foreign currency balances at subsequent balance sheet dates
- the treatment of any foreign exchange gains and losses, and
- the recording of the settlement of foreign currency receivables and payables when they come due

Any foreign currency transaction has two components: the monetary component and the nonmonetary component. In the case of the purchase of equipment, the monetary component would be cash or accounts payable, and the nonmonetary component would be the equipment.

There are many different combinations involved in the solution of these four problems, but we will identify a few of the major combinations as illustrated in the purchase of equipment:

1.   Two transactions, recognize gains and losses
2.   Two transactions, defer gains and losses
3.   One transaction, recognize gains and losses

The first approach is the most common, and it involves recording the equipment and accounts payable amounts at the spot rate on the transaction date. The philosophy is that the transaction is divided into two parts: (1) the purchase of the equipment and (2) the decision to finance through an accounts payable rather than by paying cash immediately. At subsequent balance sheet dates, the equipment remains at its historical cost, but the accounts payable value changes to reflect the new spot rate. Any difference between the previous and new spot rate is a gain or loss recognized in the current accounting period. The assumption under this approach is that the gain or loss should be reflected in the period in which the exchange rate change occurs rather than be deferred to future periods. Also, a change in the liability value should be reflected as a financing decision, much like interest expense, rather than affect the value of the equipment.

The second approach differs from the first in that the gain or loss is deferred until the liability is finally settled. Thus, the gain or loss is recognized only at the settlement date. The assumption is that exchange rates move up and down, so it is best to wait until the settlement date to reflect the net gain or loss rather than have unrealized gains in one period eliminated by losses in the next.

In the third approach, the equipment and accounts payable accounts are intertwined. A change in one account is reflected by a change in the other. If the liability increases in value as the exchange rate changes, the equipment account would also increase. The loss arising from the increased value of the liability is reflected by a higher asset value that will be depreciated over the life of the asset rather than in the period in which the exchange rate changes.

International Accounting Standards

The first time the IASC dealt with foreign exchange issues was in International Accounting Standard 21 (IAS 21), *Accounting for the Effects of Changes in Foreign Exchange Rates,* which was issued in March 1983. IAS 21 provided more options for accounting for foreign currency transactions than did comparable U.S. standards. However, IAS 21 was revised in 1993 as part of the IASC's Comparability of Financial Statements project and is effective for financial statements covering periods beginning on or after January 1, 1995. As is the case with most standards around the world, IAS 21 requires transactions to be initially recorded at the spot rate on the date of the transaction. At subsequent balance sheet dates, monetary items should be recorded at the closing rate (the same as the spot rate on the balance sheet date, known as the "current rate" in U.S. terminology), nonmonetary items carried at historical cost should be recorded at the historical exchange rate (the spot rate in effect when the transaction was initially recorded), and nonmonetary items carried at fair value should be recorded at the rate in effect when the fair values were determined.

The major departure in IAS 21 from U.K. and U.S. standards comes in the recognition of foreign exchange gains and losses. The preferred IASC treatment for exchange differences arising from the settlement of monetary items or from reporting monetary items at rates different from those at which they were initially recorded during the period should be to recognize them as income or as expenses in the period in which they arise. However, IAS 21 also has an alternative treatment for exchange differences.

> Exchange differences may result from a severe devaluation or depreciation of a currency against which there is no practical means of hedging and that affects liabilities which cannot be settled and which arise directly on the recent acquisition of an asset invoiced in a foreign currency. Such exchange differences should be included in the carrying amount of the related asset, provided that the adjusted carrying amount does not exceed the lower of the replacement cost and the amount recoverable from the sale or use of the asset.

The alternative treatment allowed for exchange differences resulting from a severe devaluation of a currency is clearly a response to the needs of the developing countries that have weak currencies and that purchase much of their capital equipment in hard currencies. However the alternative treatment identifies six limitations on its use:

- The enterprise must not report in the currency of a hyperinflationary economy.
- The exchange difference must arise from a severe devaluation or depreciation of a currency. This is something significant and unexpected, not merely continued erosion of a currency.
- There must be no practical means of hedging against this devaluation or depreciation. There may be no forwards or futures available for the currencies involved. Also, impractical does not mean impossible. If hedging is possible only at an uneconomic cost, it may be considered impractical.
- It is not presently possible to settle the liability involved.
- The acquisition of the assets must have been recent. "Recent" is not defined, but it is obviously not appropriate to continue deferring exchange differences indefinitely on the liability.
- The amount deferred should not result in the adjusted carrying amount of the asset exceeding the lower of replacement cost and recoverable amount.

It is clear that the alternative treatment, while available, it not easy to qualify for. Whereas the alternative treatment is permitted in some countries, it is not allowed in others, such as the United States, Canada, Australia, Japan, and several European countries.

Comparative National Differences

The accounting standard under which the United States operates for the purposes of accounting for foreign currency is the Statement of Financial Accounting Standards No. 52, *Foreign Currency Translation,* issued by the Financial Accounting Standards Board (FASB) in December 1981. The approach required by Statement 52 is the two transactions perspective, where the underlying asset is carried at its historical cost, and the gain or loss arising from the change in value of the monetary item is taken directly to income in the period in which it occurs.

The Canadian approach is similar to the first approach. However, in the case of long-term items, the resulting gains or losses are deferred and amortized over the term of the underlying transaction (such as the purchase of a fixed asset).

The Japanese approach is similar to the first approach. However, long-term assets and liabilities are carried at the exchange rate in effect at the transaction date. That results in deferring gains or losses on the monetary items until the date they are settled.

The French take a relatively conservative approach. It is common to recognize foreign exchange losses, but gains are deferred until the settlement date. Companies have more flexibility than do U.S. companies in that they have the option to recognize gains and losses currently or defer and amortize them over the life of the underlying transaction.

The Germans are similar to the French in that foreign exchange losses are recognized. If the change in value due to the new exchange rate results in a gain, the Germans tend to carry the items at the historical exchange rate rather than value them at the new exchange rate. This has the effect of deferring the gains until the receivable or payable is settled.

In May 1983, the Accounting Standards Committee of the United Kingdom issued Statement of Standard Accounting Practice 20 (SSAP 20), *Foreign Currency Translation.* SSAP 20 is quite similar to the first approach in the way it deals with foreign currency transactions and thus is similar to what is practiced in the United States. However, it does permit the deferral and write-off of gains and losses that arise from long-term monetary items, which is similar to the Canadian practice.

Illustration: Accounting for Sales and Purchases Denominated in a Foreign Currency

The following entries illustrate the method required by the two transactions approach, the one most commonly used, including the preferred method in IAS 21 and the required method in FASB Statement 52. Assume that a U.S. firm imports equipment from Germany on March 1 for DM1 million when the exchange rate is $.4700 per deutsche mark. Payment in DM does not have to be made until April 30.

Assume that on March 31, the exchange rate is $.4800 and on April 30 is $.4750. Also, assume that the firm's books are closed at the end of the calendar quarter.

March 1	Purchases	470,000	
	Accounts payable		470,000
	DM1,000,000 × .4700		
March 31	Foreign exchange loss	10,000	
	Accounts payable		10,000
	1,000,000 (.4800 − .4700)		
April 30	Accounts payable	480,000	
	Foreign exchange gain		5,000
	Cash		475,000

Under the second approach described earlier, gains and losses are deferred instead of recognized in the period in which they occur. Thus the foreign exchange loss of $10,000 on March 31 would be a deferred loss and would be netted with the gain on April 30 so that a net foreign exchange loss of $5,000 would be recognized on April 30, the date that the liability is liquidated. However, purchases still remain at $470,000, and the amount of cash paid is $475,000.

Under the third approach described earlier, any increase or decrease in accounts payable adjusts the purchases account. On March 31, purchases would be increased by $10,000 instead of foreign exchange loss, and on April 30, purchases would be reduced by $5,000 instead of foreign exchange gain. Thus purchases would end up being $475,000 instead of $470,000. However, the amount of cash paid would still be $475,000—the same in all three situations.

Thus the approach you use determines the timing of the foreign exchange gain or loss and whether it appears as an adjustment to purchases—and therefore cost of goods sold—or period expenses in "other income/other expenses" on the income statement.

Accounting for the purchase of fixed assets is similar to that described and illustrated previously. The difference is that if the foreign exchange gain or loss becomes part of the base value of the asset (the third alternative described in the conceptual issues section and permitted as an alternative treatment by IAS 21), depreciation expense will change to reflect the new asset base.

Using the same information provided previously but assuming a sale instead of a purchase, the journal entries would be as follows according to Statement 52 and IAS 21:

March 1	Accounts receivable	470,000	
	Sales revenues		470,000
March 31	Accounts receivable	10,000	
	Foreign exchange gain		10,000
April 30	Cash	475,000	
	Foreign exchange loss	10,000	
	Accounts receivable		480,000

Illustration: Accounting for Debt Incurred in a Foreign Currency

Due to interest rate availability or other factors, a firm may incur debt in a foreign currency with an obligation to repay principal and interest in the foreign currency. The general rules applied above apply here as well: the debt is initially recorded in dollars (assume a U.S.-based company for purposes of illustration) at the spot rate. At subsequent balance sheet dates, the debt must be restated into dollars at the new exchange rate, and any resulting foreign exchange gain or loss must be recorded in the income statement immediately. The challenge becomes the payment of interest expense, which we will assume is paid every six months for the sake of illustration. Since interest expense accrues over a period of time but is paid on a specific date, a foreign exchange gain or loss could arise from the difference between the exchange rate on the payment date and the average exchange rate over the period during which interest accrues. The following entries illustrate how to account for principal and interest.

On January 1, assume that a U.S. firm borrows 2 million Swiss francs (SwFr) for five years at 3 percent interest paid semiannually in Swiss francs. The principal does not have to be repaid until the end of the loan. Assume also that the loan is adjusted for any exchange rate change every six months. Assume the following exchange rates for the first year:

January 1	$.5800
June 30	$.5850
December 31	$.5840

The average exchange rate for the first six months was $.5825 and for the second six months was $.5860. The Swiss franc rose sharply at the end of the year after having fallen to a low of $.5900 in November. Using this information, the journal entries for the first six months would be as follows:

January 1	Cash	1,160,000	
	Notes payable		1,160,000
June 30	Foreign exchange loss	10,000	
	Notes payable		10,000
	(SwFr.5850–.5800) × SwFr 2million		
	Interest expense	17,475	
	Foreign exchange loss	75	
	Cash		17,550
	SwFr2,000,000 × (.03/2) = 30,000 × .5825 = $17,475		
	SwFr30,000 × .5850 = $17,550		
December 31	Notes payable	2,000	
	Foreign exchange gain		2,000
	(SwFr.5850–.5840) × SwFr2million		
December 31	Interest expense	17,580	
	Cash		17,520
	Foreign exchange gain		60
	SwFr30,000 × .5860 = $17,580		
	SwFr30,000 × .5840 = $17,520		

Notice that the average exchange rate is used to compute the interest expense and that the foreign exchange gain or loss is the difference between the interest expense and the cash actually paid in interest.

Hedging Strategies and Accounting for Derivatives

As illustrated in the previous examples, a firm can incur a foreign exchange loss as the exchange rate changes. For that reason, firms may choose to hedge or protect a foreign currency exposure against possible future loss. Of course, a foreign currency transaction can also result in a gain, but a firm may still enter into a hedging strategy to stabilize its future cash flows, even though that may result in forgoing a potential foreign exchange gain. The problem is that it is impossible to forecast future currency movements, so a hedge stabilizes cash flows and allows a firm to engage in foreign currency transactions with the assurance that it can protect its cash flows at a level that makes sense to do business.

Firms can use a variety of derivative financial instruments, such as forward contracts, swaps, and options, to hedge an exposure, and there are unique ways to account for them depending on the nature of the derivative and what it is used for. In the earlier examples, we assumed that an actual transaction had taken place, such as the purchase or sale of inventory, the acquisition of fixed assets, and borrowing in foreign currency. Accounting for the hedging of these types of transactions is relatively straightforward. However, international business is more complicated, and so is the accounting for their hedges. A company can enter into a firm commitment to purchase or sell inventory or capital equipment at some point in the future. Some companies do a significant amount of business abroad and are able to forecast their future sales, even though no firm commitment to sell has taken place. They may prefer to hedge a certain percentage of their estimate of future sales. Also, many companies bid in foreign currency on large projects and may want to enter into a hedge to protect the bid in case it is awarded to them. In this case, an option is widely used, because the bid is uncertain and the option need not be exercised.

There are two key standards that deal with accounting for derivatives: IAS 39: Financial Instruments: Recognition and Measurement and FASB Statement No. 133: Accounting for Certain Derivative Instruments and Certain Hedging Activities. IAS 39 was approved by the Board in December 1998 and is effective for financial statements for financial years beginning on or after January 1, 2001. Statement No. 133 was supposed to have been applied no later than January 1, 2000, but an amendment of the standard was being considered at the time of the writing of the text with the proposed application being January 1, 2001, if approved. Both standards seem to be relatively close in most matters, although there are some differences.

Derivatives have an underlying and a notional value. For purposes of this discussion, the underlying is foreign exchange, although the underlying for other derivatives could be something else, such as an interest rate or commodity like gold or silver. The notional amount is the number of units of foreign currency that will be traded. For example, if a U.S. firm owes a Japanese supplier ¥100,000,000 and enters into a forward contract to hedge the liability, the underlying for the forward contract would be Japanese yen, and the notional amount would be ¥100,000,000.

Statement 133 deals with a variety of derivative financial instruments, not just derivatives whose underlying is foreign exchange. Basically, both IAS 39 and Statement 133 require that all entities recognize derivatives as assets or liabilities in the statement of financial position and that they subsequently measure them at fair values. Changes in fair value from one period to the next are recorded in the income statement.

- Derivative instruments can be designated as a fair-value hedge, a cash flow hedge, or a foreign-currency hedge.

- Fair-value hedge—a hedge of the exposure to changes (that are attributable to a particular risk) in the fair value of (1) a recognized asset or liability or (2) an unrecognized firm commitment

- Cash flow hedge—a hedge of the exposure to variability (that is attributable to a particular risk) in the cash flows of (1) a recognized asset or liability or (2) a forecasted transaction.

- Foreign-currency hedge—a hedge of the foreign-currency exposure of (1) an unrecognized firm commitment, (2) an available-for-sale security, (3) a forecasted transaction, or (4) a net investment in a foreign operation.

The importance of qualifying for hedge accounting provisions according to Statement 133 is that the statement provides for a symmetrical matching of timing of the recognition of the gain or loss of the derivative with the gain or loss on the underlying transaction. In the case of the yen liability above, a rise in the value of the yen would cause the dollar equivalent of the yen liability to rise, resulting in a foreign exchange loss. However, if the firm enters into a forward contract to receive yen from the bank, a rise in the yen receivable would result in a foreign exchange gain, offsetting the loss on the liability. That is the symmetrical nature of hedge accounting.

Illustration: A Forward Contract to Hedge a Foreign Currency Transaction

Prior to the issuance of Statement No. 133, Statement No. 52 contained provisions for accounting for the hedge of a foreign currency denominated asset or liability. Statement No. 133 basically retains the provisions of Statement No. 52, which says that derivative hedging instruments, such as a forward contract, are measured at fair value, with changes in fair value recognized in current earnings. Those changes would basically offset the foreign exchange gains or losses from the underlying assets or liabilities.

Assume the following information for a U.S. company purchasing inventory from a German supplier on March 1 and incurring a liability of DM1,000,000 that must be paid on April 30.

$.4700	spot rate on March 1
$.4800	forward rate quoted on March 1 for delivery on April 30
$.4800	spot rate on March 31
$.4850	forward rate quoted on March 31 for delivery on April 30
$.4850	spot rate on April 30

Normally, a forward contract is not actually recorded, but the company would keep track of its changes in value over time. We will include the entries as if actually made so as to facilitate the understanding of what happens during the life of the transaction.

March 1	Purchases	470,000	
	Accounts payable		470,000
	to record the purchase at the spot rate of $.4700		

	Forward contract	480,000	
	Dollars due to bank		480,000
	to record the commitment to the bank to		
	deliver dollars at the forward rate of $.4800		
	and receive DM1 million		
March 31	Foreign exchange loss	10,000	
	Accounts payable		10,000
	DM1 million × (.4700–.4800)		
	Forward contract	5,000	
	Foreign exchange gain		5,000
	DM1 million × (.4850–.4800)		
April 30	Dollars due to bank	480,000	
	Cash		480,000
	to pay foreign exchange trader at		
	original forward rate		
	Foreign currency	485,000	
	Forward contract		485,000
	to receive FX from FX trader at bank at		
	April 30 spot rate		
	Accounts payable	480,000	
	Foreign exchange loss	5,000	
	Foreign currency		485,000

In this case, without a forward contract, the firm would have given up $485,000 to settle the liability. The forward contract resulted in giving up only $480,000. The forward contract established the exact amount of cash the company needed to settle the transaction, so they could plan to raise the cash when needed.

Illustration: A Forward Contract to Hedge a Firm Commitment

The new rules to account for a forward contract to hedge a firm commitment are significantly more complex than under the old GAAP rules. However, the end result is basically the same. The forward contract sets the value of the cash that the firm will pay, no matter what happens to the future spot rate. An example of a firm commitment would be where a U.S. company enters into a commitment to purchase capital equipment for £1,000,000 from a British manufacturer with delivery and payment to take place on April 30 and payment to be made on May 31. Due to instability in foreign exchange markets, the importer is exposed to a possible foreign exchange loss. As a result, they enter into a forward contract with the foreign exchange trader at a bank to hedge the commitment. The contract hedges both the commitment period and the period until the payment is made. Because the forward contract is a hedge of the fair value of an accounts payable with the British manufacturer, it is treated in the same way as a fair value hedge. As such, the contract is recognized as an asset and marked to market. Changes in value are taken to the income statement. Changes in the value of the firm commitment are also taken to the income statement, so the changes in the forward contract and the changes in the firm commitment should effectively offset each other, which is the objective of the hedge.

Assume that the relevant spot exchange rates are as follows:

$1.4900	March 1
$1.5200	March 31
$1.5500	April 30
$1.5950	May 31

Assume that the relevant forward exchange rates for May 31 delivery are as follows:

$1.5700	March 1
$1.5850	March 31
$1.5900	April 30
$1.5950	May 31

No entry is made on March 1, because there is a fixed future commitment rather than an actual contract. However, on March 31, the forward contract must be marked to market, and the resulting gain or loss taken to income. Assume that an appropriate discount rate is 6 percent per annum. The amount of the gain or loss on the contract is determined as follows:

$$\$1.5850 - 1.5700 = .015 \times 1,000,000 = \$15,000/(1 + .06/4) = \$14,778$$

Thus the fair value of the contract would increase by $14,778 on the balance sheet, and the same amount would be recognized in other comprehensive income. At the same time, the firm commitment would fall by a corresponding amount, resulting in a loss being recognized in other comprehensive income. Similar entries would be made at other balance sheet dates.

The bottom line, however, is that the amount of cash that the importer has to pay is set by the forward contract entered into on March 1 – $1,570,000. No matter what happens to the future spot rate or the market value of the forward contract at successive balance sheet dates, the amount set by the contract still determines what the importer must pay. The accounting for the derivative may have changed under Statement 133, but the cash flow remains the same as before. However, now the forward contract will be carried at fair market value.

Illustration: A Forward Contract to Hedge a Foreign-Currency Forecasted Sale

One of the benefits of Statement 133 is allowing hedge accounting for a foreign-currency forecasted sale or purchase. Many companies doing business abroad have developed enough experience to have a good idea what their export sales volume will be during a given time period. They have not sold anything yet or even entered into a firm commitment to sell, but they still have a good idea how much they will sell. Rather than wait for the sale to take play to enter into a hedge, they can enter into one at any time and still be able to use hedge accounting.

Assume that XYZ company assesses its exposed position periodically and determines monthly hedging strategies for the coming quarter. On March 1, XYZ estimates that it will sell £1,000,000 of inventory to British customers effective April 30. At that time, XYZ enters into a forward contract to hedge the British pounds receivable. The relevant exchange rates are:

Date	Spot Exchange Rate ($/£)	Forward Exchange Rate for Settlement on May 31
March 1	$1.4772 per £	$1.4900
End of quarter	$1.4950	$1.5050
Date of sale	$1.5100	$1.5100

Based on these exchange rates, the forward contract needs to be updated to fair market value with gains and losses going into income. Also, it is important to note that the contracts need to be adjusted at an appropriate discount rate, which we assume to be 6 percent for this example. The nominal value of the adjustment is the difference between the original forward rate quoted on March 1 and the rate quoted at the end of the quarter as well as the actual rate on the date of sale, since the value of the forward contract equals the spot rate on the date of sale when the forward contract comes due.

Date	Nominal Value	Fair Value	Gain or Loss for the Period
March 1	0	0	0
March 31	($15,000)	($14,778)	($14,778)
April 30	($20,000)	($20,000)	($ 5,222)

The fair value adjustment on March 31 is computed as follows:

$$15,000/[1+(.06/4)] = 14,778$$

The adjustment is negative, because the original contract will yield $1,490,000 on the sale. At the new forward rate at the end of the quarter, the exporter could have earned more cash on the contract, so the old contract is not worth as much as a new contract would have been.

Given the previous information, the journal entries for the hedge and forecasted sales are as follows:

March 1	No entry		
March 31	Other comprehensive income	14,778	
	forward contract		14,778
April 30	Other comprehensive income	5,222	
	forward contract		5,222
	Foreign currency	1,510,000	
	Sales		1,510,000
	To record the sale to the importer and receipt of British pounds at the spot rate on April 30.		
	Forward contract	20,000	
	Cash	1,490,000	
	Foreign currency		1,510,000
	To record the delivery of foreign currency to the bank at the April 30 spot rate, the closing out of the forward contract, and the receipt of dollars at the forward rate.		
	Sales	20,000	
	Other comprehensive income		20,000
	To transfer the loss on the forward contract from comprehensive income to earnings through sales revenues at the time of sale.		

The entries on April 30 were given to show the actual flow of cash and subsequent adjustments. What hedge accounting does is allow the firm to record sales revenues at the same rate as the cash received—the forward rate on the contract entered into on March 1. Granted, XYZ would have been better off not entering into the forward contract, because it would have received $1,510,000 on April 30 at the spot rate. But on March 1, there was no guarantee that the pound would strengthen against the dollar, generating higher dollar receivables. That is the chance you take with a forward contract.

Illustration: An Options Contract to Hedge a Foreign-Currency Forecasted Sale

Instead of using a forward contract, XYZ could use a put option to hedge the receivable from forecasted sales in British pounds. Assume that XYZ enters into a put option for £1,000,000 on March 1 at a strike price of $1.4900 and a premium of $20,000. The sale is expected to take place on June 30, the same time that the options contract expires. As is the case with a forward contract, the value of the options contract changes over time. On March 1, the following entry is made:

Foreign-currency options	$20,000	
Cash		$20,000

to reflect the payment of the premium to the writer of the contract. This will be written off as a loss on hedging activities over the life of the option.

The option will also be adjusted to its fair value, and the adjustment will go to comprehensive income. When the sale is finally recorded, these adjustments will be taken from other comprehensive income and used to adjust the amount of sales. The bottom line is that sales revenues and cash received will be at least the strike price, or $1,490,000. If the pound strengthens against the dollar, the option will not be exercised, and XYZ will convert the pounds into dollars at the spot rate.

SUMMARY

1. An exchange rate is the amount of one currency that must be given to acquire one unit of another currency. The spot rate refers to a quote on current transactions.

2. Foreign exchange is quoted direct (the number of units of your currency for one unit of the foreign currency) or indirect (the number of units of the foreign currency for one unit of your currency).

3. The cross rate is the exchange rate between two nondollar currencies.

4. A derivative is a contract, the value of which changes in concert with the price movements in a related or underlying commodity, such as foreign exchange. The most important foreign currency derivatives are forwards, swaps, futures, and options.

5. A forward contract is a contract between a foreign currency trader and client for future sale or purchase of foreign currency. A swap is a simultaneous spot and forward transaction. An option is the right, but not obligation, to trade foreign currency in the future at an agreed-upon rate.

6.   The daily foreign exchange market activity is approximately $1.5 trillion. The most important markets in foreign exchange are London, New York, and Tokyo, and the most widely traded currencies are the U.S. dollar, the German deutsche mark, the Japanese yen, the British pound, and the Swiss franc, with the euro coming on strong.

7.   The International Monetary Fund (IMF) was organized in 1944 to promote exchange stability. The IMF classifies exchange rate regimes accordingly: currencies that are pegged to a currency or composite of currencies, currencies whose exchange rates have displayed limited flexibility compared with either a currency or group of currencies, and countries whose exchange rates are more flexible.

8.   Foreign currency transactions are transactions whose terms are denominated in a currency other than the entity's reporting currency.

9.   For foreign currency transactions, the IASC and FASB require that the original transaction be translated into dollars at the exchange rate in effect on that date. Amounts receivable or payable in a foreign currency are translated at the current exchange rate at subsequent balance sheet dates. Foreign exchange gains and losses are taken to income immediately.

10.   As an alternative treatment, the IASC permits exchange differences that result from a severe devaluation of a currency to be included in the carrying amount of the related asset, as long as several strict conditions are met. This is not permitted in the United States.

11.   Firms can choose to hedge or protect a foreign currency exposure against possible loss. Firms typically use one of several different derivative financial instruments to hedge an exposure. Examples of derivative financial instruments are forward contracts, swaps, and options.

12.   Two key standards that deal with accounting for derivatives are IAS 39: Financial Instruments: Recognition and Measurement, and FASB Statement No. 133: Accounting for Certain Derivative Instruments and Certain Hedging Activities.

13.   Derivatives have an underlying and a notional value. For purposes of this chapter, the underlying is foreign currency, and the notional value is the number of units of the foreign currency.

14.   The accounting for a hedge of a foreign currency transaction is still covered by FASB Statement No. 52. SFAS No. 133 covers the following foreign-currency hedges: (1) an unrecognized firm commitment, (2) an available-for-sale security, (3) a forecasted transaction, and (4) a net investment in a foreign operation.

Problems

1.   Assume the following spot exchange rates between the U.S. dollar and the British pound sterling:

March 1	$1.4470
March 31	$1.4200
April 30	$1.4000

On March 1, XYZ, a U.S. company, sells goods to a British importer for £1,000,000. Payment is to be made on April 30, and XYZ adjusts its financial statements quarterly. What are the journal entries on March 1, March 31, and April 30?

2.   Assume the following spot exchange rates between the U.S. dollar and the British pound sterling:

March 1	$1.4470
March 31	$1.4650
April 30	$1.4750

On March 1, XYZ, a U.S. company, sells goods to a British importer for £1,000,000. Payment is to be made on April 30, and XYZ adjusts its financial statements quarterly. What are the journal entries on March 1, March 31, and April 30?

3. Assume the following spot exchange rates between the U.S. dollar and the British pound sterling:

March 1	$1.4470
March 31	$1.4200
April 30	$1.4000

On March 1, XYZ, a U.S. company, buys goods from a British supplier for £1,000,000. Payment is to be made to XYZ on April 30, and XYZ adjusts its financial statements quarterly. What are the journal entries on March 1, March 31, and April 30?

4. Assume the following spot exchange rates between the U.S. dollar and the British pound sterling:

March 1	$1.4470
March 31	$1.4650
April 30	$1.4750

On March 1, XYZ, a U.S. company, buys goods from a British supplier for £1,000,000. Payment is to be made on April 30, and XYZ adjusts its financial statements quarterly. What are the journal entries on March 1, March 31, and April 30?

5. On January 1, XYZ, a U.S. firm, borrows DM1,000,000 from a German bank for five years at 6 percent interest paid semiannually in deutsche marks. Principal does not have to be paid until the end of the loan. The principal is adjusted for any exchange rate changes every six months. Assume the following exchange rates for the first year of the loan:

January 1	$.4640
June 30	$.4540
December 31	$.4400

Assume that the average exchange rate for each six-month period is the simple average for that period. What are the journal entries for January 1, June 30, and December 31?

6. On January 1, XYZ, a U.S. company, purchased inventory from a Japanese supplier for ¥100,000,000, with payment to be made on February 28. At the same time, it decided to enter into a forward contract to hedge the yen liability. Assume the following exchange rates relative to the transaction:

¥110 per $	January 1 spot rate
¥108	forward rate quoted on January 1 for delivery on February 28
¥109	spot rate on January 31
¥109	forward rate quoted on January 31 for delivery on February 28
¥112	spot rate on February 28

How many dollars would XYZ have to pay the Japanese supplier, and what would be the dollar value of the sale?

Discussion Questions

1. In May 2000, Nissan announced that it was closing some factories in Japan and shifting production to the United States to shelter itself from foreign exchange risks that it faces when exporting cars to the United States. Describe the risk that Nissan is concerned about. Describe the pros and cons of using forward contracts to hedge Nissan sales to the United States and whether or not they are a better solution than moving production to the United States.

2. Pick a foreign currency of your choice and graph the value of that currency against the U.S. dollar over the past 12 months. Based on what has happened to that exchange rate, describe the financial challenges facing an exporter from the country or an exporter to that country.

3. In the chapter, we discussed how companies can use derivative financial instruments to hedge against a potential loss on a foreign currency receivable or payable. If there are possible losses from denominating receivables and payables in a foreign currency, why don't firms insist that receivables and payables always be in their own currency instead of a foreign currency?

Case: RadCo International

RadCo International, a U.S.-based software company, has sold software to a Japanese distributor for years, but the sales have always been denominated in U.S. dollars so that RadCo didn't have to worry about foreign exchange risk. In 2000, however, RadCo's sales staff finally convinced RadCo senior management to denominate export sales in Japanese yen. However, the finance staff noted that now RadCo would be exposed to possible foreign exchange gains and losses, and the accounting staff had to figure out how to record the transaction.

On January 1, RadCo switched its invoicing to yen. Although sales for the first four months had already been committed in dollars, the sales staff responsible for Japanese sales estimated that they would deliver approximately ¥10,000,000 of software to the distributor on May 31. With that information, the finance staff began discussions with Citibank to determine how it could deal with the foreign exchange risk. As part of the discussions, the relevant exchange rates provided by Citibank were as follows:

¥110   the yen/dollar spot rate on January 1
¥107   the forward rate on January 1 quoted for May 31 delivery
¥110   the strike price for a put option for May 31 delivery; the premium
        on the option is $.0002 per yen.

As the year progressed, Citibank delivered the following relevant exchange rate information to the finance staff:

¥109   the spot rate on March 31
¥108.5 the forward exchange rate for settlement on May 31
¥105   the spot rate on May 31

On May 31, RadCo delivers software priced at ¥10,000,000 to the distributor as estimated, and the distributor wires the cash to RadCo's account in Citibank. Armed with this information, the accounting staff now has to make the proper journal entries.

Questions

1. If RadCo decides not to hedge the transaction, what would the journal entries be on January 1, March 31, and May 31?

2. If they hedge the transaction with a forward contract, what would the journal entries be on January 1, March 31, and May 31? Assume that the discount rate is 6 percent per annum. Be sure to prepare a table showing fair values and period gains or losses.

3. Compare the net cash receipts from the transaction on May 31 assuming
   a. no hedge
   b. a forward contract hedge
   c. an options hedge

4. What are the pros and cons of each of the three approaches in question 3?

5. Given the financial and accounting complexities of shifting from a dollar to a yen-based transaction, should top management have allowed the sales staff to invoice in yen?

6. What have you learned about internal coordination when making decisions about which currency to use to denominate a foreign sale?

Selected References

Bank for International Settlements. 1999. *Central Bank Survey of Foreign Exchange and Derivatives Market Activity.* BIS: Basel, Switzerland (May): 69.

"Banks Retaliate in Dealing-Room War." 1993. *Euromoney* (May): p. 87.

Barkley, Tom. 2000. "Dollar Rises Against Most Currencies, Consolidating Gains After Rate Boost," *The Wall Street Journal* (May 18): C8.

Beaver, W. H. and M. A. Wolfson. 1992. "Foreign Currency Translation and Changing Prices in Perfect and Complete Markets," *Journal of Accounting Research* (Autumn): 528–50.

Claiden, R. 1997. "Accounting for Derivative Products," in *International Accounting and Finance Handbook,* edited by F. D. S. Choi. New York: John Wiley.

Coopers & Lybrand. 1996. *Understanding IAS: Analysis and Interpretation.* London: The Bath Press (September): 21-9–21-10.

Copeland, T. and Y. Joshi. 1996. "Why Derivatives Don't Reduce FX Risk," *The McKinsey Quarterly* (1): 66–79.

Dufey, G. and I. H. Giddy. 1995. "Uses and Abuses of Currency Options," *Journal of Applied Corporate Finance,* 8 (3): 49–57.

Eiteman, D. K., A. I. Stonehill, and M. H. Moffett. 1998. *Multinational Business Finance.* Reading, MA: Addison-Wesley.

Froot, K. A., D. S. Scharfstein, and J. Stein. 1993. "Risk Management: Coordinating Corporate Investment and Financing Policies," *Journal of Finance* (December): 1629–58.

Gastineau, G. L. 1992. *Dictionary of Financial Risk Management.* Chicago: Probus Publishing Company.

Houston, C. O. 1990. "Translation Exposure Hedging Post SFAS No.52," *Journal of International Financial Management and Accounting,* 2 (2, 3): 145–69.

International Accounting Standards Committee, IAS 21. 1993. *Effects of Changes in Foreign Exchange Rates.*

Janowski, D. 1999. "Global Pricing/Risk Management Techniques," *TMA Journal,* 19 (5) (September/October): 20–29.

Kawaller, I. 1998. "Capitalizing on Change: Preparing for the Euro," *TMA Journal,* 18 (5) (September/October): 32–35.

Lee, Peter. 1992. "Foreign Exchange: Bye-Bye Brokers," *Euromoney* (April): 14.

Lessard, D. R. and J. B. Lightstone. 1986. "Volatile Exchange Rates Can Put Operations at Risk," *Harvard Business Review* (July/August): 107–14.

Logue, D. E. and G. S. Oldfield. 1997. "Managing Foreign Assets When Foreign Exchange Markets Are Efficient," *Financial Management* (Summer): 16–22.

Moffett, M. H. and J. K. Karlsen. 1994. "Managing Foreign Exchange Rate Economic Exposure," *Journal of International Financial Management and Accounting* (June): 157–75.

Perrottet, C. 1998. "Don't Hide From Risk—Manage It," *Journal of International Business Strategy*, 19 (5) (September/October): 9–12.

Phillips, Michael M. and Peter Landers. 1999. "Japan Continues Solo Intervention to Hold Down Yen," *The Wall Street Journal* (July 21): A15.

PricewaterhouseCoopers. 1998. *A Guide to Accounting for Derivative Instruments and Hedging Activities* (July 31): 2.

Reed, Stanley, David Fairlamb, Susan Berfield, and Frederik Balfour. 2000. "The Sick Money of Europe," *Business Week* (May 15): 60–61.

Sesit, Michael R., Christopher Rhoads, and Jon E. Hilsenrath. 2000. "Why Can't the Euro Keep Up With the Yen?," *The Wall Street Journal* (May 10): A21.

Smith, W. S., Jr. 1995. "Corporate Risk Management: Theory and Practice," *Journal of Derivatives*, 2 (4).

Wallace, J. 1998. "Best Practices in Foreign Exchange Risk Management," *TMA Journal*, 18 (6) (November/December): 48–55.

CHAPTER TEN

FOREIGN CURRENCY TRANSLATION

Chapter Objectives

- Differentiate between the process of foreign currency conversion and the process of translation
- Compare the different foreign currency translation methodologies: the current/noncurrent method, the monetary/non-monetary method, the temporal method, and the current rate or closing rate methods
- Present the translation methodologies recommended by the International Accounting Standards Committee (IASC)
- Describe the basic dimensions of FASB Statement 52 and how that standard compares with previous GAAPs in the United States
- Illustrate the temporal and current-rate methods of translating foreign currency financial statements
- Examine the different translation methodologies in use in different countries

INTRODUCTION

In January 2000, McDonald's Corporation reported its results for 1999 and discussed the impact of foreign operations on earnings. In particular, it noted that operating income in the Asia/Pacific region rose 10 percent in constant currencies for the year. It also reported that the devaluation in Brazil and the resultant economic conditions in several markets hurt results in Latin America. Finally, sales rose in France, Germany, Spain and the United Kingdom in constant currency terms.

How could a devaluation in Brazil hurt McDonald's consolidated results? What does it mean to have sales and income rise in constant currency terms? We will answer those questions in this chapter.

In Chapter 9, we discussed how to account for foreign currency transactions, whether you are denominating sales or purchases in a foreign currency or borrowing money in a foreign currency. In Chapter 10, we move beyond foreign currency transactions and look at the accounting complexities facing a company like McDonald's which has invested all over the world and must report those results in its consolidated financial statements. The complexity is that a foreign subsidiary's financial statements, which are expressed in the currency of the country where it is located, must be translated into the reporting currency of the parent company, or U.S. dollars in the case of McDonald's. The process of translation implies that one currency is expressed, remeasured, or restated in terms of another currency. We do that all the time with the temperature. For example, 21 degrees Celsius is the same as 70 degrees Fahrenheit. To get the temperature in Fahrenheit, you just take the temperature in Celsius, multiply it by 1.8, and add 32. So, $21 \times 1.8 + 32 = 70$. We haven't changed the weather; we have just remeasured the temperature from Celsius to Fahrenheit.

Why should translation occur in the first place? Sometimes financial statements are restated or translated from one currency into another to assist the reader of the financial statements. For example, a French investor wishing to invest in a U.S. company may want to see the financial statements in euros rather than dollars. The management of an MNE may wish to see the results of a foreign operation stated in the parent currency in order to facilitate cross-national comparisons. If an MNE is to prepare consolidated financial statements, it must express the statements of its different operations in a common currency before combination or consolidation can occur.

KEY DEFINITIONS

The discussion in this chapter highlights the importance of making sure that we are consistent in terminology. Several terms important to the discussion of translation are *functional currency, reporting currency, foreign currency,* and *local currency.* The functional currency is the currency of the primary economic environment in which the company operates. The reporting currency is the currency in which the parent company prepares its financial statements. The foreign currency is any currency other than the functional currency of a company. The local currency is the currency of a particular country being referred to. The functional currency could be either the reporting currency or a foreign currency.

To illustrate these terms, let's assume that a U.S.-based MNE has an operating subsidiary in France that does some importing from Germany. The functional currency of the subsidiary would be the French franc, assuming that the company is relatively autonomous from the parent company and that most of its cash flows are in French francs. The local currency of that subsidiary would also be the French franc, the German deutsche mark would be a foreign currency to the French subsidiary, and the U.S. dollar would be the reporting currency of the consolidated enterprise. Both the franc and the deutsche mark would be foreign currencies to the parent company in the United States. If the French operation were an extension of the parent company and relatively dependent on the parent company for inventory, cash flows, and so on, the functional currency might be considered the reporting currency (the U.S. dollar).

Because the French subsidiary imports merchandise from Germany, it may have accounts payable that are denominated in deutsche marks. This implies that the amount of the liability is actually fixed in marks because that is the currency in which the liability must be settled. For financial statement purposes, however, the mark liability must be measured in francs or it could not be included with the franc liabilities on the balance sheet. A franc liability would be both measured and denominated in francs. The process of translation involves restating an account from one country to another. If the exchange rate used to translate the account from one currency to another were the rate in effect when the original transaction took place (such as the acquisition of property, plant, and equipment), that rate would be called the *historical* exchange rate. If the exchange rate used were the one in effect at the balance sheet date, it would be considered the *current* or *closing* rate.

As we will point out in this chapter, the translation of financial statements involves dealing with two key issues: the exchange rates at which various accounts are translated from one currency into another (translation methods) and the subsequent treatment of gains and losses. First, we will discuss the major translation methodologies that have been used historically, including the two most widely used methodologies today—the current rate and temporal methods. Next, we will describe the process required for use by the International Accounting Standards Committee and the U.S. Financial Accounting Standards Board. With those standards as a base, we will illustrate the translation process, and finally show how other countries translate financial statements.

TRANSLATION METHODOLOGIES: AN OVERVIEW

In the process of translation, all foreign currency balance sheet and income statement accounts are restated in terms of the reporting currency by multiplying the foreign currency amount by the appropriate exchange rate. The four major methods that have been used historically in the translation process are the current/noncurrent, the monetary/nonmonetary, the temporal, and the current rate methods.

Current/Noncurrent Method

Under the current/noncurrent method, as shown in Exhibit 10.1, current assets and liabilities are translated at current exchange rates, and noncurrent assets and liabilities and stockholders' equity are translated at historical exchange rates. This method was generally accepted in the United States from the early 1930s until FASB Statement 8 was issued in October 1975.

The current/noncurrent method is based on the assumption that accounts should be grouped according to maturity. Anything due to mature in one year or less or within the normal business cycle should be translated at the current rate,

Exhibit 10.1 Exchange Rates Used to Translate Selected Assets and Liabilities

	Current Noncurrent	Monetary Nonmonetary	Current Rate	Temporal
Cash, current receivables, and payables	C[a]	C	C	C
Inventory	C	H	C	C or H
Fixed assets	H[b]	H	C	H
Long-term receivables and payables	H	C	C	C

[a] C = current exchange rate.
[b] H = historical exchange rate.

whereas everything else should be carried at the rate in effect when the translation was originally recorded.

Monetary/Nonmonetary Method

The attitude of the U.S. accounting profession toward translation began to change in the 1950s when it was suggested that accounts be translated according to their nature rather than their date of maturity. Accounts are considered as either monetary or nonmonetary rather than current or noncurrent. Under this method, monetary assets and liabilities are translated at the current rate, and nonmonetary assets and liabilities and stockholders' equity are translated at historical rates. This approach was a radical departure from the current/noncurrent method in the areas of inventory, long-term receivables, and long-term payables.

The philosophy behind this approach is that monetary or financial assets and liabilities have similar attributes in that their value represents a fixed amount of money whose reporting currency equivalent changes each time the exchange rate changes. Monetary accounts should therefore be translated at the current exchange rate. In the current/noncurrent method some current assets are monetary (such as cash) and some are nonmonetary (such as inventory carried at cost), and yet all are translated at the current exchange rate. The proponents of the monetary/nonmonetary method consider it more meaningful to translate assets and liabilities on the basis of attributes instead of time.

Temporal Method

The temporal method was originally proposed in Accounting Research Study 12 by the AICPA and formally required in Statement 8. According to the temporal method, cash, receivables, and payables (both current and noncurrent) are translated at the current rate. Other assets and liabilities may be translated at current or historical rates, depending on their characteristics. Assets and liabilities carried at past exchange prices are translated at historical rates. For example, a fixed asset carried at the foreign currency price at which it was purchased would be translated into the reporting currency at the exchange rate in effect when the asset was purchased. Assets and liabilities carried at current purchase or sales exchange prices or future exchange prices would be translated at current rates. For example, inventory carried at market would be translated at the current rather than the historical rate. Under historical cost accounting, the temporal method provides essentially the same results as the monetary/nonmonetary method.

The attractiveness of the temporal approach lies in its flexibility. If a country were to change from historical cost accounting to current value accounting, the temporal method would automatically translate all assets and liabilities at current rates. The theoretical attractiveness of this approach is that the branches and subsidiaries of a parent company would be translated into the parent currency in such a way that the parent currency would be the single unit of measure.

Current Rate Method

The current rate method is the easiest to apply because it requires that all assets and liabilities be translated at the current exchange rate. Only net worth would be translated at the historical rate. This approach is easier to use than the others because a company would not have to keep track of various historical exchange rates. The current rate approach results in translated statements that retain the same ratios and relationships that exist in the local currency. For example, the ratio of net income to sales in local currency is rarely the same in dollars under other translation approaches because a variety of current, historical, and average exchange rates is used to translate the income statement. Because all accounts would be translated at a single exchange rate under the current rate method, the ratio at net income to sales would remain the same in the reporting currency as in the foreign currency.

INTERNATIONAL ACCOUNTING STANDARDS

The International Accounting Standards Committee issued IAS 21, "Accounting for the Effects of Changes in Foreign Exchange Rates" in July 1983 and later revised it in 1993. It was issued just after FASB Statement 52 (December 1981), so it was able to take advantage of the FASB deliberations in developing a standard. In addition, it was issued about the same time as the relevant Canadian and British standards, and IASC's interaction with the British, Canadian, and American standard-setters, as well as those from other parts of the world, resulted in a standard that would be widely accepted.

IAS 21 contains provisions for both transactions and translation of financial statements. In the case of translating foreign currency financial statements, the closing rate and temporal methods are used, depending on the operating characteristics of the foreign operations. When using the closing rate method and translating the income statement, the average rate must be used. Operations in highly inflationary countries must be adjusted for local inflation before translation into the reporting currency. Translation gains and losses are taken to stockholders' equity.

VIAG AG is a large German industrial concern in energy, chemicals, and telecommunications. In 1999, VIAG announced in the footnotes in its annual report that its consolidated financial statements were prepared for the first time in accordance with International Accounting Standards. A new addition to the German Commercial Code made it possible for German companies to finally issue consolidated financial statements according to IASs. In note 4, VIAG management stated the following:

> The currency translation of foreign financial statements takes place in accordance with the principle of functional currency (IAS 21). In VIAG's consolidated balance sheet, the translation of items of all foreign companies takes place accordingly at the balance sheet date, because the major foreign companies included in consolidation conduct their business independently in their national currency.... In the consolidated statement of income, the income and expense items are translated at average rates for the year.

This is the current rate method as explained in IAS 21.

HISTORICAL DEVELOPMENT IN THE UNITED STATES

We have already alluded to some of the evolutionary development of the translation standard in the United States in this chapter. In the late 1960s and early 1970s, the U.S. dollar came under severe pressure from other currencies, and in 1971 it was devalued approximately 10 percent against its official gold value. During that time, the Accounting Principles Board (APB) was studying the translation issue, and in 1972, Accounting Research Study 12, which recommended the adoption of the temporal method of translation, was issued. However, the APB was being phased out and the FASB was being organized, so nothing was done with ARS 12.

In December 1973, FASB issued Statement 1, *Disclosure of Foreign Currency Translation Information,* to stave off pressure while it deliberated on the more substantive issues of how to translate foreign currency financial statements. It is important to note that the dollar had been devalued again in early 1973 and had finally been cut loose to float freely in the spring of 1973. Thus, the translation issue became much more critical than it had been when the dollar was fixed against most major currencies. In addition, the dollar was essentially floating down in value against most of the major currencies of the industrial world.

On February 21, 1974, the board issued a Discussion Memorandum on translation that addressed a number of important issues. After public hearings were held, the issues in the Discussion Memorandum were consolidated and an exposure draft was issued. After hearing responses to the exposure draft, the board issued Statement 8 in October 1975.

FASB Statement 8

According to Statement 8, the objective of translation was as follows: "For the purpose of preparing an enterprise's financial statements, the objective of translation is to measure and express (a) in dollars and (b) in conformity with U.S. generally accepted accounting principles (GAAP) the assets, liabilities, revenues, or expenses that are measured or denominated in foreign currency."

The temporal method of translation has already been described briefly, but there are some important things about the temporal principle and Statement 8 that have not been addressed. In the income statement, for example, most revenues and expenses are translated at the average exchange rate during the year. In practice, the income statement is translated monthly, and the cumulative balance from prior months is added to the current month's balance to get the cumulative totals for the year. Accounts such as cost of sales and depreciation expense are translated at the exchange rate in effect when the assets were originally purchased.

Another important feature is that Statement 8 required that gains and losses from foreign currency transactions and the translation of foreign currency financial statements had to be taken directly to the income statement. That meant that translated earnings were fluctuating widely depending on what was happening to the exchange rate, independent of the operations of the firm. This area became a source of real contention in the corporate world and was one of the major factors that led to the downfall of Statement 8.

In addition, many firms complained about carrying inventory at historical rates in dollars for two reasons. The first reason was simply cost-benefit. The feeling was that if inventory were turning over relatively rapidly and approximating current rates, then it would be a lot easier to compute inventory values if the current rate could be used instead of having to keep track of the old historical exchange rates. The other reason had to do with timing. Managers complained that because inventory was being translated at the historical rate, it was possible for an exchange rate change in one quarter to impact earnings in a subsequent quarter when inventory flowed through the cost of goods sold. They felt that this was distorting the operating performance of each quarter. Thus a number of critics of Statement 8 felt that the statement would be improved if inventory could be carried at current rather than historical exchange rates.

A final major criticism related to the disposition of the gain or loss on long-term debt. Statement 8 required that firms translate long-term debt at current rates, a practice already followed by nearly half the U.S. multinationals prior to 1975. Because most of the foreign currency long-term debt in the 1970s was in currencies that were strengthening vis-à-vis the U.S. dollar, U.S. firms were recognizing sizable losses. Many firms felt that because the foreign currency debt was generally being liquidated by foreign currency earnings, there was really no dollar exposure. They also argued that the fixed assets purchased by the debt were a natural hedge or protection against loss since they were constantly generating earnings. Thus, they felt that they should have been able to write off the losses over the life of the assets or treat the losses as an adjustment to interest expense.

Movement to Statement 52

As a result of these and other criticisms, the board decided in May 1978 to invite comments on Statements 1 through 12. Of the 200 letters received by the board, most addressed the issues in Statement 8. In January 1979, the board decided to add a project to reconsider all or parts of Statement 8 to its agenda. In February 1979, a task force containing representatives of the IASC as well as the professional standard-setting bodies in the United Kingdom and Canada was appointed to advise the board.

In August 1980, an exposure draft was issued after 18 public board meetings and 4 public task force meetings. In December 1980, there was a public hearing held on the exposure draft, which attracted 360 letters and 47 presentations. In an unprecedented move, the board issued a revised exposure draft on June 30, 1981. This was followed by more public meetings and 260 letters of comment. Finally, in December 1981, Statement 52, *Foreign Currency Translation,* was issued.

FASB STATEMENT 52

The development of Statement 52 was not an easy matter. There were no clear-cut solutions to the problems raised in Statement 8, and the suggestions for change ranged from minor alterations of the statement to a major rethinking of the entire translation process. In the final analysis, the latter approach prevailed, but the vote for both exposure drafts and the final standard was four to three. The minority view held very strongly to Statement 8 and could not accept the changes inherent in Statement 52.

One of the major differences in the statements is that Statement 52 adopted new objectives of translation. The stated objectives are as follows:

1. Provide information that is generally compatible with the expected economic effects of a rate change on an enterprise's cash flows and equity.
2. Reflect in consolidated statements the financial results and relationships of the individual consolidated entities as measured in their functional currencies in conformity with U.S. GAAP.

Selection of the Functional Currency

The term *functional currency* is used for the first time in the translation literature in conjunction with Statement 52. Although we have already defined and illustrated what *functional currency* means, we need to refine our definition a little more. Exhibit 10.2 contains some information provided in Statement 52 on how a company can choose the functional currency.

Conceptually, it is possible for a foreign entity to have more than one functional currency. For example, the entity could sell and distribute products manufactured by the parent company so the functional currency might be that of the parent. However, it might also be manufacturing and selling products locally, so the functional currency for those functions would be the local currency. In practice, the board expected that firms would pick only one functional currency for each operation abroad. Once the functional currency of the operation has been selected, it is possible to begin the translation process. It is important to remember that the functional currency is selected on the basis of operating criteria established by management. If the firm wishes to change the functional currency, it can do so only because the operating criteria used in the initial selection have changed. This is designed so that companies won't change functional currencies capriciously to

Exhibit 10.2   Factors Influencing the Determination of the Functional Currency

a. Cash Flow Indicators

1. *Foreign Currency*—Cash flows related to the foreign entity's individual assets and liabilities are primarily in the foreign currency and do not directly impact the parent company's cash flows.

2. *Parent's Currency*—Cash flows related to the foreign entity's individual assets and liabilities directly impact the parent's cash flows on a current basis and are readily available for remittance to the parent company.

b. Sales Price Indicators

1. *Foreign Currency*—Sales prices for the foreign entity's products are not primarily responsive on a short-term basis to changes in exchange rates but are determined more by local competition or local government regulation.

2. *Parent's Currency*—Sales prices for the foreign entity's products are primarily responsive on a short-term basis to changes in exchange rates; for example, sales prices are determined more by worldwide competition or by international prices.

c. Sales Market Indicators

1. *Foreign Currency*—There is an active local sales market for the foreign entity's products, although there also might be significant amounts of exports.

2. *Parent's Currency*—The sales market is mostly in the parent's country or sales contracts are denominated in the parent's currency.

d. Expense Indicators

1. *Foreign Currency*—Labor, materials, and other costs for the foreign entity's products or services are primarily local costs, even though there might also be imports from other countries.

2. *Parent's Currency*—labor, materials, and other costs for the foreign entity's products or services, on a continuing basis, are primarily costs for components obtained from the country in which the parent company is located.

e. Financing Indicators

1. *Foreign Currency*—Financing is primarily denominated in foreign currency, and funds generated by the foreign entity's operations are sufficient to service existing and normally expected debt obligations.

2. *Parent's Currency*—Financing is primarily from the parent or other dollar-denominated obligations, or funds generated by the foreign entity's operations are not sufficient to service existing and normally expected debt obligations without the infusion

(continues)

Exhibit 10.2   (*Continued*)

of additional funds from the parent company. Infusion of additional funds from the parent company for expansion is not a factor, provided funds generated by the foreign entity's expanded operations are expected to be sufficient to service that additional financing.

f.   Intercompany Transactions and Arrangements Indicators

1.   *Foreign Currency*—There is a low volume of intercompany transactions, and there is not an extensive interrelationship between the operations of the foreign entity and the parent company. However, the foreign entity's operations may rely on the parent's or affiliate's competitive advantages, such as patents and trademarks .

2.   *Parent's Currency*—There is a high volume of intercompany transactions, and there is an extensive interrelationship between the operations of the foreign entity and the parent company. Additionally, the parent's currency generally would be the functional currency if the foreign entity is a device or shell corporation for holding investments, obligations, intangible assets, and the like, that could readily be carried on the parent's or affiliate's books.

Source: Financial Accounting Standard Board, *Statement of Financial Accounting Standards No. 52, Foreign Currency Translation* (Stamford, CT: FASB, December 1981), pp. 26–27.

take advantage of the differences in the financial statements that result from the different translation methods.

The Translation Process

The board defines the translation process in Statement 52 as the process of expressing in the reporting currency of the enterprise those amounts that are denominated or measured in a different currency. In the examples given in the balance of this chapter, the reporting currency is defined as the U.S. dollar.

The actual translation process depends on which currency the books and records of the foreign entity are kept in and on how the parent defines the functional currency of the foreign entity. Once those decisions have taken place, the translation process involves either the current rate method or the temporal method.

In a more precise discussion of the translation process, the board refers to the process of "translation" and "restatement." To understand the differences in these terms, refer to the conditions set forth in Exhibit 10.3. Note that the books and records of the foreign entity can be kept in either the foreign currency or the reporting currency of the parent company. If the books and records are kept in the reporting currency and the functional currency is defined as the reporting currency, no translation process is necessary.

If the books and records of the foreign entity are kept in the foreign currency, the translation process depends on the definition of the functional currency. If the functional currency is the foreign currency, the financial statements are translated into the parent currency using the current rate method.

Exhibit 10.3   Translation or Remeasurement of Foreign Currency Financial Statements into the Reporting Currency

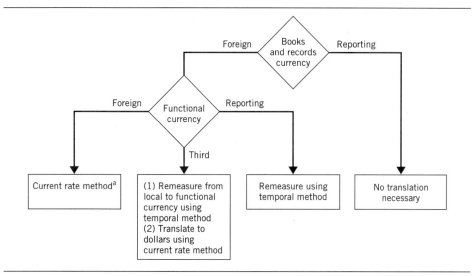

[a] In the case of a highly inflationary economy, the local currency may be the functional currency from an operating standpoint, but the dollar is considered the functional currency from a translation standpoint.

As Exhibit 10.3 shows, one exception to the functional currency rule is when the foreign entity is located in a highly inflationary economy. Highly inflationary economies are those that have a cumulative inflation rate of approximately 100 percent over a three-year period. This is equivalent to an average rate of 26 percent compounded annually. For reasons discussed later in this chapter, the temporal method must be used.

As another, although rare, possibility, the books and records are kept in the foreign currency, but the functional currency is a third currency. In that situation, the financial statements need to be remeasured from the foreign currency to the functional currency using the temporal method and then translated into the reporting currency using the current rate method. The rationale behind the concept of remeasurement is to produce the same results as if the transactions had actually taken place in the functional currency. Thus, nonmonetary assets are restated in the functional currency at the exchange rate in effect when the assets were acquired in the foreign currency.

As a final possibility, the books and records are kept in the foreign currency, but the functional currency is defined as the reporting currency. In that situation, the foreign currency financial statements are remeasured into the reporting currency using the temporal method.

The important thing to note from this discussion is that IAS 21 and Statement 52 use both the current rate method and the temporal method of translating and remeasuring financial statements from a foreign currency to U.S. dollars. The key is to know in which currency the books and records are kept and how the functional currency of the foreign entity is defined. Thus, Statement 52 has not necessarily simplified the translation process, and we cannot forget all the problems that occurred with Statement 8. Also, it is incorrect to refer to Statement 52 as the current rate method since it encompasses both methods.

The Translation Process Illustrated

Earlier in this chapter, we mentioned that the translation process has to deal with two issues: which exchange rate (current or historical) must be used to translate each individual account in the financial statements and how the resulting translation gain or loss is to be recognized in the statements.

Exhibit 10.4 contains the relevant exchange rates and basic assumptions that are needed to translate the financial statements in Exhibits 10.5 and 10.6. Note that two different retained earnings figures are given for the current rate and temporal methods. We will explain this later in the chapter. Also, note that even though taxes were paid evenly throughout the year, dividends were paid only on June 30.

The Temporal Method

Remember that the temporal method is used to remeasure financial statements from a foreign currency to the functional currency. Assume that Grover Manufacturing Plc is the British subsidiary of a U.S. firm and that the functional currency is defined as the U.S. dollar rather than the British pound. The use of the temporal method requires that we do the following:

1. Remeasure cash, receivables, and liabilities at the current balance sheet rate.

2. Remeasure inventory (which is carried at historical cost in this case), fixed assets, and capital stock at the appropriate historical exchange rates.

Exhibit 10.4   Relevant Exchange Rates

Exchange Rates	($ per £)
Rate in effect when capital stock was issued; the long-term notes payable was incurred and fixed assets were acquired	1.85
December 31, 2000	1.48
Average for 2001	1.53
December 31, 2001	1.56
Rate for December 31, 2000 inventory	1.50
Rate for December 31, 2001 inventory	1.45
Dividend rate June 30, 2001	1.55
Assume that taxes were paid evenly throughout the year	

Retained Earnings	Dollar Value
Retained Earnings 12/31/00 (current rate method)	$11,560
Retained Earnings 12/31/00 (temporal method)	$12,360

Exhibit 10.5   Pounds Sterling Balance Sheet (in thousands)

Grover Mfg. Plc		
	December 31	
	2001	2000
Assets		
Current assets		
Cash and receivables	4,000	3,000
Inventory	4,500	3,000
Total	8,500	6,000
Fixed assets		
Land	3,000	3,000
Building (cost £10,000)	7,000	8,000
Equipment (cost £10,000)	4,000	6,000
Total	14,000	17,000
Total Assets	22,500	23,000
Liabilities and Stockholders' Equity		
Current liabilities	5,500	6,000
Long-term liabilities		
Notes payable	3,000	5,000
Deferred income taxes	2,500	2,000
	5,500	7,000
Stockholders' Equity		
Capital stock	5,000	5,000
Retained earnings	6,500	5,000
	11,500	10,000
Total Liabilities and Stockholders' Equity	22,500	23,000

3. Remeasure most revenues and expenses at the average rate for the year; cost of sales and depreciation expense are translated at the appropriate historical exchange rates.

4. Take all remeasurement gains or losses directly to the income statement.

To accomplish these purposes, it is easier to remeasure the balance sheet before the income statement. Notice that in Exhibit 10.7 there is no exchange rate associated with retained earnings. This is because the December 31, 2001, retained earnings amount is the difference between total assets and liabilities less the other stockholders' equity accounts (in this case, just capital stock). Thus, the retained earnings balance must be $12,255 at the end of the year.

The remeasured statement of income and retained earnings is found in Exhibit 10.8. Notice that in the income statement cost of sales and depreciation

Exhibit 10.6 Pounds Sterling Statement of Income and Retained Earnings

Grover Mfg. Plc
Statement of Income and Retained Earnings for the Year Ended
December 31, 2001 (pounds in thousands)

Sales		18,000
Expenses:		
Cost of sales	9,000	
Depreciation	3,000	
Other expenses	2,100	14,100
Income before Taxes		3,900
Income Taxes		1,900
Net Income		2,000
Retained Earnings, December 31, 2000		5,000
		7,000
Dividends		500
Retained Earnings, December 31, 2001		6,500

Exhibit 10.7 Remeasured Balance Sheet: Temporal Method

Grover Mfg. Plc
Translated Balance Sheet (Temporal Method) December 31, 2001 (in thousands)

	Pounds	Exchange Rate	Dollars
Assets			
Cash and receivables	4,000	1.56	6,240
Inventory	4,500	1.45	6,525
Land	3,000	1.85	5,550
Building—net	7,000	1.85	12,950
Equipment—net	4,000	1.85	7,400
	22,500		38,665
Liabilities and Stockholders' Equity			
Current liabilities	5,500	1.56	8,580
Notes payable	3,000	1.56	4,680
Deferred taxes	2,500	1.56	3,900
Capital stock	5,000	1.85	9,250
Retained earnings	6,500		12,255
	22,500		38,665

Exhibit 10.8   Remeasured Statement of Income and Retained Earnings:
Temporal Method

Grover Mfg. Plc
Translated Statement of Income and Retained Earnings (Temporal Method) for the Year
Ended December 31, 2001 (in thousands)

	Pounds	Exchange Rate	Dollars
Sales	18,000	1.53	27,540
Expenses:			
Cost of sales	9,000	*a*	14,040
Depreciation	3,000	1.85	5,550
Other expenses	2,100	1.53	3,213
Translation loss (gain)			1,160
	14,100		23,963
Income before Taxes	3,900		3,577
Income Taxes	1,900	1.53	2,907
Net Income	2,000		670
Retained Earnings (12/31/93)	5,000		12,360
	7,000		13,030
Dividends	500	1.55	(775)
Retained Earnings (12/31/94)	6,500		12,255
Beginning inventory	3,000	1.50	4,500
Purchases	10,500	1.53	16,065
Goods available for sale	13,500		20,565
Ending inventory	4,500	1.45	6,525
	9,000		14,040

a Cost of sales.

expense are not remeasured at the same exchange rate as are other revenues and expenses. In the case of cost of sales, different rates are used for beginning inventory, purchases, and ending inventory. Depreciation expense is translated at the historical rate in effect when assets were purchased.

In the case of ending inventory, it is useful at this point to briefly explain more specifically how the remeasurement process works. U.S. GAAP adheres to the lower-of-cost or market concept, so those two amounts must be calculated before determining which is the correct inventory figure. Cost is determined by multiplying the historical cost in the foreign currency by the exchange rate in effect when the inventory was acquired. Market is determined by multiplying the market value in the foreign currency by the current exchange rate (actually the exchange rate in effect when market was determined). The lower-of-cost or market test is then conducted in dollars. It is important to note that the test is not performed in the foreign currency but *is* performed in the reporting currency. For example, assume that inventory cost £3,000 when the exchange rate was $1.50 per £, and market value was £3,100 when the exchange rate was $1.42. In £, cost would be lower than market, but in dollars market ($4,402) would be lower than cost ($4,500), so we would select market in dollar terms rather than cost in £ terms.

Notice in the income statement that there is a translation loss of $1,160. That figure is derived by working backward. We know from the balance sheet in Exhibit 10.7 that the ending retained earnings balance must be $12,255. Because we remeasured the dividend amount and were provided the beginning retained earnings (RE) balance, we can derive the net income figure for the year (ending RE + dividends–beginning RE = NI). All the other accounts were remeasured, so the translation gain is the amount that must be plugged in to arrive at the net income figure. The important thing to note here is that the translation gain is taken directly to the income statement rather than to the balance sheet.

The Current Rate Method

The current rate method is far easier to determine. It is used when the functional currency is defined as the foreign currency and is by far the more widely used translation method. To accomplish the translation process, the following steps must be performed:

1. Total assets and liabilities are translated at the current exchange rate.
2. Stockholders' equity accounts are translated at the appropriate historical exchange rates.
3. All revenue and expense items are translated at the average exchange rate for the period.
4. Dividends are translated at the exchange rate in effect when they were issued.
5. Translation gains and losses are taken to a special accumulated translation adjustment account in stockholders' equity.

In the current rate method, it is better to translate the income statement before translating the balance sheet because the translation gain or loss becomes a balance sheet plug figure rather than an income statement plug figure as in the temporal method. Notice that in Exhibit 10.9 all income statement accounts are translated at the average exchange rate for the period. The beginning retained earnings balance was provided in Exhibit 10.4, and dividends are translated at the exchange rate in effect when they were paid. Thus, the ending retained earnings balance is derived from the other figures rather than plugged in from the balance sheet.

In Exhibit 10.10, all assets and liabilities are translated at the current exchange rate. Capital stock is translated at the exchange rate in effect when it was issued, and retained earnings are picked up from Exhibit 10.9. All that is left is the accumulated translation adjustment, which is a $5,155 loss that makes the balance sheet balance. It is important to note that the translation adjustment is taken to stockholders' equity rather than to the income statement, as was the case under the temporal method.

Foreign Currency Transactions

In Chapter 9, we learned that gains and losses from foreign currency transactions are taken to the income statement. For example, assume that the British subsidiary

Exhibit 10.9   Translated Statement of Income and Retained Earnings: Current
Rate Method

Grover Mfg. Plc
Translated Statement of Income and Retained Earnings (Current Rate Method) for the
Year Ended December 31, 2001 (in thousands)

	Pounds	Exchange Rate	Dollars
Sales	18,000	1.53	27,540
Expenses:			
Cost of sales	9,000	1.53	13,770
Depreciation	3,000	1.53	4,590
Other expenses	2,100	1.53	3,213
	14,100		21,573
Income before taxes	3,900		5,967
Income taxes	1,900	1.53	2,907
Net income	2,000		3,060
Retained earnings (12/31/00)	5,000		11,560
	7,000		14,620
Dividends	500	1.55	775
Retained earnings (12/31/01)	6,500		13,845

Exhibit 10.10   Translated Balance Sheet: Current Rate Method

Grover Mfg. Plc
Translated Balance Sheet Current Rate Method December 31, 2001 (in thousands)

	Pounds	Exchange Rate	Dollars
Assets			
Cash and receivables	4,000	1.56	6,240
Inventory	4,500	1.56	7,020
Land	3,000	1.56	4,680
Buildings—net	7,000	1.56	10,920
Equipment—net	4,000	1.56	6,240
Total	22,500		35,100
Liabilities and Stockholders' Equity			
Current liabilities	5,500	1.56	8,580
Notes payable	3,000	1.56	4,680
Deferred taxes	2,500	1.56	3,900
Capital stock	5,000	1.85	9,250
Retained earnings	6,500		13,845
Accumulated translation adjustment	____		(5,155)
Total	22,500		35,100

suffers a foreign exchange loss of £10,000 from an import denominated in deutsche marks. The loss would be translated into dollars at the 2001 average exchange rate of $1.53, and the $15,300 loss would probably show up on the income statement under "other income/other expense." Gains and losses on foreign currency debt are often shown as an adjustment of interest expense. This is true for both the temporal and current rate methods of translation.

Intercompany Transactions

There are various types of intercompany transactions that occur between a parent and subsidiary. Some are considered long term in nature, such as when a parent company loans money to a subsidiary but does not expect to have the loan repaid. Others are short term in nature, such as when a parent lends money to a subsidiary and expects the loan to be repaid. In addition, intercompany profits can arise when the parent sells goods or services to a subsidiary, and a portion of these profits can be related to exchange rate changes.

Long-Term Investment   An intercompany transaction that is of a long-term-investment nature is one where settlement is not planned or anticipated in the foreseeable future. For example, assume that the parent company lends $500,000 to its British subsidiary on January 1, 2000, when the exchange rate was $1.48. The British subsidiary would carry the loan on its books at £337,838. At the end of the year when the exchange rate is $1.56, the loan would be worth £320,513, giving rise to a foreign exchange gain of £17,325. If the loan is expected to be paid back, the gain would be recognized in the income statement of the British subsidiary and translated into dollars at the 2001 average exchange rate for consolidation purposes. However, if the loan is considered long term in nature, the exchange gain would be taken to the separate component of stockholders' equity if the financial statements are translated by the current rate method and to the income statement if remeasured by the temporal method.

Elimination of Intercompany Profits   Intercompany profits, such as those arising from a sale from a parent to subsidiary, must be eliminated upon consolidation, combination, or the equity method, and such profits are based on the exchange rates at the dates of the sales or transfers. For example, assume that a U.S. parent company sells $100,000 in software to its British subsidiary on October 1, 2001, when the exchange rate is $1.45 and the year-end rate balance sheet rate is $1.56. The determination of intercompany profits is found in Exhibit 10.11. Notice that the inventory is carried on the subsidiary books at £68,966. When the exchange rate changes to $1.56 at the end of the year, the dollar equivalent of the inventory using the current rate method becomes $107,587. However, the parent company profit of $25,000 must be eliminated from the inventory upon consolidation, so the inventory is carried at $82,587 instead of $75,000, which was the value of the inventory when the sale was made. Under the temporal method, the inventory is carried at historical cost, so the inventory is the same at the balance sheet date as it was at the transfer date.

Exhibit 10.11   Elimination of Intercompany Profits

	Transfer	Rate	Balance Sheet	Rate
	$1.45/£		$1.56/£	
	Local Currency	U.S. Dollars	Local Currency	U.S. Dollars
Inventory Transfer Price	68,966	100,000	68,966	107,587
Parent cost		75,000		75,000
Parent Profit Component		25,000		25,000
Inventory after profit elimination		75,000		82,587

Statement of Cash Flows

The guidelines for preparing the statement of cash flows for an MNE can be found in FASB Statement 95 and are basically the same as those found in International Accounting Standard 7. IAS 7 is one of the few standards that the SEC will allow foreign firms to use when registering in the United States rather than having to reconcile to U.S. GAAP. A cash flow statement should report flows of cash and cash equivalents classified by operating activities, investing activities, and financing activities. Cash equivalents are short-term investments that are purchased and sold as part of the firm's cash management activities, rather than as part of its operating, investing, and financing activities. Using the example of our U.S. parent and British subsidiary, the following steps must be followed in preparing a Statement of Cash Flows.

- The British subsidiary first prepares its own statement of cash flows in British pounds.
- Next, the cash flows are translated into dollars using the actual exchange rate in effect when the cash flows took place or the average exchange rate for the year.
- Finally, the translated cash flows are consolidated with the parent company's cash flow statement.

Net income is the beginning point for a cash flow statement, and the consolidated income statement may carry unrealized foreign exchange gains and losses, such as those that arise from carrying a foreign currency receivable or payable. Because these gains and losses are not cash flows, they must be excluded from cash flows from operating activities. One approach would be to disclose these gains and losses as a reconciling item between net income and net cash flow from operating activities. In addition, exchange rate changes can affect foreign currency cash balances during a period. The resulting gain or loss must be reported as a separate item on the reconciliation of the change in cash and cash equivalents during the period.

Rather than disclose the effect of exchange rate changes as an adjustment to operating income, it is more common to show it as a separate component of cash flows for the period. For example, DaimlerChrysler, which was formed by the merger of DaimlerBenz, a German company, and Chrysler, a U.S. company, prepares its consolidated financial statements according to U.S. GAAP and uses the euro as the currency of its financial statements, although it also provides financial information in U.S. dollars. In its 1999 consolidated cash flow statement, it disclosed the effect of foreign exchange rate changes on cash and cash equivalents maturing within three months as a separate item after cash provided by operating, investing, and financing activities.

Disclosure of the Impact of Statement 52

Statement 52 is very specific about what needs to be disclosed:

1. The aggregate transaction gain or loss included in income.
2. An analysis of the changes during the period of the separate component of stockholders' equity, including at least the following.
   a. Beginning and ending amount of cumulative translation adjustments.
   b. The aggregate adjustment for the period resulting from translation adjustments and gains and losses from certain hedges and intercompany balances.
   c. The amount of income taxes for the period allocated to the translation adjustments.
   d. The amounts transferred from cumulative translation adjustments and included in determining net income for the period as a result of the sale or complete or substantially complete liquidation of an investment in a foreign entity.

That information can be provided in a separate financial statement, in notes to the financial statements, or as a part of a statement of changes in equity. There does not seem to be any uniform or suggested method for determining where the information is to be displayed or in which format.

Firms usually disclose their translation policies in the footnotes, as noted below in the case of DaimlerChrysler, which is a part of footnote 2, Summary of Significant Accounting Policies. As noted, DaimlerChrysler uses the current rate method for its operations in all countries except those that are highly inflationary. In addition, DaimlerChrysler provides separate information on the cumulative translation adjustment in the consolidated statements of changes in stockholders' equity, as shown in Exhibit 10.12.

One of the difficulties of this disclosure process is that the focus is on the measurable transactions and translation gains and losses. It is important for management to spend some time in the annual report explaining the rest of the impact of the translation of financial statements on the operations of the firm. In early 1999, for example, the U.S. dollar was rising against most foreign currencies, except for the Japanese yen. That strength turned to weakness in mid-1999, but the dollar again began to rise rather sharply in the first half of 2000. During these times

Exhibit 10.12   DaimlerChrysler

Foreign Currencies – The assets and liabilities of foreign subsidiaries where the functional currency is other than the euro are generally translated using period-end exchange rates while the statements of income are translated using average exchange rates during the period. Differences arising from the translation of assets and liabilities in comparison with the translation of the previous periods are included as a separate component of stockholders' equity.

The assets and liabilities of foreign subsidiaries operating in highly inflationary economies are remeasured into euro on the basis of period-end rates for monetary assets and liabilities and at historical rates for non-monetary items, with resulting translation gains and losses being recognized in income. Further in such economies, depreciation and gains and losses from the disposal of non-monetary assets are determined using historical rates.

The exchange rates of the significant currencies of non-euro participating countries used in preparation of the consolidated financial statements were as follows (prior periods have been restated from Deutsche Marks into euros using the Official Fixed Conversion Rate of #eu1 = DM1.95583):

		Exchange Rate at December 31,		Annual Average Exchange Rate		
Currency:		1999 €1 =	1998 €1 =	1999 €1 =	1998 €1 =	1997 €1 =
Brazil	BRL	1.80	1.42	1.93	1.29	1.22
Great Britain	GBP	0.62	0.70	0.66	0.67	0.69
Japan	JPY	102.73	134.84	121.25	144.96	136.20
USA	USD	1.00	1.17	1.07	1.11	1.13

CONSOLIDATED STATEMENTS OF CHANGES IN STOCKHOLDERS' EQUITY

(in millions of €)	Capital Stock	Additional Paid-in Capital	Retained Earnings	Accumulated Other Comprehensive Income			Treasury Stock	Preferred Stock	Total
				Cumulative Translation Adjustment	Available for-Sale Securities	Minimum Pension Liability			
Balance at January 1, 1997	2,444	4,210	16,581	(972)	112	(20)	–	–	22,355
Net income	–	–	6,547	–	–	–	–	–	6,547
Other comprehensive income	–	–	–	1,865	157	1	–	–	2,023
Total comprehensive income									8,570

(continues)

273

Exhibit 10.12 *(Continued)*

Issuance of capital stock	4	85	—	—	—	—	—	89
Purchase and retirement of capital stock	(59)	(1,430)	—	—	—	—	(462)	(1,951)
Dividends	—	—	(1,276)	—	—	—	—	(1,276)
Other	2	93	40	—	—	—	38	173
Balance at December 31, 1997	**2,391**	**2,958**	**21,892**	**893**	**269**	**(19)**	**(424)**	**27,960**
Net income	—	—	4,820	—	—	—	—	4,820
Other comprehensive income (loss)	—	—	—	(1,402)	259	(1)	—	(1,144)
Total comprehensive income								**3,676**
Issuance of capital stock	163	3,913	—	—	—	—	—	4,076
Purchase and retirement of capital stock	—	—	—	—	—	—	(169)	(169)
Re-issuance of treasury strock	—	538	—	—	—	—	482	1,020
Dividends	—	—	(1,086)	—	—	—	—	(1,086)
Special distribution	—	—	(5,284)	—	—	—	—	(5,284)
Other	7	(135)	191	—	—	—	111	174
Balance at December 31, 1998	**2,561**	**7,274**	**20,533**	**(509)**	**528**	**(20)**	**—**	**30,367**
Net income	—	—	5,746	—	—	—	—	5,746
Other comprehensive income (loss)	—	—	—	2,431	(181)	(8)	—	2,242
Total comprehensive income								**7,988**
Issuance of capital stock	8	83	—	—	—	—	—	67
Purchase of capital stock	—	—	—	—	—	—	(86)	(86)
Re-issuance of treasury stock	—	—	—	—	—	—	86	86
Dividends	—	—	(2,356)	—	—	—	—	(2,356)
Other	(8)	—	2	—	—	—	—	(6)
Balance at December 31, 1999	**2,565**	**7,329**	**23,925**	**1,922**	**347**	**(28)**	**—**	**36,060**

Source: DaimlerChrysler Annual Report 1999, p. 75.

of dollar strength, at the same time that many foreign economies were relatively weak as compared with the U.S. economy, many U.S. firms were experiencing a translated dollar profit squeeze. This can be illustrated by the following example:

	Income FC	**Exchange Rate**	**Dollars**
First Quarter 1999	FC100,000	$1.00	$100,000
First Quarter 2000	FC110,000	$0.25	$27,500

Income rose in foreign currency from 100,000 to 110,000 over the year, an increase of only 10 percent, due primarily to a weak economy. However, the dollar equivalent fell from $100,000 to $27,500, a drop of 72.5 percent. Thus, one can see how a foreign currency gain can be turned into a dollar loss if the foreign economy is growing slower than the foreign currency is weakening relative to the dollar. It would be important to report this type of situation to shareholders so they can better understand the reported results.

Many companies do a good job of describing how foreign exchange impacts operations. Coca-Cola, for example, provides several pieces of information in its financial review in the annual report. It noted in 1999 that it uses 20 functional currencies. It then goes on to provide the percentage change rates for several key currencies in 1997, 1998, and 1999. It also discusses its hedging strategies in a couple of locations in the annual report.

The Concept of Exposure

Although we have discussed exposure in different parts of this chapter, we will summarize the key concepts here. The concept of exposure is that the translated value of an account denominated in a foreign currency changes when the exchange rate changes. From the standpoint of the translation of foreign currency financial statements, accounts translated at the current rate are exposed to an exchange rate change; those translated at the historical rate are not.

Exhibit 10.13 illustrates the concept of exposure from the point of view of an exposed asset or liability position. An exposed asset position is one where the assets translated at the current rate exceed the liabilities translated at the current rate. An exposed liability is just the opposite. In the case of a U.S. company investing in Japan, an exposed asset position in a strong Japanese yen results in a translation gain because the dollar value of the yen assets rises as the yen appreciates against the dollar. An exposed liability position results in a translation loss because the value of the yen liabilities rises as the yen appreciates.

If the yen were weakening against the dollar, the exposed asset and liability positions would result in a loss and a gain, respectively.

The current rate method is likely to have an exposed asset position because all assets are translated at the current rate. The size of the exposed position depends on what percentage of the assets is financed by debt.

The temporal method is likely to have an exposed liability position because the only exposed assets are cash, receivables, and inventory carried at market values. If the firm uses very little debt to finance assets, it might have a small exposed liability position or be relatively balanced in its exposure.

Exhibit 10.13 Exposure

	Strong Foreign Currency	Weak Foreign Currency
Net Asset Position	Gain	Loss
Net Liability Position	Loss	Gain

Translated income is very much like an asset position, so firms are positively exposed with income earned in a strong currency country. However, income earned in a weak currency country will be depressed by the weak exchange rate.

As a result, the exposure impact on income is more consistent with the current rate method. Under the current rate method, an investment in a strong currency country will result in a translation gain that is taken to equity. At the same time, translated income will get an extra kick from the strong currency. This is also consistent with dividend flows. Dividend flows from a strong currency country will benefit from the rising exchange rate. Dividend flows from a weak currency country will lose value due to the weakening exchange rate.

However, the results under the temporal method will be mixed. If the firm has an exposed liability position in a strong currency country, the translation of the financial statements will result in a translation loss that will be taken to the income statement. However, the income statement itself will be positively benefited by the strong currency. Thus, the impact on income will be mixed and volatile, depending on the degree of movement of the exchange rate.

DaimlerChrysler provides a good example of how companies discuss exposure in their annual reports. In Exhibit 10.12, DaimlerChrysler discloses their exposed position in four specific currencies as well as their total exposed position. Then they show what impact a 10 percent appreciation of the euro would have on pre-tax cash flows in the absence of any other hedging strategies. Since the financial statements of DaimlerChrysler are presented in euro, an appreciation of the euro would be the equivalent of a devaluation of the foreign currencies of the countries where DaimlerChrysler is doing business, so an appreciation of the euro would result in weaker translated results of foreign operations. Since Daimler-Chrysler uses the current rate method, they would have an exposed asset position, and Exhibit 10.13 shows us that they should have a loss. Note that Daimler-Chrysler shows the impact of a strengthening euro rather than a weakening euro. A weakening euro would result in gains, not losses, but the Germans are very conservative and would be more likely to want to disclose the impact of a loss rather than a gain.

NON-U.S. TRANSLATION PRACTICES

Up to this point, we have described the process required by the IASC and the U.S. FASB. We noted earlier, however, that the standards in the U.K. and Canada were issued at about the same time as IAS 21 and Statement 52. IAS 21, and the influence of FASB, have done a great deal to create convergence in the translation process. In addition, it should be noted that the British pioneered the current rate method and thus had a strong influence on IAS 21 as well.

The Fourth Directive on the format and content of financial statements in the EU and the Seventh Directive on consolidated financial statements do not contain much guidance on accounting for foreign currency transactions and the translation of foreign currency financial statements. The EU, however, has agreed to allow European firms to use International Accounting Standards, so IAS 21 is rapidly becoming the norm in Europe. Prior to that, some countries had specific standards, while others did not. In addition, there was great variation in practice.

Although both the current rate and temporal methods are allowed in most European countries, most tend to use the current rate method. The notable exception is Germany, where firms tend to use a form of the temporal method. The Germans do not make a distinction in translation methodology based on the functional currency, as is the case in the United States.

The French use the temporal method for integrated foreign companies (similar to using the reporting currency as the functional currency) and the current rate method for self-sustaining foreign entities (similar to using the foreign currency as the functional currency). Gains and losses are treated in the same way as in Statement 52.

United Kingdom

In April 1983, the Accounting Standards Committee of the United Kingdom issued Statement of Standard Accounting Practice No. 20 (SSAP 20), *Foreign Currency Translation*. Prior to that time, the method of translation most widely used in the United Kingdom was the current rate method (known as the closing-rate method in the United Kingdom). However, SSAP 20 allows the use of the closing-rate method or the temporal method, depending on the operating relationship that exists between the investor and investee. This is similar to the concept of the functional currency described in Statement 52.

In spite of the similarities between the standards of the United States and the United Kingdom, some important differences also exist.

1. SSAP 20 does not deal with foreign currency transactions. It comments in the foreword to the standard that foreign currency transactions must be translated into the reporting currency, but it does not deal with many of the issues covered in Statement 52.

2. In terms of terminology, the British use closing rate rather than current rate.

3. SSAP 20 does not require the level of disclosure on translation gains and losses that is required in Statement 52. In addition, British firms do not have to set up a separate section in stockholders' equity to hold translation adjustments since they already use a reserve account for a variety of adjustments. SSAP 20 requires disclosure of the movement on reserves during the year. It requires that somewhere the net amount of exchange gains and losses included in equity and in net income for the period be disclosed.

A reading of SSAP 20 reveals two interesting points. The first is that the vast majority of firms affected by the standard did not have to change their practices materially insofar as it has been estimated that more than 90 percent of the British multinationals were using the closing rate method when the standard was adopted. The experience in the United States was just the opposite when Statement 52 was issued: essentially all firms were using the temporal method. The other point is that the British standard seems to have more flexibility built in than does the U.S. standard.

Canada

The Canadian standard on foreign currency translation was adopted in July 1983. That standard, which dealt with both transactions and translation, has elements that are similar to as well as different from the U.S. and British standards.

For translating foreign currency financial statements, the temporal and current rate methods can be used depending on the operating characteristics of the foreign operations. If the reporting enterprise is an integrated foreign operation, the temporal method for translation must be used. This is similar to defining the functional currency as the reporting currency in Statement 52. Translation gains and losses are taken to income unless they relate to long-term debt. As we noted earlier, those gains and losses can be deferred and amortized. This variance from international practice as required under IAS 21 and FASB Statement 52 is no small difference. Canadian companies are heavy borrowers of U.S. dollars, and they have traditionally not taken gains and losses to income. The elimination of this approach to dealing with gains and losses would have a significant effect on earnings volatility of Canadian companies. The Canadian Institute has been trying to bring their practice into line with the IASC and FASB since 1983, but nothing has been finalized. The practice in Canada is still to defer and amortize translation adjustments.

If the reporting enterprise is a self-sustaining foreign operation, the current rate method must be used. This is similar to defining the functional currency as something other than the reporting currency in Statement 52. Translation gains and losses are taken to a separate section in stockholders' equity rather than taken to income, which is consistent with Statement 52.

USE OF DERIVATIVES TO HEDGE A NET INVESTMENT

In Chapter 9, we showed how a derivative financial instrument could be used to hedge exposure on foreign currency transactions, but we did not discuss the use of a derivative to hedge a net investment of foreign operations. Statement 133 basically retains the same provisions that applied under Statement 52 for accounting for the hedge of a net investment. Gains and losses on a derivative used to hedge a net investment are taken to a separate component of shareholder' equity rather than taken directly to income. That assumes, of course, that the derivative is designated and is effective as a hedge of the net investment. Since the derivative used to hedge the net investment is marked to fair value at the end of each accounting period, the gain or loss may be included in the cumulative translation adjustment to the extent that the changes represent an effective economic hedge of the net investment.

DISCLOSURE OF DERIVATIVE FINANCIAL INSTRUMENTS

A final subject in this chapter is the disclosure of derivatives. In Chapter 9, we discussed the accounting for derivatives in conjunction with foreign currency transactions, but in this chapter we will only deal with disclosure. In recent years there has been a lot of publicity about losses due to derivatives, and disclosure has been relatively noncomparative due to the off-balance-sheet nature of the instruments. Most experts agree that derivatives, including foreign currency derivatives, are subject to several kinds of risk:

- Market risk—the risk of loss due to unexpected changes in interest and exchange rates
- Credit risk—the potential loss from counterparty nonperformance
- Liquidity risk—related to market liquidity of instruments held and, therefore, closely related to market risk
- Operating risk—linked to inadequate controls that ensure following a properly defined corporate policy.

The key is to determine how best to disclose the extent of the risk to users. As a result of IAS 39 and FASB Statement 133, companies are improving and standardizing their disclosures on financial instruments. At the time of the writing of this edition, neither standard had been fully implemented, but they were the only standards in the world dealing with financial instruments. By examining the financial statements of a number of companies that were early adopting either of the two standards, one can make the following observations about disclosures on financial instruments:

- The disclosures are located in the footnotes to the financial statements and are fairly comprehensive.
- They described the types of financial instruments used by the company and the types of risks they are hedging.
- They provide at least the notional principal amounts and fair values of each type of derivative financial instrument.
- They may disclose other information, such as the carrying values and maturities of the derivatives.

SUMMARY

1. Companies translate foreign currency financial statements into the parent currency to assist the readers of financial statements and to enable management to compare results across different countries.

2. The functional currency is the currency of the primary economic environment in which the company operates.

3. The current/noncurrent method translates current assets and liabilities at current exchange rates and noncurrent assets, liabilities, and stockholders' equity at historical exchange rates.

4.   The monetary/nonmonetary method translates monetary assets and liabilities at the current exchange rate and nonmonetary assets and liabilities at the historical exchange rate.

5.   The temporal method translates monetary assets and liabilities at the current rate and other accounts at current or historical exchange rate, depending on their characteristics. Assets and liabilities carried at past exchange prices (such as fixed assets carried at historical cost) are translated at the historical exchange rate. Assets and liabilities carried at current cost are translated using the current exchange rate.

6.   The current rate method translates assets and liabilities at the current rate and shareholders' equity at historical rates. Income statement items are translated at the average exchange rate.

7.   Under the temporal method, translation gains and losses go to income; under the current rate method, they go to shareholders' equity.

8.   IAS 21 and FASB Statement 52 require financial statements to be translated using either the temporal or the current rate methods.

9.   Exchange gains and losses that arise from foreign currency transactions are translated at the average exchange rate for the period.

10.   Foreign exchange gains and losses are reported in the statement of cash flows as a reconciling item between net income and net cash flow from operating activities or as a separate component of cash flows for the period.

11.   In their annual reports, companies typically disclose the translation method they use and the amount of the translation gain or loss for the period. The latter information is usually disclosed in the statements of shareholders' equity for companies that use the current rate method to translate financial statements. In addition, they often disclose the impact of foreign exchange on operations.

12.   If a foreign subsidiary has a net exposed asset position in a strong currency country, it will usually report a translation gain; the opposite is true if operating in a week currency country. This is usually the case when translating using the current rate method.

13.   According to IAS 39 and FASB Statement 133, companies generally disclose the types of financial instruments they use, their notional principal amounts, and their fair values. In addition, they may disclose other information, such as carrying values and maturities of the derivatives.

Problems

1.   Rouse Company, a developer of major shopping centers, built two shopping centers in Canada and financed more than 90 percent of the cost with a loan from Canadian lenders. The loan would be paid off with rental income from the shopping centers with no recourse to Rouse Company.

a.   Assume that Rouse treated the U.S. dollar as the functional currency for translation purposes and that the Canadian dollar was weakening against the U.S. dollar. What do you think would have been the impact of that situation on the income statement?

b.   Rouse argued to the FASB that its operations in Canada constituted a natural hedge and that it should not have to reflect any translation gains or losses in income. What do you think they meant by a "natural hedge," and what is your opinion about their contention?

    c. How would your answer in question a differ if Rouse treated the Canadian dollar rather than the U.S. dollar as the functional currency?

    d. Given the assumptions in the case, which currency should be the functional currency?

2. The following is an example of a U.S. company with a U.K. subsidiary:

	First Quarter 2001			First Quarter 2002		
	Pound Sterling	U.S. Dollar Equivalent per Pound	U.S. Dollars	Pound Sterling	U.S. Dollar Equivalent per Pound	U.S. Dollars
Net sales	£5,020	1.60	$8,032	£5,390	1.45	$7,816
Cost of sales	3,320	1.55	5,146	3,465	1.50	5,198
Gross profit	1,700		2,886	1,925		2,618
Operating expenses	1,170	1.60	1,872	1,315	1.45	1,907
Pretax results	530		1,014	610		711
Income taxes	310	1.60	496	315	1.45	457
Net earnings	£ 220		$ 518	£ 295		$ 254

    a. Was the U.S. dollar stengthening or weakening against the pound from the fourth quarter of 2000 to the first quarter of 2001? from the first quarter of 2001 to the first quarter of 2002?

    b. Was the temporal method or the current rate method used to translate this income statement?

    c. Analyze the effect of translation on reported sales and earnings from one year to the next and compare the dollar and pound changes.

    d. Assume that the average exchange rate for the first quarter of 2001 was $1.60 and the average exchange rate for the first quarter of 2002 was $1.45. If the income statements had been translated at the average exchange rate, what would have been the impact on your answer for question c?

3. RadCo International is a U.S. firm with a wholly owned subsidiary in France. The basic assumptions involved in the French subsidiary and its interaction with the parent company are as follows:

Relevant Exchange Rates (US$/FF)

December 31, 2000	.1500
December 31, 2001	.1380
Historical Rate	.1600
Average during 2001	.1450
Average during fourth quarter, 2000	.1510
Average during fourth quarter, 2001	.1400

Balance Sheet (in French francs; in thousands)

	12/31/00	12/31/01
Cash	1,000	2,000
Accounts receivable	3,900	4,725

(continues)

Inventories	3,600	4,700
Fixed assets	27,500	27,500
Accumulated depreciation	(2,750)	(5,500)
Total	33,250	33,425
Accounts payable	6,500	6,000
Long-term debt	12,500	10,800
Capital stock	6,200	6,200
Retained earnings	8,050	10,425
Total	33,250	33,425

Income Statement (in French francs)	
Sales	31,500
Expenses	
Cost of goods sold	(18,000)
Depreciation	(2,750)
Other	(4,500)
Taxes	(1,500)
Net income	4,750
Dividends	2,375

a. The functional currency of the subsidiary is the French franc, and the financial statements have been recast in U.S. GAAP to assist in the translation process.
b. Capital stock was issued and fixed assets acquired when the exchange rate was FF6.3 per dollar; dividends are paid at a rate of .1450.
c. Inventories were all acquired in the previous quarter.
d. Purchases, sales, and other expenses occurred evenly throughout the year.
e. There is a zero beginning balance in the accumulated translation adjustment account.
f. Inflation in France has been in the single digits in recent years.

Exercise: Translate the financial statements into U.S. dollars.

4. RadCo International is a U.S. firm with a wholly owned subsidiary in Mexico that uses the dollar as its functional currency. The relevant facts in the case are as follows:

Relevant Exchange Rates (Pesos/US$)	
Historical Rate	5.0000
December 31, 2000	8.5000
December 31, 2001	9.4900
Average during 2001	9.0000
Average fourth quarter 2000	8.4500
Average fourth quarter 2001	9.2000

Balance Sheet (in Mexican pesos in thousands)		
	12/31/00	12/31/01
Cash	20,000	14,000
Accounts receivable	40,000	110,000
Inventories	40,000	30,000
Fixed assets	100,000	100,000
Accumulated depreciation	(20,000)	(30,000)
Total	180,000	224,000
Accounts payable	30,000	50,000
Long-term debt (U.S.$120)	1,020	1,139
Long-term peso debt	44,000	44,000
Capital stock	60,000	60,000
Retained earnings	44,980	68,861
Total	180,000	224,000

Income Statement
(in Mexican pesos in thousands)

Sales	230,000
Expenses	
Cost of goods sold	(110,000)
Depreciation	(10,000)
Other	(80,000
Taxes	(6,000)
Foreign exchange loss	(119)
Net income	32,881
Beginning inventory	40,000
Purchases	100,000
	140,000
Ending inventory	30,000
Cost of goods sold	110,000

a. Most of the transactions take place in Mexican pesos, although the subsidiary borrowed money in U.S. dollars. The financial statements have been recast into U.S. GAAP to facilitate the translation process.
b. Capital stock was issued, fixed assets acquired, and long-term dollar debt incurred when the exchange rate was 5.0000 pesos per dollar.
c. Inventories are acquired during the previous quarter.
d. Purchases, sales, and other expenses occurred evenly throughout the year.
e. Fixed assets are being depreciated on a straight-line basis over 10 years.

Exercise: Translate the peso financial statements into dollars.

Discussion Questions

1. Siemens is a German company that generates its revenues in energy, industry, information and communications, and health care. It has operations all over the world. In the notes to its financial statements, Siemens states:

   "Due to the weakness of the German mark relative to the British pound, the U.S. dollar and several Asian currencies, total assets increased DM2.7 billion upon translation of foreign currency accounts. As a result, the negative translation adjustment in shareholders' equity was substantially reduced. Net sales decreased DM1.5 billion, due to the opposite impact of annual average exchange rates on the related statement of income accounts." Explain what this means in terms of exposure and the impact of exchange rates on reported results.

2. Some might argue that Statement 52 is an international standard because FASB received a great deal of input from the IASC and from other countries while it was developing the standard. What are the strengths and weaknesses of this type of international collaboration? Does it weaken the IASC's position as an international standard-setter if it allows the United States or any other country to set a standard before it does?

3. Why do you think most U.S. companies use the current rate method as allowed under Statement 52 when the only method allowed prior to that was the temporal method or some variation of that method?

4. Imperial Chemical Industries PLC (ICI) is a British chemical company that lists ADRs on the New York Stock Exchange. In its 1999 annual report, ICI identifies its policies for dealing with foreign exchange as follows:

   "Profit and loss accounts in foreign currencies are translated into sterling at average rates for the relevant accounting periods. Assets and liabilities are translated at exchange rates ruling at the date of the Group balance sheet. Exchange differences on short-term foreign currency borrowings and deposits are included with net interest payable. Exchange differences on all other balances, except relevant foreign currency loans, are taken to trading profit. In the Group accounts, exchange differences arising on consolidation of the net investments in overseas subsidiary undertakings and associates are taken to reserves, as are differences arising on equity investments denominated in foreign currencies in the Company accounts. Differences on relevant foreign currency loans are taken to reserves and offset against the differences on net investments in both Group and Company accounts."

   Which translation methodology does ICI use? Do their policies seem consistent with what is required by FASB's Statement 52?

   Toward the end of their annual report, they also include reconciliation information consistent with Form 20-F that is required to be filed by the SEC. In that section, ICI notes that under U.K. GAAP, foreign currency differences arising on foreign currency loans are taken to reserves and offset against differences arising on net investments (if they act as a hedge) and that U.S. GAAP is more restrictive. In what way is it more restrictive?

5. XYZ Company, a manufacturer of computer peripheries, assembles a particular product line at a wholly owned facility in Singapore. The product is designed at XYZ's headquarters in the United States, but the different components used in the assembly process are manufactured throughout Asia and shipped to Singapore for final assembly. Some of the components are manufactured in multiple locations, so the customer can actually designate where XYZ should source the components. The final product is assembled in Singapore and then shipped via Emery Freight to customers throughout Asia. XYZ Singapore does not buy any components from

the United States, but it invoices all of the components purchased from Asian suppliers in U.S. dollars. In addition, it sells the product to Asian customers in U.S. dollars. However, all of its expenses in Singapore are paid in Singapore dollars. Most of the key marketing decisions are made by the U.S. marketing staff, although the Singapore staff acts as a liaison with Emery Freight personnel and deals with the local workers, most of whom come from Sri Lanka on short-term work visas.

XYZ prefers to translate the results of their Singapore subsidiary into dollars using the current rate method. What is the advantage to XYZ of using the current rate method? As their auditor, what do you think of their decision? If their decision is wrong and they should be using the temporal method, is it possible for them to change?

Case: Coca-Cola (United States)

In its 1999 annual report, Coca-Cola describes the impact of foreign exchange on its operations as follows:

"Our international operations are subject to certain opportunities and risks, including currency fluctuations and government actions. We closely monitor our operations in each country and seek to adopt appropriate strategies that are responsive to changing economic and political environments and to fluctuations in foreign currencies. We use approximately 60 functional currencies. Due to our global operations, weaknesses in some of these currencies are often offset by strengths in others. In 1999, 1998, and 1997, the weighted-average exchange rates for foreign currencies, and for certain individual currencies, strengthened (weakened) against the U.S. dollar as follows:

Year Ended December 31,	1999	1998	1997
All currencies	even	(9)%	(10)%
Australian dollar	3%	(16)%	(6)%
British pound	(2)%	2%	4%
Canadian dollar	even	(7)%	(1)%
French franc	(2)%	(3)%	(12)%
German mark	(2)%	(3)%	(13)%
Japanese yen	15%	(6)%	(10)%

These percentages do not include the effects of our hedging activities and, therefore, do not reflect the actual impact of fluctuations in exchange on our operating results. Our foreign currency management program mitigates over time a portion of the impact of exchange on net income and earnings per share. The impact of a stronger U.S. dollar reduced our operating income by approximately 4 percent in 1999 and by approximately 9 percent in 1998.

Exchange gains (losses)-net amounted to $87 million in 1999, $(34) million in 1998 and $(56) million in 1997, and were recorded in other income-net. Exchange gains (losses)-net includes the remeasurement of certain currencies into functional currencies and the costs of hedging certain exposures of our balance sheet."

Questions

1. Which translation methodology or methodologies does Coca-Cola use?

2. Given the methodology they use, would you expect them to have translation gains or losses in 1997? In 1998? In 1999? Can you find any information in the chapter to help determine their actual gains or losses in those years? Were your answers consistent with what actually happened to Coca-Cola during those years?

3. Explain how Coca-Cola could use the translation methodology that it does and still have exchange gains and losses that show up in income as explained by them in the last paragraph above.

Case: *Kamikaze Enterprises* (Japan)

Ray Addis, chairman of the board of Ace Inc., a medium-size airplane manufacturing company, had called Frank Anderson into his office to talk about an investment made by Ace in Japan five years ago. Ray was very upset because Ace's Japanese affiliate, Kamikaze Enterprises, owned 40 percent by Ace and 60 percent by the Bansha Group, was not doing well. He expected Frank, the CFO of Ace, to explain what was going on. Ray had been involved in marketing all his life, unlike Frank who came up through the finance route.

"How are you doing, Frank?"

"Pretty good, I guess, Ray. I gather from your note that you're not too pleased with Kamikaze Enterprises."

"That's an understatement. In our last set of statements, I noticed that we picked up a dollar loss from Kamikaze for the fifth year in a row. I wouldn't mind it so much, but that loss reduced our earnings by nearly 40 percent. Why can't we get that blasted operation in the black? I thought those Japanese were supposed to be cost-efficient. I feel like we're tapping money down a rat hole."

"I can understand your concern, Ray, but we've gotten a healthy yen dividend from Kamikaze every year since we've been in operation. Because the yen keeps strengthening, the dollar equivalent of that dividend goes up every year."

"I realize that, Frank, but we report in dollars to our shareholders, and I have to explain those foreign exchange losses at the next annual meeting. What am I going to do? I understand that the book value of our investment has been written down to practically nothing because of those losses. Either that operation becomes profitable or we cut loose. Let me know in three weeks what our plan of action should be."

"OK, Ray. I'll see what I can do."

"What a circus," thought Frank as he walked back to his office. "There's no way I can explain this situation so that he understands."

Ace Inc. had entered into the minority joint venture with the Bansha Group to produce small corporate aircraft in Japan. Ace provided the technical expertise and some equity financing. However, the Bansha Group provided most of the funds through debt financing with its bank. The investment was almost 90 percent debt financed.

Kamikaze Enterprises had actually been quite profitable, increasing yen profits by nearly 25 percent a year. Sales were growing at about the same rate. This growth and high profitability allowed Kamikaze to declare sizable dividends each year. When translated into dollars, however, the yen profits turned into losses, which reduced Ace's equity investment in Kamikaze. Frank had spoken to the managers of Kamikaze, who did not appear to understand the problem or want to do anything about it. Ace had been offered $50 million for its investment in Kamikaze, which seemed ironic given that the book value on Ace's books was close to zero.

Frank's major concern was that he was afraid the problem stemmed from Ace's accounting policies not their finance strategies. He decided to talk to his controller to find out what the problem might be and how they could correct it.

Questions

1. Which translation methodology did Ace use to translate Kamikaze's financial statements into dollars? Explain how you know that.

2. Assume that Ace uses the other translation methodology allowed by FASB's Statement 52. How would that change the facts in the case?

3. Which translation methodology do you think Ace should use, and why?

Selected References

Accounting Standards Committee. 1983. "Foreign Currency Translation," *Statement of Standard Accounting Practice No. 20,* London, U.K.: ASC.

Ayres, F. L. and J. L. Rodgers. 1994. "Further Evidence on the Impact of SFAS 52 on Analysts' Earnings Forecasts," *Journal of International Financial Management and Accounting* (June): 120–41.

Bartov, E. 1997. "Foreign Currency Exposure of Multinational Firms: Accounting Measures and Market Valuation," *Contemporary Accounting Research,* 14 (4) (Winter): 623–52.

Bartov, E. and G. M. Bodnar. 1995. "Foreign Currency Translation Reporting and the Exchange-Rate Exposure Effect," *Journal of International Financial Management & Accounting,* 6 (2) (Summer): 93–114.

Beaver, W. and M. Wolfson. 1982. "Foreign Currency Translation and Changing Prices in Perfect and Complete Markets," *Journal of Accounting Research* (Autumn): 528–50.

Choi, F. D. S. and R. R. Gunn. 1997. "Hyperinflation Reporting and Performance Assessment," *Journal of Financial Statement Analysis,* 2 (4) (Summer): 30–38.

Cohen, E. 1999. "The Euro and Its Impact on the European Economy: A View from Europe," *Journal of International Financial Management & Accounting,* 10 (2) (Summer): 143–51.

Demirag, I. S. 1987. "A Review of the Objectives of Foreign Currency Translation," *International Journal of Accounting* (Spring): 69–85.

Financial Accounting Standards Board. 1975. "Accounting for the Translation of Foreign Currency Transactions and Foreign Currency Financial Statements," *Statement of Financial Accounting Standards No. 8.* Stamford, CT (October).

Financial Accounting Standards Board. 1981. "Foreign Currency Translation" *Statement of Financial Accounting Standards No. 52.* Stamford, CT (December).

Goldberg, Stephen R., Charles A. Tritschler, and Joseph H. Godwin. 1995. "Financial Reporting for Foreign Exchange Derivatives," *Accounting Horizons* 9 (2) (June): 5.

Harris, T. S. 1997. "European Currency Transactions and Translation," in *International Accounting and Finance Handbook,* chapter 13, 2nd edition, edited by F. D. S. Choi. New York: John Wiley.

Hepworth, Samuel R. 1956. *Reporting Foreign Operations.* Ann Arbor: University of Michigan.

Houston, C. O. 1989. "Foreign Currency Translation Research: A Review and Synthesis," *Journal of Accounting Literature,* 8, pp. 25–48.

International Accounting Standards Committee. 1993. IAS21. *The Effects of Changes in Exchange Rates.*

Lorensen, Leonard. 1972. *Accounting Research Study No. 12,* "Reporting Foreign Operations of U.S. Companies in U.S. Dollars." New York: AICPA.

Nobes, Christopher. *Interpreting European Financial Statements: Towards 1992.* London: Butterworths, 96–102.

Pourciau, S. and T. F. Schaefer. 1995. "The Nature of the Market's Response to the Earnings Effect of Voluntary Changes in Accounting for Foreign Operations," *Journal of Accounting, Auditing & Finance*, 10 (1) (Winter): 51–70.

PriceWaterhouseCoopers 1998. *The New Standard on Accounting for Derivative Instruments and Hedging Activities.* New York: PriceWaterhouse Coopers.

PricewaterhouseCoopers. 1998. *A Guide to Accounting for Derivative Instruments and Hedging Activities* (July 31).

Rotenberg, W. 1998. "Harmonization of Foreign Currency Translation Practices: Canadian Treatment of Long Term Monetary Items," *The International Journal of Accounting*, 33 (4): 429.

Soo, B. S. and L. Gilbert Soo. 1994. "Accounting for the Multinational Firm: Is the Translation Process Valued by the Stock Market?" *Accounting Review* (October): 617–37.

Wilson, A. C. and S. Stanwick. 1995. "Alternatives to Current Accounting for Derivative Instrument," *CPA Journal*, 65 (12) (December): 48–49.

CHAPTER ELEVEN

INTERNATIONAL ACCOUNTING FOR PRICE CHANGES

Chapter Objectives

- Identify the major ways that companies and their financial statements are impacted by inflation
- Compare general purchasing power and current value approaches to inflation accounting
- Review the International Accounting Standards on accounting for price changes and inflation
- Examine inflation regulations and practices in different countries, with special emphasis on approaches to inflation accounting in South America and the Netherlands

Inflation has been a persistent worldwide phenomenon that has had a devastating impact on the economies of many countries over the years. Argentina, Brazil, Israel, Mexico, and Russia have been among the worst sufferers of hyperinflationary conditions. Annual rates of inflation in these countries have often exceeded 100 percent and have been as high as 2,000 percent in Brazil and Russia. Even in the major industrialized countries, inflation reached double figures in the mid-1970s, and in the United Kingdom it went up to a high of 25 percent. Not surprisingly, there has been increasing concern in the countries most affected to adopt "inflation accounting" systems, which will remedy the defects of conventional historical cost accounting and reveal the impact of price changes and inflation on earnings and assets.

In this chapter, we analyze alternative approaches to accounting for price changes and inflation internationally and review international harmonization initiatives.

IMPACT OF INFLATION ON THE CORPORATION

The effect of inflation on the financial position and performance of a corporation can result in inefficient operating decisions by managers who do not understand its impact. In terms of financial position, financial assets such as cash lose value during inflation because their purchasing power diminishes. For example, if a business holds financial assets such as cash during a period when inflation rises by 10 percent, that cash has 10 percent less purchasing power at the end of the period than at the beginning. Conversely, holding financial liabilities is beneficial because the business will pay its obligations in the future with cash that has lost some of its purchasing power. The caveat here is that financial liabilities, such as short- and long-term bank loans, often carry very high interest rates in inflationary economies.

The effect of inflation on nonmonetary assets is reflected in both the income statement and the balance sheet. During a period of rising prices, current sales revenues are matched against inventory that may have been purchased several months earlier and against depreciation computed on the historical cost of property, plant, and equipment that may have been purchased several years ago, despite the fact that replacing inventory and fixed assets has become more expensive.

These income statement and balance sheet effects could lead the corporation into liquidity problems as the cash generated from revenues is consumed by the ever-increasing replacement cost of assets. The overstatement of income that results from matching old costs with new revenues could lead to demands from shareholders for increased dividends and from employees for higher wages, even though the corporation is watching its cash dwindle.

Much has been said in recent years about how conventional accounting misrepresents a corporation's real financial position. The concern is that analysts and investors cannot make informed financial decisions without understanding the impact of inflation. Accordingly, the type of accounting measurement system used as well as its interpretation is an essential issue to all user groups. The measurement of income is also relevant to a wide range of concerns including share prices, business stability, wages, job security, and economic growth. In the context of the MNE, these concerns are heightened by the existence of user groups with constituencies located in different countries with different traditions of accounting measurement.

While there may be some recognition of the necessity to introduce a system of accounting for price changes or inflation accounting, except in countries such as Germany where it is considered likely to institutionalize inflation, the term *inflation accounting* covers a variety of possible methods. The major alternative approaches are "general purchasing power accounting" and "current value accounting."

ACCOUNTING MEASUREMENT ALTERNATIVES

General purchasing power accounting includes all systems designed to maintain the real purchasing power of capital or shareholders' equity in the corporation by accounting for changes in the *general level of prices* (i.e., the general purchasing power of money). This is the strict meaning of the term *inflation,* though the term *inflation accounting* is generally used in a very broad sense. Variations on the term *general purchasing power accounting* include "constant dollar accounting" or "general price level accounting" in the United States and "current purchasing power account-ing" (CPP) in the United Kingdom.

Current value accounting, on the other hand, includes all systems designed to account for current values or changes in specific prices. These include "current cost accounting" and "replacement value accounting" systems, which aim to main-tain the physical capital, productive capacity, or operating assets of the corporation; and "current exit (or selling) price accounting," which aims to maintain share-holders' equity but in terms of the selling prices of the corporation's net assets. While there is a wide range of alternatives proposed within each of these broad clas-sifications—together with "real value" systems, which combine elements of both—the use of inflation accounting systems in practice is not well developed.

In essence, therefore, there are two philosophies about how to account for inflation. General purchasing power accounting is concerned that the value of money has gone down or up, whereas current value accounting is concerned that the cost of specific assets has gone up or down. It is possible to apply these approaches to all items in the financial statements that can be adjusted or to only some of the items. Furthermore, the approaches can be used separately or in con-junction with each other. Whatever the approach, it is necessary to identify which accounts are to be adjusted, what is to be the basis for the adjustment (such as an index), and where the adjustment is to be reflected in the financial statements.

General Purchasing Power Accounting

The general philosophy supporting general purchasing power accounting is to report assets, liabilities, revenues, and expenses in units of the same purchasing power. The approach here is that the monetary unit of measure should be uniform while retaining the basis of measurement used in the financial statements (e.g., his-torical cost).

In most countries, financial statements are prepared on a historical cost-nom-inal currency basis. This means that the statements are not adjusted for changes in the general price level. Under GPP accounting, the nonfinancial items in the financial statements (inventory, plant, and equipment) are restated to reflect a common purchasing power, usually at the ending balance sheet date. For example, assume that a firm purchased a machine on January 1, 2001, for $10,000 and that the general price level, as measured by the consumer price index, increased by 15 percent during the year. On December 31, the machine would appear on the bal-ance sheet at $11,500 ($10,000 + [$10,000 × 0.15]) from which depreciation would be deducted, adjusted in GPP terms, to be charged against income. This implies that it would take $11,500 of end-of-year purchasing power to buy what $10,000 bought on January 1. For the year-end financial statements, the financial assets and liabilities (cash, receivables, payables) would not be adjusted because they are already stated in terms of December 31 purchasing power, but all other assets (including inventory), liabilities, revenues, and expenses (including depreciation) would be adjusted. When the 2000 and 2001 financial statements are compared, however, all the items in the 2000 accounts—including the financial assets and lia-bilities—would be restated to December 31, 2001, purchasing power to ensure com-parisons with the 2001 financial statements.

It has been suggested that GPP accounting should be applied to financial assets and liabilities as well. Cash, for example, loses purchasing power during an inflationary period because it cannot purchase as much at the end of the period as it did at the beginning. Debtors benefit during inflation, however, because they can pay their debts at the end of the period with cash whose purchasing power has fallen. Therefore, a firm that has increased its net financial asset position during an inflationary period suffers a loss in purchasing power, whereas a firm that has increased its net financial liability position enjoys a gain in purchasing power. The GPP accounts would reflect this loss or gain in a separate monetary items adjustment.

A further issue concerns the nature of the index to be used to make the GPP adjustments. As we noted earlier, the consumer price index is the one most widely used around the world to measure inflation. It measures the changes in prices for a wide range of consumer goods and services that are purchased for final consumption. However, because the index is consumer oriented, it may not necessarily reflect the change in prices that directly affect a given corporation.

Current Value Accounting

As we have already noted, *current value accounting* is concerned with the rise or fall in the cost or value of specific assets, not with the overall loss of purchasing power of a currency. Under this concept, income is not considered to be earned until the corporation has maintained its capital in current value terms. Under current value accounting, a new basis for valuing assets replaces the traditional historical cost approach.

There are two major approaches to current value accounting: current cost (or replacement cost) and current exit price (selling price or net realizable value). *Current cost accounting,* the most widely accepted method, is used for most classes of nonmonetary assets. Under this approach, assets are valued at what it would cost to replace them. However, whether the value should reflect the same asset being replaced or a similar asset performing the same function with a newer technology has been the subject of considerable discussion. *Current exit price accounting,* on the other hand, values assets, especially finished goods inventory, at what they could be sold for, less costs to complete and sell the items. In Dutch *exit value theory,* a further distinction is made between liquidation, value, and the going-concern concept. Under the *going-concern concept,* the asset is valued at the estimated sales price on normal completion of production.

Current value accounting results in holding gains and losses when nonmonetary assets are revalued. This is the gain or loss during the period the asset is held by the corporation. The gains and losses involved can either be taken into the income statement or reflected on the balance sheet as a capital adjustment account. A further issue concerns the determination of current values. For inventory, suppliers' lists are most commonly used because they reflect the most current prices for the items. Fixed assets are more complex. Property and plant are usually revalued according to a specific index, such as a construction cost index. Equipment may be revalued on the basis of a supplier list or engineering estimates—especially for machinery that is custom designed and built. Appraisal values are also a possibility for fixed assets. Current value accounting is obviously more complex to administer because it requires a mixture of actual prices, estimates, appraisal values, and indices for homogeneous groups of assets.

To see the impact that the use of current value accounting can have on income, assume that a corporation had sales revenues of $1,000,000, current cost of goods sold of $900,000, and historical cost of goods sold of $700,000. Under current cost accounting, operating gross profit (i.e., the difference between sales revenues and current cost of goods sold) would be $100,000. Under historical cost accounting, gross profit would be $300,000 (i.e., the difference between sales revenues and historical cost of goods sold). However, some of the historical cost profit was derived from holding inventory during a period when its specific price was increasing. Thus, the difference between the current cost of goods sold and the historical cost of goods ($900,000 – $700,000 = $200,000) can be considered a realized holding gain. It is realized because the assets were actually sold during the period.

Current Value: GPP Accounting

Although we have discussed GPP and current value accounting separately, many accountants and economists believe that the two should be combined in a *real value accounting system*. Assume, for example, that an asset was acquired at the beginning of the year for $150,000 and that at the end of the year the current value of the assets was $190,000, but the asset measured in end-of-year GPP terms was $165,000. The total holding gain of the asset would be:

$$\begin{array}{r} \$190,000 \\ \underline{-150,000} \\ \$40,000 \end{array}$$

However, the "real" holding gain (the gain net of the impact of inflation) would be only $25,000:

$$\begin{array}{r} \$190,000 \\ \underline{-165,000} \\ \$25,000 \end{array}$$

It is important to note that changes in the general level of prices (i.e., inflation) will tend to differ from changes in specific prices (current values) relevant to the corporation. Indeed, even zero inflation may be the outcome of a number of specific price changes, which, on average, show that no inflation has occurred. The impact that matters, from the corporation's perspective, is the net impact of prices directly affecting the corporation relative to the average level of prices affecting the GPP of money.

INTERNATIONAL ACCOUNTING STANDARDS

The first reaction of the IASC to inflation accounting came in 1977 in IAS 6, *Accounting Responses to Changing Prices*. At that point, however, there was no definitive standard in either the United States or the United Kingdom, and there was substantial uncertainty as to how the inflation accounting issue would be resolved in those two countries.

IAS 6 was very brief because the IASC attempted to set standards that are essentially a narrowing of available options and had to rely on a consensus of its member organizations. In 1977, inflation accounting was a hot topic, but no clear-cut consensus had emerged. Therefore, the IASC decided to do the next best thing—require disclosure of the methods being used.

A more definitive inflation standard did not emerge until 1981 with IAS 15, *Information Reflecting the Effects of Changing Prices,* which replaced IAS 6. By that time, the FASB had issued SFAS 33, *Financial Reporting and Changing Prices,* in September 1979, and the Accounting Standards Committee (ASC) in the United Kingdom had issued SSAP 16, *Current Cost Accounting,* in April 1980. With the influence and support of those two countries, the IASC was ready to issue a more definitive standard.

Rather than require one specific way to account for inflation, the IASC recognized that a difference of opinion still existed as to how inflation should be accounted for in the financial statements. As IAS 15 pointed out:

> There is not yet an international consensus on the subject. Consequently, the International Accounting Standards Committee believes that further experimentation is necessary before consideration can be given to requiring enterprises to prepare primary financial statements using a comprehensive and uniform system for reflecting changing prices. Meanwhile, evolution of the subject would be assisted if enterprises that present primary financial statements on the historical cost basis also provide supplementary information reflecting the effects of price changes. (para. 18)

The standard discussed the merits of each of the two major philosophical approaches to accounting for inflation, the GPP approach and the current cost approach, but it did not attempt to take a stand. The following major types of information reflecting the effects of changing prices are recommended for disclosure by IAS 15.

1. The amounts of the adjustment to or the adjusted amount of depreciation of property, plant, and equipment.

2. The amount of the adjustment to or the adjusted amount of cost of sales.

3. The adjustments relating to monetary items, the effect of borrowing, or equity interests when such adjustments have been taken into account in determining income under the accounting method adopted.

4. The overall effect on results (income) of the adjustments as well as any other items reflecting the effects of changing prices that are reported under the accounting method adopted.

5. When a current cost method is adopted, the current cost of property, plant and equipment, and inventories.

6. The method adopted to compute the information called for in the preceding items, including the nature of any indices used.

While the IASC encourages corporations to disclose the information described in these six items, they have decided that such disclosures are not necessary to conform with international accounting standards because "the international consensus … that was anticipated when IAS 15 was issued has not been reached."

IAS 15 is important, however, because it recognizes the need for information to be disclosed about the impact of price changes and inflation and gives some specific guidelines that companies can follow to improve the quality of disclosure. The fact that the underlying information from country to country may differ, of course, is a problem, but the accounting profession clearly cannot agree on a universal solution. This is not surprising given the lack of evidence to support one system over another.

Indeed, the available evidence concerning, for example, the utility of current cost accounting is not encouraging. However, more disclosures will assist financial statement users worldwide. The guidelines may also be beneficial for countries concerned about inflation accounting and wishing to develop their own accounting standards. The guidelines are flexible enough to incorporate current value or GPP approaches but precise enough to encourage useful disclosures.

IAS 15 was supplemented in 1989 by IAS 29 on financial reporting in hyperinflationary economies, which requires restatments for GPP changes in hyperinflationary countries regardless of whether the financial statements of the enterprise concerned are based on a historical cost or current value approach.

IAS 16, on property, plant, and equipment, revised in 1998, is also relevant in that a current value accounting approach is permitted specifically as an alternative to historical cost. The basis to be used is "fair value," which is usually market value for existing use in the case of land and buildings and market value determined by appraisal or, if specialized assets, at depreciated replacement cost for plant and equipment. Regular revaluations are required so that book values do not differ materially from fair values at the balance sheet date.

COMPARATIVE NATIONAL REGULATION AND PRACTICE

The practice of inflation accounting varies throughout the world and to a considerable extent is a function of the rate and impact of inflation. Substantial experience of inflation accounting has been gained following the hyperinflation experienced in South America, most notably in Argentina, Brazil, and Chile. The hyperinflationary conditions experienced by South American countries would appear to explain the relatively rapid adoption of inflation accounting systems compared to other countries

Inflation Accounting in the United Kingdom, United States, and Continental Europe

In the United Kingdom, the accounting profession introduced SSAP 16 in 1980 after long debate, which required current cost accounting financial statements either as supplementary statements or as the main accounts, with the proviso that historical cost accounts must also be provided. However, SSAP 16 was officially withdrawn in 1988 following declining inflation levels and criticism from business. Currently, only a few companies provide voluntary current cost disclosures. At the same time, many companies make periodic revaluations of their land and buildings to market values (approximating exit or selling prices).

In the United States, regulation was first introduced with a legal requirement imposed by the SEC in 1976 (Accounting Series Release 190) to disclose replacement cost information relating to depreciation, cost of sales, fixed assets, and inventory. Subsequently, in 1979, the FASB issued Statement of Financial Accounting Standards No. 33, requiring supplementary disclosures on both a GPP and a current cost basis. However, by 1986, with SFAS 82 and SFAS 89, SFAS 33 was no longer mandatory after a cost-benefit analysis of its requirements and a decline in the rate of inflation rendered it obsolete.

Both GPP and current cost disclosures were required by SFAS 33. In addition to adjusted income disclosures, the current costs of inventory, plant, and equipment were required to be disclosed along with increases or decreases in current costs adjusted for GPP changes (i.e., net of inflation). A further required item of disclosure was the purchasing power gain or loss on net monetary items. The noteworthy feature of this standard was its experimental nature; it made available an array of information prepared using different inflation accounting systems. An example of the required disclosures is provided by Nabisco Brands in its 1983 annual report (see Exhibit 11.1).

In contrast, the current cost accounting system in the United Kingdom provided for four adjustments—depreciation, cost of sales, monetary working capital, and gearing. The gearing adjustment, which abated the other operating adjustments by the proportion of debt financing, was a matter of some controversy in that it incorporated an element of the GPP approach by recognizing that there was a gain to be derived from holding net monetary liabilities in a period of inflation.

In Australia, Canada, and New Zealand, developments were much more tentative than in the United Kingdom and the United States. The accounting professions in those countries issued recommendations based essentially on the current cost accounting system required in the United Kingdom and the United States but with some local variations, especially with regard to the treatment of monetary items.

In continental Europe, there has been much less enthusiasm for introducing inflation accounting despite official recommendations on the subject—for example, in France and Germany. In some countries, there have nevertheless been instances in which periodic revaluations were required or permitted, for example, in France in the late 1970s when revaluations using government indices were required for all long-term or fixed assets. However, these revaluations did not impact on earnings for tax purposes, as any additional depreciation was canceled out by a credit transfer from the revaluation reserves. While the Netherlands is renowned for the development of replacement value accounting, there is no compulsion to use the system, nor even professional standards on the subject. In Sweden, there are no requirements on inflation accounting but some notable voluntary disclosures have been made by companies such as Astra (see Exhibit 11.2). Similarly, Switzerland has no requirements but some interesting cases of current value accounting in practice (e.g., Nestlé uses current replacement costs for tangible fixed assets in its main accounts).

Taken overall, regulatory developments worldwide have been few and relatively recent. The major alternative inflation accounting systems of GPP accounting and current value accounting have both been in evidence, although current cost accounting, for a time, was the more popular system in a number of Anglo-American countries before losing favor altogether as inflation levels fell and the costs of

Exhibit 11.1   Nabisco Brands: Adjustments for Changing Prices

Consolidated Statement of Income Adjusted for the Effects of Changing Prices
Year Ended December 31, 1983

(In Millions, Except per Share Data)	Historical Basis	Adjusted for Changes in Specific Prices (Current Cost)
Net sales	$5,985.2	$5,985.2
Cost of sales	3,650.8	3,669.1
Depreciation expense	131.1	206.7
Other expenses	1,560.4	1,560.4
Interest expense	76.8	76.8
Provision for income taxes	243.5	243.5
Net income	$322.6	$228.7
Net income per common share	$4.86	$3.45
Gain from decline in purchasing power of net monetary liabilities		$34.4
Increase in specific prices of inventories and property, plant, and equipment held during the year[a]		$34.2
Less effect of increase in general price level		(113.1)
Excess of increase in general price level over changes in specific prices		$(78.9)
Foreign currency translation adjustment		$(107.9)

[a] At December 13, 1983, the current cost of inventory was $759.6 million and the current cost of property, plant, and equipment, net of accumulated depreciation was $2231.2 million.

Five-Year Comparison of Selected Supplementary Financial Data Adjusted for the
Effects of Changing Prices

(Dollars in Millions, Except per Share Data)	1983	1982	1981	1980	1979
Net Sales—Total					
Historical cost	$5,985.2	$5,871.1	$5,819.2	$5,587.2	$4,975.3
Constant dollar	5,985.2	6,060.1	6,377.1	6,755.5	6,829.2
Net Sales—Ongoing Businesses					
Historical cost	$5,985.2	$5,463.4	$5,049.7	$4,848.8	$4,349.7
Constant dollar	5,985.2	5,639.3	5,533.8	5,862.8	5,970.6
Net Income					
Historical cost	$322.6	$314.7	$266.3	$234.8	$186.5
Current cost	228.7	254.0	157.0	114.8	100.0

(continues)

Exhibit 11.1   *(Continued)*

(Dollars in Millions, Except per Share Data)	1983	1982	1981	1980	1979
Net Income per Common Share					
Historical cost	$4.86	$4.83	$4.21	$3.73	$2.97
Current cost	3.45	3.90	2.48	1.82	1.59
Net Assets at Year-End					
Historical cost	$1,710.8	$1,835.9	$1,522.8	$1,344.1	$1,200.3
Current cost	2,386.4	2,639.2	2,579.5	2,472.6	2,483.5
Excess of Increase in General Price Level over Changes in Specific Prices	$(78.9)	$(196.6)	$(43.9)	$(110.4)	$(96.5)
Gain on Net Monetary Liabilities	$34.4	$41.1	$88.7	$115.6	$134.5
Cash Dividends Declared per Common Share					
Historical cost	$2.28	$2.05	$1.77	$1.60	$1.45
Constant dollar	2.28	2.12	1.94	1.93	1.99
Market Price per Common Share at Year End					
Historical cost	$41.00	$36.75	$31.00		
Constant dollar	40.31	37.51	32.86		
Average Consumer Price Index (1967 = 100)	298.4	289.1	272.3	246.8	217.4

Source: Nabisco, 1983 Annual Report.

compliance exceeded benefits. While voluntary current cost disclosures are still encouraged, there appears to be little regard for their usefulness among corporations and financial analysts.

Inflation Accounting in South America

With hyperinflation rampant in recent years in a number of South American countries, notably Brazil and Argentina, it is not surprising that there have been pressures to adopt "inflation accounting" systems.

In Brazil, inflation accounting adjustments were used as early as the 1950s, but a new company law in 1976 required a general indexation approach to restate historical costs in terms of current purchasing power as of the date of the financial

Exhibit 11.2   Astra (Sweden): Impact of Inflation

It is difficult, both theoretically and practicably, to calculate the impact of inflation on an international group that is affected by changes in exchange rates, when inflation rates vary sharply between countries in which the subsidiaries are located. However, Astra has chosen, each year since 1975, to present an approximate calculation of the effect of inflation on group earnings. Since 1981 the calculations generally follow a draft recommendation in favor of current cost accounting issued by the Swedish Institute of Authorized Public Accountants (FAR). This means, among other things, that all costs of a sold product are restated to reflect the cost situation at the time of sale: the costs of goods, as well as depreciation, are expressed in current costs. In addition, increases in value of inventories and fixed assets—whether realized or not—shall be shown in the year's earnings. In the adjoining calculation, the simplified assumption has been made that the increases in value conform to the Swedish rate of inflation, which means that any real change in value has not been taken into account. The company's monetary working capital has been affected by inflation during the year. The change in purchasing power of the monetary working capital has been calculated on the basis of the change in the consumer price index during the year in Sweden. In the same way, the effect of inflation on financial receivables and liabilities has reduced the interest income and interest expense shown. Similarly, the change in purchasing power has been calculated on the deferred tax liability.

			Amounts in SEK m.
	Conventional Accounting	Current Cost Accounting	Difference
Operating income	23,755	23,755	—
Operating expenses	(16,393)	(16,485)	(92)[1]
Operating earnings	7,362	7,270	(92)
Depreciation	(862)	(1,060)	(198)
Operating earnings after depreciation	6,500	6,210	(290)
Nonoperating income	1,393	996	(397)[2]
Nonoperating expenses	(125)	(57)	68[3]
Minority interest	50	50	—
Pretax earnings	7,818	7,199	(619)
Taxes	(1,726)	(1,726)	—
Change in purchasing power of deferred tax liability	—	57	57
Net earnings	6,092	5,530	(562)
Earnings per share, SEK	9.92	9.01	(0.91)

[1] Change in purchasing power of noninterest-bearing operating receivables and liabilities, SEK 47 m, and change in price of goods sold, calculated in local currency and translated at year-end exchange rates, SEK (139) m.

[2] Change in purchasing power of nonoperating receivables.

[3] Change in purchasing power of nonoperating liabilities.

Ten-Year Summary
The table shows that inflation did not have any appreciable effect on Astra's conventionally adjusted net earnings. Real earnings averaged about three-quarters of conventionally adjusted earnings and had an insignificantly lower rate of growth.

In real terms, Astra's net earnings increased annually at an average rate of 35 percent during the period 1984–93.

(continues)

Exhibit 11.2 *(Continued)*

Value at Each Year's Prices	1984	1985	1986	1987	1988	1989	1990	1991	1992	1993
CONVENTIONAL ACCOUNTING										
Net earnings, SEK m	383	554	597	635	747	991	1,432	2,182	3,527	6,092
Earnings per share, SEK	0.62	0.90	0.97	1.03	1.21	1.62	2.38	3.60	5.76	9.92
CURRENT COST ACCOUNTING										
Net earnings, SEK m	299	425	468	480	570	752	977	1,745	3,246	5,530
Earnings per share, SEK	0.49	0.69	0.76	0.78	0.93	1.22	1.59	2.83	5.27	9.01

Value at 1993 Prices	1984	1985	1986	1987	1988	1989	1990	1991	1992	1993
CONVENTIONAL ACCOUNTING										
Net earnings, SEK m	639	860	888	905	1,008	1,262	1,640	2,312	3,668	6,092
Earnings per share, SEK	1.04	1.40	1.44	1.47	1.64	2.05	2.73	3.81	5.99	9.92
CURRENT COST ACCOUNTING										
Net earnings, SEK m	499	661	698	684	769	957	1,119	1,849	3,376	5,530
Earnings per share, SEK	0.81	1.07	1.13	1.11	1.25	1.55	1.88	3.06	5.51	9.01

Source: Astra, 1993 Annual Report.

statements. The index used was defined by law as the index recognized by the government for the purpose of adjusting its own debt. All corporations were required to restate their balance sheets with respect to property, plant and equipment and related depreciation, investments, and deferred costs and shareholders' equity. The net effect of these adjustments was included in income for the year. However, with dramatically reduced levels of inflation, these requirements were withdrawn with effect from January, 1996.

In Argentina, inflation accounting systems were introduced primarily through the initiative and involvement of the accounting profession. In 1972, a statement was issued recommending the publication of supplementary GPP financial statements. While compliance was initially modest, it increased in the 1980s to the extent that most major companies produced inflation-adjusted accounts. However, in 1995, the GPP adjustment requirements were removed following a period of low inflation.

Current Value Accounting in the Netherlands

In the Netherlands, the Dutch have been aware of current value accounting for a long time. The extensive training of accountants in business economics has resulted in an accounting philosophy that is concerned with current values and costs, and with sound business-economic principles and practices. While there are no set requirements for the use of current value accounting, as either primary or supplementary information, there is significant though dwindling support for its use. While some firms use current cost statements as their primary statements, it is more common to see partial current cost statements or historical cost statements with supplementary disclosures.

If there are no requirements for current cost or GPP accounting, why focus on the Netherlands? The first reason involves the theories of Professor Theodore Limperg, who is often called the father of replacement value theory because of his pioneering work in the Netherlands in the 1920s and 1930s. He focused on the strong relationship between economics and accounting and believed that income should not be earned without maintaining the source of income of the business from a going-concern or continuity standpoint. Therefore, income is a function of revenues and replacement values rather than historical costs. In addition, he maintained that current value information should be used by all decision makers—management as well as shareholders. The second reason for looking at the Netherlands is to learn from the experience of the large Dutch multinational Philips, which was a pioneer preparer of current value financial statements. In fact, Philips first used this approach in 1936 for internal cost accounting purposes and introduced it in 1952 into its primary accounts for financial reporting purposes. But in 1992 the company decided to revert to historical cost accounting on the grounds that it would improve communications to shareholders, considerably simplify accounting systems and procedures, and be more in line with international accounting practices (see Exhibit 11.3).

Nevertheless, Philips is an interesting and valuable example of the application of current value accounting in practice. In its current value financial statements, Philips used current replacement values together with a gearing adjustment to reflect the extent to which there were benefits accruing from financing assets from loan

Exhibit 11.3   Philips (Netherlands): Accounting Policies

Changes in the Preparation of the 1992 Annual Report

In the 1991 annual report reference was made to a reappraisal of our policies and procedures within the framework of Operation Centurion. This reappraisal included close scrutiny of our accounting policies and our financial reporting in order to:

- improve communication with the shareholders;
- considerably simplify our accounting systems and procedures;
- be more in line with current international accounting practices.

In view of the above, it has been resolved with effect from January 1, 1992:

1. to replace current cost accounting with historical cost accounting;

2. to replace the local currencies in highly inflationary countries with a functional currency, generally the U.S. dollar;

3. to capitalize the amounts of goodwill arising from acquisitions made as from January 1, 1992, and to amortize these amounts over a period not exceeding 40 years. In previous years goodwill was charged directly to stockholders' equity;

4. to capitalize certain software development costs when it is determined that the resulting software products will be marketable over an extended period. The amortization period will depend on the nature of the product involved but in no event will exceed three years. For reasons of prudence no expenditures were capitalized in 1992.

Additionally, it has been resolved to apply the American standard (FAS 106) with regard to postretirement health care benefit plans. This means that in accordance with this standard a provision covering such costs will be created over a 20-year period, beginning January 1, 1993, for the United States and January 1, 1995, for all other countries.

To simplify the accounting procedures, costs of basic research and general and administrative expenses in the corporate centers and the national organizations are no longer allocated to the specific product sectors.

With regard to the transition from current cost to historical cost accounting and the use of the U.S. dollar as functional currency in highly inflationary countries the 1991 information has been restated for purposes of comparability. The effects of the change in accounting for goodwill and changes in consolidation are reflected in the notes to the 1992 financial statements. Income from operations per product sector for 1991 has been adjusted in line with the change in allocation of general costs.

Source: Philips, 1992 Annual Report.

rather than equity capital. Under its current value accounting system, both the balance sheet and income statement were adjusted. While current value was generally considered to be equal to replacement value, in certain instances the lower business value (or net realizable value) was taken as the current value. For inventory, standard costs were determined at the start of each year. As prices changed during the year, an index was developed by the purchasing department for homogeneous groups of assets and applied to the standard cost to yield the current value. The indices were prepared quarterly or bimonthly in situations in which inflation was more extreme. Current values were determined by the purchasing department for fixed assets (either individually or in homogeneous groups), by the engineering department for specially designed pieces of equipment, and by the building design and plant engineering department for buildings. As in the case of inventory, indices were often used to update current values of homogeneous groups of assets. The increase (or decrease) in value of inventory and fixed assets due to specific price changes was credited (debited) to a revaluation surplus account in the balance sheet rather than to the income statement. The effect of current value changes showed up in the income statement as a higher or lower cost of goods sold (as a result of increases or decreases in inventory prices) and higher or lower depreciation expense.

However, as Brink (1992) has shown, Philips tended for some years to apply replacement value accounting in a way that was far from conservative and designed to enhance profits. The treatment of inventory value reductions and the gearing adjustment in hyperinflationary countries, for example, was especially controversial, quite apart from accounting policies relating to foreign currencies, goodwill, and intangibles in general. Against this background, Philips's surprise loss in 1990 of 4.24 billion guilders would seem to have led to some serious questioning of the usefulness of the current replacement value accounting system and to its eventual demise.

PROBLEMS AND PROSPECTS

The existence of significant levels of inflation and price volatility in many countries suggests that the need for and use of inflation accounting systems is likely to remain the subject of some controversy in the foreseeable future.

Although GPP accounting has been in use in some hyperinflationary South American countries, no examples of current cost accounting standards or regulations in the United Kingdom and the United States at the national level have survived the demise of the inflation accounting experiments of the mid-1980s. Nevertheless, some European companies are making voluntary current value disclosures.

Controversy remains, however, over many aspects of current cost accounting, particularly with respect to the gearing adjustment and the treatment of gains and losses on monetary items. Other problems include the use of indices, particularly with respect to foreign subsidiaries, and the verification of current costs for corporations in industries experiencing rapid technological change.

It is hoped that there will be some further experimentation with various types of inflation accounting systems including a real value approach, which combines both the GPP and current cost approaches. There may also be a growing appreciation of the circumstances under which each alternative may or may not be feasible or useful in measuring profits and assets. The usefulness of exit or selling prices in the context of recessionary conditions, particularly with regard to the value of property and investments, may also be better appreciated. There also seem to be opportunities for using other relevant sources of information such as cash flows.

SUMMARY

1. Inflation is a worldwide phenomenon with varying impact in different countries. In recent years, countries, such as Argentina, Brazil, Chile, Israel, Mexico, and Russia have been among the worst sufferers of hyperinflationary conditions.

2.   Under inflationary conditions, where prices are continually changing, traditional historical cost accounting becomes defective and misleading as a basis for decision making.

3.   The major alternative approaches to accounting for price changes and inflation are GPP accounting and current value accounting. GPP accounting includes all systems designed to maintain the current (constant) purchasing power of the corporation's equity. Current value accounting, on the other hand, includes all systems designed to account for changes in specific prices such as current cost (or replacement value) accounting and current exit (or selling) price accounting. Real value accounting systems, which combine elements of both of the major approaches involved, are also available.

4.   The IASC has adopted a disclosure approach whereby companies are encouraged to experiment, provided the accounting methods used and amounts involved are disclosed in sufficient detail to inform users.

5.   At the national level, experience with inflation accounting systems is varied, with the hyperinflationary countries of South America using GPP accounting while the Anglo-American countries, with more moderate rates of inflation, experimenting with current cost accounting. Significantly, as the rate of inflation has declined in the Anglo-American countries, so has the support for current cost accounting.

6.   Interesting cases of voluntary disclosures by MNEs can be found in a number of countries, notably the Netherlands, Sweden, Switzerland, and the United Kingdom.

7.   Given the countinuing presence of inflation, albeit at varying rates around the world, it is likely that the subject of inflation accounting will continue to be important and controversial. Further experimentation seems desirable given the lack of knowledge about the usefulness of the various alternatives.

Discussion Questions

1.   How do price changes and inflation affect the financial position and performance of a corporation? What operational problems does inflation create for management?

2.   Compare and critically comment on the philosophies behind the following:
   a.   General purchasing power
   b.   Current value accounting
   c.   Current value–general purchasing power (real value) accounting

3.   Explain how Philips (the Netherlands) determined current costs for its financial reports. What were the reasons given for reverting to historical cost in 1992? Was this decision justifiable in your opinion?

4.   Under what circumstances are corporations likely to voluntarily disclose the impact of price changes and inflation?

5.   To what extent is a disclosure approach to inflation accounting likely to overcome problems of comparability internationally?

6.   Inflation in Russia and China has been relatively high in recent years, and yet no inflation accounting systems have been introduced. Should inflation accounting be required, and, if so, which approach would you recommend be used?

7. In Germany, there is a resistance to any form of inflation accounting and a concern to maintain a strictly historical cost approach. Why is this, and can such an approach be justified on theoretical grounds?

Case: BP Amoco

BP Amoco is one of the world's largest petroleum and petrochemical groups. BP Amoco has well-established operations in Europe, the United States, Australasia, and parts of Africa and is expanding into other regions, notably Southeast Asia, America, and the countries of the former Soviet Union.

For some years now, BP has incorporated a replacement cost accounting approach into the presentation of its group income statement and the results of its individual business and geographical areas (see Exhibit 11.4)

Exhibit 11.4. BP AMOCO—Financial Statements

Group income statement

For the year ended 31 December	Note	1999	$ million 1998
Turnover		**101,180**	83,732
Less: Joint ventures		**17,614**	15,428
Group turnover	1	**83,566**	68,304
Replacement cost of sales		**68,615**	56,270
Production taxes	2	**1,017**	604
Gross profit		**13,934**	11,430
Distribution and administration expenses	3	**6,064**	6,044
Exploration expense		**548**	921
		7,322	4,465
Other income	4	**414**	709
Group replacement cost operating profit	5	**7,736**	5,174
Share of profits of joint ventures	5	**555**	825
Share of profits of associated undertakings	5	**603**	522
Total replacement cost operating profit	5	**8,894**	6,521
Profit (loss) on sale of businesses	6	**(421)**	395
Profit (loss) on sale of fixed assets	6	**84**	653
Restructuring costs	6	**(1,943)**	–
Merger expenses	6	**–**	(198)
Replacement cost profit before interest and tax	5	**6,614**	7,371
Stock holding gains (losses)	5	**1,728**	1,391

(continues)

Exhibit 11.4.   (*Continued*)

Historical cost profit before interest and tax		**8,342**	5,980
Interest expense	7	**1,316**	1,177
Profit before taxation		**7,026**	4,803
Taxation	11	**1,880**	1,520
Profit after taxation		**5,146**	3,283
Minority shareholders' interest		**138**	63
Profit for the year		**5,008**	3,220
Distribution to shareholders	12	**3,884**	4,121
Retained profit (deficit) for the year		**1,124**	(901)
Earnings per ordinary share—cents			
Basic	13	**25.82**	16.77
Diluted	13	**25.68**	16.70
Replacement cost results			
Historical cost profit for the year		**5,008**	3,220
Stock holding (gains) losses		**(1,728)**	1,391
Replacement cost profit for the year		**3,280**	4,611
Exceptional items, net of tax	6	**2,050**	(652)
Replacement cost profit before exceptional items		**5,330**	3,959
Earnings per ordinary share—cents			
On replacement cost profit before exceptional items	13	**27.48**	20.62

Notes on accounts

5 Analysis of replacement cost profit $ million 1999

Profit	Group replacement cost operating profit[a]	Joint ventures	Associated undertakings	Total replacement cost operating profit[a]	Exceptional items[b]	Replacement cost profit before interest and tax
By business						
Exploration and Production	**6,718**	**175**	**301**	**7,194**	**(1,097)**	**6,097**
Refining and Marketing	**1,337**	**380**	**123**	**1,840**	**(334)**	**1,506**
Chemicals	**561**	–	**125**	**686**	**(257)**	**429**
Other businesses and corporate	**(880)**	–	**54**	**(826)**	**(592)**	**(1,418)**
	7,736	**555**	**603**	**8,894**	**(2,280)**	**6,614**

Exhibit 11.4. (*Continued*)

Profit	Group replacement cost operating profit[a]	Joint ventures	Associated undertakings	Total replacement cost operating profit[a]	Exceptional items[b]	Replacement cost profit before interest and tax
By geographical area						
UK[c]	**2,063**	**(1)**	**49**	**2,111**	**(237)**	**1,874**
Rest of Europe	**548**	**381**	**238**	**1,167**	**(258)**	**909**
USA	**2,803**	**13**	**185**	**3,001**	**(983)**	**2,018**
Rest of World	**2,322**	**162**	**131**	**2,615**	**(802)**	**1,813**
	7,736	**555**	**603**	**8,894**	**(2,280)**	**6,614**
						1998
By business						
Exploration and Production	2,987	65	179	3,231	396	3,627
Refining and Marketing	1,712	760	92	2,564	394	2,958
Chemicals	950	–	150	1,100	43	1,143
Other businesses and corporate	(475)	–	101	(374)	17	(357)
	5,174	825	522	6,521	850	7,371
By geographical area						
UK[c]	1,796	127	8	1,931	(39)	1,892
Rest of Europe	345	633	271	1,249	106	1,355
USA	2,506	31	94	2,631	511	3,142
Rest of World	527	34	149	710	272	982
	5,174	825	522	6,521	850	7,371

Stock holding gains (losses)	1999	1998
By business		
Exploration and Production	**(1)**	(17)
Refining and Marketing[d]	**1,613**	(1,228)
Chemicals	**116**	(146)
	1,728	(1,391)

(continues)

Exhibit 11.4.   (*Continued*)

Stock holding gains (losses)	1999	1998
By geographical area		
UK	**151**	(136)
Rest of Europe	**494**	(283)
USA	**839**	(720)
Rest of World	**244**	(252)
	1,728	(1,391)

[a] Replacement cost operating profit is before stock holding gains and losses and interest expense, which is attributable to the corporate function. Transfers between group companies are made at market prices taking into account the volumes involved.

[b] Exceptional items comprise profit or loss on the sale of businesses and fixed assets and termination of operations and in addition for 1999 include restructuring costs and for 1998 merger expenses.

[c] UK area includes the UK-based international activities of Refining and Marketing.

[d] Includes $547 million stock holding gains in respect of joint ventures and associated undertaking (1998 $330 million losses).

Accounts
Accounting policies (excerpt)

Accounting standards

These accounts are prepared in accordance with applicable UK accounting standards. The group has adopted Financial Reporting Standard No. 12 "Provisions, Contingent Liablities and Contingent Assets" (FRS12) and Financial Reporting Standard No. 13 "Derivatives and Other Financial Instruments: Disclosures" (FRS13) with effect from January 1, 1999. The financial information for 1998 has been restated to comply with the requirements of FRS12.

Accounting convention

The accounts are prepared under the historical cost convention. Historical cost accounts show the profits available to shareholders and are the most appropriate basis for presentation of the group's balance sheet. Profit and loss determined under the historical cost convention includes stock holding gains or losses and, as a consequence, does not necessarily reflect underlying trading results.

Replacement cost

The results of individual businesses and geographical areas are presented on a replacement cost basis. Replacement cost operating results exclude stock holding gains or losses and reflect the average cost of supplies incurred during the year, and thus provide insight into underlying trading results. Stock holding gains or losses represent the difference between the replacement cost of sales and the historical cost of sales calculated using the first-in first-out method.

Questions

1. Why do you think BP would want to introduce replacement information into the presentation of its results?

2. What is the meaning and significance of the stock holding gains of $1,728 million identified for 1999?

3. What is the meaning and significance of the stock holding losses for 1998 of $1,391 million?

4. To what extent is BP's replacement cost information likely to give a better insight into its underlying trading results and future prospects than historical cost information? Discuss this question with respect to the results:

a. of the group

b. by business, and

c. by geographical area

5. Do you think BP should extend its replacement cost approach to the balance sheet? If so, why? If not, why not?

6. Discuss whether more MNEs should be encouraged to follow BP's lead in disclosing replacement cost information.

7. What different approaches to measurement could be considered today by MNEs as desirable alternatives or supplements to historical cost?

Selected References

Brink, H. L. 1992. "A History of Philips' Accounting Policies on the Basis of its Annual Reports," *European Accounting Review* (December).

Choi, F. D. S. 1987. "Resolving the Inflation/Currency Translation Dilemma," *Management International Review*, 27 (2): 26–34.

Choi, F. D. S. and R. R. Gunn. 1997. "Hyperinflation Reporting and Performance Assessment," *Journal of Financial Statement Analysis* (Summer): 30–38.

Goudeket, A. 1966. "An Application of Replacement Value Theory," *Journal of Accounting* (July).

International Accounting Standard Committee, IAS 16. *Property, Plant and Equipment.* London: IASC (revised 1998).

International Accounting Standards Committee. 1981. International Accounting Standard 15, *Information Reflecting the Effects of Changing Prices.* London IASC (November; reformatted 1994).

International Accounting Standards Committee. 1989. IAS 29, *Financial Reporting in Hyperinflationary Economies* (reformatted 1994).

Kirkman, P. 1985. *Inflation Accounting in Major English-Speaking Countries* (Englewood Cliffs, NJ: Prentice-Hall

Lee, T. A. 1985. *Income and Value Measurement,* 3d ed. New York: Van Nostrand Reinhold.

Mey, A. 1966. "Theodore Limperg and His Theory of Values and Costs," *Abacus* (September).

Muis, Jules S. 1975 "Current Value Accounting in the Netherlands: Fact or Fiction," *Accountant* (November).

Mumford, M. 1979. "The End of a Familar Inflation Accounting Cycle," *Accounting and Business Research* (Spring).

Schmidt, F. 1930. "The Impact of Replacement Value," *Accounting Review* (September): 235–42.

Sweeney, H. W. 1927. "Effect of Inflation on German Accounting," *Journal of Accountancy* (March): 180–91.

Van Offeren, D. H. 1990. "Accounting for Changing Prices in Dutch Annual Reports," *Advances in International Accounting,* 3: pp. 87–106.

Whittington, Geoffrey. 1983. *Inflation Accounting.* New York: Cambridge University Press.

Whittington, Geoffrey. 1984. "The European Contribution to Inflation Accounting," in *Congress Proceedings, European Accounting Association, Sixth Annual Congress 1983, University of Glasgow,* Scotland.

Zeff, S. A. and H. Z. Ovando. 1975. "Inflation Accounting and the Development of Accounting Principles in Chile," *Accountant's Magazine* (June).

CHAPTER TWELVE

INTERNATIONAL AUDITING ISSUES

Chapter Objectives

- Discuss important factors influencing the quality of the accounting and auditing profession
- Discuss the nature of global audit services and examine the challenges of auditing across borders
- Describe the strategies of the global public accounting firms in servicing clients worldwide
- Provide a comparative international analysis of audit standards
- Explain the role of the International Federation of Accountants (IFAC) in harmonizing auditing standards worldwide
- Review recent developments including the establishment of the International Forum on Accountancy Development (IFAD)

INTRODUCTION

Auditors are increasingly practicing internationally, both as individuals and as firms. The main impetus behind this movement has been the globalization of business, which has accelerated especially in recent years. As enterprises became multinational, they asked that their financial advisers be equally multinational. As a result, professional accountants have organized themselves into global organizations, providing a wide range of services throughout the world. This chapter examines the role of the external auditors in its interaction with the multinational. It also examines the largest auditing firms in their role as global service corporations and some of the unique problems they experience.

The external auditor is an independent professional who works closely with clients to provide global value-added services such as tax advice, training, review of financial control systems and, in more remote locations, basic accounting services. Given that audit firms often have offices and correspondents in a larger number of countries than any single multinational firm, external auditors have also become repositories of information about operating conditions for firms wishing to move into a location.

THE ACCOUNTING AND AUDITING PROFESSION

According to Arens and Loebbecke (1994), "auditing is the accumulation and evaluation of evidence about quantifiable information of an economic entity to determine and report on the degree of correspondence between the information and the established criteria." There are three key dimensions to this definition: quantifiable (and verifiable) information; established criteria (or auditing standards); and a competent, independent person.

Even as these issues must be addressed in the domestic setting, they must also be addressed in the international setting. There are differences worldwide in the way one becomes an auditor, the form and content of the financial statements, and auditing standards. Besides the difficulty of solving these problems in a national setting, there is also the problem of crossing national boundaries. For example, is it possible for the auditor of the German company BMW to rely on the opinion of a U.S. auditor for a subsidiary of BMW in the United States, given that GAAP are different in the United States, that the qualifications of a U.S. auditor are different from those of a German auditor, and that the auditing standards in the United States are different from those in Germany?

The quality of the auditing profession is a function of several factors, such as the reputation of the accounting and auditing profession, the quality of the educational system, and the certification process. Reputation is important because it determines whether or not the profession is able to attract competent people.

Educational systems vary with respect to the specific training they provide potential candidates for the accounting profession. In some countries, such as the United States, a high value is placed on the university experience in the education of students, and firms that recruit at the universities are familiar with the backgrounds students will have when they graduate. In other countries, especially the developing countries, accounting education may not be that important or even available. Accounting is often viewed as a discipline within economics, and little attention is paid to accounting education. That type of educational system might not prepare students for careers in accounting in quite the same way as would be expected in an industrialized country. The educational system might also be influenced by the role an accountant is expected to play. In Germany, for example, there is an emphais on tax accounting.

Finally, the licensing process is carried out by the private sector in some countries and the public sector in others. In the United States, each state is empowered to certify a candidate, and the states vary in terms of educational and experience requirements. However, the National Uniform CPA exam is prepared by the Board of Examiners of the American Institute of CPAs (AICPA), a private sector organization. Certification in the United Kingdom is also a private sector process. In Germany and France, however, the government is much more involved in the certification process. In Germany, the government certifies a candidate only after following a series of steps, including a government-regulated admission and examination procedure.

The certification or licensing process is also a function of several other factors, such as the identity of the candidate, educational requirements, experience requirements, and examination. An additional aspect of certification is the issue of reciprocity, or the ability of a certified accountant in one country to practice in another. This will be discussed in more detail later.

GLOBAL AUDIT SERVICES AND THE INTERNATIONAL AUDITING CHALLENGE

While each firm differs, the services provided by the global audit firm include:

1. Audit/Attestation and Assurance Services
2. Tax Advisory and Compliance Service
3. Consulting/Management Advisory Services

The services described in Exhibit 12.1 provide a broad taxonomy that applies equally well to domestic and global firms. What is different about the global corporation is the complexity of these functions and the number of potential audit locations. Procter and Gamble operates in 140 countries each with their own unique reporting rules, currency, and taxes. Their auditors have to review their operations in each of these countries, plus file a tax return in many of them. They also have to prepare a consolidated return in P&G's home base in the United States.

Exhibit 12.1 Attestation, Assurance, Consulting/Tax

	Attestation	Assurance	Consulting/Tax
Result	Written conclusion about the reliability of the written assertions of another party	Better information for decision-makers. Recommendations might be a by-product	Recommendations based on the objectives of the engagement. Tax documents for the government. Tax advice
Objective	Reliable information	Better decision making	Better outcomes
Independence	Required by standards	Included in definition	Not required
Substance of Auditor Output	Conformity with established or stated criteria	Assurance about reliability or relevance of information. Criteria might be established, stated, or unstated	Recommendations; not measured against formal criteria
Form of Auditor Output	Written	Some form of communication	Written or oral

Although audit responsibilities are similar for international and domestic operations, there are some unique challenges in the foreign environment, such as local accounting practices, foreign currency, local legal and business practices, language and customs, and distance. Although most large companies attempt to standardize their accounting practice worldwide, it does not happen everywhere. Local records may be kept according to local accounting procedures, which makes it difficult to use a standardized audit package. Also, the infrequency of audits (because of distance) may mean that there is insufficient accounting data to provide a clear audit trail. Some of the factors making auditing a challenging task include:

1. Local business practices and customs
2. Differences in currency, language, and law between countries
3. Distance and organizational issues
4. Availability of suitable personnel

Audit Challenges: Local Business Practices and Customs

Audit and assurance procedures employed by audit firms are designed to confirm past transactions, assess the quality of the control system, and determine future areas of risk. Local business practices and customs can create challenges in simply confirming what has happened, as well as in assessing future risks. Examples of such challenges include:

1. *Predominance of cash.* Although paying expenses by cash, rather than check, is common practice in many countries (particularly emerging market economies), it makes record keeping of expenses and revenue control difficult. Japan provides a good example of some of the challenges that arise in cash management. It is very common for the Japanese to use cash instead of checks for some transactions. To send cash in the mail, they use money envelopes carried in special pouches by the mail carrier. Larger businesses use checks, but banks often provide only computerized lists of transactions rather than canceled checks. This makes it difficult to check the signature and authorization of actual checks during the audit. Because of the interlocking nature of the banks, many payments are made by bank transfers directly from one bank account to another. The only verification of the transfers is a computer printout. Some firms use a variety of transfers to keep the government from verifying earnings for a tax base.

2. *Inability to confirm accounts receivable.* In most cases, the confirmation letter itself must be translated into another language. Relying on the customer to return the confirmation is another challenge because foreign customers lack experience with confirmations. It may not be customary for local auditors to send confirmations for accounts receivable or even to confirm year-end bank balances. The mail service may also be inefficient and unreliable, and it may take weeks before the customer receives the confirmation letter, if the customer receives it at all. In emerging markets where qualified staff are rare, audit confirmations are often seen as an

intrusion and responded to with caution. This is particularly true in some countries where auditors must by practice or law report to the government without necessarily telling their client.

Audit Challenges: Currency, Language, and Law

Foreign Currency Foreign currency restrictions and transfer requirements should be known for each country in which the auditor works. In addition, the auditor must be aware of corporate procedures for translating financial statements and recording foreign currency transactions so that reports sent to the parent in its own currency are prepared properly. Management must determine which translation methodology is to be used, and the auditor needs to determine if the choice is based on the right criteria, using the appropriate accounting standard.

Language and Culture Ignorance of the local language can be a fatal handicap when the auditor deals with bilingual personnel. Having to rely on a translator may mean that the auditor is not getting the full story. In many countries, the financial statements must be kept in the local language and currency, so knowledge of that language is essential. Sometimes, knowing the language can be useful for getting information in touchy situations. For example, two auditors of the Brazilian subsidiary of a large multinational energy company noticed that a purchasing agent was driving a relatively expensive car. Because the two auditors spoke the local language, they were able to go to the man's home and interview his father. They found out from the proud father that his son was so important he received a 5 percent commission on everything he bought for the company. Needless to say, the purchasing agent did not last long in his position.

Interaction of Home Country and Local Law Home countries occasionally have laws that extend to subsidiaries of their domestic companies that operate abroad. These laws may contradict or conflict with laws in the host country. Examples include boycotts on doing business with certain countries or anti-boycott legislation where the auditor must certify no country is being discriminated against. Other examples include human rights or other social disclosure. Perhaps one of the most intrusive of such extraterritorial laws is the U.S. Foreign Corrupt Practices Act, which not only forbids most forms of bribes but also specifies what minimum accounting controls must be in place.

Audit Challenges: Distance and Organization for Providing Audit Services

The auditor of a large multinational corporation has a very difficult time organizing the firm's services properly. For example, Coca-Cola, the American beverages company based in Atlanta, Georgia, has operations all over the world. Its auditor, Ernst & Young, also has an office in Atlanta, which is responsible for the audit. One of the partners in the Atlanta office is assigned as the partner in charge of the worldwide audit. That partner must decide on the scope of the audit, taking into consideration such factors as

1. The countries where Coca-Cola has subsidiaries;
2. The materiality of each subsidiary vis-à-vis the corporation as a whole;
3. The existence of a branch, subsidiary, or correspondent of the auditor in the country or city of each major subsidiary; and so on.

A major challenge of auditing outside the home base is distance. Far-flung operations are not audited as frequently or as thoroughly as the domestic operations, which makes the foreign audit even more difficult. It is often impossible to conduct pre-audit and post-audit visits, so most communication has to be by telephone, e-mail, fax, or mail. The earlier example on confirming accounts receivable illustrates the difficulty of distance. When post-audit problems arise, it may be impossible to get an answer quickly or to communicate adequately.

Given the need to cover clients in widely dispersed areas, how do public accounting firms service their multinational clients? The simplest way is for a professional to travel from the home office to service a client abroad. This would be sufficient as long as the foreign sector was a small part of the client's overall operations. However, this approach is unsatisfactory in the long run because of the complexity of the international audit and tax environments and the increasing internationalization of most of the firm's larger clients.

Beyond the traveling auditor approach the firm must make increasing commitment to physical or legal presence on the ground overseas. The lowest level of commitment uses a variety of relationships with host country correspondent firms. These can range from very weak to very strong.

At one end of the scale, the local correspondent may be a representative who performs services for more than one accounting firm. A very loose operating relationship may exist. At the other end of the scale, a very strong correspondent relationship may exist in which the local firm performs services exclusively for one foreign public accounting firm. Whether an auditing firm expands abroad through strong or weak correspondent relationships, the partners in other countries remain separate, autonomous organizations. Unlike a corporation, which retains equity control over its far-flung operations, these partnerships are built on mutual benefit and service. There are situations in which an auditing firm in one country owns operations in other countries, but those are the exception rather than the rule.

A stronger presence abroad is to be part of a global alliance of firms that share technology, clients, and sometimes staff. These alliances may be separate legal entities that use the parent firm's name or a derivative thereof. The partnership in individual countries retains its separate identity, but a more cohesive cooperative effort exists among the firms through the international partnership. With one exception all the global audit firms operated in this manner until the mid 1990s and still do so in many countries. Ernst & Young, for example, trades as Ernst & Young in the United States, Canada, and other large English-speaking countries but becomes Ernst & Young—Henry Martin, Lisdero y Asociados in Argentina and Ernst & Young—Punongbayan & Araullo in the Philippines. This arrangement allows for local knowledge plus global clients, but without the tight control of a single firm.

The strongest presence for any global firm would be a single entity with common equity holdings. This can be achieved by expanding outward through branches of the original firm or by the merging of previously independent entities. Home office personnel often fill the important positions in foreign branches until domestic personnel can be trained to take over. In some cases, local firms are acquired; in others, new firms are established. The branch concept, coupled with strong central management, provides for tighter control over services. Arthur Andersen, for example, has always operated as a single entity expanding as and when required by new branches. KPMG by contrast is the descendant of a number of very strong local firms and has only relatively recently established a common presence and brand name globally.

Audit Challenges: Audit Impediments from International Diversity, Availability, and Training of Auditors

If the audit firm should choose to open a branch rather than rely on correspondents, it faces the challenge of getting staff on the ground with which it is satisfied. These challenges include problems of reciprocity for its expatriate staff being transferred in, lack of local audit staff, and a variety of training models for preparing staff for the audit function. We now examine the profession and the firms that it serves.

The Supply of Auditors   The number of accountants also depends on barriers to entry to the profession, such as strict educational and testing requirements. In Exhibit 12.2 we compare the number of accountants in a country by computing a ratio of the number of accountants in the country to the population, that is, the accountants per capita. It is interesting to note that the emerging market countries such as Kenya and Korea have a small number of accountants per capita compared with the high-income countries. Also, countries with a tradition of standards designed to service the government (Code law countries) have a relatively smaller number of accountants. For example, the United Kingdom, with roughly the same population as France, has eight times France's number of accountants.

International Differences in Training of Practicing Auditors   Not only do numbers of accountants vary between countries but also the training of potential audit professionals can vary considerably. In some countries, such as the United States, a high value is placed on the university education of students, and firms that recruit at universities are familiar with the background of students when they graduate. The educational system might also be influenced by the role an accountant is expected to play (e.g., managerial accounting, tax accounting). Like many of the learned professions, preparation to become a practicing accountant includes the timeless elements of formal education, experience, and examination.

There are essentially three different models of accounting education leading to certification. The three models are:

1. The **apprenticeship** approach, patterned after the British experience, which does not require specific university training in Accounting
2. The **university**-based model for certification, similar to the approaches used in the United States and Germany.

Exhibit 12.2   Accounting Professionals

Country	Population 1994 (millions)	Number of Accountants	Number of Accountants per Thousand of Population
Canada	29.141	101,800	3.49
Egypt	61.636	384	0.006
France	57.747	26,200	0.45
Germany	81.278	21,225	0.26
Hong Kong	5.838	6,559	1.12
India	918.57	77,700	0.08
Italy	57.157	63,000	1.1
Japan	124.815	12,559	0.1
Kenya	27.343	1,500	0.05
Korea, Republic of	44.563	3,100	0.07
Mexico	91.858	13,700	0.15
Netherlands	15.397	8,000	0.52
Nigeria	108.467	7,339	0.07
South Africa	40.555	14,598	0.36
United Kingdom	58.091	205,458	3.54
United States	260.631	439,000	1.68

Source: International Federation of Accountants; United Nations.

3.   The **dual track** model, found in the Netherlands and France, which permits either approach.

While each model has its strength, auditors may be unfamiliar with the competence level of staff in all countries. In the apprenticeship model, even after several years of study, staff with significant experience may not yet be qualified, in a professional sense. One may often get staff that are relatively junior for many years. In the university model, staff may be qualified and yet not as fully experienced as one would like. One solution for the global firm is to concentrate on developing a stronger human capital base through common global training and internship or foreign residency programs. It is common to find accountants in various stages of their careers, usually from the manager level up, working in foreign offices to learn the challenges of audits in those countries and to train local accountants in the ways of the international firm. When these accountants return to their home countries, they can more effectively perform local subsidiary audits that comply with the requirements in countries where the client's parent company is located. This in turn allows the engagement partner for the parent to express an opinion.

Reciprocity   As we saw earlier, the number of accountants available in any particular country varies significantly. It would therefore seem natural that if international business activity grows in a country with relatively few accountants, auditors would move from relative surplus countries such as the United States and the

United Kingdom to countries in need. Even between surplus countries, it would often seem to be a reasonable conclusion that such intra-country flows would speed up the global audit process. However, as the International Federation of Accountants noted in a 1995 Statement of Policy:

> National professional institutes and national regulatory authorities have been reluctant to accept the professional qualifications of foreign accountants for regulated services. Conditions of residence, citizenship, special educational criteria and examinations have been set, conditions which are, in many cases, impossible to meet. Moreover, some of these criteria do not pertain to the professional qualifications. Given the international scope of the accountancy profession, professionally qualified accountants, both as individuals and firms, are increasingly seeking to be recognized in foreign countries, and often see these barriers as unreasonable.
>
> The demand for recognition of foreign accountancy qualifications has been given special impetus by the successful completion of the Uruguay Round of trade negotiations, and the General Agreement on Trade in Services (GATS). The GATS addresses regulatory obstacles to international trade and foreign investment in service industries, including the cross-border practice of accountancy and other professions. It sets out a series of rules to discipline government intervention in the marketplace, to ensure that foreign or internationally-affiliated service providers, firms and professionals enjoy the same privileges as their domestic counterparts or competitors with respect to government regulation and to remove discriminatory obstacles to market entry and practice by persons from other countries. Signatories to the GATS and its provisions bind their national and sub-national regulatory authorities. (Recognition of Professional Accountancy Qualifications Statement of Policy of Council par 3–4)

Thus the multilateral agreement, the General Agreement on Trade in Services (GATS), addresses these problems of qualifying to practice in other countries in two ways. First, it requires countries to administer their licensing rules in a reasonable, objective, and impartial manner, and forbids using them as disguised barriers to trade. Countries are also required to establish specific procedures for verifying the competence and credentials of professionals from other countries. Second, it encourages countries to recognize other countries' qualifications, either autonomously or through mutual recognition agreements.

Reciprocity has varied in practice over time. At one time British accountants could and did have a valid global certificate to practice. This changed most dramatically in the United States but also in Canada and Australia in the 1970s. Further, fairly open reciprocity in the United States disappeared with a 1977 court decision. In the 1990s, regional economic integration has begun a return to reciprocity. The free trade agreement signed between the United States and Canada in 1989 initiated a closer degree of economic cooperation between the two largest trading partners in the world, and it also created closer cooperation in accounting. On September 1, 1991, a memorandum of understanding entitled "Principles for Reciprocity" was signed between the AICPA, the NASBA, and the Canadian Institute of Chartered Accountants (CICA). According to the agreement, a professionally qualified accountant in one country could ask for the other country's qualification, subject to taking an exam on the local tax and legal framework. This special exam eliminated the need for Canadian accountants, for example, to take the Uniform CPA exam. This short-form exam has been extended to members of the Institute of

Chartered Accountants of Australia who similarly take the short-form IQEX exam. IQEX is an acronym for the International Uniform Certified Public Accountant Qualification Examination. The Examination is one of the requirements used to assess the professional competence of Australian and Canadian Chartered Accountants who wish to obtain the CPA certificate.

In a similar regional reciprocity situation, the European Union issued a series of directives that must be incorporated into national law in each country. The Eighth Directive, as adopted by the Council of Ministers of the European Union in 1984, deals with the qualifications of statutory auditors. Within the EU auditors from one country are allowed to practice in another member country if two conditions are met. The conditions are:

1. The auditor must have obtained qualifications that are deemed to be equivalent to the reviewing authorities in the host country.

2. The auditor must demonstrate that they understand the laws and requirements for conducting statutory audits in the host country.

The rules for reciprocity are relatively flexible in several other countries. In the Netherlands, for example, the Ministry of Economic Affairs may issue a license to a foreign accountant on the grounds of proof of suitable qualifications obtained abroad and satisfactory moral standing. The French recognize foreign diplomas from countries that grant reciprocal treatment once the candidate has passed an oral examination administered by the Ministry of Education covering French law, tax and accounting, and ethics. However, the Germans and British are as strict as the United States in not granting reciprocity easily. In the early 1990s, there were discussions between the United States and the European Union about granting reciprocity, but as of 2000 there were still too many challenges to resolve. As a result, the British and American professions were discussing a bilateral reciprocity that would involve requiring knowledge of local laws before accountants were allowed to practice.

GLOBAL ACCOUNTING FIRMS

Strategies of the Global Audit Firm

As a global firm as well as a global service provider, public accounting firms have traditionally expanded abroad to better service their clients and to provide a line of defense against other global accounting firms that might be tempted to encroach on their client base. Companies that have switched from small or medium-size auditors to more international auditors often give the following reasons for the switch:

1. The need to reflect the increasing size of our overseas business.

2. The need to have one firm auditing all companies within the group.

A good example of global strategy was the battle over the expanding Varity audit. In 1990, KPMG took over the audit engagement of Varity Corporation, which had three business groups: Massey-Ferguson, a tractor manufacturer; Perkins, a diesel engine manufacturer; and Kelsey-Hayes, a wheel and brake components manufacturer. When Varity acquired Kelsey-Hayes in 1989, it decided to submit its audit work to open bid, and KPMG won out over Deloitte & Touche, Ernst & Young, and Price Waterhouse. As KPMG developed its bid, the partner chosen to coordinate the engagement visited 30 Varity locations throughout the world and prepared a bid based on KPMG's strength worldwide. The partner felt that his global experience, especially his work with British clients, given Varity's significant British operations, was a key factor in the decision.

One of the major reasons for the mergers discussed below is the increasing globalization of business. Large audit firms have increasingly become multinational firms in the mold of Unilever or GM rather than a loose alliance of related service providers. This has been especially true in Europe, where the implementation of the Fourth Directive has required more firms to be audited than had been the case previously. Further, the European Union's expansion and elimination of most of the remaining barriers to free trade and investment by the end of 1992 caused these firms to look more closely at their ability to service clients outside their home markets.

Many other markets were opening up to mergers, acquisitions, and to new foreign investment in the early and mid 1990s. In 1991, for example, India decided to open up its market and allow foreign firms to have a majority equity position in Indian companies, something that had been restricted in the past. This international expansion also opens up the market to the auditing firms. The 1993 NAFTA treaty and its predecessor the U.S./Canada free trade agreement also opened continent-wide markets. It was clear at that point that the auditors had to follow the lead of their clients to provide adequate service. Given that most of the large corporations in the world are in the United States, Canada, Europe, and Asia, the auditing firms began to look at ways to strengthen their presence in each of those major markets.

Structure of the Audit Industry

As in business generally, there are large and small audit firms. In the United States alone, there are more than 45,000 CPA firms. However, the world's largest public accounting firms conduct the audits of most of the world's largest corporations. Figure 12.1 identifies the top five firms in 1999 by revenues and provides the revenue data of those firms in the United States. These firms are: Arthur Andersen, Deloitte Touche Tohmatsu, Ernst & Young, KPMG, and PriceWaterhouseCoopers.

A major development since the early 1980s with respect to the competitive position of the major public accounting firms is merger activity. In 1989, in rapid succession, Deloitte Haskins & Sells and Touche Ross announced they would merge into a new U.S. firm, Deloitte & Touche (DT), and Ernst & Whinney and Arthur Young announced the formation of a new U.S. firm, Ernst & Young (EY). Although discussions took place between Arthur Andersen (AA) and Price Waterhouse, a merger did not result. It is very difficult for such large firms to mesh together, especially where there are significant differences in organizational culture. In 1998, Price Waterhouse successfully merged with Coopers and Lybrand to form PricewaterhouseCoopers (PWC). Attempts to merge Ernst & Young and KPMG were stymied by regulators.

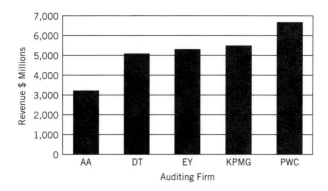

Figure 12.1 U.S. Revenues of Global Audit Firms 1999

Another trend for public accounting firms is to organize around industry. For example, in 1995 KPMG announced it was going to organize the firm around five national integrated industry-focused teams. Each team consists of assurance (auditing), tax, and consulting professionals and each team focuses on one of the five industries, with a shared top and bottom-line. Thus, bottom-line responsibility would no longer rest on the traditional functional and geographical organizations. This model of organizational structure is similar to the Global Product Organization further discussed in Chapter 13. The teams are health care and life sciences; information, communications, and entertainment; public services; financial services; and manufacturing, relating, and distribution. The result is more of a matrix form of organization, with the industry as the primary focus and functional organizations as a secondary focus.

From a manager's point of view both the strategy and structure of audit firms indicate that they have in many ways achieved high levels of success. On the one hand, they provide value to their clients and yet unlike many other service agencies, they do this through a structure and strategy that is suitable to their role as global corporations and from which they no doubt learn how to serve their clients more effectively. All of this has been achieved in an industry that is nationally regulated and where the supply of skills in no way matches the pattern of global growth. The mission statement of Arthur Andersen provides an interesting insight into the strategy and organization of the global audit firm (see Exhibit 12.3).

AUDIT STANDARDS

The growth of national and international capital markets has turned the spotlight on the auditor as an important credibility link between the corporation and investor-creditor. Outsiders are interested in an objective, independent view of the financial statements of a firm. National corporations—especially in countries where the auditing profession has not achieved an international reputation—are turning increasingly to global accounting firms to certify their financial statements and thereby attract international investors. The use of international auditors emphasizes that auditing standards and practices, like accounting standards and practices,

Exhibit 12.3   A Mission Statement from a Global Audit Firm—Arthur Andersen

Who We Are Is What We Do

Arthur Andersen is a global, multidisciplinary professional services organization that provides clients, large and small, all over the world, the thing they need most to succeed: knowledge. Our work is to acquire knowledge and to share knowledge—knowledge of how to improve performance in management, business processes, operations, information technology, finance, and change navigation—so that our clients can grow and profit. This knowledge comes from three source: experience, education, and research. In all three, Arthur Andersen excels.

Who We Are Is How We Work

Arthur Andersen is a global organization, with 382 offices in 81 countries. But for us, global is more than a worldwide presence; it's also an attitude. With a unique organizational structure, common methods, and shared values, Arthur Andersen is able to serve its clients, wherever they are located, as "one firm." Our team of over 70,000 people work together—across boundaries of competencies, functions, and geographies—to deliver to each client a multidisciplinary, complete solution.

Who We Are Is Where We Came From

When Mr. Arthur Andersen founded the firm in 1913, he said, "We want to measure our contribution more by the quality of the service rendered than by whether we are making a good living out of it." Today, quality is still our number one focus, as we strive continuously to understand, accept, meet, and exceed our clients' needs and expectations.

Source: http://www.arthurandersen.com

vary considerably from country to country. The major factors we need to discuss here are sources of audit guidelines and audit requirements, differences in audit standards, and audit opinions.

The development of auditing standards in a given country is a complex dynamic of cultural, legal-political, and economic variables, so one would not expect total uniformity. Auditing standards come from the public (government) sector, the private sector, or a combination of the two. The first source of influence—the public sector—is prevalent in developing countries where the accounting profession is not well organized or sufficiently strong. The government often takes the lead by incorporating audit requirements and, to a lesser extent, standards into law. This thrust is also evident in industrialized countries such as Germany, which is legalistic and prescriptive and whose auditing profession has historically been established and regulated by law. The German case is interesting because the accounting profession there makes recommendations on audit standards that are then incorporated into law by the government.

This approach can be contrasted with that of the United States, where the SEC requires that an audit be conducted but does not say how. This is left to the accounting profession through auditing standards developed by the AICPA. A similar approach is followed in the United Kingdom and Canada.

There are wide differences in the requirements for audits worldwide. Here, however, we are specifically discussing compliance audits rather than operational or other kinds of audits. A compliance audit is one that is undertaken to determine if the auditee is following procedures or guidelines established by a higher authority. In the United States, annual independent audits are required of firms traded on a national exchange as well as firms with more than 500 shareholders and assets of more than $5 million. However, most other large companies have audits, and many banks and regulatory agencies require them. In Canada, public corporations, private corporations meeting certain tests of size, municipalities, universities, hospitals, and most nonprofit organizations are required to be audited. In the United Kingdom, all limited companies must be audited.

The Fourth Directive of the European Union, which we discussed earlier in the context of accounting standards, is also a source of auditing requirements. Although the Fourth Directive does not deal with audit standards and practices or the qualifications of auditors—which is left up to the Eighth Directive—it does require that firms that fall under the guidelines of the Fourth Directive be audited. That is an important legal consideration, because most countries in the European Union have incorporated the Fourth Directive into their national law. Basically, the Fourth Directive requires the publication and audit of public companies. However, it allows countries to exempt small and, in some cases, medium-size companies from the audit requirement. Because of the long tradition of auditing financial statements in the United Kingdom, small companies there are still required to be audited. Germany, however, has decided to exempt small companies from the audit requirement.

Just because a large number of countries require an audit does not mean that all audits are done the same way. Financial statements come from the firms' books and records, which reflect the underlying transactions the firm engages in. The term *audit* could mean that the financial statements accurately reflect the books and records of the firm. The audit would entail tracing the data from the books and records to the financial statements, a relatively simple process. The auditor would rely primarily on the honesty of management and would not be as concerned as his or her counterpart in the United States or United Kingdom with confirming inventory taking or bank balances.

A more extensive audit would determine whether the books and records accurately reflect the original transactions. This would involve a more extensive investigation of the internal control system to make sure that corporate procedures for recording transactions are clearly established, communicated, and followed. It would also involve more extensive tests of original transactions and tracing their eventual flow through the records to the financial statements.

There are many reasons why audit standards vary from country to country. In the United States and the United Kingdom, there are broadly based capital markets and a highly qualified accounting profession. The capital markets require that financial statements be independently verified, and the profession has developed and refined audit standards over time. The air of skepticism has encouraged fairly rigid tests.

Culture often plays a part as well. In Japan, bank deposits and loans payable are obtained from the company rather than by independent confirmation, because the latter would show too much distrust in company personnel, which could mean a loss of face.

A comparative international analysis of audit standards with respect to the audit function, ethical standards and enforcement, and audit reports is shown for a selection of countries in Exhibit 12.4.

Exhibit 12.4 Comparative International Audit Standards

PANEL A

	THE AUDIT FUNCTION			
	Required to Be Audited	Election of Auditor	Objective or Purpose of Audit	Sources of Auditing Standards

North and South America

Argentina	An independent audit is required by Argentinean legal control authorities like Inspeccion General de Justicia, Taxes Departments, Central Bank, etc.	Appointed by the board of directors or by the shareholders at the annual meeting for the period subject to review, so as to increase the reliability of accounting information	To issue a technical opinion as to whether the statement presents fairly the entity's financial position and results for the period subject to review, according to Professional Accounting Standards so as to increase the reliability of accounting information.	Professional Auditing Standards are issued by the professional organizations. The Argentinean GAAS are similar to U.S. GAAS.
Mexico	Every company registered with the Comision Nacional de Falores (National Securities Commission), all companies filing a consolidated tax return and for tax purposes all companies with income of Pesos 2,412,000 or more than 300 employees in the previous fiscal year.	Generally appointed by the general manager, the board of directors, or the shareholders.	The objective of an audit is to express an opinion regarding the company's financial statements. The purpose of an audit of a small company would include providing financing, tax and social security services and meeting the requirements of the National Securities Commission. The general law of commercial companies requires all corporations to appoint at least one statutory auditor or (comisario), who is required to submit an annual report to the shareholders on accounting and administrative matters	Set forth in technical bulletins issued by the Comision de Normas y Procedimiemto de Auditoria of the Mexican Institute of Public Accountants, and summarized and classified in the publication *Auditing Standards and Procedures*, issued by the Mexican Institute of Public Accountants.
United States	Companies traded on a national stock exchange, companies that have over 500 shareholders and assets of over $5 million (amounts vary depending on applicable state laws),	Recommendation by the audit committee or board of directors and approved by the shareholders.	The expression of an opinion on the fairness with which the financial statements presents fairly, in all material respects, financial position, results of operations, and its cash flows in conformity with generally accepted accounting principles.	Statements on Auditing standards are issued by the Auditing Standards Board, the senior technical body of the AICPA designated to issue pronouncements on auditing matters.

	and certain types of financial service industries (if required to file with the Securities and Exchange Commission or regulated or funded by federal agencies).			
Europe				
The Netherlands	All public companies, private companies, cooperative societies, and mutual guarantee associations if they meet at least two of the following criteria; assets exceed 7.5 million guilders; net turnover exceeds 15 million guilders; average number of employees exceeds 49. All insurance companies and institutions registered under Dutch Credit System Supervision Act and investment companies under Dutch Investment Companies Supervision Act.	Appointed by shareholders at the annual meeting or by the supervisory board of the board of directors.	To ensure that balance sheets and accompanying notes present a true and fair view of the financial position; and that profit and loss statements and notes give a true and fair view of the results of operations of a company for the fiscal year under review.	NIVRA has adopted International Standards on Auditing issued by IFAC. They have been translated to the Dutch with specific modifications as necessary.
United Kingdom	All limited companies above a specified size limit. Small companies may request audit; separate requirements exist for charities; other bodies/interested parties may request "audit"	Appointed/reappointed annually by shareholders' majority vote at annual general meeting; in exceptional circumstances casual vacancies may be appointed by Secretary of State for Trade and Industry	An independent examination and opinion, for shareholders, on whether the financial statements give a true and fair view of the state of the company's affairs as at the balance sheet date and of the profit and loss for the year then ended and have been properly prepared in	The Auditing Practices Board (APB) established in 1991 by the Consultative Committee of Accountancy Bodies (CCAB) comprising the six principal accountancy bodies in the UK and Republic of Ireland

(continues)

Exhibit 12.4 (Continued)

PANEL A

THE AUDIT FUNCTION

	Required to Be Audited	Election of Auditor	Objective or Purpose of Audit	Sources of Auditing Standards
	service for a wide range of enterprises.		accordance with the Companies Act 1985.	
Italy	In Italy there are two bodies charged with auditing: The Board of Statutory Auditors (*Collegio Sindacale*) and the Auditing Firm. The first is composed of three to five members and it is compulsory for all companies in the legal form of Stock Company and for Limited Liability Companies that have a capital above 200 million liras. However, a board is required also if, in two consecutive financial years, the company exceeds two of the following limits: (a) assets—4.70 million liras, (b) earnings from sales and provisions of services—9.500 million liras; average staff employed during the financial years—50 units. The Auditing Firm is compulsory for listed companies and other entities that operate in	Proposed by the board of directors and elected by the general meeting of shareholders.	To ensure that the financial statements taken as a whole give a true and fair view of the financial position and results in compliance with the civil code.	Auditing standards are issued by the Dottori Commercialisti and the Ragionieri Collegialisti; and approved by the National Association of Auditors' Firms (ASSIREVI) and by CONSOB. Similar to International Standards on auditing.

	particular economic sectors. A recent decree specifies the regulation concerning appointments for the Board of Statutory Auditors and for Audit firms in listed companies. Particularly: Auditing firms are in charge of the independent audit of financial statements (and some additional financial information); Statutory Auditors have to control the behavior of directors and the internal control systems of the company.			
France	The following are required to be audited: public limited companies, some limited companies, and some nonprofit organizations (associations, football leagues, political parties, etc.)	Elected or reelected by the shareholders for a six-year term.	To certify that all reports and financial statements conform to existing rules and regulations and give a fair and true view.	Companies Act of 1966 and standards published by the Compagnie Nationale des Commissaires aux Comptes, (CNCC). These standards are in accordance with IFAC's standards (IAPC)
Germany	Public companies (including cooperatives), and stock corporations, insurance companies, banks, and government-directed enterprises, audits provided by disclosure law, special audits of relations with affected companies, Small companies are exempted.	Elected by shareholders at annual meeting in case of statutory audit.	To determine that financial statements comply with the company's status under legal regulations (German Law) and give a true and fair view.	Commercial laws and jurisdiction are the primary basis, but the Institute of Wirtschaftsprüfers issues professional standards and guidelines.

(continues)

Exhibit 12.4 (Continued)

PANEL A

	THE AUDIT FUNCTION			
	Required to Be Audited	Election of Auditor	Objective or Purpose of Audit	Sources of Auditing Standards
Sweden	Any company with limited liability status. This includes limited liability companies, branches of foreign companies, cooperative units, and banks	The Companies Act requires appointment of at least one auditor by the shareholders.	To satisfy requirements of the Companies Act and to determine if a company's accounts are fairly presented.	The Companies Act states that the audit should be carried out in accordance with generally accepted auditing standards. SBPA recommendations and sections of the Companies Act are the main sources of the auditing standards. These standards are much less detailed than U.S. standards and professionals rely on judgment when applying specific standards
Asia and Pacific				
Australia	All public and "large" entities have to be audited. A company is "large" if it has two of the following three attributes: consolidated gross revenue of $10 million; consolidated gross assets of $5 million; 50 or more employees.	Board of directors with shareholders' approval; client's management; or Auditor General; and at the choice of the body to be audited.	Corporation Law requires that accounts show a true and fair view and comply with the Accounting Standards and the Corporation Regulations; accounts should be presented fairly and be in accordance with the trust deed.	Auditing shandards (AUS) and guidelines (AUG) approved by the ICAA and ASCPA
Japan	Corporations with more than 500 million yen in capital stock or more than 20 billion in liability stocks; public stock and debentures exceeding 500	Under the commercial Law Code, the auditor and auditing officer are appointed at the stockholders' general meeting. Under the Securities and Exchange Act, the auditor (CPA or corporate) is	The commercial Law Code does not specify the purposes of an audit; the Securities and Exchange Act specifies that it is to protect indirectly public interests and investors, to confirm that the financial statements	No Commercial Law Code; the Auditing Standards require: (1) experience, ability, independence; (2) a fair, impartial attitude; (3) due care; (4) refusal to use or

	million yen; stocks registered for the stock exchange or over the counter; plans to list on the exchange; and labor unions and educational institutions receiving a subsidy from governmental bodies; corporations applying for financing from the Small Business Investment Development Corporation.	appointed by the board of directors.	fairly and appropriately show the financial position and results, and that they are prepared in conformity with accounting principles.	reveal confidential information; (5) sufficient evidence for a reasonable basis for an opinion; (6) planning, execution; and (7) audit procedure, timely and extent of tests based on internal controls, materiality and audit risk.
Hong Kong	All companies incorporated and registered under the companies Ordinance except certain private companies.	Appointed by the shareholders at the annual meeting.	Show a true and fair view at the balance sheet date and of profit and loss for the financial year and compliance with the Companies Ordinance, certain private companies must show a true and correct view.	Statements of Auditing-Standards of the HKSA regulations of the Companies Ordinance.
Singapore	All incorporated companies, both public and private.	Appointed by the shareholders at the annual meeting.	To determine whether accounts give a true and fair view of the company's affairs in accordance with provisions of the Companies Act.	Statements of Auditing Guidelines and Practices of the Institute of Certified Public Accountants of Singapore. Closely follow international standards.

PANEL B	ETHICAL STANDARDS AND ENFORCEMENT			
	Ethical Standards	Enforcement	Legal Liability	Responsibility for Detection of Fraud
North and South America				
Argentina	Argentinean Code of Ethics issued by the FACPCE, which aims to safeguard the public	A disciplinary court elected by the direct vote of all registered professionals.	Failure by an auditor to perform his or her duties, with regard to the examination of financial statements, may lead to monetary, criminal,	An auditor may be held criminally responsible, not necessarily for the perpetration of crimes, but rather for com-

(continues)

Exhibit 12.4 (*Continued*)

PANEL B

ETHICAL STANDARDS AND ENFORCEMENT

	Ethical Standards	Enforcement	Legal Liability	Responsibility for Detection of Fraud
	against careless or unscrupulous professionals.		professional, or other consequences applicable under the regulations of the control authorities involved. Due to negligence by the auditor, in the event of deception or fraud, the auditor may be responsible for paying damages to the client or another party.	plicity or concealment, such as providing false or misleading examinations of financial statements.
Mexico	The Mexican Institute of Public Accountants has issued a code of ethics to guide its members in moral conduct and to declare its intentions to serve society with trust, diligence, and self-respect.	The Mexican Institute Public . Accountants	The auditor may be sued if the audit is not conducted according to the standards and procedures issued by the Mexican Institue of Public Accountants and a third party is affected.	A statutory auditor is responsible for the vigilance of the company and the administration.
United States	The bylaws of the AICPA require that members adhere to the Rules of Code of Professional Conduct. These Principles of the Code of Professional Conduct of the AICPA express the profession's recognition of its responsibilities to the public, to clients, and to colleagues. They guide members in the performance of their professional responsibilities and express the basic tenets	The Council of the AICPA is authorized to designate bodies to promulgate technical standards under the Rules, and the bylaws require adherence to those Rules and Standards Compliance with the code or Professional Conduct depends primarily on members' understanding and voluntary actions, secondarily on reinforcement by peers and on public opinion, and, ultimately, on disciplinary proceedings, when necessary, against members who fail to comply with the rules.	The auditor may be held legally and professionally liable when he or she fails to apply due professional care in the application of the required auditing standards.	The auditor should assess the risk that fraud may cause the financial statements to contain a material misstatement. Based on that assessment, the auditor should design the audit to provide reasonable assurance of detecting errors and irregularities, due to fraud that are material tot he financial statements.

Europe			
The Netherlands	of ethical and professional conduct. The Rules of Conduct for accountants (GBA) prohibit discrediting the profession, the use of information for one's own gain. They require preserving records of evidence and keeping information about a client confidential. Key issues addressed are impartiality, confidentiality quality of work, and independence.	Complaints received by the Disciplinary Board and the Board of Appeal.	Criminal and civil liability for criminal offense (fines to imprisonment), for negligence, acts discrediting the profession; the latter part is enforced by the Disciplines Board, not by the law; for violating professional rules (resulting in written warning, written reprehension, suspension (maximum 6 months), and expulsion).	In principle, management bears responsibility for the financial statements; however, auditors can also be taken to court if they fail to detect errors. Auditors are not responsible for irregularities (intentional distortions of financial statements) if they have performed their audit with due and professional care. Material fraud that is detected, but not redressed, must be reported to the authorities.
United Kingdom	Each RSB has an ethical guide; all stress integrity, objectivity, independence, professional competence and due care, professional behavior, and confidentiality.	Each RSB must have rules for enforcing compliance with SASs; penalties may include withdrawal of registration so that person becomes ineligible to perform company audits. Monitoring is carried out, for example, by the Joint Monitoring Unit of the ICAEW/ICAS.	Rule of "joint and several" liability means that auditors may carry the full cost of negligence even where this is partly the fault of directors; liability to third party exists at common law where loss is clearly attributable to reliance on a report prepared negligently and the party preparing the report knew (or should have known) it would be relied upon.	Required to plan audit so as to obtain sufficient evidence to give reasonable assurance that the financial statements are free from material misstatement, whether caused by fraud or other irregularity or error.
Italy	The rules of association of the Ordine Nazionale del Dottori Commercialisti and of the Collegio Nazionale dei Ragionieri include specific ethics requirements relating to independence and competence. Auditing	Ethical standards are enforced by the professional associations.	The auditor is legally and professionally liable only when he or she fails to apply, or incorrectly applies, the required auditing standards.	No specific requirements. According to the ISA, the auditor is not responsible for failure to detect fraud or illegal acts if the auditing procedures appropriate in the circumstances have been competently performed.

(continues)

Exhibit 12.4 *(Continued)*

PANEL B

| | ETHICAL STANDARDS AND ENFORCEMENT | | | |
	Ethical Standards	Enforcement	Legal Liability	Responsibility for Detection of Fraud
	Standard No. 1 of the Consiglio Nazionale del Dottori Commercialisti specifies the following requirements for the auditor: Competence as a condition for acceptance of the auditor's work, exercise of due professional care in the conduct of the audit, integrity, and independence.			
France	Set both by law and the Code of Professional Ethics adopted by the Compagnie Nationale, including rules on independence, incompatible functions, advertising, use of title or firm name, relationships with colleagues, connection between predecessor and successor.	Penalties are set by law, and in several cases by the Compagnie Nationale des Commissaires aux Comptes, which may take disciplinary action.	Violation of laws that regulate the profession are subject to Penal Code. Requirements are stated by law. Auditors are required to carry liability insurance.	No responsibility, but liable to client and third parties for fraud and negligence; must report known illegal acts by client to government authorities and/or public prosecutor.
Germany	A code of ethics covers legally required audits. Detailed guidelines issued by the Institute of CPAs, and by the Chamber of Auditors include independence, professional care, partial responsibility, discretion, impartiality,	A self-regulated body can warn, reprimand, fine, or expel an auditor who is guilty of not performing duties in accordance with professional law and standards.	Unlimited liability to clients and third parties for false statements or other intentional violations. Liability is limited in case of negligence. Breach of confidentiality is a criminal offence.	Expected to conduct the examination in an impartial and conscientious manner. Liable if failure to discover fraud results from negligence.

Sweden	professional conduct, and elimination of incompatible duties. The FAR has developed rules of professional ethics similar to those followed by U.S. CPAs.	Sanctions may be imposed by the Supervisory Board by Public Accountants.	The auditor can be held liable for client damages that were intentional or caused by carelessness.	The auditor is responsible for fraud only if the failure to detect it was intentional or caused by carelessness.
Asia and Pacific				
Australia	Code of Professional Conduct (CPC) of the ICAA and ASCPA	Disciplinary committees in the . profession	The ethical standards per se do not give rise to legal liability. However, under the Corporation Law, criminal sanctions may be invoked against dishonest auditors, and de-registration may be a remedy against inappropriate conduct. Civil remedies for auditors' negligence are also available.	The auditor has no responsibility for reporting on control structures, other than reporting significant problems in the management letter to the Board or Audit Committee on a timely basis. Specific requirements to see and detect fraud do not at present exist.
Japan	The CPA law and the JICPA code prohibit the impairment of trust and require independenc, secrecy and restrictions of advertising. Punishment may be administered for false and unreasonable attestation	Under CPA Law, the Minister of Finance is empowered to investigate violations and to assess penalties, including warning, suspension, or withdrawal from registration. The CPA has the right to vindicate himself or herself. The JICPA Punishment Committee also enforces ethical standards. The president of the JICPA determines penalties according to the views of the committee and the board.	Under the Securities and Exchange Act, if investors lose because of material errors in audited financial statements, the auditor or firm must compensate for an error unless they can prove lack of intention and the use of due care. Under the Commercial Law Code, the auditor must compensate client for breach of contract and for materiality false items in an audit report if the auditor cannot prove due care.	The auditor must use due care to detect causes of material difference in financial statements. The auditor must report actions that contradict the directors' duties to the statutory auditors of the client.
Hong Kong	The Hong Kong Society of Accountants has issued statements of professional ethics originally based on those issued by the Institute of Chartered Accountants in the United Kingdom, but	The Hong Kong Society acts as the disciplinary body.	Criminal liability for auditors who willfully make untrue statements in the prospectus or who induce another person by fraudulent or reckless misrepresentation to invest money. The auditor is liable for damages to the client and in some cases to third parties for negligence	The auditor is not expected to search for fraud but must be aware of the possibility of it and investigate fully if there are grounds for suspicion.

(continues)

Exhibit 12.4 *(Continued)*

PANEL B	ETHICAL STANDARDS AND ENFORCEMENT		
	Ethical Standards	Enforcement	Legal Liability	Responsibility for Detection of Fraud
	in some cases updated based on AICPA's professional conduct.		resulting in financial loss. Negligence may also be treated as a criminal offense.	
Singapore	The rules of the Accountants Act call for integrity and confidentiality, and prohibit incompatible functions, advertising, encroachment on the business of others, certification of estimates, acceptance of benefits from service for clients wihtout consent, and acts discreditable to the profession. The standards on independence parallel those set by the United Kingdom.	The Disciplinary Committee of the ICPAS and PAB may censor, expel, or suspend a member. It may also issue fines of up to $5,000 and the costs of an investigation.	There is liability for damages to the client and in some cases third parties for negligence in performing an audit, and criminal liability for willfully making untrue statements in a prospectus. Negligence may also bring criminal liability.	The auditor is expected to seek reasonable assurance that material fraud has not occurred; if material fraud has taken place, the auditor must ensure that the error is corrected or that its effect is indicated in the financial information. The Companies Act also requires reporting of fraud under certain circumstances to the Ministry of Finance.

PANEL C	AUDIT REPORTS
	Reporting Requirement

North and South America

Argentina   Standard audit report formats have been issued by the Buenos Aires CPCE. Although not mandatory, they are generally used. The FACPCE sets the minimum data that must be included in an audit report. The important elements are:

1. The name of the reports audited and the related periods and the name of the companies.

2. The conduct of the audit in accordance with auditing standards.

3. The auditing standards.

4. The opinion as to fairness of statements.

5. Statements presented in accordance with professional accounting standards.

6. The name of those requiring audit or services.

Mexico

In all cases in which the name of the public accountant is associated with financial statements or information, he or she should express in a clear and unmistakable manner

1. The nature of his or her relation with such information.

2. His or her opinion on the same.

3. The important limitations, when applicable, that were imposed on the examination, the qualifications derived from them, the important reasons why an adverse opinion is expressed, or the reasons why a professional opinion cannot be expressed after an examination is performed in accordance with auditing standards.

The auditor, when rendering his or her opinion on financial statements, should observe that

1. They were prepared in accordance with generally accepted accounting principles.

2. Such principles were applied on a consistent basis.

3. The information presented therein and in the related notes is adequate and sufficient for its reasonable interpretation.

USA

In a standard three-paragraph report, the auditor first identifies the company and financial statements being audited and states the responsibilities of management and the auditor. Second, the auditor must indicate the scope of the examination and whether or not the audit complies with generally accepted auditing standards and that this is a sufficient basis for an opinion. Third, he or she must state whether the financial statements are presented fairly in accordance with GAAP. The auditor must express an opinion on the financial statements as a whole or assert that an opinion cannot be expressed.

Europe

The Netherlands

The wording is not specified by law. According to ISA 700 "The Auditors' Report on Financial Statements" which has been adopted by NIVRA, the auditors' report includes among others both scope and opinion paragraphs. In the scope paragraph reference is made to the ISAs. In the opinion paragraph the auditor clearly states as to whether the financial statements give a true and fair view in accordance with the financial reporting framework and, where appropriate, whether the financial statements comply with statutory requirements.

United Kingdom

The auditor's report sets out respective responsibilities of directors and auditor's scope of audit; basis of opinion and statement of opinion. By statute it must cover the balance sheet, profit and loss account and related notes; by auditing standards it extends to other financial statements prescribed by accounting standards, such as the cash flow statement. The opinion is stated on whether the financial

(continues)

Exhibit 12.4 (*Continued*)

AUDIT REPORTS

PANEL C	
Country	Reporting Requirement

statements give a true and fair view and comply with statutory requirements. The scope section explains that auditors read other information contained in the audit report, including the corporate governance statement, and consider the implications for their report if they become aware of inconsistencies. The scope section also explains the auditor's responsibilities in relation to the directors' report, the accounting records, information and explanations required, and rules regarding the disclosure of directors' remuneration.

Italy
The auditor's report consists of four main paragraphs. The first identifies the financial statements and defines the responsibilities of both the Directors and the Auditors. The second (or scope) paragraph includes the source of accounting standards used, the parts of the director's report necessary for a clear understanding of the responsibility. The third paragraph identifies any material departure or deviation from generally accepted accounting standards. The fourth paragraph is the opinion paragraph. A fifth paragraph might be present for emphasis on significant matters.

France
The auditor must certify the financial statements or qualify the report following a standard format based on International Auditing Standard. A second report is required, detailing agreements entered into between the company and legally defined related parties. There is also a standard format for this second report.

Germany
According to the German Commercial Code the auditor's report to the corporation must contain a description of the process and the result of the audit, including management's report, an estimation of future development, a statement of compliance with legal regulation, and a statement explaining the company's risk management system.

The auditor must also provide a summary that covers the content, type, and volume of the audit; an evaluation of the audit result; and statements as to whether or not the financial statements and management's report present a true and fair view.

Sweden
Chapter 10 of the Companies Act states that the auditor's report should include statements about

1. The preparation of the annual report in accordance with the Act.

2. The adoption of the balance sheet and income statement.

3. The proposal included in the administration report for disposition of the unappropriated earnings or deficit.

4. The discharge from the liability of members of the board of directors and the managing director.

Asia and Pacific

Australia

The standards report has the following format:

We have audited the accounts of X Limited on pages _____ to _____, and the Statement by Directors in accordance with Australian Auditing Standards" (scope paragraph).

In our opinion the accounts of X Limited are properly drawn up in accordance with the provisions of the Companies (XXX) Code and so as to give a true and fair view of:

(i) The state of affairs of the company at — 19— and the profit of the company for the year ended on that date; (ii) the other matters required by Section 269 of the Code to be dealt with in the accounts; and are in accordance with applicable approved accounting standards and Australian Accounting Standards (opinion paragraph).

Japan

The auditor's report must outline the scope of the audit performed and state in opinion on the financial statements, expressing whether the statements fairly present the financial position, results of operations and cash flows. It must also state matters that are also reported in the financial statements but that the auditor wants to call attention to.

Hong Kong

The auditor's report must state whether the balance sheet and profit-and-loss account have been prepared properly in accordance with the Companies Ordinance and whether they give a true and fair view of the state of affairs at the year's end and of the profit or loss for the year. The report must also express an opinion as to whether proper books of account have been kept, whether proper returns have been received from the branches, and whether the accounts agree with the books and returns. The report should be modified if the auditor has not received all reuired information and if disclosures about officers' and directors remunerations are inadequate.

Singapore

The auditor's report must state whether the accounts and, when relevant, consolidated accounts give a true and fair view. The report must also express an opinion as to whether the accounting and other records, including the registers, have been kept properly for a fair presentation and for compliance with stipulations on disclosure in the Companies Act. Reference is made to statements of auditing standards in a similar format to International Auditing Standards.

Source: Adapted from Belverd E. Needles, Jr. (2000), "Taxonomy of Auditing Standards" in Choi, F.D.S. (ed.). *International Accounting and Finance Handbook.* (New York: John Wiley & Sons), 2nd edition, Chapter 5.

INTERNATIONAL HARMONIZATION OF AUDIT STANDARDS

While multinationals, audit firms, and governments attempt to standardize their practices and permit the cross-national transfer of audit services there will still be obstacles to auditing. Much as the IASC, now IASB, is attempting to harmonize financial reporting practices, IFAC is attempting to harmonize audit standards and audit professions globally (see Exhibit 12.5).

IFAC grew out of the International Coordination Committee for the Accounting Profession (ICCAP), which was organized in 1972 at the International Congress of Accountants in Sydney, Australia. The purpose of establishing the ICCAP was to lay the groundwork for more formal organizations to help achieve the goals of accounting harmonization. This was accomplished with the establishment of the International Accounting Standards Committee (IASC) in 1973 and the IFAC in Munich at the 1977 international congress. IFAC's membership comprises representatives of 153 national professional accountancy bodies from 113 countries, representing more than two million accountants.

To accomplish its objectives, IFAC issues guidance in six key areas: auditing and related services, education, ethics, financial and management accounting, information technology, and public sector accounting. In regard to auditing, the International Audit Practices Committee of the IFAC has been very active, having issued many international standards on auditing (ISA) plus related practice statements.

There are a number of major benefits of developing and enforcing internationally acceptable auditing standards:

1. The existence of a set of international auditing standards, which are known to be enforced, will give readers of audit reports produced in other countries justifiable confidence in the auditor's opinion. By thus lending credibility to the work of the foreign auditor they enable that auditor to lend credibility to the financial statements upon which he or she is reporting.

2. International auditing standards will reinforce the benefits that are already flowing from the existence of international accounting standards by providing readers with greater assurance that the accounting standards are being adhered to.

3. By adding strength to international accounting standards, international auditing standards will assist readers in making international financial comparisons.

4. International auditing standards will provide further incentives to improve and extend the set of international accounting standards.

5. The existence of international auditing standards will aid in the flow of investment capital, especially to developing economies.

6. The development of an international set of standards will make it easier for developing countries to produce domestic auditing standards, and this will benefit them.

7. Effective and credible auditing is necessary in all instances where there is a separation between management (which produces financial reports) and outsiders (who use the reports). The need is all the greater in the case of MNEs because management is separated from the outsiders by

Exhibit 12.5   International Federation of Accountants (IFAC)

International Federation of Accountants

Organization Overview

IFAC is an organization of national professional accountancy organizations that repreent accountants employed in public practice, business and industry, the public sector, and education, as well as some specialized groups that interface frequently with the profession. Currently, it has 153 member bodies in 113 countries, representing 2 million accountants. IFAC's structure and operations provide for representation of its diverse member organizations.

Objective

IFAC strives to develop the profession and harmonize its standards worldwide to enable accountants to provide services of consistently high quality in the public interest. IFAC will fulfill this objective within the framework of its new Constitution.

Primary Activities

IFAC's leadership, its committees and task forces work with member bodies to achieve this objective by:

- **Serving as international advocates**. IFAC develops and promotes high quality technical, professional and ethical publications and guidance for use by accountants employed in every sector.

- **Acting as agents for change**. IFAC provides leadership on emerging issues, the impetus for the liberalization of accountancy services, and a universal voice for the world's accountants on issues of public and professional concern. Much of this is accomplished through outreach to numerous organizations that rely on or have an interest in the activities of the international accountancy profession.

- **Facilitating the development of a harmonized worldwide accountancy profession**. IFAC fosters the advancement of strong national professional accountancy organizations. It works closely with regional accountancy organizations and outside agencies to accomplish this.

Source: www.ifac.org

greater differences in culture, political and economic systems, geographical boundaries, and the like. Thus, international auditing standards are, in this respect, even more important than national ones.

Following criticism of its global effectiveness in enforcing audit standards, IFAC agreed to a restructuring plan in May 2000 where, as part of the restructuring, IFAC and the large international accounting firms have undertaken a major new initiative. This is designed to raise standards of financial reporting and auditing globally in an effort to protect the interests of cross-border investors and promote international flows of capital. A key aspect of this effort is the establishment of a new IFAC-sponsored grouping of accounting firms that will work closely with IFAC in developing and encouraging implementation of international accounting and auditing standards.

The new IFAC grouping or forum of firms will be open to participation by any firm with offices in more than one jurisdiction or that have, or intend to have, transnational clients and are willing to comply with rigorous quality obligations that include:

- Having policies and practices in compliance with ISAs and the IFAC Code of Ethics
- Maintenance of appropriate internal control procedures including intra-firm practice review
- Agreement to implement training on international accounting and auditing standards including the Code of Ethics
- Agreement to subject assurance work to periodic external quality assurance
- Agreement to support the development of the professional bodies and implementation of international standards of accounting and auditing in developing countries

It would seem that the most important of these obligations is the agreement to subject all the firm's offices in all jurisdictions to independent quality assurance reviews. While peer review on a national basis has taken place in several countries such as the United States and Canada, this will represent the first effort to implement global peer review and look at each of the large firms as one entity throughout the world. Membership in the forum will be conditional on compliance with these reviews. The new IFAC Forum of Firms will work alongside the new International Forum on Accountancy Development (IFAD), spearheaded by IFAC, to improve the quality of global accounting and auditing. In addition, an independent Public Oversight Board will see to it that the activities of IFAC and its Forum of Firms are in the public interest. The IFAC grouping of firms will primarily be funding by participating firms that will also contribute additional resources to strengthen IFAC's audit standards and monitoring work.

IFAD was established following the Asian financial crisis in heeding a 1997 call from James Wolfensohn, president of the World Bank. The accounting profession was criticized for not doing enough to enhance the accounting capabilities of developing and emerging nations. Following discussions between the World Bank and IFAC, it was agreed to form IFAD, representing an alliance of accountancy groups and firms across the world. IFAD is intended to be a means by which regulators, international financial institutions, investors, and representatives of the accountancy and auditing profession come together to ensure economic downturns such as the Asian financial crisis are not repeated (see Exhibit 12.6).

Exhibit 12.6   International Forum on Accountancy Development

Objectives of IFAD

1. Promote understanding by national governments of the value of transparent financial reporting, in accordance with sound corporate governance

2. Assist in defining expectations as to how the accountancy profession (in both the public and private sectors) should carry out its responsibilities to support the public interest

3. Encourage governments to focus more directly on the needs of developing countries and economies in transition

4. Help harness funds and expertise to build accounting and auditing capacity in developing countries

5. Contribute to a common strategy and framework of reference for accountancy development

6. Promote cooperation between governments, the accountancy and other professions, the international financial institutions, regulators, standard setters, capital providers and issuers

IFAD has provided a mechanism through which those with an interest in raising reporting and auditing practices can communicate and can develop the partnerships necessary to promote change in an effective and efficient manner.

Source: www.ifad.net

IFAD has been undertaking country-by-country reviews of accounting standards, ethics and disciplinary procedures, corporate governance, banking, and company law. IFAD has benchmarked information collected through these individual country reviews against international standards and will finance consultants to visit countries to help close the gaps wherever these may be identified. IFAD is firmly committed to encouraging conformity and consistency of national accounting standards with IAS.

The key to global acceptance and enforcement of International Accounting Standards depends very much on the successful implementation of IFAC's and IFAD's new initiatives. In particular, IFAD needs to promote education addressing IAS, ISA, and IFAC's Code of Ethics on a global basis. IFAC's Forum of Firms also needs to insist on the comparable implementation of accounting and auditing standards on a global basis.

Only time will tell if the efforts of IFAD and IFAC can overcome national, cultural, and other barriers and achieve global acceptance and enforcement of IAS and International Standards of Auditing (ISA) in countries around the world. In the meantime, IFAC's Forum of Firms should take the lead by upgrading their quality standards to a consistent worldwide level and ensure compliance with IAS and ISA as well as IFAC's Code of Ethics throughout their global networks.

SUMMARY

1.   The quality of the auditing profession is a function of several factors, such as the reputation of the accounting and auditing profession, the quality of the edu-

cational system, and the certification process. The certification or licensing process for an auditor is a function of several factors, such as the identity of the candidate, educational requirements, experience requirements, and examination.

2. Auditors can service their global clients by sending auditors from the home office to foreign locations; by establishing correspondent relationships with foreign auditing firms; or by investing in a foreign auditing practice through a branch office, a joint venture with a local auditing firm, or a wholly owned company.

3. Auditing in the international context is a challenging task because of the differences in local business practices and customs; currency, language and law; distance and organizational issues; and the availability of suitable personnel.

4. An important issue for the auditing profession worldwide is reciprocity or the ability of a certified accountant in one country to practice in another.

5. The Big Five, the world's largest accounting firms, are responsible for auditing most of the largest MNEs. A major development in the global strategies of the world's largest auditing firms in recent years has been the merger of firms such as Deloitte Haskins & Sells with Touche Ross, Arthur Young with Ernst & Whinney, and Price Waterhouse with Coopers and Lybrand to form larger auditing firms better able to audit global corporations.

6. National audit standards differ from country to country for a variety of reasons including the stage of development of capital markets, the maturity of the accounting profession, and the cultural environment.

7. The International Federation of Accountants (IFAC) is attempting to harmonize auditing standards and practices so financial statement users worldwide can be confident of the accuracy and reliability of the underlying financial statements.

8. The International Forum on Accountancy Development (IFAD) was established in 2000 to promote the accounting capabilities of developing and emerging nations.

Discussion Questions

1. Discuss the personal qualifications, educational requirements, and experience requirements of three different countries. Develop a matrix that includes countries down one side and the three dimensions just described across the top so you can compare and contrast the different countries.

2. If you were a certified accountant in your home country and wanted to practice as an auditor in another country, it is unlikely that you would be allowed to practice right away. Why do these barriers to entry exist? What strategies could you pursue to service your clients in markets where you are not allowed to practice?

3. What are some of the challenges global auditing firms face in trying to service their clients?

4. Why are the audits of most of the largest global companies done by the Big Five accounting firms?

5. You have the opportunity to work on an internship in a foreign country for an audit firm with an office in that country. What would be the pros and cons of such an experience, and what would you do to prepare for that experience?

6. It was mentioned in the chapter that KPMG has reorganized itself around five national industry-focused teams that consist of assurance, tax, and consulting pro-

fessionals concentrating on each industry. Why do you think KPMG moved to this type of organizational structure rather than remain organized by service (assurance, tax, and consulting services)? What do you think some of the challenges might be in switching to this type of structure? Given that KPMG is a global company, are there any unique global challenges to this structure?

7. The IFAC is attempting to harmonize auditing standards and practices. What do you think are some of the barriers to this harmonization effort? What are the benefits of their work being successful?

8. What are the prospects of IFAC achieving its goal of worldwide reliability of financial statements? Will IFAC's Forum of Firms work? How will IFAD help?

Case: *Bell Canada Enterprises* (BCE)

BCE (Bell Canada Enterprises) is a household name in Canada and is well known around the world. It is a descendant of the Bell Telephone Company of Canada, which was formed in 1880 for the original purpose of operating Canada's entire telephone system by employing the patented inventions of AT&T, the mammoth U.S. firm founded in 1877 with the patent of Alexander Graham Bell. The firm of Philip S. Ross was appointed to audit and certify the company's first financial statements. This firm later affiliated itself with the accounting firm of Touche, taking the name Touche Ross in Canada. The relationship between the auditor and company has continued unbroken since 1880.

By 1970, revenues for the Bell Canada group reached $936 million while assets topped $3.3 billion. The group consisted of Northern Electric (now known as Northern Telecom) and Bell Canada. In 1983, Bell Canada Enterprises (known as BCE) superseded Bell Canada as the parent company of the group.

By 1988, the BCE group was the largest of Touche Ross's Canadian clients and one of its largest worldwide. In 1988, its revenues exceeded $15 billion, and assets exceeded $28 billion. This would have placed BCE in twenty-first place in the Fortune 500. Moreover, these figures do not include BCE's 49 percent interest in Trans Canada Pipe Lines Limited's (TCPL) $3.5 billion in revenues and $6 billion in assets. BCE's investment in TCPL was accounted for on the equity basis. Net income for BCE in 1985, 1986, and 1987 exceeded $1 billion but fell to $882 million in 1988.

In 1988, BCE employed more than 116,000 employees worldwide in businesses ranging from telecommunications operations to real estate development and international consulting. The operations included many industry and geographic segments. Central to BCE's business are their telecommunications operations and telecommunications equipment manufacturing. Other operations include R & D, international consulting, and communication and information services, such as the publishing of telephone directories and the Canadian domestic satellite network.

BCE Client Engagement

In 1988, Touche Ross audited every substantive BCE subsidiary (more than 50 percent owned) in the world and also many of their related companies. In cases where other auditors were responsible, the audit team had to be totally knowledgeable about all business, financial reporting, and audit issues. Each operation has different problems and is managed by different executives, and the audit team has to be responsive to management in each operation.

In 1988, for financing or regulatory reasons, Touche Ross also undertook a quarterly review of most of the major companies in BCE. The audit team was present in many client engagements. In addition, BCE uses Touche Ross to provide additional services beyond the statutory audit requirements, such as providing information to securities regulators and the capital markets. The Canadian regulator of Bell Canada's telephone arm also requires an annual price study of the $1 billion in goods and services Northern Telecom supplies to Bell Canada. The CRTC requires that the transactions be extensively reviewed because the two companies are related. In addition, Touche Ross must audit the $7.5 billion in BCE's pension funds, the largest private pool of funds in Canada. Dozens of funds and the real estate ventures in which these funds have been invested must be audited annually. Other audit functions include opinions on royalty agreements and accounting opinions in foreign countries. For example, in the audit of Northern Telecom, offshore revenues represent only 10 percent of total revenues. However, offshore is a larger element in the audit effort because of local statutory requirements.

The BCE client service team also provides income tax and consulting services. Touche Ross was the principal tax adviser to BCE in 1988, providing corporate tax services to more than 120 company groups and personal tax services to more than 250 executives and senior managers. It also provided financial counseling and exit interviews. Touche Ross is also involved in the purchase investigation of every investment BCE makes and performs valuations of business segments. Consulting engagements encompass anything from information systems to personnel recruitment.

Each subsidiary and sub-business within the BCE group is operated as an individual corporation or division. Lines of authority and responsibility on the audit engagement team generally parallel those of BCE's business structure. There are about two dozen operational audit committees within the group.

The BCE engagement is organized around the core team, a small group of partners responsible for each major component of the BCE engagement. This group uses five principles as guidelines for providing services:

1. Quality service delivered on budget and on time to all companies.

2. Continuous dialogue with executives and managers of all companies.

3. Prompt identification and resolution of client and technical issues and service difficulties for all companies.

4. Consistency throughout the group in the total relationship.

5. Practice development through the sale of appropriate extended services where required.

Those charged with managing the entire engagement have the responsibility to influence team selection for each subsidiary and each special assignment in all locations around the world. The capacity of core team partners to determine team selection is essential if an international engagement is to be properly serviced. Part of the team consists of affiliate accounting firms that are not members of the Touche family. Team selection ultimately becomes the foundation on which the entire client relationship flows.

Team selection for the BCE group takes place as if the individual company were a standalone client and not just another subsidiary obtained as a matter of right. Each company must believe that the most appropriate professionals have been assigned to its account. A matching process involving knowledge level, skills, age, language, cultural background, and personality must be employed, and a team of auditors and tax specialists is selected based on these characteristics and the size and complexity of the company. A service team for a single engagement or special assignment is frequently drawn from multiple offices.

The task of the core team is to ensure that the local service team will provide BCE with quality, timely, and friendly service. The core team and service team must agree on basic issues in the engagement, which are the following:

1. *Understand the task:* Know what is to be done, by whom, by when, and for how much, and know how the service team will manage itself.

2. *Understand the client culture:* A telephone company is generally more conservative than a real estate company. Boundaries in each subsidiary must be agreed upon.

3. *Special requirements:* A tough CEO may require special care, or poor profits may suggest a more careful review.

4. *Client interface:* Work with client personnel who are handling the engagement.

5. *Special assignments:* Assess and communicate areas where Touche can assist management.

As we have previously noted, the linkages structured into the audit attempt to parallel linkages in the business. For example, the audit partner in charge of Tele Direct Publication reports to the audit partner responsible for Bell Canada, just as the CEO of Tele Direct reports to the CEO of Bell Canada. This process winds its way up to the core partners, and the international structure of the firm allows these relationship to function throughout the world. Linkages must be minimized when establishing internal interfaces so nothing gets lost in the communication process. In addition, it is not uncommon for partners to be involved in dual or multiple activities within the group (i.e., two different companies in the same city being served by the same engagement team).

The purpose of these linkages is to ensure that each partner in the BCE engagement ends up with a clearly defined service role and an understanding of the expectations for internal interface requirements. Team selection, team operation, and team structure must be planned because these roles can be composed of many elements. Planning is critical to ensure that the overall engagement meets its objectives.

The strength of communications before and during any client service function determines the success of the assignment. The first rule of Touche Ross is to talk—communication between audit partner and tax partner, between the audit partner responsible for the subsidiary and the audit partner responsible for the parent, and between partners and client. The core team insists on regular planning and progress meetings. Talking ensures that everybody is kept up to date and that problems are identified and resolved. Interactive, ongoing, continual dialogue is critical to service in an international engagement such as BCE.

Talk alone cannot run a client engagement, however. Written communication, such as memos of instructions, memos on results, and memos on problems, is encouraged. The writers of these memos are directed to send copies to other team members who may have an interest in the subject. These are sent via fax, telex, and e-mail. In addition, a newsletter directed to the key partners servicing the BCE team is published twice a year. It gives each partner some idea of what's going on in the group and lets everyone know who's who on both the Touche side and the BCE side of the engagement. This newsletter is circulated to some of the 225 partners worldwide who are involved with the BCE service team.

Questions

1. What are some of the major problems Touche Ross might have encountered in performing the audit of BCE in 1988?

2. What are the major elements in the audit process that Touche Ross followed during its audit of BCE?

3. In 1989, Touche Ross merged with Deloitte Haskins & Sells to form Deloitte & Touche. What kinds of concerns might BCE have had when the merger was announced?

Selected References

AAA. 1973. *A Statement of Basic Auditing Concepts.* Committee on Basic Auditing Concepts (Studies in Accounting Research No. 6). Sarasota, FL: American Accounting Association.

Arens, A. and J. Loebbecke. 1994. *Auditing. An Integrated Approach,* 6th ed. Englewood Cliffs, NJ: Prentice-Hall.

Carmichael, D. R. 1985. "International Harmonization of Auditing Standards," in Belverd E. Needles, Jr. (ed.), *Comparative International Auditing Standards,* pp. 165–82.

CICA/AICPA. 1999. *Continuous Auditing.* Research Report commissioned jointly by the Canadian Institute of Chartered Accountants and the American Institute of Certified Public Accountants. Toronto, Ontario: CICA.

IFAC Handbook. 2000. *IFAC Technical Pronouncements.* New York: International Federation of Accountants.

Ivancevich, S. H. and A. Zardkoohi. 2000. "An Exploratory Analysis of the 1989 Accounting Firm Megamergers," *Accounting Horizons,* 14 (4): 389–402.

International Federation of Accountants. www.ifac.org

International Forum on Accountancy Development. www.ifad.net

Klaassen, J. and J. Buisman. 1995. "International Auditing," in Nobes, C. & R. Parker, *Comparative International Accounting.* Hertfordshire, UK: Prentice-Hall, pp. 440–65.

Needles, Jr., B. E., ed. 1985. *Comparative International Auditing Standards.* Sarasota, FL: American Accounting Association.

Needles Jr., B., T. McDermott, and R. Temkin. 1991. "Taxonomy of Auditing Standards," in *Handbook of International Accounting,* chapter 6, edited by F. D. S. Choi. New York: John Wiley.

Needles, Jr., B. E. 2000. "Taxonomy of Auditing Standards" in *International Accounting and Finance Handbook,* edited by F. D. S. Choi. New York: John Wiley, chapter 5.

Needles, Jr., B. E., S. Ramamoorti, and S. W. Shelton. 2000. "The Role of International Auditing in the Improvement of International Financial Reporting," in *International Accounting and Finance Handbook,* edited by F. D. S. Choi. New York: John Wiley.

North American Trade Pacts and CA Free Trade Given Recognition Bonus. 1992. *World Accounting Report.* (April): 2, 6.

PAR. 1998. "U. N. Criticizes CPAs for Role in Asian Crisis," *Public Accounting Report* (Nov. 15): 4.

Pomeranz, F. 1986. "Auditing International Operations," in *Cashin's Handbook for Auditors,* 2nd ed., edited by J. A. Cashin, P. D. Neuwirth, and J. F. Levy. Englewood Cliffs, NJ: Prentice-Hall, pp. 23-1–23-17.

Roussey, R. S. 1999. "International Accounting and Auditing Standards in Practice," presentation at the 34th *International Accounting Conference* sponsored by the Center for International Education and Research in Accounting (CIERA), University of Illinois at Urbana-Champaign (April 22–24).

Smith, A. 1995. "The United States-Canada Bilateral Agreement on Reciprocity from an U.S. Perspective," IFAC *Newsletter.* 19(1) March: 1–3.

Stamp, E. and M. Moonitz. 1979. *International Auditing Standards.* Englewood Cliffs, NJ: Prentice-Hall.

Street, D. L., S. J. Gray, and S. M. Bryant. 1999. "Acceptance and Observance of International Accounting Standards: An Empirical Study of Companies Claiming to Comply with IASs," *The International Journal of Accounting,* 34 (1): 11–48.

Street, D. L. and S. J. Gray. 2001. "Observance of International Accounting Standards: Factors Explaining Noncompliance" The Association of Chartered Certified Accountants, 2001.

Turner, L. 1998. Remarks by Lynn Turner, Chief Accountant, United States Securities and Exchange Commission, at the *Twenty-Sixth Annual National Conference on Current SEC Developments.*

Walker, Norman R. 1997. "Managing the Audit Relationship in an International Context," in *Handbook of International Accounting,* chapter 6, edited by F. D. S. Choi. New York: John Wiley, 21.1–21.26.

CHAPTER THIRTEEN

MANAGEMENT ORGANIZATION AND CONTROL OF GLOBAL OPERATIONS

Chapter Objectives

- Show how different organizational structures and philosophies toward decision making and control in MNEs can influence the information system that the firm establishes
- Identify key aspects of a global information system
- Discuss how the international business environment influences the internal audit function and show how internal auditing is an important element in the control process
- Examine the Foreign Corrupt Practices Act and its impact on the internal control system of U.S.-based MNEs

INTRODUCTION

Decisions about which businesses to be in, where to locate operations, and how to be competitive are all part of a firm's strategy. Strategy is also the firm's response to changes in the global business environment or its attempts to predict, preempt, and exploit future environmental changes for its own benefit.

In this chapter we outline how strategic change is reflected in changes to the firm's organizational structure and control system. The accounting and information systems of a firm, in turn, are presented as an integral part of the firm's control system. These systems are also affected by changes to the firm's organizational structure and will change as structure and strategy change.

ORGANIZATIONAL STRUCTURE

The managerial challenge of the twenty-first century is to coordinate the growing network of interdependent international activities. There are two major classifications of mechanisms for coordinating activities in MNEs: (1) structural and formal mechanisms, and (2) informal and subtle mechanisms.

In practice, control is shifting from the formal to the more informal ways of coordinating activities. To understand the transition from structural to informal and subtle control mechanisms, it is important to better understand the structural issues. As a domestic firm evolves into an MNE, numerous pressures, both internal and external to the firm, put strains on the firm's organizational structure. Some responsibilities are shifted, new ones are created, and occasionally, existing ones are eliminated. As responsibilities change, so do the reporting and communication flows. Furthermore, the degree of control, both exercised and exercisable, changes over time as the firm grows in size, geographic spread, and product lines, and as changes occur in countries' sociopolitical and socioeconomic environments. New opportunities arise, as do new threats, and thus a firm's organization is constantly evolving. Failure to properly adjust the organizational structure to the changing environments may result in internal conflict and poor performance. Internal conflict and poor performance also create pressure for organizational change.

Domestic Structure

Consider the typical evolution of a multinational firm from its beginning as a purely domestic firm. The first evolutionary stage involves export activities in the form of occasional, unsolicited orders from foreign buyers. Typically, no one in the purely domestic company has much, if any, knowledge about these matters. External experts, such as export management companies and freight forwarders, are used to develop an export strategy.

As exports grow in volume, the use of external experts can become increasingly expensive, and the firm may, and typically does, decide to internalize the export activities by hiring new personnel for what becomes an export department, thereby also gaining greater control over its export activities. As Figure 13.1 shows, this first is typically a subgroup of the firm's marketing division, with only advisory or clerical capacity and no authority to commit resources.

As foreign market opportunities and sales increase, this export group grows, commensurately in size and sophistication. Foreign sales representatives may be added, leading ultimately to the establishment of foreign sales offices to better identify new customers and better serve all customers. By this stage, several internal strains have occurred. The first concerns responsibility for exports. Does the export group only advise domestic divisions, or is it empowered to make commitments? In the advisory situations, the export group feels constrained and seeks greater authority. In the commitment situation, domestic divisions feel a loss of power. In addition, there are strains related to internal pricing and profit allocations. The export group wants low transfer prices from the domestic division so it can obtain larger profits on its export sales, whereas the domestic division seeks higher transfer prices on goods it sells to the export group so that it can capture more of the

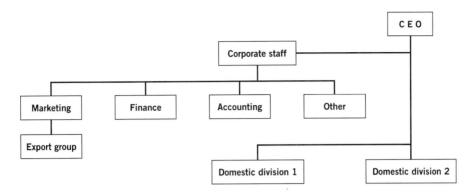

Figure 13.1   Domestic Organization with Initial Export Group

profit. Furthermore, the export group may need to rely on the product and technical expertise of the larger domestic divisions, which, if obtained, puts pressure on the domestic staff and also leads them to request greater compensation.

International Division Structure

At a later stage, it often becomes advisable to establish foreign production facilities. For example, it may become cheaper to produce abroad, or foreign governments may restrict imports or raise tariffs. Once foreign production is established, be it by a licensing agreement, a joint venture, or a wholly owned subsidiary, some existing organizational pressures abate while others arise. Specifically, many of the previous disputes over production allocation, scheduling, product adaptations, and transfer pricing diminish because previous export markets are now served by foreign rather than domestic production. What arise are new problems of responsibility and control. Someone or some group must take responsibility for the growing foreign operations, and control becomes more difficult because changes occur in at least two operating environments (domestic and foreign). Typically, because of the growing diversity of international operations, an international division replaces the old export division (see Figure 13.2). Further, because foreign activities are still a rather insignificant percentage of total corporate sales, substantial autonomy is given to the new division. As foreign operations expand further, however, the international division itself must exercise tighter control over its numerous operations and activities. To do so, it adds staff and, therefore, complexity. It also begins to fight harder for more corporate resources, which puts it into conflict with domestic divisions that also want greater resources. In essence, the firm can become split into two rival factions, and suboptimization can result.

Global Structure

To minimize conflicts and potential suboptimization, the firm typically undergoes a major reorganization, adopting a global product structure or global geographic

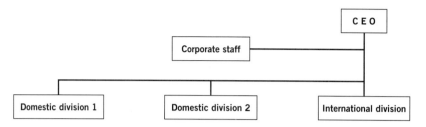

Figure 13.2   International Division

structure (see Figures 13.3 and 13.4). In the former, previous distinctions between domestic and international divisions are eliminated, and product division managers are given responsibility and control over the worldwide production and sale of their products. In the global geographic structure, existing domestic and international operations become part of one of several geographic divisions.

Firms typically select one of these structures based on a number of criteria related to their products and markets. For example, companies with narrow, relatively simple, and stable product lines often choose the global geographic structure, particularly when their products require many local adaptations or expert knowledge of local consumption practices, government policies, and so on. In short, a geographic structure works best when country or regional expertise is more important than product knowledge and expertise.

Conversely, when the product line is wide or when the products are complex and subject to rapid technological change (i.e., product knowledge and expertise are more important), the global product structure is often chosen. PepsiCo, with such diverse product lines as beverages (Pepsi) and restaurants (Pizza Hut, Taco Bell, and KFC) is organized along product lines. Global product structures are also more likely to emerge when there is a greater need for production and logistical coordination, as in vertically integrated firms or firms pursuing international production rationalization. The Procter and Gamble case at the end of the chapter presents an opportunity for you to analyze a recent restructuring decision, its source, and implications.

Yet, as was the case with organizational changes, some former problems and pressures abate while others arise. In the global product structure, old battles

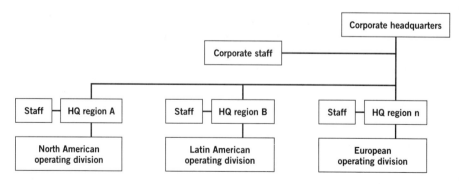

Figure 13.3   Global Geographically Oriented Organization

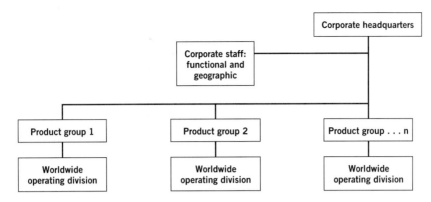

Figure 13.4   Global Product-Oriented Organization

between domestic and foreign divisions are reduced, but battles between product divisions are accentuated. As product lines gain worldwide market share, there is a need to develop regional expertise for the product lines. In the geographic structure, new battles emerge between geographic divisions as they fight for the latest in product developments and for resources for expansion.

To better coordinate and control global operations, still another organizational structure emerged—that of the global grid/matrix structure (see Figure 13.5). In this three-dimensional structure, product divisions, geographic areas, and functional areas share power and responsibilities. For example, a proposed expansion of sales of industrial equipment in the Far East involved an MNE's industrial equipment group, its Far East regional group, and finance and marketing groups at headquarters. Through such a combination, the company management hoped there

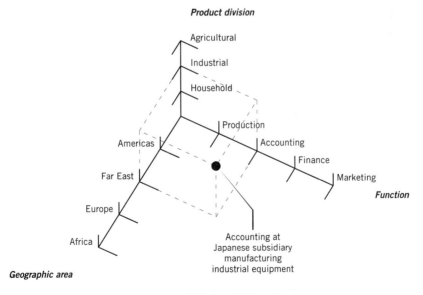

Figure 13.5   Global Grid Organization

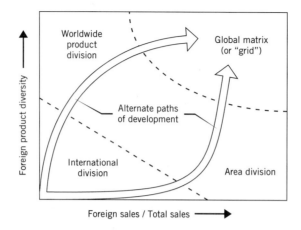

Figure 13.6   Stopford and Well's International Structural Stages Model

would be better coordination of global activities by taking a more holistic and less suboptimal approach.

In some respects, the global matrix was designed to bring the product line and geographic dimensions of the organization back together. This is illustrated in the classic Stopford and Well's stages of development of international organization, as adapted by Bartlett and Ghoshal (1989), shown in Figure 13.6. However, the matrix has not turned out to be the solution to organization dilemmas. As Bartlett and Ghoshal (1989) note, there are numerous shortcomings to the matrix:

> In practice, however, the matrix proved all but unmanageable especially in an international context. Dual reporting led to conflict and confusion; the proliferation of channels created informational logjams as a proliferation of committees and reports bogged down the organization; and overlapping responsibilities produced turf battles and a loss of accountability. Separated by barriers of distance, language, time, and culture, managers found it virtually impossible to clarify the confusion and resolve the conflicts.

The solution to the organizational dilemma is more complex than organizational structure; it involves the attitude toward the role between the parent company and the different affiliates worldwide (the centralization/decentralization dilemma) as well as the frame of mind of top management (the informal and subtle mechanisms). These organizational issues strongly influence the managerial accounting system of the firm, from the nature of the information system and the establishment of accounting policies, to the internal controls established to ensure compliance and the evaluation of the performance of foreign operations and their managers.

CENTRALIZATION VERSUS DECENTRALIZATION

As discussed in the previous section, in addition to the base structural issues in designing a global organization, a company must decide to what extent decision making should be held in a few key centers (centralized) or distributed to a large number of business units. The problem with centralization versus decentralization is that the very terms connote a mutually exclusive situation—decision making must be *either* centralized or decentralized. However, the global environment is too complex for such a simple dichotomy. Companies can be described as either multi-domestic or global in their approach to world markets, with the multi-domestic approach allowing individual subsidiaries to compete independently in different domestic markets and the global approach pitting the entire worldwide system of product and market position against the competition.

Hout, Porter, and Rudden (1982) suggest that companies that are more likely to adopt a multi-domestic strategy are those that have products that differ greatly from country market to country market. Such companies also have high transportation costs or their industries lack sufficient scale economies to yield the global competitors a significant competitive edge. Economies of scale may be too modest; R&D closely tied to a specific market; transportation costs and government barriers to trade too high; and distribution systems fragmented and too hard to penetrate. A global strategy is more likely when significant benefits gained from worldwide volume—in terms of either reduced unit costs or superior reputation or service—are greater than the additional costs of serving that volume. These volume advantages may come from larger production plants or runs, more efficient logistics networks, higher volume distribution networks, or high levels of investment in R&D. The relationship between multi-domestic/global dichotomy and centralization/decentralization is that as a company becomes more global, the emphasis shifts toward greater centralization. As countries increase in importance, they must be brought within the global manager's reach. However this is not a given: compare the fairly centralized U.S. firm Procter and Gamble and the much more decentralized Anglo-Dutch firm Unilever.

The term *global* can mean different things. Hamel and Prahalad (1992) differentiate between global competition, global businesses, and global companies. Global competition occurs when companies cross-subsidize national market share battles in pursuit of global brand and distribution positions. Rather than focus strictly on the home national market, global competition requires firms to attack competition in markets worldwide, including the home market of the foreign competitor. The first and still ongoing example of this would be the global trade in agricultural products. A more modern example would be the U.S. auto industry, which, placed under threat in the 1980s, had to react by going global. Similar battles have been fought in the airline industry.

Global businesses are those in which the minimum volume required for cost efficiency is not available in the company's home market, forcing those companies to pursue markets overseas, possibly supplying the market from domestic production. A good example might be the steel industry or the international textiles industry. Another example would be the aircraft industry where Boeing and Airbus attempt to spread their very high R&D costs across global markets to achieve breakeven and above volumes. In the 1990s one has seen a decline in the number of producers of large commercial aircraft, and an increase in cross-industry mergers as the cost and risk of designing a single new aircraft became higher and higher.

Global companies have distribution systems in key markets that enable cross-subsidization, international retaliation, and world-scale volume. Again the key players in the airline industry such as British Airways, KLM, and American come to mind. More recently one may need to go beyond the concept of companies to strategic alliances such as One World (British Airways, American Airlines, Cathay Pacific, and Qantas) or Star Alliance (United Airlines, Lufthansa, SAS, Air Canada and Thai) where global alliances have distribution systems in key markets that enable cross-subsidization, international retaliation, and world-scale volume.

Bartlett and Ghoshal (1989) identify three global imperatives that influence organizational structure, the degree of centralization of decision making, and the organizational culture of the firm:

1. *Forces for global integration:* The need for efficiency. Companies need to achieve economies of scale in such areas as product lines, parts design, and manufacturing operations. These economies are driven by cost factors as well as by the more harmonized tastes and preferences of consumers.

2. *Forces for local differentiation:* The need for responsiveness. Government interference and different market structures and consumer preferences require closer attention to local differences.

3. *Forces for worldwide innovation:* The need for learning. This imperative involves developing and diffusing worldwide innovations and linking and leveraging knowledge.

The problem for firms is that they need to deal with all three imperatives rather than focus on just one. For example, it is possible for a company to have to focus on integrating some areas while still needing to be responsive to different markets in different countries.

Bartlett and Ghoshal (1989) believe that firms need to move to a transnational strategy rather than a multi-domestic or global strategy to deal most effectively with the three imperatives just described. In this approach, corporate assets are dispersed, interdependent, and specialized. This contrasts with multi-domestic companies, which are decentralized and independent, or global companies, which are highly centralized and globally scaled.

In terms of the role of overseas operations, national units make differentiated contributions to integrated worldwide operations in what is termed a transnational organizational structure (see Figure 13.7). In other words, each national unit plays a different role, and these roles vary from country to country. One overseas operation may be a manufacturing facility, whereas another might define its role on the need to service its local market. On the other hand, multi-domestic firms exploit local opportunities, whereas global firms simply implement parent company strategies.

Knowledge is developed jointly and shared worldwide. This contrasts with multi-domestic firms, which develop and retain knowledge in each local unit, or global firms, which develop and retain knowledge at the center.

FIRM STRUCTURE AND THE ACCOUNTING FUNCTION

Centralization, Strategy, and the Accounting Function

As discussed earlier in the chapter, accounting and control derive their value from what they can provide to the firm's strategy, and are affected by the structure of the firm. For example, the degree of centralization may also affect the nature of the

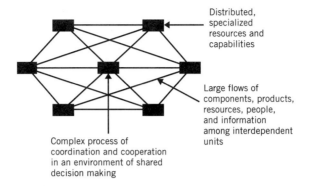

Distributed, specialized resources and capabilities

Large flows of components, products, resources, people, and information among interdependent units

Complex process of coordination and cooperation in an environment of shared decision making

Figure 13.7   Transnational Organization

accounting and control function. At its simplest level some types of accounting/ record keeping may be fairly easily centralized. Thus many U.S. firms use a central location to process all basic data; for example, several large insurance companies in the U.S. use facilities in Bangalore, India to process the myriad of accounting associated with policy accounting.

There is, however, an argument for the decentralization of control. For example, multi-domestic firms face local differences in environmental constraints, which can be cultural, legal, political, and economic. These differences require that they adapt to the way business is done, which is different from the parent country. Sharp and Salter (1997) argue that even the fundamental beliefs about behavior on which control systems are based in the United States and Canada are not valid in Asia. Bartlett and Ghoshal's (1989) transnational organizational philosophy also would influence the accounting function. To be globally competitive and flexible in the multinational arena, management needs to legitimize diverse perspectives and capabilities and develop multiple and flexible coordination processes. Thus, it would appear that the MNE would need an information system that provides a significant flow of information from parent to affiliate, from affiliate to parent, and between affiliates. Such a system is very different from either a highly decentralized or a highly centralized operation.

A strong case is made to disaggregate financial accounting as reporting standards vary considerably from country to country, and sometimes governments control the way the books and records of the firm are kept, thus leading to the decentralization of the accounting function. On the other hand, it may be important to centralize the accounting function because of the parent firm's need to consolidate its worldwide operations according to the GAAP of the parent company's country. Local differences may cause a different set of books to be kept, but the parent company will probably still require that a set of books be kept according to parent company GAAP. Coca-Cola, for example, uses policy manuals to extend a more centralized philosophy to the accounting function. In the mid-1980s, Coca-Cola's management developed a comprehensive, easy to reference accounting manual to help maintain strong financial controls over operations. A universal chart of accounts was established so that each account in the balance sheet and income statement would be consistent worldwide. Based on the chart of accounts, definitions of each account were written and policies and procedures governing the use of each account and the flow of information into the financial statements were developed. A separate section was written about translating financial statements from local currencies into U.S. dollars.

The Use of Informal Controls

As noted earlier, the matrix organizational structure was developed to deal with the global complexities involved in product lines and geographic areas. However, it was also noted that the matrix often did not work for a variety of reasons. As one manager pointed out, the challenge is not so much to build a matrix structure as it is to create a matrix in the minds of our managers. The key is to develop a corporate culture that allows the firm to be competitive globally. Three key methods used by successful managers to develop a global orientation are the following:

1. Develop and communicate a clear and consistent corporate vision.
2. Manage human resource tools effectively to broaden individual perspectives and develop identification with corporate goals.
3. Integrate individual thinking and activities into the broad corporate agenda by means of a process called co-option—that is, pulling people out of their narrow and isolated areas of responsibility and helping them to develop a broader, more global perspective.

These rules are as true in accounting as they are in marketing or any other function. Accountants need to understand the information requirements of the MNE to avoid the narrow parent company perspective so common in globally centralized firms. Several years ago, the authors met with financial managers of a few British subsidiaries of U.S. MNEs, who describe their frustration with home office accounting personnel. Because of a lack of international experience and expertise, home office personnel had a difficult time relating to the specific problems of the British subsidiaries. This was especially true of any issue related to foreign exchange.

Bartlett and Ghoshal (1989) point out the following with respect to managers (which can be generalized to accountants): "One pervasive problem in companies whose leaders lack this ability [to pull individual managers together] or fail to exercise it, is getting managers to see how their specific responsibilities related to the broad corporate vision." To involve accountants in this global vision, it is important to recruit, select, and train accountants for the global environment. This involves understanding local accounting issues as well as the global demands of the MNE. In addition, accountants must understand the global vision of the firm. It is not enough to be technically competent; the accountant also must understand the global imperatives of the firm and the ways he or she can contribute to these imperatives through a good information system.

MANAGEMENT INFORMATION SYSTEMS AND THE GLOBAL FIRM

As discussed previously, the accountant must also understand the global imperatives of the firm and the ways he or she can contribute to these imperatives through a good information system. The transfer of data has become a crucial element for global integration. The use of satellite links has dramatically increased the flow of technology. Through satellite hookups, an athletic shoe company in the United States can design a product and demonstrate it through video technology to a manufacturer in South Korea instantaneously. Satellite technology is also used to transmit messages through modems so computers, virtually anywhere in the world, can transfer electronic mail (or e-mail). In addition, with the use of scanners documents can be transferred through e-mail.

Developments in information technology are dramatically affecting the speed and form in which information is transmitted. Local area networks (LANs) connect computers within a building, allowing them to share software and databases, send e-mail, and work simultaneously on documents, schedules, projects, and the like. Through a private branch exchange (PBX), computers in company headquarters can communicate with computers in other sites, including other countries. In addition, companies can communicate with customers, suppliers, and other interested third parties through wide area network (WAN), such as the Internet. The Internet, a worldwide network of computers linked together by telephone lines, has emerged as a revolutionary and rapid way to span companies and time zones.

As well as communications with the outside world, the Internet is also being used for internal corporate communications. Sterling Software Inc., a U.S.-based software maker, uses the Internet to keep its 3,600 employees in 75 worldwide offices in touch with headquarters as well as customers. It uses the Internet to distribute e-mail, keep its sales offices connected to its R&D laboratories, and perform interactive demonstrations of software with clients. Management estimates that it saves $10 million a year using the Internet instead of dedicated phone lines for day-to-day business functions. Similarly, PriceWaterhouseCoopers, a global audit firm, uses Lotus Notes to permit several offices to work on a single set of audit documents. However, the Internet has been slow to penetrate developing countries because telephone lines there are too scarce, unreliable, and expensive to support the high-speed communication demanded by Internet applications.

Innovations in information technology are also allowing videoconferencing by computer to take place worldwide. This technology allows companies to combine visual communication with telephone communication and computer links to transfer information and images and conduct meetings and interviews around the world.

Theories and Realities of Global Information Processing

Egelhoff (1991) identifies four dimensions or types of information processing that are relevant for MNEs:

1. *Routine:* Inputs are frequent and homogeneous. It is appropriate to have rules and programs, standard operating procedures, and so on.
2. *Nonroutine:* This type of information is relatively unique and infrequent.
3. *Sequential:* Information flows in a predetermined direction across parties to an information-processing event.
4. *Reciprocal:* Information flows back and forth between parties in a kind of give-and-take manner not previously determined.

In general, accounting information for MNEs tends to be relatively routine and sequential. Accounting information tends to be electronically integrated at the parent company level, and it must have extensive reach within the information technology (IT) platform (i.e., the technology of computers, software telecommunications, and office technology, including the telephone, fax, e-mail, and so on). *Reach* refers to the number of locations that the IT platform can link together. Obviously, reach is much more difficult in the international arena. The key is to determine how to share information across organizational lines internationally.

MNEs pull together operations in different countries through mergers, acquisitions, and strategic alliances, for example, and it is not uncommon for the various companies to use different software and hardware, resulting in what is known as a *heterogeneous network*. This makes the standardization of the IT platform a nightmare. However, a new category of software designed to solve this problem is called middleware. Middleware mediates between the different kinds of hardware and software found on large networks and gives a network the appearance of harmony, even though the individual components change and expand over time.

MNEs and Transborder Data Flows

The free flow of information across national borders is vital to the successful operation of an MNE's management information system (MIS) and, by extension, the operation of the MNE itself. Furthermore, the management of this information flow is as important as the management of company assets and production. The ability of an MNE's computers to communicate with each other in a transnational network allows information to be stored, processed, retrieved, and used in decision making with great efficiency, and it facilitates communications, planning, strategy formulation, and control. However, many countries have enacted legislation that affects transborder (transnational) data flows. For these and a number of other reasons, in the future MNEs will be confronted with increased risks related to transborder flows.

Foremost among the many concerns of nation-states over transborder data flows (TBF) are privacy, economics, and national security. Privacy concerns deal with employee information such as religious and political affiliations, family background, race, sex, and employment history. Economic concerns center on industrial espionage involving corporate data piracy and the impact of TBF on local data processing industries and MNEs decision-making processes. By restricting TBF, some governments have sought to force MNEs to use local processing industries and thereby increase their size and sophistication. Others have hoped that by restricting TBF, more autonomy in decision making would be given to subsidiaries because headquarters would have less information on which to make decisions for subsidiaries. These economic concerns are also related to national security concerns. Countries seek limitations on TBF to protect against political espionage and theft of industrial properties and designs and other economic data that could weaken their security. Satellite communication nets pose a major control problem in this respect.

Governments also affect the flow of information through the infrastructure of the Information Superhighway. It makes no sense for companies to invest millions of dollars to establish an internal network that combines data, video, and voice communications when the system grinds to a halt outside the building. Local telephone lines are the primary carriers of information. The transmission speed on these lines often causes data flow to slow dramatically, from 10 million bits per second within the building, to only 56,000 bits per second outside the building. Governments can respond to this challenge by investing huge amounts in building the infrastructure or in deregulating the communication sector so competition will bring in investment, drive service, and drive down costs. However, the deregulation game is not an easy one in that governments worry about the public policy ramifications of any decision.

Management Information Systems and the Strategy of the Firm: Some Final Thoughts

Drawing on the work of Bartlett and Ghoshal (1989), we pointed out that in approaching the global market firms can adopt a transnational or decentralized (multi-domestic) approach. Firms that take more of a multi-domestic approach tend not to integrate their IT platforms to the same extent as firms that have a more global orientation. MNEs that follow the Bartlett and Ghoshal (1989) transnational model tend to be more interactive. This implies a flow of information that is more reciprocal than sequential, a situation especially common in the budgeting process.

Another alternative is to view this interaction between administrative units of the company using the approach of Gupta and Govindarajan (1991), which is illustrated in Figure 13.8. As this figure shows, knowledge flows can be grouped along two different dimensions: the outflow of knowledge from the subsidiary to the rest of the corporation and the inflow of knowledge from the rest of the corporation to the subsidiary. These flows of knowledge result in four generic subsidiary roles: global innovator, integrated player, implementer, and local innovator.

As a global innovator, the subsidiary provides knowledge for other units. Information flows would be sequential, according to the Egelhoff model, but the information would flow from, rather than to, the subsidiary.

As an integrated player, the subsidiary creates knowledge that is shared with other units in the company, but it also receives knowledge. Information flows would be reciprocal rather than sequential.

As an implementer, the subsidiary does not generate much knowledge for the rest of the units, but it receives knowledge from other units, principally from the parent company. This is the more traditional MNE, where power and knowledge are centralized.

As a local innovator, the subsidiary innovates locally, but its innovations are of little value to the rest of the firm. This would be more like a multi-domestic firm where local differences overwhelm common knowledge. Thus, the information flows are kept to a minimum.

INTERNAL CONTROL AND THE INTERNAL AUDIT

All these issues are closely tied together. A firm's information system is designed to provide information that is consistent with its organizational structure and the

Figure 13.8   Variations in Subsidiary Strategic Contexts: A Knowledge Flows-Based Framework

degree of centralization/decentralization of the organization. Once the structure and the information system are in place, the firm must ensure that rules and procedures are followed and that assets are safeguarded. This is the purpose of internal controls and a strong internal audit.

The Internal Audit

All large corporations are concerned that employees operate in a manner consistent with corporate policy. Corporate policy and procedures in all areas of the business—personnel, marketing, and production as well as accounting—are normally communicated to personnel through codes of conduct and procedures manuals. A good control system starts with these codes of conduct and standard operating procedures, but the firm needs to determine whether these codes and procedures are being followed. The internal audit function is one of the cornerstones of the process of determining compliance.

Problems of the Internal Auditor in a Foreign Operating Environment

Although the internal audit responsibilities are the same for international and domestic operations, there are some unique problems in the foreign environment, such as local accounting practices, foreign currency, local legal and business practices, language and customs, and distance. Although most large companies attempt to standardize their accounting practice worldwide, it does not happen everywhere. Local records may be kept according to local accounting procedures, which makes it difficult to use a standardized audit package. Also, the infrequency of audits (because of distance) may mean that there is insufficient accounting data to provide a clear audit trail.

Alternatives to the Traveling Auditor

These comments refer primarily to a traveling auditor. However, there are other possibilities: a resident auditor who is a local national; a resident auditor who is an expatriate from the headquarters country or is a third-country national (TCN) (that is, someone from a country other than the headquarters or local operation); or a traveling team of auditors. Local nationals obviously have an edge in knowledge of the language, culture, and business customs, but the expatriate is more familiar with headquarters' procedures. The TCN can be a cross between the two but is still considered a foreigner in the host country.

Although it is possible to use domestic auditors on temporary assignment to perform internal audits, they tend to be more specialized than regular international internal auditors. The latter need to be generalists, with skills in operational as well as financial audits. Also, the need for language skills and cultural adaptability makes it advisable to identify a cadre of international internal auditors where possible. The smaller multinationals tend to use home office auditors for foreign duties, but some larger firms are frequently using regionally based auditors.

One recommended approach for organizing the international internal audit is to establish a pyramid structure of three levels. Level 1 is the head office audit department where the director of internal audit is located. Level 2 is an area or regional audit team. For example, Miami might be the location for the Latin American region of a U.S-based MNE, or Brussels might be the location for the area or regional head for Europe. Level 3 involves a unit or entity auditor or audit team. The in-charge auditor at each entity reports directly to the head of the area or regional audit team. The nature of the structure might depend on the organizational structure that the MNE employs, as we discussed earlier. The determination has to be made based on whether the area audit team is established on the basis of geographic area or product line. The more dissimilar the product lines of the MNE, the more likely the firm is to establish an internal audit team based on product line. However, a geographically dispersed firm with a few product lines might organize the area or regional audit team by geographic area.

The Foreign Corrupt Practices Act

The Foreign Corrupt Practices Act (FCPA) is designed to eliminate two problems: poor internal controls and their product, in part, bribery. Whether influence is bought with baksheesh (Middle East), mordida (Mexico), dash (West Africa), or bustarella (Italy), it can be very costly indeed for U.S. firms because of the FCPA of 1977, which was amended in 1988. In investigating Watergate and its aftermath, the SEC was astounded at the extent to which corporate executives and employees falsified books and records and circumvented internal control systems (where they existed) to make foreign bribes. The SEC response—the FCPA—is affecting the way companies operate abroad and account for and control those operations.

Bribery itself has been termed everything from extortion to just another part of the marketing mix in international business. The problem for the MNE is that it operates in a variety of countries with different business practices and laws and competes with companies from other countries that also have different sets of business law and customs. Bribes are usually paid because the receiver of the bribe has a strong market position or has control over an aspect of the environment that can have a strong impact on the firm's operations. Payments are made to get an edge on competitors, to cause government officials to bend or ignore laws, to grease normal channels, to support the political process, and to try to ensure the firm's ability to continue operating. Sometimes the payments are made in countries where such payments are accepted business practice, and other times they are made in countries where the payments are illegal. Sometimes they are initiated by the company and other times by the recipient.

An added complication is that payments could be made without headquarters' approval. It is virtually impossible to do business in many Middle Eastern countries except through a local agent. If a fee is paid to the agent to expedite business, who is to say what the fee is used for? Similarly, a local subsidiary, staffed by local nationals attuned to their environment, may play the payments game like everyone else.

In essence, the FCPA made it illegal to pay or offer to pay money or anything of value to a foreign government official to get them to abuse their power to benefit the firm for business purposes. This does not include "grease payments."

Impact of FCPA on U.S. Firms   In a 1983 poll of 1,200 large U.S. corporations, a number of interesting things were found. Although 78 percent of the executives felt that the FCPA made it difficult to sell in countries where bribery is a way of life, 55 percent felt that unless the law was tough, small grease payments would turn into major bribes of government officials. Indeed, the law is tough, with penalties including a fine of up to $1 million for a company and up to $10,000 and five years in prison for an individual convicted of being in violation of the FCPA. In 1988, the law was modified to assess only civil rather than criminal penalties for negligent or unintentional violators of the law, while violators convicted of an intent to deceive would still be guilty of criminal liability.

The 1988 amendments to the law clarify grease payments as payments to foreign officials if they have little decision-making authority and if they have little impact on the relations between the United States and the local government, assuming that the payments are to expedite trade. Also, the parent company is exonerated from the actions of a non–wholly owned subsidiary if it can be shown that the parent tried to get the foreign corporation to comply with the FCPA.

Accounting Implications   Clearly, bribery is illegal and could have an impact on the way some firms market their goods and services in certain countries. But what does that have to do with accounting and internal auditing? A good control system is designed to safeguard corporate assets, and the internal auditor is responsible for testing compliance with the system. During its investigation of foreign bribes, the SEC found that firms were falsifying records in order to disguise improper transactions, were failing to disclose the true purpose of some transactions, and were simply not recording some transactions.

There are two accounting implications of many of the cases uncovered by the SEC. First, books and records were not being kept properly, so financial statements did not accurately reflect underlying transactions. Second, firms were encouraging the corrupt practices or had such a poor control system that the practices were going on in spite of corporate policy to the contrary. As a result, the FCPA added two other provisions to the one on bribery: one dealing with record keeping and the other with internal controls. The record-keeping provisions are to "make and keep books, records, and accounts, which, in reasonable detail, accurately and fairly reflect the transactions and dispositions of the assets of the issuer."

The second accounting implication relates to internal accounting controls. According to this provision, each firm is to devise and maintain a system of internal accounting controls sufficient to provide reasonable assurances that (1) transactions are executed in accordance with management's general or specific authorization; (2) transactions are recorded as necessary to permit preparation of financial statements in conformity with GAAP or any other criteria applicable to such statements and to maintain accountability for assets; (3) access to assets is permitted only in accordance with management's general or specific authorization; and (4) the recorded accountability for assets is compared with the existing assets at reasonable intervals and appropriate action is taken with respect to any differences.

It has always been assumed that management would require that good records be kept and would design and implement an adequate internal control system. However, this is the first time that violation of these principles could lead to civil liability and criminal prosecution. In addition, the accounting provisions of the FCPA may be violated even though no foreign bribes are paid. Most firms did not realize this when the law went into effect, but the government has legislated accounting procedures in an area into which they had never before ventured. As a result, firms are paying much closer attention to the design and implementation of their control systems.

The 1988 amendments clarified the record-keeping provisions by allowing a cost-benefit decision to be made in establishing internal controls. The assumption was that there would be no liability for inadvertent errors. Prosecution can still take place under the 1988 amendments, but there almost has to be proof of knowingly circumventing internal controls.

Compliance with the FCPA   In order to comply with the FCPA, a firm needs strong support from four levels: management, the internal auditors, the external auditors, and the board of directors. Top management needs to set the proper atmosphere for compliance with the FCPA by agreeing to abide by its provisions, formulating a written policy, communicating that policy to employees, and making sure the policy is understood and adhered to.

The internal audit staff is concerned about much more than the FCPA, and a cost-benefit analysis would preclude adding enough auditors to eliminate all risk of noncompliance. The role of the external auditor has been discussed in more detail in Chapter 12, but it is appropriate to look at this role in relation to the FCPA now. There is the feeling on the part of the general public that independent auditors should be able to detect fraud and noncompliance with the FCPA. However, generally accepted auditing standards as developed by the American Institute of Certified Public Accountants (AICPA) call for an examination of the books and records to locate problems that may have a material effect on the financial statements. Although the auditors are always keeping an eye out for questionable or illegal acts, they are concerned with those that have a material effect, whereas the FCPA is concerned with those leading to any effect. This creates some obvious problems. For both the internal and external auditor, greater attention must be paid to the types of transactions and geographical areas where there is a high probability of illegal acts. This is why a general and specific risk analysis is so critical. As one auditor pointed out, "specific skepticism naturally focuses on companies that have large sales to foreign governments, significant operations or sales in countries with traditionally relaxed commercial standards, or companies that are subject to capricious governmental regulation, which can create a strong temptation to lubricate the wheels with a bit of grease."

The final group directly concerned and able to affect the internal control system as it relates to the FCPA is the board of directors. It is up to management to design and implement an action plan in relation to the FCPA, but it is up to the board to monitor the timeliness and execution of the plan. A good example of this action involves Baxter International, the hospital supply company. In 1989, it was revealed that Baxter might have violated the antiboycott laws and the FCPA by doing business in the Middle East, so the audit committee of the board of directors hired an outside law firm to investigate the situation.

SUMMARY

1. The managerial challenge of the twenty-first century is to coordinate the increasing number of dispersed and yet interdependent international activities.

2. There are two ways to coordinate the activities of MNEs: through structural and formal mechanisms and through more informal and subtle mechanisms.

3. There are five major structural and formal mechanisms: departmentalization of organizational units, centralization versus decentralization of decision making, formalization and standardization of policies and procedures, planning, and output and behavior control.

4. When firms first begin exporting, they may rely on external experts or an export department as a unit of the domestic marketing division.

5. When a firm begins to move significantly from exporting to foreign production, an international division is established to deal with foreign transactions, and substantial autonomy is given the new division.

6. The firm may then move to a global product structure, where product division managers are given responsibility and control over worldwide production and sale of their products.

7. Alternatively, the firm may adopt the global geographic structure, where existing domestic and international operations become part of one of several geographic divisions.

8. In a global grid or matrix structure, an attempt is made to coordinate the activities of product, geographic, and functional organizations.

9. An alternative approach, the transnational organizational form, attempts to deal with the complexities of the international environment by dealing with the forces of global integration, differentiation, and worldwide innovation in a relatively flexible manner.

10. The finance and accounting functions tend to be more centralized than the personnel and marketing functions. Many companies standardize their accounting function in order to get more comparable information worldwide.

11. A sound management information system is required to provide the information that is needed in the more formal reporting structure and to provide information that makes the informal and subtle control systems work.

12. The internal audit function is to promote compliance with corporate policy and procedures in all areas of the business.

13. Some of the unique problems that arise from conducting an internal audit in the international business environment are local accounting practices, foreign currency, local legal and business practices, language, and customs and distance.

14. The Foreign Corrupt Practices Act in the United States was established to eliminate the bribery of government officials, to ensure that books and records are kept properly, and to establish good internal controls.

Discussion Questions

1. The implication from the discussion in this chapter is that as a company becomes more global, it concentrates more on the informal and subtle mechanisms for controlling global operations than it does the structural and formal mechanisms. Why is this so? Do you think structural and formal mechanisms are becoming obsolete? Discuss your reasons.

2. Look at the annual report of an MNE. As you read about the product lines and geographical operations, what kind of organizational structure would you guess the company has?

3. What challenges would your chosen MNE face in designing an effective management control system?

4. What role does MIS play? Do they have a Chief Information Officer? Do they have a Web site? How in depth do you consider it? You may wish to compare it with other sites.

5. What are some of the major ways that information technology is helping MNEs overcome the problems of time and space?

6. How important is the internal audit function?

7. Are "grease payments" unethical? Should MNEs refuse to pay them?

Exercises

1. United Airlines entered into a strategic alliance with Thai Airways to develop and market airline services. Would you characterize this strategic alliance as a global innovator, an integrated player, a local innovator, or an implementer from the standpoint of United? What is your logic for your choice? What are some of the problems that United might face in establishing appropriate informal and subtle control mechanisms for the strategic alliance?

2. Hoeschst is a German chemical company operating in different product lines and different geographic areas. Its major business areas are chemicals (23 percent of sales), fibers (15 percent), polymers (17 percent), health (24 percent), engineering and technology (15 percent), and agriculture (6 percent). Across these product lines, Hoeschst produces products as diverse as phosphorus and phosphates used in detergents, textile dyes, polyester auto tire cords, cellulose acetate fibers for cigarette filters, polyvinyl chloride (PVC), automotive paints, pharmaceuticals, cosmetics, offset printing plates, engineering ceramics, herbicides, and animal vaccines. Most of Hoeschst's product lines face significant global competition. On the geographic side, Hoeschst sells products in the European Union (51 percent of total sales); other European countries (7 percent); North America (21 percent); Latin America (7 percent); and Africa, Asia, and Australasia (14 percent).

What type of an organizational structure makes the most sense for Hoeschst, and what would be some of the major international accounting problems Hoeschst might face?

Case: *Procter & Gamble* 2005

Read the news release below and review related material at P&G's Web site: www.pg.com to answer the following questions:

Questions

1. What are the nature and history of P&G's business activities?
2. How has P&G's interaction with the global business environment changed over time?
3. Who are P&G's major competitors? (*Hint:* You may wish to visit Unilever's Web site www.unilever.com)
4. What caused P&G to change their strategy?
5. How did the strategy change P&G's organizational structure?
6. Does the structure match any of the organizational models proposed in the chapter?
7. What were the costs and benefits of the proposed change?
8. How does the organizational structure compare with P&G's competitors such as Unilever?
9. What implications does this proposed organization have on the control system of P&G?

Organization 2005 Drive for Accelerated Growth Enters Next Phase
June 9, 1999
Changes will lead to greater stretch, innovation, and speed

CINCINNATI, June 9, 1999 – The Procter & Gamble Company today announced details of the next phase of Organization 2005, P&G's far-reaching, strategic initiative to accelerate the company's growth. Overall, P&G expects Organization 2005 to increase long-term annual sales growth to 6–8 percent and accelerate earnings per share growth (excluding program costs) to 13–15 percent in each of the next five years, through fiscal 2004.

The Organization 2005 program will cost $1.9 billion after tax and affect 15,000 jobs worldwide over this time period, beginning this fiscal year. The program is anticipated to generate annual after-tax savings of approximately $900 million by fiscal 2004.

Program elements include: standardizing production lines and aligning manufacturing capacity with the new global business units to increase speed to market; implementing P&G's new Global Business Services organization to standardize systems, reduce internal transactions and better serve global customers; and simplifying P&G's organization structure to reduce hierarchy and speed decision making.

"The cost of Organization 2005 is well-justified by both the ongoing operational benefits of our new structure and the substantial financial benefits it will generate for our shareholders," said P&G's Chief Executive Durk I. Jager. "The redesign of our organizational structure, work processes and culture will pay off in bigger innovation, faster speed to market and greater growth."

Organization 2005

Under Organization 2005, P&G is moving from four business units based on geographic regions to seven Global Business Units (GBU) based on product lines—a change that will drive greater innovation and speed by centering strategy and profit responsibility globally on brands, rather than geographies. It also involves new Market Development Organizations (MDO), which will tailor the global programs for local markets and develop market strategies to build P&G's entire business based on superior local consumer and customer knowledge.

With Organization 2005, P&G also has created Global Business Services (GBS). This new organization brings together business activities such as accounting, human resource systems, order management, and information technology into a single global organization to provide these services to all P&G business units at best-in-class quality, cost, and speed. Lastly, P&G has redefined the role of corporate staff. Most corporate staff have moved into the new business units, with the remaining staff refocused on developing cutting-edge new knowledge and serving corporate needs.

The company has been transitioning to the new organization design over the past nine months and will officially begin managing and reporting the business on the new basis effective July 1, 1999.

"Organization 2005 marks the most dramatic change to P&G's structure, work processes and culture in the company's history," said Jager.

"The design efforts undertaken around the world since our announcement last September have identified more opportunities than we originally imagined to simplify work processes and streamline our operations. The result will be bigger innovation, faster speed to market and greater growth."

Organization 2005 Impacts

Of the approximately $1.9 billion after tax in costs associated with the Organization 2005 program, approximately $400 million after tax will be incurred in the current year, and approximately $1.0 billion after tax over the next two fiscal years. The remaining costs are expected to be incurred in fiscal years 2002–2004; however, these costs are expected to be more than offset by savings from the program.

The program is anticipated to begin generating significant savings by fiscal 2001, reaching annual going savings of approximately $900 million after tax by fiscal 2004. The company anticipates that of the 15,000 jobs affected over the next six years beginning this year (approximately 13 percent of P&G's work force worldwide), 10,000 positions will be eliminated through fiscal 2001 with a further 5,000 after 2001.

"We have always said that Organization 2005 is about accelerating growth, not cutting jobs. These job reductions are principally an outgrowth of changes, such as standardizing global manufacturing platforms, to drive innovation and faster speed to market," said Jager. "As always, we have considered these decisions very carefully with deep concern for the impact on our people."

"We will carry out the changes with maximum respect and attention to the welfare and future of our employees," Jager continued. "To that end we will make maximum use of normal attrition and retirements, hiring reductions, re-locations, job retraining, and voluntary separations to help reduce the number of potential involuntary separations."

"In cases of involuntary separations, we will work with our people and offer them financial assistance to help them bridge to new careers. We will continue to set a high standard in supporting and respecting our employees' futures at this time of major change."

Program Details

Key elements of the program include:

Product Supply: P&G's Organization 2005 initiative has provided the opportunity to look at the company's product supply organization from a truly global perspective. Of the program costs associated with the changes to product supply, the majority relate to global simplification and standardization of production lines to deliver greater flexibility and reduce the time required to convert production equipment to support new initiatives. The remaining costs involve aligning the company's manufacturing operations with the needs of the new global business units. These changes will translate to faster speed to market and lower costs.

The program involves the intent to close about 10 plants, as well as a number of individual production modules, resulting in the elimination of 6,700 positions globally over the next six years. While P&G has specific plans for standardization and realignment projects, there is still more detailed sourcing work to be completed to validate the current direction. Impacted organizations will be given information regarding closures with adequate time to allow for a smooth transition and shorten any period of uncertainty.

Global Business Services (GBS): The implementation of GBS involves the move of currently dispersed business activities to regionally based centers to leverage scale and standardize work processes to simplify transactions, provide better service and reduce costs. The GBS service centers will be in the following locations:

- North America and Latin America: Cincinnati (U.S.), San Jose (Costa Rica)
- Europe, Middle East, Africa: Newcastle (U.K.), Brussels (Belgium), Prague (Czechoslovakia)
- Asia: Kobe (Japan), Manila (Philippines), Guangzhou (China), Singapore

The implementation of this new organization is expected to result in the elimination of 3,900 current positions globally with the majority of these impacts occurring three to five years from now.

Other 2005 Costs: The remaining costs and work force reductions relate to aligning the organization with the new global structure. This includes reducing hierarchy to speed decision making, streamlining organizations to reflect external changes such as global trade customer consolidation, and other organization simplification to deliver the Organization 2005 design. In total, this part of the program will result in the elimination of 4,400 positions over the next six years.

This element also includes the costs for relocation to the new regional GBU center in Geneva, the co-location of the regional management of all Latin American GBU operations in Caracas, Venezuela.

Regional Impact

Of the total work force reduction anticipated, approximately 42 percent will occur in Europe, Middle East, and Africa; 29 percent will occur in North America; 16 percent in Latin America; and 13 percent in Asia. Specific facilities and businesses will not be identified publicly until specific plans have been validated and affected employees have been notified.

Focus on Growth

"Organization 2005 is focused on one thing: leveraging P&G's innovative capability. Because the single best way to accelerate our growth—our sales, our volume, our earnings growth— is to innovate bigger and move faster consistently and across the entire company," said Jager.

"The cultural changes we are making will also create an environment that produces bolder, more stretching goals and plans, bigger innovations and greater speed. For example, we have redesigned our reward system to better link executive compensation with stretch business goals and results. This will help encourage more breakthrough results and stronger growth."

Procter & Gamble markets approximately 300 brands to nearly five billion consumers in over 140 countries. They include Tide, Ariel, Crest, Pantene Pro-V, Always, Whisper, Pringles, Pampers, Oil of Olay, Vicks, and Didronel. Based in Cincinnati, Ohio, P&G has on the ground operations in over 70 countries and employs more than 110,000 employees worldwide.

Case: Autoparts Inc.

Autoparts Inc. is a large U.S.-based multinational with production operations in some 20 countries. In April the company acquired a small Italian firm that had been family owned and operated for more than 20 years. The Italian management had reacted strongly and negatively to the new parent company's plan to revamp the Italian firm's accounting system to bring it in line with that of other Autoparts affiliates.

The Two Systems

Six years before the Italian acquisition, Autoparts implemented a complex, standardized internal reporting system for all its subsidiaries. A major objective of the system was to provide headquarters with directly comparable accounting information in a precise and timely fashion. Headquarters believed that such a system was necessary to facilitate the aggregation and disaggregation of financial data for reporting to its many constituencies and for internal management decision making. Headquarters also believed that the sophisticated system forced managers to plan better, think in terms of the U.S. impact of their operations, and maintain better control over their operations. All reports were to be prepared by the affiliates in English, in dollars, and according to U.S. GAAP. Thirty basic items related to the income statement were due at headquarters by noon on the first Monday of each month, and 40 data items related to the balance sheet were due at headquarters on the following Wednesday. More extensive data were due quarterly, including trial balances with more than 1,000 lines of data and narrative comments. Complete data were due at year-end, along with extensive comments regarding performance in local currency, in dollars, and through comparisons with budgets and plans.

Autoparts decided that it would adopt a uniform computer platform utilizing the Macintosh. It made extensive use of e-mail and data transfer by modem.

The Italian firm's existing accounting staff did not measure up to that of Autoparts, to put it mildly. The former owner had required only sporadic internal reports and had made even fewer external reports. The Italian accounting staff consisted of eight people, only two of whom had much formal accounting background, and none of whom spoke English or had any understanding of U.S. GAAP. The firm had also been using a computer system installed by Olivetti, using MS-DOS as their operating system.

Resistance to the New System

The Italian staff believed that the proposed reporting requirements were burdensome, and neither necessary nor feasible. They had gotten along without them for years, and—more to the point—they were not capable of preparing the reports according to Autoparts's require-ments. Furthermore, because they were not accustomed to such procedures, complying with the strict deadlines and rules would pose significant difficulties and hardships on them. They also argued that much of the data required by headquarters was of little value to the sub-sidiary and of no value to the accounting reports they were required to prepare by Italian law. They were also concerned that the Italian government, and particularly the tax author-ities, might question them on why the reports submitted to Autoparts's headquarters would show significantly different results from those submitted in Italy.

Questions

1. Is the Autoparts system of standardized reporting an intelligent one? What considera-tions support it and argue against it?

2. Is the Autoparts policy of no exceptions, no excuses, a logical one? What factors argue for this policy and against it?

3. Based on your answers to questions 1 and 2, should the Italian subsidiary be forced to adopt the Autoparts system as is, with modifications, or not at all?

Selected References

Allen, T. J. and M. S. Scott-Morton, eds. 1994. *Information Technology and the Corporation of the 1990s: Research Studies.* New York: Oxford University Press.

Baden-Fuller, C. and M. Pitt. 1977. *Strategic Innovation: An International Casebook on Corpora-tions for Value Creation.* San Francisco: Jossey-Bass.

Bartlett, C. K. and S. Ghoshal. 1989. *Managing Across Borders* Boston, MA: Harvard Business School Press.

Birkenshaw, J. M. and A. J. Morrison. 1995. "Configurations of Strategy and Structure in Sub-sidiaries of Multinational Corporations," *Journal of International Business Studies*, 28 (4): 729–53.

Crainer, S., ed. 1995. *The Financial Times Handbook of Management.* London: FT/Pitman Pub-lishing.

Egelhoff, W. G. 1991. "Information-Processing Theory and the Multinational Enterprise," *Journal of International Business Studies*, 22: 341–68.

Ghoshal, S. 1996. *Fast Forward: The Best Ideas On Managing Business.* Boston, MA: Harvard Business School Press.

Gupta, A. K. and V. Govindarajan. 1991. "Knowledge Flows and the Structure of Control Within Multinational Corporations," *Academy of Management Review*, 16(4): 768–92.

Hamel, G. and C. J. Prahalad. 1992. "Do You Really Have a Global Strategy?" in *Transnational Management*, C. Bartlett and S. Ghoshal, eds. Homewood, IL: Richard D. Irwin.

Hofstede, G. 1984. "Cultural Dimensions in Management and Planning," *Asia-Pacific Journal of Management* (January): 81–99.

Hout, T., M. E. Porter, and E. Rudden. 1982. "How Global Companies Win Out," *Harvard Business Review* (September–October).

Mintzberg, H. and J. B. Quinn. 1996. *The Strategy Process: Concepts, Contexts, Cases.* Upper Sad-dle River, NJ: Prentice-Hall.

Nohria, N. and S. Ghoshal. 1997. *The Differentiated Network: Organizing Multinational Corpora-tions for Value Creation.* San Francisco: Jossey-Bass.

Sharp, D. and S. Salter. 1997 "Project Escalation and Sunk Costs: A Test of the International Generalizability of Agency and Prospect Theories," *Journal of International Business Studies*, 28 (1): 101–121.

CHAPTER FOURTEEN

INTERNATIONAL BUDGETING AND PERFORMANCE EVALUATION

Chapter Objectives

- Identify the major stages in the strategic control process
- Describe different ways to evaluate the performance of managers and companies in the international context
- Present the results of different studies on performance evaluation by U.S. and non-U.S. firms
- Discuss how foreign currencies impact on the budgeting and performance evaluation process
- Review the problems involved with setting intra-corporate transfer prices
- Analyze costing issues including target costing
- Examine the major issues and trends in performance evaluation

INTRODUCTION

In this chapter we look at some of the special problems faced by management in controlling the multinational enterprise. As with control in a domestic environment, control in the global environment begins with a strategic objective and includes all elements of planning and monitoring the success of a global strategy to meet those objectives. The focus of the planning process is to give strategic direction to the firm and then an operational plan to get the firm to achieve the strategic direction. The role of the management accountant in this planning process is to work with top management to identify the necessary performance criteria and then to monitor achievements against these criteria.

THE STRATEGIC CONTROL PROCESS

In a study of European MNEs by Gupta and Govindarajan (1991), the following stages in a formal strategic control system were identified:

1. Periodic strategy reviews for each business, typically on an annual or less frequent basis.
2. Annual operating plans, which increasingly include nonfinancial measures along with the traditional financial ones.
3. Formal monitoring of strategic results, which may be combined with the budget monitoring process.
4. Personal rewards and central intervention.

Having too rigid a strategic control system can be difficult for a company that is in a rapidly changing industry, but there are some distinct benefits from a formal process:

1. Greater clarity and realism in planning.
2. More "stretching" of performance standards.
3. More motivation for business unit managers.
4. More timely intervention by central management.
5. Clearer responsibilities.

For such a system to work, it is necessary to select the right strategic objectives based on an analysis of the competition and the strengths of the firm. Then suitable targets need to be set according to the strategy of the firm. Many firms attempt to benchmark their performance based on key competitors, but it is often difficult to get good data on global competitors. The system needs to be tight enough and demanding enough to put pressure on management to perform. It is common to find strategic plans that are too general, so there is a real challenge to take the plans and targets and use them to push management. Finally, it is important not to let the process get so big, complicated, and bureaucratized that it gets in the way of creative thinking and solid performance.

Trying to implement this concept in a global environment is not easy. Different operating environments make it difficult and complicated to establish and implement a strategic control system. Such operating environments include culture; legal systems (which may limit a strategic objective to increase market share or become the market leader); political differences that could influence the role the firm is allowed to play in the country; and economic systems, including inflation and market size and growth. An example of strategic objectives is given by Procter & Gamble (Exhibit 14.1).

EMPIRICAL STUDIES OF DIFFERENCES IN MANAGEMENT ACCOUNTING AND CONTROL PRACTICES ACROSS NATIONS

Setting Objectives: A Global Overview

A great deal has been written on strategy for the corporation. As it relates to multi-nationals, the setting of strategic objectives usually requires managers to focus on

Exhibit 14.1   Procter & Gamble Annual Report 1998

Extract from Management Letter to Shareholders on Future Strategy

Faster, Bigger Innovation

These results are good, yet we can and must do better. In particular, we are not satisfied with our rate of volume and sales growth. We must significantly accelerate our progress if we are to achieve the goals we've reported here in previous years:

- To double our business in 10 years,

- To grow shares in categories representing the majority of our volume, and

- To remain consistently among the top third of our peer companies in TSR performance.

We know the key is faster, bigger innovation in every part of our business. And we've made important strides in the past year to strengthen our pipeline of innovations on established brands and on new brands entering test market. But there is much more we intend to do. We must bring even better products to more markets with greater speed than ever before. And we must release the untapped power of our organization.

Important Changes to Accelerate Growth

For some time, we've been examining how our organization should evolve, and in the coming weeks, we will announce details of a comprehensive plan to simplify the way we're structured and to strengthen how we operate. The changes, while consistent with the direction in which we've been growing, are significant and will improve our ability to create and build even more profitable leadership brands around the world.

Four changes, in particular, are worth noting here:

- We will move from our current regional business units to product-based, global business units—a direction we've been heading since the late 1980s with the start of Global Category Management.

- We will strengthen our already-strong, country-based organizations to provide even deeper knowledge of local consumers and stronger partnerships with our customers. These local market organizations will be essential to bringing our product initiatives to consumers with the highest impact possible.

- We will create a new Global Business Services organization to support the global business units and the local market organizations. This move will bring together business services that are currently dispersed throughout the organization. It will also help us achieve significant economies of scale, while improving the overall quality and speed of these services.

- And finally, we will streamline our corporate staff. We will align many corporate resources with the business units and refocus others on developing the cutting-edge, functional knowledge and innovation important to our future growth and success.

To support these new structural advantages, we are also making important changes in our culture and in our reward system—all to encourage greater speed, innovation and flexibility in the organization.

Taken together, we believe these improvements will enable us to build stronger global brands; achieve faster, bigger innovation; produce accelerated business growth; and result in greater satisfaction for our people. These are the kinds of changes we've made throughout P&G's 161-year history—changes always designed to get us closer to consumers and to keep our business growing at a level we—and you—have every right to expect, given the extraordinary caliber of the men and women of Procter & Gamble.

---

choosing a suitable numeric target. Objectives can be quantified in terms of a particular budget number or financial ratio and seem to vary considerably from country to country. Possible targets include:

1. return on investment
2. sales
3. cost reduction
4. quality targets
5. market share
6. profitability
7. budget to actual

Each of these methods has its value. The most appropriate method to be used in a multinational is, in theory, best defined by the focus of the unit for which the target is being set. Sales or market share is particularly relevant for a unit that has no control over its input costs and whose primary purpose is to sell the goods of some other unit. Profitability, measured as a ratio or some other measure, is most appropriate for a fully fledged strategic business unit (i.e., a unit of a group of companies which makes its own business decisions at all levels—for example, a major division or subsidiary). In addition, targets for a unit should be linked not only to its objective, but also to that part of its operations which it controls. This theoretical concern aside, there is considerable evidence that the core objective of the corporation differs from country to country or culture. The studies that follow illustrate this point.

Studies of U.S. Multinationals

In one of the first important studies of the objectives of MNEs, Robbins and Stobaugh (1973) studied nearly 200 U.S.-based MNEs, representing almost all major U.S. industries with investments abroad and ranging in size of annual foreign sales from $20 million upward. With regard to measures of financial performance, the main conclusions from their research were as follows:

1. The many tangible and intangible items that entered into the original investment calculations were rarely taken into account in evaluating the foreign subsidiaries' performance. For example, the value or cost of a parent company's loan guarantee for a subsidiary, cost of safety stocks of inventory for foreign and U.S. operations, or the potential cost of being excluded from a market by a competitor who moves first.

2. Foreign subsidiaries were judged on the same basis as domestic subsidiaries.

3. The most utilized measure of performance for all subsidiaries was return on investment (ROI).

4. Because of the inherent limitation and problems of calculating ROI equitably for all subsidiaries, nearly all the multinationals used some supplementary device to gauge foreign subsidiaries' performance.

5. The most widely used supplementary measure was comparison to budget.

Exhibit 14.2   Evaluating Foreign Subsidiaries and Foreign Subsidiary Managers

	Percent of the Total 64 MNEs	
Financial Measures	Foreign Subsidiary (%)	Foreign Subsidiary Manager (%)
Return-on-investment (ROI)	74	67
Profits	78	66
Budgeted ROI compared to actual ROI	66	64
Budgeted profit compared to actual profit	86	87
Other measures	36	36

Source: W. Abdallah and D. Keller, "Measuring the Multinational's Performance," *Management Accounting* (1985): 28.

Additional support for the findings of this study continues even though some 25 years have passed since the original study. In a sample of 70 U.S. chemical multinationals (see Morsicato, 1980) it was found that multiple measures were used, including in descending order of use, profit, ROI, and budgeted versus actuals for profit and sales. Abdallah and Keller (1985) in a survey of 64 U.S. MNEs identified four key factors (see Exhibit 14.2). As with other studies, budgets, profits, and ROI dominate the list.

After the initial studies of U.S. corporate performance objectives a variety of studies have examined practices in other countries. Some of the countries are quite similar culturally to the United States.

Studies of U.K. Multinationals

Appleyard, Strong, and Walton (1990) studied the performance objectives of 11 British MNEs and found that the British companies preferred to use budget/actual comparisons, followed closely by some form of ROI. In the ROI measure, the profit measure used was either profit before interest and tax or profit after interest but before tax, even though tax rates vary significantly from country to country. In addition, they found that British firms tended to use the same ROI measure for foreign subsidiaries that they do for domestic subsidiaries.

Studies of Japanese Multinationals

Studies in countries whose cultures differ significantly from the United States often produce very different results. Shields, Chow, Kato, and Nakagawa (1991) reviewed the objectives used by Japanese and U.S. MNEs as found in the literature of the two countries and identified several important performance objectives used to evaluate divisional managers. As Exhibit 14.3 shows, there are some major differences between the two countries. The Japanese tend to rely on sales as their most important criterion by far, whereas U.S. firms prefer ROI.

Exhibit 14.3 Criteria Used for Evaluating Divisional Managers

Sources	Japan A (%)	United States A (%)
Sales	69	19
Sales growth	28	28
Market share	12	19
Asset turnover	7	13
Return-on-sales	30	26
ROI	7	75
Controllable profit	28	49
Residual income	20	13
Profit minus corporate costs	44	38
Manufacturing costs	28	13
Other	8	17

Source: Michael Shields, Chee W. Chow, Yutaka Kato, and Yu Nakagawa, "Management Accounting Practices in the U.S. and Japan: Comparative Survey Findings and Research Implications, *"Journal of International Financial Management and Accounting* 3, no. 2 (Spring 1991): 68.

Similarly, Bailes and Assada (1991) studied and compared the objectives of 256 Japanese and 80 U.S. MNEs. The respondents were asked to identify the first, second, and third goals for division managers; their answers are summarized in Exhibit 14.4. Bailes and Assada (1991) found that most Japanese firms (86.3 percent) preferred to use sales volume as their overall objective, with net profit after corporate overhead being a poor second (44.7 percent). American companies, by contrast, tend to use ROI most often as the divisional budget goal (68.4 percent) followed by controllable profit (51.8 percent). It is important to note how unimportant ROI appears to be to the Japanese firms. Demirag (1994) found that Japanese companies in the U.K. tended to use sales and market share targets over the longer term.

Exhibit 14.4 Top Budget Goals for Division Managers

	Japan (%)	United States (%)
Sales volume	86.3	27.9
Net profit after corporate overhead	44.7	35.0
Controllable profit	28.2	51.8
Profit margin on sales	30.7	30.5
Sales growth	19.4	22.4
Return on investment (ROI)	3.1	68.4
Production cost	40.7	12.4

Source: Jack C. Bailes and Takayuki Assada, "Empirical Differences between Japanese and American Budget and Performance Evaluation Systems," *International Journal of Accounting* 26, no. 2 (1991): 137.

Studies of APEC Multinationals

Looking at East Asia, research by Merchant, Chow, and Wu (1995) found little evidence suggesting a link between national culture and firms' goals in Taiwan. However, the sample consisted of only four firms. Comparing the perspectives of more than 400 managers in Australia, the United States, Singapore, and Hong Kong, Harrison and Harrell (1994) simply concluded that Anglo-American managers prefer shorter term but more quantitative objectives. These studies will be discussed further in the budgeting section.

Taken together these studies find that the objectives of companies from various nation-states vary considerably. It is interesting to note that the Asian nations, which are less individualistic and by and large more long-term oriented, tend to pick objectives that less directly reflect immediate returns, choosing those objectives that fit a longer-term market dominance profile.

The Budget Process Across Countries: Basics

The budget process involves taking the firm's objectives and setting them out in a series of formal plans, both short and long term. The issues that generally need to be resolved are:

1. Is there a formal budget-setting process?
2. Who participates in the budget process and how?
3. What style of communication (formal versus informal) should be used?
4. How are the budget objectives set?

Other more general issues of concern are, for example:

5. What time period should be covered (short versus long term)?
6. Should there be a specific monetary objective for the plan or would a nonquantitative objective be more appropriate?

Cross National Studies of Participation in Budgeting

Much of the Anglo-American practice in budgeting assumes that the budget process is improved through the participation of the persons involved in carrying out the budget. If managers are permitted to participate in setting their own budget targets, they not only feel better about them (satisfaction) but also tend to perform better. This type of behavior was documented in a series of experiments by Brownell (1982) who suggests that for participation to work fully, managers must feel like insiders (i.e., that their participation will actually influence decisions and have some impact on the outcome). This concept of insider/outsider is described as "locus of control."

This concept of the value of participation in budgeting may be uniquely Anglo-American. It implies first that managers at all levels care that their opinions are sought and feel that they can make a contribution without retribution. Frucot and Shearon (1991), for example, conducted a study using Mexican managers to test this proposition.

Studies of Mexican Companies   Given that Mexico is a high power distance/low individualism culture, Frucot and Shearon (1991) anticipated that Mexican managers might not favor participation even given insider status (i.e., they would rather be dictated to).

Frucot and Shearon (1991) tested their hypotheses on a sample of 83 Mexican managers in both indigenous firms and subsidiaries of U.S. multinationals. The results were initially surprising. Overall, the *performance* of the Mexican managers in indigenous firms was related to participation and locus of control. Therefore, it appeared initially there was no difference between the behavior of Mexican managers and typical U.S. managers.

Unlike U.S. managers, however, the insider/outsider dimension did not affect the *satisfaction* levels of Mexican managers (in indigenous firms). The managers of the firms studied initially appeared to be happier and motivated by a higher level of participation regardless of whether they saw themselves as running the show. However, when the sample of Mexican managers was divided by company rank, lower-level managers seemed to prefer a less participative style.

What is of greatest concern to MNEs is that Mexican managers of entirely foreign owned subsidiaries showed almost no desire to participate in the budgeting process. Unlike their American counterparts, they regarded themselves as powerless and the process as alien. An American or, for that matter, a British firm, would receive a rude shock when it realized that its employees in Mexico had little commitment to the budget process and that they might well tell their managers merely what they expected them to hear.

Studies of APEC Multinationals   A similar series of experiments was conducted, comparing Australia (low Power Distance/high Individualism) and Singapore (high Power Distance/low Individualism). Harrison (1992) anticipated that there would be a significant international difference in the ability of budget participation to explain levels of satisfaction among managers. Coming from a relatively authoritarian culture, the Singaporeans were expected to dislike or perhaps feel uncomfortable with budget participation. Harrison (1992) hypothesized that Singaporeans, therefore, would prefer a lower level of participation than their Australian counterparts. In fact, there was no significant relationship between national origin and participation, interaction and satisfaction. Overall, both groups seemed to prefer a participative style of budgeting. Harrison therefore argues that budgetary participation universally enhances job satisfaction regardless of culture. It should be noted that Harrison makes no comments about performance, which after all is the objective of participation. Harrison does not attempt to stratify his sample as Frucot and Shearon (1991) did. We therefore do not know if Asian senior managers take a different perspective from those in the junior ranks, a key concept when one is trying to argue that the power structure affects the desire to participate. Overall, the research to date appears to indicate that some of the Western participative budgetary techniques are transferable, but one must be very careful at what level they are transferred.

Other Issues in the Budgeting Process

The previous section discussed the role of participation in the budget process. While this is certainly important, it is only one facet of the process. This section goes on to look at other key variables such as how communication takes place (formal versus informal), the time frame for budgets (long versus short), and the objectives.

Research into the budget process as it unfolds in different countries has primarily focused on differences between Anglo-American and Asian cultural groups. More recently, research in this area, while continuing to focus on Asia, has switched to the ASEAN region in what has colloquially been referred to as the "Five Dragon" or "Mini Dragon" area. This includes Hong Kong, Singapore, Taiwan, Malaysia, and possibly Thailand and Indonesia. While this group is not monolithic in culture structure, it is generally seen as sharing common Confucian values which include long-term orientation and an unwillingness to "lose face." This Asian culture tends to be collectivist in that citizens of most countries in the group tend to subjugate individual rights to group needs and are moderate to high on the Power Distance scale.

U.S./Japan Comparisons   Some of the implications of these cultural differences appear in studies of the budgeting process which compare Asian and Anglo-American countries. Bailes and Assada (1991) compared the budgetary behavior of 80 U.S. and 256 Japanese listed companies. Their results indicated that more than 90 percent of companies in both countries prepared master budgets. However, they found that the process of arriving at this master budget varied. Among the points that are statistically significant are the following:

1. The average length of time spent preparing annual budgets was nearly 12 days longer for the American companies (69.72 days) than the Japanese companies.

2. As previously discussed, the primary budget objective arising from the Japanese process was increased sales volume or market share. From the U.S. companies, the primary budget objective was, overwhelmingly, ROI.

3. Division managers in American firms are more likely to participate in budget committee discussions and influence the budget committee than are their Japanese counterparts.

4. Japanese companies also tended to follow a bottom-up approach, where all levels participated in the planning, though much of the contribution was informal. Formal meetings tended to be infrequent and while managers' wishes were considered, they were less important in the process than group consensus.

5. Japanese managers are more likely to use budget variances to recognize problems on a timely basis and to use budgets to improve the next period's budget.

6. American managers are more likely to be evaluated by the budgets.

7. The bonus and salary of an American manager are much more likely to be influenced by budget performance than are those of Japanese managers.

These differences are very interesting. American managers tend to be more involved in the budgeting process, are evaluated by budgets, and are rewarded or penalized by budgets. Japanese managers tend to look at budget variances as a way to improve performance. Between the Americans and the Japanese, there is clearly a national difference in budgeting.

Ueno and Sekaran (1992) also compared U.S. and Japanese budgeting practices, framing their discussion more formally within Hofstede's cultural paradigm. Using a sample of controllers and other senior managers at manufacturing companies, they found several culturally predictable phenomena. As found in Bailes, and Assada (1991), U.S. managers used more formal meetings, communication and coordination in budget planning. Put in its cultural context, Ueno and Sekaran (1992) interpret this control process as the natural outcropping of individualism. Thus the process of budgeting becomes one of drawing together the diverse and often conflicting interests that manifest themselves in an individualist society.

Some of the other budgetary trends found in Ueno and Sekaran (1992) also appear to have cultural roots. U.S. budget makers tended to create more "slack," which was ascribed to individuals trying to enhance their own power bases and self-esteem. This calculating behavior of creating slack, which in turn created comfortable goals and more easily achievable targets, was linked to the Individualism dimension and the individual reward structure of most U.S. companies. Finally, as would be expected from a country high on the Confucian dimension, Japanese managers tended to care less about identifying controllability of items and tended to measure performance over a longer time horizon than U.S. managers. A few of the findings of Ueno and Sekaran (1992) run contrary to the view of Bailes and Assada (1991). Despite having a longer performance reward period, Japanese managers did not have an appreciably longer planning horizon than U.S. managers. One must remember, however, that much long-term planning takes place outside of the formal numeric atmosphere of a budget.

Studies of APEC Multinationals

Harrison, McKinnon, Panchapakesan, and Leung (1994) examine the budgetary and planning systems of Australia and the United States, and then Singapore and Hong Kong. They drew on the national cultural dimensions of power distance, individualism, and Confucian dynamism to predict and explain differences in philosophies and approaches to organizational design, management planning, and control systems in Asian and Anglo-American countries. Data was gathered by survey questionnaires mailed to senior accounting and finance executives in 800 organizations.

The results of Harrison et al. (1994) were largely as predicted and, in general, provide support for the importance of national culture in influencing organizational design and management planning and control systems. In particular, the cultural values of Anglo-American society relative to East Asian society are associated with a greater emphasis on decentralization, and responsibility centers in organizational design and quantitative and analytical techniques in planning and control. By contrast, the cultural values of East Asian society are associated with a greater emphasis on long-term planning and on group-centered decision making.

CHALLENGES OF CONTROL IN THE GLOBAL FIRM

Planning and Budgeting Issues

Multinational corporations contend with an array of external factors, internal considerations, and other forces that influence budget policies, composition, and control. Budgeting in a global business environment calls for an enhanced level of coordination and communication through the company because of the variety of powerful components that affect organizational performance. While multinationals need to be concerned about cultural differences and their impact on national budgeting practices, there are additional considerations in the budgeting process of these companies. Of particular importance is the impact of foreign exchange differences on cross-border operations.

Indeed, the major international issue surrounding the establishment of a budget for an MNE is to determine the currency in which the budget should be prepared: the local currency or the parent currency. For a Swiss MNE, for example, is it better to evaluate all its foreign operations in terms of the local currency results or the results translated into francs? This choice can be highly significant if major changes occur in the exchange rates. It is possible for a profit in local currency to become a loss in the parent company's currency, and vice versa. If a Swiss company's Mexican subsidiary earned a profit in pesos but a loss when translated into francs, should the subsidiary's performance be evaluated favorably or unfavorably? Most firms resolve this dilemma by considering the main purpose of the foreign operations. If it is to provide a return to parent company shareholders that maximizes their domestic purchasing power, then typically an "after-translation" basis is used. A "before-translation" basis is more likely to be used by a firm that truly considers itself a multinational firm seeking global optimization or one that leaves considerable autonomy to each foreign operation.

The foreign currency issue also raises the issue of controllability. Whether a currency rises or falls in value and by how much is clearly beyond the control of a single MNE or any one of its parts. Therefore, because proper performance evaluation should exclude the impact on results of events over which the unit or person had no control, one can argue that the before-translation basis is better than the after-translation basis. In the case of the Swiss-Mexican situation, if the peso profits become translated into franc losses, the Mexican manager should not be penalized for a result out of his or her control. On the other hand, if the Mexican manager is given the authority and responsibility to hedge against potential foreign exchange losses, then he or she could be evaluated in terms of translated profitability.

The value of establishing the budget in the local currency is that management operates in that currency, and the local currency is more indicative of the overall operating environment than the present currency would be. In addition, the exchange rate is something over which local management has no control, so it would be unwise to have a key uncontrollable item as part of the budgeting and evaluation process.

Conversely, it is often difficult for top management in the parent country to understand budgets generated in different currencies. This is especially true for a geographically diverse firm such as Coca-Cola, which might have budgets generated in 100 or more different currencies. Translating the budgets into the parent currency allows top management to consolidate the budgets into a firm-wide view of the coming year. Also, because top management has to report to shareholders in the parent currency, they might want the strategic business unit (SBU) or subsidiary management to think in terms of parent country profitability as well.

There are three possible approaches in dealing with foreign exchange in the budgeting process as it relates to performance evaluation of managers:

1. Allow operating managers to enter into hedge contracts with corporate treasury so they can "contract away" their exposures.

2. Adjust the actual performance of the unit for variations in the real exchange rate after the end of the period.

3. Adjust performance plans in line with variations in the real exchange rate.

Ways to Bring Foreign Exchange into the Budgeting Process

Lessard and Lorange (1997) identify the different ways that firms can translate the budget from the local currency into the parent currency and then monitor actual performance (see Exhibit 14.5). Three different exchange rates are used in Exhibit 14.5. The first is the actual exchange rate in effect when the budget was established, the second is the rate that was projected at the time the budget was established in the local currency, and the third is the actual exchange rate in effect when the budgeted period actually takes place. The attractiveness of the first exchange rate is that it is an objective spot rate that actually exists on a given day. It is a reasonable rate to use in a stable environment, but it may be meaningless in an unstable foreign exchange environment. The projected rate is an attempt on the part of management to forecast what it thinks the exchange rate will be for the budgeted time period. For example, management might project in June 2000 that the exchange rate between the U.S. dollar and the British pound will be $1.6500 during December 2000, so that would be the projected exchange rate used in the budgeting process. The actual exchange rate found in cell E-3 is an update of the exchange rate that was in effect when the budget was established. It provides the actual exchange rate in effect when the time period takes place.

These three exchange rates need to be considered for both the establishment of the budget as well as the monitoring of performance. In cells A-1, P-2, and E-3, the exchange rate used to establish the budget and monitor performance is the same, so any variances will be due to price and volume, not the exchange rate. The value of P-2 over A-1 and E-3 is that it forces management to think initially of what its performance will be if the forecast is reasonably accurate. A-1 never takes into account what the exchange rate will be, and it does not attempt to reconcile the

Exhibit 14.5   Possible Combinations of Exchange Rates in the Control Process

Rate Used for Relative Determining Budget ╲ Rate Used to Track Performance to Budget	Actual at Time of Budget	Projected at Time of Budget	Actual at End of Period
Actual at time of budget	A-1	A-2	A-3
Projected at time of budget	P-1	P-2	P-3
Actual at end of period (through updating)	E-1	E-2	E-3

Source: Donald R. Lessard and Peter Lorange, "Currency Changes and Management Control: Resolving the Centralization/Decentralization Dilemma," *Accounting Review* 52 (July 1977): 630.

budget from the original rate with that of the actual rate. Given the instability in exchange rates, however, some would argue that a forecast exchange rate is no more accurate than any other exchange rate. E-3 does take into consideration what performance is at the actual exchange rate, but it does not force management to be forward thinking during the budget process.

A-3 and P-3 result in a variance that is a function of operating results and exchange rate changes. Under A-3, the budget is established at the initial exchange rate, but actual performance is translated at the actual exchange rate. Thus, there is an exchange rate variance that is the difference between the original and the actual rate. P-3 results in a variance that is the difference between what management thought the exchange rate would be and what it actually was at the end of the operating period. If management's forecast was reasonably accurate, P-3 should result in a very small foreign exchange variance. If the exchange rate between the parent and local currency is relatively stable, A-3 should also result in a relatively small foreign exchange variance. However, it is important to realize that the use of A-3 and P-3 means that someone (usually local management) will be held accountable for exchange rate variances.

A more complex example of a flexible budget that involves foreign exchange is provided in Exhibit 14.6. Assume that this budget is established in British pounds for the British subsidiary of a U.S. firm. The budget is established in pounds, but U.S. management wants the budget and actual performance translated into dollars for evaluative purposes. The budget for April 2000 is established at a sale price of £150 per unit and a variable cost of £100 per unit. The actual selling price is £155 per unit, and the actual variable cost is £110 per unit. The budgeted volume is 6,000 units, and the actual number of units sold is 5,500.

There are three important (hypothetical) exchange rates for this example:

$1.7000   The actual exchange rate on October 1, 1999, when the budget was established

$1.6000   The projected exchange rate for April 2000

$1.6300   The actual average exchange rate for April 2000

Following the budget and actual results in British pounds are the translated versions of the financial statement and variance analysis according to the approaches outlined in Exhibit 14.5: A-1, P-2, E-3, A-3, P-3.

For approaches A-1, P-2, and E-3, there is no exchange rate variance because the same exchange rate is used to translate the budget and actual results from British pounds into U.S. dollars. Column 3 is the same as column 1 because the exchange rate for budget and actual results is the same. Thus, there are no exchange rate variances in column 2.

Under approach A-3, columns 3 through 7 are translated at the exchange rate in effect on October 1, 1999, and column 1 is translated at the actual average rate for April 2000. Under approach P-3, columns 3 through 7 are translated at the projected exchange rate, and column 1 is translated at the actual average exchange rate for April 2000. The important point to emphasize is that under the latter two approaches, there is an exchange rate variance that arises because the budget and the actual results are translated at different exchange rates. Thus the difference between flexible budget and actual performance is a function of an exchange rate variance and operating budget variance.

Exhibit 14.6 The Flexible Budget—A Foreign Currency Analysis

The Flexible Budget in British Pounds

	(1) Actual Results	(2) (1)−(3) Exchange Rate Variance	(3) Actual Results at Budget Rate	(4) (1)−(5) Flexible Budget Variances	(5) Flexible Budget	(6) (5)−(7) Sales Volume Variances	(7) Static (Master) Budget
Units Sold	5,500			0	5,500	(500)	6,000
Sales Revenues	852,500			27,500	825,000	(75,000)	900,000
Variable Costs	605,000			(55,000)	550,000	50,000	600,000
Contribution Margin	247,500			(27,500)	275,000	(25,000)	300,000
Fixed Costs	200,000			0	200,000	0	200,000
Operating Income	47,500			(27,500)	75,000	(25,000)	100,000

Total Sales Volume Variance (7–5) 25,000 Unfavorable

Total Flexible-budget Variances (5–1) 27,500 Unfavorable

Total Static-budget Variances (7–1) 52,500 Unfavorable

The Budget Translated into Dollars at A-1

	(1) Actual Results	(2) (1)−(3) Exchange Rate Variance	(3) Actual Results at Budget Rate	(4) (1)−(5) Flexible Budget Variances	(5) Flexible Budget	(6) (5)−(7) Sales Volume Variances	(7) Static (Master) Budget
Units Sold	5,500			0	5,500	(500)	6,000
Sales Revenues	1,449,250			46,750	1,402,500	(127,500)	1,530,000
Variable Costs	1,028,500			(93,500)	935,000	85,000	1,020,000
Contribution Margin	420,750			(46,750)	467,500	(42,500)	510,000
Fixed Costs	340,000			0	340,000	0	340,000
Operating Income	80,750			(46,750)	127,500	(42,500)	170,000

Total Sales Volume Variance (7–5) $42,500 Unfavorable

Total Flexible-budget Variances (5–1) $46,750 Unfavorable

Total Static-budget Variances (7–1) $89,250 Unfavorable

The Budget Translated into Dollars at P-2

Units Sold	5,500	0	5,500	(500)	6,000
Sales Revenues	1,364,000	44,000	1,320,000	(120,000)	1,440,000
Variable Costs	968,000	(88,000)	880,000	80,000	960,000
Contribution Margin	396,000	(44,000)	440,000	(40,000)	480,000
Fixed Costs	320,000	0	320,000	(40,000)	320,000
Operating Income	76,000	(44,000)	120,000	(40,000)	160,000

Total Sales Volume Variance (7–5) $40,000 Unfavorable
Total Flexible-budget Variances (5–1) $44,000 Unfavorable
Total Static-budget Variances (7–1) $84,000 Unfavorable

The Budget Translated into Dollars at E-3

Units Sold	5,500	0	5,500	(500)	6,000
Sales Revenues	1,389,575	44,825	1,344,750	(122,250)	1,467,000
Variable Costs	986,150	(89,650)	896,500	81,500	978,000
Contribution Margin	403,425	(44,825)	448,250	(40,750)	489,000
Fixed Costs	326,000	0	326,000	0	326,000
Operating Income	77,425	(44,825)	122,250	(40,750)	163,000

Total Sales Volume Variance (7–5) $40,750 Unfavorable
Total Flexible-budget Variances (5–1) $44,825 Unfavorable
Total Static-budget Variances (5–1) $85,575 Unfavorable

(continues)

Exhibit 14.6 (Continued)

The Flexible Budget in British Pounds

	(1) Actual Results	(2) (1)–(3) Exchange Rate Variance	(3) Actual Results at Budget Rate	(4) (1)–(5) Flexible Budget Variances	(5) Flexible Budget	(6) (5)–(7) Sales Volume Variances	(7) Static (Master) Budget
The Budget Translated into Dollars at A-3							
Units Sold	5,500		5,500	0	5,500	(500)	6,000
Sales Revenues	1,389,575	(59,675)	1,449,250	46,750	1,402,500	(127,500)	1,530,000
Variable Costs	986,150	42,350	1,028,500	(93,500)	935,000	85,000	1,020,000
Contribution Margin	403,425	(17,325)	420,750	(46,750)	467,500	(42,500)	510,000
Fixed Costs	326,000	(14,000)	340,000	0	340,000	0	340,000
Operating Income	77,425	(3,325)	80,750	(46,750)	127,500	(42,500)	170,000

Total Sales Variance (7–5) $42,500 Unfavorable
Total Flexible-budget Variances (3–5) $46,750 Unfavorable
Exchange Rate Variances (1–3) $ 3,325 Unfavorable
Total Static-budget Variances (7–1) $92,575 Unfavorable

	(1) Actual Results	(2) (1)–(3) Exchange Rate Variance	(3) Actual Results at Budget Rate	(4) (1)–(5) Flexible Budget Variances	(5) Flexible Budget	(6) (5)–(7) Sales Volume Variances	(7) Static (Master) Budget
The Budget Translated into Dollars at P-3							
Units Sold	5,500		5,500	0	5,500	(500)	6,000
Sales Revenues	1,389,575	25,575	1,364,000	44,000	1,320,000	(120,000)	1,440,000
Variable Costs	986,150	(18,150)	968,000	(88,000)	880,000	80,000	960,000
Contribution Margin	403,425	7,425	396,000	(44,000)	440,000	(40,000)	480,000
Fixed Costs	326,000	6,000	320,000	0	320,000	0	320,000
Operating Income	77,425	1,425	76,000	(44,000)	120,000	(40,000)	160,000

Total Sales Volume Variance (7–5) $40,000 Unfavorable
Total Flexible-budget Variances (3–5) $44,000 Unfavorable
Exchange Rate Variances (1–3) $ 1,425 Favorable
Total Static-budget Variances (7–1) $82,575 Unfavorable

Budgeting and Currency Practices

What do MNEs actually do? In the Robbins and Stobaugh study (1973), fewer than half the firms surveyed judged subsidiary performance in terms of translated dollar amounts, and only 12 percent used both standards. Morsicato (1980) found that a significant number of firms in her sample used both dollar and local currency budgets compared to actual profits and actual sales.

In his study of British subsidiaries of Japanese firms, Demirag (1994) noted that the "companies indicated that financial statements presented in sterling (local currency) provided them with better understanding of the performance of their companies' operations and their management.... None of the companies translated their profit budgets into yen for performance evaluation purposes ... [and] none of the parent companies sent a copy of the translated yen statements." The parent currency financial statements were sent to Japan for translation into yen at a company fixed standard exchange rate. In essence, subsidiary managers were unaware of their performance in parent currency terms.

Capital Budgeting

Capital budgeting is the longer-term relation of the operational budgeting discussed previously. However, many of the considerations discussed, particularly as they relate to economic exposure, continue to apply. As in short-term planning or budgeting, long-range planning or capital budgeting must take into consideration anticipated exchange rate movements for discounting cash flows. This becomes part of the risk factor involved in discounting future cash flows, along with any environmental uncertainty. Environmental uncertainty can be mild, such as the risk of unexpected heavier taxation, or severe, such as the risk of expropriation. In general, the risk effect is greater in less developed countries than in wealthier countries, but even in the latter, there are many adverse events that are unpredictable.

Whether or not standardized reporting practices are used in a multinational company, there is a real issue as to whether foreign operations and their managers can be evaluated on a global basis or merely on a national basis. It was noted earlier that comparing ROIs is a primary method used to evaluate both individual operations and individual managers on a standardized or global basis. But can effective decisions be arrived at in this manner? Sometimes, when environmental factors are used in long-term strategic decisions, the outcome may appear to be at odds with the quest for strong ROIs on a year-to-year basis. Therefore, capital budgeting may require even more judgment than operational budgeting.

INTRACORPORATE TRANSFER PRICING

One of the additional elements of management of the multinational is intra-corporate transfer pricing. This refers to the pricing of goods and services that are transferred (bought and sold) between members of a corporate family—for example, parent to subsidiary, between subsidiaries, from subsidiaries to parent, and so on. As such, internal transfers include raw materials, semifinished and finished goods, allocation of fixed costs, loans, fees, royalties for use of trademarks, copy-rights, and other factors. In theory, such prices should be based on production costs, but in reality often they are not.

One of the important reasons for arbitrarily establishing transfer prices is tax-ation. However, taxation is only one of a number of reasons why internal transfers may be priced with little consideration for market prices or production costs. Com-panies may underprice goods sold to foreign affiliates, and the affiliates can then sell them at prices that their local competitors cannot match. If tough antidumping laws exist on final products, a company could underprice components and semi-finished products to its affiliates. The affiliates could then assemble or finish the final product at prices that would have been classified as dumping prices had they been imported directly into the country rather than produced domestically.

High transfer prices might be used to circumvent or significantly lessen the impact of national controls. A government prohibition on dividend remittances could restrict a firm's ability to maneuver income out of a country. However, over-pricing the goods shipped to a subsidiary in such a country would make it possible for funds to be taken out. High transfer prices would also be of considerable value to a firm when it is paid a subsidy or earns a tax credit on the value of goods it exports. The higher the transfer prices on exported goods, the greater the subsi-dies earned or tax credit received.

High transfer prices on goods shipped to subsidiaries might be desirable when a parent wishes to lower the apparent profitability of its subsidiary. This might be desirable because of the demands of the subsidiary's workers for higher wages or greater participation in company profits; because of political pressures to expro-priate high-profit, foreign-owned operations; or because of the possibility that new competitors might be lured into the industry by high profits. There might also be inducements for having high-priced transfers go to the subsidiary when a local part-ner is involved, the inducement being that the increase in the parent company profits will not have to be split with the local partner. High transfer prices may also be desired when increases from existing price controls in the subsidiary's country are based on product costs (including high transfer prices for purchases).

Matching Price to Market Conditions

The particular conditions that firms use to utilize a particular level of transfer price are summarized in Exhibit 14.7. The maximum advantage would be gained when all these conditions line up on a country basis. For example, the parent operates from a country whose characteristics call for high transfer prices coming in and low transfer prices going out, while the conditions of the subsidiary's country call for the opposite.

Consider the left column of Exhibit 14.7. If the parent sells at low prices to the subsidiary and buys from it at high prices, income is shifted to the subsidiary, less-ening the overall tax burden. At the same time, the impact of a high ad valorem tar-iff in the other country is lessened. In addition, the impact of foreign exchange rationing on imports from the parent and dividend payments to the parent are less-ened, the subsidiary's ability to penetrate its local market is enhanced, the parent is less affected by its government's restrictions on capital outflows, and so on.

Exhibit 14.7   Conditions in Subsidiary's Country Inducing High and Low Transfer Prices on Flows Between Affiliates and Parent

Conditions is Subsidiary's Country Inducing *Low Transfer Prices* on Flows from Parent and *High Transfer Prices* on Flows to Parent	Conditions in Subsidiary's Country Inducing *High Transfer Prices* on Flows from Parent and *Low Transfer Prices* on Flows to Parent
High ad valorem tariffs	Local partners
Corporate income tax rate lower than in parent's country	Pressure from workers to obtain greater share of company profit
Significant competition	Political pressure to nationalize or expropriate high-profit foreign firms
Local loans based on financial appearance of subsidiary	Restrictions on profit or dividend remittances
Export subsidy or tax credit on value of exports	Political instability
Lower inflation rate than in parent's country	Substantial tie-in sales agreements
Restrictions (ceilings) in subsidiary's country on the *value* of products that can be imported	Price of final product controlled by government but based on production cost
	Desire to mask profitability of subsidiary operations to keep competitors out

Source: Jeffrey S. Arpan, *Intracorporate Pricing: Non-American Systems and Views* (New York: Praeger, 1972).

Under this set of conditions, the subsidiary country gains somewhat more than the parent country: more funds, more taxable income, greater economic growth of the subsidiary, and more export revenues. It loses somewhat in other areas, however, as local competitors may suffer adversely, have lower profits, pay less taxes, and lay off workers if the foreign subsidiary actively pursues a market penetration strategy. The government pays greater subsidies or gives more tax credits because of the subsidiary's artificially high value of exports and, like the government of the other country, its national control is lessened.

Unfortunately for firms, conditions seldom line up as nicely from their standpoint as either column of Exhibit 14.7 depicts. It is far more likely that a country will simultaneously experience conditions from both sides of the table. Thus, it is difficult to determine whether the firm will receive a net benefit from high or low transfer prices. For example, a country experiencing balance-of-payments difficulties typically would be restricting dividend outflows and the amount or value of imports. A company using high transfer prices on sales to its subsidiary in such a country would gain with respect to taking out more money than it might otherwise have been able to get out but would lose by having to decrease the quantity of imported materials its affiliate needs to compete. Alternatively, a country may have high ad valorem tariffs and high income tax rates. Underpricing goods shipped to an affiliate in such a country lessens the duties and increases subsidiary profits as a result of lower input costs, resulting in higher taxes for the subsidiary. Therefore, in situations in which conditions in a country resemble those from both columns of Exhibit 14.7, the company must weigh the gains and losses from utilizing a particular level of transfer prices.

Allocation of Overhead

As with transfer pricing of goods, the allocation of overhead has national and cross-national implications. On the cross-national side, firms must determine what to do with corporate overhead. For example, IBM's world headquarters is located in New York, but its operations are located worldwide. How does IBM allocate those costs to its operations in different countries, and what are the tax implications of this issue? This becomes a real issue for performance evaluation, because the allocation of corporate overhead directly reduces operating profit, which reduces return on invested capital, potentially pushing that return below the company's cost of capital. On the purely national side, companies struggle with the general concept of allocating overhead and the ways that affects product costs.

Cross-Border Allocation of Expenses

If it were not for differences in tax rates worldwide, companies could allocate corporate overhead based on sales revenues in each subsidiary or on some other basis. However, different tax rates complicate the situation. For companies headquartered in high tax countries, there is an incentive to charge as many expenses as possible against parent company income. However, this practice tends to overstate expenses, understate income, and understate taxes in the parent country.

In the United States, for example, the Internal Revenue Service (IRS) allocates and apportions all of a firm's expenses, losses, and other deductions to specific sources of income (sales, royalties, dividends) and then apportions the expenses between domestic and foreign source income. The IRS provides specific guidelines on how to allocate expenses between domestic and foreign source income.

The problem with using tax law to allocate overhead is that it likely eliminates any possibility for the firm to select an allocation basis that is consistent with its manufacturing strategy. When tax implications are ignored, overhead is allocated differently. The Japanese, for example, have established a direct link between allocating overhead and corporate goals.

As Hiromoto (1988) shows, Japanese managers are less concerned about how allocation techniques measure costs than they are about how the allocation techniques motivate employees to drive down costs. An example involves Hitachi, the Japanese electronics firm. In one highly automated plant, the Hitachi cost accounting system allocates overhead based on direct labor hours, which does not seem to make sense in a highly automated environment. However, Hitachi management is trying to reduce direct labor as a way to reduce cost, so allocating overhead based on direct labor encourages management to automate faster.

Another important aspect of overhead we have learned from the Japanese is that overhead cannot be reduced over the long run by simply cutting costs; the entire manufacturing process needs to be redesigned. Mark Blaxill and Thomas Hout point out that as automation and organizational complexity increase—a real problem for MNEs—so too does overhead. However, MNEs find that they have to struggle to pick up or maintain market share against global competitors. In addition, the high-tech companies have to devote more and more of their scarce resources to R&D, so there is pressure on management to react. The reaction usually comes in one of two ways: prices are dropped and costs are cut, or the firm gets out of certain product lines and develops a niche. What we have learned from the Japanese is that companies can lower overhead permanently and remain competitive only if they design controllable and highly integrated manufacturing processes. For example, through redesigning its manufacturing process, Toyota has been able to maintain a 90 percent machine uptime in one of its leading-edge forging cells, compared with the 50 percent uptime for U.S. competitors. In addition, Toyota's overhead cost averages one person per $1 million in sales, compared with five people per $1 million in sales for its U.S. competitors. Thus, the amount of overhead that is allocated can be affected dramatically by changes in the production process.

COSTING

Traditionally, prices are a function of costs and market conditions. As barriers to trade have come down in most of the industrialized markets, there is strong competition for sales, causing firms to price very aggressively. In many cases, price competition has made it difficult to generate large profit margins. Many multiproduct firms, such as General Electric (GE) in the United States, have determined that they do not want to be in any business that has a profit margin below a certain level. That is one of the reasons why GE sold its household products division. If it is not possible to drive down costs or keep market share and prices high enough to earn a good margin, it may not be possible to stay in a particular line of business.

Thus, the relationship between pricing and cost is very important. One of the ways that MNEs have been able to drive down costs is to source production offshore. Such outsourcing can be achieved by another firm producing parts and components or by setting up one's own production facilities abroad. Offshore production is often attractive because of lower labor costs. For example, the hourly wages in manufacturing in the United States are much higher compared to those in Mexico in the Mexican *maquiladora* industry along the border with the United States.

However, offshore production can also create a number of problems. If a British company were to purchase components manufactured in China and pay for the parts and components in Chinese currency, the company would face a foreign exchange risk. This makes it very difficult to determine a standard cost. Moreover, transportation costs and distance can create problems not only in direct cost but also in the necessity of holding a larger inventory as a safety stock.

One approach that firms use to attempt to control production costs is to use standard costing. Quantity and cost standards are established as benchmarks for performance. They are typically based on engineering estimates, forecasted demand, worker input, time and motion studies, and the type and quality of direct materials. Standards can be used to prepare budgets and to evaluate the performance of firms and individuals. They can also be used to help establish appropriate selling prices. To be useful, standard costs need to be realistic and practical. The standards need to be tight but attainable, allowing for normal inefficiencies. Variances established by comparing actual performance with standards can be used to identify problems that occur outside of normal inefficiencies and that need to be corrected.

Although standard costs can be very helpful in determining inventory values and the like, MNEs need to determine if the standard cost of a product should be the same in different production sites around the world. Given that standards are based on such factors as the quality of available materials, the degree of capital intensity used in the production process, and the skill level of workers and managers, it is difficult to imagine that a cost standard developed for a product in the United States would be the same as that used in Brazil. However, identifying standard costs in a consistent manner using a consistent philosophy would be possible.

Caterpillar, the largest, U.S.-based heavy equipment manufacturer, uses standard costing for inventory valuation. Caterpillar has developed a managerial product costing system that is separate from its standard cost system, and it uses the same system worldwide. The objective of Caterpillar's cost system, which is an activity-based costing system, is to "identify the activities consumed by products and through a logical, reliable, and consistent process assign the related costs properly to each [product]." Thus, product costs are based more on cost rates for different activities that the product must pass through than on standard costs for materials, labor, and overhead. This does not mean that the cost rates are exactly the same from country to country, just that all subsidiaries use the process of establishing cost rates and assigning them to products.

Target Costing

Another approach to developing costs is a market-driven system, often called target costing. Target costing, which was developed by the Japanese, differs from engineering-driven costing in that it determines the product cost by establishing a competitive market price and then subtracting a profit margin that is consistent with the company's long-range strategy. Target costing more broadly refers to the process of reducing the time for developing products, defining quality for a new product, and containing cost generally.

Once the cost is determined, the departments that contribute to the production of the product determine their standard cost, assuming no innovation. Somewhere between these two estimates is the target cost the firm shoots for. As production begins, each department tries to ratchet down its costs so that the target cost moves closer to the ideal. Thus, production processes need to be altered and adjusted to move down the target cost. This is very different from the typical standard costing system. Daihatsu, the auto company that learned this process from Toyota, tightens its monthly costs by using a cost-reduction rate based on short-term profit objectives.

Target costing is very similar to an ideal-standard cost system, where the standard can be attained only in ideal conditions. Variances include both normal inefficiencies and abnormal inefficiencies, which are usually the target of control. There is a difference of opinion as to whether these ideal standards motivate workers and managers. The target costing described here is more a function of prices than of ideal standards, but the target cost established for production managers is very similar to an ideal standard.

In 1992, Toyota Motor Company (TMC) installed the target costing system it developed in Japan at its factory in the United Kingdom. The target cost for the autos manufactured in the U.K. facility (TMUK) is determined by TMC with significant input from TMUK. The target price for the autos is determined by consulting Toyota's marketing and engineering division in Europe. The target cost cannot be the same in the United Kingdom as it would be in Japan because there are trade rules in the European Union that determine the local content of autos, requiring TMUK to get 60 to 70 percent of its parts from Europe. TMC implements the following steps in its target costing system: (1) set the target cost for each vehicle; (2) set the target cost for each component; (3) implement value engineering; (4) check achievement of targets; and (5) provide continual feedback to design engineers. The purchasing department of TMUK identifies European producers of subcomponents that meet TMC's strict product specifications. Then TMUK expects the suppliers to reduce costs and improve operations as part of TMUK's efforts to achieve its target costs. TMUK's purchasing department and technical support team visit suppliers to examine the layout of their plant and facilities to help them drive down costs.

QUALITY

Another way to drive down costs is to improve quality. There have been some significant changes in recent years in the attitude of management toward defects. The assumption had always been that production processes needed to be designed to keep the amount of defects at a tolerable level, known as the acceptable quality level (AQL). The prevailing wisdom was that if you try too hard to eliminate all defects, you will end up with a more costly manufacturing process.

The Japanese once again shattered that myth with the concept of total quality management (TQM). TQM is the process a firm follows to achieve quality. It does not mean "cheap" because some things that a firm must do to achieve high quality might be expensive. The goal under TQM is to eliminate all defects.

The difference between the Japanese and others can be found in the attitude toward quality, which is what TQM is trying to achieve. In a Western setting, quality occurs when a product meets or exceeds engineering standards. In Japan, quality is defined in the following way: "The product is so good that the customer wouldn't think of buying from anyone else." The goal of TQM is to simplify and establish a strong focus on everything the firm does. TQM also implies a proactive strategy. Firms that benchmark the industry leaders and attempt to emulate what they do will always be in second place. TQM implies that you try to be the best at whatever you do.

There are four main costs identified with TQM: prevention costs, appraisal costs, internal failure costs, and external failure costs. U.S.-based Texas Instruments, one of the largest electronics firms in the world, identified several dimensions to their cost of quality. Prevention costs include quality engineering, receiving inspection, design engineering, and quality training. Appraisal costs include design analysis and product acceptance. Internal failure costs include scrap and rework costs. External failure costs include the net cost of returned products, repairs, travel costs related to quality problems, and liability claims. The easiest to identify are the prevention costs, the appraisal costs, and the internal failure costs. The most difficult to identify are the external failure costs, but they might be the most important.

Kaplan (1983) points out that executives who have adopted the philosophy of zero defects claim that long-run production costs decrease as defects decrease. He also describes three important aspects of the discussion of TQM. The first is determining what percentage of production makes it all the way through the production process without rework. Many firms do not even keep that statistic, but it is a crucial one for the Japanese, who are trying to eliminate all defects. A second key is determining the impact of an increase in quality and a decrease in defects on the cost of manufacturing. Finally, it is important to include in the capital equipment purchase decision the savings in manufacturing cost that lead to the improvement in quality and the decrease in defects that will occur if the equipment is purchased.

PERFORMANCE EVALUATION ISSUES

Budgets, both long and short term, are in essence, plans. Transfer prices and target costing can affect prices. In the end these plans must be implemented. With the help of these techniques, whether singly or as a combined plan, managers must perform if the firm is to survive. The performance of those carrying out the plan thus needs to be measured and rewarded. Properly measuring the performance of an individual, a division, or even a company as a whole is never simple or easy. One reason for this is that different bases of measurement result in different measures of performance. Moreover, the individual or unit being evaluated does not control many events affecting performance. Strategic differences in subsidiaries may also result in different performance evaluation measures.

For example, Gupta and Govindarajan (1991) identify several issues surrounding performance evaluation that are complex in the global environment. Subsidiaries can be global innovators, integrated players, implementers, or local innovators. Global innovators and integrated players tend to be high transferors of knowledge to other units. Gupta and Govindarajan propose that units that are global innovators and integrated players need performance evaluation systems that are relatively flexible compared with the other two groups. They tend to rely more on behavioral controls (i.e., those involving surveillance of the manager's decisions and actions) and less on output controls (i.e., end results of performance) than do the other two groups. Global innovators also tend to need more autonomy than do implementers, with integrated players and local innovators somewhere in between. In addition, Gupta and Govindarajan propose that global innovators tend to rely more on internal control of their performance than on external control—the control of powerful others, luck, and so on. These major differences in the strategic objectives of subsidiaries can obviously influence performance evaluation dramatically.

A variety of events that affect performance evaluation are out of the control of managers or subsidiaries. First, let us consider the basis of measurement. There are many possible criteria against which to judge performance. Furthermore, no single basis is equally appropriate for all units of an MNE. For example, a production unit is more appropriately evaluated on cost reduction, quality control, meeting shipment targets (dates and quantities), and other measures of efficiency. For a sales subsidiary, however, these measures are less appropriate (if appropriate at all) than such measures as market share, number of new customers, or other measures of effectiveness. Similarly, profitability may be appropriate for a subsidiary that is a true profit center but inappropriate for a subsidiary in a high tax rate country that, for global tax minimization purposes, is instructed to minimize profits or even maximize losses. These situations suggest the desirability and advisability of using multiple bases for performance measurement—that is, different ones for different kinds of operations in different countries. Yet even multiple measures have their problems. First, it is more difficult to compare the performance of different units measured under different criteria. Second, it is more expensive to set up and operate a multiple-criteria system. Thus, the decision must be based on a cost-benefit analysis.

Complicating matters even more are the interdependencies of an MNE's operations. For example, a multinational automobile company may produce its steel in Japan, have it stamped in the United States, have its tires made in Canada, its axles in Mexico, its engines in Germany, and its radios in Taiwan, all for final assembly in the United States. If any one part of its far-flung operations experiences performance problems, that operation's problems will spread to the other operations. Thus, a dock strike in Germany could affect the performance of the German subsidiary, the U.S. assembly plant, and all sales subsidiaries worldwide. Proper performance evaluation would have to eliminate these uncontrollable impacts for the interdependent subsidiaries as well as for the German subsidiary. Furthermore, if other than arm's-length transfer prices were used on any of the intercorporate sales, the reported results would not be within the control of either the selling or buying subsidiary (unless they both agreed to the transfer price), and, in any case, would not reflect real performance.

Separating Managerial and Subsidiary Performance

It is also difficult but important to separate managerial performance from subsidiary performance. It is possible to have good management performance despite poor subsidiary performance, and vice versa, again largely as a result of noncontrollables. In other words, a manager may have done a superb job in the face of real adversities largely beyond his or her control even though the subsidiary's performance did not measure up to expectations. Similarly, a subsidiary's good performance may have been due to considerable luck or occurred despite poor managerial performance. Thus, in order to properly reward and keep good managers and not inadvertently reward poor managers, the evaluation system must be able to separate subsidiary and managerial performance.

Gupta and Govindarajan (1991) point out that some subsidiary managers are better able to cope with the uncertainty inherent in the foreign environment than are others. In particular, they propose that managers in charge of companies that are global innovators and integrated players are better able to deal with ambiguity than are managers of companies that are implementers and local innovators.

Properly Relating Evaluation to Performance

One of the more curious aspects of empirical studies discussed earlier in the chapter was the finding that multinationals from Western countries especially rely on ROI as the major or one of the most important measures of performance. Where intercorporate transfers are significant and are not at arm's-length prices, the ROI income numerator is highly arbitrary and, in one sense, fictitious. Also, a subsidiary manager whose evaluation is based on ROI may choose to borrow heavily in the local currency. This in turn affects the borrowing capacity of the entire firm and potentially the price of its stock and possibly subjecting the parent's consolidated financial statements to significant foreign currency losses if the borrowings are in hard currencies. Perhaps most important, ROI is not appropriate for some foreign operations, such as subsidiaries producing only for other subsidiaries, sales subsidiaries buying all their products from other subsidiaries, or subsidiaries striving to break into highly competitive, low margin markets. The problems related to using ROI as a standard measure of performance apply to other measures as well.

The need for standardization brings us back to the one method of performance evaluation that can meet most criteria without undue limitations: the comparison of performance with plan. This method permits each affiliate to be judged on its own, according to the plan it was given, and can be used to compare subsidiary performances. However, it is a reasonable basis of performance measurement only if the original plans were logical and reasonable. Therein lies one danger of the comparison to plan technique. The other danger is that subsidiary managers' inputs to the plan may be tempered by their desire to surpass the plan's expectations. For example, they might deliberately project a bleak picture. However, if the planning and budget process is sufficiently deliberative, participative, iterative, and honest, both of these dangers can be minimized.

Emerging Trends in Performance Evaluation

The restructuring of companies in the 1980s and 1990s has resulted in a focus on more specific strategies, such as quality, global efficiency, productivity improvement, and the building of critical mass. One important change is the movement from subsidiaries as a major focus of evaluation to strategic business units (SBUs). Using the SBU as the key profit center for the firm allows it to concentrate on global competitors in that same line of business.

The shift to an SBU focus has resulted in the use of the following three major trends in indicators: more use of ratios, more use of cash flows, and more use of nonfinancial criteria. Although profits are identified as the most important indicator of performance for U.S.-based MNEs, ratios such as return on sales (ROS), return on assets (ROA), return on equity (ROE), and return on investment (ROI) are once again being utilized heavily. This may not be true of Japanese firms, but it is true of U.S. firms.

Cash flows are important because they are the basis for the calculation of shareholder value (i.e., the value of the firm's equity stock, an important characteristic that raiders monitor). The focus is on long-term cash flows, discounted in the same way as with capital budgeting. Nonfinancial criteria are also increasing in importance. Some of the important measures that are being used are market share, volume, productivity, and quality.

ECONOMIC VALUE ADDED

A relatively recent tool that companies are using to measure performance is economic value added (EVA), something economists call economic profit. Basically, EVA is after-tax operating profit minus the total annual cost of capital. It is a measure of the value added or depleted from shareholder value in one period. A positive EVA requires that a company earn a return on its assets that exceeds the cost of debt *and* equity, thus adding to shareholder value. EVA is an actual monetary amount of value added, and it measures changes in value for a period. EVA is also used primarily for performance evaluation and compensation rather than for capital budgeting purposes. EVA is calculated as follows:

ROIC Return on invested capital: operating profit minus cash taxes paid divided by average invested capital

CofC Weighted average cost of capital: (net cost of debt × % debt used) + (net cost of equity × % equity used)

AIC Average invested capital: Average stockholders equity + average debt

$$EVA = [ROIC - CofC] \times AIC$$

As an example of EVA, assume the following data:

Total revenues	$6,500 (million)
Total costs	4,000
Total operating expenses	1,800
Cash taxes paid	230
Stockholders Equity (Average)	1,500
Debt (Average)	2,370
After-tax cost of debt	5.5%
% debt used	40%
Cost of equity	15%
. % equity used	60%

Operating profit = 6500 − 4000 − 1800 − 230 = 470

$$AIC = 1,500 + 2,370$$
$$ROIC = 470/3870 = 12.1\%$$
$$C \text{ of } C = (5.5\% \times .40) + (15\% \times .60) = 11.2\%$$
$$EVA = (12.1\% - 11.2\%) \times 3870 = 34.83$$

Although EVA is not a large number in this example, ROIC is greater than Cost of Capital, so the company is adding to shareholder value. As former Coca-Cola CEO Roberto Goizueta noted, "we raise capital to make concentrate, and sell it at an operating profit. Then we pay the cost of that capital. Shareholders pocket the difference." Some companies now disclose EVA in their annual reports—an interesting example is given by Infosys Technologies from India (see Exhibit 14.8).

THE BALANCED SCORECARD

The concept of the "balanced scorecard" is another approach to performance measurement increasingly being used by companies especially in the United States and Europe. This approach endeavors to more closely link the strategic and financial perspectives of a business. Developed by Kaplan and Norton (1992), this approach takes a broader view of business performance. The balanced scorecard provides a framework to look at the strategies giving rise to value creation from the following perspectives:

Exhibit 14.8   Infosys (India)—Economic-Value-Added (EVA) Statement

Economic-Value-Added measures the profitability of a company after taking into account the cost of all capital including equity. It is the post-tax return on capital employed (adjusted for the tax shield on debt) minus the cost of capital employed. It is those companies which earn higher returns than cost of capital, that create value. Those companies which earn lower returns than cost of capital are destroyers of shareholder value.

Economic Value-Added Analysis

Year ending March 31	1999	1998	1997	1996
1. Average capital employed (Rs. in lakhs)	245,41.61	142,89.67	98,46.75	76,44.80
2. Average debt/Total capital (%)	–	–	2.16	6.93
3. Beta variant	1.48	1.48	1.48	1.48
4. Risk-free debt cost (%)	12.00	12.15	13.60	14.00
5. Market premium	9.00	10.00	10.00	10.00
6. Cost of equity (%)	25.32	26.95	28.40	28.80
7. Cost of debt (post tax) (%)	–	–	7.70	7.70
8. Weighted Average Cost of Capital (WACC) (%)	25.32	26.95	27.97	27.36
9. PAT as a percentage of average capital employed (%)	54.16	42.24	33.91	27.48
10. Economic-Value-Added (EVA) (Rs. in lakhs)				
Operating profit (PBT excluding extraordinary income)	155,85.54	65,86.33	38,93.03	25,32.00
Less: Tax	22,94.00	5,50.00	5,54.00	4,31.00
Less: Cost of capital	62,13.94	38,51.07	27,54.34	20,91.59
Economic Value Added	70,77.60	21,85.26	5,84.69	9.41
				355,67.10
11. Enterprise Value (Rs. In lakhs)				
Market value of equity	9672,79.95	2963,42.20	731,04.17	
Less: Cash and cash equivalents	416,65.91	51,14.20	28,77.82	29,78.31
Add: Debt	–	–	–	4,26.06
Enterprise value	9256,14.04	2912,28.00	702,26.35	330,14.85
12. Ratios				
EVA as a percentage of average capital employed (%)	28.84	15.29	5.94	0.12
Enterprise value/average capital employed	37.72	20.38	7.13	4.32

Notes:

1. The cost of equity is calculated by using the following formula:
   Return on risk-free investment + expected risk premium on equity investment/adjusted for the average beta variant for software stocks in the U.S.
2. The figures above are based on Indian GAAP financial statements.

1. Financial—growth, profitability, and risk from the perspective of share-holders

2. Customer—value and differentiation from the customer perspective

3. Internal business processes—the priorities for various business processes that create customer and shareholder satisfaction

4. Learning and growth—the priorities to create a climate supporting organizational change, innovation, and growth.

Although the focus is still ultimately on financial performance, the balanced score-card approach reveals the drivers of long-term competitive performance. The challenge is to clearly identify these drivers, to agree on relevant measures, and to implement the new system at all levels of the organization. The significant aspect, about this measurement approach, however, is that it also creates a focus for the future because the measures used communicate to managers what is important. Thus Kaplan and Norton (2001) have refined the balanced scorecard concept into a strategic management system which replaces the traditional focus on the budget as the center for the management process (see Figure 14.1).

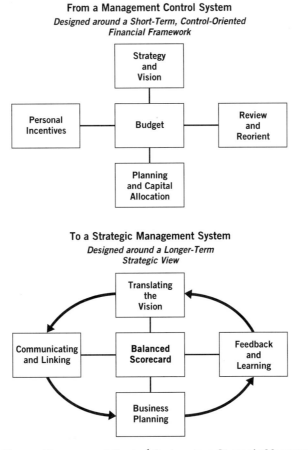

Figure 14.1 From a Management Control System to a Strategic Management System

SUMMARY

1. A major aspect of establishing a good management control system is to have a thorough understanding of the purpose of a strategic business unit or overseas subsidiary.
2. The role of the management accountant in the strategic planning process is to identify the criteria for performance and to monitor achievements against these criteria.
3. It is important to determine if performance evaluation measures should be developed in the local currency or the parent currency. The local currency is fairer to the local manager, but the parent currency is important because top management needs to answer to shareholders based on parent currency performance.
4. Several studies have been conducted on the performance evaluation measures of global companies. They tend to conclude that MNEs use multiple measures to evaluate performance, but budgets and ROI are especially popular forms of evaluation. Major differences exist from one country to another. Japanese managers tend to rely more on sales data and relatively little on ROI in contrast to U.S. managers.
5. In establishing the budget and monitoring performance, management can use the exchange rate in effect when the budget was established, a projected exchange rate, and the exchange rate in effect when actual performance has occurred.
6. Highly integrated MNE operations create problems for foreign subsidiaries because of transfer pricing problems and the different purposes underlying the existence of the subsidiaries.
7. It is important to separate managerial performance evaluation from that of the subsidiary because a profitable subsidiary can exist independent of good management and a good manager can work in a tough, unprofitable environment.
8. Recent trends in performance measurement include economic value added, which takes account of the cost of capital used in generating revenues.
9. The balanced scorecard approach to performance goes beyond financial measures to provide a number of linked perspectives relevant to strategy.

Discussion Questions

1. How can management accounting play a role in the strategic planning process?
2. MNEs often transfer their domestic performance evaluation systems into the international environment. Why is that the case? What problems could they encounter by using the same system?
3. Should the local currency or the parent currency be used for performance evaluation? Explain your answer.
4. Which of the methods for setting the budget and monitoring performance as discussed by Lessard and Lorange eliminate the impact of foreign exchange variances? Which of those approaches would you prefer to use and why?

5. Most companies use the same reports to evaluate the performance of the subsidiary and of subsidiary management. What are some of the dangers in doing this?

6. What are some of the national similarities and differences in performance evaluation techniques?

7. What is EVA, and how can it be used in a global context?

8. Discuss the advantages and problems of using the "Balanced Scorecard" approach to performance measurement.

Exercises

1. MultiCorp is a French-based company with operations in the United Kingdom. In determining the budget for 2001, MultiCorp looks at its historical performance in the United Kingdom and notes that for March 2000, its operations were as follows:

Number of units sold	5,000
Direct cost of materials and labor	£400,000
Fixed manufacturing costs	£350,000
Selling price	£100 per unit

In trying to establish the budget in British pounds for March 2001, MultiCorp does not anticipate a change in fixed costs, but its direct cost of materials and labor is expected to rise 10 percent, and its selling price is expected to rise by 15 percent.

At the time the budget is established, the spot rate (hypothetically) is FF7.6 per pound, and the projected average exchange rate for March 2001 is FF7.5 per pound.

At the end of March 2001, MultiCorp's management looked at actual results and discovered the following: the actual average exchange rate was FF7.7, the selling price £112, and the cost per unit of direct materials and labor was £90 per unit. A total 4,800 units were sold.

Determine the sales volume variances, the flexible budget variances, the foreign exchange variances, and the total static budget variances in British pounds for the following budget translation techniques according to the Lessard and Lorange model:

a. A-1

b. A-3

c. P-2

d. P-3

e. E-3

2. Use the data and questions in Exercise 1, but change the exchange rate as follows:

FF7.6	Exchange rate when the budget was established
FF7.8	Projected exchange rate
FF7.5	Actual exchange rate during March 2001
	5,200 units actually sold

Case: Niessen Apparel

Juan Valencia was upset. As general manager of the Niessen Apparel Peruvian assembly plant, he believed that his performance over the past two years was not being evaluated fairly.

He had recently sent a memo to parent company headquarters itemizing his complaints and asking for an immediate response. Charles Niessen, president of the company, asked his son Chuck to review the matter and report back to him immediately because he did not want to risk losing Valencia (who had threatened to quit).

Background

Niessen Apparel was a medium-size U.S. manufacturer of women's and children's clothing. Because of rising domestic production costs, Niessen had investigated the possibilities of sewing the garments outside the United States, after which they would be shipped back and sold in the United States. In this manner, they could lower overall production costs and be in a better position to compete with both domestic and imported products. This could be achieved by utilizing cheaper labor in a developing country for the most labor-intensive part of the production process—assembly—and taking advantage of a favorable section of the U.S. tariff code. This section allowed U.S. companies to export components to a foreign operation, then import the finished products, paying duty only on the value added outside the United States rather than on the full value of the product. Thus, a product imported from a Peruvian operation would have a smaller tariff than one imported from a strictly Peruvian company. This, of course, would give a U.S. company an advantage over a foreign company not owned by a U.S. corporation. For example, a product costing $100 imported from Peru might have a tariff of $20 levied against it (20 percent of its value). However, if the product had $50 worth of U.S. components in its value, then under the code the U.S. tariff would be $10 (20 percent of the value added outside the United States). Thus, the full import price would be $110, compared with the $120 import price of the nonqualifying imports.

The Method of Performance Evaluation

To justify the Peruvian sewing plant, Niessen believed that it should be evaluated as a profit center. This would allow the operation's profitability to be compared to the next best alternative use of funds. Valencia was to be responsible for the profitability of the Peruvian operations and was to be evaluated and rewarded on that basis. In addition, Niessen believed that the subsidiary's performance should be evaluated in terms of U.S. dollars rather than local Peruvian currency because its value to him and his company was its contribution to U.S. earning power.

Problems with the Operations and Systems

Initially, a transfer pricing system was established on an arm's-length basis for all intercompany shipments. This was consistent with the profit center concept in that any other method would result in artificial profits. However, over the past two years the transfer prices on components shipped to Peru had been increased, and the transfer prices on finished goods shipped back to the United States had been decreased. These changes were made to take better advantage of the special tariff provisions (i.e., to pay less import duty) by increasing the U.S. content and decreasing the foreign value added to the finished product. This change in strategy was considered desirable by the U.S. marketing people, who wanted to sell more competitively in the United States, and by the treasurer, who wanted to save on import duties. In order to avoid problems with U.S. and Peruvian government agencies, the transfer prices had been adjusted gradually but steadily each month. Helping to conceal this procedure was the continued decline of the Peruvian currency relative to the U.S. dollar. This, in itself, increased Peruvian import (purchasing) costs while lowering U.S. import prices (costs).

Although the effects of the new transfer prices and currency values worked out very well for the U.S. marketing manager (whose profits increased significantly), just the opposite occurred for Valencia. The performance evaluation of its subsidiary's operations deteriorated to the point where one member of the U.S. staff who was unaware of what had been going on suggested that Valencia be fired or the Peruvian operation be terminated. In addition, Valencia's annual salary bonus had virtually disappeared because it was based largely on his subsidiary's profit performance. To make matters worse, slower than anticipated U.S. sales growth had caused a cutback in shipments to and from Peru, idling much of the Peruvian capacity. And because the Peruvian subsidiary sold only to the U.S. parent, it could not use its surplus production capacity, causing its costs to rise further and its profits to decrease further.

Questions

1. What were the strengths and weaknesses of Niessen Apparel's original method of performance evaluation?

2. What factors should Niessen consider in deciding whether to change the company's method of performance evaluation?

3. Should the old evaluation method be changed for the Peruvian operation? If so, why and how?

Case: Uplift International Ltd. (United Kingdom)

Uplift International Ltd., which manufactures forklifts, is a multinational based in the United Kingdom. The forklift engines are designed and manufactured in its Manchester plant and then shipped to subsidiaries in Brazil and Canada, where the forklift bodies are made. These subsidiaries, in turn, sell the finished forklifts worldwide. In 1995 Uplift introduced a line of forklifts featuring a new engine, which it had spent several years and millions of dollars developing.

To spread out and recapture the R&D costs of the new engine, Uplift had increased the transfer price of the engines sold to its Brazilian and Canadian subsidiaries. In both cases, however, it had encountered problems with government agencies.

First, the Brazilian government had stated that the new transfer price included, in effect, a hidden royalty payment from the subsidiary to the parent. Such payments were illegal by Brazilian law, and hence the new transfer price was unacceptable. The Canadian Inland Revenue Department also was unhappy with the new transfer price because it would result in higher expenses and lower taxes for the Canadian affiliate. This effect had not gone unnoticed by the Brazilian government either. Both governments were also concerned about the headquarters overhead allocation component in the transfer price. In their eyes, the parent had little justification for charging the subsidiaries for overhead, which they did not really benefit from.

In 1996, Uplift lowered its transfer prices on engines shipped to Brazil (eliminating the R&D allocation) to comply with the Brazilian government's ruling. At that point, the Canadian, British, and Brazilian governments all became upset. The Canadians felt that if the Brazilian subsidiary was not going to be charged for R&D, the Canadian subsidiary should not be charged either. The British government was upset because it felt that Uplift should have been collecting R&D fees from its subsidiaries (which were obviously benefiting from it). Furthermore, by not collecting R&D fees, Uplift was shifting taxable income out of the United Kingdom and into Brazil. Meanwhile, the Brazilian customs authority had become upset because, as a result of the lower transfer prices, it was receiving less duty (tariffs) than before.

In sum, Uplift seemed to be in a position in which it could please no one.

Questions

1. Was Uplift justified in attempting to allocate to its subsidiaries, through increased transfer prices, the development costs of the new engines? Would it be justified in allocating to its subsidiaries R&D costs of projects that ultimately did not result in any commercial application by the company?

2. If a company is justified in allocating overhead, R&D, and other similar expenses to its subsidiaries, what would be the most equitable method of doing so?

3. In situations in which some countries will not allow subsidiaries to pay the parents for such allocations, how should a parent handle these "debts"? How should it handle the complaints of the other governments, such as those of Canada in this specific case, which do allow the allocation but object to the nonuniform pricing policies?

4. What can Uplift International Ltd. do to resolve the intra-Brazilian government conflict between the tax and customs authorities?

Case: Global Telecom (United States)

Ryan Louw, a summer intern at Global Telecom (GT), is thinking about some of the major problems that GT is facing in evaluating the performance of foreign operations. One of his assignments is to identify as many problems as he can and recommend some policy considerations.

GT is a U.S.-based telecommunications company committed to helping customers solve their communications and information needs. It came into being with the deregulation of the telecommunications industry and has risen rapidly to become one of the largest players in the industry. Mirroring the product lines of AT&T, the major competitor in the global market, GT's major lines of business are computer and network equipment, communications services (voice, data and video communications services nationally and internationally over cable, satellite, and mobile systems), and network systems.

In the 1980s, GT expanded rapidly in the U.S. market but has only recently begun to expand abroad. However, top management believes that the international market has a great deal to offer. GT's initial markets were in the United Kingdom and Canada, but it has begun to expand rapidly into other European countries, Latin America, and Asia, especially China.

GT is primarily a product line organization with a strong focus on finance. To keep up with AT&T and other global competitors, GT believes it needs to raise more capital and invest significant funds in R&D to develop new product lines. It is concerned that its current product line focus may change significantly as it adds new products and businesses.

GT initially tried to expand overseas with greenfield investments, but it became immediately obvious that countries jealously guarded their telecommunications sectors. As a result, GT was forced to enter into a variety of strategic alliances with relatively strong, independent partners. In addition, GT's growth in international business forced top management to reorganize the company and add a new layer of management responsible for markets in Europe, Latin America, the United States and Canada, and Asia. At this point, foreign revenues are only 20 percent of total revenues but are expected to grow to 35 percent by the end of the decade.

In order to control costs, GT realized that it needed to improve labor and investment productivity, so it had selected return on sales (ROS) and return on assets (ROA) as its major financial targets. It also used other targets for market share, quality, and so on. The target-setting process is similar to one used by Ford Motor Company:

1. *Identify key trends and critical issues:* During this stage, the product groups and geographic area groups work with top management to determine the key environmental variables that will affect the firm over the next 5 to 10 years.

2. *Assemble industry and competitive data:* Once the issues and strategies are resolved, local managers prepare five-year business plans. The new matrix structure with product groups and geographic areas is complicating this process significantly. In addition, the industry is moving quickly, and possible changes in government regulations make it difficult to know what businesses GT may be in in five years and who its competitors will be.

3. *Agree on competitive targets:* Specific targets are set for each SBU with heavy involvement at the corporate controller's level. There is a strong functional linkage between headquarters and SBU personnel, even at the international level.

4. *Prepare detailed plans to achieve targets:* During the fall, after targets are finalized, the budgeting process takes place for each product group, region, and country. Each reporting unit prepares detailed profit center budgets, which are expected to result in their assigned ROS and ROA targets. Top management reviews the budgets and helps to resolve matrix conflicts before finally signing off on the budget.

5. *Track performance to plan:* After budgets are finalized, actual results are compared to the plan on a monthly basis. Both ROS and ROA targets are set and tracked in dollars according to U.S. GAAP. A forecast rate is used to set the budget, and actual results are translated into dollars at the actual exchange rate.

GT's experience in Mexico in 1994, however, caused it to rethink its approach to performance evaluation. Top management had projected a year-end exchange rate of 3.2 pesos per dollar, but the peso devaluation forced the peso down to 5.325 pesos per dollar, with the average for the year at 3.6 pesos per dollar. That clobbered GT's results and caused significant unfavorable variances as a result of foreign exchange. Subsidiary management in Mexico argued that it shouldn't even have to be evaluated for dollar results since it had no control over the peso/dollar exchange rate.

GT was also considering adopting EVA after benchmarking AT&T's approach to performance evaluation. This approach was described by CFO Alex Mandl in AT&T's 1992 annual report:

> In 1992 we began measuring the performance of each of our units with an important new management tool called "Economic Value Added"—"EVA" for short. In financial shorthand, EVA measures returns in excess of the cost of capital. That is how we created value for you, the owners of our business.
>
> • Investors provide us money by purchasing AT&T debt and stock. We use that money to purchase equipment, to make investments, and for a variety of other needs. Our balance sheet might be viewed as a status report on the uses we made of that money.

- In exchange for the use of their money, investors expect a return on investment. Bondholders expect interest payments, and shareowners expect divident payments and a rising stock price. The return these investors expect depends on market conditions—such as the levels of interest rates and stock prices—and their views about the riskiness of investing in AT&T's future performance.

- With our targeted mix of debt and equity financing, our cost of meeting investor expectations—our "cost of capital"—generally ranges between 11 and 14 percent of the money investors have supplied. The EVA for each of our management units is the dollar amount by which its after-tax operating profit exceeds its cost of capital.

- Shareowners can judge for themselves whether or not AT&T is creating shareowner value by keeping track of their total return on investment over time. EVA gives our managers a way to also track the creation of shareowner value in individual AT&T units.

EVA is truly a system of measurement. It supplements traditional accounting measures of performance, giving us additional insight into our business and helping us to identify the factors that affect our performance. We have made it the centerpiece of our "value-based planning" process. And we are linking a portion of our managers' incentive compensation to performance against EVA targets for 1993.

In summary, our performance planning, measurement and reward programs are now fully aligned with the interests of shareowners. And I believe what gets measured gets done.

The treasury staff noted that GT's cost of debt in the United States was 5.5 percent and cost of equity was 15 percent; 35 percent of operations are funded by debt and 65 percent by equity. Currently, GT does not sell shares on any foreign stock exchanges, although it heard that some foreign investors had purchased GT stock on the Nasdaq. Also, GT management isn't sure how to apply EVA to its foreign operations and wonders if an EVA focus would have helped foresee anything in Mexico.

GT-Mexico results for 1994 were as follows:

	Thousands of Pesos
Total revenues	6,300
Total costs	3,800
Total operating expenses	2,300
Cash taxes paid	80
Total assets	5,300
Cash	2,100
Total liabilities	4,000
Short-term debt	700
Long-term debt	1,000

The Mexican peso was the functional currency for GT-Mexico. Ryan was curious about the impact of the peso devaluation on GT-Mexico's EVA relative to what it was in pesos and what it would have been at the projected rate.

Selected References

Abdallah. W. and D. Keller. 1985. "Measuring the Multinational's Performance," *Management Accounting* 67 (4): 26–30.

Appleyard, A., N. Strong, and P. Walton. 1990. "Budgetary Control of Foreign Subsidiaries," *Management Accounting (U.K.)* (September): 44–45.

Arpan, J. 1972. *Intracorporate Pricing: Non-American Systems and Views.* New York: Praeger.

Bailes, J. and T. Assada. 1991. "Empirical Differences between Japanese and American Budget and Performance Evaluation Systems," *International Journal of Accounting,* 26 (2): 131–42.

Blaxill, M. and T. Hout. 1991. "The Fallacy of the Overhead Quick Fix," *Harvard Business Review.* (July/August): 93–101.

Borkowski, S. C. 1999. "International Managerial Performance Evaluation: A Five Country Comparison," *Journal of International Business Studies,* 30 (3): 533–55.

Brownell, P. 1982. "A Field Study Examination of Budgetary Participation and Locus of Control," *The Accounting Review,* 57 (4): 66–77

Chow, C. W., M. D. Shields, and A. Wu. 1999. "The Importance of National Culture in the Design of and Preference for Management Controls for Multinational Operations," *Accounting, Organizations, and Society,* 24 (5/6) (July/August): 441–61.

Demirag, I. S. 1994. "Management Control Systems and Performance Evaluations in Japanese Companies: A British Perspective," *Management Accounting (U.K.)* (July–August): 18–20, 45.

Demirag, I. and A. Tylecote. 1996. "Short-term Performance Pressures on British and Scandinavian Firms: Case Studies," *European Management Journal,* 14 (2) (April): 201–06.

Eiteman, D. K. 1997. "Foreign Investment Analysis," in *International Accounting and Finance Handbook,* 2nd ed., edited by F. D. S. Choi. New York: John Wiley.

Frucot, V. and W. Shearon. 1991. "Budgetary Participation, Locus of control, and Mexican Managerial Performance and Job Satisfaction." *Accounting Review* 66 (1): 80–99.

Gupta, A. and V. Govindarajan. 1991. "Knowledge Flows and the Structure of Control Within Multinational Corporations," *Academy of Management Review,* 32 (2): 768–92.

Harrison, G. 1992. "The Cross-Cultural Generalizability of the Relation between Participation, Budget Emphasis and Job Related Attitudes," *Accounting Organizations and Society.* 17 (1): 1–15.

Harrison, G., J. L. McKinnon, S. Panchapakesan, and M. Leung. 1994. "The Influence of Culture on Organizational Design and Planning and Control in Australia and the United States Compared with, Singapore and Hong Kong," *Journal of International Financial Management & Accounting,* 3: 242–61.

Harrison, P. and A. Harrell. 1994. "An Incentive to Shirk, Privately Held Information and Managers' Project Evaluation Decisions." *Accounting, Organizations and Society* 19 (7): 569–77.

Hassel, L. G. 1991. "Performance Evaluation in a Multinational Environment," *Journal of International Financial Management and Accounting,* 3 (1): 17–38.

Hiromoto, T. 1988. "Another Hidden Edge—Japanese Management Accounting," *Harvard Business Review* (July/August): 22–26.

Hofstede, G. 1984. "Cultural Dimensions in Management and Planning," *Asia Pacific Journal of Management.*

Hofstede, G. 1991. *Cultures and Organizations: Software of the Mind.* London: McGraw-Hill.

Ito, K. and K. R. Macharzina. 2000. "Strategic Planning Systems," iin *International Accounting and Finance Handbook,* 2nd ed., edited by F. D. S. Choi. New York: John Wiley.

Kaplan, R. 1983. "Measuring Manufacturing Performance: A New Challenge for Managerial Accounting Research," *Accounting Review,* 58 (4): 687.

Kaplan, R. and D. Norton. 1992. "The Balanced Scorecard—Measures that Drive Performance," *Harvard Business Review* (January–February): 71–79.

Kaplan, R. S. and D. P. Norton. 2001. *The Strategy-Focused Organization.* Cambridge, MA: Harvard Business School Press.

Lessard, D. 1996. "International Financial Markets and the Firm," *The Journal of Finance,* 51 (2) (June).

Lessard, D. and S. Zaheer. 1996. "Breaking the Silos: Distributed Knowledge and Strategic Responses to Volatile Exchange Rates," *Strategic Management Journal,* 7 (7) (July).

Lessard, D. and P. Lorange. 1977. "Currency Changes and Management Control: Resolving the Centralization/Decentralization Dilemma," *Accounting Review* (July).

Merchant, K. A., C. W. Chow, and A. Wu. 1995. "Measurement, Evaluation, and Reward of Profit Center Managers: A Cross-Cultural Field Study," *Accounting, Organizations, and Society,* 20 (7/8) (October/November): 619–38.

Morsicato, H. 1980. *Currency Translation and Performance Evaluation in Multinationals.* Ann Arbor, MI: UMI Research Press.

Robbins, S. and R. Stobaugh. 1973. "The Bent Measuring Stick for Foreign Subsidiaries," *Harvard Business Review* (September–October).

Shields, M., C. Chow, Y. Kato, and Nakagawa, Y. 1991. "Management Accounting Practices in the U.S. and Japan: Comparative Survey Findings and Research Implications," *Journal of International Financial Management and Accounting,* 3 (1): 61–77.

Ueno, S. and U. Sekaran. 1992. "The Influence of Culture on Budget Control Practices in the USA and Japan: An Empirical Study," *Journal of International Business Studies,* 23 (4): 659–74.

Wijewardena, H. and A. De Zoysa. 1999. "A Comparative Analysis of Management Accounting Practices in Australia and Japan: An Empirical Investigation," *International Journal of Accounting,* 34 (1): 49–70.

CHAPTER FIFTEEN

INTERNATIONAL TAXATION ISSUES

Chapter Objectives

- Identify the major factors that influence the different tax systems used worldwide
- Discuss the role that the tax credit and tax treaties play in avoiding double taxation when firms earn income in different countries
- Explain how income from controlled foreign corporations may be taxed differently than income from noncontrolled foreign corporations
- Compare the tax treatment and book treatment of foreign exchange gains and losses due to foreign currency transactions and the translation of foreign currency financial statements
- Discuss the tax dimensions of intracorporate transfer pricing
- Illustrate how international tax planning can influence cash flows

INTRODUCTION

The game between tax authority and corporation or individual is an ancient one played with all the gusto of any natural rivalry. As the tax authority sets up a new defense to plug the gaps, the corporation adjusts its strategy and tries to open up a new hole or take advantage of existing ones. For the MNE, every taxing authority around the world has its own set of defenses that must be adjusted to.

The challenge is significant, and home office tax accountants must work with specialists in tax law from each country in which the firm operates as well as technical advisers in exchange controls and cash flow possibilities. This chapter considers the philosophy of tax systems and taxation, especially as that philosophy relates to foreign source income and taxes related to revenues and earnings from international operations.

Although tax systems vary around the world, it is commonly accepted that each country has the right to tax income earned inside its borders. That is where the similarity stops. Opinions diverge as to the classes of revenue considered taxable, how expenses are determined, and what kinds of taxes should be used (such as direct or indirect). Moreover, there are differences in adherence to tax laws based on cultural differences and attitudes toward enforcement.

DIRECT TAXES

Corporate Income Tax

The two approaches to taxing corporate income are the classic and the integrated systems. The classic system used in the United States, Belgium, the Netherlands, and Luxembourg, for example, taxes income when it is received by each taxable entity. Thus, the earnings of a corporation are taxed twice—when the corporation earns them and when they are received as dividends by shareholders.

The integrated system tries to take taxation of both the corporation and the shareholder into consideration in order to eliminate double taxation. In most cases, there is only partial rather than full integration, so double taxation is not completely eliminated. There are two ways to integrate a system:

1. Through a split rate as in Germany, in which the normal tax rate for most companies is 45 percent; the rate is reduced, however, to 30 percent for profits that are distributed.

2. The second and dominant approach to integration is imputation, which involves taxing earnings at the same rate whether remitted as a dividend or not, but allowing a partial or full tax credit for the shareholders. This is the approach followed by most of the remaining countries in the European Union, as well as such non-EU countries such as Canada, Australia, New Zealand, and Japan—but with different results. Most of the European countries using the integrated approach have adopted a system of giving partial credits to shareholders on tax paid by the corporation when income is distributed to the shareholder. This is the approach followed in the United Kingdom where the corporate tax rate is a flat 31 percent. When shareholders are taxed on their dividends, a portion of the corporate income tax paid by the corporation is imputed to the shareholders so the income is not double taxed. Other countries, like Italy and France, have a full imputation system in which shareholders get a tax credit that eliminates their tax burden.

It is interesting to note that in general corporate tax rates have been coming down in recent years, notably in the OECD and EU (see Figure 15.1).

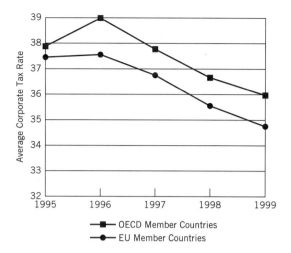

Figure 15.1   OECD and EU Average Corporate Tax Rates—1995–1999

What Income Is Taxable?

Even without leaving home a corporation may begin to interact with the nuances of different tax systems: income derived from the export of goods and services as well as from a foreign branch or foreign corporation. Worldwide foreign source income from the export of goods and services is taxable when earned. Tax incentives, such as the Foreign Sales Corporation in the United States, may be used to encourage exports, however, and these incentives have the effect of taxing foreign source income differently from domestic income.

Taxing the earnings of foreign branches and foreign corporations is more complex. Two different approaches to the taxation of foreign source income are the territorial approach and the worldwide approach. The territorial approach as used in Hong Kong, for example, asserts that only income earned in Hong Kong should be taxed there; foreign source income should be taxed in the country where it is generated, not in Hong Kong.

The worldwide approach, as used in the United States, taxes both domestic and foreign source income. This has the potential to lead to double taxation because that income may be taxed in two different countries. The two major ways to minimize double taxation where foreign source income is taxed is through the tax credit (allowing the company a direct credit against domestic taxes for the foreign income taxes already paid) and tax treaties. In addition, some countries that use the worldwide approach do not tax earnings of foreign subsidiaries until the parent receives a dividend. This is known as the deferral of taxation of foreign source income.

Within a given country, the tax authorities normally tax income on earnings of all corporations, even when foreign investors own them. For example, the German subsidiary of General Motors is taxed like all corporations in Germany. The domestic branch of a foreign corporation is normally taxed at the same rate as domestic corporations.

Determination of Expenses

Another factor that causes differences in the amount of taxes paid is the way countries treat certain expenses for tax purposes. Expenses are usually a matter of timing. If R&D expenses are capitalized, for example, their impact on taxable income will be spread over the period in which they are written off. If they are treated as expenses in the period in which they are incurred, the impact will be immediate.

Opinions also differ from country to country as to the useful life of an asset. If one government allows a company to write off an asset in 5 years, whereas in another country the same asset has a taxable useful life of 10 years, the tax burdens in the two countries will be quite different. In addition, there may be a big difference between a country's statutory and effective tax rate. A high statutory tax rate with a liberal determination of expenses may result in a relatively low taxable income and thus low effective tax rate, and this is the rate that is of concern to the investor. A good example of this is that when the United States passed the Tax Reform Act (TRA) of 1986, the U.S. government lowered tax rates, but it broadened the base of taxable income so it would continue to collect roughly the same amount of revenue. Thus, the effective tax rate did not change as much as did the statutory tax rate. This same effect spread throughout most of the other OECD countries during the late 1980s where rates were reduced and the tax base broadened. A few exceptions are France, Germany, and Italy, where tax rates were reduced but the base was not broadened.

Withholding Tax

The income earned by the foreign subsidiary or affiliate of a multinational is taxable in the foreign country, and the tax is levied against the foreign corporation, not against the parent. However, the actual cash returns to the parent in the form of dividends, royalties (payments made by the foreign corporation to the parent for the use of patents, trademarks, processes, and so on), and interest on intracompany debt are taxable to the parent. Normally a country levies a withholding tax on payments to the nonresident investor. This tax varies in size from country to country and depends on whether the country has a tax treaty with other countries.

INDIRECT TAXES

Value Added or Goods and Services Taxes

In some countries, such as the United States, the individual direct income tax is the most important source of revenue for the government. In other countries, like France, indirect taxes are very important. Examples of indirect taxes are consumption taxes (such as the sales tax in the United States), the VAT, excise taxes, estate and gift taxes, employment taxes, and different kinds of user fees.

In Europe, the VAT, sometimes referred to as the TVA, is a source of considerable government income and is also the major source of revenue for funding the operations of the European Union. The basic concept behind the VAT is that a tax is applied at each stage of the production process for the value added by the firm to goods purchased from the outside, which have been subject to the VAT. The tax is charged by businesses on the value of their sales, but the tax burden eventually falls on the consumer because a company that pays VAT on its own expenses can reclaim that tax already paid. The major method for computing the VAT and the one required in the European Union is the subtractive method. Exhibit 15.1 demonstrates how to compute the VAT in the United Kingdom where the VAT rate is 17.5 percent. The VAT differs from a sales tax in that the entire sales tax appears at the retail level rather than at each stage of the process. In addition, the VAT is not listed separately to the consumer. For example, the consumer would not pay the retailer £23.50 plus a VAT of £4.11. The £23.50 that the consumer pays the retailer includes the VAT.

THE AVOIDANCE OF DOUBLE TAXATION OF FOREIGN SOURCE INCOME

Credits and Deductions

The foreign branches and subsidiaries of MNEs are subject to a variety of taxes, both direct and indirect, in the countries where they operate. The problem is that the income earned in the foreign country may be subject to income taxes twice: when the earnings are realized in the foreign location and when they are realized in the parent country. In the United States, for example, income from foreign corporations is usually taxed when a dividend is remitted to the parent company. The company may choose to treat the taxes paid as a credit that can be applied against their tax liability, or it can deduct the tax from income to reduce taxable income.

The simple illustration in Exhibit 15.2 demonstrates the difference in U.S. tax liability that arises from double taxation, a tax deduction, and a tax credit. In the double taxation column, the foreign source income is taxed at 30 percent in the foreign country and at 35 percent in the United States (using the U.S. federal rate). Thus, the total tax paid is $65, the net income after all taxes is only $35, and the effective

Exhibit 15.1   The Value-Added Tax

Calculation	Manufacturer	Wholesaler	Retailer	Consumer
Net cost of goods	£0.00	£10.00	£14.00	£23.50
Markup		£4.00	£6.00	
Net selling price	£10.00	£14.00	£20.00	
VAT chargeable (17.5% × Net selling price)	£1.75	£2.45	£3.50	
Gross selling price	£11.75	£16.45	£23.50	
Accounting for VAT				
Due to Customs and Excise	£1.75	£2.45	£3.50	
Recoverable from Customs and Excise	£0.00	£1.75	£2.45	
Net Vat Paid	£1.75	£0.70	£1.05	

Exhibit 15.2   Treatment of Foreign Corporate Income Tax

	Double Taxation	Deduction	Credit
Income earned by the foreign corporation	$100.00	$100.00	$100.00
Foreign tax at 30% on $100	30.00	30.00	30.00
Net income after tax	$70.00	$70.00	$70.00
U.S. tax at 35% on $100	35.00		
U.S. tax at 35% on $70		$24.50	
U.S. tax at 35% on $100 less foreign tax at 30% on $100			5.00
Net income after taxes in U.S.	$35.00	$45.50	$65.00
Effective tax rate	65%	54.5%	35%

tax rate is thus 65 percent. In the deduction column, the U.S. tax rate of 35 percent is levied on the income that results from deducting the foreign income tax from the gross income of the foreign corporation. Thus, the U.S. tax is only $24.50, the total tax paid is $54.50, and the net income after tax in both countries is $45.50, definitely better than in the double taxation situation. Notice that under the tax credit column, U.S. income tax of $5.00 is assessed against the foreign source income because the tax rate in the foreign country (30 percent) is lower than it is in the United States (35 percent). In U.S. tax law, an excess credit (if the foreign tax rate exceeds the U.S. tax rate) can be carried back and applied against foreign source income of prior years or carried forward to be applied against foreign source income in future years.

A key point to grasp is that a tax must be considered an income tax to be creditable; the VAT described earlier would be eligible for deduction but not for the credit. In determining the tax credit in the United States, for example, the predominant nature of the foreign tax must be that of an income tax as defined in the United States. Thus, a tax might be considered an income tax in one country but still not be eligible for the credit if that tax is deemed something else from the perspective of the IRS in the United States.

It should be noted that in the United States the tax credit is available only for taxes on income paid directly by the U.S. corporation (e.g., the withholding tax on dividends) or deemed to have been paid by it. The deemed direct tax is the corporate income tax actually paid by the foreign corporation to the foreign government and deemed to have been paid by the U.S. parent.

Tax Treaties

As we have noted, with the spread of business worldwide, income earned in one country may be subject to taxation in other countries. Philosophical differences about how income should be taxed have given rise to treaties between countries to minimize the effect of double taxation on the taxpayer, protect each country's right to collect taxes, and provide ways to resolve jurisdictional issues. In the area of double taxation, treaties can specify that certain classes of income would not be subject to tax, can reduce the rate on income and/or withholding taxes, and can specifically deal with the issue of tax credits. Although the latter point could be considered a duplication of the Internal Revenue Code, its specification in a tax treaty would simply strengthen the tax credit concept. It could also deal with specific types of taxes that could be considered creditable, and so on. Among other things, tax treaties tend to reduce or eliminate the taxes on dividends, interest, and royalty payments.

A pattern of tax treaties was developed by the OECD in 1963 and subsequently amended and reissued. That pattern, initially resisted by the U.S. government, was accepted in principle in the model tax treaty approved by the United States in 1977. The treaty contains 29 articles dealing with such issues as the taxes covered, the persons and organizations covered, relief from double taxation, the exchange of information between competent authorities of contracting nations, and the conditions under which a treaty may be terminated. The model treaty also deals with issues such as who is allowed to tax income, how income is to be characterized, how expenses are to be allocated, what rights exist to certain types of deductions, and how rates of tax on foreign investors can be reduced.

Sometimes treaties are comprehensive; other times they amend existing treaties or deal with specific issues. In 1994, for example, the United States and Canada signed an agreement resulting in significant reductions in tax rates on cross-border payments of dividends, interest, and royalties. The rate on direct investment dividends would be reduced to 5 percent from 10 percent; the rate on interest would fall to 10 percent from 15 percent; and the rate on most royalties would drop to zero from 10 percent.

U.S. TAXATION OF FOREIGN SOURCE INCOME

The Tax Haven Concept

A tax haven is a phenomenon that has emerged from the philosophy that foreign source income should not be taxed at all or should be taxed only when declared a dividend. A tax haven may be defined as a place where foreigners may receive income or own assets without paying high rates of tax upon them. Tax havens offer a variety of benefits, including low taxes or no taxes on certain classes of income. Because of these benefits, thousands of so-called mailbox companies have sprung up in such exotic places as Liechtenstein, Vanuatu (formerly New Hebrides), and the Netherlands Antilles.

Some examples of types of tax haven countries are as follows:

1. Countries with no income taxes, such as the Bahamas, Bermuda, and the Cayman Islands.
2. Countries with taxes at low rates, such as the British Virgin Islands.
3. Countries that tax income from domestic sources but exempt income from foreign sources, such as Hong Kong, Liberia, and Panama.
4. Countries that allow special privileges; generally their suitability as tax havens is limited.

To take advantage of a tax haven, a corporation would ordinarily set up a subsidiary in the tax haven country through which different forms of income would pass. The goal is to shift income from high tax to tax haven countries. This is normally accom-

Exhibit 15.3 Article from *The Economist*, January 29, 2000

As globalization ebbed and flowed, the taxman's share of economic output went relentlessly up, despite warnings from politicians that globalization would make it harder for government to collect taxes and thus to provide public services. But now a new factor has entered the equation: the Internet. It epitomizes borderlessness, and the irrelevance of being in a particular physical location. By being everywhere and nowhere at once, it seems certain to speed up globalization. And in doing so, according to the Organization for Economic Cooperation and Development, it might damage tax systems so badly that it could "lead to governments being unable to meet the legitimate demands of their citizens for public services."

Shopping Around

The Internet has dawned just as tax collectors are getting worried about another aspect of globalization: tax competition. Both the European Union and the OECD have declared war on "harmful" low-tax policies used by some countries to attract international businesses and capital. The OECD says that tax competition is often a "beggar-thy-neighbor policy" which is already reducing government tax revenues, and will start to be reflected in the data during the next couple of years. The Internet has the potential to increase tax competition, not least by making it much easier for multinationals to shift their activities to low-tax regimes, such as Caribbean tax havens, that are physically a long way from their customers, but virtually are only a mouse-click away. Many more companies may be able to emulate Rupert Murdoch's News Corporation, which has earned profits of £1.4 billion ($2.3 billion) in Britain since 1987 but paid no corporation tax there.

Source: The Economist, January 29, 2000.

plished by using the tax haven subsidiary as an intermediary. For example, a British manufacturer could sell goods directly to a dealer in Germany and concentrate the profits in Britain. It could equally well sell the goods to a tax haven subsidiary at cost and then sell the goods to the German dealer at a profit, thus concentrating the profits in the tax haven corporation.

Many countries are naturally concerned about minimizing the opportunities for using tax havens where they are likely to be disadvantaged. The OECD, for example, plans to impose sanctions on countries offering "harmful" tax competition (see Exhibit 15.3).

The Controlled Foreign Corporation

As we noted earlier, a U.S. corporation may choose to produce and sell in the foreign country through a branch of the parent or through a foreign corporation in which the parent has an equity interest. The tax implications of these situations are interesting. The income or loss of a foreign branch must be combined with parent income for tax as well as book purposes in the period in which the income or loss occurs. In the case of a foreign corporation, however, a U.S. parent does not declare income from a foreign corporation for tax purposes until it actually receives a dividend. This is the principle of deferral—the income is deferred from U.S. taxation until it is received as a dividend. As mentioned earlier, the deferral principle is a basic tenet of the taxation of foreign source income.

The deferral principle works most of the time, but an exception is made for a certain class of income (i.e., Subpart F income) of a certain type of corporation (i.e., a controlled foreign corporation). In general, Subpart F income is not deferred but must be declared by the U.S. parent corporation as soon as it is earned by the foreign corporation. However, we first must define a controlled foreign corporation (CFC). A CFC is a foreign corporation in which "U.S. shareholders" hold more than 50 percent of the voting stock. A U.S. shareholder, for tax purposes, is a person or enterprise that holds at least 10 percent of the voting stock of the foreign corporation.

Subpart F Income

Why does it make a difference for tax purposes whether a foreign corporation is a CFC? As Figure 15.2 shows, if the foreign corporation is not a CFC, its income is automatically deferred until remitted as a dividend to the shareholders. If the foreign corporation is a CFC, the deferral principle may not apply to certain kinds of income. To understand this, it is necessary to go back in history a few years. As mentioned earlier, sometimes U.S. corporations do business in tax haven countries and therefore benefit from low or nonexistent income taxes. If a tax haven corporation was actively involved in the production and sale of goods and services, there was no problem. However, the U.S. government noticed that many companies were setting up tax haven corporations just to avoid paying U.S. tax. Therefore, the Revenue Act of 1962 minimized the tax avoidance practices of multinationals. The Act allowed a U.S. corporation to apply the deferral principle to its portion of income derived from the active conduct of a trade or business of a CFC, but it could not defer its portion of passive income, referred to as Subpart F income in the Internal Revenue Code.

Subpart F income is divided into eight groups: (1) insurance of U.S. risks, (2) foreign-base company personal holding company income, (3) foreign-base company sales income, (4) foreign-base company services income, (5) foreign-base company shipping income, (6) foreign-base company oil-related income, (7) boycott-related income, and (8) foreign bribes.

The first category of Subpart F income, insurance of U.S. risks, arose because many U.S. corporations were setting up a foreign insurance subsidiary in a tax haven country and paying insurance premiums to the subsidiary on U.S. and foreign risks. The parent could deduct the premiums as expenses, and the subsidiary was paying little or no tax on the premium income. After the Revenue Act of 1962 the income from the premiums is taxable to the parent when earned by the CFC.

Foreign-based company personal holding company income includes dividends, interest, royalties, and similar income that arises from holding rights rather than from actually producing or selling goods and services. However, the income must be derived from sources outside the country where the CFC is organized. For example, if Multicorp established a holding company in Switzerland that owned Multicorp's subsidiaries in France and Spain, the dividends received by the holding company would be considered Subpart F income to Multicorp.

Foreign-based company sales income arises from the sale or purchase of goods produced and consumed outside the country where the CFC is incorporated. For example, a U.S. company could sell merchandise to an unaffiliated buyer in France but have the paperwork go through a tax haven CFC in Switzerland. On paper, the U.S. company would sell to the Swiss Company (probably a wholly owned subsidiary), which would sell to the French company. Prices would be set to concentrate profits in the Swiss company. However, that income would be considered Subpart F income under the 1962 law and would have to be declared by the U.S. company. It should also be noted that the income is considered Subpart F income as long as the CFC in Switzerland is not actively involved in selling and servicing the product with its own staff. If that were to happen, the income would be active rather than passive (see Figure 15.2).

Foreign-based company services income arises from contracts utilizing technical, managerial, engineering, or other skills. For example, a U.S. hotel management firm could enter into a contract to manage a hotel for an investor in the Middle East and have the management fee billed to a tax haven subsidiary in Switzerland. That fee would be considered Subpart F income to the U.S. firm.

Foreign-based company shipping income arises from using aircraft or ships for transportation outside the country where the CFC is incorporated.

The inclusion of bribes and boycotts as Subpart F income resulted from the TRA of 1976. To penalize companies that supported the Arab boycott of Israel, congress decided to classify income from operations resulting from countries involved in certain international boycotts as Subpart F income. In addition, the income from those operations does not enjoy the full benefit of the tax credit.

Bribes paid to foreign government officials as explained in the Foreign Corrupt Practices Act (FCPA) of 1976 are considered a new class of Subpart F income, even though the bribes are not really a form of income to the parent and the bribes are not deductible expenses. These two twists of the law have nothing to do with tax avoidance like the other dimensions of Subpart F income; they were included simply to punish offenders of other laws.

In summary, there are several implications of Subpart F income. For foreign corporations that are not CFCs, income is not taxable to the U.S. shareholder (the parent corporation) until a dividend is declared. For CFCs active income is also deferred, but passive or Subpart F income must be recognized by the parent when earned, regardless of when a dividend is declared. The only major exception to the rule is that if the foreign-based company income of a CFC is less than 5 percent of gross income of $1 million, none of it is treated as Subpart F income. If the foreign-

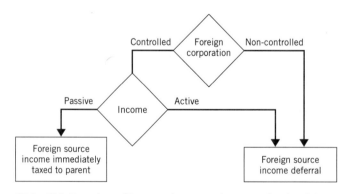

Figure 15.2 U.S. Taxation of Income from Foreign Branches and Corporations

based company income exceeds 70 percent of gross income, all the company's income is treated as Subpart F income.

The United States, like most industrialized countries, uses the worldwide approach, which means that the IRS taxes U.S. residents on their worldwide income. However, the situation just described, of CFCs and Subpart F income, is a uniquely American philosophy. The industrialized countries that tax worldwide income generally tax the income only if a dividend is declared to the parent company.

TAX EFFECTS OF FOREIGN EXCHANGE GAINS AND LOSSES

In Chapters 9 and 10, we discussed the accounting requirements in FASB Statement No. 52 for translating foreign currency transactions and foreign currency financial statements into the parent currency (hereafter referred to as dollars). We noted that FASB prefers to recognize the impact of an exchange rate change when the event takes place rather than defer that impact into the future. Therefore, transaction gains and losses are recognized in income when the rate changes, not when the transaction is finally settled. In the case of financial statements, gains and losses that arise under the current rate method are taken directly to a separate component of stockbrokers' equity, whereas gains and losses that arise under the temporal method are taken directly to income.

The treatment of these gains and losses for tax purposes is not consistent with the requirements of Statement No. 52. Generally, gains and losses from foreign currency transactions are treated as ordinary income on loss and are recognized only when realized; gains or losses cannot be recognized while foreign currency balances are being held.

Foreign Currency Transactions

The IRS treats foreign currency transactions from the two-transactions perspective just as Statement No. 52 does. However, it does not recognize gains and losses until the financial obligation has actually been settled. Assume that a U.S. importer purchases a piece of equipment on credit from a German supplier for DM1 million on December 1 when the rate is $0.64/DM. On December 31, the rate moves to $0.65, and on January 31 when the supplier is paid by the importer, the rate is $0.67. For financial reporting and tax purposes, the original transaction would be recorded at $640,000. On December 31, the firm would recognize a loss of $10,000 (1,000,000 × [0.65 − 0.64]) for financial statement purposes to reflect the higher value of the liability, and on January 31 it would recognize a loss of $20,000 (1,000,000 × [0.67 − 0.65]) to reflect the increase in value of the liability.

For tax purposes, however, the firm would wait until January 31 when it settles the financial obligation to determine the gain or loss. In this case, it would recognize a loss of $30,000 (1,000,000 × [0.67 − 0.64]) to reflect the difference between the amount at which the liability is initially recorded and the amount at which it is settled.

Branch Earnings

U.S. tax law has introduced the concept of a qualified business unit (QBU), which is a trade or business for which separate books are kept. For tax purposes, the earnings of a QBU can be divided into two parts: earnings that have been distributed back to the home office and earnings that are retained in the foreign location. In the case of a branch, both types are taxable to the home office. The amount of earnings distributed to the home office is translated at the exchange rate in effect on the date of the transfer, and branch profits are translated at the average exchange rate.

This translation approach is called the profit-and-loss approach by the IRS, which requires that the profit-and-loss statement of the branch be translated into dollars at the average exchange rate for the year. A difference between the average exchange rate and the exchange rate when the distribution is made can give rise to a gain or loss, as illustrated in Exhibit 15.4. Because branch tax was paid at the end of the year instead of evenly throughout the year, it must be translated at the year-end rate instead of at the average rate. The foreign exchange gain is the amount of the distribution times the difference between the average rate (at which branch profits are already translated) and the exchange rate when the distribution is made. Thus, the total amount of branch profits included in parent income includes the foreign exchange gain. The tax credit is computed by translating the actual branch profits tax at the exchange rate in effect when the taxes were paid.

Exhibit 15.4   Determination of Taxable Income on a Foreign Branch

Branch profits before tax		FC 130,000
Tax[a]		<u>30,000</u>
Branch profits after tax		FC 100,000
12/31 distribution		FC 50,000
Average exchange rate		$0.55 per FC
12/31 exchange rate		$0.58 per FC
Branch profits included in U.S. taxable income:		
Branch profits after tax @ $0.55		$55,000
Branch tax @ $0.58		17,400
Distribution @ $0.58	$29,000	
Distribution @ $0.55	<u>27,500</u>	
Foreign exchange gain		<u>1,500</u>
		$73,900
Tax credit:		
FC 30,000 @ $0.58 = $17,400		

Note: FC = foreign currency.

[a] Assume taxes are paid at the end of the year.

Taxable Earnings from Foreign Corporations

Earlier in this chapter when we discussed the recognition of earnings from a foreign corporation and the related tax credits, we assumed that the amounts were translated into dollars. Now we need to show how dividends and tax credits are translated into dollars for tax purposes. The recognition of earnings of a foreign corporation depends on whether the corporation is a CFC. When the foreign corporation is not a CFC, income is not recognized by the U.S. parent until a dividend is distributed. In such a case, the tax credit formula, as we discussed earlier, is as shown in Exhibit 15.5.

Assume that a British corporation earns £500,000, pays corporate income tax of £165,000 evenly throughout the year, and declares two dividends to the U.S. investor of £100,000 each (on June 30 when the exchange rate was $1.55 and on December 31 when it was $1.50). The average rate for the year was $1.54. In this case, the taxable income and tax credit would be computed as shown in Exhibit 15.5. The dividends are translated at the rate in effect when they are paid, and income taxes, for purposes of computing the deemed direct tax, are translated at the rate when they were paid. Because the foreign subsidiary is not taxed until a dividend is declared, the parent company does not have to translate the financial statements into dollars for tax purposes.

Controlled Foreign Corporation

As we discussed earlier, a CFC has two types of income: non-Subpart F income and Subpart F income. The non-Subpart F income is not taxed to the parent company until a dividend has been distributed, so the same rules as described earlier apply for the non-CFC situation. In the case of Subpart F income, the IRS assumes that a constructive dividend has been declared at the end of the year, so it is necessary to translate the financial statements of the firm into dollars. The profit-and-loss statement is translated into dollars at the average exchange rate for the year, as for branch earnings.

Exhibit 15.5 Determination of Taxable Income on the Tax Credit on Earnings from a Foreign Subsidiary

Earnings before foreign tax	£500,000
Foreign income tax paid	165,000
Earnings after foreign tax	£335,000

Dividends paid: £100,000 @ $1.55 = $155,000
£100,000 @ $1.50 = $150,000

Tax credit:

£200,000/335,000 × £165,000 = £98,507

£98,507 × $1.54 = $151,701

Grossed-up dividend: $155,000 + $150,000 + $151,701 = $456,701

Dividends/Profits × Foreign taxes paid = Tax credit

TAX INCENTIVES

For the purposes of this chapter, tax incentives are of two major types: incentives by countries to attract foreign investors and incentives by countries to encourage exports of goods and services.

Tax incentives to invest usually involve tax holidays of one form or another. The Brazilian government provides a 10-year tax holiday for companies that invest in the impoverished northeast and Amazon regions of the country. Mexico does not offer a tax holiday for foreign investors, but it does provide tax credits for companies that invest in counties located outside the metropolitan areas, such as in Baja and along the border with the United States.

Another popular form of incentive involves exports. In the European Union, many export products are zero-rated, which means that exports are not assessed to VAT. This allows firms to offer their products at a lower price than they otherwise could. Both Japan and Mexico also have an internal VAT but do not apply the VAT against exports.

Within the United States and United Kingdom many local authorities can and do offer reductions in or the elimination of local property taxes. U.S. cities and states can often be persuaded to waive state and city income taxes for a major investment. At the U.S. federal level there are de facto reductions of earnings from export income through the Foreign Sales Corporation (FSC).

Foreign Sales Corporation

The Foreign Sales Corporation Act of 1984 was signed into law on July 18, 1984, as a part of the TRA of 1984, and the new law was designed to replace the Domestic International Sales Corporation (DISC) legislation that had been in existence in the United States since 1972.

The DISC was established in the 1970s to encourage exports by U.S. firms. Although the DISC was not a taxable entity, its income was taxed to its shareholders (generally the MNE that established the DISC) at a reduced tax rate. However, the DISC was just a paper shell rather than an operating company, so it violated subsidy rules established by GATT. The Foreign Sales Corporation (FSC) was established in response to the criticism from GATT members. The changes in the tax laws have eliminated many of the privileges, but there are still a number of U.S. companies that have DISCs organized under the new legislation. They are still allowed to defer a portion of DISC undistributed profits but not to the extent previously allowed.

Organization of the FSC To deal with the concerns of GATT, now WTO, a qualified FSC must satisfy the following requirements:

1. It must be incorporated in and have its main offices in a foreign country or U.S. possession (except Puerto Rico).

2. It must have economic substance rather than just be a paper corporation.

3. The export services that it performs for its parent company or companies must be performed outside the United States.

4. Up to 25 shareholders may own an FSC, which permits export trading companies to set up FSCs if they desire.

Tax Benefits of the FSC   If a foreign corporation qualifies as a FSC, the following tax benefits accrue to the U.S. exporter that owns the FSC:

- A portion of the FSC income is exempt from U.S. corporate income tax
- Special transfer pricing rules allow the exporter to sell goods or services to the FSC at less than an arm's-length price
- A dividends-received deduction is permitted

Because the FSC is owned by a U.S. exporter and could be established in a tax haven country, arbitrary transfer pricing methods may be used to reduce the U.S. tax liability. Thus, the IRS requires the exporter to use an arm's-length transfer pricing method or an administrative transfer pricing method. Under the administered transfer pricing rules, the FSC can have profits no greater than 1.83 percent of foreign trading gross receipts. The gross receipts less administered profit and related expenses determine the transfer price from the exporter to the FSC. Once the profit is determined, a portion of that profit is exempt from U.S. taxation. If the profit is determined by the administered transfer pricing rules, 17/23 of the income is exempted from U.S. tax. If the profit is determined by the arm's-length transfer pricing rules, 34 percent of the income is exempted from U.S. taxation.

The U.S. Internal Revenue Code identifies the different types of income that are considered to be foreign trading gross receipts and thus under the tax reduction provisions of the code. For the transactions to count as foreign trading gross receipts, economic processes and the management of the transactions must take place outside of the United States. The major economic processes that qualify for the conditions are (1) advertising and sales promotion, (2) processing customer orders and arranging for delivery, (3) transportation, (4) determination and transmittal of a final invoice or statement of account and the receipt of payment, and (5) the assumption of credit risk.

For a transaction to qualify as a foreign trading gross receipt under the economic processes concept, 50 percent of the total direct costs of the transaction must take place in a foreign location. Alternatively, the transaction qualifies if 85 percent of the total costs in any two of the preceding five economic process categories takes place outside the United States.

Although the FSC appears to be complicated, it does offer some definite tax savings. Because many smaller firms could also benefit from the FSC, some states have established FSCs that smaller firms can join.

TAX DIMENSIONS OF EXPATRIATES

Most countries tax the earnings of their residents. However, the United States goes further than many industrialized countries by taxing the worldwide income of its citizens. A survey by *Business International* revealed that of eight major Western countries, the United States is the only one that taxes its expatriates on worldwide income. The United States does, however, provide some relief for citizens who have been residents, outside the United States for an uninterrupted period that includes an entire taxable year.

INTRACORPORATE TRANSFER PRICING

Internal pricing, also known as intracorporate transfer pricing or transfer pricing, refers to the pricing of goods and services that are transferred (bought and sold) between members of a corporate family—for example, parent to subsidiaries, between subsidiaries, from subsidiaries to parent, and so on. As such, internal transfers include raw materials, semifinished and finished goods, allocation of fixed costs, loans, fees, royalties for use of trademarks, copyrights, and other factors. In theory, such prices should be based on production costs, but in reality they often are not. As discussed in Chapter 14, transfer pricing is also a management control tool and tax minimization may clash with the objective of motivating management to enhance profitability.

Although industrial countries such as the United States have been concerned about the transfer pricing policies of their own domestic firms, they are now becoming concerned about the transfer pricing policies of foreign investors. In 1992, there was significant discussion in the United States over possible transfer pricing violations by Japanese auto firms. The concern was that the Japanese were under-invoicing the import of parts and components used in U.S. assembly operations, thus minimizing customs duties and giving the firms a competitive advantage over U.S. manufacturers. Exhibit 15.6 shows the results of a survey by Tang (1992) of factors influencing the transfer pricing decisions of Fortune 500 companies in 1977 and 1990. The consistently most important factors besides corporate profitability were differential tax rates, restrictions on repatriation of profits or dividends, and the competitive position of foreign subsidiaries.

Tax Considerations in Transfer Pricing Decisions

In an article entitled "The Corporate Shell Game," *Newsweek* magazine gave an overly simplistic, hypothetical example of a U.S. company that manufactured goods through its German subsidiary and sold them to its Irish subsidiary, which in turn sold the goods back to the U.S. parent company. The goods were manufactured at a cost of $80 by the German subsidiary and sold for the same amount to the Irish subsidiary. Even though the tax rate in Germany is 45 percent, there is no tax on the transaction. The Irish subsidiary then sells the goods to the U.S. parent for $150, earning a profit of $70. Because the tax rate in Ireland is only 4 percent for that transaction, the Irish subsidiary pays only $2.80 in tax. The U.S. parent then sells the goods for $150, earning no profit and paying no tax, even though the U.S. tax rate is 35 percent. Thus, the U.S. company ends up paying only $2.80 in income taxes, and this amount is paid in Ireland.

U.S. Rules

In the United States, Section 482 of the Internal Revenue Code governs transfer-pricing rules. The Code section permits the IRS to distribute, apportion, or allocate

Exhibit 15.6 Importance of Environmental Variable Influencing International Transfer Pricing Behavior

Ranking of Average Importance Score			Average Importance Score	
1990	1977	Variables	1990	1977
1	1	Overall profit to the company	4.04	3.94
2	4	Differentials in income tax rates and income tax legislation among countries	3.45	3.06
3	2	Restrictions imposed by foreign countries on repatriation of profits or dividends	3.32	3.24
4	3	The competitive position of subsidiaries in foreign countries	3.31	3.16
5	6	Rate of customs duties and customs legislation where the company has operations	3.04	2.99
6,7,8	8	Restrictions imposed by foreign countries on the amount of royalty or management fees that can be charged against foreign subsidiaries	2.90	2.85
6,7,8	11	Maintaining good relationships with host governments	2.90	2.75
6,7,8	9	The need to maintain adequate cash flows in foreign subsidiaries	2.90	2.83
9	7	Import restrictions imposed by foreign countries	2.71	2.89
10	5	Performance evaluation of foreign subsidiaries	2.69	3.01
11	16	The need of subsidiaries in foreign countries to seek local funds	2.61	2.40
12	12	Devaluation and revaluation in countries where the company has operations	2.44	2.71
13,14	15	Antidumping legislation of foreign countries	2.38	2.45
13,14	20	Antitrust legislation of foreign countries	2.38	2.14
15	17	The interests of local partners in foreign subsidiaries	2.36	2.30
16	10	Rules and requirements of financial reporting for subsidiaries in foreign countries	2.34	2.78
17	14	Volume of interdivisional transfers	2.31	2.53
18	13	Rates of inflation in foreign countries	2.24	2.57
19	19	Risk of expropriation in foreign countries where the company has operations	2.01	2.23
20	18	U.S. government requirements on direct foreign investments	1.94	2.27

Source: R. Y. W. Tang, "Transfer Pricing in the 1990s," *Management Accounting* (February 1992).

gross income, deductions, credits, or allowances between related enterprises if it feels that tax evasion is taking place. The IRS prefers that all transfers among related enterprises take place at "arms's-length" prices, which are defined as the prices that would be obtained between unrelated entities. As a result, the IRS is concerned about monitoring transfers in the following five areas: loans and advances, performance of services, use of tangible property, use of intangible property, and sale of tangible property.

In making the allocations, the key for the IRS is to try to establish what an arm's-length price should be. For the sale of tangible property, that price can be determined in one of six ways as the comparable uncontrollable price method, the resale price method, the comparable profits method, the cost-plus method, the profits split method, and other methods. The first method uses the concept of a market price to determine the transfer price. Of course, an external market for the same or very similar product must exist for this method to be used. The IRS also allows for differences resulting from reductions in variable expenses (such as selling expenses).

If it is impossible to use the comparable uncontrollable price method, the firm must then use the resale price method. Assume that the manufacturer in the United States sells a product to an independent distributor in Hong Kong, which sells the product directly to any other firm. The IRS would then take the price established by the distributor to outside customers and back out any costs to completion plus a normal profit margin to determine the transfer price from the manufacturer to the distributor.

The cost-plus method involves the costs of manufacturing the product plus a normal profit margin from the sales of similar products. Obviously, it is difficult to justify costs and normal profit margins. The other three methods are less common and are used as a last resort.

TAX PLANNING IN THE INTERNATIONAL ENVIRONMENT

As we have seen, the tax dimensions of international operations are very complex. The tax environment is unique in each national setting, and the advice of competent local staff who understand the tax situation is essential. In spite of the individual nature of each country, we can nevertheless use some general concepts as tax planning guides.

Choice of Methods of Servicing Foreign Markets

There are a variety of ways in which a firm can choose to service its foreign markets: exports of goods and services and technology, branch operations, and foreign subsidiaries.

Exports   When exporting goods and services, a firm must decide whether to service the products from the parent country or from a foreign location. A U.S. firm needs to consider the benefits of operating through a sales office abroad. A Foreign Sales Corporation (FSC) provides such an opportunity and can provide substantial tax benefits if the operations are legitimate ones that result in active rather than passive income. If the income is active, it makes sense to set up the sales office in a tax haven country where income can be sheltered. When the firm decides to license technology abroad, it must be aware of the withholding taxes and relevant tax treaties.

Foreign Branches   Operating abroad through a branch has several distinct benefits. Because branch profits and losses are not subject to deferral, it is often beneficial to open a branch when first operating abroad since the initial years are normally loss years. The home office could use branch losses to offset home office income for tax purposes. Branch remittances are usually not subject to withholding taxes as are dividends from subsidiaries. For example, in Belgium there is a withholding tax on branch remittances, but a tax treaty with the United States eliminates that tax. Natural resource companies like to operate through branches abroad because the IRS allows branches to use the depletion allowance and other tax benefits relating to natural resources. These benefits come back directly to the parent company.

Foreign Subsidiaries   A major tax benefit of operating abroad through a subsidiary is that its income is usually sheltered from taxation in the home country until a dividend is remitted. In the United States, that is true for all subsidiary income except the passive income of a CFC. This underscores the importance of making sure the operations of a CFC in a tax haven country are legitimate so the firm does not have to worry about the Subpart F provisions. The major problem with operating through a subsidiary is that any losses sustained cannot be recognized by the parent company. Thus, the subsidiary form of organization is much more valuable after the start-up years, when the operations become profitable.

Location of Foreign Operations   The location of foreign operations is influenced by three major tax factors: tax incentives, tax rates, and tax treaties. The importance of tax incentives was emphasized in the Brazilian and Mexican examples in the tax incentives section of this chapter. The existence of tax incentives can materially reduce the cash outflow required for an investment project, which will increase the net present value of the project. That tax effect could change the timing of an investment decision.

Because the determination of revenues and expenses for tax purposes is a function of tax law in most countries, it is important to be intimately familiar with local tax laws. Because this is almost impossible for someone in corporate headquarters, it is necessary to have competent tax and legal help in each local country.

Tax treaties have a critical impact on the cash flows related to withholding taxes on dividends, interest, and royalties. Strict attention to tax treaties can help investors choose the location of their legal operations wisely (which may or may not be the same as the location of their managerial operations). For example, the withholding tax between the United States and the United Kingdom is 15 percent according to a bilateral treaty, whereas both countries have a 5 percent withholding agreement with the Netherlands. A U.S. company would be better off establishing a holding company in the Netherlands to receive dividends from its British operations, subject to a 5 percent withholding tax. The Dutch holding company could then remit a dividend to the U.S. parent subject to a 5 percent withholding tax, which would be better than the 15 percent withholding tax between the United States and the United Kingdom. This is just one example of the ways tax treaties can be used to improve the cash flows of foreign investors.

Transfer Pricing

As we discussed earlier, transfer pricing is a method of equalizing taxes globally. This ability is limited by the increasing vigilance of tax authorities, particularly those of the United States, but possibilities exist. Care needs to be taken (as with other strategic issues) that in the final decision tax considerations do not crowd out important management control and other essential issues.

SUMMARY

1. The territorial approach to taxing income asserts that foreign source income should be taxed where earned and not mixed with domestic source income. The worldwide philosophy treats all income as taxable to the parent. This leads to double taxation, which can be minimized by the tax credit and tax treaties.

2. Under the deferral concept, earnings of foreign subsidiaries are not taxed until remitted as a dividend.

3. Tax laws in different countries often allow an accelerated recovery of the cost of assets in order to encourage economic growth.

4. The classic system of corporate income taxation taxes income when it is received by each taxable entity, which leads to double taxation. The integrated system of taxation tries to eliminate double taxation through a combination of a split-rate system and tax credits.

5. Countries often collect a withholding tax on dividends, interest, and royalties paid to foreign investors. These levies can be reduced through tax treaties.

6. The value-added tax (VAT) is an indirect tax that is an important source of revenue in many countries, especially in Europe. It is applied at each stage of the production process for the value added by the firm to goods purchased from the outside.

7. The IRS allows U.S. companies a credit against their U.S. tax liability for income taxes paid to a foreign government. A company can choose to treat those taxes, along with all other direct and indirect taxes that they might incur, as a deduction to arrive at taxable income.

8. Tax treaties can specify that certain classes of income would not be subject to tax, reduce the rate on income and/or withholding taxes, and specifically deal with the issue of tax credits.

9. A tax haven is a country that has no income tax, taxes income at low rates, or exempts from taxation income from foreign sources.

10. In the United States, a controlled foreign corporation (CFC) is any foreign corporation that is majority-owned by U.S. shareholders.

11. Income from a non-CFC is not taxed until a dividend is sent to the U.S. investor. Active income from a CFC also qualifies for the deferral privilege and is not taxed until remitted as a dividend.

12. Passive income (Subpart F income) is income not derived from the active conduct of a trade or business. It is taxable to the parent when earned and the deferral principle does not apply.

13. For tax purposes, foreign exchange gains and losses on foreign currency transactions are not recognized until the financial obligation has been settled.

14. Branch remittances are translated at the exchange rate in effect when the remittance is sent to the home office. Remaining branch earnings

are translated using the profit-and-loss method, where they are translated at the average exchange rate for the year.

15. Dividends from subsidiaries are translated into dollars at the exchange rate in effect on the date that the dividend is paid. The different elements in the tax credit are also translated at that same exchange rate.

16. The Foreign Sales Corporation (FSC) provides tax advantages to exporters, but it requires exporters to set up a sales office abroad.

17. Some countries provide tax holidays, such as the forgiveness of income taxes for a period, to attract foreign investors.

18. U.S. expatriates are allowed a foreign-earned income exclusion, a foreign housing cost exclusion and/or deduction, and a foreign tax credit in determining their U.S. tax liability.

19. International tax planning requires that a firm take taxes into consideration when determining the type of operation to be followed in servicing international markets (exporting, licensing, branches, or subsidiaries) and the location of the operation (by considering tax incentives, tax rates, and tax treaties).

Discussion Questions

1. A company has subsidiaries in host countries A and B. Country A has a statutory corporate tax rate of 30 percent, whereas Country B's is 40 percent. What are some specific reasons that Country B's effective tax rate might actually be more favorable to the firm?

2. Assume that a U.S. company wishing to shelter its foreign source income from U.S. taxes uses the Netherlands Antilles. Using a review of the literature outside the text, answer the following questions:

   a. Why is the Netherlands Antilles such a good tax haven country?

   b. What problems does the Netherlands Antilles face as a tax haven country?

   c. What impact could the repeal in the United States of the 30 percent withholding tax on interest from securities have on the use of the Netherlands Antilles as a tax haven country?

3. How does the existence of classic and integrated corporate tax systems affect the financing decisions of multinational corporations?

4. Why and how do tax authorities get involved in the transfer-pricing situation?

5. According to the survey mentioned in this chapter, what are the most important factors companies consider in establishing transfer prices? What might cause this survey to provide less than accurate reasons for actual practices?

6. The North American Free Trade Agreement (NAFTA) includes the United States, Canada, and Mexico, with the possibility that Chile might be added as the next member. What are some of the questions that must be addressed if their tax systems are to be harmonized? What stands in the way of harmonization?

7. You have just been hired by a small start-up company that is expanding quickly overseas. What tax advice would you give them as they explore different ways to penetrate foreign markets?

Exercises

1. Assume a VAT situation where the tax rate is 15 percent, with export sales exempt. The manufacturer does not purchase inputs on which VAT has been paid, and its net selling price to the wholesaler before VAT is £250. The wholesaler adds value of £300, and the retailer adds value of £500 to the consumer.

    a. What are the gross and net selling prices at the manufacturer, wholesaler, and retailer levels?

    b. How much in VAT is paid to the tax authorities at each level?

    c. What is the final amount that the domestic consumer pays, and how much of that is VAT?

    d. Would your answer to item c be the same if the retailer were to export the goods instead of selling them to a domestic consumer?

2. ABC Company has income from the following countries:

Country	Type of Operation	Gross Earnings	Income Tax Rate
United States	Parent	500,000	40%
X	Branch	(10,000)	25%
Y	Distribution	120,000	5%
Z	100%-owned	400,000	45%

    ABC's subsidiary in Z declares a 40 percent dividend; Z's withholding tax on dividends is 5 percent. Both the branch and the distribution facility, which is wholly owned, retain all earnings. The distribution earnings are considered to be foreign-based company sales income. What is ABC's final U.S. tax liability?

3. Puerto International has a branch in Mexico that manufactures a garage door alarm for people with mountain bike racks that fit on the top of their cars. The subsidiary earned $800,000 in 2000 before tax, with Mexican corporate tax rates at 40 percent. Taxes were paid evenly throughout the year. How much income did Puerto have to include in its U.S. taxable income in 2000, and what was the tax credit?

4. In 2000 San Fernando Drilling shipped 300 diamond drill bits to its subsidiary in Ecuador. The drill bits were shipped at San Fernando's cost of $1 million each to avoid Ecuador's duty of 20 percent. In 2000 Ecuador's income tax on foreign subsidiaries was 35 percent and the U.S. corporate tax rate was 35 percent. In 2001 Ecuador proposes to raise the corporate tax rate to 45 percent, eliminate duties, and impose a 10 percent VAT. The U.S. rate will remain the same.

    Required:

    1. What action (if any) should San Fernando take on its export pricing?

    2. What possible U.S. government action may result from your decision in 1?

5. As a U.S. congressman from South Carolina you are considering proposing a bill to eliminate a state income tax of 7 percent and a sales tax of 5 percent and replace it with a value added tax of 10 percent. Discuss the pros and cons of such an action. You should note that a typical South Carolina family spends about 80 percent of its taxable income on goods and services that would be covered by this tax.

Case: Belgian Coordination Center (Belgium)

When the United States Tax Reform Act (TRA) of 1986 was enacted, the basic corporate tax rate in the United States dropped from 46 to 34 percent. At that time, corporate tax rates in Europe ranged from 35 to 56 percent. Since then, corporate tax rates in some European countries had fallen, but they were generally higher than in the United States.

To attract significant high-level foreign investment, Belgium enacted several favorable tax provisions in the late 1980s. Belgium is an interesting country. With 10 million people, it is only the eighth largest country in the European Union. However, it is the sixth largest in per capita GNP, second in population density (and eleventh in the world), and first in the European Union in urbanization. In 1988, 66 percent of Belgium's GNP was in services, 32 percent in manufacturing, and only 2 percent in agriculture.

One important tax attraction is the possibility of establishing a coordination center. A coordination center can be established for one or more of the following activities: development and centralization of advertising; supply and gathering of information; insurance and reinsurance; R&D; relations with national and international authorities; financial; accounting and administrative services; currency hedging; and other related activities. Most coordination centers are financial and accounting in nature.

The activities of the center are free from Belgian exchange controls and are virtually tax free. Taxes are based on a small percentage (usually 8 percent) of expenses, except for salary costs and finance charges. Any dividends paid by the center to its parent company are exempt from paying withholding tax.

A coordination center can hold title to assets that it can lease to other members of the corporate group both inside and outside Belgium. The center can also be used to finance operations in other countries. For example, a member of the corporate group in Germany could borrow money from the coordination center and pay all interest to the center.

Questions

1. How does the establishment of the coordination center impact the tax liability of companies that lease assets from the center and companies that finance asset acquisitions through the center?

2. What would be the impact on the tax liability of the parent company of the activities listed in question 1?

3. Other than the issues identified in question 2, what are some other reasons why a U.S. company might want to establish a coordination center in Belgium? What must it do to gain the maximum tax benefits from operating in Belgium?

Case: Midwest Uniforms

Midwest Uniforms Inc. manufactures and sells cloth and disposable uniforms. The company also launders and delivers uniforms to hospitals, medical laboratories, and doctors' offices. The corporation is organized in the state of Michigan and operates three plants there—one that manufactures disposable uniforms and related supplies such as caps and masks; one that manufactures reusable cloth uniforms; and a plant that launders, presses, and delivers clean uniforms.

The company is owned by the Fulton family. Daniel Fulton, age 60, and his wife, Lauren, age 59, jointly own 40 percent of the corporation's one vote per share common stock. The Fultons' son, Michael, owns 20 percent of the common stock, their daughter, Meghan, owns 20 percent of the stock, and a family trust holds the remaining 20 percent for five grandchildren. Daniel manages the plant that manufactures disposable uniforms while Michael runs the cloth uniform plant, and Meghan manages the plant that launders and delivers uniforms.

During the early 1980s, the bulk of the demand for the company's disposable and cloth uniforms came from the Midwest. In the late 1980s, the company saw increased demand for its disposable uniforms from outside the region and outside the United States. In the past few years, the company has started to supply disposable uniforms to companies in the hazardous waste cleanup industry. It expects its sales of disposable uniforms to hazardous waste companies to triple during the 1990s. The corporation had $4 million of revenue in 1992, of which $1,500,000 was attributable to the sale of disposable uniforms.

Midwest Uniforms' manufacturing plants are working at near capacity. The company has considered closing its laundering facility and converting it to a manufacturing plant. Many of its cloth uniform customers have indicated, however, that the company's ability to launder and deliver clean uniforms is one of the reasons they purchase uniforms from Midwest. The company also has considered expanding each of the manufacturing plants, since it has adequate land at each location. Because the demand for its cloth uniforms is still predominantly from the Midwest while the demand for the disposable uniforms is becoming worldwide, Daniel Fulton has suggested that the company consider converting the disposable uniform plant to a cloth uniform plant and building a new disposable uniform manufacturing facility elsewhere.

Daniel would like the company to build a disposable uniform plant in Puerto Rico. He and his wife are nearing retirement age and feel that if they located to a warmer climate, they would be able to work well beyond the age of 65. His estimates indicate that it would be less expensive to build the plant in Puerto Rico than in the Midwest and that labor costs could be reduced by at least 25 percent and operating costs could be reduced by at least 20 percent.

The facility in Puerto Rico would operate as a branch of Midwest Uniforms. The raw materials would be shipped to Puerto Rico from the supplier in the United States and the uniforms, caps, masks, etc., that are manufactured would be shipped directly from the plant to customers worldwide. Daniel's research indicates that taxes are lower in Puerto Rico and that the United States provides a tax credit for foreign income taxes.

Michael Fulton is concerned about the potential labor unrest in Puerto Rico. He wants the company to organize a subsidiary in Hungary and call it Global Uniforms Inc. Since Hungary left socialism, it has been forced to deal with terrible pollution problems, as have other countries in the former eastern bloc. In fact, the pollution problems of these countries are a major obstacle to joining the European Community (EC) since they must first comply with the environmental rules of the EC. Michael feels that by locating a plant in eastern Europe, the corporation will be able to take advantage of the emerging markets in that area and, as a result, more than triple its sales of disposable uniforms and supplies. His research also indicates that the corporation could cut labor costs by 30 percent and operating costs by 25 percent by locating in Hungary.

Michael is particularly interested in sheltering income from taxation so that the grandchildren in the family will have adequate funds to attend college and graduate school. He believes that organizing a foreign subsidiary would save the corporation taxes since his research indicates that a foreign corporation's U.S. shareholders are not taxed on the corporation's income until it is distributed to the shareholders as a dividend. He would like, if

Exhibit 1   Current and Project Revenue and Expenses

Plant	1992	1993	1994	1995
Disposable uniforms				
Revenues	$1,500,000	$2,000,000	$2,750,000	$3,500,000
CGS	400,000	550,000	745,000	945,000
Operating expenses	500,000	666,000	915,750	1,165,500
Cloth uniforms				
Revenues	2,000,000	2,500,000	2,750,000	3,000,000
CGS	600,000	750,000	825,000	900,000
Operating expenses	500,000	625,000	688,000	750,000
Laundry				
Revenues	500,000	550,000	600,000	650,000
CGS	100,000	110,000	120,000	130,000
Operating expenses	200,000	220,000	240,000	260,000

possible, to leave all the foreign earnings in the foreign company until the grandchildren are ready to attend college. He proposes that 20 percent of the stock of the subsidiary be owned by the family trust and 80 percent by Midwest Uniforms Inc.

Meghan, on the other hand, would like the corporation to expand the two existing manufacturing plants and continue to manufacture the disposable products in the United States. She is concerned that the U.S. taxation of worldwide income would actually result in a higher overall tax liability for the corporation. She believes that the corporation can increase its exports through sales offices located in foreign countries.

The current and projected revenue and expenses of Midwest Uniforms are included in Exhibit 1. The estimates assume that the plants will remain in the United States.

Tax Considerations of Doing Business in Puerto Rico[1]

In Puerto Rico, a corporation is considered to be a domestic corporation if it is organized under the laws of Puerto Rico and a foreign corporation if it is organized under the laws of another jurisdiction. A corporation is considered to be a resident of Puerto Rico if it is incorporated under the laws of Puerto Rico or, in the case of a foreign corporation, it if is engaged in a trade or business in Puerto Rico. A Puerto Rican corporation is taxed on its worldwide income. A resident foreign corporation is taxed on all Puerto Rican source income and certain foreign income connected with Puerto Rican operations.

A corporation can use either a calendar or fiscal year in calculating its tax liability. Corporate tax is imposed at a flat rate of 22 percent. A surtax is imposed on taxable income, after a deduction of $25,000, at the rates indicated in Exhibit 2. There is no provision in Puerto

[1] *Sources:* Price Waterhouse, New York (1991). *Corporate Taxes, A Worldwide Summary, and Coopers & Lybrand (1991).* 1991 International Tax Summaries, A Guide for Planning and Decision. New York: Wiley.

Exhibit 2 Corporate Surtax Rates in Puerto Rico

Surtax Net Income			
Over	Not Over	Tax on Column 1	Percentage on Excess
0	$75,000	—	6
$ 75,000	125,000	$ 4,500	16
125,000	175,000	12,500	17
175,000	225,000	21,000	18
225,000	275,000	30,000	19
275,000[a]		39,500	20

[a] In the case of a corporation whose net income subject to tax exceeds $500,000 for any taxable year, a tax of 5 percent of net income subject to tax in excess of $500,000 is imposed to phase out the benefits of the graduated tax rates.

Rico for filing consolidated returns. A controlled or affiliated group of corporations is limited to one surtax exemption that must be allocated among the members of the group.

A branch operating in Puerto Rico is taxed at the same rates as a corporation and is entitled to the same deductions and credits. Branches of foreign corporations are subject to income tax only on their Puerto Rican source income and on income effectively connected with a trade or business within Puerto Rico. In addition, foreign corporations doing business in Puerto Rico are subject to a branch profits tax (BPT). The BPT is 25 percent (10 percent for hotel, manufacturing, or shipping operations) and is applied to amounts deemed to be repatriated from the branch in Puerto Rico. The deemed dividend will generally be triggered if the branch has earnings and profits generated in Puerto Rico that are *not* reinvested in Puerto Rico. The BPT is not applicable to those corporations deriving at least 80 percent of their gross incomes from Puerto Rican sources.

To encourage industrialization in Puerto Rico, certain activities (basically manufacturing, export, maritime freight transportation, and certain service industries) may obtain partial exemption from income and property taxes and 60 percent exemption from municipal license taxes. The municipal license taxes are 0.3 percent of gross receipts. The exemption can be obtained for a period of 10 to 25 years depending on the location of the business within the island. For purposes of the partial income exemption, Puerto Rico has been classified into four industrial zones. The periods and rates of exemption are included in Exhibit 3. In addition, the two principal harbors in Puerto Rico have been classified as foreign trade zones and foreign or domestic goods may be entered without a formal U.S. customs inspection and without the payment of any duties or excise taxes.

Exhibit 3 Periods and Rates of Exemptions from Puerto Rico Taxes

Industrial Zones	1–5 years	6–10 years	11–15 years	16–20 years	21–25 years
1. High industrial development	90%	90%	None	None	None
2. Intermediate industrial development	90%	90%	90%	None	None
3. Low industrial development	90%	90%	90%	90%	None
4. Vieques and Culebra	90%	90%	90%	90%	90%

Tax Considerations of Doing Business in Hungary[2]

A company is considered a resident of Hungary if it is incorporated in and has its head office in Hungary. A foreign company cannot trade through a branch in Hungary, but it can open a representative office, a service office, or a construction site.

Resident corporations are taxed on their worldwide incomes. A business profits tax of 40 percent is levied on all Hungarian business entities. The tax rate is affected by tax incentives that are intended to encourage foreign investment in manufacturing corporations. The incentives are in the form of rebates. The tax rates after the rebates are included in Exhibit 4.

Entities subject to the business profits tax are not subject to other income taxes. Business entities of foreign ownership, however, are subject to an additional 4.5 percent levy on the business profits tax base.

A foreign company that trades in Hungary is subject to a corporate tax of 40 percent of the taxable income. The taxable income of a representative office is deemed to be 90 percent of the total of 6 percent of Hungarian sales made by its parent company and 90 percent of 5 percent of sales made outside Hungary if the representative office was involved.

Points for Discussion

1. If the corporation builds a plant in Puerto Rico, can it use the foreign tax credit for any foreign taxes that it pays? Can the credit be used for taxes paid to Hungary?

2. If the corporation decides to build a plant in Puerto Rico, is there any other U.S. tax provision that it can use in lieu of or in addition to the foreign tax credit?

3. If the corporation organizes a subsidiary in Hungary, will the income of the corporation be subject to U.S. taxation? If so, when and how? Will the controlled foreign corporation rules apply to a subsidiary organized in Hungary?

4. What are the benefits of organizing a foreign sales corporation?

Exhibit 4   Business Profits Tax Rates in Hungary

Type of Entity	Rate
Standard rate for corporations	40%
Manufacturing entity owned more than 30% by foreigners	
First 5 years	16%
Second 5 years	24%
Manufacturing entity owned more than 30% by foreigners in a priority industry	
First 5 years	0
Second 5 years	16%

[2] Same sources as in note 1.

Selected References

Arpan, J. 1972. *Intracorporate Pricing: Non-American Systems and Views.* New York: Praeger.

Avi-Yonah, R. 1995. "The Rise and Fall of Arm's Length: A Study in the Evolution of U.S. International Taxation," *Virginia Tax Review.* 15(1) (Summer).

Baker, A., M., Carsley, and R. O'Connor. 1997. "Two Approaches – One Result," *International Tax Review.*

Bodner, P. 1997. "International Taxation," in *International Accounting and Finance Handbook,* 2nd ed., edited by F. D. S. Choi. New York: John Wiley, pp.39:1–21.

Borkowski, S. C. 1997. "Factors Affecting Transfer Pricing and Income Shifting: Between Canadian and U.S. Transnational Corporations," *The International Journal of Accounting,* 32 (4): 391–415.

Borstell, T. 1997. "Introduction to Transfer Pricing," *International Tax Review* (April).

Bovenberg, A. L., S. Crossen, F. Vanistendael, and J. Westerburgen. 1992. *Harmonization of Company Taxation in the European Community: Some Comments on the Ruding Committee Report,* Kluwer.

Burns, J. 1980. "Transfer Pricing Decisions in U.S. Multinational Corporations," *Journal of International Business Studies* (Fall): 23–39.

Cavusgil, S. 1996. "Transfer Pricing for Global Markets," *Journal of World Business,* 31 (4) (Winter).

Commerce Clearing House. 1999. Standard Federal Tax Reports. Chicago: CCH.

Eberhartinger, E. L. E. 1999. "The Impact of Tax Rules on Financial Reporting in Germany, France, and the U.K.," *The International Journal of Accounting,* 34 (1): 93–119.

James, S. R. and C. W. Nobes. 1999. *The Economics of Taxation.* Englewood Cliffs, NJ: Prentice-Hall.

Klassen, K., M. Lang, and M. Wolfson. 1993. "Geographic Income Shifting by Multinational Corporations in Response to Tax Rate Changes," *Journal of Accounting Research,* 31 (Supplement): 141–173.

KPMG Global Tax Services. www.tax.kpmg.netLamb, M. 1995. "When Is a Group a Group? Convergence of Concepts of 'Group' in European Union Corporation Tax," *European Accounting Review,* 4 (1): 33–78.

Lamb, M., C. W. Nobes, and A. D. Roberts. 1998. "International Variations in the Connections Between Tax and Financial Reporting," *Accounting and Business Research* (Summer) 28 (3): 173–188.

Nobes, C. W. 1980. "Imputation Systems of Corporation Tax in the EEC," *Accounting and Business Research* (Spring). 10 (38): 221–231.

O'Connor, W. 1997. "International Transfer Pricing," in *International Accounting and Finance Handbook,* 2nd ed., edited by F. D. S. Choi. New York: John Wiley, pp. 38: 1–38.

Picciotto, S. 1992. *International Business Taxation.* London: Weidenfeld and Nicolson.

Plasschaert, S. 1994. "The Multiple Motivations for Transfer Pricing Modulations in Multinational Enterprises and Governmental Counter-Measures: An Attempt at Clarification," *Management International Review* (34) First Quarter.

Ruchelman, S. C., L. Schneidman, and F. B. Voght. 1998. "The Good, The Bad, and The Ugly: Recent Cases Addressing International Tax Transactions," *The International Tax Journal,* 24 (2) (Spring).

Tang, R. Y. W. 1992. "Transfer Pricing in the 1990s," *Management Accounting* (February): 22–26.

Tate, C. 1998. "Transfer Pricing: The New Tax Minefield," *Australian CPA,* 68 (6) (July).

Turner, R. 1998. "Proceed with Caution," *CA Magazine,* 131 (6) (August).

Yancey, W. F. and K. S. Cravens. 1998. "A Framework for International Tax Planning for Managers," *Journal of International Accounting Auditing and Taxation,* 7 (2): 251–72.

NAME AND COMPANY INDEX

H

I

J

K

L

Z

Subject Index

A